African
Americans in
Pennsylvania

The Pennsylvania Railroad employed African Americans not only as pullman porters and conductors but also in mechanical trades. Here PRR equipment engineer Dennis McCloud of Philadelphia oils a crane he operated in laying track. The photograph, by an unknown photographer, dates probably from the late 1960s. (Courtesy of the Pennsylvania State Archives)

African Americans in Pennsylvania

Shifting Historical Perspectives

Edited by
Joe William Trotter Jr.
and
Eric Ledell Smith

The Pennsylvania Historical and Museum Commission
and
The Pennsylvania State University Press

Library of Congress Cataloging-in-Publication Data

African Americans in Pennsylvania : shifting historical perspectives / edited by Joe
William Trotter, Jr. and Eric Ledell Smith.
    p.   cm.
    Includes bibliographical references and index.
    ISBN 0-271-01686-8 (cloth : alk. paper)
    ISBN 0-271-01687-6 (paperback : alk. paper)
    1. Afro-Americans—Pennsylvania—History. 2. Pennsylvania—Race
relations. I. Trotter, Joe William, 1945– . II. Smith, Eric Ledell, 1949– .
F160.N4A37   1997
974.8′00496073—dc21   97-5210
                                                 CIP

Printed in the United States of America
Published by The Pennsylvania State University Press,
University Park, PA 16802-1003
and The Pennsylvania Historical and Museum Commission,
P.O. Box 1026, Harrisburg, PA 17108-1026

It is the policy of the Pennsylvania State University Press to use acid-free paper for the
first printing of all clothbound books. Publications on uncoated stock satisfy the minimum
requirements of American National Standard for Information Sciences—Permanence of
Paper for Printed Library Materials, ANSI Z39.48-1992.

*For the African American people of Pennsylvania
and for the historians who have diligently worked
to tell their story*

Contents

Foreword

Brent D. Glass, Executive Director,
Pennsylvania Historical and Museum Commission

One of the central themes of writing about American history in the past quarter-century has been the need to call attention to social groups, particularly minorities, that had received little or no attention from historians. Underlying this effort to expand the reach of our profession is the recognition that the everyday lives of Americans reveal important historical information that offers new perspectives on major events and adds a new dimension to questions relating to continuity and change over time.

In spite of some notable successes in making the historical presence of minorities more visible and in careful examination of the historical experiences of ordinary citizens, I am convinced that we have only scratched the surface of possibilities. At the same time, we may be too easily caught up in the rhetoric of modern-day culture wars—the clamor for more inclusive scholarship and multicultural education, and the countervailing demand for "standards" that reinforce traditional interpretations of the past. As a result, we can easily lose sight of the rich and significant body of work that has evolved in recent decades which addresses significant gaps in our historical consciousness.

What strikes me as most impressive about the essays and articles collected in this volume is not that African Americans have had a prominent role in Pennsylvania's history but that the scholarship documenting their presence is extensive and exceptional. This research and writing about African Americans is not limited to Pennsylvania's big cities, but ranges widely into such subjects as small-town life and military history.

Perhaps one challenge in making African Americans more visible in our history is the need to reach wider audiences with the work already produced. Certainly, one of the central reasons for the Pennsylvania Historical and Museum Commission's role as co-publisher of this book is its desire to bring the work of a generation of historians to an audience that usually is not reached through academic journals and magazines.

Another benefit of collecting these articles in a single publication is to examine the wide range of issues that have received attention over the years and to compare the perspectives of leading scholars in the field. Conversely, the subjects not included may indicate gaps where we must encourage new scholarship in the future. In recent years, for example, the contributions of African Americans to our cultural history—in religion, education, literature, and the arts—are beginning to receive the kind of scholarly attention once reserved for more traditional subjects like political, military, and economic history.

The Pennsylvania Historical and Museum Commission's commitment to building new audiences for history extends beyond publications such as this one. For twenty years, the Commission has attempted to illuminate topics in African American history through a variety of formats. The most successful and innovative of these endeavors is the Annual Conference on Black History in Pennsylvania. Each year the conference draws hundreds of participants for two days of scholarship and fellowship. A different city is selected for each conference, and a community group serves as host and coordinates local arrangements.

The collective support of many partners is evident throughout the conference. Statewide organizations—the Pennsylvania Humanities Council, the Pennsylvania Historical Association, and the Pennsylvania Federation of Museums and Historical Organizations—organize presentations on a wide range of topics, and the Pennsylvania Arts Council customarily sponsors an artistic event. Students from the community are provided special programs with assistance from the Pennsylvania Department of Education.

In many other significant ways, the Commission has made notable progress in promoting the understanding of African American history. Development of a thematic guide to the African American holdings of the State Archives, special exhibits at The State Museum, state historical markers, feature articles in *Pennsylvania Heritage* magazine, and living history programs at Pennsylvania's historic sites and museums are among the many ways we have attempted to tell this story. My expectation is that this program will continue to grow.

Throughout the past two decades, a remarkable group of citizen volunteers has guided the Commission's African American history programs. The Commission's Black History Advisory Committee consists of historians, teachers, librarians, archivists, community leaders, journalists, legislators, and public officials. They generously give their time, intellect, and creative energies to shape each and every activity undertaken by the Commission. As a result, the Commission has had access to a rich variety of opinion and experience that reflects the intellectual and educational leadership of the African American community. Any success we have enjoyed over the years is due directly to the very special interaction between the committee and our Commission members and staff. In many ways, this book is a product of this partnership, and a tribute to its legacy.

Editors' Preface

Since its inception in 1913, the Pennsylvania Historical and Museum Commission (PHMC) has acknowledged the role of African Americans in the state's history. From the outset, the State Archives collected various manuscripts that indirectly documented the role of slaves and the abolitionist movement in Pennsylvania. Yet, only during the upsurge of black activism during the late 1960s and early 1970s did the agency broaden its interest in black history into a fuller commitment. In 1976, the agency established the Black History Advisory Committee and soon launched its Annual Black History Conference. According to a recent PHMC status report, the annual conference represents the Commission's "most sustained commitment to black history."

Held at a different site each year, the annual conference energetically promotes "scholarship and local programming" on the state's African American past. Partly as a result of the Annual Black History Conference as well as the PHMC's growing commitment to research on the state's black population, interest in Pennsylvania's black history has dramatically expanded over the past two decades. As the PHMC status report concludes, however, the "very visibility" of the black history conference "has also at times obscured the need for other Commission programs to engage African American subjects and audiences."

Despite the recent proliferation of scholarship on the state's black history, we lack a comprehensive synthesis of Pennsylvania's African American experience. The existing scholarship is widely scattered in a variety of specialized monographs and scholarly essays in local, regional, and national journals. Recent studies remain largely inaccessible to the average reader, who seeks a broad understanding of the state's black history from its beginnings in the colonial era to recent times. Yet, the available scholarship on the subject is simply too rich to remain hidden from the general reader. Thus, we here offer a single-volume anthology that pulls together scholarly essays on a variety of topics, time periods, and locales. Such a volume, we believe, fills an important gap in our understanding of the state's history.

In addition to meeting the needs of the general reader, *African Americans in Pennsylvania* promises to address the needs of academic, public, civic, professional, and community leaders. By providing resources for developing courses, units, and projects on the state's black history, this volume should prove indispensable to college, university, and secondary school teachers.

Moreover, as a work of historical scholarship, this book should also help community leaders and public policy professionals understand key changes in African American life over the past 300 years. Above all, by bringing together a selection of the most carefully conceptualized, researched, and argued essays, it is our hope that this volume will deepen our historical consciousness, stimulate new research, and facilitate the writing of a new synthesis of the state's African American experience.

The anthology opens with a critical review of the existing scholarship. Here we assess the strengths and weaknesses of prevailing studies, pinpoint the principal contributions of essays selected for this volume, and conclude that the recent scholarship provides a foundation for a new history of African Americans in the Keystone State.

The volume itself is divided into four parts, each marked by important shifts in the state's economy. Part I documents the transformation of enslaved Africans into free African Americans, accenting the growth and expansion of African American communities and the rise of new forms of political, institutional, and cultural expression in the wake of the American Revolution. Part II assesses the impact of early industrialization, urbanization, and emancipation on the state's black population. This section illuminates the connection between early pre–Civil War emancipation in the North and later post–Civil War emancipation in the South.

Part III examines Pennsylvania's African American history during the triumph of industrialism, the expansion of the de facto racial segregationist order, and the massive inflow of South, Central, and Eastern European immigrants into the state's expanding cities. Essays in this section also analyze the impact of the two world wars, the Great Migration, and the Great Depression on Pennsylvania's black community, emphasizing the emergence of new forms of interracial and intraracial conflict and cooperation. Finally, Part IV traces the impact of the civil rights and Black Power movements and analyzes the impact of deindustrialization, rising unemployment, and the spread of urban poverty during the late twentieth century.

A number of people helped to make this book possible. First and most important, we wish to thank the Pennsylvania Historical and Museum Commission, the Pennsylvania State University Press, particularly editor Peter Potter, and the Department of History at Carnegie Mellon University. These institutions provided necessary resources for bringing the project to completion. At the PHMC, we are indebted to Brent Glass, Bob Weible, Diane Reed, and Linda Shopes for their ongoing commitment and support of our work. At Carnegie Mellon, we owe special debts to Steven Schlossman, Chair of the Department of History; Peter N. Stearns, Dean of the College of Humanities and Social Science; Mark Kamlet, Dean of the H. John Heinz III School of Public Policy and Management; Provost Paul Christiano, President Emeritus Richard M. Cyert; and Former President Robert M. Mehrabian.

We are also indebted to members of the PHMC's Black History Advisory Committee, which gave us critical comments on the overall focus of the project and helped us avoid crucial errors. Among the many members of the Committee, we are especially grateful to James Trotman and Ruth Hodge for their helpful input. For his critical comments on the book, we wish to thank our friend Laurence Glasco at the University of Pittsburgh. Larry's insightful criticisms and encouragement are deeply appreciated. Likewise, the perceptive reading of two anonymous reviewers for the Pennsylvania State University Press greatly enhanced our efforts and we are in their debt. To these diligent scholars, we extend our sincere thanks. Although we found it difficult to act on all of the important suggestions that we received, we believe that this is a better collection as a result of the careful comments of our colleagues and friends.

This project also benefited from the careful work of our clerical and administrative assistants. For her careful typing of the manuscript, we extend our special gratitude to Elaine Burrelli, administrative assistant at Carnegie Mellon University's Center for Africanamerican Urban Studies and the Economy (CAUSE). In addition, Joe Trotter wishes to thank his wife LaRue and his many sisters, brothers, nieces, and nephews for their ongoing encouragement and support.

Finally, we thank the African American people who made Pennsylvania's black history, and the many scholars who have diligently worked to tell their story. To them, we respectfully dedicate this book.

NOTE: Except for occasional mechanical changes and the addition of some photographs, the essays and articles are reprinted in their original form.

Pennsylvania's African American History:

A Review of the Literature

Joe W. Trotter Jr.

Scholarship on Pennsylvania's black history mirrors the larger study of African Americans in U.S. society. Until the era of the modern civil rights movement, historians largely ignored the role of blacks in the development of the state and the nation.[1] Fortunately, the state's black history received substantial attention in the general histories of nineteenth-century black historians—Robert Benjamin Lewis, William Wells Brown, James C. Pennington, Martin R. Delany, and George Washington Williams, among others. As noted elsewhere, these pioneers included ministers who used the Bible as both source material and inspiration to combat charges of racial inferiority. Like their white counterparts, however, early black historians wrote narrative histories and advanced theological interpretations of the black experience.[2]

Under the growing impact of professionalization during the late nineteenth and early twentieth century, a new generation of university-trained historians of black history emerged. Whereas the nineteenth-century pioneers used history to combat prevailing racist notions that God or "nature" had ordained a lowly position for blacks in American society, the new black writers and their white allies used history to counteract an even more destructive claim—that scientific evidence proved the intellectual, social, and cultural inferiority of blacks. The first generation of professional historians not only accented the destructive impact of racism on the lives of African Americans, but also noted their achievements and contributions to the nation's history despite adversity. Propertied, educated, and elite blacks, particularly men, gained substantial attention in these studies.[3]

Only during the onset of the modern civil rights and Black Power movements and their aftermath would scholars of the black experience produce a broader and more inclusive class and gender history of African Americans. The late-twentieth-century studies not only focused on the lives of ordinary, poor, and working-class black men and women, but also emphasized how they shaped their own lives as well as the institutions, politics, and culture of their communities. At the same time that such studies helped to revise the old story, they also introduced new chronological, regional, and topical dimensions to the subject.[4]

In order to place this collection within a broader scholarly context, this Introduction examines the transformation of the state's black historiography from its early beginnings to the present. Specifically, it explores the pioneering works of the nineteenth century; the contributions of professional historians during the early to mid-twentieth century; and, in recent times, studies of the civil rights and post–civil rights eras. Although a variety of doctoral dissertations and master's theses enrich the study of African Americans in Pennsylvania, this Introduction focuses on selected books and articles published in scholarly journals.[5]

Nineteenth-Century Pioneers

During the early to mid-nineteenth century, as elsewhere in American society, Pennsylvania's black history was closely intertwined with the struggle against slavery in the South, on the one hand, and the fight against reenslavement, deportation, and disfranchisement in the North, on the other. The nineteenth-century pioneers responded to these struggles by producing studies that defended blacks against charges of inferiority and justified emancipation. While these pioneers take the nation as their focus, they treat Pennsylvania's African American community as a major key to the history of blacks in the United States. Equally important, they also illustrate the strong religious commitments of early black historians.

As suggested above, the early-nineteenth-century scholars wrote narrative histories and framed their accounts in biblical terms. They emphasized the "fatherhood of God" and the "brotherhood of man."[6] Both implicitly and explicitly, these writers responded to the proslavery arguments of southern slaveholders, to popular beliefs about the white man's "manifest destiny" to subjugate the continent, and to widespread notions about the racial inferiority of African peoples.[7] In his brief *Text Book of the Origin and History of the Colored People,* for example, clergyman J. W. C. Pennington of New York initiated his study with the biblical creation story. He emphasized one source of the human family and refuted the notion that blacks were doomed by a divine curse to live their lives as drawers of water and hewers of wood for their white counterparts. Supplementing his biblical sources with events in the lives of blacks in Africa and the New World, Pennington condemned slavery and color prejudice as a sickness that abhorred the truth and threatened to carry "the total nation down to a state of refined heathenism." Indeed, according to Pennington, whites required the sympathy and prayers of blacks because of the destructive impact of their illness.[8]

Other pioneer black historians supported the arguments of Pennington. In *The Black Man,* William Wells Brown highlighted the lives of "individuals, who, by their own genius, capacity, and intellectual development" surmounted the obstacles of "slavery and prejudice" and "raised themselves to positions of honor and influence."[9] Brown believed that countless other blacks could reach similar heights if only the barriers to their advance were removed. As he put it, "All I demand for the black man is that the white people shall take their heels off his neck, and let him have a chance to rise by his own effort."[10] Like Pennington, Brown also emphasized the hand of God in human affairs, arguing that "civilization is handed down from one people to another, its great fountain and source being God our Father."[11]

Even more so than Brown and Pennington, Martin R. Delany highlighted discrimination against blacks and defended them against charges of inferiority. Born near Charles Town, Virginia (now West Virginia) around 1812, by the mid-1820s Delany had moved with his family to the Pittsburgh region, where he was educated and later established the black newspaper *The Mystery* in 1843. In his *Condition, Elevation, Emigration, and Destiny of the Colored People of the United States,* Delany emphasized the connection between the slavery of blacks in the South and the status of free blacks in the North.[12] He believed, with few exceptions, that black "freemen in the non-slaveholding States" occupied the "very same position, politically, religiously, civilly, and socially . . . as the bondman" of the slave states.[13] Although Delany also believed in the hand of God in history, he criticized blacks for expecting "Him to do that for them, which it is necessary they should do themselves."[14] Delany asserted that "there are no people more religious in this country, than the colored people, and none so poor and miserable as they."[15] In his effort to develop a program for the full emancipation of slaves and free blacks, Delany hoped to combine what he called the spiritual, moral, and physical laws of God and nature. In conclusion, however, he

despaired and sought solutions to the problems of free blacks outside the
United States. Until the onset of the Civil War, he became a staunch advocate
of free black emigration to Central and South America to establish a beach-
head for the liberation of slaves in the South.[16]

George Washington Williams wrote the most comprehensive study of the
black population during the nineteenth century. Born in 1849 in Bedford,
Virginia, Williams moved with his family to western Pennsylvania in 1850,
first to Johnstown and then to New Castle just north of Pittsburgh, where he
lived until he enlisted in the Union Army during the Civil War. In his two-
volume *History of the Negro Race in America*, Williams reinforced themes
first established in studies by Pennington, Brown, Nell, and others. Trained
as a Baptist minister at the Newton Theological Institution near Boston, Williams opened his study by emphasizing the divine "unity of mankind"—
"one race," "one blood," and "one language." Although he suggested that
belief in the curse of Canaan receded following the Civil War, he concluded
that "the folly of the obsolete theory should be thoroughly understood by the
young men of the Negro race who, though voting now, were not born when
Sumter was fired upon."[17] Like his nineteenth-century counterparts, Williams
affirmed his belief in the Bible and concluded that in the "interpretation of
History the plans of God must be discerned," but unlike his earlier contemporaries he moved substantially beyond a religious interpretation of the black
experience. Even in his effort to refute the charge of the biblical curse, he
acknowledged a growing dependence on scientific as well as biblical knowledge: "I am alive to the fact, that, while I am a believer in the Holy Bible, it
is not the best authority on ethnology. . . . Whatever science has added I have
gladly appropriated."[18]

Pennsylvanians figured prominently in the writings of the nineteenth-century pioneers. William Wells Brown's biographical sketches and narratives
included Charlotte L. Forten, William Still, George Vashon, William Douglas, and Robert Purvis. Brown approvingly quoted at length from Robert
Purvis: "In the matter of rights there is but one race, and that is the *human
race*. 'God has made of one blood all nations to dwell on all the face of the
earth. . . .' Sir, this is our country as much as it is yours, *and we will not
leave it.*"[19] For his part, Delany discussed Pennsylvania blacks' contributions
to the Revolutionary War and business, agricultural, mechanical, and professional pursuits.[20] More important, he pinpointed Pennsylvanians—Richard
Allen, James Forten, and others—as key figures in the political struggles of
blacks in the nation, particularly their rejection of the American Colonization
Society (ACS) effort to colonize free blacks in Africa. Delany also suggested
that Pennsylvania blacks not only played a role but also took the lead in the
antislavery movement. "Anti-Slavery took its rise among *colored men*. . . .

Our Anti-Slavery [white] brethren were converts of the colored men, in be-half of elevation."[21]

In his study of blacks in the Revolutionary War and the War of 1812, William Cooper Nell covered the experiences of black Pennsylvanians at home and at war.[22] His study illuminates the experiences of such Pennsylvania soldiers as Major Jeffrey, John Johnson, John Davis, and James Derham, and, on the home front, Bishop Allen and Absalom Jones.[23] Nell also discussed the Christiana riot, where blacks killed one white slave catcher and mortally wounded another. His account shows how several white townspeople supported blacks and were consequently tried for levying war against the federal government along with blacks, but all were acquitted in what was the nation's largest mass indictment for treason.[24] Similarly, in his two-volume study, George Washington Williams emphasized the tensions that the reality of slavery and the preachings of liberty caused for the commonwealth: "When England began to breathe out threatenings against her contumacious dependencies in North America, the people of Pennsylvania began to reflect upon the probable outrages their Negroes would, in all probability, commit. They inferred that the Negroes would be their enemy because they were their slaves. This was the equitable findings of a guilty conscience."[25]

Although nineteenth-century black historians faced an uphill battle against racism, some white abolitionists encouraged the work of black writers. In her introduction to William Cooper Nell's *Colored Patriots of the American Revolution*, Harriet Beecher Stowe acknowledged that blacks were "generally considered by their enemies, and sometimes even by their friends, as deficient in energy and courage." She then concluded that Nell's book would "redeem the character of the race from this misconception."[26] Similarly, Wendell Phillips supported the black historian's effort "to stem the tide of prejudice against the colored race." He added, "The white man despises the colored man, and has come to think him fit only for the menial drudgery to which the majority of the race has been so long doomed."[27]

Although some nineteenth-century whites supported the findings of nineteenth-century black pioneers, it would take another generation of black historians and their white allies to bring the state's black history under detailed analysis. The achievements and limitations of this scholarship are the subject of the next section.

Early-Twentieth-Century Professionals

The nineteenth-century pioneers gave way to a new generation of professional historians during the late nineteenth and early twentieth century. These scholars offered more rigorous, systematic, and analytical contributions to the state's black history than their nineteenth-century predecessors did. The new historians emphasized the positive contributions of African Americans to Pennsylvania and to American society, pinpointed the artificial barriers they had to overcome, and sanctioned the equal participation of blacks and whites in the life of the Commonwealth. Although the state's black population continued to gain treatment within the larger studies of blacks in America,[28] this period ushered in more specialized studies of Pennsylvania's history.

State-level studies by Edward Raymond Turner and Richard Wright epitomized the emergence of the new history. Turner and Wright moved beyond efforts to discern the hand of God in human affairs and emphasized the impact of social forces.[29] Focusing on the colonial origins through the Civil War, Turner aimed "to give a complete account of the legal, social, and economic history of the Pennsylvania Negro in his rise from slavery to freedom."[30] Written under the direction of Johns Hopkins University professor James Curtis Ballagh, Turner's book made extensive use of manuscript collections, statistical data, and newspapers among other primary accounts— that is, the hallmarks of the emerging historical profession.

Although Turner acknowledged the role that blacks played in shaping their own experience, he stressed the role of the attitudes and behavior of whites toward blacks. He related the relatively small numbers of blacks in the early development of the state "to economic and industrial causes, and also to the effective opposition of many of the white people" to slavery.[31] When the state passed a gradual abolition act in 1780, the first of its kind in the nation, he emphasized "economic causes," the role of the Quakers, and "the enthusiasm attending upon the Revolutionary War."[32] In the aftermath of the gradual emancipation law and the slow but steady increase of free blacks in the state, Turner again accented the role of the Friends, the abolitionists, and the antislavery advocates: "They helped and encouraged the Negro, they protected him, and upheld his rights. To them largely was due the abolition of slavery, the suppression of the local slave trade, and the management of the underground railroad."[33]

On the other hand, like the early pioneers, Turner recognized barriers that whites erected against the full participation of African Americans in the life of the state. He argued that the first blacks shared a status of servitude with whites but that "as time went on there arose differences and discriminations, the inevitable incidents of life service, which tended to make the status decidedly inferior."[34] Even after attaining freedom, Turner concluded that "the growth of race prejudice" prevented progress.[35] Such prejudice persisted, "so that in Pennsylvania there was none of the race equality which was assumed by Reconstruction statesmen in the solution of Southern problems after the Civil War."[36] Yet, even as Turner emphasized the incidence of race prejudice, he related the intensification of such prejudice to the increasing "influx of Negroes from the South, the apparent deterioration in character, the immense increase in crime, and the rising pretensions of the Negroes themselves."[37]

The historian Richard R. Wright Jr. also advanced a new "scientific" history of the state's black population.[38] Wright received his Ph.D. degree from the University of Pennsylvania in 1911 and later became a bishop in the African Methodist Episcopal Church. In 1912 he published his dissertation, *The Negro in Pennsylvania: A Study in Economic History.* More so than Turner, however, Wright described the "Negro problem" as a problem of white racism and stressed the role of whites in creating both a caste and class system. "The 'Negro Problem'—that condition which is peculiar to Negroes, and common to them—is rather found in the attitudes of the white race toward the Negro; an attitude of a majority which seeks to shut out a minority from the enjoyment of the whole social and economic life. It is an attitude which . . . only complicates the general problems of crime, of ignorance, of poverty, etc., among Negroes, which some mistake for the 'Negro Problem.' "[39] On the one hand, in contrast to Turner, Wright believed that the migrants of the pre–Civil War years represented "many of the best of the Southern Negroes."[40] On the other hand, however, Wright argued that the Civil War disrupted this positive stream of black migrants and brought to Pennsylvania many of the "ex-slaves of the more ignorant type."[41] Yet, Wright shows how these migrants established the foundations for the rise of a new black professional and business class during the Reconstruction years. "It is upon these incoming Negroes and these alone, that the Negroes begin to rise and to diversify their occupations."[42] At the same time that Wright emphasized dimensions of intraracial class formation, he also advanced a class analysis of racism. He argued that discrimination increased as one ascended the social ladder from poor to elite blacks. "In the economically and intellectually lowest stratum—that of the pauper and criminal—there is but little race problem."[43]

While emphasizing the role of Pennsylvania in establishing a caste and class system, Wright nonetheless documented the state's role in destroying the system of slavery. Describing the state as "the parent of the movement for the abolition of Negro slavery," he gave Pennsylvania credit for providing leadership in the crusade against human bondage: "For not only was the first protest against slave trade in this country made here, but here the underground railroad was probably started; here the first anti-slavery society was

organized; here was the first trial of gradual abolition by law, and here numerous pioneer movements for the emancipation of the slaves and the betterment
of the condition of the freedmen found fertile soil and vigorous growth."[44]

A variety of regional, county, and local studies reinforced the insights of
Turner and Wright. These studies unfolded in three interrelated clusters. One
set focused primarily on slavery, abolition, and the Underground Railroad.
Compared with slavery in the South, these studies emphasized the minor role
of slaves and slavery in the commercial economy of Pennsylvania. Such studies also accented the very positive role of Pennsylvania whites, particularly
Quakers, in the abolition of slavery in the state and the nation.[45] A second
cluster of studies analyzed specific aspects of African American community
life—business, religious, civil rights, and political institutions and leadership.
Studies of black community life illuminated the ways that African Americans, particularly black elites, developed their own responses to racial proscription.[46] Finally, while most of the first and second groups were explicitly
historical in approach, a third set was primarily urban sociological studies
with secondary historical components. These included studies by Ira Reid,
Clara Hardin, and W. E. B. Du Bois, whose *Philadelphia Negro* emerged as
the first and most influential of these works.[47]

In *The Philadelphia Negro*, Du Bois articulated his commitment to a scientific—that is, "objective"—approach to his subject. He assessed a variety of
sources and even criticized some of those generated by friends and sympathizers as too biased to be taken alone: "Unfortunately, however, the Friends'
investigations are not altogether free from suspicion of bias in favor of the
Negro, the census reports are very general and newspaper articles necessarily
hurried and inaccurate. This study seeks to cull judiciously from all these
sources and others, and to add to them specifically collected data for the
years 1896 and 1897."[48]

Based upon a solid corpus of primary and secondary documents, including
legislative acts and his own doctoral dissertation on the suppression of the
African slave trade, Du Bois placed the study of Philadelphia blacks within
the larger historical context of the rise of slavery and the transition to freedom
in Pennsylvania. According to Du Bois, the city's black population made
progress in the aftermath of emancipation during the late eighteenth and early
nineteenth century, followed by a period of decline during the 1820s and
1830s. He emphasized not only the destructive impact of immigrant competition and prejudice against blacks, but also the negative influence of new
black migrants on the city's established black residents. Comparing the two
periods, he concluded:

> If, as in 1790, the new freedmen had been given peace and quiet and
> abundant work to develop sensible and aspiring leaders, the end

would have been different; but a mass of poverty-stricken, ignorant fugitives and ill-trained freedmen had rushed to the city, swarmed in the vile slums which the rapidly growing city furnished, and met in social and economic competition equally ignorant but more vigorous foreigners. These foreigners outbid them at work, beat them on the streets, and were enabled to do this by the prejudice which Negro crime and the anti-slavery sentiment aroused in the city.[49]

In the aftermath of the Civil War, Du Bois argued that a brief period of material progress was again disrupted. Again, he stressed the influence of the increasing migration of newly emancipated slaves from the South, as well as the impact of white racial hostility and economic competition. "Thus we see that twice the Philadelphia Negro has, with a fair measure of success, begun an interesting social development, and *twice through the migration of bar-barians* [black and white] *a dark age has settled on his age of revival* [italics added]."[50]

The Philadelphia Negro not only advanced scholarship on the city and state's black history. It helped to launch the fields of American and African American urban sociology and established the intellectual foundations for the growth of black urban history as a field. Yet *The Philadelphia Negro* and other sociological studies offered an attenuated view of history that served mainly as a backdrop to the story of contemporary black Pittsburgh and Philadelphia. Moreover, like the early-twentieth-century historical scholarship, the sociological studies documented African American contributions to the growth of the state as well as the impact of racism, but neglected important class and gender dimensions of the black experience. They offered little insight into the ways that the black poor, workers, and women experienced the impact of racial restrictions and devised their own responses to such barriers. Fortunately, the new social, political, and intellectual movements of the 1960s and 1970s would dramatically change perspectives on African Americans in the state and nation.

Civil Rights and Black Power Era Studies

Under the impact of the modern civil rights, Black Power, and social history movements, studies of Pennsylvania's black history proliferated. Unlike the earlier scholarship, the new studies emphasized the perspectives, ideas, and activities of African Americans themselves. Civil rights and Black Power era scholarship deepened our understanding of slavery and abolition, added studies of small black communities like those in Harrisburg and Steelton, and placed increasing emphasis on the role of black workers and the poor. Historical research and writing on the state's black history also became much more specialized than before. Although some brief general studies emerged,[51] scholars increasingly carved out aspects of the eighteenth, nineteenth, and twentieth centuries as their distinct areas of expertise. Taken together, these new historical studies complemented earlier approaches and illuminated how African Americans shaped their own history from the colonial era through the mid-twentieth century. Still, important cultural issues, the role of women, and the dynamics of gender relations only slowly gained attention. It is in these areas that much work remains to be done.

Colonial Origins

African American life during the colonial era received substantial attention. Studies of the colonial period supplemented traditional sources with new quantitative techniques and data, demonstrated how slavery was a significant rather than negligible factor in Pennsylvania's history, reinterpreted the role of Quakers in the slave trade and the abolitionist movement, and comprehended the experiences of bondage and freedom from the vantage point of African Americans.[52] In his study of slavery in Philadelphia (Chapter 1 in the present volume), social historian Gary B. Nash used a variety of records—death, burial, baptism, shipping, and tax records, along with other traditional sources—to establish a more precise estimate of the extent and use of slave labor in the colony.[53] Unlike previous studies, Nash concluded that Quaker involvement in the slave trade was greater than previously assumed. Slave artisans and craftsmen were particularly important to the urban economy. Despite the efforts of Quaker abolitionists like John Woolman and Anthony Benezet, according to Nash, only the increasing availability of "cheap" white servants led to the Quakers' abandonment of slavery during the late eighteenth century.

Research by Darold D. Wax anticipated as well as reinforced Nash's emphasis on the significance of the slave trade and slavery to Pennsylvania's early commercial economy.[54] More than 1,200 slaves entered the Delaware River valley area between 1759 and 1765, about 75 percent directly from Africa. Moreover, according to Wax the intensification of the slave trade in these years represented a continuity of developments from the late seventeenth century, although before the 1750s most slaves entered the state via the West Indies and South Carolina rather than directly from Africa. Wax concluded that by the American Revolution slavery was well established in eastern Pennsylvania and that "white residents grew accustomed to a black presence and the many exterior signs [advertisements for both the sale of slaves and the recapture of runaways] that theirs was a slave society."[55]

By accenting the significance of slavery to the colonial economy, studies of this period also highlighted occupational diversity among slaves. Nash emphasized the role of skilled slave craftsmen in the commercial economy of Philadelphia; Wax documented the regional use of slave labor in manufacturing, shipping, and agriculture; and Joseph Walker focused on the use of slaves in the charcoal iron industry in Berks, Chester, Montgomery, Lancaster, Dauphin, and York counties.[56] In Berks County, Richard Johnson also noted that "quite a few blacks became skilled workers, mastered several languages, and held responsible positions." Conversely, in his study of Lancaster, Jerome Wood concluded that blacks were mainly domestic servants and "were never a factor in the economic life of the borough." As he put it, "They served rather as advertisements of their owners' high economic and social status."[57] Alan Tully's study of slaveholding in Chester and Lancaster counties reinforced Wood's conclusions: "In the rural society of early Southeastern Pennsylvania the value of a slave, like the value of various pieces of personal property depended, in part at least, on his role as a status conferring possession."[58] Tully and Wood undoubtedly underplayed the economic use of slaves in rural areas, but their focus on domestic slavery helped to underscore the diverse uses of slave labor in colonial Pennsylvania.

Along with expanding knowledge of slavery and race as integral parts of the state's colonial beginnings, scholars deepened our understanding of slavery and freedom from the vantage point of bondsmen. Civil rights and post–civil rights era studies documented a great deal of diversity and complexity in the demographic, economic, social, and institutional experiences of blacks. Earlier studies had compared slavery in Pennsylvania and other northern states to southern plantation slavery and concluded that it was a relatively mild experience, but the new writers gave significant attention to slave mortality and fertility rates, emphasizing the inability of slaves to reproduce themselves when heavy imports ceased. According to Nash, writing in 1973, life was quite deadly for northern urban workers, free and slave, white and black alike.[59] A decade later, however, Susan Klepp reexamined quantitative evidence on mortality rates by race and concluded that black slaves "faced substantially higher risks of death in Philadelphia than did free or dependent whites."[60] More specifically, Klepp argued that race intensified for Africans "the customary treatment" of the so-called "inferior persons" by their "social superiors."[61]

Revolutionary and Early Nineteenth Century

As scholars of the civil rights era deepened our perspective on slavery and race during the colonial era, they also expanded our knowledge of the abolitionist movement and development of free African American communities in the wake of the American Revolution and the growth of the new nation. Studies by Carl Oblinger, Theodore Hershberg, G. S. Rowe, Leslie C. Patrick-Stamp, and others illuminate changes in the socioeconomic position of blacks during and following the process of gradual emancipation.[62] While the emancipation of blacks in the wake of the Revolution represented a real achievement, these scholars argue that such freedom was offset by the pressures of racial discrimination, the rising numbers of Irish immigrants, and the proximity of two slave states. Carl Oblinger examined the lives of some 15,000 poor blacks in Lancaster and Chester counties between 1780 and 1860. According to Oblinger, free blacks often became "transient paupers" who faced imprisonment, the almshouse, family breakup, and the loss of their children. Such pressures led nearly 25 percent of the black men and women that Oblinger studied into severe poverty.[63]

The second generation of professional historians criticized the sources, methodology, and theoretical perspectives of existing studies. In his seminal essay "Free Blacks in Antebellum Philadelphia" (Chapter 4 in this volume), Theodore Hershberg advanced perhaps the sharpest critique of his predecessors. With a few notable exceptions, he argued that the literature "lacks a solid empirical base, a sophisticated methodological and theoretical approach, and a focus on the black community itself."[64] Based upon extensive quantitative analysis of abolitionist, Quaker, and U.S. censuses, and on W. E. B. Du Bois's *Philadelphia Negro,* Hershberg concluded that urban social conditions created special problems for blacks over and beyond those produced by slavery. He found more poverty among Philadelphia-born free blacks than among recent ex-slave migrants to the city. Thus, he called for a theoretical reconceptualization of black urban life—one that would connect some aspects of Philadelphia's black experience to "the processes of urbanization, industrialization and immigration, occurring in a setting of racial inequality, rather than to slavery."[65]

Civil rights era scholars gradually reexamined the statutes regulating black life in the early republic and reinterpreted the issue of black criminality. Focusing on sixteen counties and the city of Philadelphia between 1780 and 1800, G. S. Rowe concluded that "theft lay at the heart of the eighteenth-century black criminal experience."[66] For Rowe, however, it was "theft born of need" rather than any moral or character defects or even "a calculated revenge against Philadelphia's propertied classes."[67] According to Rowe, blacks were also prosecuted for their offenses in rising numbers because propertied white elites were developing a broader American preoccupation with "safeguarding property and property rights."[68] By emphasizing the way poverty underlay theft within the larger context of an evolving oppressive capitalist economy, Rowe not only helped to shift attention away from black crime as evidence of their inferiority and low moral character, but also modified recent efforts to reinterpret theft as a deliberate and calculated mode of resistance to economic and racially based exploitation. As he put it, "Generally, blacks . . . stole life necessities, clothing, food, small amounts of money or items like watches which could quickly be converted to cash."[69]

While Rowe responded to both the old and the new scholarship, early studies framed social historian Leslie C. Patrick-Stamp's work on class, race, and crime during the Revolutionary and early national period. In her essay on blacks in Philadelphia's Jail and Penitentiary House at Walnut Street, the state's and nation's first prison, Patrick-Stamp not only criticized Turner for his assertion that "black people were averse to work and prone to criminality," but challenged Du Bois's argument that newcomers from the South accounted for the bulk of black criminal behavior in the city.[70] Based upon the dockets of the Walnut Street facility, Patrick-Stamp demonstrates that class and racial factors played important roles in the disproportionate incarceration rates of African Americans. Moreover, she concludes that "not all black immigrants to Pennsylvania came from Southern states." Some came to Pennsylvania from other northern states, from the Caribbean, and from the continent of Africa itself. Furthermore, according to Patrick-Stamp, "upon arriving in Pennsylvania, or even if they had been born in the state, these black people encountered impediments to supporting or sustaining themselves."[71]

If studies of black criminality revealed the destitution and poverty of African Americans in the face of adversity, research on black institution-building, political, and civil rights activities unveiled their resilience and creativity.[72] Such studies demonstrate that the black population developed its own strategies for dealing with class and racial subordination. In his book *Forging Freedom*, Gary B. Nash examines the experiences of Philadelphia blacks from their enslavement during the seventeenth century through the early national period. His story revolves around the notion of "tragedy and triumph"—the failure of Pennsylvania to live up to its promise to produce an equitable multiracial society, on the one hand, and the extraordinary success of Philadelphia blacks in forging a community ("not only a geographic clustering of former slaves but also a community of feeling and consciousness"), on the other. As such, *Forging Freedom* is partly a story of leaders—"some inspired, others frail; but it is also a reckoning of ordinary people making choices, searching for solutions to their own problems, and determining the course of their own lives as best they could."[73]

Other studies documented the responses of blacks to their status, from disfranchisement in 1837 through the difficult years of the Fugitive Slave

Law in the 1850s. A series of case studies emphasized the role of blacks rather than whites in the activities of the Underground Railroad. In his study of Robert Purvis and the formation of the Philadelphia Vigilance Committee in 1837, for example, historian Joseph Borome shows how blacks organized "to protect fugitives as well as free Negroes from slave catchers and kidnappers." Similarly, R. J. M. Blackett analyzed the response of Pittsburgh blacks to the Fugitive Slave Law of 1850 (see Chapter 5 in this volume). Although Pittsburgh's black community did not develop a vigilance committee, as their Philadelphia counterparts did, the city's black Philanthropic Society (formed during the 1830s) "acted as the defensive arm of the community" and helped fugitives escape to freedom.[74] Of course, as Blackett put it, some of the society's functions overlapped with other aspects of black community life. The African American community itself was "one of resistance to racial aspersion and the development of institutions to cater to needs of blacks in a rapidly expanding industrial economy." Historian Charles Blockson played a key role in popularizing the scholarly shift from emphases on whites to the role of blacks in the state's Underground Railroad. Blockson argued forcefully that African Americans developed their own underground resistance movement.[75]

While some historians focused on the activities of the Underground Railroad, others examined African American responses to racial proscription and violence against Pennsylvania's own free black population. Social historian Emma Jones Lapsansky elaborated upon black institution-building activities and helped to revamp our understanding of racial violence in nineteenth-century Pennsylvania and America (see Chapter 3). According to Lapsansky, Philadelphia's black community and its leaders developed a set of interlocking ideas of their own: economic security, public safety, and social status. The dynamic interplay of these factors made the causes of antiblack violence and tensions quite complex (there were five major riots against the black community between 1834 and 1849). In each of the major riots, the mobs attacked one of the following symbols of "success": churches, meeting halls, and property of outstanding black leaders. At a certain level, Lapsansky concludes that "while the white mobs were expressing their frustrations at their own social immobility black people [particularly black elites] for their part were concerned with publicly exhibiting the proof of their progress toward the respectable life."[76]

Lapsansky's point is well taken. Philadelphia's black community was internationally known as the most vibrant intellectually, economically, and politically active free black community in the nation at the time. In her study of Philadelphia's black elite, for example, Julie Winch emphasized the ways that this elite derived its power from "a complex network of autonomous black organizations, which offered able and articulate men and women within the community a basis for extending their authority and developing the skills they would require to oversee city-wide and, in some cases, national organizations."[77] Moreover, according to Winch, unlike the white elite, for whom wealth and influence were quite synonymous, skill and commitment to the cause of racial uplift were more important for black elites than wealth. Such criteria, according to Winch, created a structure that was more fluid and permeable for blacks from the poor and working classes to obtain access.[78] Although Winch undoubtedly exaggerates the influence of noneconomic factors in the rise of the black elite, her study demonstrates in convincing detail its dynamic leadership role between 1787 and 1848.

Some studies of race relations, education, and politics linked antebellum, Reconstruction, and late-nineteenth-century black Pennsylvania. Leroy T. Hopkins not only analyzed the experiences of Lancaster's blacks during the Civil War years but placed those experiences within the broader context of the antebellum era (see Chapter 7). He shows how the black community faced disfranchisement, the "Columbia race riots" of 1834–35, and mounting racial hatreds following the "Manheim Tragedy," which involved the execution of two black men for the rape and murder of two white women of German descent. Lancaster's hostile antebellum racial climate stiffened white resistance to black participation in the Civil War as citizens and as soldiers. Thus, for Hopkins, the "Columbia race riots" and the hostility of whites were more characteristic of white racial attitudes and practices than the "Christiana Riot," in which local whites helped fugitive slaves escape to freedom.[79]

Edward Price analyzed the complicated transition from exclusion to segregation in the state's public school system. During the long period of exclusion before the Civil War, Price shows how blacks responded with a plethora of self-help educational activities. In the wake of the Civil War and Reconstruction, however, African Americans mobilized politically on the local and state levels and demanded equal access to public education. In 1881, the state legislature passed a law eliminating all distinctions based on color or race. Rather than initiating the full and equal access of blacks to education in the state, however, Price shows how the law ushered in a new era of de facto racial segregation.[80] Focusing on nineteenth-century Pittsburgh, Ann G. Wilmoth reinforced emphasis on early self-help traditions but stressed how blacks viewed education as a key "to upward mobility and as a means through which they could secure their civil rights." Harry C. Silcox confirms Wilmoth's point in his essay on Octavius V. Catto, a teacher at Philadelphia's Institute for Colored Youth and a victim of Election Day violence in October 1871[81] (see Chapter 8). Other studies also suggest the relationship between education and black politics.[82]

Unlike most studies that bridged the early and late nineteenth century, Gerald G. Eggert's essay (Chapter 9 in this book) focuses on black life in Harrisburg, a medium-sized rather than large urban center. While Harrisburg showed important similarities with larger cities across time, Eggert emphasized unique features. The migration of southern blacks to Pittsburgh and Philadelphia escalated during the post–Civil War years and intensified during the era of the Great Migration, while Harrisburg's black population increased notably in the first few years after the Civil War but thereafter dropped as a proportion of the city's population through the mid-twentieth century. Moreover, the city itself shifted from an industrial base during the late nineteenth century to an increasingly governmental and administrative city. Compared with larger cities in the state and nation, Eggert concludes, there were few opportunities for a black industrial proletariat to emerge and for the small segregated black community to develop into a huge ghetto.[83] Eggert's comparative insights are largely confirmed by a close analysis of late-nineteenth- and twentieth-century scholarship.

Late Nineteenth and Early Twentieth Century

Migration, work, and the transformation of black urban communities emerged at the core of scholarship on the late nineteenth and early twentieth century. Such studies emphasized the comparative experiences of black and white workers, particularly those of new immigrant origins; the impact of southern black migration on interracial and intraracial class relations; and especially the emergence of new social, political, and cultural movements as southern blacks dramatically increased their number and percentage of the state's black population. Although Pittsburgh and Philadelphia retained the spotlight, small centers of black population also gradually gained attention. John E. Bodnar examined the impact of the new immigrant workers on blacks in Steelton between 1880 and 1920 (see Chapter 10). He showed that industrial communities like Steelton had attracted black laborers before the onset of the New Immigration, mainly Southern Slavs and a few Italians.[84]

According to Bodnar, African Americans achieved their highest occupational advances by 1905. They had fewer of their numbers in unskilled jobs than white immigrants, but they had established three churches and a newspaper. Thereafter, however, under the increasing influx of new immigrants, African Americans started to lose their foothold. Indeed, of all ethnic groups only blacks experienced a decline in numbers between 1890 and 1910. As Bodnar put it, black workers "were not only losing semiskilled occupations to Slavs and Italians but, consequently, [were] being forced to leave their Northern homes, presumably in search of work, at an increasing rate." Although World War I would curtail European immigration and usher in a new era of black migration, Bodnar concluded that the newcomers would have "to start their economic climb over again—from the bottom."[85]

Complementing Bodnar's study is Dennis C. Dickerson's examination of black steelworkers in western Pennsylvania between 1875 and 1980 (Chapter 16). "Race, not class," Dickerson argues, fundamentally shaped the status of black workers and created "the poverty and unemployment which perennially afflicts them."[86] Drawing upon a broad range of secondary and primary sources, including oral interviews of surviving steelworkers, Dickerson documents the persistence of racial discrimination in the hiring, promotion, and job assignment of black workers. Although the first generation of black iron and steel workers enjoyed a relatively high status, marked by employment in a variety of skilled positions, Dickerson, like Bodnar, concludes that they failed to gain the economic and social security necessary for the advancement of succeeding generations of black migrants. Management, foremen, unions, technological changes, and rank-and-file white workers, all working in tandem, relegated blacks to the most difficult, hot, low paying, and insecure rungs of the industrial ladder.[87] Indeed, he suggests, "After more than a century as steel employees, Black workers in Pittsburgh, Homestead, Braddock, Clairton, Johnstown, and many other mill communities finally attained equality with whites as they stepped together into local unemployment lines."[88]

Dickerson's book is not only the story of persistence and change in the economic status of black steelworkers. It is also the story of the complex interplay between changes in the labor market experience of black workers and their larger institutional, social, and political life. Dickerson provides substantial insight into black steelworkers' religious, fraternal, political, civil rights, and leisure activities, especially for the era of Great Migration. His *Out of the Crucible* includes illuminating analyses of black steelworker preachers, baseball teams (such as the Homestead Grays), and the unusual appeal of the Garvey Movement, not only among working-class blacks but also among members of the small black elite as well: "The versatile Reverend J. C. Austin of Ebenezer Baptist Church and president of the Pittsburgh NAACP was the best-known backer of Marcus Garvey" and, moreover, "the pastor of John Wesley African Methodist Episcopal Zion Church . . . identified his church with the UNIA [Universal Negro Improvement Association], an organization that his parishioners deemed relevant to their quest for social and economic equality."[89]

Historian Peter Gottlieb both reinforced and moved well beyond the insights of Dickerson and Bodnar. Drawing upon the theoretical insights of social science research as well as recent studies by social historians, including oral interviews as well as statistical accounts, Gottlieb analyzed the black migration to Pittsburgh "as a social process" (see Chapter 11 of the present volume). Through "seasonal migration and temporary industrial work within the South," he demonstrates how African Americans "prepared themselves for geographic movements further afield," ultimately leading to their migration to northern industrial centers like Pittsburgh.[90] Based upon numerous oral interviews, company records, newspapers, and a variety of other primary and secondary sources, Gottlieb reconstructs the premigration status of blacks in southern industry and agriculture, as owners, as tenants, and as farm laborers. At the core of the study, however, is the notion of black migration and black working-class formation as "a process of self-transformation," reflected most clearly in the emergence and expansion of black kin, friend, and communal networks.[91]

Gottlieb shows how the prior demographic and economic experiences of rural blacks interacted with the changing socioeconomic conditions of the industrial city and influenced their patterns of work, spatial mobility, and cultural consciousness. In addition to heavy labor and extensive geographic mobility, he accents the persistence of southern attitudes and consciousness among black newcomers to Pittsburgh. Like peasant migrants to industrial cities throughout the world, he concludes that black migrants sought northern wages in order to sustain a traditional "Southern" way of life. Even blacks who settled permanently "in fact lived, worked, socialized, and worshipped primarily among other blacks from the South."[92] Only future generations would become "wholly" northern urban-industrial men and women. Although Gottlieb emphasized the persistence of southern patterns and the role of black workers in shaping their own industrial experiences, he nevertheless recognized important aspects of change and documented a variety of impediments to the occupational mobility of black workers. Using their kinship and communal networks, black migrants fought back, sometimes in dramatic ways, against the forces that would suppress them.[93]

In his analysis of black migration to Philadelphia (Chapter 12 of this volume), Frederic Miller reinforced the principal conclusions of Gottlieb's book. Based upon the 1924 Philadelphia survey of 510 black migrant families, Miller shows that "black migration in the 1920s was a complex process in which broad social and economic forces interacted with personal and family situations."[94] Like Gottlieb, Miller illuminates how blacks came to the city from a variety of regional, occupational, and social backgrounds; even more than Gottlieb, he also shows how migrant experiences in the city "varied by neighborhood, ranging from residential mobility and job turnover in white immigrant South Philadelphia to relative stability, or stagnation, in the traditional ghetto around South Street."[95] Although black migrants gained access to improved educational facilities and a better climate of race relations, Miller's analysis shows that more than 50 percent were "planning or seriously considering returning South."[96] Thus, Gottlieb's emphasis on the continuing pull of the South on black migrants who shifted back and forth between Pittsburgh and their southern homes gains support in evidence from Philadelphia.

Several studies examined the intensification of racial conflict during the industrial transformation of the state's economy. Studies by Dennis Downey, Raymond Hyser, David McBride, Richard Sherman, and V. P. Franklin, among others, deepened our understanding of the causes, meaning, and consequences of racial violence in Pennsylvania and elsewhere during the early twentieth century. Downey and Hyser explored the 1911 lynching of Zachariah Walker in the small industrial town of Coatesville in eastern Pennsylvania. Describing the Coatesville lynching as "a multilayered tragedy, an enduring tragedy at the heart of American life, during the industrial era," Downey and Hyser concluded that the lynching was not a "random act by anonymous individuals," but partly the product of a culture of violence activated by a growing sense of insecurity as blacks migrated to the city and took industrial jobs in rising (though slight) numbers.[97] Like their white southern counterparts, when news that a black man had killed a white company coal and iron policeman, whites invoked a central feature of their culture—"a code of honor and an understanding of manhood that fostered a peculiar notion of chivalry in matters of racial etiquette."[98] In short, according to Downey and Hyser the lynching of Zachariah Walker was no aberration in the state's history but part of a national phenomenon whose roots were deeply planted in Pennsylvania as well as elsewhere.

The new studies demonstrated that state and local governments and the courts heightened racial animosities. Historian David McBride offers an insightful analysis of the state courts' interpretations of Pennsylvania's civil rights laws, which prohibited racial discrimination in public accommodations. While the Pennsylvania courts upheld the state's law, they responded to the U.S. Supreme Court's *Plessy v. Ferguson* decision (which sanctioned separate and unequal treatment of blacks) by restricting interpretations of the law and weakening its impact on racial practices. In other words, before the 1930s Pennsylvania courts emphasized the need to preserve the "integrity of common law, property rights, and the United States Supreme Court's restrictive construction of the fourteenth amendment."[99] During the 1930s, however, the court broke with precedent and "developed a fundamental opposition to the Plessy doctrine" of "separate but equal."[100]

Richard Sherman also emphasizes "the national character of American racial problems" and the role of the government in the Johnstown exodus of

1923. When a black migrant killed two white policemen and mortally wounded another, he shows how the mayor issued an order barring the entry of new blacks and requiring all blacks with fewer than seven years' residence to leave the city. The newly formed branch of the Ku Klux Klan reinforced the mayor's proclamation by intimidating of black residents. Although the city's black population had reached nearly 3,000 by 1923, an estimated three-quarters of blacks soon vacated their homes in the city's Rosedale section. According to Sherman, only the spotlight of national publicity created a sympathetic response among some members of the city's white community.[101] Similarly, V. P. Franklin analyzed the Philadelphia Riot of 1918. He offered an extensive critique of prevailing studies of riots in the urban North at the time. Such studies stressed black victimization both during and after the events. Unlike existing studies, rather than retreating into a period of quiescence, Franklin shows how Philadelphia's black community mobilized, formed the Colored Protective Association, and succeeded in getting the offending white commander and officers removed to another district.[102]

Although most civil rights era scholars emphasized the creative responses of Pennsylvania blacks to growing racial hostility, they acknowledged the incidence of intraracial friction. As the black southern migrant population increased, the black community itself experienced growing tensions. As V. P. Franklin points out (Chapter 13), only the failure of black police officers to testify against their white colleagues seemed to block the convictions of white officers for wrongdoing in the 1918 riot. Moreover, in Pittsburgh and elsewhere, longtime residents expressed displeasure with the growing southern black population. In his study of Philadelphia's African Methodist Episcopal Church, historian Robert Gregg concludes that Robert J. Williams, the church's wartime minister, lost his church under the impact of social tensions generated by the rapid growth of the city's southern black population. The church put its efforts into recruiting the most economically viable of the new residents and neglected the needs of the masses of poor and working-class blacks. According to Gregg, large numbers of the new black Philadelphians turned away from the mainstream black churches like "Mother Bethel" toward "the cults."[103]

Dickerson, Gottlieb, Gregg, and others demonstrate that, despite such tensions, which often pitted northern-born and southern-born workers and elites against each other, black business, professional, and working-class people bridged the class gap and created relatively cohesive (though precarious) black urban communities. A variety of black institutions—newspapers, churches, fraternal orders, social clubs, and civil rights, political, business, professional, leisure time, and labor organizations—reflected the dynamics of racial solidarity. In the fight against discrimination and subordination in the larger socioeconomic, cultural, and political life of Pennsylvania and the United States, black Pennsylvanians of different class, gender, and regional backgrounds often joined forces to advance the interests of the group. The study of black education in Philadelphia by V. P. Franklin is an excellent illustration of this process.

Franklin's book illuminates not only the formal and informal public and community-based aspects of black education, but also the role of the black middle class and elites in fostering educational demands that cut across class lines. Indeed, although he eschews a systematic class analysis of his data, Franklin suggests that cross-class unity characterized African American demands for segregated black schools before the 1930s, as well as demands for desegregation thereafter. "Many middle-class teachers and lower-class black workers were among the supporters of voluntary segregation for black social advancement [during the 1920s]. . . . During the 1930s, however, when public school desegregation was in their best interest, most black teachers supported the campaigns of . . . other middle- and lower-class blacks who lobbied for a change [desegregation] in public school policies and practices."[104] Covering the first fifty years of the twentieth century, Franklin's book offers a useful transition to scholarship on the mid-twentieth century.

The Depression, World War II, and the Civil Rights Era

Research on the Depression, World War II, and the civil rights and Black Power eras is less well developed than research on the nineteenth and early twentieth century. Much of our knowledge of these periods, particularly since World War II, relies on journalistic, literary, sociological, anthropological, political science, and public policy accounts.[105] Yet, historians of Pennsylvania's black history are beginning to chart the very complex and ambiguous transition of the state's black population from the early period of exclusion and segregation to the late-twentieth-century era of integration. Pivotal factors in studies of this transition are the rise of the New Deal coalition of Franklin D. Roosevelt, the Depression, World War II, and the increasing militance of Pennsylvania blacks themselves. Studies by Viscount Nelson, V. P. Franklin, Charles T. Banner-Haley, Alexa Benson Henderson, Constance A. Cunningham, and others illuminate the myriad responses of blacks under the impact of hard times and the emergence of new social welfare programs.[106] For his part, Merl E. Reed analyzes black workers, defense industries, and the federal Fair Employment Practices Committee (FEPC) during the war years (Chapter 15 in the present volume). Reed documents the wartime experiences of African Americans in steel mills, shipyards, the U.S. Postal Service, telephone companies, and other public and private firms and agencies.

According to Reed, only the emergence of wartime conditions and the ongoing protest of black workers themselves brought positive changes in the policies and practices of the unions, the state, and industries alike. Although weak, the FEPC enabled black workers to gain a new and better foothold in public transportation, iron and steel, and shipbuilding industries.[107]

Several studies document the state's institutional transition from segregation to integration. Analyses of black sports, health care, housing, and neighborhood change suggest that the emergence of integration was a bittersweet experience, filled both with hope and with a great deal of disappointment. For the city of Philadelphia, David McBride examined the growth of the segregated black medical establishment during the early 1900s, the rise of a desegregation movement during the late 1940s and 1950s, and the actual integration of blacks into the city's larger medical system by the mid-1960s. McBride concludes that integration produced a "shortage" of black medical practitioners that continues to this day. In Pennsylvania, as elsewhere in America, African Americans found it difficult to move from their earlier segregated but powerful positions in black medical institutions to full participation in predominantly white ones.[108]

In his groundbreaking study of black sports history, Rob Ruck shows how baseball facilitated the creation of a more cohesive black community in Pittsburgh during the era of the Great Migration. Sports helped to bridge the gap between migrant and old resident as well as between classes. Still, similar to blacks in the health professions, the era of the Great Migration and the Depression witnessed the expansion of segregated black baseball, resulting in the rise of black professional teams like the Homestead Grays and the Pittsburgh Crawfords. This pattern would persist through World War II. Thereafter, along with pressure from the commercialization of community-based sports in general, the integration of black players into the previously all-white professional leagues would bring the Negro Leagues to an end. As with medical care, integration was again a bittersweet victory. As Ruck put it,

> Black sandlot ball, along with white sandlot ball, fell victim to a new emphasis on televised commercial sport, a change that ushered in a new era for the black athlete and heightened the perception of sport as an economic passport for black youth. But the cost was high; the black community lost control over its sporting destiny. In the 1960s, sport for black Pittsburgh entered a new phase in which integrated schools, colleges, and pro leagues replaced the sandlots and the Negro leagues. The once-segregated sporting life was largely history.[109]

The bitter side of the transition from segregation to integration is further explored in recent essays by a policy historian, a sociologist, and a social historian. In their essay on Philadelphia's Richard Allen Homes, John Bauman, Norman P. Hummon, and Edward K. Muller examine the impact of poverty on the lives of black low-income housing residents and conclude that integration failed (see Chapter 18 in this volume). According to Bauman and associates, from as early as the 1950s, federal housing and urban renewal policies intensified the impact of neighborhood segregation, labor market exclusion, inadequate education, and poor social services on the lives of the black poor. Such experiences increased over time, but Bauman and others emphasize its early post–World War II roots rather than the explosive growth of concentrated urban poverty during the 1970s and 1980s.[110]

Sociologist Elijah Anderson offers a contemporary analysis of the changes that are currently transforming two neighborhoods in North Philadelphia, called "Village–Northton" (see Chapter 19). While Northton is predominantly black and low income, the Village is presently a racially mixed area undergoing transition from a working-class and middle-class neighborhood to an increasingly white middle- and upper-class one. Anderson analyzes how the persistence of race and racial animosities are "increasingly compounded by considerations of social class" in the late twentieth-century. He also laments the passage of what he sees as an earlier more cohesive cross-class, pre-1960s black community, where "old heads," described as stable men who worked hard for self, family, and church, represented a repertoire of much respected wisdom and advice. According to Anderson, the "new old head" is increasingly involved in illegal pursuits if he works at all and exhibits little of the stability and sage advice of the earlier "old heads."[111] Although Anderson's portrait suffers from an ahistorical view of early twentieth-century black urban life, it reveals the deep persistence of class and racial problems in the age of integration.

Historian Laurence Glasco reinforces the tragic perspective on Pennsylvania's black history in his recent essay, "Double Burden: The Black Experience in Pittsburgh" (Chapter 17 of the present volume). Based upon a wide variety of published articles, books, and essays, as well as unpublished Ph.D. and Master's theses, Glasco analyzes changes in Pittsburgh's black community from the antebellum years through the 1980s. He concludes that the city's black population labored historically under a "double burden" that, following World War I, was really a "triple" burden of racial discrimination, long-term loss of economic opportunities (through gradual deindustrialization), and a geographically widely dispersed black population, which made political mobilization especially difficult. Although Glasco is now rethinking his notion of "double burden," his essay illuminates how the changes of the nineteenth century gave way to the urban-industrial transformation of the state's black population during the twentieth century. Both implicitly and explicitly, his essay challenges historians to document not only how the changes of the depression and World War II gave rise to the events of the 1950s and 1960s, but also how the state's black history was shaped by the civil rights and Black Power movements, by deindustrialization, and by the emergence of new national and international trends in politics, culture, and the economy.[112] Indeed, few studies offer us the long view of historical changes as this one.

The Post–Civil Rights Era: Toward New Gender and Cultural Perspectives

Civil rights and Black Power era scholarship transformed historical research on African Americans in Pennsylvania and in the nation. As discussed above, such studies emphasized the perspectives and volition of African Americans themselves. Although scholars retained a keen interest in the role of black elites, they treated the black experience itself from the bottom up, giving working-class blacks and the poor increasing attention. Yet, even as civil rights era scholars revamped our knowledge of each phase of the black experience, they made few efforts to systematically explore the dynamics of gender as well as class and race. Fortunately, beginning during the early 1980s, scholars, particularly women historians, turned toward the role of black women in the state's history.

Recent scholarship on black women reveals neglected aspects of Pennsylvania history from the colonial era through recent times. Although several scholars documented the diverse use of slave labor in colonial Pennsylvania, for example, such studies focused on men, not women. In her essay on black women in colonial Pennsylvania (Chapter 2), historian Jean R. Soderlund shows that the lives of slave women varied by specific circumstances and social settings but that the nature of their work, mainly domestic and personal service, varied little.[113] Other scholars of the colonial era recognized the special role of women in reproducing and nurturing both the slave labor force and the African American family and community.[114] Hence, under the impact of black women's studies, the importance of the ratio of female to male slaves gained increasing attention.

Women's historians are also slowly recasting our knowledge of both the antebellum and postbellum eras. As suggested above, black men figured prominently in the new scholarship on the abolitionist movement, aid to fugitives, and increasing resistance to racial attacks on black Pennsylvanians themselves. The limitations of this scholarship became increasingly apparent during the 1980s. As Janice Sumler-Lewis notes in her work on the Forten-Purvis women (Chapter 6 in this volume), "We cannot hope to know the complete story of reform in this nation until the role of black women also comes to light. . . . As black females in a racist-sexist society, they brought a unique perspective to their work . . . [and] contributed importantly to the directions of change in the country."[115] In her groundbreaking essay on the social and political activist Charlotte Forten, Emma Jones Lapsansky shows how Philadelphia's black community was influenced by gender as well as by class and race.[116] Unlike black men and white women, she says, African American women pursued a dual mission of "public betterment" of their race and sex.

Research on black migration, urban communities, and workers gave more attention to the role of women than other fields. As Peter Gottlieb and Frederic Miller note (Chapters 11 and 12, respectively), for example, black women were key to the operation of black kin and communal networks that helped to bring migrants to the cities, facilitated their settlement, and linked them to essential institutions and services. Yet, even here, scholars neglected the role of gender as opposed to simply women in the development of such networks. As historian Darlene Clark Hine argues in her critique of the literature, scholars failed to differentiate the gender-specific threads of southern black migration to the state from the peculiarly racial and class ones.[117] According to Hine, "many black women quit the South out of desire to achieve personal autonomy and escape from sexual exploitation both within and outside their families and from sexual abuse at the hands of southern white as well as black men." In her study of black migrant women and Pittsburgh's medical establishment, Carolyn Leonard Carson addresses an important dimension of Hine's concern (Chapter 14 of this volume). Carson shows how the Pittsburgh Urban League and black public health nurses were instrumental in helping southern black women make the increasing transition from their previous childbearing traditions (including midwives) to new professional medical services. Although she does not examine the extent of black midwifery in the industrial North, black infant and maternal mortality rates nonetheless gradually improved.[118]

Under the editorship of Darlene Clark Hine, Elsa Barkley Brown, and Rosalyn Terborg-Penn, *Black Women in America: An Historical Encyclopedia* (1993) offers the single most comprehensive source of scholarship on black women in Pennsylvania and the nation. Especially illuminating in this volume are essays on the Forten sisters of Philadelphia; the Shaker minister Rebecca Cox Jackson; Fanny Jackson Coppin and the Institute for Colored Youth; the economist and lawyer Sadie Tanner Mossell Alexander; and the

black sculptor Meta Vaux Warrick Fuller, among many others. In her introduction to the volume, Hine argues that it is no longer tenable to rationalize
the exclusion of black women from African American experience or from
the experience of women more generally. "We cannot accurately comprehend
either our hidden potential or the full range of problems that besiege us until
we know about the successful struggles that generations of foremothers
waged against virtually insurmountable obstacles."[119]

Historian Edna McKenzie also urges us to pay close attention to the role
of women in black institutions, civil rights, and political organizations. In
her essay on Daisy Lampkin, McKenzie suggests how Pennsylvania's black
women played a key role in the political and civil rights struggles of the years
between the two world wars and of the 1950s. Daisy Lampkin served as vice-
president of the Pittsburgh Courier Publishing Company and was also on the
staff of the Pittsburgh Urban League and NAACP. She also served as regional
and national field secretaries of the NAACP during the period.[120]

As scholars turned toward gender issues during the 1980s and 1990s, other
important aspects of black culture, leisure time, and community life nonetheless remained insufficiently explored. Middle-class and elite forms of expression in music, novels, poems, plays, paintings, and photography, and
working-class and popular expressions in a variety of sports, games, music,
dances, folklore, and oral traditions—all need systematic and close analysis.
To be sure, since the mid-1980s even these areas received increasing attention
in scholarly essays, doctoral dissertations, and articles in popular publications.[121] Still, the chronological coverage, depth, and breadth of such studies
are quite thin. Even for the premiere black cultural institution—the church—as
suggested by C. James Trotman, we have few studies outside the African
Methodist Episcopal denominations.[122]

While elements of black culture undoubtedly represent the most important
gaps in our knowledge, other, more conventional, topics also warrant additional research. First, despite our expanding knowledge of socioeconomic
and class issues, we still need more studies of blacks in business, the professions, and a variety of occupations beyond the mass production industries of
coal, steel, and shipbuilding during the industrial era. Even for such mass
production industries, however, the pivotal importance of local chapters of
the National Urban League awaits detailed study. Second, although emphasis
on the development of the ghetto is prominent in recent research, our knowledge of black housing and neighborhood development in cities and towns
outside Pittsburgh and Philadelphia is quite deficient.

Third, for all of the emphasis on the civil rights and political struggles of
Pennsylvania blacks, we do not have systematic studies of the NAACP, the
Garvey Movement and, surprisingly, electoral politics, covering a long period

of time and acknowledging variations and similarities from city to city and from region to region within the state.[123] Fourth, black historical biography advanced little beyond Andrew Buni's fine study of Robert L. Vann, editor of the *Pittsburgh Courier*.[124] The state's history is replete with figures of local, state, national, and even international significance. Fifth, with the exception of collections on the antebellum era, we have few anthologies of primary documents on various aspects of the state's black experience.[125]

Finally, as a means of heightening the prospects of research on the state's black history, we need in-depth studies of the role of community-based individuals and organizations in the collection, preservation, and dissemination of vital historical materials. We need studies of the relationship between these local efforts and the work of larger, more richly endowed, private and public historical societies. In his essay "Locating Rare Materials on Black History and Genealogy," historian Charles Blockson calls attention to this issue. Blockson notes how some community-based collections found their way into established university and historical society archives, but he laments that "whole collections disappeared after the death of the collector." More recently, in his book *William Dorsey's Philadelphia and Ours,* historian Roger Lane uses the papers of the American Negro Historical Society and illuminates the problems and prospects of community-based historical collections. Lane's book suggests a need to document the work of other William Dorseys and their individual and collective activities throughout the commonwealth.[126] By addressing such remaining blind spots and connecting social, economic, political, and cultural issues, we will be able to achieve a more accurate portrait of the state's black history.[127]

Pennsylvania's African American history and historiography will no doubt continue to change with the emergence of new social trends. Each generation reveals the ongoing connection between historical writing, changes in the academy, and transformations in society, politics, culture, and the economy. Whether scholars responded to a world of religious or scientific convictions, or more recent concerns with gender and cultural issues, they faced the persistent problems of racial and class bias in both the writing and the experience of Pennsylvania history. Thus, as we seek to create a fuller and more inclusive history of the state's black experience, an appreciation of the nineteenth-century pioneers and the first generation of professional historians is no less significant than their late-twentieth-century counterparts.

Still, it is the civil rights and post–civil rights era scholarship that moves us well beyond the class and gender limitations of the earlier writers and establishes the intellectual foundations for a fresh new synthesis of the state's black history. Since the late 1960s, scholars of Pennsylvania's black history have focused increasing attention on social transformations of the commercial, industrial, and, increasingly, the postindustrial eras. Such studies broadened the temporal, spatial, and topical scope of the state's black history by examining western as well as eastern Pennsylvania; small and medium-sized as well as large urban centers; and the role of workers, the poor, and increasingly women, as well as elite and middle-class black men.

By building upon existing scholarship, a new study of Pennsylvania's African American experience would not only foster a better understanding of the state and nation, but pinpoint remaining gaps and help to set a new and more fruitful research agenda for the twenty-first century. It is in this spirit that we offer this anthology of recent writings on Pennsylvania's African American experience.

Notes

1. For the national context, see Earl Lewis, "To Turn as on a Pivot: Writing African Americans into a History of Overlapping Diasporas," *American Historical Review* 100 (June 1995): 765–87; Darlene Clark Hine, ed., *Afro-American History: Past, Present, and Future* (Baton Rouge, La., 1986); August Meier and Elliott Rudwick, *Black History and the Historical Profession* (Urbana, Ill., 1986); Joe W. Trotter, "African-American History: Origins, Development, and Current State of the Field," *OAH Magazine of History* 7 (Summer 1993): 12–18. Excellent guides to the state's history are Dennis B. Downey and Francis J. Bremer, eds., *A Guide to the History of Pennsylvania* (Westport, Conn., 1993); Norman B. Wilkinson, comp., *Bibliography of Pennsylvania History,* 2nd ed. by S. K. Stevens and Donald Kent (Harrisburg, Pa., 1957); Carol Wall, ed., *Bibliography of Pennsylvania History: A Supplement* (Harrisburg, Pa., 1976); John B. B. Trussell Jr., comp., *Pennsylvania Historical Bibliography*, Additions 1–6 (Harrisburg, Pa., 1979–89); and Roland M. Baumann, ed., *Dissertations on Pennsylvania History, 1886–1976: A Bibliography* (Harrisburg, Pa., 1978). For general studies of Pennsylvania that neglected the place of blacks, see, among others over a long period of time, Thomas F. Gordon, *The History of Pennsylvania . . . to . . . 1776* (Philadelphia, 1829); William Carpenter, *History of Pennsylvavnia* (Philadelphia, 1854); William Cornell, *The History of Pennsylvania* (New York, 1879); J. Thomas Scharf and Thompson Wescott, *History of Philadelphia, 1609–1884,* 3 vols. (Philadelphia, 1884); Howard Jenkins, *Pennsylvania, Colonial and Federal: A History 1608–1903* (Philadelphia, 1903); Samuel W. Pennypacker, *Pennsylvania, The Keystone: A Short History* (Philadelphia, 1914); George P. Donehoo, *Pennsylvania: A History* (New York, 1926); John F. Watson, *Historic Tales of Olden Time* (Philadelphia, 1933); Wayland F. Dunaway, *A History of Pennsylvania,* 2nd ed. (New York, 1948); Paul A. Wallace, *Pennsylvania: Seed of a Nation* (New York, 1962); Sylvester K. Stevens, *Pennsylvania: The Keystone State,* 2 vols. (New York, 1956), and *Pennsylvania: The Heritage of a Commonwealth,* 4 vols. (West Palm Beach, Fla., 1968). Only gradually did blacks gain attention in general histories of the state. See Thomas C. Cochran, *Pennsylvania: A Bicentennial History* (New York, 1978); Philip Klein and Ari Hoogenboom, *A History of Pennsylvania* (University Park, Pa., 1980).

2. Excellent discussion of these early studies are found in Clarence E. Walker, "The Ameri-

can Negro as Outsider, 1836–1935," *Canadian Review of American Studies* 17, no. 2 (Summer 1986): 137–54. See also John Hope Franklin, *George Washington Williams: A Biography* (Chicago, 1985); Earl Thorpe, *Black Historians: A Critique* (New York, 1971).

3. W. E. B. Du Bois, *The Negro* (1915; reprint, New York, 1970) and *Black Folk Then and Now* (New York, 1939); Carter G. Woodson, *The Negro in Our History,* 2nd ed. (1922); Benjamin Brawley, *A Social History of the American Negro* (1921; reprint, New York, 1970); E. Franklin Frazier, *The Negro in the United States* (New York, 1957); John Hope Franklin, *From Slavery to Freedom* (New York, 1947).

4. See note 1 above: Lewis, Hine, Meier and Rudwick, and Trotter.

5. For a comprehensive listing of Ph.D. dissertations, master's theses, books, and scholarly essays, see bibliographies compiled by Eric Ledell Smith, Ancella Livers, and Matt Hawkins.

6. Robert Benjamin Lewis, *Light and Truth; Collected from the Bible and Ancient and Modern History; Containing the Universal History of the Colored and the Indian Race, From the Creation of the World to the Present Time* (1836; reprint, Portland, Me., 1844); James W. C. Pennington, *A Text Book of the Origin and History of the Colored People* (Hartford, Conn., 1841); William Cooper Nell, *Colored Patriots of the American Revolution* (Boston, 1855); William Wells Brown, *The Black Man, His Antecedents, His Genius, and His Achievements* (1874; reprint, New York, 1969), and *The Rising Son; or, the Antecedents and Advancement of the Colored Race* (Boston, 1874); Martin Robinson Delany, *The Condition, Elevation, Emigration and Destiny of the Colored People of the United States* (Philadelphia, 1852); George Washington Williams, *History of the Negro Race in America, 1619–1880,* vols. 1 and 2 (1883; reprint, New York, 1968); Joseph T. Wilson, *Black Phalanx: A History of the Negro Soldiers of the United States in the Wars of 1775–1812, 1861–1865* (1890; reprint, New York, 1968).

7. See David Roediger, *The Wages of Whiteness: Race and the Making of the American Working Class* (London, 1991); George M. Frederickson, *The Black Image in the White Mind: The Debate on Afro-American Character and Destiny, 1817–1914* (Middletown, Conn., 1971).

8. Pennington, *A Text Book of the Origin and History of the Colored People*, 85.

9. Brown, *The Black Man,* 5–6.

10. Ibid., 6, 48.

11. Ibid., 30.

12. Delany, *Condition, Elevation* . . . , 10.

13. Ibid., 14.

14. Ibid., 38.

15. Ibid., 39.

16. Ibid., 187.

17. Williams, *History of the Negro Race,* vi; John Hope Franklin, *George Washington Williams,* 2–3.

18. Williams, *History of the Negro Race,* vi, 552.

19. Brown, *The Black Man,* 259.

20. Delany, *Condition, Elevation* . . . , 10, 14, 26, 30, 36, 38, 39, 146, 187.

21. Ibid., 26. Although he favored emigration to other parts of the western hemisphere, Delany opposed the ACS's effort to remove free blacks from America to Africa.

22. Nell, *Colored Patriots,* 9.

23. Ibid., 166–97.

24. Ibid., 311–12, 349–50.

25. Williams, *History of the Negro Race,* 315.

26. Nell, *Colored Patriots,* 5.

27. Ibid., 7.

28. Du Bois, *The Negro* and *Black Folk Then and Now*; Woodson, *The Negro in Our History;* Brawley, *A Social History of the American Negro;* Frazier, *The Negro in the United States;* John Hope Franklin, *From Slavery to Freedom.*

29. See Edward Raymond Turner, *The Negro in Pennsylvania: Slavery, Servitude, Freedom, 1639–1861* (Washington, D.C., 1911), and *Slavery in Pennsylvania* (Baltimore, 1911); Richard Wright, *The Negro in Pennsylvania: A Study in Economic History* (Philadelphia, 1912); and Richard R. Wright Jr., "Property Holding of Negroes in Pennsylvania," in *Commonwealth of Pennsylvania, Annual Report of the Secretary of Internal Affairs,* part 3 (Harrisburg, Pa., 1910), 54–108. See also Carter G. Woodson, "The Negro in Pennsylvania," *Negro History Bulletin* (hereafter cited as *NHB*) 12 (April 1949): 150–51; Rufus Gibson, "The Negro in Pennsylvania," *NHB* 5 (December 1941): 52–58.

30. Turner, *The Negro in Pennsylvania,* viii.

31. Ibid., 250.

32. Ibid.

33. Ibid., 251.

34. Ibid., 250.

35. Ibid., 251.

36. Ibid.

37. Ibid.

38. Wright, *The Negro in Pennsylvania,* 182.

39. Ibid., 12, 186–87.

40. Ibid., 12, 53.

41. Ibid., 53.

42. Ibid., 199.

43. Ibid., 187.

44. Ibid., 131, 200–201.

45. Joseph H. Smith, "Some Aspects of the Underground Railway in the Counties of Southeastern Pennsylvania," *Montgomery County Historical Society Bulletin* 3 (1941): 3–19; Robert Brewster, "The Rise of the Antislavery Movement in Southwestern Pennsylvania," *Western Pennsylvania Historical Magazine* (hereafter cited as *WPHM*) 22 (March 1939), 1–18; Irene E. Williams, "The Operation of the Fugitive Slave Law in Western Pennsylvania from 1850–1860," *WPHM* 4 (July 1921): 150–60; Edward Burns, "Slavery in Western Pennsylvania," *WPHM* 8 (October 1925), 204–14; Edward Turner, "The Underground Railroad in Pennsylvania," *Pennsylvania Magazine of History and Biography* (hereafter cited as *PMHB*) 36 (July 1912), 309–18; Harmon Yerkes, "Anti-Slavery Days—Experiences of Fugitives," *Bucks County Historical Society Papers* 3 (1909): 504–12; W. U. Hensel, *The Christiana Riot and the Treason Trials of 1851; An Historical Sketch* (Lancaster, Pa., 1911); Herbert Aptheker, "The Quakers and Negro Slavery," *Journal of Negro History* (hereafter cited as *JNH*) 25 (July 1940): 331–62; Richard I. Shelling, "William Sturgeon, Catechist to the Negroes of Philadelphia and Assistant Rector of Christ Church, 1747–1766," *Presbyterian Episcopal Church History Magazine* 8 (1939): 338–401. County studies include Paul N. Schaffer, "Slavery in Berks County," *Berks County Historical Society Review* 6 (July 1941): 110–15; William Worner, "The Columbia Race Riots," *Lancaster County Historical Society Papers* 26 (October 1922): 175–87; Sarah Christy, "Fugitive Slaves in Indiana County," *PMHB* 18 (December 1935); Ruth Nuermberger, *The Free Produce Movement: A Quaker Protest Against Slavery* (Durham, N.C., 1942); Norman B. Wilkinson, "The Philadelphia Free Produce Attack upon Slavery," *PMHB* 66 (July 1942); Edwin Bronner, *Thomas Earle as a Reformer* (Philadelphia, 1948); Thomas Drake, *Quakers and Slavery in America* (New Haven, 1950); Wayne Homan, "The

Underground Railroad," *Historical Review of Berks County* 23 (Fall 1958): 112–18. On women, see Judith Anderson, "Anna Dickinson, Antislavery Radical," *Pennsylvania History* (hereafter *PH*) 3 (July 1936); Samuel Sillen, *Women Against Slavery* (New York, 1955).

46. Henry Minton, *Early History of Negroes in Business in Philadelphia* (Nashville, Tenn., 1913); Charles Wesley, *Richard Allen: Apostle of Freedom* (Washington, D.C., 1935); Bella Gross, "The First National Negro Convention," *JNH* 31 (October 1946, 435–43); Ray Allan Billington, "James Forten: Forgotten Abolitionist," *NHB* 13 (November 1949): 31–45; Woodson, "The Negro in Pennsylvania" (see note 29); Frederick Binder, "Pennsylvania Negro Regiments in the Civil War," *JNH* 37 (October 1952): 383–417; George L. Davis, "Pittsburgh's Negro Troops in the Civil War," *WPHM* 36, no. 1 (March 1953): 101–13.

47. W. E. B. Du Bois, *The Philadelphia Negro: A Social Study* (1899; reprint, New York, 1967); Clara A. Hardin, *The Negroes of Philadelphia: The Cultural Adjustment of a Minority Group* (Bryn Mawr, Pa., 1945); Ira Reid et al., *Social Condition of the Negro in the Hill District of Pittsburgh* (Pittsburgh, 1930); H. A. Tucker, "Negroes in Pittsburgh," *Charities* 21 (1909): 599–608.

48. Du Bois, *The Philadelphia Negro,* 44.

49. Ibid., 30–31.

50. Ibid., 10–11.

51. See Ira V. Brown, *The Negro in Pennsylvania History* (Gettysburg, Pa., 1970); Charles L. Blockson, *Pennsylvania's Black History* (Philadelphia, 1975), and *African Americans in Pennsylvania: A History and Guide* (Baltimore, 1994); David McBride, ed., *Blacks in Pennsylvania History: Research and Educational Perspectives* (Harrisburg, Pa., 1983); Emma Jones Lapsansky, *Black Presence in Pennsylvania: "Making It Home,"* Pennsylvania History Studies, no. 21 (University Park, Pa., 1990); Bettye Collier-Thomas, *Freedom and Community: Nineteenth-Century Black Pennsylvania* (Philadelphia, 1992); Leroy T. Hopkins and Eric Ledell Smith, *The African Americans in Pennsylvania* (Harrisburg, Pa., 1994); Patricia Mitchell, *Beyond Adversity: African-Americans' Struggle for Equality in Western Pennsylvania, 1750–1990* (Pittsburgh, 1993). In this teaching program, Mitchell emphasizes the achievements of African Americans and how some moved well "beyond adversity."

52. Gary B. Nash, "Slaves and Slave Owners in Colonial Philadelphia," *William and Mary Quarterly* (hereafter cited as *WMQ*), 3rd series, 30 (April 1973): 223–56; Gary B. Nash and Jean Soderlund, *Freedom by Degrees: Emancipation in Eighteenth-Century Philadelphia* (New York, 1990). See also Darold D. Wax, "Quaker Merchants and the Slave Trade in Colonial Pennsylvania," *PMHB* 86 (April 1962): 143–59; Manning Marable, "Death of the Quaker Slave Trade," *Quaker History* 63 (Spring 1974): 17–33; Jean R. Soderlund, *Quakers and Slavery: A Divided Spirit* (Princeton, 1985).

53. Nash, "Slaves and Slave Owners."

54. Darold D. Wax, "The Negro Slave Trade in Colonial Pennsylvania" (Ph.D. diss., University of Washington, 1962); "Negro Imports into Pennsylvania, 1720–1766," *PH* 32 (July 1965): 254–87; "The Demand for Slave Labor in Colonial Pennsylvania," *PH* 34 (October 1967): 331–45; "Negro Import Duties in Colonial Pennsylvania," *PMHB* 97 (January 1973): 22–44; and "Africans on the Delaware: The Pennsylvania Slave Trade, 1759–1765," *PH* 50 (January 1983): 38–49.

55. Wax, "Africans on the Delaware," 38; William M. Wiecek, "The Statuary Law of Slavery and Race in the Thirteen Mainland Colonies of British America," *WMQ*, 3rd ser., 34 (April 1977): 258–80; Richard Johnson, "Slaves and Indentured Blacks in Berks County Before 1800," *Historical Review of Berks County* 37 (December 1971): 8–14; Paul Crawford, "A Footnote on Courts for Trial of Negroes in Colonial Pennsylvania," *Journal of Black Studies* 5, no. 2 (December 1974): 167–74.

56. Joseph Walker, "Negro Labor in the Charcoal Iron Industry of Southeastern Pennsylvania," *PMHB* 93 (October 1969): 466–86; Johnson, "Slaves and Indentured Blacks."

57. Jerome H. Wood Jr., "The Negro in Early Pennsylvania: The Lancaster Experience," in Elinor Miller and Eugene D. Genovese, eds., *Plantation, Town, and County: Essays on the Local History of American Slave Society* (Urbana, Ill., 1974), 452.

58. Alan Tully, "Patterns of Slaveholding in Colonial Pennsylvania: Chester and Lancaster Counties, 1729–1758," *Journal of Social History* (hereafter cited as *JSH*) 6 (March 1973): 284–305.

59. Nash, "Slaves and Slave Owners," 238.

60. Susan Klepp, "Seasoning and Society: Racial Differences in Mortality in Eighteenth-Century Philadelphia," *WMQ,* 3rd ser., 51 (July 1994): 473–506.

61. Ibid., 474.

62. Carl D. Oblinger, "Alms for Oblivion: The Making of a Black Underclass in Southeastern Pennsylvania, 1780–1860," in John Bodnar, ed., *The Ethnic Experience in Pennsylvania* (Lewisburg, Pa., 1973), 94–119; and idem, *Freedoms Foundations: Black Communities in Southeastern Pennsylvania Towns, 1780–1860* (Maryville, Mo., 1972); Theodore Hershberg, "Free Blacks in Antebellum Philadelphia: A Study of Ex-Slaves, Freeborn, and Socioeconomic Decline," *JSH* 5 (December 1971): 183–209; G. S. Rowe, "Black Offenders, Criminal Courts, and Philadelphia Society in the Late Eighteenth Century," *JSH* 22 (June 1989): 685–712; Leslie C. Patrick-Stamp, "Numbers That Are Not New: African Americans in the Country's First Prison, 1790–1835," *PMHB* 119 (January and April 1995): 95–128. Cf. Debra Newman, "They Left with the British: Black Women in the Evacuation of Philadelphia, 1778," *Pennsylvania Heritage* 4 (December 1977): 20–23; Donald J. D'Elia, "Dr. Benjamin Rush and the Negro," *Journal of the History of Ideas* 30 (July 1969): 413–22; Todd L. Savitt, "Lincoln University Medical Department: A Forgotten Nineteenth-Century Black Medical School," *Journal of History of Medicine and Allied Sciences* 140 (January 1985): 42–65; Betty L. Plummer, "Benjamin Rush and the Negro," *American Journal of Psychiatry* 2 (1970); Roger A. Bruns, "Anthony Benezet and the Natural Rights of the Negro," *PHMB* 96 (January 1972): 104–13; Jean S. Straub, "Anthony Benezet: Teacher and Abolitionist of the Eighteenth Century," *Quaker History* 57 (1968): 3–16; Charles E. Wynes, "Dr. James Durham, Mysterious Eighteenth-Century Black Physician: Man or Myth?" *PMHB* 103 (July 1979): 325–33; Nancy Slocum Hornick, "Anthony Benezet and the Africans' School: Toward a Theory of Full Equality," *PMHB* 99 (October 1975): 399–421; Owen S. Ireland, "Germans Against Abolition: A Minority's View of Slavery in Revolutionary Pennsylvania," *Journal of Interdisciplinary Studies* 3 (March 1973): 685–706; William E. Juhnke, "Benjamin Franklin's View of the Negro and Slavery," *PH* 41 (October 1974): 375–88. See also the recent essay by Billy G. Smith, "Runaway Slaves in the Mid-Atlantic Region During the Revolutionary Era," in Ronald Hoffman and Peter J. Albert, eds., *The Transforming Hand of Revolution: Reconsidering the American Revolution as a Social Movement* (Charlottesville, Va., 1996), 199–230.

63. Oblinger, "Alms for Oblivion" and *Freedoms Foundations.*

64. Hershberg, "Free Blacks," 183.

65. Ibid., 201.

66. Rowe, "Black Offenders," 685.

67. Ibid.

68. Ibid.

69. Ibid., 691. Still, we need not dismiss the notion that at least for some poor and working people such actions were pursued quite consciously as part of a larger sense of class and racial inequality.

70. Patrick-Stamp, "Numbers That Are Not New" (note 62 above), 96–97, n. 3.

71. Ibid., 127.

72. Gary B. Nash, *Forging Freedom: The Formation of Philadelphia's Black Community, 1720–1840* (Cambridge, Mass., 1988); Charles L. Blockson, *The Underground Railroad in Pennsylvania* (Jacksonville, N.C., 1981), and "A Black Underground Resistance to Slavery, 1833–1860," *Pennsylvania Heritage* 4 (December 1877): 29–33; Joseph Borome, "The Vigilant Committee of Philadelphia," *PMHB* 92 (July 1968): 320–51; Richard J. M. Blackett, "Freedom, or the Martyr's Grave; Black Pittsburgh's Aid to the Fugitive Slave," *WPHM* 61 (April 1978): 117–34; Emma Jones Lapsansky, "Since They Got Those Separate Churches: Afro-Americans and Racism in Jacksonian Philadelphia," *American Quarterly* 32 (Spring 1980): 54–78; Julie Winch, *Philadelphia's Black Elite: Activism, Accommodation, and Struggle for Autonomy, 1787–1848* (Philadelphia, 1988); Winch, "Philadelphia and the Other Underground Railroad," *PMHB* (January 1987); cf. John L. Myers, "The Early Antislavery Agency System in Pennsylvania, 1833–37," *PH* 31 (January 1964); Charles D. Spotts, *The Pilgrims' Pathway: The Underground Railroad in Lancaster County* (Lancaster, Pa., 1966); Ira Brown, "Miller McKim and Pennsylvania Abolitionism," *PH* 30 (January 1963), and "An Anti-Slavery Agent: C. C. Burleigh in Pennsylvania, 1836–37," *PMHB* 105 (January 1981); Stanley I. Kutler, "Pennsylvania Courts, the Abolition Act, and Negro Rights," *PH* 30 (1963): 14–27; Joseph C. Burke, "What Did the Prigg Decision Really Decide?" *PMHB* 93 (1969): 73–85; Melvin H. Buxbaum, "Cyrus Bustill Addresses the Blacks of Philadelphia," *WMQ,* 3rd ser., no. 29 (January 1972): 99–108; John Stephens Durham, "Black Philadelphian: At Home and Abroad," *PMHB* 106 (October 1982): 527–37; and Charles E. Wynes, "Ebenezer Don Carlos Bassett, America's First Black Diplomat," *PH* 51 (July 1984): 232–40.

73. Nash, *Forging Freedom,* 5; Borome, "Vigilant Committee of Philadelphia," 370; Blackett, "Freedom, or the Martyr's Grave," 118–19. See also Arthur B. Fox, "Arthurville: An Antebellum Black Settlement," *Pittsburgh Heritage: The Newsletter of the Committee on Pittsburgh Archaeology and History* 6 (September 1990): n.p.; Ann G. Wilmoth, "Pittsburgh and the Blacks: A Short History, 1780–1875" (Ph.D. diss., The Pennsylvania State University, 1975), and idem, "Toward Freedom: Pittsburgh Blacks, 1800–1870," *Pennsylvania Heritage* 4 (December 1977): 14–19.

74. Blackett, "Freedom, or the Martyr's Grave," 118–19; Blockson, *Underground Railroad,* "A Black Underground Resistance"; and *Pennsylvania Black History;* Charles Blockson, "The History of the Black Man in Montgomery County," *Bulletin of the Historical Society of Montgomery County* 18, no. 4 (1973): 337–62.

75. See Blackett, "Freedom," and both studies by Blockson cited in note 74, above. On the widespread existence of racial conflict, see Roderick W. Nash, "William Parker and the Christiana Riot," *JNH* 46 (January 1961): 24; Richard Grau, "The Christiana Riot of 1851: A Reappraisal," *Journal of Lancaster County Historical Society* (hereafter cited as *JLCHS*) 68, no. 4 (September 1964): 147–75; Jonathan Katz, *Resistance at Christiana: The Fugitive Slave Rebellion, Christiana, Pennsylvania, September 11, 1851* (New York, 1974); Margaret Hope Bacon, *Rebellion at Christiana* (New York, 1975); Thomas P. Slaughter, *Bloody Dawn: The Christiana Riot and Racial Violence in the Antebellum North* (New York, 1991). On racial violence, see John Runcie, "Hunting the Nigs in Philadelphia: The Race Riot of August 1834," *PH* 39 (April 1972): 187–218; Elizabeth M. Geffen, "Violence in Philadelphia in the 1840s and 1850s," *PH* 36 (October 1969): 381–410; Willis L. Shirk, "Testing the Limits of Tolerance: Blacks and the Social Order in Columbia, Pennsylvania, 1800–1851," *PH* 60 (January 1993): 35–60. See also Roderick W. Nash, "William Parker and the Christiana Riot," *JNH* 46, no. 1 (January 1964): 24; Grau, "The Christiana Riot of 1851: A Reappraisal"; Bacon, *Rebellion at Christiana;* Slaughter, *Bloody Dawn.*

76. Lapsansky, "Since They Got Those Separate Churches." Cf. Dee Andrews, "The African Methodists of Philadelphia, 1794–1802," *PMHB* 108 (October 1984): 471–86; Charles L. Coleman, "The Emergence of Black Religion in Pennsylvania, 1776–1850," *Pennsylvania Heritage* 4 (December 1977): 24–28; Roberta A. Day, "Some Facts About St. Paul's A.M.E. Church, Bellefonte," *Centre County Heritage* 17 (September 1981): 10–12; Carol George, *Segregated Sabbaths: Richard Allen and the Rise of Independent Black Churches, 1760–1840* (New York, 1973); Richard G. Johnson, "The Founding of Reading's Bethel African Methodist Church," *Historical Review of Berks County* 45 (Fall 1980): 132–35, 144, 151; Richard G. Johnson, "The Meaning of Old Bethel," *Pennsylvania Heritage* 6 (September 1980): 26–27; Clarence Walker, *A Rock in a Weary Land: The African Methodist Episcopal Church During the Civil War and Reconstruction* (Baton Rouge, La., 1982). Essays by C. James Trotman suggest the need to broaden our perspective to include other denominations. C. James Trotman, "Matthew Anderson: Black Pastor, Churchman, and Social Reformer," *American Presbyterians* 66 (March 1988): 11–21; C. James Trotman, "Race, Reform, and Religion in the Life of Matthew Anderson," *Princeton Seminary Bulletin* 9 (January 1988): 143–55. For insight into the African colonization movement, see Kurt Lee Kocher, "A Duty to America and Africa: A History of the Independent African Colonization Movement in Pennsylvania," *PH* 51 (April 1984): 118–53; Eli Seifman, "The United Colonization Societies of New York and Pennsylvania and the Establishment of the African Colony of Bassa Cove," *PH* 35 (January 1968): 23–44; Leroy T. Hopkins Jr., "No Balm in Gilead: Lancaster's African-American Population and the Civil War Era," *JLCHS* 95, no. 1 (Winter 1993): 20–31.

77. Winch, *Philadelphia's Black Elite* (note 72 above), 2.

78. Ibid.

79. Hopkins, "No Balm in Gilead."

80. Edward Price, "School Segregation in Nineteenth-Century Pennsylvania," *PH* 43 (April 1976): 121–37.

81. Ann G. Wilmoth, "The Nineteenth-Century Education of Afro-Americans in Pittsburgh and Allegheny City: Path Toward Equality?" in McBride, *Blacks in Pennsylvania History* (note 51 above); Harry C. Silcox, "Nineteenth-Century Philadelphia Black Militant: Octavius V. Catto (1839–1871)," *PH* 44 (January 1977): 53–76; Harry Silcox, "Delay and Neglect: Negro Public Education in Antebellum Philadelphia, 1800–1860," *PMHB* 97 (October 1973): 444–64; Harry Silcox, "Philadelphia Negro Educator: Jacob C. White, Jr., 1837–1902," *PMHB* 97 (January 1973): 75–98.

82. Emma Jones Lapsansky, "Discipline to the Mind: Philadelphia's Banneker Institute, 1854–1872," *PMHB* 117 (January 1993): 83–103; Horace Mann Bond, *Education for Freedom: A History of Lincoln University, Pennsylvania* (Princeton, 1976); Catherine M. Hanchett, "George Boyer Vashon, 1824–1878: Black Educator, Poet, Fighter for Equal Rights," *WPHM* 68 (July 1985): 209–19; Joel Schor, "The Southern Background: Meaning of Black Land Grant Education to the Urban North," in McBride, *Blacks in Pennsylvania History*. David McBride, "Africa's Elevation and Changing Racial Thought at Lincoln University, 1854–1886," *JNH* 62 (October 1977): 363–77; David McBride, "Solomon Porter Hood, 1853-1943: Black Missionary, Educator and Minister to Liberia," *JLCHS* 84 (January 1980): 2–9; Edward Price, "The Black Voting Rights Issue in Pennsylvania, 1780–1900," *PHMB* 100 (July 1976): 356–73; Ira V. Brown, "Pennsylvania and the Rights of the Negro, 1865–1887," *PH* 28 (January 1961): 45–57; David McBride, "Black Protest Against Racial Politics: [Charles W.] Gardner, [Fredrick A.] Hinton and Their Memorial of 1838," *PH* 46 (April 1979): 149–62; Wynes, "Ebenezer Don Carlos Bassett, America's First Black Diplomat," 232–40; Henry C. Silcox, "The Black 'Better Class' Dilemma," *PMHB* 113 (January 1989): 45–66; H. E. Cox, "Jim

Crow in the City of Brotherly Love: The Segregation of Philadelphia Horse Cars," *NHB* 26 (1962): 119–23; Philip S. Foner, "The Battle to End Discrimination Against Negroes on Philadelphia Streetcars," *PH* 40 (July 1973): 261–90; Silcox, "Nineteenth-Century Philadelphia Black Militant." Cf. Wilmoth, "Nineteenth-Century Education of Afro-Americans."

83. Gerald G. Eggert, "Two Steps Forward, a Step-and-a-Half Back: Harrisburg's African American Community in the Nineteenth Century," *PH* 58 (January 1991): 1–36; Gerald G. Eggert, "The Impact of the Fugitive Slave Law on Harrisburg: A Case Study," *PMHB* 109 (October 1985): 537–69; Mary D. Houts, "Black Harrisburg's Resistance to Slavery," *Pennsylvania Heritage* 4 (December 1977): 9–13.

84. John E. Bodnar, "The Impact of the 'New Immigration' on the Black Worker, Steelton, 1880–1920," *PMHB* 97 (April 1973): 214–229; John Bodnar, "Peter C. Blackwell and the Negro Community of Steelton, 1880–1920," *PMHB* 97 (April 1973): 199–209; Cf. John Bodnar, Roger Simon, and Michael P. Weber, *Lives of Their Own: Blacks, Italians, and Poles in Pittsburgh, 1900–1960* (Urbana, Ill., 1982), which treats blacks as pathological compared with other groups, Italians and Poles.

85. Bodnar, "The Impact of the 'New Immigration,' " 228–29.

86. Dennis Dickerson, *Out of the Crucible: Black Steelworkers in Western Pennsylvania, 1875–1980* (New York, 1986); Peter Gottlieb, *Making Their Own Way: The Southern Blacks' Migration to Pittsburgh* (Urbana, Ill., 1987); Peter Gottlieb, "Migration and Jobs: New Black Workers in Pittsburgh, 1916–1930," *WPHM* 61 (January 1978): 1–15; Laurence Glasco, "Double Burden: The Black Experience in Pittsburgh," in Samuel P. Hays, ed., *City at the Point: Essays on the Social History of Pittsburgh* (Pittsburgh, 1984); Constance A. Cunningham, "Homer S. Brown: First Black Political Leader in Pittsburgh," *JNH* 66 (December 1981): 304–17; Joe T. Darden, *Afro-Americans in Pittsburgh* (Lexington, Mass., 1973); Carl Oblinger, "Southern-born Blacks in Harrisburg, 1920–1950," *Pennsylvania Heritage* 4 (December 1977): 64–68. Cf. Ronald Lewis, *Black Coal Miners in America: Race, Class, and Community Conflict, 1780–1980* (Lexington, Ky., 1987); and Linda Nyden, "Black Miners in Western Pennsylvania, 1925–1931: The National Miners Union and the United Mine Workers of America," *Science and Society* 41 (March 1977): 69–101.

87. Dickerson, *Out of the Crucible*, 1.

88. Ibid., 251. See also Dennis C. Dickerson, "The Black Church in Industrializing Western Pennsylvania, 1870–1950," *WPHM* 64 (October 1981): 329–44.

89. Dickerson, *Out of the Crucible*, 80–81. See also Dickerson, "The Black Church."

90. Gottlieb, *Making Their Own Way.*

91. Ibid.

92. Ibid.

93. Ibid., 210.

94. Frederic Miller, "The Black Migration to Philadelphia: A 1924 Profile," *PMHB* 108 (July 1984): 315–50. See also Allan B. Ballard, *One More Day's Journey: The Making of Black Philadelphia* (New York, 1984). In a recent essay, urban geographer Joe T. Darden concluded that a "type of color caste system" existed in Pittsburgh's housing and job markets during World War I and its early aftermath. "It was apparently racial discrimination rather than recent migrant status that forced blacks into separate occupations and neighborhoods, and the war apparently did not alter this fact to any significant degree." (Joe T. Darden, "The Effect of World War I on Black Occupational and Residential Segregation: The Case of Pittsburgh," *Journal of Black Studies* 18 [March 1988]: 297–312.)

95. Miller, "The Black Migration to Philadelphia," 349.

96. Ibid., 350.

97. Dennis B. Downey and Raymond M. Hyser, *No Crooked Death: Coatesville, Pennsylvania, and the Lynching of Zachariah Walker* (Urbana, Ill., 1991), 7–9. Cf. Dennis B. Downey and Raymond M. Hyser, "A Crooked Death: Coatesville, Pennsylvania, and the Lynching of Zachariah Walker," *PH* 54 (April 1987): 85–102; William Ziglar, "Community on Trial: The Coatesville Lynching of 1911," *PMHB* 106 (April 1982): 245–70.

98. Downey and Hyser, *No Crooked Death,* 8.

99. David McBride, "Mid-Atlantic State Courts and the Struggle with the Separate but Equal Doctrine, 1880–1939," *Rutgers Law Journal* 17 (Spring–Summer 1986): 569–89.

100. Ibid., 571.

101. Richard B. Sherman, "Johnstown v. the Negro: Southern Migrants and the Exodus of 1923," *PH* 30 (October 1963).

102. Vincent Franklin, "The Philadelphia Race Riot of 1918," *PMHB* 99 (July 1975): 336–50.

103. Ibid., 347–50; Robert S. Gregg, "The Earnest Pastor's Heated Term: Robert J. Williams's Pastorate at 'Mother' Bethel, 1916–1920," *PMHB* 113 (January 1989): 67–88; Robert S. Gregg, *Sparks from the Anvil of Oppression: Philadelphia's African Methodists and Southern Migrants, 1890–1940* (Philadelphia, 1993), 88. See also Roger Lane, *Roots of Violence in Black Philadelphia, 1860–1900* (Cambridge, Mass., 1986), and *William Dorsey's Philadelphia and Ours: On the Past and Future of the Black City in America* (New York, 1991). In *Roots of Violence,* Lane analyzes the patterns of black violent criminal behavior in Philadelphia between 1850 and 1900 and concludes that the emergence of a black criminal subculture ("the product of a peculiar and bitter history") best explains the long-term persistence of black crime at the same time that violent crimes decreased for "the white population as a whole" (4). Lane's book offers an example of how some scholars soon returned to earlier and more pathological portraits of black life in the city. However, Lane analyzes the records of the American Negro Historical Society (called the William Henry Dorsey papers in honor of their "custodian") and shifts his perspective on black life. In *Dorsey's Philadelphia and Ours,* Lane concludes: "The thirty-five or forty years between the Emancipation Proclamation and roughly the turn of the century were by any measure the most hopeful in the history of black Americans. And while for the great rural majority the joy which greeted the death of slavery was tempered by political and social reverses later in the period, there were no such obvious setbacks among those who moved to Northern cities" (xi–xii).

104. Vincent P. Franklin, *The Education of Black Philadelphia: The Social and Educational History of a Minority Community, 1900–1950* (Philadelphia, 1979). Cf. Judy Jolley Mohraz, *The Separate Problem: Case Studies of Black Education in the North, 1900–1930* (Westport, Conn., 1979); John G. Ramsey, "The Education of Black Philadelphia: The Social and Educational History of a Minority Community, 1900–1950," *Urban Education* 15 (July 1980): 251–54.

105. For the national pattern, see Kenneth L. Kusmer, "African Americans in the City Since World War II: From the Industrial Era to the Post-Industrial Era," *Journal of Urban History* 21 (May 1995): 458–504. Citations on the Pennsylvania experience are found in Ancella Livers, "Selected Bibliography of African Americans in Western Pennsylvania," *Pittsburgh History* 78 (Winter 1995–96): 198–201.

106. H. Viscount Nelson, "The Philadelphia NAACP: Race Versus Class Consciousness During the Thirties," *Journal of Black Studies* 5 (May 1975): 255–76; V. P. Franklin, "Voice of the Black Community: The Philadelphia Tribune, 1912–1941," *PH* 51 (October 1984): 261–84; Charles T. Banner Haley, "To Do Good and Do Well: Middle-Class Blacks and the Depression, Philadelphia, 1929–1941" (Ph.D. diss., State University of New York, 1980); Constance A.

Cunningham, "Homer S. Brown: First Black Political Leader in Pittsburgh," *JNH* 66 (December 1981): 304–17; Rob Ruck, "Black Sandlot Baseball: The Pittsburgh Crawford," *WPHM* 66 (January 1983): 49–68; Rob Ruck, *Sandlot Seasons: Sport in Black Pittsburgh* (Urbana, Ill., 1987); David K. Wiggins, "Wendell Smith, the Pittsburgh Courier-Journal and the Campaign to Include Blacks in Organized Baseball, 1933–1945," *Journal of American Sports History* 10 (June 1983): 5–29.

107. Merl E. Reed, "Black Workers, Defense Industries, and Federal Agencies in Pennsylvania, 1941–1945," *Labor History* 27 (June 1986): 356–84.

108. David McBride, *Integrating the City of Medicine: Blacks in Philadelphia Health Care, 1910–1965* (Philadelphia, 1989).

109. Ruck, *Sandlot Seasons.*

110. John F. Bauman, Norman P. Hummon, and Edward K. Muller, "Public Housing, Isolation, and the Urban Underclass," *Journal of Urban History* 17 (May 1991): 264–92.

111. Elijah Anderson, "Race and Neighborhood Transition," in Paul E. Peterson, ed., *The New Urban Reality* (Washington, D.C., 1985): 99–127. Cf. Lenora E. Berson, *Case Study of a Riot: The Philadelphia Story* (New York, 1966); Emma J. Lapsansky, *Before the Model City: An Historical Exploration of North Philadelphia* (Philadelphia, 1969); Lane, *William Dorsey's Philadelphia and Ours;* Carl Husemoller Nightingale, "It Makes Me Wonder How I Keep from Going Under: Young People in Poor Black Philadelphia, and the Formation of a Collective Experience, 1940–1990" (Ph.D. diss., Princeton University, 1992). Key sociological and anthropological works on this period include Roger D. Abrahams, *Deep Down in the Jungle . . . Negro Narrative Folklore from the Streets of Philadelphia* (Chicago, 1970); Roger Abrahams, *Negro Folklore from South Philadelphia: A Collection and Analysis* (Philadelphia, 1961); John F. Szwed, "Black Folk Culture in Pennsylvania: Ongoing Bibliography of Pennsylvania Folklore and Related Materials," *Keystone Folklore* 19 (June 1974): 113–19; Melvin D. Williams, *On the Street Where I Lived* (New York, 1981); Anderson, *Streetwise;* Dan Rose, *Black American Street Life: South Philadelphia, 1969–1971* (Philadelphia, 1987).

112. Glasco, "Double Burden: The Black Experience in Pittsburgh" (note 86 above). Cf. Mitchell, *Beyond Adversity* (note 53 above). Museum Programs Division, Historical Society of Western Pennsylvania, 1993). In this teaching program, Mitchell emphasizes the achievements of African Americans and how some moved well "beyond adversity."

113. Jean Soderlund, "Black Women in Colonial Pennsylvania," *PMHB* 107 (January 1983): 49–68.

114. In his 1983 article, "Africans on the Delaware," for example, Wax called attention to the social and cultural processes by which Africans became African Americans, noting the role of language and the importance of the ratio of male and female slaves, blacks and whites, and American-born and African-born blacks (281). A somewhat earlier effort is Merle G. Brouwer, "The Negro as a Slave and as a Free Black in Colonial Pennsylvania" (Ph.D. diss., Wayne State University, 1973), and "Marriage and Family Life Among Blacks in Colonial Pennsylvania," *PMHB* 99 (July 1975): 368–72.

115. Janice Sumler-Lewis, "The Forten-Purvis Women of Philadelphia and the American Antislavery Crusade," *JNH* 66 (December 1981): 281–88.

116. Emma Jones Lapsansky, "Feminism, Freedom and Community: Charlotte Forten and Women Activists in Nineteenth-Century Philadelphia," *PMHB* 113 (January 1989): 3–19; Emma Jones Lapsansky, "Friends, Wives, and Strivings: Networks and Community Values Among Nineteenth-Century Philadelphia Afro-American Elites," *PMHB* 108 (January 1984): 3–24. Other studies on the role of women in the early-nineteenth-century black community include Margaret Hope, "One Great Bundle of Humanity: Frances Ellen Watkins Harper, 1825–

1911," *PMHB* 113 (January 1989): 21–43; Debra L. Newman, "Black Women in the Era of the American Revolution in Pennsylvania," *JNH* 61 (July 1976): 276–89.

117. Darlene Clark Hine, "Black Migration to the Urban Midwest: The Gender Dimension, 1915–1945," in Joe W. Trotter, ed., *The Great Migration in Historical Perspective: New Dimensions of Race, Class, and Gender* (Bloomington, Ind., 1991), 127–46.

118. Carolyn Leonard Carson, "And the Results Showed Promise. . . . Physicians, Childbirth, and Southern Black Migrant Women, 1916–1930; Pittsburgh as a Case Study," *Journal of American Ethnic History* 14 (Fall 1994): 32–64. Cf. Arthur J. Edmunds, *Daybreakers: The Story of the Urban League of Pittsburgh: The First Sixty-five Years* (Pittsburgh, 1983).

119. Darlene Clark Hine, Elsa Barkley Brown, and Rosalyn Terborg-Penn, eds., *Black Women in America: An Historical Encyclopedia*, vols. 1 and 2 (Bloomington, Ind., 1993), 1:xix.

120. Edna McKenzie, "Pittsburgh's Daisy Lampkin, NAACP National Field Secretary: Her Life, a Labor of Love and Service," *Pennsylvania Heritage* 9 (June 1983): 9–12.

121. Maurice Shipley, "Black Cultural Development in Pennsylvania (Since 1990)," *PH* 4 (December 1977): 48–51; Richard D. Beards, "His Eye Was on the Positive," *Pennsylvania Heritage* 16 (December 1990): 4–11, on photographer John Moseley; Stephen May, "The Resurrection of Henry Ossawa Tanner," *Pennsylvania Heritage* 28, no. 1 (December 1992): 22–29; Myron Schwartzman, "Romare Bearden: Pittsburgh Memories Inspire a Lifetime of Art," *Pittsburgh Magazine* (June 1992): 32–33; Eileen Southern, "Musical Practices in Black Churches of New York and Philadelphia, ca. 1800–1844," *Afro-Americans in New York Life and History* 4 (January 1980): 61–77; Fredrick Jerome, "The Philadelphia Tribune and Black Music and Musicians in Philadelphia, 1912–1932," *Western Journal of Black Studies* 16 (March 1992): 39–48; Neil Lanctot, "Fair Dealing and Clean Playing: Ed Bolden and the Hilldale Club, 1910–1932," *PMHB* 117 (January 1993): 3–49; Judith E. Stein, "Pippin," *Pennsylvania Heritage* 20 (Spring 1994): 22–29; Robert F. Ulle, "Popular Black Music in Nineteenth Century Philadelphia," *Pennsylvania Folklife* 25 (Winter 1975–76): 20–28; Judith Kerr Nina, "God-Given Work: The Life and Times of Sculptor Meta Vaux Warwick Fuller, 1877–1968" (Ph.D. diss., University of Massachusetts, 1986); Vincent Jubilee, "Philadelphia's Afro-American Literary Circle and The Harlem Renaissance" (Ph.D. diss., University of Pennsylvania, 1980); Eric Ledell Smith, "Pittsburgh's Black Opera Impressario: Mary Cardwell Dawson," *Pennsylvania Heritage* 21 (Winter 1995): 4–11.

122. Exceptions include Trotman's research on Presbyterian minister Matthew Anderson and Dennis Dickerson's study of a variety of denominations in western Pennsylvania. See note 89 above and accompanying main text.

123. Important components of a broader historical study of blacks and electoral politics do exist. See Miriam Ershkowitz and Joseph Zikmund, eds., *Black Politics in Philadelphia* (New York, 1971); Richard A. Keiser, "The Rise of a Biracial Coalition in Philadelphia," in Rufus P. Browning, Dale Rogers Marshal, and David H. Tabb, eds., *Racial Politics in American Cities* (New York, 1990), 49–72; David McBride, "Black Protest Against Racial Politics: Charles W. Gardner, Fredrick A. Hinton and Their Memorial of 1838," *PH* 46 (April 1979): 149–62; J. Whyatt Mondesire, "Politics of Black, White and Gray" (on politician William Gray III), *Philadelphia Magazine* 84 (January 1993): 49–55; Edward J. Price Jr., "The Black Voting Rights Issue in Pennsylvania, 1780–1900," *PMHB* 100 (July 1976): 356–73; Bruce Ransom, "Black Independent Electoral Politics in Philadelphia: The Election of Mayor W. Wilson Goode," in Michael Preston, Lenneal Henderson Jr., and Paul Puryear, eds., *The New Black Politics*, 2nd ed. (New York, 1987), 256–89; Henry C. Silcox, "The Black 'Better Class' Dilemma," *PMHB* 113 (January 1989): 45–66; Eric Ledell Smith, "Asking for Justice and Fair Play: African American State Legislators and Civil Rights in Early Twentieth Century Pennsylvania" *Pennsylvania History* 63 (Spring 1996): 169–203.

124. Andrew Buni, *Robert L. Vann of the "Pittsburgh Courier": Politics and Black Journalism* (Pittsburgh, 1974).

125. Charles Blockson, *The Underground Railroad: First Person Narratives of Escape to Freedom in the North* (New York, 1987); Billy G. Smith and Richard Wojtowicz, eds., *Slaves Who Stole Themselves: Advertisements for Runaways in the Pennsylvania Gazette, 1728–1790* (Philadelphia, 1989); Dorothy Sterling, *Speak Out in Thunder Tones: Letters and Other Writings by Black Northerners, 1787–1865* (New York, 1973); Maxwell Whiteman, *The Kidnapped and the Ransomed: The Narrative of Peter and Vina Still After Forty Years of Slavery* (Philadelphia, 1970).

126. Lane, *William Dorsey's Philadelphia and Ours;* Blockson, in McBride, *Blacks in Pennsylvania.*

127. The author is indebted to the PHMC Black History Advisory Committee for bringing this dimension of the state's history to the fore.

PART ONE

THE COMMERCIAL ECONOMY

The Transformation of Africans into
African Americans, 1684–1840

For Sale.

The time of a stout, healthy NEGRO
boy, eighteen years of age, to serve until
he is twenty-eight, late the property of
John Kelso, deceased.

H. B. KELSO, *Adm'r.*

Erie, March 31, 1821.

The Kelso family of Erie were well-known slave owners in northwestern Pennsylvania.
This notice illustrates the impact of the Gradual Abolition Act, which affected African
Americans throughout the state, including Erie. The individual for sale had to serve for
ten more years before he became free. (Courtesy of Erie County Historical Society)

Pennsylvania's first African Americans lived in the Delaware River Valley
region as early as 1639. Small in numbers, these early Africans were enslaved
by the Swedes, the Dutch, and the Finns. It was not until 1684, three years
after the first Quakers arrived in Pennsylvania, that the ship *Isabella* landed in
Philadelphia carrying 150 Africans. Thereafter, the state's black population
expanded considerably.

Although slavery existed in colonial Pennsylvania, the Keystone State developed a commercial rather than plantation economy. Philadelphia merchants handled most of the imports from England, exports to the West Indies, and short-haul commerce among American cities and small coastal towns and inland settlements. Integral to this commercial economy were the iron, gunmaking, and shipbuilding industries, which were dominated by individual entrepreneurs rather than companies.

African Americans in the commercial economy typically worked in a variety of occupations. They worked in agriculture, including raising cereals and grains and tending livestock (for commercial and noncommercial purposes), and they worked as charcoal-iron workers, sailmakers, longshoremen, and mariners; street vendors, domestic servants, and common laborers; and in various arts and crafts. Following the renowned slave insurrection in New York in 1712, the Pennsylvania Assembly passed an act to prohibit the importation of slaves by setting an extraordinarily high importation tax. Although the British Crown repealed the nonimportation law, the number of slaves coming to Pennsylvania gradually declined until the onset of the French and Indian War.

Resistance to the institution of slavery by both Pennsylvania blacks and whites led to a ban on slave importation and passage of the Gradual Abolition Act of 1780. Under the impact of the American Revolution, the size of the African American community in Pennsylvania grew from nearly 3,000 in 1750 to 10,300 in 1790 to 48,000 by 1840, representing the second largest concentration of African Americans in the northern states. The changes of these years involved not only shifts in the size of the black population but also the transformation of enslaved Africans into free African Americans. Whereas in 1750 most blacks were slaves, by the 1840s most African Americans in Pennsylvania were free people.

As the free black population increased, religious traditions and the church emerged at the heart of African American institutional, social, cultural, and political life. In this section, three chapters illustrate how Pennsylvania blacks made the transition from Africans to African Americans. Gary B. Nash analyzes the significance of slaves and slavery in the early growth and development of the commonwealth; Jean Soderlund gives a rare view of the situation and role of African American colonial women; and Emma Jones Lapsansky demonstrates the pivotal role of the black church in African American community life.

CHAPTER ONE

Slaves and Slave Owners in Colonial Philadelphia

Gary B. Nash

Although historians have recognized the importance of slavery in the social and economic life of colonial America, they have associated the institution primarily with the plantation economy of the southern colonies. Textbooks in colonial history and black history rarely mention urban slavery in the northern colonies, or take only passing notice of the institution and conclude that the small number of slaves in northern cities served as domestic servants, presumably in the households of the upper class.[1] The history of slavery in the colonial period is particularly obscure for Philadelphia, the largest city in British North America on the eve of the Revolution. In the extensive literature on William Penn's colony, the inquiring student finds only the most impressionistic information regarding the number of slaves in the city, the pattern of slave ownership, the use of slaves, and the interplay of demand for black and white bound labor. None of the historical accounts of Philadelphia published in the last century deals directly with slavery, thus leaving the impres-

This chapter was first published in the *William and Mary Quarterly*, 3rd ser., 30 (April 1973): 223–56. Reprinted by permission of the Institute of Early American History and Culture. The author wants to thank Peter Ball, Sharon Salinger, and Billy Smith for their comments and research assistance, as well as James A. Henretta, University of New South Wales; Richard S. Dunn, University of Pennsylvania; and Lutz Berkner, University of California Los Angeles, for their critical suggestions.

sion that the institution was incidental to the development of Philadelphia as an urban center.[2]

To some extent this gap in our knowledge can be explained by the traditional dependence of historians upon literacy evidence. In the case of Philadelphia they have been unusually handicapped by the fact that not a single official census was taken in the city during the colonial period. Although census data revealing the racial composition of the population are intermittently available for New York from 1698 to 1771 and for Boston from 1742 to 1770, historians of colonial Philadelphia have had to rely on the widely varying comments of residents and travelers to estimate the slave population.[3] Thus, the opinion of Governor William Keith, who reported in 1722 that Pennsylvania had few slaves "except a few Household Servants in the City of Philadelphia," and the view of Andrew Burnaby, who recorded nearly forty years later that "there are very few Negroes or slaves" in Philadelphia, and the comment of Benjamin Franklin, who wrote in 1770 that in the northern cities slaves were used primarily as domestic servants and that in North America as a whole "perhaps, one family in a Hundred . . . has a slave in it," have taken on unusual weight in the historical record.[4] To be sure, visitors to Philadelphia occasionally conveyed a different impression. For example, after visiting the city in 1750, Peter Kalm, the Swedish botanist, noted that in earlier decades slaves had been bought "by almost everyone who could afford it, the Quakers alone being an exception." Kalm added that, more recently, Quakers had overcome their scruples "and now . . . have as many Negroes as other people."[5] But Kalm's view seems to have been regarded as a minority report and is seldom cited by historians.

Despite the absence of census data, other kinds of evidence are available to indicate that slaveholding in Philadelphia was far more extensive than has generally been believed. It is known, for example, that in December 1684, just three years after the coming of the Quaker founders of the colony, a shipload of 150 African slaves arrived in Philadelphia. Transported by a Bristol mercantile firm, the slaves were eagerly purchased by Quaker settlers who were engaged in the difficult work of clearing trees and brush and erecting crude houses in the budding provincial capital. So great was the demand for the slaves, according to one prominent settler, that most of the specie brought to Philadelphia by incoming settlers was exhausted in purchasing the Africans.[6] Thus, at a time when the population of Philadelphia was probably about 2,000, some 150 slaves became incorporated into the town's social structure. Although little evidence is available to indicate the extent of slave importation in the next few decades, a survey of inventories of estates from 1682 to 1705 reveals that about one in fifteen Philadelphia families owned slaves in that period.[7]

It is unlikely that slaves entered the city at more than a trickle in the next few decades, at least in part because of high import duties imposed after 1712. But the reduction of the import duty to £2 per head in 1729 and the lapse of any duty after 1731 seem to have triggered a significant increase in slave importations. Although most Quaker merchants withdrew from the trade in the 1730s after a period of controversy within the Society of Friends regarding the morality of importing and trading slaves, merchants of other religious persuasions gladly accommodated the growing demand for slave labor.[8] Some indication of this new importance of slavery can be inferred from the burial statistics which were recorded in Philadelphia in 1722, 1729, 1731–32, and 1738–44 and published annually beginning in 1747.[9] Whereas only 26 Negroes died in Philadelphia in 1722, some 97 were buried there in 1729, 102 in 1731, and 83 in the following year. These figures tend to confirm the observation of Ralph Sandiford, an early Quaker abolitionist who wrote in 1730: "We have *negroes* flocking in upon us since the duty on them is reduced to 40 *s per* head for their importation."[10] Indeed, the proportion of black deaths in the annual death toll during the early 1730s was the highest in the city's history (Tables 1.1 and 1.2).

Following a period of relatively heavy imports in the early 1730s, the traffic in slaves seems to have slackened considerably. Correspondingly, the number of black deaths declined in the late 1730s and did not again reach the level of the period from 1729 to 1732 until after 1756. This leveling off of the slave trade at a time when the city was growing rapidly cannot be satisfactorily explained in economic terms since the high import duties of the earlier period had not been reinstituted. Instead, it must be attributed to a preference for German and Scotch-Irish redemptioners and indentured servants who flooded into Philadelphia between 1732 and 1754. Although these immigrants had been attracted to Pennsylvania in substantial numbers since 1716, their numbers increased dramatically beginning in 1732.[11] The relative de-

Table 1.1. Burials in Philadelphia, 1722–1755

| Year | Average Burials per Year | | |
	White	Black	% Black
1722	162	26	13.8
1729–32	396	94	19.2
1738–42	418	51	10.9
1743–48[a]	500	64	11.3
1750–55	655	55	7.7

[a]Based on details registered in 1743–44 and 1747–48; the bills of mortality for 1745–46 are not extant.

cline in black deaths between 1732 and 1755 suggests that city dwellers with sufficient resources to command the labor of another person usually preferred German or Scotch-Irish indentured servants to black slaves when the former were readily available, even though indentured labor was probably somewhat more expensive.[12]

The beginning of the Seven Years' War in 1756 marked the onset of a decade in which slavery and slave trading reached their height in colonial Philadelphia. This can be explained largely by the sudden drying up of the supply of indentured German and Scotch-Irish laborers who had disembarked at Philadelphia in record numbers between 1749 and 1754.[13] Historians have never made clear the reasons for this stoppage, although most have implied that the wartime disruption of transatlantic traffic put an end to the Palatine and Scotch-Irish emigration.[14] The answer, however, originates on land, not on sea. Beginning in the fall of 1755, the English commanders in the colonies began recruiting indentured servants in order to bolster the strength of the British units, which were reeling under attacks of the French and their Indian allies on the western frontier.[15] About 2,000 Pennsylvania servants had been recruited by the end of 1755, according to one estimate, and the problem was serious enough by early 1756 to warrant a strong message from the Assembly to the governor, warning: "If the Possession of a bought Servant . . . is . . . rendered precarious . . . the Purchase, and Of Course the Importation, of Servants will be discouraged, and the People driven to the Necessity of pro-viding themselves with Negro Slaves, as the Property in them and their Ser-vice seems at present more secure."[16] Rather than reversing the policy of luring servants into the British army while offering partial financial recom-pense to their owners, Parliament legitimized and extended the practice in a law which was carried to the colonies in July 1756 by Lord Loudoun, the new British commander-in-chief. By this time Benjamin Franklin was issuing firm warnings to the English government and predicting what had already happened. The continuing enlistment of servants, he wrote, "will . . . intirely destroy the Trade of bringing over Servants to the Colonies, either from the British Islands or Germany."[17] As Franklin explained, "no Master for the future can afford to give such a Price for Servants as is sufficient to encourage the Merchant to import them" when the risk of losing a newly purchased servant to the British army remained so great.[18] With little hope for a reversal of English policy, Pennsylvanians seeking bound labor turned to black slaves. According to one of Philadelphia's largest merchants, writing in September 1756, "all importations of white Servants is ruined by enlisting them, and we must make more general use of Slaves."[19] If those with capital to invest in human labor had heretofore preferred white indentured labor to black slave labor, even at some economic disadvantage, by late 1756 their options had

Table 1.2. Burials in Philadelphia, 1756–1775

Year	Average Burials per Year		
	White	Black	% Black
1756–60	917	91	9.2
1761–65	990	87	8.1
1766–70	856	87	9.2
1771–75	1,087	87	7.4

been narrowed and they turned eagerly, in the face of the rising cost and unpredictability of white labor, to African slaves.

The shift to black slave labor is reflected both in the shipping records and in the annual bills of mortality in Philadelphia. Importation of slaves, which according to a recent study had averaged only about twenty a year in the 1740s and about thirty a year in the early 1750s, began to rise sharply. Although precise figures are not available, it appears that at least 100 slaves entered Philadelphia in 1759. By 1762, probably the peak year of slave importations in the colony's history, as many as 500 slaves may have arrived, many of them directly from Africa. In each of the following four years, between 100 and 200 embarked.[20]

Corroborating evidence of this rapid expansion of slavery is provided by the burial statistics of blacks during these years. Burials had averaged 51 a year from 1738 to 1742, 64 a year from 1743 to 1748, and 55 a year from 1750 to 1755, when unprecedented numbers of slaves were sold in the city, and remained steady at an average of 87 a year in the next three five-year periods (Table 1.2).

What makes this rapid growth of slavery in Philadelphia especially noteworthy is that it occurred at precisely the time the pre-Revolutionary abolitionist movement, centered in Philadelphia and led by John Woolman and Anthony Benezet, was reaching its climax.[21] Attempting to end the slave trade through appeals to conscience at a time when white indentured labor was becoming unreliable and expensive, these ideologues found their pleas falling on ears rendered deaf by sudden changes in the economics of labor market.

The rapid wartime growth of the slave trade ended as fast as it had begun. By the beginning of the 1760s, with the war subsiding and British recruiting sergeants no longer at work, the influx of German and Scotch-Irish redemptioners and servants recommenced. As indicated in Table 1.3, the Scotch-Irish immigration, which throughout the colonial period flowed predominantly through Philadelphia, had begun an upward swing in 1760; within three years, ships crowded with Palatine immigrants were also disgorging

Table 1.3. Number of immigrant ships arriving in Philadelphia,[22] 1750–1775

Year	German	Irish	Total	Year	German	Irish	Total
1750	15	6	21	1763	4	15	19
1751	16	0	16	1764	11	8	22
1752	19	3	22	1765	5	10	15
1753	19	5	24	1766	5	20	25
1754	19	5	24	1767	5	13	18
1755	2	2	4	1768	4	7	11
1756	1	1	2	1769	4	11	15
1757	0	6	6	1770	7	12	19
1758	0	3	3	1771	9	19	28
1759	0	2	2	1772	8	15	13
1760	0	7	7	1773	15	17	32
1761	1	8	9	1774	6	15	21
1762	0	10	10	1775	2	13	15

NOTE: The number of German ship arrivals is probably quite accurate. The Scotch-Irish arrivals are based mainly on shipping advertisements, but because the newspaper files are not complete, the figures for these may be too low.

their passengers on the Philadelphia docks. Concurrently the slave trade tapered off. The import duties, reported annually to the Assembly by the customs officer at Philadelphia, indicate that from September 1764 to September 1768, when German and Scotch-Irish immigration had almost reached prewar levels, slave imports dropped to an annual average of 66. Between 1768 and 1770, they declined to less than 30 per year,[23] and by the end of the latter year the Pennsylvania slave trade had all but ceased.[24] Given the choice once more between black slaves and white indentured servants, Philadelphians and other Pennsylvanians chose the latter to satisfy their requirements for bound labor.

For the years from 1767 to 1775, the size and composition of the black population in Philadelphia can be charted with unusual precision because abundant records with which the social historian can work have survived: transcripts of the tax assessors' reports for 1767, 1769, 1772, and 1774, and enumeration of taxable slaves in the city in 1773, and constables' returns for 1775.[25] Unlike earlier tax lists, which indicate only the total rateable estates of the city's inhabitants, the assessors' reports for these years record each category of assessable wealth, including land, buildings, ground rents, slaves, servants, and livestock. In addition, the constables' returns of 1775 list all heads of households and include for each house the number—and in most cases the ages—of all tenants, hired and bound servants, slaves, and children. As specified by law, the tax assessor listed only slaves between 12 and 50 and servants between 15 and 50 years of age as assessable property,[26] so the totals obtained from these lists must be adjusted to account for slaves and servants outside of these age limits.

The tax assessors' reports of 1767 indicate a total of 814 slaves between the ages of 12 and 50 in the city of Philadelphia. If we include as a part of urban Philadelphia the district of Southwark, which lay along the Delaware River immediately south of the city and contained many of the shipyards, ropewalks, tanneries, sail lofts, and ship chandlers' offices associated with the maritime commerce of the city, the number of slaves is swelled to 905.[27]

To this number we must add slaves who were under 12 or over 50 years of age. Unfortunately, almost no data for determining the age structure of the slave population in Philadelphia are available for the years before 1775. It is virtually certain, moreover, that by 1775 the age distribution had changed markedly after a decade of declining importations. It is reasonable, however, to infer the age distribution of Philadelphia slaves for coeval census data for New York City slaves. In the enumerations of 1731 and 1737, some 23.5 percent and 25.3 percent, respectively, of the slaves in New York City were under 10 years of age. In the census reports of 1746, 1749, 1756, and 1771, the black population was divided into those 16 and over and those under 16. The under-16 segment was, respectively, 48.7, 43.7, 41.2, and 36.2 percent of the whole slave population. These figures indicate that the proportion of children was declining and that Negroes 12 years or younger made up about 25 to 30 percent of the slave population of New York City in the decade before the Revolution. Census data for eight counties of New Jersey between 1726 and 1772, and for the entire province of New York between 1703 and 1771, show a fairly low range of variation in the age distribution of slaves and thus reinforce one's confidence in estimating that about 30 percent of the slaves in Philadelphia were too young to be included in the tax assessors' reports in 1767.[28]

Slaves over 50 years of age are estimated to have constituted 5 percent of the Philadelphia slave population in 1767. The Philadelphia constables' reports of 1775, which give the ages of most of the city's slaves, reveal that 7.6 percent of the slaves were over 50. Because the age structure of the slave population probably advanced from 1767 to 1775 as a result of a low birth rate and a marked decrease in slave importations, this figure was probably nearer 5 percent for the former year. Comparable data from New York City show that 6.7 percent of male slaves were over 60 in 1746, 3.7 percent in 1749, 6.0 percent in 1756, and 2.8 percent in 1771.[29]

After adjusting the total of 905 taxable slaves to account for those of non-taxable ages, we can estimate that in 1767, at a point only a few years after

Table 1.4. Slave population in Philadelphia, 1767–1775

Year	Slaves Age 12–50	Estimated Slave Population[a]	Approx. Total Population	% Slave
1767	905	1,392	16,000	8.8
1769	856	1,270	16,850	7.9
1772	774	1,069	18,225	5.9
1773	669[b]	945	18,700	5.1
1774	658	869	19,175	4.5
1775	450	672[c]	19,650	3.4

[a]Based on estimates that 30% of the slave population were under 12 and 5% were over 50 in 1767 and that these ratios changed steadily for the next eight years, by which time those under 12 composed 15% and those over 50 were 7.6% of the slave population.[32]
[b]The Galloway report indicated 608 slaves for the city. This number has been increased by 10% to include Southwark, where in 1772 and 1774 slaves represented 10.4% and 9.7% of the total number of slaves in the city.
[c]The total for the city has been increased 10%, to include Southwark. The number of slaves of all ages in the city was 611, of whom 418 were between 12 and 50 years of age, as reported on the constables' returns.

what was probably the apogee of slaveholding in the colonial period, almost 1,400 slaves served their masters in Philadelphia. In a total population of about 16,000, slaves represented one-twelfth of the city's inhabitants.[30]

As importations of black slaves subsided following the reopening of the white indentured servant trade, the slave population in Philadelphia entered a period of substantial decline. Between 1767 and 1773 the number of slaves between 12 and 50 years old in Philadelphia decreased from 905 to 669, and the approximate total number of slaves from 1,392 to 945. The number of slaves dropped again, although slightly, in 1774 and then decreased sharply in the following year (Table 1.4).

How is one to explain this precipitous decline of the slave population, which between 1767 and 1775 reduced the number of slaves in the city by more than half? Given the intensity of the abolitionist campaign during these years, one might suspect that the manumission of slaves was the major factor. Benjamin Rush's assertion in May 1773 that three-quarters of his fellow Philadelphians "cry out against slavery" seems to confirm such a view.[31] But even among Quakers, the only vigorous opponents of slavery in Philadelphia, manumissions were rare until late in 1775, a year after the Yearly Meeting of the Society of Friends took a strong stand against slaveholding and began systematic visitations to Quaker slaveholders in order to encourage private manumissions. In fact, as the carefully kept Quaker records reveal, only eighteen slaves were manumitted in Philadelphia between 1766 and 1775, and of these fourteen belonged to "persons not in Membership with Friends."[33]

The real explanation of the rapidly declining number of slaves was the inability of the slave population to reproduce itself in a period when slave importations had virtually ceased. This is made manifest by correlating the data from the annual mortality bills and the constables' reports of 1775. The mortality bills reveal that between 1767 and 1775 some 679 blacks, almost all of them slaves, were buried in the "Strangers Burialground"—an average of about 75 per year. In an era when slave importations were inappreciable, one side effect of this heavy death toll was to alter the age structure of the slave population. Many female slaves passed beyond the age of fertility and were not replaced by younger slave women. This further depressed a fertility rate, which even in periods of substantial importation was far below the white birth rate for two major reasons. First, male slaves outnumbered female slaves in almost all places and times during the colonial period, and Philadelphia, so far as can be ascertained from the limited data, was no exception.[34] Second, in a city where more than half of the slaveholders owned only a single adult slave, sexually mature male and female slaves infrequently lived together under the same roof, thus further reducing the incidence of conception.[35]

The low fertility rate of slave women in the northern regions in general was noted by several eighteenth-century amateur demographers. Franklin, for example, remarked in 1751 that only by constant importation was the African population maintained.[36] Edward Wigglesworth, professor of divinity at Harvard, ventured the same opinion in 1775, writing that "a large annual importation from Africa [was required] to keep the stock good."[37] That these impressions of knowledgeable observers applied with special force to Philadelphia after slave importations dropped off in the late 1760s is evident from the age structure of slaves listed on the constables' report of 1775. These lists give the ages of 89 percent of the city's slaves, of whom only 10.7 percent were under 10 years of age. Data for other areas indicate approximately the same age structure.[38] From 1767 to 1775, when the slave population averaged about 1,000, some 679 blacks had been buried in Philadelphia, and fewer than 100 black children had been born and survived infancy. This excess of deaths over births can only be explained by an extremely low birth rate, a drastically high infant mortality rate, or a combination of the two.[39]

While the slave labor force was contracting rapidly, the number of free blacks in Philadelphia grew slowly. Free blacks had lived in the city at least as early as 1717, when the Anglican church recorded the baptism of a free black woman.[40] Although it is extremely difficult to trace the growth of the free black community during the next half-century, some scattered evidence is available to throw a glimmer of light on these Philadelphians. Between 1748 and 1752, fourteen free blacks, some adults and some children, were baptized in the Anglican church.[41] And in 1751 the *Pennsylvania Gazette* printed the complaint of one Philadelphian who upbraided a number of free blacks who "have taken Houses, Rooms, or Cellars, for their Habitations" for creating disorders with "Servants, Slaves, and other idle and vagrant Persons."[42] By 1768, eight free black children were attending an Anglican school established ten years before for the education of blacks, and in 1770 a Quaker school for blacks had enrolled thirty-six children of free blacks.[43] Twenty-seven free blacks are mentioned in the Anglican baptism records between 1756 and 1765, and in the following decade forty-one additional free blacks were cited.[44] From this scattered and incomplete evidence, it seems likely that the free black population was about 150 in 1770. Occasional manumissions in the early 1770s may have swelled the number of free blacks to about 250 on the eve of the Revolution.[45]

These population estimates can be combined with the statistics compiled from the bills of mortality to approximate a crude death rate for 1767, when slavery was near its peak in Philadelphia. By calculating the slave population at 1,392 (Table 1.4) and adding 100 free blacks, an estimated black population of 1,492 is obtained. With black burials averaging 102 annually in Philadelphia in the five-year period 1765–69, this indicates a crude death rate of 68.4. Although this figure seems startlingly high, it is not out of range with the death rate of Negroes in pre-Revolutionary Boston, where between 1742 and 1760 the crude mortality rate varied between 54 and 67.[46] Moreover, there is good reason for the black mortality rate in Philadelphia to have exceeded that of Boston: despite Benjamin Franklin's vigorous denials, Philadelphia seems to have been an unusually unhealthy island in the middle of the generally salubrious northeast coastal plain.[47]

By examining the tax assessors' reports of 1767, it is also possible to draw a collective profile of slave-owning Philadelphians for that year. The assessors' reports disclose that, of the 3,319 taxpayers in the city, 521 (15.7 percent) owned slaves. Because taxpayers who owned only slaves under 12 or over 50 years of age do not appear on the assessors' returns as slave owners, this total must be increased somewhat. The constables' reports of 1775 show that almost 14 percent of the slave owners in that year owned only slaves whose ages fell outside the taxable limits. If this pattern applied in 1767, more than 70 slave owners would not be revealed by the assessors' returns and the total number of slave owners should be increased to about 590.[48] A still more accurate measurement of how extensively slavery permeated the social structure can be made by keeping in mind that the number of taxpayers and the number of householders were by no means the same. Of the 3,319 taxpayers in 1767, some 337 were assessed a poll tax, indicating that they were single freemen, usually living at the home of their parents or renting lodging in the house of another. Others—perhaps as many as 10 percent—were tenants.[49] It is clear from the tax assessors' reports that very

Table 1.5. Pattern of slave and servant ownership in Philadelphia, 1767

No. of Taxable Slaves or Servants	No. of Slave Owners	% of Slave Owners	No. of Servant Owners	% of Servant Owners
1	297	57	169	72
2	136	26	55	24
3	56	11	6	3
4 or more	32	6	3	1
TOTAL	521		233	

few tenants or persons assessed a poll tax owned slaves. By conservative estimate, then, the number of householders could not have numbered more than about 80 percent of the number of taxpayers. Calculating the number of households in Philadelphia at about 2,655 (80 percent of the total number of taxpayers) and the number of slave owners at about 590, we can estimate that slaves resided in the homes of more than one in every five families in Philadelphia in 1767.

To understand how many Philadelphians participated in the institution of slavery, one must also take into account the shifting composition of the slave-owning group in the city. Although only fragmentary evidence remains by which to trace the sale or transfer after death of slaves, some indication of the turnover in slave ownership can be inferred by comparing the tax assessors' reports of 1767 and 1769. On the 1769 list, 125 persons appeared as slave owners who had not been assessed for slave property in 1767. Including these "new" owners, more than 700 Philadelphia families, representing about one-quarter of the households in the city, were involved in slavekeeping in the closing years of the 1760s. However moderate the treatment of slaves, and whatever the quasi-familial status of some bondsmen and women, the master-slave relationship and the ownership of other human beings as chattel property were extensively woven into the fabric of city life. If John Woolman was correct in believing that slaveholding, even by the kindliest of masters, did "yet deprave the mind in like manner and with as great certainty as prevailing cold congeals water," and that the absolute authority exercised by the master over his slave established "ideas of things and modes of conduct" that inexorably molded the attitudes of children, neighbors, and friends of slaveholders, then Philadelphia, at least for a brief period, was indeed deeply involved in the "peculiar institution."[50]

In sharp contrast to the towns of the colonial South, most slave owners in Philadelphia held only one or two adult slaves. Of the 521 slave owners appearing on the 1767 tax list, 57 percent owned only a single slave between 12 and 50 years of age, and another 26 percent owned but two (Table 1.5). If slaves under 12 and over 50 years of age were included, these figures would be somewhat, but probably not significantly, changed. In all likelihood, this pattern of ownership reflects the limited possibilities for employing slaves in gang labor in a city where most of the productive labor, outside of shipbuilding and a few enterprises such as bakeries, brickyards, and ropewalks, was still carried out in the small shop of the individual artisan.

That slave-owning in Pennsylvania was predominantly an urban phenomenon is made apparent by comparing the number of slaves in the city with figures for outlying rural areas. In Chester and Lancaster counties, the most densely populated and agriculturally productive areas in the colony, slaves numbered only 289 and 106 respectively on the assessors' lists of 1759. Only 4.2 percent of the taxpayers in Chester County, and 1.2 percent in Lancaster County, owned slaves in that year.[51] Although it might be expected that the large importations of the early 1760s would have increased the incidence of slaveholding somewhat in these areas, this did not in fact happen. By 1773–74 the number of slaves reported by the tax assessors in Chester and Lancaster counties had dropped to 237 and 52 respectively, while the number of taxable white inhabitants was increasing sharply between 1760 and 1770—from 4,761 to 5,484 in Chester County and from 5,635 to 6,606 in Lancaster County.[52]

Even in Philadelphia County, immediately to the north and west of the city, slaveholding never approached the level obtained in the city. In 1767 only 206 of 5,235 taxpayers (3.9 percent) owned a total of 331 taxable slaves.[53] Thus the incidence of slaveholding in the city was about four times that of the surrounding countryside. No tax lists for Philadelphia County are extant before 1767, making it impossible to determine whether slaveholding was increasing or decreasing at this time. But it appears that slaveholding was near its peak in 1767; by 1772 the number of slaves had dropped from approximately 502 to 457, and two years later had declined to 410 (Table 1.6).[54]

Table 1.6. Composition of the unfree labor force in Philadelphia, 1767–1775[55]

	Philadelphia City				Philadelphia County			
Year	Slaves	Servants	Total	% Slaves	Slaves	Servants	Total	% Slaves
1767	1,392	395	1,787	77.9	502	422	924	54.3
1769	1,270	482	1,752	72.5	536	443	979	54.7
1772	1,069	558	1,627	65.7	457	389	846	54.0
1773	945	673	1,618	58.4	440	426	866	50.8
1774	869	767	1,636	53.1	410	467	877	46.7
1775	673	869	1,542	43.6	—	—	—	—

The tax assessors' lists also reveal that slaves composed more than three-quarters of the unfree labor in the city in 1767 and that slaveholders outnumbered servant holders more than two to one (Tables 1.5 and 1.6). The five-year period between 1755 and 1760, when almost no indentured servants entered the colony and most of those already there completed their terms of servitude, serves to explain this emphasis on black labor. That 104 ships arrived in Philadelphia with Scotch-Irish and German immigrants in the six intervening years before the tax list of 1767 was drawn[56] suggests that for at least a brief period in the early 1760s slaves may have represented as much as 85 to 90 percent of the city's bound laborers. After 1767, however, with slave importations reduced to a trickle and white indentured servants crowding into the city, the composition of the unfree labor force underwent equally sudden changes, reverting to what was probably the pre-1755 pattern. By 1775, white servants, who less than a decade before were less than one-quarter of the unfree labor force, constituted 56 percent of Philadelphia's bound workers (Table 1.6).

A different pattern prevailed in the rural areas outside Philadelphia, as indicated in Table 1.6 by the figures for Philadelphia County. Whereas white indentured servants made up only 22 percent of the unfree labor force in 1767 in the city, they constituted almost half the bound laborers in the surrounding county. Seven years later, this pattern had changed only slightly in Philadelphia County, where the incidence of both servantholding and slaveholding was always much lower than in the city.

What also claims our attention is the fact that, at a time when the population of the city was growing rapidly, the demand for bound labor, either black or white, was shrinking. Between 1767 and 1775, when urban Philadelphia grew from approximately 16,000 to 20,000, the number of servants and slaves declined from 1,787 to 1,542. Whether this was a long-range trend reflecting changes in the organization of work and the growing profitability of wage versus bound labor is impossible to determine without examining a series of postwar assessors' reports.[57] But it is possible that on the eve of the Revolution a plentiful supply of free wage laborers, created by rural overpopulation in the hinterland, decreased the demand for bound labor in Philadelphia, or the sources of indentured labor in Germany and Ireland may have been drying up. Whatever the reasons, those with money to invest in human labor were turning more and more in the last third of the eighteenth century from the bound to the wage labor.

By analyzing the 1767 tax list, it is also possible to establish the correlation between economic status, as measured by assessable wealth, and slave ownership. As might be expected, slave owners were concentrated in the upper wealth bracket. Only 5 percent of Philadelphia's 521 slave owners in 1767

Table 1.7. Economic status of Philadelphia and Boston slaveholders

	No. and % Slaveholders			
Position Among All Taxables	Philadelphia, 1767		Boston, 1771	
Bottom 50%	26	5.0%	17	5.4%
Upper middle 25%	151	28.9	70	22.0
Top 25%	344	66.1	231	72.6
TOTAL	521		318	

came from the bottom half of the white wealth scale, and these 26 individuals owned only 28 of the 905 taxable slaves in the city. Almost two-thirds of the slave owners had sufficient wealth to place them in the top quarter of the property owners, and one-third of them, holding 44 percent of the city's slaves, came from the wealthiest tenth of the population. This unsurprising correlation between wealth and slave ownership parallels the Boston pattern of 1771 (Table 1.7).[58]

Slave owners in the city were distributed through the top half of the social scale to a far greater degree than in the rural areas. Whereas the top 10 percent of the taxpayers in Philadelphia owned 44 percent of the city's slaves, the upper tenth in Philadelphia County owned 77 percent of the slaves, in Chester County 58 percent, and in Lancaster County 60 percent.[59] The tendency for slaveholding to be heavily concentrated in the upper reaches of rural society but to be diffused through the middle strata of urban society is probably best explained by the greater prosperity enjoyed by those at the middling levels of city life. In Philadelphia County, for example, the top one-tenth of the wealth holders included all those with estates of £24 or more. In the city, by contrast, a taxpayer needed at least £60 of taxable property to count himself or herself in the wealthiest tenth of the community. Put differently, more people in the city than in the country had amassed sufficient wealth to afford a slave, and it seems likely that this contributed to the much higher incidence of slaveholding and servantholding in Philadelphia than in outlying areas.

The correlation between wealth and slave ownership can be misleading, however. At first glance it seems to indicate that slaveholding was restricted to the elite in Philadelphia and thus, like the building of stately townhouses and the flourishing of the arts in the third quarter of the eighteenth century, was a part of cultivating the genteel life. This view is reinforced by scanning the list of slaveholders, which is studded with names of prominent pre-Revolutionary Philadelphians—merchants, professionals, proprietary officeholders, and political magnates such as John Baynton, Thomas Bond, Thomas Cadwalader, Benjamin Chew, John Dickinson, Benjamin Franklin, Joseph

Table 1.8. Occupations of Philadelphia slaveholders in 1767

Occupational Group	No. and % of Slave Owners		No. and % of Taxable Slaves Owned	
Merchants and retailers	161	31.2%	291	32.2%
Professionals (including doctors, lawyers, officeholders)	39	7.5	95	10.5
Service trades (including tavernkeepers, barbers, printers)	30	5.6	48	5.2
Wood, metal, and stone workers	66	12.6	104	11.5
Cloth and leather workers	56	10.7	97	10.7
Food processors (including butchers, bakers, brewers, millers)	31	6.0	70	7.7
Maritime trades (including captains, mariners, shipwrights, and sail, rope, and blockmakers)	75	14.2	122	13.3
Miscellaneous (including widows)	31	6.1	44	4.9
Unknown	32	6.1	34	3.8
TOTAL	521		905	

Galloway, Thomas Lawrence, Samuel McCall, Samuel Mifflin, Robert Morris, Edward Pennington, Edmund Physick, Edward Shippen, Joseph Shippen, Robert Waln, Thomas Wharton, and Thomas Willing. But an analysis of the occupations of slave owners reveals that slaves were owned by a wide range of artisans—and even by mariners and carters, who commanded little leverage in the social and political life of the city and could hardly be considered proto-aristocrats.

As Table 1.8 indicates, about one-third of the taxable slaves in the city were owned by merchants and shopkeepers. Many of these slaves were doubtless household servants, while others were being held for sale by merchants engaged in the slave trade or were contracted out for day labor. Ninety-five slaves (10.5 percent) were held by thirty-nine "professional" men—sixteen doctors, ten lawyers, nine officeholders, two conveyancers, a clergyman, and a teacher. Innkeepers or tavernholders owned thirty-four slaves, and widows and "gentlemen" accounted for thirty-one more.

Nearly half of the city's slaves are included in these categories, but the other half were owned by artisans, men associated with maritime enterprise, or, in a few cases, by laborers. Almost every occupational category in the city included at least one slaveholder and some, such as bakers, metalworkers, woodworkers, and ropemakers, were heavily represented.

That slave labor was used extensively by artisans and craftsmen is also

Built in 1702, the London Coffee House was located on South Front Street in what is now Center City Philadelphia. It was a meeting place for local merchants, mariners, and bankers. Equipped with a platform for displaying captive Africans, the London Coffee House was one of colonial Philadelphia's major marketplaces for the sale and purchase of slaves. (Courtesy of the Historical Society of Pennsylvania)

revealed by the small number of Philadelphians who held four or more slaves of assessable age—men, in other words, who were employing labor on a fairly large scale by pre-Revolutionary standards. Only 32 of 521 slaveholders in Philadelphia were included in this group. Of these, eight were merchants, including such prominent figures of Philadelphia society as William Allen, perhaps the wealthiest man in Philadelphia, Isaac Coxe, Samuel Howell, John Hughes (later appointed stamp collector), Archibald McCall, Samuel McCall, Samuel Mifflin, and Thomas Willing. Six lawyers, including John Dickinson (whose eleven slaves made him the second-largest slave-holder in the city), John Ross, and John Lawrence, were also among this group, as were two proprietary officials, James Tilghman and Benjamin Chew. But among the other large slaveholders were five bakers, three rope-makers, a sailmaker, a goldsmith, and a ferryman, whose slaves apparently operated the ferries that plied the Delaware River between Philadelphia and Burlington, New Jersey. The largest slave owner in Philadelphia was John Phillips, whose thirteen slaves manned the city's largest ropewalk in Southwark.[60]

Perhaps most surprising is the large number of ship captains and mariners who owned slaves. Almost 10 percent of the slave owners were men whose work took them to sea. It is possible that these Philadelphians purchased female slaves to assist their wives with household tasks while they were away. But given the racial attitudes of colonial Americans and the general appre-hension of slaves that existed in all urban centers, it is more likely that most of these seagoing Philadelphians purchased slaves to work on board ship. The substantial number of mariners and ship captains who owned slaves suggests that the American merchant marine may have been far more heavily manned by black labor than has been previously recognized.[61] It is especially likely that slaves owned by mariners were black sailors. The constable reports reveal that all but two of thirty-two mariners owning slaves were married, but twenty-three of them owned no house, renting their quarters from others. Nine of them had no taxable assets other than their slaves, suggesting that these mariners, who were generally located in the lower reaches of society, had used the small amount of capital they possessed to purchase a slave and thus increase their share of the profits from Atlantic voyages.

Mariners were not alone in preferring slave labor to real estate as a field for investment. Of the 521 slave owners, only 190 (36.4 percent) owned a house or property in Philadelphia. The other 331 rented their dwellings, pre-ferring to put excess capital into the acquisition of a slave or two rather than purchasing or building a house. Of course, the incidence of both slave ownership and home ownership increased with the level of wealth in Phila-delphia, so that many men in the top echelon owned both real estate and human property. But for a significant number of middle-class Philadelphians with limited capital to invest, acquisition of slaves took precedence over the purchase of a house. Indeed, for one-eighth of slaveholders their human prop-erty represented their only taxable assets. Typical of these Philadelphians were men and women like Charles Jenkins, a mariner living in Southwark; John Dowers, a sailmaker in Mulberry Ward; William Benning, a staymaker in Walnut Ward; and Widow Sinclear, who kept a tavern in Walnut Ward.

Thus a great many of Philadelphia's slave owners appear to have been small entrepreneurs who lacked the assets to purchase or maintain a slave merely for the social prestige it would confer. Instead, most of these city dwellers seem to have purchased slaves, particularly after the white indentured labor supply became uncertain, as a means of carrying on their crafts and small-scale industries and thereby improving their fortunes.

Correlations between slave ownership and religious affiliation are difficult to establish because church membership records are incomplete for the pre-Revolutionary period. But the Society of Friends was assiduous in record keeping, and therefore it is possible to identify almost all of the Quaker slaveholders and determine whether the incidence of slaveholding among Friends differed from that of non-Friends. This is of special significance, because for Quakers buying, selling, or even owning a slave involved a direct conflict of economic interest and ideology. Whereas an Anglican, Presbyterian, German Lutheran, Methodist, or member of any other religious group in Philadelphia could participate in the institution of slavery secure in the knowledge that it was justified both by his church and by the prevailing philosophies of the Western world, Quakers could not. Since the 1690s, individual Quakers had been developing piecemeal the argument that slave-owning was sinful and that only by dissociating themselves from it could they cleanse themselves of impurities.[62] Individual arguments of this kind were followed by official action. Periodically after 1730, the Philadelphia Yearly Meeting advised its members not to buy or sell slaves. More important, prodded by the tireless work of John Woolman, the Yearly Meeting agreed in 1758 to exclude Friends who bought or sold slaves from meetings for business and to refuse their contributions as tainted money. Although it would not institute a policy of disownment, as Woolman urged, the Yearly Meeting appointed a committee which, with the assistance of Friends appointed by various Quarterly Meetings, was to visit all slaveholders and convey the message that slave ownership, although not yet cause for disownment, was no longer consistent with the Quaker view of just relations among the brotherhood of man. Woolman himself took up the task of making independent visits to dozens of Philadelphia slave owners, asking them to look into their hearts to ascertain whether their ownership of slaves did not reveal an immoral lust for gain.[63] These visitations, together with the official pronouncements of the Yearly and Quarterly Meetings, involved every Quaker slaveholder by the late 1750s in a situation where economic interest and ideology were in direct conflict. Increasing the tension was the fact that the uncertainties and rising price of white bound labor, owing to the recruitment of indentured servants by the British army beginning in late 1755, created new inducements for the purchase of black labor at the very time that the Quaker leaders were taking fresh steps to end the involvement of Friends in the institution of slavery.

The best method of estimating the size of the Quaker segment of the entire Philadelphia population, in order to lay a basis for comparing the ratio of Quakers to non-Quakers on the list of slave owners in 1767, is to establish the number of Quaker and non-Quaker deaths during this era. On the annual bills of mortality, Quaker burials represented between 12.4 and 13.9 percent of the total number of white burials in the city for every five-year period from 1755 to 1774; for the period as a whole, Quaker burials represented 12.8 percent of the same total. In the list of slave owners in 1767, it is possible to identify 88 members of the Society of Friends, or 16.9 percent of the total of 521.[64] Although the burial statistics indicate only the approximate size of the Quaker community, it seems safe to conclude that Friends were somewhat overrepresented among Philadelphia slaveholders in proportion to their numbers. Confirmation of this extensive involvement by Friends in slavekeeping can be found in Quaker documents themselves. To be sure, a prominent Philadelphia Quaker, James Pemberton, wrote in 1762 that the "In[i]quetous [slave] traffic heavy of late [has] lamentably Increas'd here, tho' the members of the Society Appear entirely clear of being Concerned in the Importation and there are few Instances of any purchase of them."[65] But only three months earlier the Philadelphia Yearly Meeting had regretfully noted an "increase of Slaves among the members of our religious Society" in its report to the London Yearly Meeting.[66] And among the slave owners identified in the 1769 assessors' reports are the names of at least seven Quakers who had not owned slaves two years before. The evidence is substantial, then, that when faced with a direct choice between forgoing the human labor they needed or ignoring the principles enunciated by their leaders, and officially sanctioned by the Society through its Quarterly and Yearly Meetings, the rank and file of Philadelphia Friends chose the latter course. More than twenty years of abolitionist campaigning by men such as Woolman and Benezet, and the increasing commitment of the Society of Friends to ending slavery, culminating in the decisions of 1758, failed to stem the influx of slave labor into Philadelphia, to bring about more than a handful of manumissions, or even to prevent an increase in slave ownership among Quakers. Not until about 1764, by which time white bound labor had become as available as before the war, did Quakers stop buying slaves, and not until the eve of the American Revolution was the ideological commitment of the Quaker leadership able to prevail over the membership at large in the matter of manumission.

The religious affiliations of non-Quakers cannot be readily identified, given the fragmentary state of church records for several groups, such as the Baptists, Roman Catholics, and Swedish Lutherans. But an analysis of surnames in the list of 521 slaveholders indicates that at least one group eschewed slaveholding to a remarkable degree. This was the German element in Philadelphia, composed of German Lutherans and German Calvinists. German Lutherans ranked just behind the Anglicans as the largest religious group in the city and, combined with German Calvinists, accounted for 23 percent of the burials in Philadelphia between 1765 and 1769, a five-year period bracketing the tax assessment of 1767. Although they contributed virtually nothing to the antislavery literature of the period, they seem to have had a strong aversion to slaveholding. Only 17 of the 521 (3.3 percent) slave owners can be identified as Germans—an incidence of slaveholding that clearly distinguishes them from all other ethnic and religious groups in the city. This abstinence from slaveholding can only partly be explained in economic terms, for while it is true that the Philadelphia Germans were concentrated in the lower half of the wealth structure, thus putting ownership of a slave beyond the means of many, a sizable number of Germans enjoyed a modest affluence. Perhaps of equal importance was the aversion to slaveholding which the immigrants from the Palatinate expressed, beginning with the Germantown Petition of 1688 against slavery and continuing through Christopher Sauer, the advertisements for runaway slaves, or slave sales in his German-language newspaper at a time when Benjamin Franklin had no compunction about printing them in the *Pennsylvania Gazette*.[67] The Philadelphia Germans had no reservations about purchasing indentured servants, most of whom were their countrymen, but they drew the line there and only rarely ventured to purchase African slaves.[68]

On the eve of the American Revolution, the slave population was dwindling as a result of a small number of private acts of manumission and, more important, because of the virtual cessation of the slave trade and through natural decrease. As the Second Continental Congress convened in Philadelphia, slavery was moving slowly into its twilight period in the largest city in British North America.[69] But the long history of slavery in the city and the wholesale substitution of black for white bound labor in the late 1750s and early 1760s demonstrate that even in the center of colonial Quakerism the appeals of antislavery ideologues went largely unheeded whenever they interfered with the demand for bound labor. In an era of economic expansion, Philadelphians, including Quakers, avidly sought slave labor when their manpower requirements could not be otherwise met, and not until white indentured laborers became available in sufficient number to supply the needs of the city did the abolitionist appeals produce more than a few dozen manumissions.

Notes

1. Of the five current textbooks in colonial history, Max Savelle's *History of Colonial America,* rev. ed., by Robert Middlekauff (New York, 1964), and O. T. Barck and H. T. Lefler's *Colonial America,* 2nd ed. (New York, 1968), make no mention of urban slavery in the northern colonies; Curtis Putnam Nettels, *The Roots of American Civilization: A History of American Colonial Life* (New York, 1938), states that "Negroes were profitable only in regions where they could labor as gangs at a common task" and were found mostly in domestic service in New England (325–26). This view is repeated in David Hawke, *The Colonial Experience* (Indianapolis, Ind., 1966), 472–73. Oliver P. Chitwood, *A History of Colonial America,* 3rd ed. (New York, 1961), mentions slaves in New York City without comment (348).

The following general accounts of Afro-American history ignore slavery in Philadelphia or intimate that the institution never took firm root in Pennsylvania: Lerone Bennett Jr., *Before the Mayflower: A History of the Negro in America, 1619–1964,* 3rd ed. (Baltimore, 1966); John Hope Franklin, *From Slavery to Freedom: A History of Negro Americans,* 3rd ed. (New York, 1969); August Meier and Elliott M. Rudwick, *From Plantation to Ghetto: An Interpretive History of American Negroes,* rev. ed. (New York, 1970), and Sauders Redding, *They Came in Chains: Americans from Africa* (Philadelphia, 1950). In *Pennsylvania: The Keystone State* (New York, 1956), [former] State Historian Sylvester K. Stevens makes no reference to blacks in his chapter, "The Peopling of Pennsylvania."

2. See, for example, Ellis Paxon Oberholtzer, *Philadelphia: A History of the City and Its People: A Record of 225 Years* (Philadelphia, 1912); J. Thomas Scharf and Thompson Westcott, *History of Philadelphia, 1609–1884,* vol. 1 (Philadelphia, 1884); John F. Watson, *Annals of Philadelphia and Pennsylvania . . . ,* vol. 3 (Philadelphia, 1857); Carl and Jessica Bridenbaugh, *Rebels and Gentlemen: Philadelphia in the Age of Franklin* (New York, 1942); Carl Bridenbaugh, *Cities in Revolt: Urban Life in America, 1743–1776* (New York, 1955); Horace Mather Lippincott, *Early Philadelphia: Its People, Life, and Progress* (Philadelphia, 1917); and Struthers Burt, *Philadelphia: Holy Experiment* (New York, 1945).

3. Edward Turner, the most thorough student of slavery in Pennsylvania, concluded that it is "almost impossible to obtain satisfactory information as to the number of Negroes in colonial Pennsylvania" and made no attempt to calculate the slave population of Philadelphia at any point in the colonial period except by inference, such as in stating that "when fairs were held in Philadelphia as many as a thousand Negroes sometimes gathered together for carousal and barbaric rejoicing." Edward R. Turner, "Slavery in Colonial Pennsylvania," *Pennsylvania Magazine of History and Biography* (hereafter *PMHB*) 35 (1911): 143, 149. On the eve of the Revolution, two independent estimates placed the slave population of Pennsylvania as high as 10,000 and as low as 2,000. Evarts B. Greene and Virginia D. Harrington, *American Population Before the Federal Census of 1790* (New York, 1932), 114. The latest population estimates make no mention of Philadelphia but set the number of slaves in the colony at 6,000 in 1770. U.S. Census Bureau, *Historical Statistics of the United States: Colonial Times to 1957* (Washington, D.C., 1960), 756.

4. Keith to Board of Trade, December 18, 1722, Board of Trade Papers, Proprieties, II, R. 42, Historical Society of Pennsylvania, Philadelphia (hereafter HSP) and cited in Edward Raymond Turner, *The Negro in Pennsylvania: Slavery–Servitude–Freedom, 1639–1861* (Washington, D.C., 1911), II, n. 40; Andrew Burnaby, *Travels Through the Middle Settlements in North America in the Years 1759 and 1760 . . . ,* 2nd ed. (Ithaca, N.Y., 1960), 57; [Benjamin Franklin], "A Conversation between an ENGLISHMAN, a SCOTCHMAN and an AMERICAN on the Subject of

SLAVERY" (1770), in Vernet W. Crane, "Benjamin Franklin on Slavery and American Liberties," *PMHB* 62 (1938): 5. Gottifried Achenwall, a professor at the University of Göttingen,
based his "Some Observations on North America and the Colonies of Great Britain There"
(1767) on information gleaned from conversations with Franklin. On slavery, presumably following Franklin's comments, he wrote that there were very few slaves in Pennsylvania because
of a distaste for the institution and the absence of suitable agricultural work. Slavery in the
cities was not mentioned. A full translation of "Observations" appears in Leonard W. Labaree
et al., eds., *The Papers of Benjamin Franklin* (New Haven, Conn., 1959), 13:348–77.

5. Adolph B. Benson, ed., *Peter Kalm's Travels in North America: The English Version of
1770*, rev. ed., (New York, 1964), 1:206.

6. Nicholas More to William Penn, December 1, 1684, Albert C. Myers Collection, box 2,
no. 6, Chester County Historical Society, Chester, Pennsylvania.

7. Gary B. Nash, *Quakers and Politics: Pennsylvania, 1681–1726* (Princeton, N.J., 1968),
278 n. 69. The inventories are in Philadelphia Wills and Inventories, Book A (1682–99) and
Book B (1699–1705), photocopies at HSP.

8. Turner, *The Negro in Pennsylvania*, 4–6; W. E. B. Du Bois, *The Philadelphia Negro: A
Social Study* (Philadelphia, 1899), 411–18, where the legislation concerning import duties is
listed; Darold D. Wax, "Negro Imports into Pennsylvania, 1720–1766," *Pennsylvania History*
32 (1965): 256 n. 9; and Wax, "Quaker Merchants and the Slave Trade in Colonial Pennsylvania," *PMHB* 86 (1962): 145. For early Quaker controversy concerning the slave trade, see
Thomas E. Drake, *Quakers and Slavery in America* (New Haven, Conn., 1950), 34–47.

9. The figures for 1722, 1729, and 1731–32 were printed in the *American Weekly Mercury*
and are summarized, except for 1729, in Samuel Hazard et al., eds., *Pennsylvania Archives*,
8th ser. (Harrisburg, Pa., 1931), 4:3517. The figures for 1738–44 are reproduced in Labaree et
al., *Papers of Franklin* 3:439. Bills of mortality, which distinguished race and religious affiliation, were published annually between 1747 and 1775 by the Anglican church in Philadelphia
and are available, except for 1749 and 1750, on microcard as listed in Charles Evans, *American
Bibliography: A Chronological Dictionary of All Books, Pamphlets and Periodical Publication
Printed in the United States, . . . 1639 . . . 1820* (Chicago and Worcester, Mass., 1903–59).

10. *The Mystery of Iniquity: In a Brief Examination of the Times . . . with Additions*, 2nd
ed. (Philadelphia, 1730), 5.

11. Seventeen ships carrying German immigrants had entered Philadelphia between 1727,
when records are first available, and 1731. In the next two years, eighteen ships arrived, and
after a three-year period in which arrivals dropped to two or three a year, the greatest influx in
the colony's history began. For the next seventeen years, from 1737 to 1754, an average of
eleven ships a year, carrying about 40,000 German immigrants, left their passengers at Philadelphia. The number of ships arriving each year, and calculations of the average number of
immigrants per ship, are given in Ralph Beaver Strassburger and William John Hinke, *Pennsylvania German Pioneers: A Publication of the Original Lists of Arrivals in the Port of Philadelphia from 1727 to 1808*, Pennsylvania-German Society Publications 42–44 (Norristown, Pa.,
1934), 1:xxix, xxxi. Abbot Smith presents evidence indicating that Strassburger and Hinke
underestimated the Palatine immigration by about 15 percent. See Abbot Emerson Smith, *Colo-
nists in Bondage: White Servitude and Convict Labor in America, 1607 to 1776* (Chapel Hill,
N.C., 1947), 320–23. Of the Palatine immigrants, about one-half to two-thirds were redemptioners or indentured servants, according to the estimates of Cheesman A. Herrick, *White Servitude in Pennsylvania: Indentured and Redemption Labor in Colony and Commonwealth*
(Philadelphia, 1926), 176–77, and Karl Frederick Geiser, *Redemptioners and Indentured Servants in . . . Pennsylvania* (New Haven, Conn., 1901), 40–41. While most of these Palatines

made their way to rural areas north and west of Philadelphia, that a substantial number remained in the city is evident from the sharp increase of deaths listed in the annual mortality bills for "Dutch Calvinists," "Dutch Reformed," and "Strangers." The number of arriving Irish and Scotch-Irish indentured servants is much less certain. Some inflated estimates, based on highly suspect evidence, have been made by Michael J. O'Brien, "Shipping Statistics of Philadelphia Custom House, 1733 to 1744, Refute the Scotch-Irish Theory," *Journal of the American Irish Historical Society* 22 (1923): 132–41, where it is estimated that 126,000 immigrants arrived from Ireland between 1735 and 1750. A far more informed recent study puts the figure below 30,000. See R. J. Dickson, *Ulster Emigration to Colonial America, 1718–1775* (London, 1966), 59.

12. Darold D. Wax's examination of sale prices leads him to conclude that servants, presumably with a full term to serve, were sold at about half the price of the average slave. "The Demand for Slave Labor in Colonial Pennsylvania," *Pennsylvania History* 34 (1967): 344. Turner estimates that slaves cost about three times as much as white servants (*The Negro in Pennsylvania,* 10–11). The relative profitability of slave as opposed to indentured labor in a colonial urban environment has never been calculated, to my knowledge. Presumably a slave would work at least twice as long as an indentured servant and in most cases, barring an early death, from four to six times as long. Moreover, the offspring of slaves became additional assets of the owner. The most careful estimates of the cost of indentured servants set the price at mid-century at £3 to £4 per year of indenture. When this is compared with the price of slaves, which varied widely but for full-grown blacks seems to have averaged about £40 to £50, it becomes apparent that the average slave needed to work only about three to six years longer than a servant with a seven-year indenture to make up the price differential. For prices of slaves and indentured servants, see ibid., 10–11 n. 38, and Arthur Zilversmit, *The First Emancipation: The Abolition of Slavery in the North* (Chicago, 1967), 40–46. Although further investigation of the economics of slave and indentured labor is badly needed, I tentatively conclude that indentured labor was somewhat more expensive than slave labor.

13. At least twenty-two ships crowded with German and Scotch-Irish immigrants had reached Philadelphia in each year between 1752 and 1754. But from 1755 to 1760 an average of only four ships a year carrying German and Scotch-Irish immigrants arrived in Philadelphia (Table 1.3). Strassburger and Hinke, *German American Pioneers,* 1:xxx, and Dickson, *Ulster Emigration,* Appendix E. That the general transatlantic traffic continued to flow is evident from the statistics on the import and export of goods at Philadelphia and from the fact that the city's merchants had no difficulty importing slaves. Imports from England declined 40 percent in 1755 from the previous two-year level, but from 1757 to 1760 were at all-time highs. Exports declined about one-third from 1756 to 1760, partially as a result of the war in some of the wheat-producing areas of Central Pennsylvania, but still remained high enough to indicate that the Atlantic traffic was far from halted. The shipping data are from *Historical Statistics of the U.S.,* 757.

14. Geiser, *Redemptioners and Indentured Servants,* 39, and C. Henry Smith, *The Mennonite Immigration to Pennsylvania in the Eighteenth Century,* Pennsylvania-German Society Publications 30 (Norristown, Pa., 1929), 204, 217.

15. Stanley McCrory Pargellis, *Lord Loudoun in North America* (New Haven, Conn., 1933), 105–8, 116–19.

16. The estimate was by William Peters in a letter to Thomas Penn, proprietor of Pennsylvania. Cited in Labaree et al., *Papers of Franklin* 6:397 n. 2 For the plea of the Assembly, see ibid., 397–98.

17. Pargellis, *Lord Loudoun,* 116–23, and Franklin to Sir Everard Fawkener, July 27, 1756, in Labaree et al., *Papers of Franklin,* 6:472–76.

18. Franklin to Fawkener, July 17, 1756, in Labaree et al., *Papers of Franklin,* 6:472–76. In addition to the inadequate compensation made by the British army for enlisted servants, the Pennsylvanians complained that they were unable to replace their servants at such critical points in the agricultural cycle as harvest or seedtime when they were lured away by the British recruiting sergeants. Thus, it was the undependability as well as the cost of indentured servants that led to the transition to slave labor.

19. Thomas Willing to Coddrington Carrington, September 3, 1756, Willing and Morris Letter Book, 221, HSP, quoted in Darold Duane Wax, "The Negro Slave Trade in Colonial Pennsylvania" (Ph.D. diss., University of Washington, 1962), 32.

20. Wax, "Negro Slave Trade," 47–48. In 1761, twenty-four Philadelphia merchants petitioning the governor to withhold his approval of a £10 per head duty passed by the Assembly referred to the continuing scarcity of labor owing to "near a total Stop to the importation of German and other white Servants." The petition is published in William Riddell, "Pre-Revolutionary Pennsylvania and the Slave Trade," *PMHB* 52 (1928): 16–17. That heavy importations continued from 1762 to 1766 in spite of the imposition of what the Assembly meant to be a prohibitory £10 duty testifies to the insistent demand for labor, white and black, at this time. Some merchants may have managed to circumvent the tariff by landing their cargoes duty free across the Delaware River in western New Jersey or lower down the river in Delaware. See Wax, "Negro Imports into Pa.," 258, and Henry Schofield Cooley, *A Study of Slavery in New Jersey,* Johns Hopkins University Studies in Historical and Political Science 14 (Baltimore, 1896), 16. Cooley notes that in 1761 the New Jersey Assembly took cognizance of the fact that many slaves were "landed in this Province each year in order to be run into New York and Pennsylvania." Given the apparent prevalence of illegal entries, all official importation figures for Pennsylvania based on customs accounts must be regarded as underestimates.

21. For extensive treatments of the abolitionist campaign, none of which attempts to measure the success of the abolitionists in bringing about private manumissions of slaves, see Drake, *Quakers and Slavery,* chaps. 3 and 4; Zilversmit, *First Emancipation,* chap. 3; and David B. Davis, *The Problem of Slavery in Western Culture* (Ithaca, N.Y., 1966), chap. 10.

22. The number of German ship arrivals is given in Strassburger and Hinke, *German American Pioneers,* 1:xxx, and can be regarded as nearly accurate since Pennsylvania law required the registration of all alien arrivals. The Scotch-Irish arrivals, based primarily on shipping advertisements in the *Belfast News Letter,* are tabulated in Dickson, *Ulster Emigration,* Appendix E. The newspaper files are incomplete from about 1750 to 1775, so the figures for these may be too low.

23. Slave importation from 1761 to 1771, as calculated from the customs accounts, are tabulated in Wax, "Negro Slave Trade," 48. Thomas Riche, a Philadelphia merchant, was a few years premature in asserting in 1764 that "the time is over for the sale of Negroes here." Riche Letter Book, 1764–71, HSP, quoted in Wax, "Negro Imports into Pa.," 255.

24. According to Benezet, more slaves were exported than imported in Philadelphia by 1773. Benezet to Granville Sharp, February 18, 1773, Sharp Letter Book, Library Company of Philadelphia, cited in Wax, "Negro Imports into Pa.," 255.

25. Transcripts of the 1767 assessors' reports are at the Van Pelt Library, University of Pennsylvania, Philadelphia. Transcripts of the 1769 and 1774 lists are published in Hazard et al., *Pennsylvania Archives,* 3rd ser., 14 (Harrisburg, Pa., 1897), but servants and slaves are lumped together. I have used microfilm copies of the original transcripts, which distinguish between slaves and servants, deposited at the Pennsylvania State Archives, Harrisburg, Pennsylvania, and available at HSP, where a transcript of the 1772 assessors' reports is also deposited.

The constables' returns of 1775 are in the Philadelphia Archives, City Hall (hereafter cited as constables' returns of 1775). A facsimile of the 1773 report, from Joseph Galloway to the Earl of Dartmouth, is in B. F. Stevens, *Facsimiles of Manuscripts in European Archives Relating to America, 1773–1783* . . . (London, 1889–95), 24:2086. The Galloway report also tabulates the number of taxable servants and slaves for each county in Pennsylvania in 1773.

26. The basic tax law governing the assessment for servants and slaves was passed in 1764 and continued in force throughout the pre-Revolutionary period. White servants of 15–20 years of age were valued at 30*s*; slaves of 12 to 50 years of age were valued at £4. James T. Mitchell and Henry Flanders, comps., *The Statutes at Large of Pennsylvania from 1682 to 1801, 6:1759 to 1765* (Harrisburg, Pa., 1899), 358.

27. Southwark's urban character and rapid growth enabled it to become a municipality with powers equivalent to those of the counties by an act of the Assembly in May 1762. Scharf and Westcott, *Philadelphia,* 256–57. See also Margaret B. Tinkcom, "Southwark, a River Community: Its Shape and Substance," *American Philosophical Society Proceedings* 114 (1970): 327–42.

28. The New York census data are in Greene and Harrington, *American Population,* 97–102. The New Jersey data are summarized by J. Potter, "The Growth of Population in America, 1700–1860," in D. V. Glass and D. E. C. Eversley, eds., *Population in History: Essays in Historical Demography* (London, 1965), 656–57. Data for Newport, Rhode Island, in 1755 show that 39.5 percent of slaves were under age 16, if one interprets the designations "boys" and "girls" as referring to persons under 16 and the designations "men" and "women" as referring to persons over 16. Greene and Harrington, *American Population,* 67. In New Haven and New London, Connecticut, in 1774, 48 percent of the slave population were under the age of 20. Charles J. Hoadly, *Public Records of the Colony of Connecticut, from October 1772 to April 1775, Inclusive* (Hartford, Conn., 1887), 14:483–92.

29. Constables' returns of 1775. The New York City figures are derived from Greene and Harrington, *American Population,* 99–102.

30. Although no census was taken in the city during these years, a series of enumerations of houses and taxable inhabitants allows for calculations of crude population levels of 7,800 in 1740 and 10,700 in 1755. Actual counts of houses that were made in 1749 and 1769 are given in Watson, *Annals of Philadelphia,* 3:236; the number of houses for 1760 is also recorded in James Mease, *A Picture of Philadelphia* . . . (Philadelphia, 1811), but no source for the figure is given in Watson, *Annals of Philadelphia,* 3:235–36, and has been calculated for 1756 from the tax list of that year reprinted by Hannah Bender Roach, comp., "Taxables in the City of Philadelphia, 1756," *Pennsylvania Genealogical Magazine* 22 (1961): 34–41. The ratio of taxables to inhabitants and houses to inhabitants, the basis for establishing crude population levels for 1740 and 1755, has been derived from Sam Bass Warner's recent calculation of the city's population in 1775: *The Private City: Philadelphia in Three Periods of Its Growth* (Philadelphia, 1968), 12, 225–26.

31. Rush to Granville Sharp, May 1, 1773, in L. H. Butterfield, ed., *Letters of Benjamin Rush* (Princeton, N.J., 1951), 1:81.

32. Ages are given or can be inferred for 88.7 percent of the slaves on the 1775 constables' returns. Of this sample, 15 percent were below 12 years of age, and 7.6 percent were above 50. The approximate total slave population in various years in Table 1.4 is based on this changing age structure, as estimated in the table below. The age structure for 1767 has been estimated from the data cited in note 28. By far the most important factor in the changing age distribution was the rapid decline in slave importations after 1766.

Age Structure of Slaves in Philadelphia, 1767–1775

Year	% Below 12	12–50	Above 50
1767	30	65.0	5.0
1769	27	67.4	5.6
1771	23	70.8	6.2
1773	19	74.1	6.9
1775	15	77.4	7.6

33. Fifty-three slaves, all belonging to Quakers, were emancipated in 1776. These manumissions and others by non-Quakers are recorded in Papers of Manumission, 1772–90, C27 and C28, Philadelphia Quarterly Meeting (Orthodox), Pennsylvania Department of Records, Philadelphia, and in some cases are also listed in Manumission Book A, Papers of the Pennsylvania Abolition Society, HSP. Slave children who were promised their freedom when they reached adulthood are not included in this number.

34. The ratio of male to female slaves and the percentage of females of childbearing ages in the slave population can only be approximated. The 1775 reports of the constables indicated the sex of slaves only in Chestnut and the eastern half of Mulberry Ward. Among the 55 slaves for whom both sex and age were given, 33 were males and 22 females. Fourteen of the females were between 15 and 35 years of age. This ratio is approximately borne out by Philadelphia inventories of estates in 1774 that listed 22 slaves—11 male, 8 female, and 3 whose sex was unspecified. I am indebted to Alice Hanson Jones of Washington University, St. Louis, Missouri, for this information. Among the 73 slaves 18 years or older who were manumitted in Philadelphia between 1767 and 1777, some 38 were male, 31 female, and 4 undetermined. These data are compiled from the Papers of Manumission, 1772–90, C27 and C28 (note 33 above). In the three censuses for New Jersey and the six for New York, covering the years 1703–72, males varied from 52 to 56 percent of the black population. Potter, "Growth of Population," 653, 659. In Massachusetts in 1764 and in Connecticut in 1774, male slaves represented 57.6 percent and 56.5 percent, respectively, of the slave population. U.S. Census Bureau, *A Century of the Population Growth from the First Census of the United States to the Twelfth, 1790–1900* (Washington, D.C., 1909), 161–69.

35. The constables' returns of 1775 from Chestnut and Mulberry wards indicate that adult male and female slaves were living together in only 5 of 55 slave owners' houses.

36. "Observations on the Increase in Mankind," in Labaree et al., *Papers of Franklin*, 4:231.

37. *Calculations on American Population, With a Table for estimating the annual Increase . . . in the British Colonies . . .* (Boston, 1775), 13.

38. Southwark, for which no constables' reports are extant, is not included in the calculations for the city. For the New York data, see note 28. In Connecticut in 1774, some 32.1 percent of the population was under 10 years of age (U.S. Census Bureau, *A Century of Population Growth,* 168–69). In Bristol, Rhode Island, in the same year, 27.6 percent of the men and 26.9 percent of the women were in this age bracket. John Demos, "Families in Colonial Bristol, Rhode Island: An Exercise in Historical Demography," *William and Mary Quarterly,* 3rd ser., 25 (1968): 53.

39. Fifty-eight children ages 1 to 9 are listed in the constables' reports. A few more were undoubtedly among those for whom ages were not given. The baptismal records of the Anglican church reveal that between 1767 and 1775 some 63 black infants, 50 belonging to slaves and 13 belonging to freedmen, were baptized. We can be sure that some of these died in

infancy, which explains why the count on the constables' returns is lower than this figure. Only the Anglican church, so far as is known, welcomed black Philadelphians to baptism. Given the commitment of the Anglicans to religious and educational training for blacks in Philadelphia, a policy pursued from the early 1750s, it is likely that most slaves, regardless of the religion of their owners, took their children to the Anglican church for baptism. The demographic decline inherent in such an age structure is made clear in E. A. Wrigley, *Population and History* (New York, 1969), 23–28, 62–76; T. H. Hollingsworth, *Historical Demography* (London, 1969), 98–102, 345–49; and Michael Drake, *Population and Society in Norway, 1735–1865* (Cambridge, 1969), 42–46, 157. Philip D. Curtin has argued that in tropical America in the eighteenth century an annual excess of deaths over births of 20–50 per 1,000 can be attributed to a low fertility rate caused by excess males over females and by the high morality rate attributed to the "disease environment" ("Epidemiology and the Slave Trade," *Political Science Quarterly* 83 [1968]:213–14). The United States, Curtin argues, was "a striking exception to this pattern of natural decrease among the slave population" because of the more balanced ratio of female and male slaves, a consequently higher fertility rate, and a more favorable "disease environment." Ibid., 214 n. 43; and Curtin, *The Atlantic Slave Trade: A Census* (Madison, Wis., 1969), 73. Whatever the situation elsewhere in America, the demographic pattern for slaves in Philadelphia, and perhaps for other northern cities in the eighteenth century, appears to have been much closer to that of the Caribbean islands than to that of the American South.

40. Edward Raymond Turner, "The Abolition of Slavery in Pennsylvania," *PMHB* 36 (1912): 132. On September 8, 1719, the commissioners of the County of Philadelphia exacted rent from Peter, a free black, living on a lot in Philadelphia owned by "the City and County." *Journal of the Proceedings of the Commissioners of the County of Philadelphia, 1718–1751,* Philadelphia City Archives, City Hall.

41. Register Books of Christ Church: Marriages, Christenings, and Burials, 1 (January 1, 1719–March 1750); 2 (March 1750–December 1762), HSP.

42. *Pennsylvania Gazette,* March 5, 1750.

43. Zilversmit, *First Emancipation,* 79–80; [Society of Friends], *A Brief Sketch of the Schools for Black People . . .* (Philadelphia, 1867), cited in Du Bois, *Philadelphia Negro,* 84.

44. Register Books of Christ Church, 2 (1750–62); 3 (1763–1810), HSP.

45. The 1774 tax assessors' reports, which indicate rents received by house owners leasing their property to others, show seventeen free black householders. I have found no way to determine whether the assessors identified all black renters or to calculate the size of their families and the number of free blacks renting rooms.

46. Using five-year averages, John B. Blake calculates a death rate in Boston between 1705 and 1775, including the black population, that varied from 32 to 45 (*Public Health in the Town of Boston, 1630–1822* [Cambridge, Mass., 1959], 250). My calculation of the crude mortality rate for blacks is based on black burial totals as given in Lorenzo Johnston Greene, *The Negro in Colonial New England, 1620–1776* (New York, 1942), 348–49, and in the *Boston Gazette* after 1752, and on the enumerations of black inhabitants as given in Greene, *Negro in Colonial New England,* 84–85. However, the black population of 989 for 1755 cited in Greene includes only blacks 16 years old and above and thus should be raised to about 1,640 if the age distribution of black Bostonians paralleled that of blacks in other areas in the colonies. Slave mortality rates are badly in need of investigation. A few preliminary words on the subject are offered by Potter, "Growth of Population in America," 568–659. Robert R. Kuczynski, a pioneering student of demographic trends in the British colonies, concluded on the basis of unstated evidence that the mortality rate of whites in North America was greater than that of slaves. See Robert R. Kuczynski, *Population Movements* (Oxford, 1936), 17.

47. Although the two cities were roughly equal in population in the mid-eighteenth century, Philadelphia buried an average of 977 persons annually while Boston interred 538. (Boston deaths are tabulated in Blake, *Public Health in the Town of Boston,* and the Philadelphia totals are derived from the annual bills of mortality.) Three explanations can be suggested for this difference. First, Boston began an inoculation program to control smallpox in 1720, a full decade before Philadelphia. Second, Boston was largely spared "ship fever" (variously identified as typhus, diphtheria, yellow fever, and throat distemper), which apparently accompanied the steady flow of Palatine immigrants through Philadelphia. Third, the Philadelphia death count was swelled in some years by large numbers of Palatines who had contracted ship fever during the Atlantic crossing and died shortly after arrival in Philadelphia, the main distributing point for German immigrants. In 1754, for example, when nineteen ships bearing Palatines arrived, 253 immigrants who succumbed to "ship fever" were buried in the city. For Franklin's defense in 1764 of Philadelphia's healthful climate, which had been called into question in George Whitefield's mind by what Franklin called "bugbear Boston Accounts," see his letter to Whitefield, June 19, 1764, in Labaree et al., *Papers of Franklin,* 11:231–32. In his almanac for 1750, Franklin had ventured that the mortality rate computed by "political Arithmeticians" for healthy countries of one death per thirty-five people annually could be applied to *Philadelphia: Poor Richard Improved on for . . . 1750* (ibid., 439). There is no study of public health in Philadelphia to parallel Blake's *Public Health in the Town of Boston* and John Duffy's *A History of Public Health in New York City, 1625–1866* (New York, 1968).

48. In 1775, some 58 of 423 slave owners (13.7 percent) held only slaves under 12 or over 50 years of age. Eight years earlier a somewhat larger number probably held only slaves too old or not old enough to be counted as assessable property. Prospective slave buyers preferred slaves not yet physically mature, perhaps because they were more tractable or adaptable to a new master. In 1767, when the era of large slave importations was ending, the age structure of the slaves was probably somewhat lower and the percentage of slave owners holding nontaxable slaves somewhat higher. For a discussion of the desirability of young slaves, see Wax, "Demand for Slave Labor in Pa.," 337. Indicative of this preference was Thomas Willing's request for "A Parcell of healthy [Negro] Boys about 10–12 years old [which] will undoubtedly sell to good advantage" (Willing to Coddrington Carrington, September 3, 1756, Willing and Morris Letter Book, 221, HSP).

49. In the Middle Ward of Philadelphia in 1774, according to a recent analysis, almost 23 percent of the taxpayers lived with other families. Warner, *Private City,* 15, table 3.

50. *Some Considerations on the Keeping of Negroes, Part Second* (1762), in Phillips P. Moulton, ed., *The Journal and Major Essays of John Woolman* (New York, 1971), 237. Woolman wrote the second part of his widely circulated essay during the period when the slave trade in Pennsylvania was at its height, completing the manuscript in November 1761 (ibid., 195). Another Friend, Thomas Nicholson, wrote in 1767 of his concern that slave-owning proved "a Snare to Friends' Children by being made use of as Nurseries to pride, Idleness and a Lording Spirit, over our Fellow Creatures" ("On Keeping Negroes," manuscript dated June 1, 1767, Society Miscellaneous Collection, Box 11-A, HSP).

51. I am indebted to James T. Lemon of the University of Toronto for this information, compiled from the manuscript tax returns of Chester and Lancaster counties at Chester County Courthouse, Chester, Pennsylvania, and Lancaster County Court House, Lancaster, Pennsylvania.

52. The 1773 figures have been compiled from tax lists in Hazard et al., *Pennsylvania Archives,* 3rd ser. 12 and 17. The number of taxables is tabulated in Samuel Hazard, ed., *The Register of Pennsylvania . . . IV* (Philadelphia, n.d.), 12.

53. Compiled from the 1767 tax assessors' reports, excluding Southwark.

54. Southwark is not included in these totals.

55. The figures have been adjusted to include Southwark with the city and to reflect the approximate number of servants and slaves not included in the tax lists because their age excluded them as taxable property in the assessors' reports. Servants between the ages of 15 and 50 were taxable. The constables' returns of 1775 show that 27 percent of the servants were under 15 or over 50 years old. I have raised the number of servants listed in the tax reports to account for these "missing" servants.

56. Strassburger and Hinke, *Pennsylvania German Pioneers,* 1:xxix, and Dickson, *Ulster Emigration,* Appendix E.

57. In 1783, when the city's population had grown to about 24,500, the number of servants and slaves had dropped to about 725. This decline may have been caused primarily by a stoppage in the importation of servants during the Revolutionary years and the concurrent release from servitude of all those indented before the war. The 1783 figure is extrapolated from the number of servants and slaves of taxable age on the tax assessors' lists for that year (data for Mulberry Ward are missing). I am indebted to John Daly of the Philadelphia City Archives for providing the 1783 data.

58. The figures for Boston are taken from James A. Henretta, "Economic Development and Social Structure in Colonial Boston," *William and Mary Quarterly,* 3rd ser., 22 (1965): 85 n. 18.

59. The Philadelphia County figures are derived from the 1767 tax list. The Chester and Lancaster county figures are taken from Alan Tully, "Patterns of Slaveholding in Rural Southeastern Pennsylvania, 1720–1758" (paper presented at meeting of the Association for the Study of Negro Life and History, October 18, 1970).

60. Evidence that slaves were employed extensively as artisans is confirmed by advertisements in the Philadelphia newspapers of this period. In a two-year period bracketing the 1767 tax list, the *Pennsylvania Gazette* carried a number of advertisements listing slaves who were qualified as carpenters, millers, distillers, bakers, shipbuilders, blacksmiths, sailmakers, and manager of a bloomery. In one advertisement, four black sailmakers were offered for sale with the note that "as the sailmakers here are stocked with Negroes, they will be ready at any time for what other market may have a call for them" (*Pennsylvania Gazette,* May 19, 1768). See also Leonard Price Stavisky, "Negro Craftsmanship in Early America," *American Historical Review* 54 (1949): 315–25; Zilversmit, *First Emancipation,* 35–40; and Wax, "Demand for Slave Labor in Pennsylvania" 355–56.

61. Wax, "Demand for Slave Labor in Pennsylvania," 334–35; Jesse Lemisch, "Jack Tar in the Streets: Merchant Seamen in the Politics of Revolutionary America," *William and Mary Quarterly,* 3rd ser., 25 (1968): 375 n. 19; and Harold D. Langley, "The Negro in the Navy and Merchant Service, 1798–1869," *Journal of Negro History* 52 (1967): 273–86, provide a few references to seagoing slaves.

62. The early activities of individual Quaker opponents of slavery are best described in Drake, *Quakers and Slavery,* 1–47, and Davis, *The Problem of Slavery,* 291–326.

63. Drake, *Quakers and Slavery,* 48–67, and Sydney V. James, *A People Among Peoples: Quaker Benevolence in Eighteenth-Century America* (Cambridge, Mass., 1963), 130–40.

64. The Quaker slaveholders have been identified primarily from the following sources: birth, death, and marriage records for the Philadelphia Monthly Meeting, as compiled in William Wade Hinshaw, ed., *Encyclopedia of American Quaker Genealogy* (Ann Arbor, Mich., 1936–1950); "Directory of Friends in Philadelphia, 1757–1760," *Pemberton Papers* 14, HSP, printed in *PMHB* 16 (1892): 219–38; Philadelphia Monthly Meeting, Membership Lists,

1759–62 and 1772–73; and Papers of Manumission, 1772–90, C27 and C28, Philadelphia Quarterly Meeting (Orthodox), Pennsylvania Department of Records. Not included in the total of 88 are 7 slave owners disowned by the Society of Friends between 1760 and 1767, and four slave owners for whom identical names were found in both Quaker and Anglican records.

65. Pemberton to Joseph Phipps, December 13, 1762, Dreer Collection, HSP, quoted in Wax, "Quaker Merchants and the Slave Trade," 159.

66. Philadelphia Yearly Meeting Minutes, 1747–79, 174–75, quoted in Wax, "Negro Slave Trade in Colonial Pa.," 31.

67. The most recent consideration of the Germantown Petition is J. Herbert Fitz, "The Germantown Anti-Slavery Petition of 1688," *Mennonite Quarterly Review* 33 (1959): 42–59. On Sauer, see William R. Steckel, "Pietist in Colonial Pennsylvania: Christopher Sauer, Printer, 1738–1758" (Ph.D. diss., Stanford University, 1950), 116.

68. It is also possible that the German immigrants, perhaps the most ethnocentric of all Philadelphians before the Revolution, were too anti-Negro to buy slaves. I am indebted to Richard S. Dunn for this suggestion.

69. At the time of the first federal census in 1790, some 239 slaves remained in Philadelphia. U.S. Census Bureau, *Heads of Family at the First Census of the United States Taken in the Year 1790: Pennsylvania* (Washington, D.C., 1908), 10.

CHAPTER TWO

Black Women in Colonial Pennsylvania

Jean R. Soderlund

Sometime before 1750, and perhaps as early as 1720, Rachel Pemberton, the wife of long-term assemblyman and Quaker leader Israel Pemberton Sr., offered freedom to her slave Betty. The black woman refused the offer, preferring to remain with the family.[1] Later in the century, in the spring of 1776, another wealthy Quaker couple, Provincial Councilor William Logan and his wife, Hannah, discussed freedom with their slave Dinah. In this case, however, the black woman broached the subject. According to William and Hannah, Dinah asked them to set her free. The Logans had already freed her daughter Bess, but they seem to have been saddened by Dinah's request because she had been in Hannah's family since she was a child and they considered her a part of their family. She was a grandmother, and perhaps the Logans thought she should remain under their protection. But Dinah wanted the status of a free black, and in the end the Logans agreed to give her "full Liberty to go and live with whom & Where She may Chuse."[2] Dinah elected to stay in the household as a hired servant, though both Hannah and William Logan soon

This chapter was first published in *The Pennsylvania Magazine of History and Biography* 107 (January 1983): 69–83. Reprinted by permission. The author is grateful to P. M. G. Harris, Department of History, Temple University, for his encouragement and helpful criticism, and to the Philadelphia Center for Early American Studies for financial support while she did much of the original research for this chapter.

died, and she is the woman who is supposed to have saved Stenton, their
Germantown mansion, from being burned by the British in 1777.[3]

The contrasting ways in which the Pembertons' slave Betty and the Logans' black woman Dinah faced the prospect of freedom, or indeed viewed
their condition as slaves, may have resulted from individual differences. Betty
was perhaps more timid or less skillful than Dinah. Nevertheless, the periods
of Pennsylvania history in which these two women lived were likely to have
influenced their decisions as well. Earlier on, when Betty turned down manumission, slavery was at its height in Philadelphia and very few blacks lived
in the city. By the time Dinah demanded her freedom, a substantial number
of freed men and women resided in the town nearby. Some owned property
and were married in the Anglican and Lutheran churches, and many had
learned to read and write. While Betty's husband and children, if she had
any, were almost certainly enslaved, we know that Dinah's daughter Bess,
and perhaps other family members as well, were already free. Thus, leaving
aside any personal differences, life as a free black woman in Philadelphia
would have been much more problematic for Betty before 1740 than for
Dinah in 1776.

Slavery had existed on the Delaware, and African women had lived in the
region since before William Penn came in 1682. The largest numbers of
blacks were imported relative to the local population during the first two
decades of the eighteenth century.[4] Some Pennsylvanians worried about this
influx, especially after the New York slave revolt of 1712. The Pennsylvania
Assembly in that year placed a prohibitive tariff of £20 on each black imported into the colony, but the Crown disallowed the law.[5] While during the
years 1711–16 Quakers from Chester County pressed the Philadelphia Yearly
Meeting (the central body of Friends in the Delaware Valley) to prohibit
members from buying imported blacks, the Yearly Meeting, influenced by
Philadelphia merchants and other slaveholders, refused to do more than caution Friends not to buy blacks lately brought into the province.[6] In 1726, in
order to control the relatively large local slave population and to discourage
owners from freeing their slaves, the Assembly passed a black code that
required a £30 surety bond for manumission, forbade intermarriage between
whites and blacks, and restricted the freedom of both slaves and free blacks
to travel, drink liquor, and carry on trade. The law also empowered justices
to bind out free black children with or without the consent of their parents,
boys until they reached the age of 24 years and girls until they were 21.[7]

Unlike the sugar colonies of the West Indies and the tobacco regions of
the Chesapeake, where plantation owners became increasingly dependent on
black labor as the colonial period progressed, slaves remained a rather small
proportion of the labor force in Philadelphia. Pennsylvania attracted large

numbers of white immigrants after 1720; German and Scots-Irish servants and free laborers supplied much of the labor required by Pennsylvanians. Slavery reached a peak in Philadelphia around 1720, when slave prices were relatively low and white labor was quite scarce. With a more abundant supply of Europeans after 1720, however, Philadelphians who needed labor and wanted to avoid using slaves now had a greater choice. Thus slaveholding declined in Philadelphia after the second decade of the eighteenth century. Increasing numbers of Quakers and Presbyterians either manumitted their slaves or simply did not buy any. By the 1770s, even several slave owners who were affiliated with the Church of England, the religion most resistant in Philadelphia to antislavery reform, freed their slaves. Abolitionism was strongest and earliest in the city among wealthy Quaker merchants and professionals, who, because they used Africans and Afro-Americans mainly for personal service, could view involuntary bondage as a form of ostentation rather than as a necessary source of labor. Quaker craftsmen, in contrast, were much less willing to give up their blacks because they needed them to keep their shops going. Slaves became especially desirable once again during the Seven Years' War, when the supply of white servants dried up; but they were always valuable to craftsmen, who invested a considerable amount of money and time to buy and train them. By the 1770s, however, slaveholding was much less common among all groups of Philadelphians, even craftsmen. Poor economic conditions and a glut of free white workers after the end of the Seven Years' War undercut the demand for slaves.[8]

In rural Pennsylvania, most slave owners were wealthy farmers, although some craftsmen and innkeepers also held blacks. Analysis of probate records for eastern Chester County, as well as tax lists for all of Chester, Philadelphia, and Lancaster counties, show that a much smaller percentage of rural inhabitants owned slaves than did Philadelphians throughout the period before 1770. Slavery, nevertheless, did not decline among Pennsylvania farmers after 1720, as it did among Philadelphia residents. To the contrary, in the 1770s the institution actually showed signs of growing in rural Pennsylvania. However, this expansion was retarded by the Pennsylvania Assembly's passage of the Gradual Abolition Act of 1780 and by the decision of the Philadelphia Yearly Meeting in 1776 to disown all slave owners.[9]

Except in the kind of work they did, which for most was domestic service, black women in colonial Pennsylvania had a wide range of experiences depending on where and in what time period they lived. In Philadelphia, they were close to other blacks and had certain benefits, such as schooling, that the city could provide. On the other hand, most blacks in rural areas like eastern Chester County were thinly scattered across the countryside. The situation for all African and Afro-American women in Pennsylvania changed

over time as increasing numbers achieved freedom. Thus, black women of
the 1760s and 1770s had several advantages over their mothers and grandmothers who had lived thirty or forty years before; many of their owners
were more amenable to arguments that they should be free, and if they lived
in Philadelphia they could rely on a fairly large community of free blacks for
support.

Both of the slave women mentioned earlier, Betty and Dinah, worked for
families of rich Philadelphia Quaker merchants, and therefore their lives were
substantially different from the situation of sisters living in the plantation
areas to the south, or even of black women working in rural Pennsylvania. In
the West Indies, South Carolina, and the Chesapeake, the large majority of
black women worked from sunup to sundown in the fields growing sugar,
rice, tobacco, and grain. In the West Indies, most lived on large plantations
with fifty or more slaves. But even though many blacks lived in close proximity to one another on the islands, their family life was disrupted because
mortality was high and women on the average had few children. In Virginia
and Maryland, the mean number of laborers on plantations was smaller than
in the West Indies: most blacks lived in slave groups of fifteen or more.
Although many planters transferred husbands and teenage children to other
quarters or separated families by sale, blacks in the pre-Revolutionary Chesapeake usually lived near their immediate families and kin.[10]

In Philadelphia throughout the colonial period, owners held an average of
only about 2.4 slaves.[11] This meant that entire black families, including
mother, father, and several children, rarely lived under the same roof. While
the sex ratio of adult blacks was fairly even in the city, according to the
probate inventories, at most only two in five black women lived in the same
household with an adult black man (see Table 2.1). Only 3 percent were listed
in the probate records with men who were described specifically as their
husbands. The relationship of the rest of the men to the women is unknown;
they could have been husbands or mates, prospective mates or friends, men
to whom the women had no attachment, or men whom they detested or
feared. Records of black marriages in Christ Church and St. Peter's Church,
Philadelphia, also indicate that relatively few married slave couples lived
together. Between 1727 and 1780 some 64 black couples were married at the
Anglican churches (all but 8 after 1765). In one-quarter of these marriages,
both partners were free, and another 14 percent were marriages between a
free black and a slave. Twenty-nine (45.3 percent) were marriages in which
both the husband and wife were slaves; of these slave couples, fewer than
one-fourth (7 of the 29) were owned by the same master.[12]

That so few of Philadelphia's black women lived in the same households
with their husbands was perhaps less disruptive of family life than it seems,

Table 2.1. Black women and men in Philadelphia, 1682–1780

Years	Sex Rate		Black Women				Black Men		
	No.	Adult Men per Adult Woman	No.	% Listed with Black Man	% Listed with Child Specified as Theirs	% Listed with Child Who Could Be Theirs	No.	% Listed with Black Women	% Listed with Child Who Could Be Theirs
1682–90	22	1.40	5	100.0	0	20.0	7	71.4	42.8
1691–1700	77	0.88	8	37.5	50.0	0	7	42.8	42.8
1701–10	104	1.05	21	33.3	9.5	33.3	22	31.8	22.7
1711–20	165	1.33	24	37.5	50.0	4.2	32	28.1	46.9
1721–30	182	0.61	18	16.7	33.3	22.2	11	27.3	36.4
1731–40	207	0.93	27	33.3	25.9	14.8	25	36.0	36.0
1741–50	353	1.11	46	39.1	28.3	19.6	51	35.3	35.3
1751–60	378	1.33	43	48.8	27.9	18.6	57	36.8	26.3
1761–70	512	1.17	66	48.5	25.8	21.2	77	41.6	36.4
1771–80	401	0.90	40	45.0	30.0	15.0	36	50.0	33.3
1682–1789	2,401	1.09	298	41.9	28.5	18.1	325	38.5	34.5

(46.6)

SOURCE: Probate inventories.

because most husbands probably lived close by. Philadelphia, which as late as the 1770s reached only as far back from the Delaware as Seventh Street,[13] had a fairly large black population throughout the eighteenth century. For instance, in 1750, when the population of Philadelphia was about 15,000, as many as 1,500, or one-tenth, of the city's residents were black.[14] Evidence from other sources suggests that the number of blacks living in the city was large enough to make white Philadelphians uneasy. The whites complained on a number of occasions about slaves and free blacks gathering in groups in the evenings and on Sundays. In 1696 the Philadelphia Yearly Meeting urged its members to restrain their slaves "from Rambling abroad on First Days or other Times."[15] The Pennsylvania Assembly passed a law in 1706 prohibiting blacks from meeting together "in great companies," but this statute evidently had limited effect because a number of Philadelphians, seemingly unaware that this law was on the books, petitioned in 1723 for a similar ban. In 1750 another petition from inhabitants of Philadelphia County protested to the Assembly about the custom of shooting off guns at New Year's; they complained that such revelry had been introduced into the county by immigrant Germans and was now practiced by servants and blacks. The behavior they found disagreeable included excessive drinking, firing guns into houses, and throwing lighted wadding into houses and barns.[16] And the historian Edward Turner claimed (albeit without giving the source of his information) that as many as 1,000 blacks gathered for festivals on the outskirts of town.[17] Thus, while few black women lived in the same house with their husbands, there was a large slave population living in what we would now consider a small city, and hence there was a good chance that their mates lived nearby.

Of course, even this tenuous link between family members could be broken at any time by the owner. Slave-owning fathers sometimes gave a young slave to their children when they married,[18] and most testators either divided their blacks among the heirs or directed that the slaves be sold upon their deaths.[19] While the white family members who received the blacks might live fairly close together, an owner's demise could bring about a painful separation for slaves. No testators stipulated that their slaves be sold together.[20] Philadelphia newspaper advertisements also provide evidence that many owners sold husbands away from wives, and children away from their parents; most indicated no concern about the consequences for the slaves. Merle G. Brouwer found in his survey of newspaper advertisements of slaves for sale in Pennsylvania that masters rarely specified that a slave should be kept in the neighborhood of his or her kin. Indeed, runaway notices indicate that slave families were broken up and husbands or wives taken to other colonies. The first place masters thought to look for their runaway slaves was in the vicinity of their former residence and with the family from whom they had been separated.[21]

While slave women throughout Pennsylvania faced the prospect of being cut off from their families by sale or by the death of the master, Philadelphia black women were even less likely to live with their children than were adult females in rural areas. According to the probate inventories, which show the slaves' lives at only one point in time, only 28.5 percent of slave women in Philadelphia had children described as their own living in the same household (see Table 2.1). In most cases a woman had only one child who was specifically described as hers. Another 18 percent (for a combined total of almost one-half) were listed on their owners' inventories with black children who *could* have been theirs but were not described as such. The number of city women who actually lived in the same household with their children was almost certainly lower than Table 2.1 suggests. Some of the children listed on their owners' inventories, especially those over age 5, were hired out to other families.[22]

Rural black women in Pennsylvania were much more likely to live with their families than were urban slaves. In eastern Chester County (now Delaware County), 70 percent of the women were listed on inventories with black children who were theirs or who could have been, and as many as 48 percent lived with adult men (see Table 2.2).[23] Life was more difficult for Chester County women in another way, however, because many fewer blacks lived there and the distance between plantations on which other slaves lived were quite far. The situation for men in eastern Chester County was especially bad in the years from 1721 to 1740 and in the 1770s because, according to the inventories, men outnumbered women at those times by a considerable margin. Over the colonial period, at most only one-third of the black men in Chester lived with a black woman, and even fewer lived with a black child (Table 2.2).[24] Some blacks in Chester apparently conquered their loneliness by establishing sexual partnerships with whites. In the 1760s and 1770s, some 13.5 percent of the slaves listed in Chester area inventories were mulattoes. By contrast, in Philadelphia, where the chance of obtaining a black companion was better, only 3.2 percent of the slaves listed in inventories during those decades had mixed parentage. Data from Quaker manumissions show a similar pattern. Mulattoes were 30 percent of the slaves freed by members of four Chester County meetings, but only 5.4 percent of those emancipated by Philadelphia Friends.[25] Almost 16 percent of the slaves registered by Chester County slaveholders in 1780 were mulattoes.

Two factors may explain why fewer black women in Philadelphia than in Chester lived with children. One reason is that infant mortality in the city

Table 2.2. Black women and men in eastern Chester County, 1682–1780

Years	Sex Rate		Black Women				Black Men		
	No.	Adult Men per Adult Woman	No.	% Listed with Black Man	% Listed with Child Specified as Theirs	% Listed with Child Who Could Be Theirs	No.	% Listed with Black Women	% Listed with Child Who Could Be Theirs
1682–90	6	—	0	—	—	—	0	—	—
1691–1700	10	1.00	2	100.0	100.0	0	2	100.0	100.0
1701–10	18	0.67	3	33.3	66.7	0	2	50.0	50.0
1711–20	30	0	1	0	0	100.0	0	—	—
1721–30	42	6 to 0	0	—	—	—	6	0	0
1731–40	55	1.80	5	60.0	20.0	60.0	9	33.3	33.3
1741–50	82	1.00	4	50.0	25.0	25.0	4	50.0	25.0
1751–60	84	1.00	6	50.0	0	16.7	6	50.0	0
1761–70	104	1.00	5	20.0	40.0	40.0	5	20.0	40.0
1771–80	79	1.86	7	57.1	57.1	28.6	13	30.8	38.5
1682–1780	510	1.42	33	48.5	39.4	30.3	47	34.0	29.8

(69.7)

SOURCE: Probate inventories.

was very high. Susan E. Klepp found in her study of white families that almost half the children born to mothers in colonial Philadelphia died before they reached the age of 15, and one-fourth died during the first year. No one has done an equivalent study of infant mortality in Chester County, but evidence from elsewhere in colonial America suggests that mortality among the total population was lower in rural areas than in the cities.[26] The other reason is that owners sold black children to other families. Raising a child could be expensive, especially when food had to be purchased, and her or his service was possibly less useful to a city family than on a farm. Black girls and boys in Philadelphia were more likely to be the only slaves living in their households than were children in Chester. According to the probate inventories, 20.1 percent of girls and 27.5 percent of boys in Philadelphia were their owners' only slaves, while just 9.1 percent of girls and 22.2 percent of boys in Chester lived apart from other blacks.

The evidence on the kinds of work black women performed suggests that most did domestic labor. While there are a few references to slave women working in shops, such as one woman listed in the "still house," even these women could have performed menial tasks usually assigned to females. Also, a few Pennsylvania owners kept as many as ten or fifteen blacks on their plantations; women in these groups were more likely to work in the fields.[27] Like most adult female slaves in Philadelphia, the Pembertons' Betty and the Logans' Dinah belonged to men who were merchants, shopkeepers, or craftsmen.[28] These two women probably worked under the supervision of their owners' wives. Although black men also worked as domestics in Philadelphia, the kinds of slaves owned by persons of various occupations suggest that the roles of men and women were dissimilar. As shown in Table 2.3, based on the Philadelphia inventories, innkeepers and widows, whose slaves would do most domestic labor, owned more women than men when they

Table 2.3. Gender and age of blacks owned by women and men of various occupations in Philadelphia, 1682–1780

	No. Blacks Owned	Women	Men	Girls	Boys	Unknown	Total
Widows and single women	96	39.6%	21.9%	17.7%	10.4%	10.4%	100.0%
Innkeepers	37	35.2	24.3	13.5	18.9	8.1	100.0
Mariners	78	30.8	26.9	10.3	17.9	14.1	100.0
Craftsmen	287	27.2	36.9	11.1	18.5	6.3	100.0
Merchants and shopkeepers	282	24.5	30.1	12.1	21.6	11.7	100.0
Gentlemen and professionals	89	23.6	36.0	14.6	23.6	2.2	100.0

SOURCE: Probate inventories.

died. Craftsmen, professionals, and merchants owned more men. Husbands and fathers, in dividing their estates among heirs, often left a black woman or girl to their wives and daughters. If the woman married, her slave normally became the property of her husband under the law of coverture,[29] but the black woman probably continued to work for the wife. Israel Pemberton clearly regarded Betty as his wife's slave, but she was his legally and he made provision for her in his will. Hannah Logan had a definite interest in Dinah, and both she and her husband signed the manumission.[30]

Most black women in colonial Philadelphia did housework. They cooked, cleaned, washed and ironed laundry, kept fires, gardened, looked after children, and served as maids. Some also sewed and made cloth. For instance, one 14-year-old girl knew housewifery, knitting, sewing, and could read.[31] Black women lived in their masters' houses and generally slept in garrets, kitchens, or rooms near kitchens. Merchants and professionals sometimes hired women and girls out by the year or by indenture,[32] and women could be lent or hired out for shorter periods to help tend the sick, put in gardens, preserve food, and wait on tables for special occasions. Girls were sometimes apprenticed to learn a trade, presumably housewifery or spinning.[33] Black women continued to do domestic labor even after they were freed, working as servants and laundrywomen.[34] In Chester County, most women also did housework, though here they would have tended larger gardens, raised poultry, milked cows, produced cloth, and helped in the fields (especially at harvest) as well.[35]

While the life conditions of slave women in Philadelphia remained essentially unchanged between 1720 and 1776 in several respects—notably in the fact that few lived with their families under one roof and in terms of the work they did—nevertheless, the situation of the Philadelphia black population as a whole altered sufficiently by 1776 that a woman like Dinah sought her freedom. Most important, a significant number of free blacks lived in the city and its environs by the 1770s. Back in the 1720s or 1730s, when Betty refused her freedom, most of the blacks in Pennsylvania had been recently imported. Few white Americans, in Pennsylvania or elsewhere, thought that slavery was wrong. Evidence of manumissions from wills, which thus far is the only source we have before the Quakers began recording manumissions in the 1770s, indicates that only nine slaves were freed by will by Philadelphians before 1720. Another nine were freed in the 1720s, and three more in the 1730s.[36] Perhaps others were released during their masters' lifetimes, but relatively few blacks were freed before 1740. The Assembly further demonstrated the proslavery climate in Pennsylvania in the 1720s when in response to a number of petitions they passed the Black Code of 1726, which stated that "tis found by experience that free negroes are an idle, slothful people

PEPPER POT.

" Pepper Pot, smoking hot."

African American colonial women were not just wives and homemakers; they were also entrepreneurs. This copy of a woodcut print by an unknown artist depicts African American female street vendors selling a Philadelphia treat: pepper-pot soup. (Courtesy of the Library of Philadelphia)

and often prove burdensome to the neighborhood and afford ill examples to other negroes."[37]

In the decade after 1740, in contrast, antislavery opinion grew in Philadelphia, especially among the Quakers and Presbyterians. In 1754 the Philadelphia Yearly Meeting issued *An Epistle of Caution,* its first forthright statement that slavery was wrong, and in 1758 Quakers forbade all members from importing or buying slaves, and appointed a committee to encourage Friends throughout the Delaware Valley to give up their blacks.[38] Though by no means all Quakers agreed with the Yearly Meeting's decisions, many Friends freed their slaves in their wills after 1740, and others emancipated their blacks during their lives. Philadelphia Presbyterians, influenced by the religious egalitarianism of the Great Awakening, began manumitting their slaves by the 1760s, and even some Anglicans freed their blacks.[39] Between 1741 and 1770, Philadelphians emancipated at least seventy-five slaves in their wills;[40] others freed their blacks before their deaths.[41] In the 1770s, the Philadelphia Monthly Meeting recorded manumissions for hundreds of slaves freed by Friends and non-Friends.[42] Gary B. Nash found a significant decrease in the number of slaves owned by Philadelphia taxpayers between the years 1767 and 1775. My study of probate records indicated the same decline, as the percentage of inventoried decedents owning slaves dropped from more than 20 percent in the 1760s to 13 percent in the 1770s.[43] Most likely, much of the decrease resulted from manumission, and by 1776 a substantial free black population was living in or near the city. Given this large-scale move toward emancipation, Dinah's request for freedom should not have been too great a surprise for the Logans.

In the early nineteenth century, Philadelphia was the center of both the white and black abolitionist movements in America. The source of white antislavery reform has been linked to the eighteenth-century Quakers; Delaware Valley Friends moved from ridding their meeting of slaveholding to helping to establish the Pennsylvania Abolition Society and lobbying for abolition in society at large. Historians have not yet traced the roots of the united and vocal black community of early-nineteenth-century Philadelphia back to the colonial period. Instead, they have focused on the founding of the Free African Society and separate churches by Richard Allen and Absalom Jones, and on James Forten's opposition to the movement for colonization of free blacks in Africa. No one has looked for the colonial beginnings on which these later developments rested.[44] Actually, Philadelphia became the center of the black abolitionist movement of America after 1790 because already in the 1770s a relatively large and sophisticated free black population lived there. Many could read and write and had learned trades. They married at the Anglican and Lutheran churches and attended Quaker meetings (though they could not join the Society).[45] While the majority held menial jobs and few free blacks are noted on the tax lists, at least some owned property, and most supported themselves and their families in freedom.

Both the Society of Friends and the Anglican church took an interest in educating Africans and Afro-Americans. Antislavery Quakers hoped to train blacks to be useful and moral citizens. As early as 1696 the Philadelphia Yearly Meeting urged its members to bring their slaves to meetings and to watch over their behavior. Beginning in the 1750s the Yearly Meeting continually reminded slave owners to teach blacks to read and write, to educate them in the principles of Christianity, and to train them in an occupation in preparation for freedom.[46] Most local meetings believed that their members were not doing enough in these respects, but quite a few blacks did learn to read and write.[47] John Woolman mentioned in 1762 that many slaves could read, and the Shrewsbury Monthly Meeting in East Jersey found in 1775 that at least five of the twenty-four slaves still held in bondage by meeting members, including two adults and three children, had been taught to read.[48] Many testators who directed that their young slaves be freed at a future date specified that they be apprenticed to a trade first.[49]

Several schools opened in Philadelphia to educate blacks. A "Mr. Bolton" was taken to court for teaching them in his school in 1740. Reverend William Sturgeon, assistant to Dr. Robert Jenney, rector of Christ Church, started catechizing Afro-Americans in 1747, and in 1750 Anthony Benezet began holding evening classes for blacks in his home. In 1758, Bray's Associates opened a school at Christ Church for free blacks, and in 1770 Benezet convinced the Philadelphia Monthly Meeting to open an "African School" of their own. The first class included twenty-two girls and boys, evenly divided in gender. Later, older black men and women also came. All of the children studied reading, writing, and arithmetic. The girls learned sewing and knitting from a mistress, while boys did more advanced academic work. Though the school had trouble keeping schoolmasters and also had difficulty in maintaining regular attendance of pupils who often had to help support their families, a total of 250 black students received some instruction between 1770 and 1775.[50]

Not very much is known about the economic status of free blacks in the late colonial period, but we do have a few clues. According to the Quaker committees that in the late 1770s and early 1780s checked on the welfare and behavior of blacks freed by meeting members, most freed men and women were able to support themselves. A committee of the Concord Monthly Meeting in Chester County, in a report that was more detailed than those of other meetings, found only two families who had economic problems: a mother with two young children whose husband was still a slave, and an aged couple who needed their daughter's help at home but could not provide for her education or training. It is unclear how many free black families lived in the Concord area in the 1770s, but the Quakers seemed pleased with their condition. The Friends inspected and settled accounts between the blacks and their employers and encouraged freed men and women with large families to bind out their children as apprentices in order to relieve their financial burden.[51] Quakers in other places also found that their ex-slaves prospered in freedom. Wilmington Friends were pleased that most of their liberated blacks could provide for themselves and their families "with frugality," while members

of a New Garden committee reported that most of the freed blacks continued
to live among Friends and were successful in finding jobs. Quakers of the
Philadelphia Quarterly Meeting, on the other hand, were disappointed that
few free blacks asked for their help or advice; blacks in the city and its
environs apparently had the resources to help one another over rough periods
and thus avoided the paternalistic scrutiny to which Friends generally subjected recipients of their aid.[52]

Several free black women living in the Philadelphia area were quite successful. In Pennsylvania, unlike New Jersey and New York, blacks could own
real property.[53] Three free black women died before 1780, leaving wills that
have survived. The first was Jane Row, deceased in 1766. She held real estate
on Fourth Street in Philadelphia and in Southwark and owned two slaves,
whom she wanted to sell to reasonable and good masters. Row lived with but
never married a man named Henry Hainy, who had fathered two of her sons,
John and Thomas Hainy. She had possibly been married earlier, because
another of her sons was William Row. A fourth son, John Miller, was a free
mulatto. Like so many male testators who used the same phrase in bequeath-
ing personalty to their wives, Row willed Hainy a bed and furniture as a
token of her "love and esteem." Ann Elizabeth Fortune, a single woman,
owned personal property and a black woman, Jane, whom she freed. The
third woman, Jane Linkhorn Woodby, was a widow, who had married her
deceased husband, Emanuel, in 1756 at Christ Church. She directed that her
lot and buildings in Spring Garden be sold and that the money be invested
for the support and education of her daughter, Jane.[54] While the number of
black women owning property in colonial Philadelphia is unknown, these
three wills suggest that at least some blacks were able to amass considerable
estates. Jane Row, especially, appears to have lived with a forceful independence. She certainly took advantage of the lack of societal pressure on blacks
to marry.

The names Pennsylvania blacks adopted also provide insight into their
relationships with whites and into the way in which they identified themselves within the larger white society.[55] Evidence from manumissions, marriage records, and wills indicates that before emancipation at least some
slaves used surnames, which were at best grudgingly recognized by their
masters. Most significant, they never chose the surname of their latest
owner.[56] Several examples from Quaker manumissions illustrate these points.
Joseph Pratt of Edgmont Township, Chester County, freed "a certain Negro
woman named Susanna, otherwise called Susanna Cuff," and John Hoopes
of nearby Goshen Township freed a "Negro man named Jo, otherwise called
Joseph Samuel." George Brinton, also of Chester County, referred to his
slave as "Mordica" or "Mott" but admitted that the man used an "allias,"

calling himself George Brown.[57] Mulattoes were more likely to use surnames than were slaves listed as "Negroes," and more enslaved men than women held recognized last names. Of fifty-three mulattos freed by Quakers in ten monthly meetings, twenty-eight (52.8 percent) were listed with first and last names. Surnames were given for only 61 of 383 (15.9 percent) freed "Negroes."[58] In the Christ Church marriage records for 1709–80, some 20 percent of the male slaves being married had last names but only one of thirty-eight female slaves (2.6 percent) had a surname given. More than 80 percent of the free black men and women both were listed with last names.[59]

Historians have known for a long time that slavery evolved differently in colonial Pennsylvania than in the plantation areas of the American South and the West Indies. However, the paucity of evidence stretching over the entire colonial period has hindered full understanding of the role slavery played in the Pennsylvania economy and society. New information from probate inventories places tax list and census data available for the late colonial period in better perspective. Philadelphia relied heaviest on black slave labor early in the eighteenth century; they turned to whites as European immigration increased and as abolitionism took hold. Slavery was only one of several kinds of labor that Pennsylvanians employed, and even those who chose to own slaves held relatively few. On average, slave masters in both urban and rural areas held fewer than three slaves each.

The limited nature of the institution in Pennsylvania and the spread of antislavery thought had a profound influence on the lives of both urban and rural black women. Though the work Pennsylvania women performed varied little over time or by geographic area, other circumstances of their lives differed considerably. In Philadelphia, rather few lived in the same house with their husbands and children, but their families probably lived close by. In rural areas like Chester County, more women lived with their families, but the total black population was sparse. Though women in both places had a better chance to achieve freedom as time went by, blacks in the city had an added advantage by the 1770s because they could look to a substantial free black community for support. Many free black women, men, and children in Philadelphia could read and write and had learned trades or occupations. At least some owned property, including houses and lots in or near the city. Thus, the Logans might have anticipated that Dinah would ask for her freedom in 1776; probably many blacks throughout the province approached their owners with the same request. Serving as someone's slave in a city or area where friends, neighbors, and relatives were free must have angered and hurt quite a number of blacks. As many proslavery apologists predicted, including the Pennsylvanian assemblymen of 1726 drafting the slave code, the presence of free blacks in a community had a pernicious influence on the willingness of other blacks to remain slaves.

Notes

1. Philadelphia Recorded Wills (hereafter cited as Phila. Wills), Israel Pemberton, 1754, Book K, 143; the original will has been lost. Original manuscript wills and inventories (Phila. Wills and Admins.) and books of recorded wills for Philadelphia County are located in the Register of Wills office in the basement of City Hall Annex, Philadelphia. The Chester County probate records cited below (Chester Wills) are housed in the Chester County Archives, Chester County Court House, West Chester, Pennsylvania, although most of the wills and inventories before 1715 are included with the Philadelphia records.

2. Manumission Book for the Three Philadelphia Monthly Meetings, 1772–1796 (hereafter Phila. MM mans.), Arch Street Meeting House, Philadelphia, Phila. Wills, James Logan, 1752, Book I, no. 314; Sarah Logan, 1754, Book K, no. 121; William Logan, 1776, Book Q, no. 324; Hannah Logan, 1777, Book Q, no. 339.

3. John F. Watson, *Annals of Philadelphia in the Olden Time*, rev. ed. (Philadelphia, 1905), 2:480.

4. My analysis of all 2,401 serving probate inventories, 1682–1780, for the city of Philadelphia, where a large proportion of blacks in Pennsylvania lived throughout the colonial period, showed that the relative frequency of slave ownership peaked among decedents in the second decade of the eighteenth century. Jean Ruth Soderlund, "Conscience, Interest, and Power: The Development of Opposition to Slavery Among Quakers in the Delaware Valley, 1688–1780" (Ph.D. diss., Temple University, 1981), 169–81. Population estimates in U.S. Census Bureau, *Historical Statistics of the United States, Colonial Times to 1970* (Washington, D.C., 1975), part 2, 1168, and burial statistics cited by Gary B. Nash ("Slaves and Slaveowners in Colonial Philadelphia," *William and Mary Quarterly* [*WMQ*], 3rd ser., 30 [April 1973]: 226–27, 230–31), show that as a percentage of the total population, blacks were more numerous in this region around 1720 than at any other time in the colonial period. Increased importation of Africans and West Indian blacks also occurred in the Chesapeake and in New York in the years just after 1700. U.S. Census Bureau, *Historical Statistics,* part 2, 1172–73; Paul G. E. Clemens, *The Atlantic Economy and Colonial Maryland's Eastern Shore* (Ithaca, N.Y., 1980), 60–61.

5. Darold D. Wax, "Negro Import Duties in Colonial Pennsylvania," *Pennsylvania Magazine of History and Biography* (*PMHB*) 97 (January 1973): 23–24.

6. Soderlund, "Conscience, Interest, and Power," 57–61.

7. James T. Mitchell and Henry Flanders, comps., *The Statutes at Large of Pennsylvania from 1682 to 1801* (Harrisburg, Pa., 1896–1915), 4:59–64.

8. Soderlund, "Conscience and Controversy: The Problem of Slavery in the Quaker City" (paper presented at the Annual Meeting of the Organization of American Historians, Philadelphia, April 3, 1982); Nash, "Slaves and Slaveowners," 229–56; Billy G. Smith, "The Material Lives of Laboring Philadelphians, 1750–1800," *WMQ,* 3rd ser., 38 (April 1981): 163–202.

9. Evidence from 510 surviving probate inventories, 1682–1780, for nine townships in eastern Chester County (Chester, Upper and Nether Providence, Aston, Middletown, Edgmont, Ridley, Springfield, and Marple) indicates that fewer than 17 percent of inventoried decedents

held slaves during the years 1701–70. Thirty percent owned slaves when they died in the decade 1691–1700, and 19 percent were slave owners in the 1770s. Soderlund, "Conscience, Interest, and Power," 181–204. See also Nash, "Slaves and Slaveowners," 244–45; and Alan Tully, "Patterns of Slaveholding in Colonial Pennsylvania: Chester and Lancaster Counties, 1729–1758," *Journal of Social History* 6 (Spring 1973): 284–305.

10. Richard S. Dunn, "Servants and Slaves: The Recruitment and Employment of Labor in Colonial America" (paper presented at the Conference on Colonial America at Oxford, August, 1981); Allan Kuliloff, "The Beginnings of the Afro-American Family in Maryland," in Aubrey C. Land, Lois Green Carr, and Edward C. Pepenfuse, eds., *Law, Society, and Politics in Early Maryland* (Baltimore, 1977), 171–96.

11. This average includes blacks listed in the probate inventories of decedents who had lived in the city of Philadelphia (not including Southwark and the Northern Liberties) during the years 1682–1780. I have not included blacks who are specifically noted as living outside the city. The actual mean number of blacks in each household was lower because some masters had more than one house and because they often hired out their slaves. According to the Philadelphia constables' returns of 1780 (Philadelphia City Archives, City Hall Annex), only 1.4 blacks lived in each slaveholding household. Much of the evidence for the discussion that follows comes from my analysis of probate wills and inventories for Philadelphia and for the nine townships in eastern Chester County, 1682–1780. It is assumed that the slaves listed in the probate records, aggregated by decade, represent an approximate cross section of the black population. See Soderlund, "Conscience, Interest, and Power," appendix 2, for a discussion of the potential problems in using probate data.

12. Records of Christ Church, Philadelphia, Marriages, 1709–1800, Genealogical Society of Pennsylvania (GSP) transcripts, housed at the Historical Society of Pennsylvania (HSP).

13. Sam Bass Warner Jr., *The Private City: Philadelphia in Three Periods of Its Growth* (Philadelphia, 1968), 11.

14. Billy G. Smith, "Death and Life in a Colonial Immigrant City: A Demographic Analysis of Philadelphia," *Journal of Economic History* 37 (December 1977): 863–89. Blacks probably were 8 to 10 percent of Philadelphia's population at mid-century. My estimate is based upon data from the bills of mortality analyzed by Gary Nash ("Slaves and Slaveowners," 226–27, 230–31), which show that 13.8 percent of the burials in Philadelphia in 1722 were of blacks, 19.2 percent in 1729–32, 10.9 percent in 1738–42, 11.3 percent in 1743–48, 7.7 percent in 1750–55, 9.2 percent in 1756–60, 8.1 percent in 1761–65, 9.2 percent in 1766–70, and 7.4 percent in 1771–75. My estimate would be wrong if blacks had a higher mortality rate than the total population. However, while the black death rate may have been somewhat above that of whites, especially during periods of high importation in the early eighteenth century, in the 1730s, and in the early 1760s, the difference was probably minimized by the fact that immigrants (who had higher-than-average death rates) made up a large segment of the white Philadelphia population. For example, the percentage of decedents who were black, according to the mortality statistics, in the period 1750–55 (7.7 percent) probably represents a low figure because the early 1750s was a time when few slaves were imported but was the peak period of German immigration; close to 35,000 Germans arrived in Philadelphia during the years 1749–54. See Darold Duane Wax, "The Negro Slave Trade in Colonial Pennsylvania" (Ph.D. diss., University of Washington, 1962), 46; and Marianne Wokeck, "The Flow and Composition of German Immigration to Philadelphia, 1727–1775," *PMHB* 105 (July 1981): 267.

15. Philadelphia Yearly Meeting (Men's), Minutes (hereafter: PYM mins.), July 23, 1696. These minutes and those of other Quaker meetings cited below are available on microfilm at the Friends Historical Library, Swarthmore College.

16. *Statutes at Large,* 2:236; Gertrude MacKinney, ed., *Pennsylvania Archives,* 8th ser. (Harrisburg, Pa., 1931), 2:1464; 4:3396–97.

17. Edward R. Turner, *Slavery in Pennsylvania* (Baltimore, 1911), 32–33, 42.

18. For example, George Emlen gave Dinah to his daughter Hannah Logan during his lifetime; Phila. Wills, William Logan, 1776, Book Q, no. 324.

19. For example, see Phila. Wills, George Claypoole, 1731, Book E, no. 175; Henry Dexter, 1750, Book I, no. 139.

20. No wills were found in which the testators directed their executors to keep black families together when they were sold. Masters who cared that much about their slaves' needs either emancipated them or provided for their support by giving them small farms, houses, or tools. Some owners showed little concern about the consequences of separation for their blacks. Elizabeth Fishbourn of Chester, for example, directed that a young black boy be taken from his mother as soon as he was weaned (Phila. Wills, Book C, no. 141), while others wanted their slaves sold to the highest bidders.

21. Merle G. Brouwer, "Marriage and Family Life Among Blacks in Colonial Pennsylvania," *PMHB* 99 (July 1975): 368–72.

22. Though William Masters was hardly a typical Philadelphia slave owner—he held thirty-three blacks at his death—his inventory provides valuable information on the practice of binding out black children. Of seventeen children listed in his inventory, eleven were bound out, one as far away as Wilmington (Phila. Wills, William Masters, Book M, no. 27).

23. Analysis of the Chester County Slave Register of 1780, which includes blacks registered in response to the Gradual Abolition Act of 1780 by their owners from throughout Chester County, yielded somewhat similar results. More than 64 percent of the black women were listed with black children, and as many as 42 percent lived with a black man (Chester County Slave Register, 1780, Pennsylvania Abolition Society Papers, reel 24, HSP). The author is indebted to Gary B. Nash for this reference.

24. The Chester County Slave Register of 1780 indicated an almost even adult sex ratio; thus, 43 percent of the men were listed with a black woman, about the same as the percentage of women who were listed with men. The register also listed more men with children than did the inventories—as many as 44 percent—but still this percentage was considerably lower than the percentage of women living with black children. The discrepancy between data from the slave register and the probate inventories may have resulted from the fact that different geographic areas were covered, or because the Chester probate data for the 1770s are too small to represent the black population reliably.

25. Chester Monthly Meeting, Manumissions, 1776–80; Concord Monthly Meeting, Manumissions Book, 1777–89; Goshen Monthly Meeting, Manumissions, recorded in the monthly meeting minutes, 1775–77; Kenett Monthly Meeting, Manumissions, 1776–80; all located at Friends Historical Library, Swarthmore, Phila. MM mans. Only the emancipated slaves who lived in the vicinity of the monthly meeting are counted.

26. Susan E. Klepp, "Social Class and Infant Mortality in Philadelphia, 1720–1830" (paper presented at the Philadelphia Center for Early American Studies Seminar, Philadelphia, November 6, 1981), 17–18; Smith, "Death and Life," 887–89.

27. For example, Phila. Admins., John Knight, 1729, no. 19; Phila. Wills, John Jones, 178, Book C, no. 83.

28. According to the Philadelphia probate inventories, 1682–1780, men in these occupations owned 57.7 percent of all adult black women.

29. Marylynn Salmon, "Trust Estates and Marriage Settlements" (paper presented at the Philadelphia Center for Early American Studies Seminar, November 1979).

30. Phila. Wills, Israel Pemberton, 1754, Book K, no. 143; Phila. MM mans.

31. *Pennsylvania Gazette,* January 22, 1767; "Record of Indentures of Individuals Bound Out as Apprentices, Servants, Etc. and of German and Other Redemptioners in the Office of the Mayor of the City of Philadelphia, October 3, 1771, to October 5, 1773," *Pennsylvania-German Society Proceedings and Addresses* 16 (1907): 70–71; Carole Shammas, "Mammy and Miss Ellen in Colonial Virginia" (paper presented at the Conference on Women in Early America, November 5–7, 1981, Williamsburg, Virginia); Mary Beth Norton, *Liberty's Daughters: The Revolutionary Experience of American Women, 1750–1800* (Boston, 1980), 12–23.

32. Phila. MM mans.; Phila. Wills, Thomas Lloyd, 1694, Book A, no. 105; "Record of Indentures, 1771–1773."

33. Phila. Wills, Clement Plumstead, 1745, Book G, no. 163; William Coleman, 1769, Book O, no. 235–36.

34. Phila. Wills, James Bright, 1769, Book O, no. 254; Lloyd Zachary, 1756, Book K, no. 307; James White, 1770, Book O, no. 352; James Young, 1779, Book R, no. 162; Phila. MM mans.

35. Soderlund, "Conscience, Interest, and Power," 188–90; Norton, *Liberty's Daughters,* 13–15.

36. Phila. Wills, 1682–1739.

37. *Pennsylvania Archives,* 8th ser., 2:1462, 1735; *Statutes at Large,* 4:59–64.

38. PYM mins., September 14–19, 1754; September 23–29, 1758.

39. Soderlund, "Conscience, Interest, and Power," chap. 6.

40. Phila. Wills, 1740–70.

41. For several mentioned in wills, see Phila. Wills, Samuel Preston, 1743, Book G, no. 41; Nathaniel Allen, 1757, Book L, no. 28; John Jones, 1761, Book M, no. 82; Benjamin Trotter, 1769, Book O, no. 164.

42. Phila. MM mans.

43. Nash, "Slaves and Slave Owners," 236–37; Soderlund, "Conscience, Interest, and Power," 171–81.

44. Benjamin Quarles, *Black Abolitionists* (London, 1969), 3–8; Winthrop D. Jordan, *White over Black: American Attitudes Toward the Negro, 1550–1812* (Chapel Hill, N.C., 1968), 422–26.

45. Henry J. Cadbury, "Negro Membership in the Society of Friends," *Journal of Negro History* 21 (April 1936): 151–213.

46. PYM mins., July 23, 1696; September 14–19, 1754; September 20–26, 1755.

47. In my survey of the minutes of most monthly meetings in the Philadelphia Yearly Meeting, I found that meetings generally reported in response to the query of the Yearly Meeting on slavery that their members treated their slaves decently but did not educate them as well as the meeting desired.

48. *The Journal and Major Essays of John Woolman,* ed. Phillips P. Moulton (New York, 1971), 117–18; Shrewsbury Monthly Meeting (Men's), Minutes, August 7, 1775.

49. For example, John Jones (d. 1761), a Quaker cordwainer who freed his slaves, directed in his will that Phyllis (age 13 years) remain bound to Joseph Morris, a Philadelphia merchant, until she reached age 15 and that she be sent to school long enough to learn to read well. Jones wanted his black boy James (age 7 years) to go to school to learn to read and write and to be apprenticed to a light trade such as that of joiner (Phila. Wills, John Jones, 1761, Book M, no. 82). Boys were more frequently bound out to trades before freedom than were girls, and they were apprenticed to occupations such as cordwainer, tailor, and house carpenter (Phila. Wills, Elizabeth Holton, 1757, Book K, no. 324; Robert Cross, 1766, Book O, no. 7; Anthony Fortune, 1779, Book R, no. 232).

50. Nancy Slocum Hornick, "Anthony Benezet and the Africans' School: Toward a Theory of Full Equality," *PMHB* 99 (October 1975): 399–421; Richard I. Shelling, "William Sturgeon, Catechist to the Negroes of Philadelphia and Assistant Rector of Christ Church, 1747–1766," *Historical Magazine of the Episcopal Church* 8 (December 1939): 388–401.

51. Concord Monthly Meeting (Men's), Minutes, August 4, 1779. According to the Concord MM mans., members of the Concord meeting freed at least eleven adult slaves during the period 1776–79; other free blacks who had been released earlier certainly lived in the area as well.

52. Wilmington Monthly Meeting (Men's), Minutes, July 14, 1779; New Garden Monthly Meeting (Men's), Minutes, May 5, 1781; Phila. Quarterly Meeting (Men's), Minutes, August 2, 1779.

53. William M. Wiecek, "The Statutory Law of Slavery and Race in the Thirteen Mainland Colonies of British America," *WMQ,* 3rd ser., 34 (April 1977): 279.

54. Phila. Wills, Jane Row, 1766, Book N, no. 255; Ann Elizabeth Fortune, 1768, Book O, no. 196; Jane Woodby, 1773, Book P, no. 333; Emanuel Woodby, 1773, Book P, no. 282; Records of Christ Church, Marriages, GSP, 4247.

55. See Herbert G. Gutman, *The Black Family in Slavery and Freedom, 1750–1925* (New York, 1976), 230–56, on the use of surnames by eighteenth- and nineteenth-century slaves.

56. This generalization is drawn from the minority of slaves whose surnames are given in the manumission and church records cited below; a few mentioned in wills also had last names. Further research linking free blacks to their former masters (for example, use of the Pennsylvania Abolition Society records) might reveal that some did adopt the names of their last owners.

57. Goshen Monthly Meeting (Men's), Minutes, August 11, 1775, and May 9, 1777, Concord MM mans., George Brinton, 1781.

58. See manumission records cited in note 25 above, and Bucks Quarterly Meeting, Manumissions Book, 1776–93, Chesterfield Monthly Meeting, Manumissions, 1774–96; and Exeter Monthly Meeting Manumissions, 1777–87, all in Friends Historical Library; Swarthmore and Abington Monthly Meeting, Manumissions, 1765–84, Quaker Collection, Haverford College; Burlington Monthly Meeting, Manumission Book, 1771–81, Burlington County Historical Society, Burlington, New Jersey.

59. Records of Christ Church, Marriages, GSP.

CHAPTER THREE

"Since They Got Those Separate Churches":

Afro-Americans and Racism in Jacksonian Philadelphia

Emma Jones Lapsansky

In August 1834 a mob of white Philadelphians launched a massive three-day attack on a nearby black community. This riot, the first in a series of such antiblack incidents in Philadelphia, was finally quelled by some 800 special constables and militia. However, before peace was restored, one black church had been destroyed, another defaced, and scores of black people had been injured, at least one fatally so. The incident, one of many examples of violence in Jacksonian America, attracted attention both from contemporary reporters and subsequent investigators. While observers often cited general unrest to explain such urban violence, modern historians have had more success in isolating specific community concerns that were potential causes of racial disturbances. They have subjected the riot to close scrutiny. Who were the rioters (by age, occupation, social background, etc.)? How were they organized, mobilized, viewed by society, punished?[1]

Historians who have recently examined patterns of riots and rioters in Western society over the last four centuries have reached some generaliza-

This chapter and the accompanying Figures 1–5 were first published in *American Quarterly,* Spring 1980, 54–78. Reprinted by permission of Johns Hopkins University Press. Copyright © 1980. The author would like to thank the University of Pennsylvania Bicentennial College (now the Philadelphia Center for Early American Studies) for support that facilitated the research for this work.

tions that are valid for Philadelphia's 1830s antiblack riots. First, they have concluded that the terms "riot" and "mob" carry connotations that are too suggestive of lack of direction and purpose—that often so-called "mob" action is actually a violent statement of a quite specific political objective. Second, these historians have agreed that the rioters often were not simply representing the ideas of a narrow minority, but in fact felt "legitimate" because they reflected concerns held by a wide section of a community including not just the rabble but also the "respectable" and even the well-to-do. Third, the riots of the 1830s and 1840s have been represented as the last violent gasp of a Western society making a lurching transition from government by unbridled human passion to government of laws administrated by "professionals."[2]

Using these generalizations as a beginning point, other investigators have sought to isolate more specifically the dynamics of certain types of disturbances in antebellum American cities. Usually these investigators followed the formula set forth by David Grimsted on Jacksonian riots, that they had "obvious roots in both the psychology of [their] participants and their socioeconomic situation."[3] In the case of antiblack rioting, the analyses sought to identify the characteristics which separate individuals who engaged in antiblack mob action from those who did not, and the investigators have generally concluded that certain elements of white society felt threatened by free blacks.[4] While the thrust of such investigations is not to be disputed, they usually have paid little attention to the possibility that unique qualities and actions among the riot victims may give us further insight into the dynamics of racial violence.

In his discussion of weaver riots in Philadelphia in the 1840s, David Montgomery suggested that particular qualities shared by rioters and victims alike helped to fan the flames of the attackers' hatred.[5] To date, little attention of this sort has been directed toward race riots. Except for briefly noting that middle-class blacks were often targeted for attack, most investigators described the victims of antiblack riots as the passive instruments upon which whites' tensions—frequently external or peripheral to the black community—were played out. Such issues as economic competition (for unskilled employment), spatial "turf" controversies (blacks "invading" white neighborhoods or being displaced by "reclamation"), and concerns over competition for status among upwardly (or downwardly) mobile whites are among a few of the dynamics traditionally associated with antiblack violence.[6] These issues may be considered external or peripheral to the black community in the sense that, had there been no black community or had the black community been self-contained, these issues might still have existed between various groups of whites. The presence of black people, and the fact that they touched white society at critical junctures—ranging from economic competition to the sharing of public space—created a peculiar dimension in early-nineteenth-century urban social relations.

No one would take issue with the argument that Afro-Americans have often been the instruments of white Americans' interaction with each other, the "pawns" in someone else's games. However, the question to be pursued here is the extent to which their role as instruments was passive. In what ways and to what extent did dynamics *originating within* the black community itself affect the tone and substance of the interaction *between* urban black Americans and urban white Americans? Were some black people or activities objectively "threatening," or did this "threat" exist only in the minds of white observers? Was there a consistent pattern of actions on the part of black people that triggered negative responses in whites, or were attacks purely the gratuitous and random results of whites' frustrations?

We know much about such questions with regard to slavery,[7] but we have less knowledge with respect to the antebellum urban free Negro. Several investigators have suggested that the white attackers' choices of targets might yield some insights, that institutions that signaled increasing economic progress and "status" in the black community were especially attractive targets for destruction, but no one has explored how these targets were created or examined their significance to Afro-Americans themselves.

One reason that antiblack riots have been accepted at face value is that they are "typical" of the riots of the period—that is, the victims are accepted as the social inferiors of the attackers, and the attackers were afforded public tolerance because the victims, though they had not committed crimes subject to the discipline of public authorities, had nevertheless committed breaches of a decorum that was understood by most of the community.[8] Hence the 1830s antiblack riots were unremarkable. Yet, if Afro-Americans may be looked at for a moment as an active and not passive group, as actors instead of only as acted-against, the issue of racial violence may be viewed from another perspective. Were there elements endemic to the creation or existence of certain institutions within the urban black community that contributed to whites' selection of these institutions as targets for destruction? In approaching this issue, I find it first useful to explore the more general questions of what place Afro-Americans sought in early-nineteenth-century American society, the ways in which they sought to achieve their goals, and the extent of their success.

The Philadelphia black community makes a particularly interesting case study. It was not "typical," but it was atypical in ways that tended to produce a good deal of measurable evidence of the tension between blacks and whites. The most important characteristic of the Philadelphia black community is that it was a visible presence. In 1830 its 15,000 members made it America's largest northern urban black population. Moreover, though this community represented less than 10 percent of the total city population, it reflected a 30 percent increase over the city's black population of 1820. Hence, though the number of blacks in Philadelphia was not large, black and white Philadelphians perceived an ever-increasing number of dark faces in their midst.

The Philadelphia black community was also visible because, compared with other black communities, it was economically well off. This was due partly to the progress of several decades of freedom, partly to Quaker philanthropy, and partly to the in-migration of some exceptionally talented and energetic ex-slaves. An 1838 census concluded that the aggregate wealth of the community was $977,500, or about $270 per household. Even by nineteenth-century standards this did not mean the community was wealthy, but the distribution of that wealth is significant for an understanding both of the internal dynamics of the black community and of its relationships with the larger community. While a great majority of black households had no real property and only negligible personal property, the wealthiest tenth of the population controlled 70 percent of the community's wealth. Stated another way, the black community might be seen as 14,000 poor people juxtaposed to upward of 1,000 economically "substantial" black citizens. Indeed, a survey published in 1845 listed six Afro-Americans among the city's several dozen wealthiest people. Moreover, two of these wealthy Afro-Americans had inherited their money and could not be dismissed as self-made nouveau riche.[9] For the black community, this economic disparity meant that a noticeable minority stood out, economically and socially, from the majority. For the white community, it meant the visibility of Afro-Americans who seemed to differ from upper-class or middle-class whites only in the incidental aspect of color.

The black community of Philadelphia was spatially stable and had been so for many years. In the 1790s, Bethel African Methodist Episcopal Church had been established at Sixth and Lombard Streets. Since then Afro-Americans had increasingly anchored their "turf," setting up a number of institutions—schools, insurance companies, masonic lodges, and several additional churches—within a few blocks of Bethel. As early as 1811, a black neighborhood was identifiable at the southern edge of the city, near Bethel Church, and by 1830 this neighborhood, while not devoid of whites, had become more heavily black and was expanding to the west. Though Afro-Americans and their institutions were to be found in all parts of the city and its suburbs, there was, then, an early and clearly defined intellectual, social, and economic focus for the Negro community at the southern edge of the city[10] (see Fig. 1).

This stability in the black community was enhanced by increasingly cos-

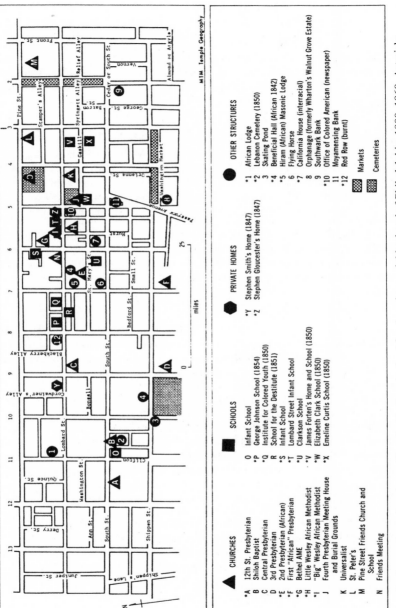

FIG. 1. Approximate locations of key institutions in the Afro-American neighborhood of Philadelphia, 1800–1860. Asterisks indicate predominantly black membership.

mopolitan contacts after 1820. Beginning in 1827 with *Freedom's Journal,* America's first black newspaper, black Philadelphia always had a distribution office for the black newspapers, as well as for Garrison's *Liberator* (usually located in the neighborhood near Bethel).[11] In addition to this formal mechanism of communication, informal connections between prominent black Philadelphians and the world outside black Philadelphia were well established and expanding through the 1820s. Francis Johnson, a musician in demand at white "society" parties all over Pennsylvania and New York, was in a position to bring the news and tastes of the outside world home to his fellow black Philadelphians. Likewise, noted black caterers like Robert Bogle had some intimacy with such white Philadelphia power figures as Nicholas Biddle.[12]

Black abolitionists, carrying out their organizing activities, traveled widely and met frequently with their wealthy and powerful patrons. Such people returned to the black community bursting with the news of their travels and of the support of their white friends. Typical was this report by John Bowers of a stopover in a Lancaster, Pennsylvania, hotel en route from an abolitionist meeting in Harrisburg:

> I finished my breakfast. . . . I rose and the [white abolitionist] friends in company (which they certainly were) gave the landlord to understand . . . that if I could not sit there, they would not, . . . thus proving to the colored men, and to the world, that they were not abolitionists in word, but in deed, and determined to carry out those principles which they profess.[13]

Such contacts of professional service and social reform with the white upper classes brought black Philadelphians comfortable incomes and information about the lives, values, and tastes of white leaders. These contacts also brought access to powerful allies in times of need. On more than one occasion, a black individual's personal, medical, or legal crisis was eased by the intervention of a powerful white friend.[14]

Many of the characteristics of the Philadelphia black community were apparent in other urban black communities in some measure and combination. In New York, for example, black leaders could draw on the resources of wealthy white abolitionists like the Tappan brothers. What made the Philadelphia community unique was that its size, wealth, stability, and access to resources in the white community were older and more pronounced than in other cities, and that it had a number of wealthy blacks as well as access to wealthy whites. If racial tensions were connected to any of these characteristics, then, these tensions should be evident in Philadelphia. Hence, Philadelphia becomes a laboratory in which to explore the interaction between mechanisms within the antebellum black community and the white communities with which it shared the city, for to the white communities of Philadelphia, black people constituted a presence not easily ignored.

To black people their spokesmen had double status: they were prominent in local black affairs, but they were "national" leaders as well. Numerous enough and informed enough to encompass a range of tastes, the black neighborhood at the south of the city had, for example, not one but two masonic lodges and a half-dozen different churches to accommodate the diversity within the black community.[15] All this added up to a highly visible group of upwardly mobile black people—to be emulated by other blacks and to be carefully and suspiciously watched by groups of whites.

White contemporaries perceived the concerns of Philadelphia blacks in terms of some of their own primary tensions: the pressing problem of economic competition, the emotional issues of "amalgamation" (cross-racial mating) and of blacks' aspirations for upward social mobility, the heightened aggressiveness of blacks in the economic sphere, and the increased belligerence of their social and political style and rhetoric.

On the question of economic competition, the white working-class community was vocal. A commission appointed to investigate the causes of the 1834 riot reported:

> Among the causes which originated the late riots, are two. . . . An opinion prevails, especially among white laborers, that certain portions of our community, prefer to employ colored people, whenever they can be had, to the employment of white people; and that, in consequence of this preference, many whites, who are able and willing to work, are left without employment, while colored people are provided with work, and enabled comfortably to maintain their families; and thus many white laborers, anxious for employment, are kept idle and indigent. Whoever mixed in the crowds and groups, at the late riots, must so often have heard those complaints, as to convince them that . . . they . . . stimulated many of the most active among the rioters.[16]

Occupational competition was certainly at the top of the list of working-class whites' concerns, but the question of amalgamation was equally important. Nor was this latter a concern only of the working classes. Among upper-class whites, there was some annoyance over the rumor that wealthy black sailmaker James Forten "was ambitious . . . and strove for a respectable platform for [his family]: and to this end it was said of him that he coveted to wed his daughter to a whiter species at some sacrifice to his fortune."[17] Liberal Quakers themselves, while supporting black "progress," were conservative in their estimate of the appropriate limits of social intercourse with blacks.[18]

Reformers concerned with promoting public morality toward black people were joined in their disapproval of racial intermixing by others who were more interested in protecting the purity of immorality. The publisher of a guide to the city's brothels questioned the limit of decorum in racial taboos:

> There is a brothel occupied by a swarm of yellow girls, who promenade up and down Chestnut Street, . . . and strange to say, they meet with more custom[ers] than their fairer skinned rivals. . . . There is no accounting for taste, however, and we have no objection to a white man hugging a Negro wench to his bosom, providing his stomach is strong enough.[19]

Statements ranging from curiosity to annoyance at the possibilities of "race mixing" were frequent among Philadelphia whites, and one riot, that of 1849, focused on the destruction of a prosperous little tavern, in the neighborhood near Bethel Church, which was owned by a mulatto man and his wife.[20] However, since numerous less prominent but no less interracial bars, gambling houses, and brothels in the neighborhood were left untouched, it is worth speculating that it was, perhaps, intermarriage for the purpose of upward mobility that was abhorred by the riotous whites, and not necessarily amalgamation per se. In any case, "race mixing" in the nineteenth-century city, and its meanings for different groups of whites and blacks, is a subject that bears further inquiry. Job competition and amalgamation were but portions of a larger issue, that blacks' rising aspirations and designs for upward mobility threatened to jostle the established social order. Even before the significant antiblack riots of the 1830s, a white Philadelphia historian expressed the widespread resentment against blacks' new values and aspirations:

> In the olden time, dressy blacks and dandy coloured beaux and belles, as we now see them issuing from their proper churches, were quite unknown. Their aspirings and little vanities have been growing since they got those separate churches. Once they submitted to the appellation of servants, blacks, or Negroes, but now they require to be called coloured people, and among themselves, their common call of salutation is—gentlemen and ladies.[21]

Ironically, "those separate churches," symbolizing black arrogance to many whites, were the result of whites' own unchristian attitudes toward their black brothers. In the 1790s, Philadelphia blacks had rebelled against segregated seating in racially mixed churches and withdrew to their own institutions.

With the exception of their masonic lodges (the leadership of which was frequently drawn from the leaders of the church), the black community had developed no other major public arena by 1830. Whereas, in the white community, church leadership was frequently drawn from among people who were leaders in other spheres, in the black community the separate church had become and remained *the* arena for developing leadership skills.

Furthermore, to fill a vacuum, the churches had expanded their jurisdiction to include political and social, as well as religious, concerns. The absence of alternative networks through which leadership might emerge (political, professional, or commercial) meant that this church leadership and its values became synonymous with the values of the entire black community. The church, then, served as both the training ground and the operating base for religious leaders such as Bethel's pastor, Richard Allen, who in turn were seen by many whites and blacks as the black community's secular leaders as well. For white rioters to attack the black church was to strike at the seat of the black community's organizational strength while simultaneously aiming at one of the symbols of black arrogance.

While this issue of symbols was not as immediate as job competition, it was no less important, and many aspects of the tangible issues cannot be fully understood without also comprehending the importance of such symbols. For example, recent analysis has shown that many antiblack rioters were not in direct economic competition with black workers, that the occupations for which they were trained were ones in which blacks did not participate.[22] Clearly, something more was at work here than simply a matter of white workers being replaced at their jobs by black workers.

Some insight into the hidden agenda in the labor controversy may be drawn from the newspaper passage quoted earlier that describes white frustration that "colored people are . . . enabled comfortably to maintain their families." At issue was not so much specific jobs as the fact that whites were jobless while blacks lived comfortably—that, in fact, sometimes blacks' comfort was had from the income of poorer whites. Thus, it is not surprising that one of the targets of the 1834 rioters, in the early stages of the riot when choice of targets appears to have been most selective, was the son of wealthy black Philadelphian James Forten, owner of a country estate and a carriage—and several rental properties occupied by less well-off whites.[23]

Available evidence on the Philadelphia riots does not provide conclusive proof that the more well-to-do blacks and their property were preferred targets. Nevertheless, certain patterns that emerged lend weight to the argument that this was so. For example, in the 1834 riot many victims were robbed of their valuables—silver, watches, etc.[24]—items which the poor would have been less likely to possess (or to convince authorities that they possessed). An additional indication that the better-off blacks made more appealing targets is that of the more than three dozen houses destroyed in the second night of this rioting, many were "substantial brick ones" from which fine furniture was thrown into the streets and destroyed, while many more easily destroyed frame houses, owned by blacks in the same streets, were left untouched.[25]

These choices of targets suggest resentment of the "have-nots" specifically against the "haves." So too does the casualty of the third night of rioting. A group of whites, claiming to have been fired upon from a house *near* the black masonic lodge, destroyed the lodge building, citing it as a place where blacks would gather, rather than attacking the house from which the alleged shots originated.[26] Similar insight may be drawn from the description of the kinds of people who were assaulted in the 1834 riot. Contemporaries expressed some outrage that the mob attacked "old, confiding and unoffending" blacks.[27] Yet this outrage is more comprehensible if one substitutes the words "middle-aged," "respectable," and "hardworking" for the description of these victims, one of whom was reportedly a onetime servant of George Washington. It then begins to appear that individuals, groups, and property which represented economic and social "success" and "respectability" were prime targets for rioters' resentments.

It seems also significant that some of the attackers had actually crossed the city, passing other concentrations of Afro-Americans, in order to reach the south end, where the greatest concentration, not just of black people but also of their organizations, was to be found. Equally informative were the continuing complaints that blacks could find work when whites could not, and the repeated reports of blacks being assaulted at work.[28]

The visibility of affluent Negroes, and the resentment of them by struggling whites, was apparent not only in the printed sources of the day but also in stage and iconographic caricature in which the Philadelphia Negro was portrayed as the prototype of the "uppity nigger." In the late 1820s, caricaturist Edward Clay introduced a series of cartoons entitled "Life in Philadelphia," many of which poked fun at the activities and aspirations of upwardly mobile blacks in the city (see Figs. 2, 3, 4, and 5). Clay, a professional man himself, ignored the doings of the lower-class and working-class blacks, who by far outnumbered the tiny elite which he chose to ridicule. Instead, he concentrated on the attempts of the black upper classes to set themselves apart from the masses, and on their conspicuous consumption of the material goods and social values associated with upper-class whites. He ridiculed their strivings by pointing to their adoption of values of family heritage, their cultivation of music, the romance languages, and the arts, and to their tendency to adopt the latest style in dress and furnishings. These caricatures, capturing as they did the essence of black "society" in Philadelphia, were immensely popular both in Philadelphia and in England, where they were copied and augmented by other cartoonists over the next several decades.[29]

Conspicuous consumption and other elements of the lifestyle of the class of Philadelphia Afro-Americans represented was a topic of general discussion for both blacks and whites of the day. Whites' comments indeed suggested the reactions expected of a class "threatened" from below—annoyance at the audacity of the lower classes in stepping out of their "places." Typical was this comment from the same historian quoted earlier on the subject of "dressy blacks and dandy coloured beaux."

> As a whole, they show an overwhelming fondness for display and vainglory in processions . . . and in the pomp and pageantry of Masonic . . . societies. . . . With the kindest feelings for their race, judicious men wish them wise conduct.[30]

Typical also is this satire of black social life, published in the *Pennsylvania Gazette:*

> A joke of no ordinary magnitude was enacted last night, by getting up a Coloured Fancy Ball, at the Assembly-Room. . . . Carriages arrived, with ladies and gentlemen of colour, dressed in "character" in the most grotesque style. . . .
> It is worthy of remark, that many of the coaches containing these sable divinities were attended by white coachmen and *white footmen.* It is indeed high time that some serious attention was paid to the conduct and pursuits of the class of persons alluded to, and it may be well to inquire if matters progress at this rate how long it will be before masters and servants change places.[31]

What were the concerns of black leaders settled securely in the city by 1830? How did they interpret the dynamics of the racist attacks? What did they see as the most effective response to the rising frequency and virulence of such attacks after 1830? Did they passively accept this as the reality of their world? Did they seek simply to escape? Did they launch or consider counterattacks? And ultimately, how effective were their strategies in reducing the hostility against them, in protecting them from its ravages, and in helping them to progress toward the places they sought in society?

Commentary by contemporary Afro-Americans on the subject of lifestyles

"How you find yourself dis hot weader Miss Chloe?"
Pretty well I tank you Mr Cesar only I aspire
too much!"

Fɪɢ. 2. Caption reads "How you find yourself dis hot weader Miss Chloe?" "Pretty well
I tank you Mr. Cesar only I aspire too much!" From the *Life in Philadelphia* series by
Edward Clay. (Courtesy of the Historical Society of Pennsylvania)

FIG. 3. A black woman plays a guitar while Mr. Mortimer sings "Quite con a Moor, as de Italians say." From the *Life in Philadelphia* series by Edward Clay. (Courtesy of the Historical Society of Pennsylvania)

Fig. 4. A black "gentleman" leaves his card for Miss Dinah, who is "petickly engaged in washing de dishes." From the *Life in Philadelphia* series by Edward Clay. (Courtesy of the Historical Society of Pennsylvania)

sheds some light on goals and values as seen from within the black community. Concerned with acceptability to the larger white society, black leaders admonished their constituents to make life choices that would convince whites of their suitability for responsible citizenship. To this end, one of the early Philadelphia meetings of the National Convention of Free People of Color—a group established in the early 1830s to address the problems of free blacks and, in later years, the problems of enslaved brothers as well—adopted a resolution advocating that the designation "African" be dropped from the titles of black organizations. Instead, the fact that black people were colored *Americans* should be stressed.[32] To this end also, they gravitated toward values which they felt would establish them as "respectable" in wider American society. An 1837 statement of goals written by a Philadelphia black leader bears the unmistakable mark of liberal Quaker influence:

> . . . We shall advocate the cause of peace, believing that whatever tends to the destruction of human life is at variance with the precepts of the Gospel. . . . We shall endeavor to promote education with sound morality, not that we shall become "learned and mighty," but "great and good." . . . We shall advocate temperance in all things, and total abstinence from all alcoholic liquors. We shall advocate a system of economy, not only because luxury is injurious to individuals, but because its practice exercises an influence on society, which in its very nature is sinful.[33]

Frugality, temperance, religion, and education, they argued, would be the keys that would result in the respectability that would open the doors of American society to black people.

Among this list of goals of the elites in the black community, perhaps the most important was education. But why? In a society where few people were formally educated, and in which the highly educated Negro was frequently frustrated by lack of opportunities to exercise his talents, how would education help them become "great and good"? For the leaders of this community, the purpose of education seemed to be twofold. For one thing, it would keep black youths off the streets, where their presence and idleness would reinforce whites' perception that Negroes were aimless, undisciplined, and untrainable. Hence the statement by one black leader that education inspired ambition, "the cornerstone of all human greatness . . . without which we become nothing—nay, we become awful nuisances to society."[34]

Equally important, educational institutions would provide the medium for socializing black youth and ex-slaves into the temperate, "orderly" lifestyle that leaders felt was so essential to their acceptance in the larger society:

(a)

FIG. 5. Captioned "At Home" (a) and "Abroad" (b), this "Sketch of Character" ridicules black lifestyles. (Courtesy of the Library Company of Philadelphia)

The age in which we live is fastidious in its taste. It demands eloquence, figure, rhetoric, and pathos; plain, honest, common sense is no longer attracting. . . . The means of ameliorating our condition . . . is by a strict attention to education. We find that those men who have

(b)

ever been instrumental in raising a community into respectability, have devoted their best and happiest years to this important object, have lived laborious days and restless nights; made a sacrifice of ease, health, and social joys and terminated their useful career in poverty, with the only consoling hope that they had done justice to their fellow men, and should in their last hours of triumphant prospect lie down on the bed of fame and live to future ages.[35]

As an accompaniment to practical education, black elites enjoyed a wide range of curricular "extras" designed to add an "eloquence" to their lives that was frequently publicized by white and black alike. Edward Clay and his followers satirized this "society," but an anonymous writer—probably a black Philadelphian named Joseph Willson—produced a more serious document on upper-class black social life. Willson in 1841 published a book describing the lifestyles of what he termed "the higher classes of colored society," mentioning "parlors . . . carpeted and furnished with sofas, sideboards, card tables, mirrors . . . and in many instances . . . a piano forte," where in prearranged formal visits black women trained in "painting, instrumental music, singing . . . and . . . ornamental needlework" visited with each other. Their men—home from concerts, lectures, or meetings of literacy, debating, and library association gatherings at their meeting halls, sometimes joined their women, bringing news of the lectures and debates they had heard or engaged in. The topics of these meetings ranged from treatises on ancient Rome to studies of medicine, but the most frequent subjects related to the plight of blacks in America. Jacob White, destined to become a public school administrator in the years after the Civil War, was one young member of this social circle whose debating skills, at one point, were turned to a defense—before a black audience—of slavery as beneficial because it brought Africans in touch with civilization![36]

Rivaling the commitment to education was the Philadelphia black leaders' concern for frugality and temperance—a concern which sometimes led to a delicate balancing act against the desire for "eloquence . . . and rhetoric." An article in the black newspaper *Freedom's Journal* denounced the *Pennsylvania Gazette*'s satire of a black "fancy ball" in Philadelphia and cautioned Afro-Americans about the damaging image of such balls:

> The obloquy and contempt which have heretofore been heaped upon us, as a body, for our much and continual dancing, will, we hope, cause many who are persons of reflection, to think some upon the propriety of spending so many valuable hours in this amusement. While we are no advocates of dancing, we do not consider it criminal to indulge in it, occasionally, once or twice a year.[37]

The writer went on to distinguish the "we [who] don't believe in balls" from the "few who do" and expressed the concern that these latter "should not be cause to ridicule a whole society."[38]

Black newspapers frequently carried articles exhorting their readers to live disciplined, frugal lives, and set before them numerous biographies—from Toussaint L'Ouverture to Paul Cuffe—of black leaders who had contributed to the progress of the race by so doing.[39] In their statements black leaders expressed this commitment to sober consumption, but in actuality they seemed to live well, making up in "style" and "culture" what they denied themselves in frivolity. Abolitionists who visited black Philadelphians' homes commented—some with disapproval—on the sumptuousness they found there.[40] And Joseph Willson described the homes of Philadelphia's black elite as "present[ing] an air of neatness and [having] the evidences of comfort, . . . quite astonishing when compared with their limited advantages for securing them." But Willson goes on to make the point that people do not seem to be living beyond their means: "Unlike fashionable people of other communities, they live mostly within their incomes . . . and hence . . . they manage to maintain even appearances."[41]

Such "even appearances" in the lives of black elites must have been particularly annoying to whites in less stable positions—the displaced skilled laborers who participated in the riots. Though it was not black competition but rather new technology and new work routines that actually caused skilled whites' job displacement, "upper-class" blacks were an acceptable target for frustration whereas upper-class whites were not.

Bruce Laurie, in his study of antebellum Philadelphia working-class whites' lifestyles and values, has suggested that among certain segments of society (the same segments that would have been involved in the riots) there was a strong resistance to temperance and punctuality—what Laurie terms the "new morality" or "new respectability"—that was necessary for the coming regimentation of the industrial work day.[42] Such an interpretation adds the potential for yet another dimension to antiblack violence, for the recipe of frugality, temperance, religion, and education—seasoned with "eloquence"—advocated by black leaders must have been given added spice to the taste of antiblack hatred in the mouths of white rioters.

Hence, the virulent attack on the black temperance parade, which triggered the race riot of 1842, emerges as something more than simple racial violence. If blackness was injury, black temperance added insult to it. Before the riot was over, a black meeting hall, erected by and named for Stephen Smith, a wealthy black merchant, was destroyed. Nor was this destruction the result of random violence, for the local authorities, pinpointing the hall as a potential target, had set up a guard around the building. Nevertheless, it and a neighboring black church were destroyed by the crowd, and a third building, a brick structure erected as a temperance meeting hall by the black community, was ordered destroyed by municipal authorities lest its presence incite more unrest.[43]

Few participants in antiblack riots were ever prosecuted, and this fact was not lost on black leaders. An article in the *Colored American* newspaper spelled out one Afro-American's perception that the black upper classes presented a target partly because the white upper classes were unavailable:

> Abolition is a mere pretext for these outbreakings. The same class of vagabonds who mob abolitionists, would as readily mob . . . the aristocracy could they do it with the same impunity.[44]

Though these leaders understood that they were the scapegoats of American society, still they continued to pursue the only strategy they could conceive: to convince that society of the Afro-American's respectability. They were proud of their restraint and their independence. They were quick to take offense to any disparagement of their character, and they responded with lengthy protestations of their temperance and industry. One such refutation, published in a white newspaper in 1832, pointed to the large number of colored benevolent societies, and the fact that none of the societies' members had ever been convicted in the court, as evidence of the respectable nature of the black community.[45]

These groups, pleased with their capacity to care for blacks both inside and outside their membership, noted how few black people were in the almshouses and then went on to point out that "in Philadelphia, far from burdening the whites with the support of . . . [black] paupers . . . [black people's] taxes, over and above the support of their own poor, furnish funds for the support of *white* paupers."[46]

A significant segment of the black elite was, then, concerned with whites' perception of the Negro. This group was committed to education and frugal, temperate living, with the intent of "rendering harmless, false and exaggerated accounts of our degraded condition by living consistent, orderly and moral lives."[47]

A small minority of Philadelphia blacks, however, grew frustrated with shaping its rhetoric and its policies to suit the tastes of a white public. Some resorted to direct confrontations with local authorities—a fact which was noted as one of the "causes" of the 1834 riots:

> The other cause [of rioting] is the conduct of certain portions of the colored people, when any of their members are arrested as fugitives from justice. It has too often happened, that . . . the colored people have not relied on the wisdom and justice of the judiciary . . . or on the active and untiring exertions of benevolent citizens, . . . but they have . . . forcibly attempted the rescue of prisoners. . . .[48]

While some took to physical force, others confined their anger to a growing belligerence in their public statements. Though forced to recognize that white allies might desert their cause if the black community exhibited too much radical spirit, these dissenters had come to understand that the elite's stride toward "respectability" had been, at best, minimally effective in bringing about significant change in the lives of most black people. As the national black organizations inched away from total commitment to pacifism and lost some of their zeal for temperance as a pressing issue for Afro-Americans, a few Philadelphia leaders reluctantly followed, with blistering statements against white slaveholders and even some mild protest about the hypocrisy of some abolitionists.[49] A few blacks as well as whites criticized the bold ones who indulged in such "measures denunciatory" of the white community, claiming such measures were ineffectual and self-defeating.[50] Yet some black leaders, disgruntled at the slowness of progress, became increasingly verbal about their exasperation as mid-century approached. Scattered among the exhortations to black Americans to improve themselves, there began to creep a note of admonition toward the white world as well. Typical was this statement, made by one black leader:

> On the one hand we see arrayed against us unblushing impiety, unholy pride, groveling sinful prejudice, and a short-sighted worldly policy. . . . *The unholy alliance must capitulate. . . .*[51]

If one response of Afro-Americans to increased racism was the redoubling of efforts to prove themselves respectable, and another was the increase in the belligerent tone of rhetoric, yet a third expression of disillusionment, frustration, and fear was to flee Philadelphia altogether—a response that contemporary observers felt was part of the design of the rioters:

> It is notorious, indeed, a fact not to be concealed or disputed, that the "object" of the most active among the rioters, was a destruction of the property, and injury to the persons, of the colored people, with intent, as it would seem to induce or compel them to remove from this district.[52]

It was possible, of course, that one individual might do all three: step up efforts to be "respectable," increase the amount of anger expressed in public statements, and leave the city. Those who left went to places as close as New Jersey and as far away as West Africa. But one of the more interesting developments in the black community through the 1830s and 1840s was the number of people who chose the first two alternatives but rejected—in fact, reversed—the third: that is, the number of vocal and militant abolitionists who moved from outside the black neighborhood or outside of Philadelphia into the area that was experiencing the riots.

While we cannot discount the external pressure (from the city's white communities) to "ghettoize" the black community, it is worth noticing that, by 1850, a number of black leaders with substantial economic power had left other neighborhoods—neighborhoods untouched by riots—and bought residences in the area in which resided black churches, newspapers, and so on. Because in 1850 all the neighborhoods of the city still had some black residents, including some black homeowners, it would seem unlikely that those black owners who moved from other neighborhoods into the riot area did so solely because of force—or at least unlikely that they were driven out of the old neighborhood simply because they were black.[53]

By 1850, the leading families of Cassey, Ayres, Forten, and Parrot were joined in the neighborhood near Bethel by the Gloucester, Bustill, Stephen Smith, Florin, and White families, each with taxable property worth from $500 to $12,000.[54] These families were typically composed of two working parents—for example, a tailor or baker father and a teacher or seamstress mother—who had one or more children in the local black schools. Seven of the thirteen black schools were located in this neighborhood, and no other schools were grouped so closely together.[55] These people's names appeared frequently as organizers of local meetings, signers of petitions, or representatives on boards of black organizations.

From this group and this neighborhood came a disproportionately large number of the public statements of the black community in the years 1834–50, when antiblack rioting was at its peak in Philadelphia. The concerns they voiced for action within the black community were handed down to the next generation of leaders, many of whom were their biological as well as their spiritual children, for Bustills, Fortens, Whites, Stills, and many other black leaders through the Civil War and late nineteenth century were second- if not third-generation organizers in the black community.[56]

The strategy of respectability, adopted in the 1830s by the majority of the influential black leaders, was the strategy carried on by the younger group of leaders that drew together in the Bethel neighborhood in the wake of the riots. The full import of the fact that the white community seemed to grow more hostile in proportion to the success of these goals seems to have been lost on these leaders. Yet each of the five major riots against the black community between 1834 and 1849 resulted not only in generalized mayhem but also in the destruction of at least one of these symbols of group "success": churches, meeting halls, outstanding black leaders' property. In 1834 it was a masonic hall and a church; in 1835 several substantial brick houses; in

1838, in addition to Pennsylvania Hall itself, rioters burned the Quaker Shelter for Colored Orphans and another black church. The temperance parade in 1842 occasioned the destruction of two meeting halls and yet another church, and in 1849 an interracial tavern went up in smoke. An examination of other inhabitants who shared the neighborhood adds further weight to the argument that the rioters chose their targets with some purpose, for all along small streets that rippled the area, rioters bypassed seats of gambling and prostitution—some of them interracial—to reach homes and meeting places of "unoffending" blacks.[57]

The differences of style and opinion between the respectable and the unrespectable within the black community are of use in gaining insight into the relationship of the total black community to the equally varied white community. Some progress has recently been made in describing objective characteristics that differentiated various levels of material progress among antebellum urban blacks.[58] Sometimes these intrablack dynamics had a dramatic effect on black-white relations. One example of what might be called a "domino" effect of intrablack tensions may be seen in the riot that occurred in the summer of 1835. A group of blacks, reflecting the widespread acceptance of the black community's adoption of "Americanization" values, ridiculed the manners and clothing of a West Indian servant, teasing him for his "African" ways and unstylish clothing. The servant, much upset, petitioned his master for better clothing. When the master refused, the servant beat him. A race riot ensued, which like the one before it was aimed at the property of comfortable black people.[59] Presenting the image of colored Americans as separate in style and dress from Africans was a highly emotional issue within some segments of the black community—important enough to inspire public ridicule and destroy at least one servant's social restraint.

Out of an examination of the black community, then, the antiblack riots of the 1830s and 1840s are given another dimension—a dimension born not only out of the peculiarities of Philadelphia's white communities but also out of the unique qualities of the black community. While the white mobs were expressing their frustration at their own social immobility, black people, for their part, were concerned with publicly exhibiting the proof of their progress toward the "respectable" life. This set of dynamics proved mutually antagonistic. Within this setting, Philadelphia's black leaders continued to focus on three goals: economic security, physical safety, and social status. With respect to the first goal, they achieved some measure of success by 1830, accentuated by the fact that a few Afro-Americans achieved some economic power and that in times of crisis both black and white wealth could be called in for support. After 1830, when changes in the geographic integration of the city, heightened competition for work, and the rise of trade guilds that excluded blacks eroded the gains made in the early years of the century, Philadelphia's black leaders still had no choice but to continue agitation for economic opportunities.[60]

On the second goal—physical security—the tactic adopted by the black community was even less successful. Since the upper-class whites, whom black leaders saw as their national allies, were themselves hated by working-class whites, black leaders' choices of allies had the effect of reinforcing their position of being attractive targets for anti–upper-class as well as anti-black attacks.

It is interesting that no major black leader conceived of a cross-racial political union among the working classes. Until well into the 1840s, black leaders steered clear of political organization completely, and their huddling together helped in forming the ghetto that made it unnecessary to attack anymore; now they could simply be isolated.

If the effectiveness of the first two strategies was limited, in the third—the pursuit of status—blacks found their goals even more thwarted. For here black leaders found that they were alone. While working people hated the idea of upward mobility in an economic way, elites supported it only as long as it stayed within certain limits—as long as it avoided measures "denunciatory" of themselves, or attempts at intermarriage. The 1838 decision of the state legislature to rescind black suffrage suggests that the rioters were indeed "legitimized" by the approval of the larger white community, as it is "respectable" citizens and not criminals who are most likely to exercise this kind of political power. The 1830s and 1840s were a critical time for Afro-Americans in a northern city. All-black organizations, only a generation or so old, found themselves working out policies and goals under the tremendous pressure of generally tumultuous urban situations in which they were under physical and psychological attack. It was too soon in the development of Afro-American organizational life for the group to move toward recognizing that its own sets of values differed from those of the major society it sought to enter. It was too soon to have accumulated the experience that might later tell them that inclusion in American society required fundamental change—not just within the black community but in the entire political and class structure of American society.

Black leaders, then, adjusted their tactics and goals to the realities of their city as it moved into the Civil War era. They gave up physical competition for the city space and retreated to the safety of their own neighborhoods, with its supportive institutions and services. Likewise, they gave up their commitment to some of the causes of white liberals, such as temperance. A few expatriated, forgoing hope of acceptance in America at all. Most, however, continued their use of their "separate churches" and lodges to cultivate and promote their leaders and their pursuits of respectability and acceptability. And on the issue of "amalgamation" they were silent. Continued resentment against the abolitionists and against blacks as the "cause" of the disruption of Civil War far outweighed the gains possible through the old strategies of preparing for full inclusion in American society by living "respectably." And though riots and rioters gradually disappeared from American cities as legitimate extralegal tools of public discipline,[61] rioting against blacks remained acceptable. But the black churches and masonic lodges remained under the leadership of the children of leaders steeped in the values of frugality, temperance, respectability, and "Americanization." As they moved into the twentieth century, such leaders found themselves more and more out of touch with a constituency that could no longer see the use of such values.

A generalized racism in the context of the riot atmosphere of the mid-nineteenth century might well have been sufficient to engender both the riots and the rioters without any "provocation" from within the black community. Nevertheless, an examination of inner dynamics may help to keep us aware that interracial tensions are a complex phenomenon.

Notes

1. See, for example, John Runcie, "Hunting the 'Nigs' in Philadelphia: The Race Riot of August 1834," *Pennsylvania History* 29 (April 1972); Leonard Richards, *Gentlemen of Property and Standing: Anti-Abolition Mobs in Jacksonian America* (New York, 1970); David Grimsted, "Rioting in Its Jacksonian Setting," *American Historical Review* 77 (April 1972): 361–97.

2. Natalie Zemon Davis, "The Rites of Violence: Religious Riots in Sixteenth-Century France," *Past and Present* 59 (May 1973): 62; Grimsted, "Rioting in Its Jacksonian Setting," 373; Pauline Maier, "Popular Uprisings and Civil Authority in Eighteenth-Century America," in Stanley Katz, ed., *Colonial America* (New York, 1971), 432; E. P. Thompson, "The Moral Economy of the English Crowd in the Eighteenth Century," *Past and Present* 50 (February 1971): 78, 112; Sam Bass Warner, *The Private City: Philadelphia in Three Periods of Its Growth* (Philadelphia, 1968), 137.

3. See, for example, David Montgomery, "The Shuttle and the Cross: Weavers and Artisans in the Kensington Riots of 1844," *Journal of Social History* 5 (Summer 1972): 411–46.

4. Grimsted, "Rioting in Its Jacksonian Setting," 161.

5. Montgomery, "The Shuttle and the Cross," 419.

6. Grimsted, "Rioting in Its Jacksonian Setting," 378; Richards, *Gentlemen of Property and Standing,* 99; Runcie, "Hunting the 'Nigs,' " 209.

7. See, for example, John Blassingame, *The Slave Community* (New York, 1972); Gilbert Osofsky, *Puttin' on Ole Massa* (New York, 1969); Eugene Genovese, *Roll, Jordan, Roll* (New York, 1976).

8. Grimsted, "Rioting in Its Jacksonian Setting," 374, 377; Thompson, "The Moral Economy," 78, 112.

9. W. E. B. Du Bois, *The Philadelphia Negro* (1899; reprint, New York, 1969); Theodore Hershberg, "Free Blacks in Antebellum Philadelphia," in E. Miller and E. Genovese, *Plantation, Town, and County* (Urbana, Ill., 1974), 421–23; Pennsylvania Society for Promoting the Abolition of Slavery, *Present State and Condition of the Free People of Color of the City of Philadelphia* (Philadelphia, 1838), 6; [J. Zieber], *Wealth and Biography of the Wealthy of Philadelphia . . . estimated to be Worth $50,000 and Upwards* (Philadelphia, 1845). Zieber's biographies admittedly "estimates" are less important for the accuracy about black wealth than for the perception that some blacks *seemed* to be among the city's wealthiest few.

10. Norman C. Johnston, "Caste and Class of the Urban Form of Historic Philadelphia," *Journal of the American Institute of Planners,* November 1966, 334–50.

11. The short-lived *Freedom's Journal,* the sporadic *Colored American,* and the *Liberator* are among the news sheets which listed this neighborhood as their Philadelphia distribution point. As of March 3, 1827, *Freedom's Journal,* the black newspaper published out of New York from 1827 to 1829, listed Francis Webb as its distribution agent in Philadelphia. When this paper failed and was later replaced by the *Colored American,* John Bowers and later Stephen Gloucester, both well-known leaders of the Philadelphia black community, were listed as the Philadelphia agents.

12. Du Bois, *Philadelphia Negro,* 34–36.

13. *Colored American,* February 25, 1837.

14. See, for example, Benjamin Quarles, *Black Abolitionists* (New York, 1969), chap. 6.

15. Emma Jones Lapsansky, "South Street Philadelphia: 'A Haven for Those Low in the World' " (Ph.D. diss., University of Pennsylvania, 1975), 199–250.

16. *Pennsylvania Register,* December 10, 1834.

17. Abraham Ritter, *Philadelphia and Her Merchants* (Philadelphia, 1860), 47–48.

18. Russell Weigley, "A Peaceful City: Public Order in Philadelphia from Consolidation Through the Civil War," in Allen Davis and Mark Haller, *The Peoples of Philadelphia: A History of Ethnic Groups and Lower Class Life, 1790–1940* (Philadelphia, 1973); Quarles, *Black Abolitionists,* 48–50.

19. Anonymous, *A Guide to the Stranger, or Pocket Companion for the Fancy, Containing a List of the Gay Houses and Ladies of Pleasure in the City of Brotherly Love and Sisterly Affection* (Philadelphia, ca. 1849), 17.

20. Lapsansky, "South Street Philadelphia," 222.

21. John Fanning Watson, *Annals of Philadelphia* (Philadelphia, 1830), 479.

22. Runcie, "Hunting the Negro," 201.

23. Lapsansky, "South Street Philadelphia," 228; Runcie, "Hunting the Negro," 191.

24. Runcie, "Hunting the Negro," 212; *Pennsylvania Register,* August 23, 1834.

25. J. Thomas Scharf and Thompson Westcott, *History of Philadelphia* (Philadelphia, 1884), 1:638.

26. Ibid., 637–38.

27. Runcie, "Hunting the 'Nigs,' " 213.

28. Ibid., 197; *Pennsylvania Register,* August 23, 1834.

29. The accompanying cartoons, produced as broadsides by Edward Clay and later caricaturists, were part of a series, titled "Life in Philadelphia," produced in Philadelphia and in London. Evidently there was in both places an audience that could appreciate the Philadelphia black community as the prototype of black aspirations. The broadsides were published by William Simpson and C. S. Hart in Philadelphia and by Tregear and several other publishing houses in London.

30. Watson, *Annals of Philadelphia,* 479.

31. *Freedom's Journal,* March 14, 1828 (reprint from the *Pennsylvania Gazette*).

32. Quarles, *Black Abolitionists,* 54.

33. William Whipper, "Minutes and Proceedings of the First Annual Meeting of the American Moral Reform Society," in Dorothy Porter, ed., *Early Negro Writing, 1760–1837* (Boston, 1971), 207.

34. William Whipper, "An Address . . . Before the Colored Reading Society of Philadelphia, for Mental Improvement," in Porter, *Early Negro Writing* 107.

35. Ibid., 115.

36. Joseph Willson, *Sketches of the Higher Classes of Colored Society in Philadelphia* (Philadelphia, 1841), 57, 97–116; Harry Silcox, "Philadelphia Negro Educator, Jacob C. White Jr.," *Pennsylvania Magazine of History and Biography* 97 (January 1973): 75–98; Broadsides of Banneker Institute, Leon Gardiner Collection, Historical Society of Pennsylvania, Philadelphia.

37. *Freedom's Journal,* March 14, 1828.

38. Ibid.

39. See, for example, *Colored American,* February 25, 1838, and August 17, 1840.

40. Jane Pease and William Pease, *They Who Would Be Free: Blacks' Search for Freedom, 1830–1861* (New York, 1972), 111.

41. Willson, *Sketches,* 94. Also, the diary of James Forten's granddaughter Charlotte L. Forten contains ample information on the "proper" education of an upper-class black Philadelphia girl. The diary has been republished: Ray Allen Billington, ed., *A Free Negro in the Slave Era* (New York, 1961). See also Silcox, "Philadelphia Negro Educator, Jacob C. White."

42. Bruce Laurie, "Nothing on Compulsion: Life Styles of Philadelphia Artisans, 1820–1850," *Labor History,* Summer 1974, 350–52. For another discussion of this resistance to workday discipline, see Montgomery, "The Shuttle and the Cross," 411.

43. Scharf and Westcott, *History of Philadelphia,* 1: 660; Quarles, *Black Abolitionists,* 99.

44. *Colored American,* June 2, 1838.

45. *Pennsylvania Register,* June 9, 1832.

46. *Pennsylvania Register,* March 12, 1831.

47. *Pennsylvania Register,* May 7, 1831.

48. *Pennsylvania Register,* December 10, 1834.

49. See Quarles, *Black Abolitionists,* chaps. 3 and 10.

50. Willson, *Sketches,* 77–78.

51. William Watkins, "Address Before the Moral Reform Society in Philadelphia . . . 1836," in Porter, *Early Negro Writing,* 166.

52. *Pennsylvania Register,* December 10, 1834; Hershberg, "Free Blacks," 421; Du Bois, *Philadelphia Negro,* 29, 48.

53. Philadelphia Social History Project, Computer Map of Black and Mulatto Residence, 1850, in Theodore Hershberg, "Mulattoes and Blacks: Intra-Group Color Differences and Social Stratification in Nineteenth-Century Philadelphia" (paper presented at the Annual Meeting of the Organization of American Historians, April 1974). Though it is possible that black people who became abolitionists were made unwelcome in their old neighborhoods, the lack of evidence on the subject suggests that this was not widespread.

54. Lapsansky, "South Street Philadelphia," 222, 240–41; Philadelphia Society of Friends, Manuscript Census of the Colored Population of Philadelphia, 1847.

55. Benjamin Bacon, "Statistics of the Colored People of Philadelphia" (Philadelphia, 1856).

56. Hershberg, "Mulattoes and Blacks," map; Emma Lapsansky, *Before the Model City* (Philadelphia, 1969), 43.

57. Lapsansky, "South Street Philadelphia," 239, 240; Warner, *Private City* (note 2 above), 79–160.

58. Hershberg, "Mulattoes and Blacks," 6.

59. *Pennsylvania Register,* August 1, 1835; Scharf and Westcott, 1:642.

60. Hershberg, "Free Blacks," 427. Though Runcie argues, plausibly, that *specific* labor competition between blacks and whites was at a minimum, Hershberg's interpretation that general competition for jobs was acutely felt after 1830 seems to fit well with available evidence.

61. Grimsted, "Rioting in Its Jacksonian Setting," 392; Maier, "Popular Uprisings," 452.

PART TWO

THE INDUSTRIALIZING ERA
The Meaning of Freedom in a Democratic State,
1840–1870

Wilkes-Barre, Pennsylvania, has always had a small but active population of African Americans; according to the U.S. Census, there were 416 blacks living there in 1870. Here, on April 26, 1870, blacks in Wilkes-Barre's public square greeted a parade celebrating the passage of the Fifteenth Amendment, which gave African Americans the right to vote. (Courtesy of the Wyoming Historical and Geological Society)

By 1850, Pennsylvania had the largest free African American population of any northern state, but blacks found the Keystone State far from a democracy. Black Pennsylvanians had been disfranchised by the 1837 state constitution, so the struggle to regain the ballot dominated the activities of black state conventions during this period. Moreover, as elsewhere in the North, passage of the federal Fugitive Slave Law in 1850 put both the free blacks and the fugitive slaves at risk and threatened to destroy the state's black community.

While some whites joined blacks in resistance activities, such as the Christiana Riot of 1850, interracial tensions intensified during the industrializing era.

Stimulated by improved transportation links such as turnpikes, canals, and railroads, Pennsylvania rapidly emerged as a leading industrial state. Its largest industries included coal, textile manufacturing, lumber, and iron. Manufacturing spread from Philadelphia and Pittsburgh to communities like Lancaster, Reading, Harrisburg, and several towns in the Monongahela and Ohio Valleys. Unfortunately, competition from immigrants, discriminatory management and labor union practices, and a dearth of white political allies excluded or relegated African Americans to the cellar of this industrial expansion. In the wake of the Civil War, African Americans not only found it difficult to secure new jobs in the expanding industrial sector but also faced displacement from skilled trades and occupations like catering, barbering, and stevedoring, where they had previously established themselves.

Although African Americans continued to face racial restrictions during the Reconstruction era, they regained the franchise with passage of the Fifteenth Amendment in 1870. The victory was bittersweet. What did freedom mean if you could vote but not work, or if you were black and female but could not vote? Still, African Americans would soon use their vote to demand equal access to all aspects of the commonwealth's socioeconomic, political, and institutional life.

The six chapters in this section represent different perspectives on the Pennsylvania African American experience during the industrializing era. Theodore Hershberg and Gerald Eggert address the socioeconomic status of blacks in two different communities: Philadelphia and Harrisburg. R. J. M. Blackett and Leroy Hopkins examine how Pittsburgh and Lancaster's black communities reacted to slavery, abolitionism, and the Civil War. Finally, we take a look at aspects of African American leadership in Philadelphia: Harry C. Silcox on Octavius Catto, and Janice Sumler-Lewis on the interplay of race, class, and sex in the activities of the Forten-Purvis women.

CHAPTER FOUR

Free Blacks in Antebellum Philadelphia:

A Study of Ex-Slaves, Freeborn, and Socioeconomic Decline

Theodore Hershberg

Afro-American history in general has received a great deal of attention from historians in the past decade. The same cannot be said about the history of black Americans who were free before the Civil War. Studies published since Leon Litwack's *North of Slavery* have considered racial discrimination in the legal tradition, the relationship between race and politics, the establishment of black utopian communities, and the role of blacks in the abolitionist movement.[1] With a few exceptions notable in the earlier studies of the free Negro by Luther P. Jackson and John Hope Franklin, the literature lacks a solid empirical base, a sophisticated methodological and theoretical approach, and a focus on the black community itself.[2] There exists an important need for new studies of the family and social structure, of the development of such

This chapter was originally read at the Annual Meeting of the Association for the Study of Negro Life and History, Philadelphia, October 1970, and was presented in revised form at the Temple University Conference on the History of the Peoples of Philadelphia, Philadelphia, April 1971. It was revised once again for publication in the *Journal of Social History* 5 (December 1971): 183–209 and is reprinted here by permission. It has benefited from suggestions offered by many individuals, and the author expresses his gratitude for this assistance. A special note of thanks must go to the Center for Metropolitan Problems of the National Institute of Mental Health. Their financial support (2R01 M1116621), which began in April 1969, made the research possible.

community institutions as churches, schools, and beneficial societies, and of migration and social mobility.[3]

Antebellum Philadelphia offers the historian an important opportunity to study each of these topics. The free-black population of the city had its roots in the eighteenth century. Its free-black population in 1860, more than 22,000, was the largest outside the Slave South and second only to Baltimore. All-black churches, schools, and voluntary societies were numerous. The National Negro Convention Movement met for the first time in Philadelphia in 1830, and the city hosted such meetings frequently thereafter. Many of the leading black abolitionists, such as James Forten, Robert Purvis, and William Still, were Philadelphians. Most significant for the historian, the data describing all facets of this history are extant. The black history collections and the papers of the Pennsylvania Abolition Society at the Historical Society of Pennsylvania and the Library Company of Philadelphia are even richer for the antebellum period than the Schomburg Collection of the New York Public Library.

In many ways this essay resembles a preliminary progress report.[4] Despite the research and analysis which remain to be done, it is appropriate to discuss several important themes that emerge early in the study of nineteenth-century black Philadelphians: the socioeconomic deterioration of the antebellum black community, the condition of the ex-slaves in the population, and the value of understanding the urban experience for the study of black history.

A Context of Decline

The decision of the Pennsylvania Abolition Society in 1837 to take a census of Philadelphia's free-Negro population was made for both a specific and a general purpose. The specific purpose was to defeat the move, already under way in Harrisburg, to write into the new state constitution the complete disfranchisement of Pennsylvania blacks. The general purpose was "to repel" those who denounced "the whole of the free colored people as unworthy of any favor, asserting that they were nuisances in the community fit only to fill alms houses and jails."[5]

The strategy employed to accomplish these ends reveals a good deal about the faith which the abolitionists had in hard fact and reasoned argument. The data from the census were presented to the delegates at Harrisburg and to the public at large in the form of a forty-page pamphlet summarizing the findings.[6] The pamphlet argued that disfranchisement should be defeated because the free-Negro population made a worthy contribution to the well-being of

Table 4.1. Church, school, and beneficial society attendance, and occupational category data from the Pennsylvania Abolition Society 1838 census (as summarized by the society)

	Total Households			
Variables	All Freeborn	Ex-Slave HHs	Ex-Slave HH HDs	Ex-Slave HH HDs Bought Selves
Church attendance				
Nonchurchgoers	17.8%	9.3%	5.4%	3.2%
White churches	5.5	5.1	5.7	7.5
Baptist	8.7	10.3	11.4	12.9
Methodist	70.7	76.5	74.1	76.3
Episcopal	7.0	4.8	4.7	2.2
Presbyterian	7.6	5.3	6.7	5.4
Catholic	4.1	1.1	1.3	1.1
Misc.	1.9	2.0	1.7	2.2
School attendance				
HH child attend	27.6	29.2	29.0	35.4
HH child not attend	22.5	25.4	15.9	22.9
Child attend	55.0	67.1	71.7	71.2
Beneficial society membership				
HH with members	56.4	56.1	60.8	64.6
Members	27.1	27.0	35.1	32.4
Occupational category				
White collar	4.0	5.4	8.2	4.9
Skilled	17.6	16.6	18.8	20.7
Unskilled	78.4	78.1	73.1	74.4

	Male-Headed Households					
		Ex-Slave HHs and Ex-Slave Heads				
Variables	All Freeborn	All	Free HDs	All	Manumitted	Bought Selves
Church attendance						
Nonchurchgoers	18.5%	10.5%	13.5%	4.8%	7.1%	3.7%
White churches	5.2	4.3	4.1	4.6	3.8	5.1
Baptist	8.1	11.0	10.0	12.7	13.9	12.8
Methodist	71.1	75.1	77.7	70.6	70.9	75.6
Episcopal	8.1	4.6	0.4	5.1	3.8	2.6
Presbyterian	7.8	5.8	4.7	7.6	7.6	5.1
Catholic	2.6	1.3	0.9	2.0	2.5	1.3
Misc.	2.3	2.2	2.4	2.0	1.3	2.6
School attendance						
HH child attend	29.7	35.9	35.3	37.2	36.5	38.3
HH child not attend	25.2	28.3	32.2	20.1	17.6	24.7
Child attend	54.9	61.4	55.7	72.7	75.0	70.8
Beneficial society membership						
HH with members	52.0	57.7	53.8	65.2	62.3	69.1
Members	25.5	26.2	22.6	34.5	34.6	33.0
Occupational category						
White collar	4.2	5.4	4.4	7.0	7.3	5.1
Skilled	17.5	15.6	14.2	18.4	17.1	20.3
Unskilled	78.3	79.0	81.4	74.6	75.6	74.7

SOURCE: *Journal of Social History* 5 (1979): 186.
HH = Household.
HD = Head (of household).

the entire community. Blacks paid considerable taxes and rents, owned property, were not disproportionately paupers and criminals, cared for their own underprivileged, and, finally, as consumers put money into the income stream of the general economy. The facts contained in the published pamphlet therefore "gave great satisfaction affording the friends of the colored people strong and convincing arguments against those who were opposed to their enjoying the rights and privileges of freemen."[7]

Although unsuccessful in the specific purpose—blacks were disfranchised in Pennsylvania until 1870, when the Fifteenth Amendment was adopted—the Abolitionists and Quakers undertook further censuses in 1847 and 1856.[8] As in 1838, these later censuses were followed with printed pamphlets which duly noted the discrimination and problems facing free Negroes and counseled patience to the "magnanimous sufferers," as they referred to their Negro brethren. The general tone of the pamphlets, however, was optimistic and pointed to important gains made in past decades. The overall optimism, however, proved unfounded when the actual manuscript censuses were submitted to computer analysis.

The "friends of the colored people," unfortunately, had been carried away by their admirable purpose. It was one thing to document that free Negroes were not worthless, that they could indeed survive outside of the structured environment of slavery, and even that they could create a community with their own churches, schools, and beneficial societies, but it was quite another thing to argue that the people and the institutions they created actually *prospered* in the face of overwhelming obstacles. It is not so much that the Abolitionists and Quakers were wrong as that they went too far. And in so doing, they obscured a remarkable deterioration in the socioeconomic condition of blacks from 1830 to the Civil War.

Beginning in 1829 and continuing through the ensuing two decades, Philadelphia Negroes were the victims of half a dozen major antiblack riots and many more minor mob actions. Negro churches, schools, homes, and even an orphanage were set on fire. Some blacks were killed, many were beaten, and others were run out of town.[9] Contemporaries attributed the small net loss in the Negro population between 1840 and 1850 in large part to riots.[10] In the same decade, the white population grew 63 percent. While it is important to maintain the perspective that the antiblack violence occurred within a larger context of anti-Catholic violence, this knowledge must have been small comfort to Philadelphia Negroes.

A victimized minority, one reasons, should organize and bring *political* pressure on local government officials. But black Philadelphians after 1838, as we have seen, were denied even this remedy. Disfranchisement of all Negroes, even citizens who owned sufficient property to vote in all elections during the previous twenty-three years, was all the more tragic and ironic because, at the same time, all white males in Pennsylvania over the age of 21 were specifically given the right to vote.

In addition to the larger, less measurable forces such as race riots, population decline,[11] and disfranchisement, black Philadelphians after 1838 suffered a turn for the worse in wealth, residential segregation, family structure, and employment.

The antebellum black community was extremely poor. The total wealth—that is, the combined value of real and personal property holdings—for three out of every five households in both 1838 and 1847 amounted to $60 or less. This fact, it can be noted in passing, precludes the use of simple economic class analysis in determining social stratification in the black community.[12] The distribution of wealth itself, moreover, was strikingly unequal within the black population. In both 1838 and 1847 the poorest half of the population owned only one-twentieth of the total wealth, while the wealthiest 10 percent of the population held 70 percent of the total wealth; at the very apex of the community, the wealthiest 1 percent accounted for 30 percent of the total wealth.[13]

Between 1838 and 1847 there was a 10 percent decrease in per capita value of personal property, and a slight decrease in per capita total wealth among Philadelphia blacks. Although the number of households included in the 1847 census was 30 percent greater than in 1838, the number of real property holders fell from 294 to 280, and their respective percentages fell from 9 percent to 6 percent. There was, in other words, despite a considerable increase in the number of households, both absolute and percentage decrease in the number of real property holders.

Another way of highlighting the decline is to create roughly equal population groups, rank them by wealth, and determine at what point in the rank order blacks ceased to include owners of real property. In 1838, owners of real property extended through the wealthiest 30 percent of the ranked population; in 1847 they extended less than half as far. In 1838, moreover, it required a total wealth holding of between $200 and $300 in order to own real property; by 1847 an individual required a total wealth holding twice as high before he could purchase land or own a home.

This statistic is complemented by a measurable rise in residential segregation over the decade. Disfranchisement (perhaps as valuable to us as a symptom of contemporary feelings about Negroes as it was a cause), a decade of race riots, and a general backlash against abolitionist activities all contributed to the creation of a social atmosphere in which it was considerably more difficult for even the wealthiest of Negroes to acquire real property. It is tempting to conclude quite simply that rising racism meant that a far higher

Table 4.2. Wealth and property holding data from the Pennsylvania Abolition Society 1838 census (as summarized by the society)

	Total Households (3,295) (12,084 persons)			
Variables	All Freeborn	Ex-Slave HHs	Ex-Slave HH HDs	Ex-Slave HH HDs Bought Selves
Total HHs	2,489	806	314	96
Total persons	8,867	3,217	1,013	358
Family size (w/o singles)	3.88	4.27	3.84	4.12
Two-parent HH (%)	77.0	79.8	79.3	90.5
Wealth categories				
$0–20 (%)	23.9	19.6	17.5	10.4
$21–40 (%)	21.1	19.6	19.7	11.5
$41–90 (%)	17.8	15.1	14.6	11.5
$91–240 (%)	18.6	21.1	18.8	25.0
$241 + (%)	18.6	24.6	29.3	41.7
Avg. TW	$252	$268	$295	$388
Avg. PP all HHs[a]	$176	$175	$191	$223
Avg. RP all HHs	$76	$93	$105	$164
Avg. RP owners only	$987	$730	$567	$527
% RP owners	7.7	12.8	18.5	31.2
Avg. rent	$48	$50	$47	$53

	Male-Headed Households (2,361) (9,609 persons)					
				Ex-Slave HHs Ex-Slave Heads		
Variables	All Freeborn	All	Free HDs	All	Manumitted	Bought Selves
Total HHs	1,760	601	394	207	85	81
Total persons	6,966	2,643	1,852	791	312	327
Family size (w/o singles)	4.06	4.40	4.70	3.99	3.80	4.72
Two-parent HH (%)	99% of all male-headed households with					
Wealth categories	2 or more persons were two-parent households					
$0–20 (%)	21.8	16.3	19.0	11.1	16.5	6.2
$21–40 (%)	18.6	18.1	19.5	15.5	16.5	8.6
$41–90 (%)	16.7	14.0	14.7	12.6	12.9	11.1
$91–240 (%)	20.9	23.0	22.6	23.7	24.7	28.4
$241 + (%)	22.1	28.6	24.1	37.2	29.4	45.7
Avg. TW	$257	$317	$284	$380	$388	$409
Avg. PP[a] all HHs	$181	$204	$180	$249	$269	$252
Avg. RP all HHs	$69	$113	$103	$131	$119	$157
Avg. RP owners only	$768	$770	$1,017	$564	$776	$472
% RP owners	9.0	14.6	10.1	23.2	15.3	33.3
Avg. rent	$53	$55	$55	$54	$49	$56

SOURCE: *Journal of Social History,* 5 (1979): 188.

[a]There is little observable difference between the average personal property for all HHs and the average personal property for owners only: 95–100% of all HHs owned personal property.

TW = Total Wealth   PP = Personal Property   RP = Real Property   HH = Household price had to be paid in order to induce a white man to sell land to a black man. Stating such a conclusion with complete confidence, however, requires further *comparative* research in order to determine whether instead this phenomenon applied equally to all ethnic groups—that is, a period of generally appreciating land values.

The actual measurement of residential segregation depends upon the use of a "grid square"—an area roughly one and a quarter blocks square—and is a vast improvement over far larger geographical entities, such as districts or wards. Each Negro household was located on detailed maps, and its precise grid square was recorded. All variables about each household, then, are observable and measurable in small, uniquely defined units.

Residential segregation is measured in two dimensions: the *distribution* of the household population, that is, the number of grid squares in which Negro households were located; and the *density* of the population, that is, the number of Negro households per grid. Residential segregation was rising in the decade before 1838, and it increased steadily to 1860. Between 1838 and 1847, average density increased 13 percent in all grid squares inhabited by blacks. More important, however, is that the percentage of households occupying the most dense grid squares (those with more than 100 black households) increased by almost 10 percent. Between 1850 and 1860 the average density changed very little, but the trend toward settlement in the more dense grids continued. By 1860 the number of households occupying the most dense grid squares reached more than one in four, an increase of 11 percent over the previous decade, and the high point between 1838 and 1880. During the Civil War decade, residential segregation fell off, but it rose again from 1870 to 1880 as migration from the South swelled the Negro population of Philadelphia to 31,700, an increase of 43 percent over both the 1860 and 1870 totals.

Data from the Abolitionist and Quaker censuses, the U.S. Census of 1880, and W. E. B. Du Bois's study of the Seventh Ward in 1896–97 indicate, in each instance, that two-parent households were characteristic of 78 percent of black families. That statistical average, however, belies a grimmer reality for the poorest blacks. There was a decline in the percentage of two-parent households for the poorest one-fifth of the population, from 70 percent in 1838 to 63 percent ten years later, and for the poorest half of the black population the decline was from 73 percent to 68 percent. In other words, among the poorest half of the community at mid-century, roughly one family in three was headed by a female.[14]

An unequal female-male sex ratio no doubt indirectly affected family building and stability. Between 1838 and 1860 the number of black females per 1,000 black males increased from 1,326 to 1,417. For whites in 1860 the corresponding figure was 1,088. Between 1860 and 1890 the sex ratio for blacks moved in the direction of parity: 1,360 in 1870, 1,263 in 1880, and 1,127 in 1890 indicates that the movement away from, and after 1860 back toward, equal distribution of the sexes was due to a change in the number of black males in the 20-to-40 age bracket. Changes in this age bracket usually result from two related factors: occupational opportunities and in- and out-migration rates. The remarkably high excess of females over males throughout the period probably reflects poor employment opportunities for black men (while the demand for black female domestics remained high) accompanied by net out-migration of young black males. The gradual improvement of industrial opportunities for young black males after 1860, accompanied by net in-migration of increasing numbers of young black men, reduced the excess of black females. The sociological consequences of such an imbalance in the sex ratios are familiar: illegitimacy, delinquency, broken homes, and such. In light of these statistics, it is surprising that the percentage of two-parent households was as high as it was.

More important for our purposes, however, is another measure of the condition of the entire black population often obscured by the debate over the matrifocality of the black family, focusing as it does on narrow statistical analysis of traditional household units: How many blacks were living outside of black households? How many were inmates of public institutions? How many were forced not only to delay beginning families, but to make lives for themselves *outside* the black family unit, residing in boarding houses as transients or living in white homes as domestic servants?[15]

The data indicate that there was a slow but steady rise in the percentage of black men and women who found themselves outside the black family. Between 1850 and 1880 their numbers nearly doubled. By 1880, some 6,000 persons—slightly less than one-third of the adult population (inmates, transients, and servants combined)—were living outside the normal family structures. One out of every five adults lived and worked in a white household as a domestic servant. That so many Negroes took positions outside their traditional family units is testimony to the strength and persuasiveness of the job discrimination which existed at large in the economy; that this occurred within a context of widening occupational opportunities for whites, a benefit of increasing industrialization and the factory system, makes it even more significant. In 1847 less than half of 1 percent of the black male work force was employed in factories. And this came at a time, it should be remembered, when thousands of Irish immigrants were engaged in factory work.

Blacks were not only denied access to new jobs in the expanding factory, but because of increasing job competition with the Irish they also lost their traditional predominance in many semiskilled and unskilled jobs. The 1847 census identified 5 percent of the black male work force in the relatively well-paying occupations of hod carrier and stevedore. The following letter to a city newspaper written in 1849 by one "P.O." attests to the job displacement:

> That there may be, and undoubtedly is, a direct competition between them (the blacks and Irish) as to labor we all know. The wharves and new buildings attest this fact, in the person of our stevedores and hod-carriers as does all places of labor; and when a few years ago we saw none but blacks, we now see nothing but Irish.[16]

"P.O." proved perceptive indeed. According to the 1850 U.S. Census, the percentage of black hod carriers and stevedores in the black male work force fell in just three years, from 5 percent to 1 percent. The 1850 Census, moreover, reported occupations for the entire country and included 30 percent more black male occupations than the 1847 Census; nevertheless, the absolute number of black hod carriers fell sharply from 98 to 28, and stevedores from 58 to 27.

A similar pattern of increasing discrimination affected the ranks of the skilled. Blacks complained not only that it was "difficult for them to find places for their sons as apprentices to learn mechanical trades,"[17] but also that those who had skills found it more difficult to practice them. The "Register of Trades of the Colored People," published in 1838 by the Pennsylvania Abolition Society to encourage white patronage of black artisans, noted that 23 percent of 656 skilled artisans did not practice their skills because of "prejudice against them."[18] The 1856 Census recorded considerable deterioration among the ranks of the skilled. The percentage of skilled artisans not practicing their trades rose from 23 percent in 1838 to approximately 38 percent in 1856. Skilled black craftsmen were "compelled to abandon their trades on account of the unrelenting prejudice against their color."[19]

Job discrimination, then, was complete and growing: blacks were excluded from new areas of the economy, uprooted from many of their traditional unskilled jobs, denied apprenticeships for their sons, and prevented from practicing the skills they already possessed. All social indicators—race riots, population decrease, disfranchisement, residential segregation, per capita wealth, ownership of real property, family structure, and occupational opportunities—pointed toward socioeconomic deterioration within Philadelphia's antebellum black community.

Ex-Slave and Freeborn

Among the 3,300 households and 12,000 persons included in the 1838 Census, about one household in four contained at least one person who although free in 1838 had been born a slave. Living in these 806 households were some 1,141 ex-slaves, or 9 percent of the entire population.

What was the condition of the ex-slave relative to his freeborn brother? Were ex-slaves in any way responsible for the socioeconomic deterioration just described? Contemporaries perceived two very different effects of direct contact with slavery. "Upon feeble and common minds," according to one view, the slave experience was "withering" and induced "a listlessness and an indifference to the future." Even if the slave somehow managed to gain his freedom, "the vicious habits of slavery" remained, "worked into the very grain of his character." But for others, "who resisted . . . and bought their own freedom with the hard-earned fruits of their own industry," the struggle for "liberty" resulted in "a desire for improvement" which "invigorated all their powers and gave energy and dignity to their character as freemen."[20] An analysis of the data permits us to determine whether both groups were found equally in antebellum Philadelphia or whether one was more representative of all ex-slaves than the other.

The richness of detail in the census schedules allows us to make several important distinctions in the data describing the ex-slave households. We know which of the 806 households were headed by ex-slaves themselves, 314, and how these 40 percent of all ex-slave households were freed—if, for instance, they were "manumitted" or if, as they put it, they had "bought themselves."

We are dealing, then, with several ex-slave categories: (1) 493 households in which at least one ex-slave lived but which had a freeborn household head; I shall refer to this group as free-headed, ex-slave households. (2) 314 households in which at least one ex-slave lived but which had an ex-slave household head; I shall refer to this group as ex-slave–headed households. In this second group of ex-slave–headed households I have selected two subgroups for analysis: (a) 146 ex-slave household heads who were manumitted, and (b) 96 ex-slave household heads who bought their own freedom.[21]

Cutting across all of these groups is the dimension of sex. The census identified household heads as males, females, and widows. There was a strong and direct relationship between family size, wealth, and male sex, so that the largest families had the most wealth and the greatest likelihood of being headed by a male. Because there was also a strong and direct relationship between sex and almost all other variables, with males enjoying by far the more fortunate circumstances, it is important to differentiate by sex in comparing the general condition of the ex-slave groups with that of the free-born population. Ex-slaves differed from their freeborn neighbors in a variety of significant social indicators:

Family Size

The family size of all ex-slave households was 10 percent larger than house-holds all of whose members were freeborn: 4.27 persons compared with 3.88. Families of ex-slave households headed by freeborn males and those headed by males who bought their own freedom were 20 percent larger: 4.70. The instances in which freeborn families were larger occurred only where female and, to a lesser extent, widow ex-slave households were involved. (This, by the way, is the general pattern in most variables; in other words, ex-slave females and widows more closely resembled their freeborn counterparts than ex-slave males resembled freeborn males.)

Two-Parent Households

Two-parent households were generally more common among the ex-slaves. Taken together, two-parent households were found 80 percent of the time among ex-slaves, while the figure for the freeborn was 77 percent. A signifi-cant difference, however, was found in the case of ex-slave household heads who bought their own freedom. In this group, 90 percent were two-parent households.

Church

For two basic reasons the all-black church has long been recognized as the key institution of the Negro community: first, an oppressed and downtrodden people used religion for spiritual sustenance and for its promise of a better life in the next world; second, with the ability to participate in the political, social, and economic spheres of the larger white society in which they lived sharply curtailed, Negroes turned to the church for fulfillment of their secular needs.

Important in the twentieth century, the church was vital to blacks in the nineteenth. Philadelphia Negroes were so closed off from the benefits of white society that church affiliation became a fundamental prerequisite for a decent and, indeed, bearable existence.[22] For this reason, nonchurch affilia-tion, rather than poverty, was the distinguishing characteristic of the most disadvantaged group in the community. Nonchurchgoers must have enjoyed few of the benefits and services which accrued to those who were affiliated with a church in some manner. The socioeconomic profile of non-churchgoers is depressing. They fared considerably less well than their churchgoing neighbors in all significant social indicators: they had smaller families, fewer two-parent households, high residential density levels, and they were disproportionately poor. Their ratios for membership in beneficial societies and for the number of school-age children in school was one-fourth and one-half, respectively, that of the larger community. Occupationally, they were decidedly overrepresented among the unskilled sectors of the work force.

In this sense, then, the percentage of households with no members attending church is a more valuable index of general social conditions than any other. Some 18 percent of the freeborn households had no members attending church; for all ex-slave households the figure was half as great. Although ex-slave households were one in four in the community-at-large, they were less than one in ten among households with no members attending church. The ratio were even lower (one in twenty) for ex-slave-headed households and lowest (one in thirty) for ex-slaves who bought themselves.

About 150 households, or 5 percent of the churchgoing population of the entire community, attended twenty-three predominately white churches. These churches had only "token" integration, allowing a few Negroes to worship in pews set apart from the rest of the congregation. Ex-slaves of all groups attended white churches in approximately the same ratio as did the freeborn—1 household in 20.

The churchgoing population of the entire community consisted of 2,776 households distributed among five religious denominations: Methodists (73 percent), Baptists (9 percent), Presbyterians (7 percent), Episcopalians (7 percent), and Catholics (3 percent). Methodists worshiped in eight and Baptists in four all-black congregations scattered throughout the city and districts. Together they accounted for more than eight of every ten churchgoers. The various ex-slave groups were found an average of 11 percent more frequently among Methodists and 30 percent more frequently among Baptists.

In any case, Methodists and Baptists differed little from each other, and to describe them is to characterize the entire community: poor and unskilled. Within each denomination, however, a single church—Union Methodist and Union Baptist—served as the social base for their respective elites. And while ex-slaves attended all the community's all-black churches, it was in these two churches that the ex-slaves were most frequently found. The ex-slave members of these two churches shared the socioeconomic and cultural characteristics of the community's elite denominations—the Episcopalians and the

Presbyterians—and it should not be surprising, therefore, to find ex-slaves of all groups underrepresented in each of these last two denominations.

Beneficial Societies

Next to the church in value to the community were the all-black "beneficial societies." These important institutions functioned as rudimentary insurance groups which provided their members with relief in sickness, aid during extreme poverty, and burial expenses at death.

There were more than 100 distinct societies in antebellum Philadelphia. They grew out of the obvious need and were early manifestations of the philosophy of "self-help" which became so popular later in the nineteenth century. Almost always they were affiliated directly with one of the all-black churches. The first beneficial society, known as the "Free African Society," was founded in 1787. A dozen societies existed by 1815, 50 by 1830 and 106 by 1847.

Slightly more than 50 percent of freeborn households were members of the various societies. Making good the philosophy of self-help half a century before Booker T. Washington, the societies found ex-slaves more eager to join their ranks than freeborn blacks. Each group of ex-slaves had a higher percentage of members, especially ex-slave–headed households (61 percent), ex-slaves who purchased their own freedom (65 percent), and the males among the latter group (70 percent).

Membership in beneficial societies varied significantly by wealth and status. Ranking the entire household population in thirty district wealth categories revealed that, beginning with the poorest, the percentage of membership rose with increasing wealth until the wealthiest six categories. For this top 11 percent of the population, however, membership in beneficial societies declined from 92 percent to 81 percent. Among the wealthiest—and this applied equally to ex-slaves—there was less need for membership in beneficial societies.

Education

One household in four among the freeborn population sent children to school. For ex-slave households, the corresponding figure was more than one in three. Ex-slave households had slightly fewer children but sent a considerably greater percentage of their children to school. For freeborn households the percentage was 55 percent; for all ex-slave households it was 67 percent; and for ex-slave–headed households the figure rose to 72 percent. To the extent that education was valuable to blacks, the ex-slaves were better off.

Location and Density

Smaller groups of ex-slaves clustered disproportionately in the outlying districts of Kensington, Northern Liberties, and Spring Garden. Some 25 percent of the entire black population of Philadelphia, they constituted about 35 percent of the black population in these areas. Most ex-slaves, however, lived in the same proportions and in the same blocks as did the freeborn population.

More interesting than the pattern of their distribution throughout the city, however, was the level of population density in which they lived—that is, the number of black neighbors who lived close by. To calculate the number of black households in a grid square of approximately one and a quarter blocks, three density levels were used: 1–20, 21–100, and in excess of 100 households per grid square.[23]

The less dense areas were characterized by larger families, greater presence of two-parent households, less imbalance between the sexes, and fewer families whose members were entirely nonnatives of Pennsylvania. In these areas lived a disproportionately greater number of wealthy families, and among them a correspondingly overrepresented number of real property owners. Here white-collar and skilled workers lived in greater percentages than elsewhere in the city, and unskilled workers were decidedly few in both percentage and absolute number. The major exceptions to the distribution of wealth and skill came as a result of the necessity for shopkeepers and craftsmen to locate their homes and their businesses in the city's more densely populated sections.

Ex-slave households were more likely than freeborn households to be found in the least dense areas (one in four, compared with one in five). Conversely, ex-slave households were less likely to be found in areas with the greatest density of black population.

Wealth

The parameters of wealth for Negroes in antebellum Philadelphia have already been described. The community was impoverished, but poverty did not touch all groups equally. In terms of average total wealth, including both real and personal property, free-headed ex-slave households differed little from the freeborn population. In considering the ex-slave–headed household, however, differences emerge. Average total wealth for this group was 20 percent greater; for males in this group it was 53 percent greater; and for males who freed themselves it was 63 percent greater.

The most significant differences in wealth by far occurred in real property holding. One household in thirteen, or slightly less than 8 percent, among the freeborn owned real property. For all ex-slave households the corresponding ratio was one in eight; for ex-slave–headed households, one in five; for males who were in this group one in four; and, most dramatic, for males who purchased their own freedom one in three owned real property. To these ex-slaves, owning their own home or a piece of land must have provided something (perhaps a stake in society) of peculiarly personal significance. Distribution of wealth, to view the matter from a different perspective, was less unequal for ex-slave households, particularly ex-slave household heads. The poorest half of the freeborn and ex-slave–headed households owned 5 percent and 7 percent respectively of the total wealth; for the wealthiest one-quarter of each group the corresponding figure was 86 and 73 percent; for the wealthiest one-tenth, 67 and 56 percent; and for the wealthiest one-hundredth, 30 and 21 percent. Overall wealth distribution, in other words, while still skewed toward pronounced inequality, was more equally distributed for ex-slave household heads in the middle and upper wealth categories.

Occupation

The final area of comparison between the ex-slaves and the freeborn is occupation.[24] Analysis of the data using the same classification schema for Negroes as for white ethnic groups confirms an earlier suspicion that, although such schemata are necessary in order to compare the Negro with white ethnic groups, they are entirely unsatisfactory tools of analysis when social stratification in the Negro community is the concern. Even though the Negroes who constituted the labor force of antebellum Philadelphia described themselves as engaged in 400 different occupations, a stark fact emerges from the analysis: there was almost no occupational differentiation.

Five occupations accounted for 70 percent of the entire male work force: laborers (38 percent), porters (11.5 percent), waiters (11.5 percent), seamen (5 percent), and carters (4 percent); another 10 percent were employed in miscellaneous laboring capacities. Taken together, eight out of every ten working men were unskilled laborers. Another 16 percent worked as skilled artisans, but fully half of this fortunate group were barbers and shoemakers; the other skilled craftsmen were scattered among the building-construction (3.2 percent), home-furnishing (1.3 percent), leather goods (1.2 percent), and metal work (1.2 percent) trades. Less than half of the 1 percent of Negroes, as pointed out in another context, found employment in the developing factory system. The remaining 4 percent of the labor force were engaged in white-collar professions. They were largely proprietors who sold food or second-hand clothing from vending carts and should not be considered "store owners."

The occupational structure for females was even less differentiated than for males. More than eight out of ten women were employed in day-work capacities (as opposed to those who lived and worked in white households) as domestic servants: "washers" (52 percent), "day workers" (22 percent), and miscellaneous domestics (6 percent). Some 14 percent worked as seamstresses and accounted for all the skilled workers among the female labor force. Finally, about 5 percent were engaged in white-collar work, which, like the males, meant vending capacities in clothing- and food-selling categories.

It should come, then, as no surprise that there were few distinctions of significance in the occupational structure of the ex-slaves and freeborn work forces. The differences in vertical occupational categories find male ex-slave household heads more likely to be in white-collar positions (7 percent, as opposed to 4 percent for the freeborn), equally distributed in the skilled trades, and slightly less represented in the unskilled occupations (75 percent as opposed to 78 percent). Within the horizontal categories, there were few important differences. Male ex-slave household heads were more likely than the freeborn to be employed as porters, carpenters, blacksmiths, preachers, and clothes dealers.

In summary, then, we find the ex-slaves with larger families, greater likelihood of two-parent households, higher affiliation rates in church and beneficial societies, sending more of their children to school, living more frequently in the least dense areas of the county, generally wealthier, owning considerably more real property, and being slightly more fortunate in occupational differentiation. By almost every socioeconomic measure, the ex-slave fared better than his freeborn brother. While ex-slaves were distributed throughout the socioeconomic scale, they were more likely to be part of the community's small middle class, which reached into both the lower and the upper strata, characterized more by their hardworking, conscientious, and God-fearing lifestyle than by a concentration of wealth and power.

An Urban Perspective

On the basis of the data presented, it is possible to state two conclusions, offer a working hypothesis, and argue for the necessity of an urban perspective. First, the relatively better condition of the ex-slave, especially the ex-

Prominent among antebellum free Philadelphia blacks was
sailmaker and social activist James Forten (1766–1842). This
reproduction of a watercolor of Forten is by an unknown artist.
(Courtesy of the Historical Society of Pennsylvania)

slave who was both a male and who had bought his own freedom, confirms
the speculations of a few historians that the slave-born Negro freed before
the Civil War was exceptional—a uniquely gifted individual who succeeded
in internalizing the ethic of deferred gratification in the face of enormous
difficulties.[25] More striking is that the socioeconomic condition of the great
majority of ex-slaves was not markedly inferior to that of the freeborn. That
ex-slaves were generally better off than freeborn blacks, however, should not
suggest anything more than relative superiority; it does not imply prosperity
and should not obscure the generally impoverished and deteriorating condition of the black community. Second, because the remaining 91 percent of
Philadelphia's antebellum black population was freeborn, the dismal and declining socioeconomic circumstances of that population cannot be attributed
to direct contact with the "slave experience." Direct contact with slavery was

undoubtedly a *sufficient* cause of low status and decay; it most certainly was not a *necessary* cause.[26]

In a very important sense the first conclusion has little to do with the second. The latter is not arrived at because those who had direct contact with slavery fared better in the city than those who were born free. The second conclusion is not based upon a recognition that slavery was less destructive or benign (although in some aspects it certainly could have been so), but rather that the antebellum northern city was destructive as well. It is significant to understand that slavery and the discrimination faced by free Negroes in the urban environment were both forms of racism which pervaded the institutions and informed the values of the larger white society.

The comparison of the freeborn and the ex-slave was undertaken in an effort to learn more about the question which students of the black experience want answered. What was the effect of slavery on the slaves? In the case of antebellum Philadelphia the ex-slaves may not be representative of the slave experience. If they were, however, our insight would necessarily be limited to the effect of the mildest slavery system as it was practiced in Maryland, Delaware, and Virginia.[27]

Deemphasizing direct contact with slavery does not imply that the institution of slavery, and the debasement and prejudice it generated, did not condition the larger context. The indirect effect of slavery cannot be underestimated. The proslavery propaganda provided the justification not only for the institution but also for the widespread discriminatory treatment of the free Negro both before and long after emancipation.

Yet, on the other hand, one must not allow this understanding, or an often overwhelming sense of moral outrage, to lead to a monolithic interpretation of the effects of the slave experience. Stanley Elkins's treatment of slavery may be in error, but few historians doubt that his urging of scholars to end the morality debate and to employ new methods and different disciplines in the study of slavery was correct and long overdue.

There is no historically valid reason to treat the slave experience as entirely destructive or entirely benign, nor, for that matter, does historical reality necessarily fall midway between the two. It may be more useful to study the problems blacks faced at different times and in different places in their history and to attempt to trace their historical origins, rather than to begin with slavery and assume that it represented in all instances the historical root. Some of the problems faced by blacks may more accurately be traced to the processes of urbanization, industrialization, and immigration, occurring in a setting of racial inequality, rather than to slavery.

One of the most significant contributions to black history and sociology in recent years presents data that suggest the postslavery, possibly urban, origins of the matrifocal black family. In groundbreaking essays on the Negro family after the Civil War, Herbert Gutman has demonstrated convincingly that traditional interpretations of slavery and its effect on the black family are seriously misleading. Examining "the family patterns of those Negroes closest in time to actual chattel slavery," Gutman did not find "instability," "chaos," or "disorder." Instead, in fourteen varied southern cities and counties between 1865 and 1880 he found viable two-parent households ranging from 70 to 90 percent.[28]

It is significant that of the areas studied by Gutman the four lowest percentages of two-parent households were found in cities: Natchez and Beaufort, 70 percent; Richmond, 73 percent; and Mobile, 74 percent. The urban experience was in some way responsible for the weaker family structure and for a whole set of other negative socioeconomic consequences, all of which are found in the Philadelphia data.

Yet the city is more than a locale. Slavery itself underwent major transformations in the urban setting.[29] Sustained advances in technology, transportation, and communication made the city the context for innovation, and the innovation, in turn, generated countless opportunities for upward mobility for those who could take advantage of them. And there was the rub. Blacks, alone among city dwellers, were excluded not only from their fair share but also from almost any chance for improvement generated by the dynamics of the urban milieu. That the exclusion was not systematic but, by and large, incidental did not make it any less effective. The city provided an existence at once superior to and inferior to that of the countryside: for those who were free to pursue their fortunes, the city provided infinitely more opportunities and far greater rewards; for those who were denied access altogether (or for those who failed), the city provided scant advantages and comforts. There were few interstices.

The data presented in this essay point to the destructiveness of the urban experience for blacks in nineteenth-century Philadelphia.[30] To proceed, data comparing the black experience with that of other ethnic groups are necessary, and they are forthcoming. Although much research remains, it is possible to offer a hypothesis. The forces which shaped modern America—urbanization, industrialization, and immigration—operated for blacks within a framework of institutional racism and structural inequality. In the antebellum context, blacks were unable to compete on equal terms with either the native-white-American worker or the thousands of newly arrived Irish and German immigrants. Philadelphia Negroes suffered in the competition with the Irish and Germans and recovered somewhat during the Civil War and Reconstruction decades, only to suffer again, in much the same circumstances, in competition with the "new" immigrant groups—this time the

Italians, Jews, Poles, and Slavs, who began arriving in the 1880s. Best characterized as a low-status economic group early in the century, Philadelphia's blacks found themselves a deprived and degraded caste at its close.

Students of black history have not adequately appreciated the impact of the urban experience. In part this is due to several problems: to the larger neglect of urban history; to unequal educational opportunities which prevented many potential black scholars from study and other students from publication; to difficulties inherent in writing history "from-the-bottom-up"; and to present reward mechanisms which place high premium on quickly publishable materials involving either no new research or shoddy and careless efforts.

There are, however, other and more important considerations, with no little sense of irony. The moral revulsion to slavery prevented development of alternative explanations of low status and decay. In the immediate postslavery decades and throughout the twentieth century, blacks and then white allies took refuge in an explanation used by many abolitionists before them— namely, that slavery and not racial inferiority was responsible for the black condition. They were, of course, not wrong; it was rather that they did not go far enough. It was, and still is, much easier to lament the sins of one's forefathers than it is to confront the injustices in more contemporary socioeconomic systems.

Although August Meier and Elliott Rudwick titled their well-known and widely used text *From Plantation to Ghetto,* and with the little data available to them subtly but suggestively wove the theme of the impact of urban environment through their pages, scholars have been slow to develop it in monographic studies. The Philadelphia data from 1838 to 1880 enable one to examine this theme in minute detail. Although 90 percent of the nation's black population in 1880 was southern and overwhelmingly rural, the key to the twentieth century lies in understanding the consequences of the migration from the farm to the city. The experience of Philadelphia Negroes in the nineteenth century foreshadowed the fate of millions of black migrants who, seeking a better life, found different miseries in what E. Franklin Frazier called the "cities of destruction."

If we are to succeed in understanding the urban experience, we must dismiss simplistic explanations which attribute all present-day failings to "the legacy of slavery" or to "the problems of unacculturated rural migrants lacking the skills necessary to compete in an advanced technology." We must understand, instead, the social dynamics and consequences of competition and accommodation among different racial, ethnic, and religious groups, taking place in an urban context of racial discrimination and structural inequality.

Notes

1. Leon Litwack, *North of Slavery* (Chicago, 1961); Arthur Zilversmit, *The First Emancipation* (Chicago, 1967); Eugene H. Berwanger, *The Frontier Against Slavery: Western Anti-Negro Prejudice and the Slavery Extension Controversy* (Urbana, Ill., 1967); V. Jacques Voegeli, *Free But Not Equal: The Midwest and the Negro During the Civil War* (Chicago, 1969); James A. Rawley, *Race and Politics* (Philadelphia, 1969); Eric Foner, *Free Soil, Free Labor, Free Men* (New York, 1970); William Pease and Jane Pease, *Black Utopia* (Madison, Wisc., 1963); Benjamin Quarles, *Black Abolitionists* (Oxford, 1969); Carleton Mabee, *Black Freedom: The Non-Violent Abolitionists, 1830 to the Civil War* (New York, 1970).

2. Luther P. Jackson, *Free Negro and Property Holding in Virginia, 1830–1860* (New York, 1942), and John Hope Franklin, *The Free Negro in North Carolina, 1790–1860* (Chapel Hill, N.C., 1943). There are, of course, many other state and local studies: W. E. B. Du Bois, *The Philadelphia Negro* (Philadelphia, 1899); Edward R. Turner, *The Negro in Pennsylvania* (Washington, D.C., 1911); John Russell, *The Free Negro in Virginia, 1830–1860* (Baltimore, 1913); John Daniels, *In Freedom's Birthplace: A Study of Boston's Negroes* (Boston, 1914); James M. Wright, *The Free Negro in Maryland* (New York, 1921); Robert A. Warner, *New Haven Negroes* (New Haven, Conn., 1940); Emma Lou Thornbrough, *The Negro in Indiana* (Indianapolis, 1957). Especially valuable articles include Carter Woodson, "The Negroes of Cincinnati Prior to the Civil War," *Journal of Negro History* 1 (January 1916); Charles S. Sydnor, "The Free Negro in Mississippi Before the Civil War," *American Historical Review* 32 (July 1927); E. Horace Fitchett, "The Origin and Growth of the Free Negro Population of Charleston, South Carolina," *Journal of Negro History* 26 (October 1941); J. Merton England, "The Free Negro in Antebellum Tennessee," *Journal of Southern History* 9 (February 1943).

3. There are, of course, important beginnings. Among them are E. Franklin Frazier's *Free Negro Family* (Nashville, Tenn., 1932), and Carter G. Woodson's *Education of the Negro Prior to 1861* (Washington, D.C., 1915), *The History of the Negro Church* (Washington, D.C., 1921), and *Free Negro Heads of Families in the United States* (Washington, D.C., 1925). Fortunately, there are studies of the free Negro currently [1970] under way, and others awaiting publication which will make important contributions to the literature. I am aware of the following: Ira Berlin, University of Illinois, Chicago Circle, on the free Negro in the Upper South; Rhoda Freeman, Upsala College, on the free Negro in New York; Carol Ann George, Oswego State College, on the free-Negro church; Laurence Glasco, University of Pittsburgh, on the free Negro in Buffalo and Pittsburgh; Floyd Miller, Hiram College, on Martin Delany and the colonization movement; Carl Oblinger, Johns Hopkins University, on free-Negro communities in southeastern Pennsylvania towns; Armisted Robinson, University of Rochester, on free Negro in Memphis; Harry Silcox, Temple University, on free-Negro education in Philadelphia and Boston; Arthur O. White, College of Education, University of Florida, on the free Negro in Boston; Marina Wikramanayaka, University of Texas, El Paso, on the free Negro in Charleston.

4. The Philadelphia Social History Project is a study of comparative social mobility in nineteenth-century Philadelphia focusing on the patterns of three distinct groups: blacks, Irish, and Germans. The research, originally funded in April 1969 by the National Institute of Mental Health, was recently expanded to include native white Americans in order to study, in the most comprehensive comparative perspective, the relationships between social mobility and social stratification, industrialization, family structure, and neighborhood.

The data are derived from three distinct sources. First, the Population Manuscript Schedules of the U.S. Census for Philadelphia County, 1850–80. From these census records enumerated decennially by the federal government, information was taken describing each of approximately

500,000 black, Irish, German, and all Irish and German males above the age of 17, a large sample of Irish, German, and native white American households, including all members of each sample household, and all black men, women, and children. The major variables listed in these census schedules include name, age, sex, color, occupation, property, and place of birth.

The second data source is the Manufacturing Manuscript Schedules of the U.S. Census for Philadelphia County, 1850–80. All places of business in the county with an annual product of $500 or more were included in the census. In all, data describing more than 24,000 individual firms, ranging from 4,700 in 1850 to 8,500 in 1880, have been recorded. Although the information included in the census varied slightly from year to year, each firm was described in terms of the following variables: company name, name of business or product, amount of capital, number of employees (males, females, youths), wages, source of power, machines, materials and product (the latter two in kinds, quantities, and value), number of months per year in operation, and so on.

The third data source consists of three unusually detailed household censuses of the entire free-Negro population of antebellum Philadelphia taken in 1838 and 1856 by the Pennsylvania Abolition Society and in 1847 by the Society of Friends. These censuses describe 11,600 households and include, in addition to those variables listed in the U.S. Census of Population, membership in a specific church, beneficial and temperance societies, income, education, school attendance, house, ground and water rent, slave birth, how freedom was acquired, the amount of property brought to Pennsylvania, and marital status. Most of the analysis included in this chapter is based on this source.

The data describing each individual, household, and firm were put into machine-readable form. When all the data are verified, a sophisticated linkage program will instruct the computer in tracing specific individuals, households, and firms from census to census and within each census. When identifications are made, it will be possible to proceed with analysis of the intra- and intergenerational aspects of the research.

5. Edward Needles, *Ten Years' Progress: A Comparison of the State and Condition of the Colored People in the City and County of Philadelphia from 1838 to 1847* (Philadelphia, 1849), 7–8.

6. Pennsylvania Abolition Society, *The Present State and Condition of the Free People of Color of the City of Philadelphia and Adjoining Districts* (Philadelphia, 1838).

7. Needles, *Ten Years' Progress,* 7–8.

8. Society of Friends, *Statistical Inquiry into the Condition of the People of Color of the City and Districts of Philadelphia* (Philadelphia, 1849); Benjamin Bacon, *Statistics of the Colored People of Philadelphia,* 2nd ed., rev. (Philadelphia, 1859).

9. Sam Bass Warner Jr., *The Private City* (Philadelphia, 1968); chap. 7, "Riots and the Restoration of Order," 125–57.

10. Society of Friends, *Statistical Inquiry,* 7.

11. There was also a net population loss of 0.17 percent for blacks between 1860 and 1870; the white population in the same decade, however, increased some 20 percent.

12. Social distinctions indispensable to the study of social stratification do exist among this 60 percent of the household population; however, they do not emerge along economic lines. Households averaging $30 of total wealth are not distinctively different from households worth $20 or $50. Important social distinctions can be determined by using specific noneconomic measures such as church affiliation or a more general noneconomic measure such as "lifestyle," which in turn is described by a number of other variables: residence, family structure, education, and occupation.

13. The unequal distribution of wealth was not unique to the black population. Stuart

Blumin, "Mobility and Change in Ante Bellum Philadelphia," in Stephen Therstrom and Richard Sennett, eds., *Nineteenth-Century Cities* (New Haven, Conn., 1969), found greater inequality among a sample of the entire Philadelphia population in the U.S. Census for 1860 than I did among all blacks in the Abolitionist and Quaker censuses in 1838 and 1847: the wealthiest 10 percent in 1860 owned 89 percent of the wealth, and the wealthiest 1 percent owned 50 percent of the wealth. Data describing the universe of black, Irish, and German property-holders in the U.S. Census for Philadelphia in 1860, however, indicate that inequality was pronounced in all three groups; in each case the wealthiest 10 percent of the population owned about 88 percent of the wealth. The Lorenz measures for the blacks, Irish, and Germans were .95, .94 and .92 respectively.

14. Some 99 percent of all male-headed households were two-parent households as well. Female-headed households in the Abolitionist and Quaker censuses were invariably one-parent households.

15. The data necessary to answer a series of important questions concerning the black men and women who lived and worked in white households as domestic servants will soon be available. Their age structure, marital status, mobility, social status, and the possibility of their families living close by will be examined. It will be valuable to know whether "live-in" service was a short-term or long-term experience and to determine its effects on family-building, family structure, and child-rearing techniques. Perhaps the most important question, and one which relates this form of employment to the experience of other ethnic groups, is whether such employment was seen by blacks as severely limiting, demeaning, and poor-paying, engaged in only because there were no other occupational alternatives.

16. *Daily Sun,* November 10, 1849. I am indebted to Bruce Laurie, who originally came across the letter in his rigorous research on ethnic divisions within the working class of antebellum Philadelphia.

17. *Register of the Trades of the Colored People in the City of Philadelphia and Districts* (Philadelphia, 1838), 1–8.

18. Appendix to *Memorial from the People of Color to the Legislature of Pennsylvania,* reprinted in *Hazard's Register, 1832,* 9:361.

19. Benjamin C. Bacon, *Statistics of the Colored People of Philadelphia,* 2nd ed. (Philadelphia, 1859), 13–15.

20. Needles, *Ten Years' Progress,* 2.

21. The data describing the ex-slaves and the freeborn, although comprehensive, are not complete; specific age, specific place of birth, and length of residence information are not included in the census. Such data will become available for a significant number of individuals only after linkage between censuses (especially between the Quaker census of 1847 and the U.S. Census of 1850) is accomplished, because in 1850 the latter began to list age and place of birth data for every individual. While no explicit data in any of the censuses describe the length of residence, linkage will provide approximation of this information, especially where in-migrants (those not listed in 1838 but found in ensuing censuses) are concerned.

David Gerber of Princeton University pointed out to me that the absence of such data in this essay may represent serious limitations, for "there may well be intervening variables which offer a better and very different interpretation of the data than the simple fact of free-birth and ex-slave status." No doubt other variables such as age and length of residence will affect some of my conclusions; however, I am of the opinion that when such information is analyzed the essential findings will remain intact. The most significant differences between the ex-slave and the freeborn are found among a specific group of ex-slaves: those who purchased their own freedom. This information makes it clear that we are dealing not with children who left slavery before its mark was firmly implanted on them, but with adults who must have worked long and hard to save the money necessary to secure their freedom. I do not believe that knowing their exact age or length of residence in the city would affect to a great degree their peculiarly high level of achievement in Philadelphia.

22. The data describing church affiliation are derived from the Abolitionist and Quaker census categories "name of religious meeting you attend" and "number attending religious meeting." These terms and very high percentage of positive respondents make it clear that we are not dealing here with formal, dues-paying church membership, but rather with a loose affiliation with a church.

23. Admittedly crude at this stage of research, the population density technique of analysis nevertheless yields interesting and important information, and with refinement it promises to be an invaluable tool for the study of neighborhood and its relation to social mobility, class, ecology, and community structure.

24. The construction of meaningful occupational categories has thus far proven to be the most difficult part of the research. While constructing such categories for the Irish, German, and native white American work force (currently under way) is certainly complex, one at least has the benefit of considerable occupational differentiation, which provides vertical distance—a prerequisite for the study of social mobility and social stratification. Some thirteen vertical categories, including white collar/skilled/unskilled, nonmanual/manual, proprietary/nonpropri- etary, and combinations of these schemata, and 102 horizontal categories including building construction, food, clothing, and domestic service were constructed for the study of the black occupational structure.

25. See the discussion of the "hiring-out system," 38–54, in Richard C. Wade, *Slavery in the Cities* (New York, 1964). It is highly likely that many of the ex-slave household heads who bought their freedom had experienced the hiring-out system firsthand and migrated to Philadelphia.

26. There is some reason to believe that the total number of ex-slaves (1.41, or one out of every 5 persons who migrated to Pennsylvania) is understated. The year 1838 was not too early for free blacks to fear being sent south illegally or legally as runaway slaves. It is understand- able, therefore, that even though Philadelphia blacks were asked by their clergymen to cooper- ate with the two census-takers (a white abolitionist, Benjamin Bacon, and the black minister of the First African Presbyterian Church, Charles Gardner), many blacks who had been born slaves reported instead that they had been born free. Although it is impossible to determine whether those who were nonnatives of Pennsylvania had been in fact slave-born or freeborn, the likelihood that ex-slaves are underestimated is further supported by the fact that 50 percent of the black population had been born outside of Pennsylvania.

Of course, the important consideration concerns the consequences of understating the actual number of ex-slaves among the black population. If the socioeconomic condition of the ex- slaves who identified themselves as freeborn was significantly worse than the actual freeborn, and if their numbers were sufficiently large enough, the conclusions offered in this chapter would to a certain extent be compromised. The problem, however, can be resolved.

Consider the following. For the same reasons that one suspects the ex-slaves are underenu- merated, it is unlikely that many blacks born free or slave in the free states migrated to Philadel- phia. It is also unlikely that more than a few elderly Pennsylvania-born blacks who had once been slaves were included in the 1838 census. Pennsylvania's gradual emancipation law had been passed in 1780. When we speak of the ex-slaves, whether or not correctly identified in the census, therefore, we can be fairly certain they were not natives of Pennsylvania but had mi- grated from the Upper South. When all freeborn migrants (read as including a significant number of unidentified ex-slaves) were compared with all freeborn natives, their socioeconomic profile was strikingly similar to that of the identified ex-slaves. In other words, the one population cohort in which unidentified ex-slaves might be found was at least as well off as the freeborn native population, and in some important respects better off.

27. To determine the effect of slavery on the slaves, as compared with blacks who were born free or who won their freedom before the Civil War, we would have to look someplace after 1865. No one has yet found any data for the post-Emancipation period which distinguishes the freed from the freeborn (or from those freed before the Civil War). We can make the assumption that because 94 percent of the blacks in the South were slaves in 1860, a significant percentage of the migrants from the South after the Civil War were ex-slaves. But even if we discount the fact that if the migrants came from Maryland, Delaware, or the District of Columbia they were more likely to have been free before the Civil War (55 percent of all blacks in these areas were free in 1860), we are still left with the problem of representativeness. To put it another way, even if we had the data which distinguished the freed from the freeborn, we would still be left with only the typical migrant, not the typical ex-slave. There is every reason to believe that Carter Woodson was correct in his observation that the migrants who came to the cities of the North before the Great Migration were not typical at all, but rather representatives of the "Talented Tenth." The migrants who came after 1910, and especially 1915, although not "typical" of the millions of southern blacks who did not migrate, were nevertheless far more representative of southern blacks than those who migrated before them. They came to the North for different reasons than did those who left the South a generation earlier, say between 1875 and 1900. The "push and pull" factors (floods, drought, and the boll weevil, and the demand for industrial labor heightened by the end of immigration from Europe) which led to the Great Migration simply were not operative in the earlier period. Those who came before 1900 were probably motivated for different reasons; the problems they faced in the South, and the opportunities they saw in the North, if not different in kind were certainly different in degree.

The logic of the situation suggests that we examine a northern city during the period of the Great Migration which had a significantly large antebellum black community and which experienced migration from the South between 1865 and 1900, hoping to identify and study three distinct groups of blacks: native-of-the-city, migrants arriving before 1900 (the "Talented Tenth"), and migrants arriving after 1900 (the "typical" migrant). The problem with this approach is twofold: first, we would no longer be dealing with the "typical" ex-slave, but with his children; second, the data necessary to distinguish the three groups among the population are not available.

28. Herbert Gutman, "The Invisible Fact: Negro Family Structure Before and After the Civil War" (paper read at the Association for the Study of Negro Life and History, Birmingham, Ala., October 1969, and in a revised form at the Organization of American Historians, Los Angeles, April 1970).

29. Wade, *Slavery in the Cities,* "The Transformation of Slavery in the Cities," 243–82.

30. A major interest of my research is to develop and make explicit for the city the characteristics of an "urban component" which distinguishes the urban from the rural experience. There is certainly general agreement that urban conditions differ from rural ones in significant dimensions: family structure, sex ratios, mortality, fertility, housing conditions, diet, educational and occupational opportunities, plus the intangibles of values and expectations. In future work, however, I hope to demonstrate that it is seriously misleading to treat these urban/rural differences monolithically. The racial discrimination and structural inequality of the city affected each ethnic group differently. The advantages of the city were never equally available for all.

CHAPTER FIVE

"Freedom, or the Martyr's Grave":
Black Pittsburgh's Aid to the Fugitive Slave

R. J. M. Blackett

> *When the sun comes back and the first quail calls,*
> *Follow the drinkin' gourd,*
> *For then the old man is a-waitin' for to carry you to freedom,*
> *If you follow the drinkin' gourd.*
>
> —*"The Drinking Gourd" (slave song)*

Follow the Drinkin' Gourd

The history of antebellum northern black urban communities is one of resistance to racial oppression and the development of institutions to cater to the needs of blacks in a rapidly expanding industrial economy. Between 1830 and 1860, black communities from Boston to Cincinnati forged, nurtured, and sustained their own institutions in their battle to survive in what in many instances were extremely hostile environments. They created their own churches as a protest against segregation in white churches, and founded black newspapers to air their views, literary societies to improve skills, temperance and moral reform societies, masonic lodges, and secret societies to protect their communities from outside encroachment. By mid-century these institutions were well developed through decades of involvement in the Negro Convention, abolitionist and anticolonization movements, and local efforts to improve the lot of black communities. It is just as well that they were, for on September 18, 1850, President Millard Fillmore signed into law the infamous Fugitive Slave Law, which guaranteed to southern slave interests the return

This chapter was first published in the *Western Pennsylvania Historical Magazine* (now called *Pittsburgh History*) 113 (January 1989): 3–19. Reprinted by permission.

of their escaped chattels. Black communities rose to the occasion and, with the support of white abolitionists, stood four-square against attempts to enforce the new law. This chapter examines the efforts employed by the black community in Pittsburgh to aid fugitives and to resist the Fugitive Slave Law.

In 1830, Pittsburgh's blacks numbered 472, and there were 1,193 in Allegheny County. By 1850 the black population of the city had increased to 1,959, and the county's rose to 3,431, representing a slight rise in number of blacks from 3.8 percent to 4.2 percent of the city's population, with the heaviest concentration in the East Ward, and 2.4 percent to 2.5 percent through the county.[1] If one could gauge the black community's cohesiveness by the number of organizations and associations catering to the needs of the black population, then the 1830s and 1840s witnessed the emergence of a relatively close-knit black community in the city.

In January 1832, blacks, disillusioned by the city's failure to provide their children with adequate schooling, came together to form the African Education Society, which aimed to disperse "the moral gloom, that has long hung around" the black community.[2] Later that year they formed the Theban Literary Society, which in 1837 joined the Young Men's Moral Reform Society, founded in 1834, to form the Young Men's Literary and Moral Reform Society. The first temperance society was formed in 1834 to eliminate "the demon booze" and aid in the moral elevation of the community. As in other communities throughout the North, black Pittsburghers were actively involved in the abolitionist and anticolonization movements in the 1830s. In 1831, a public meeting of blacks issued a stinging condemnation of the American Colonization Society's efforts at Liberian colonization and called on all blacks to remain in their native land and fight against slavery and racial prejudice.[3] The debate over immediate emancipation and colonization was well aired in southwestern Pennsylvania. Erasmus Wilson estimated that there were twenty colonization societies in the area at the end of the decade. After a rather fitful existence, local antislavery societies came together to form the Union Antislavery Society of Pittsburgh and Allegheny in January 1839.[4] In July 1838, young blacks formed the first Juvenile Antislavery Society in America.[5]

By 1837 there were four benevolent societies catering to the needs of and providing services for the black community. Toward the end of the decade, blacks formed the Philanthropic Society, which, as its name suggests, duplicated some of the efforts of the benevolent societies, but at the same time it acted as the defensive arm of the community. Evidence suggests that it was a secret society whose main objectives were the protection of the community, the abduction of slaves from slaveholders visiting the area, and a link, if not the most important arm, in the Underground Railroad in Pittsburgh and Allegheny City. The prominence of the Philanthropic Society may account for the marked absence of attacks on the black community by white mobs. In comparison with other cities like New York, Boston, Philadelphia, and Cincinnati, there were only two race riots in antebellum Pittsburgh—in 1834 and 1839. In 1830 the society and a contingent of the Mayor's Police led the defense of Hayti, as the Hill District was then called.[6]

These local activities were linked to the wider state and national activities of blacks in the 1830s and 1840s. Black societies sent representatives to state and national meetings of the Negro Convention Movement, participating in and contributing to the burgeoning efforts among blacks to forge a national movement. When in 1837–38 the Pennsylvania legislature moved to restrict the franchise to whites, local blacks convened a meeting to condemn the move and issued a memorial calling on the legislators to reconsider their actions. Although blacks were removed from the voting rolls, the Pittsburgh Memorial showed both the level of political sophistication and the cohesiveness of the community.[7] Over the next few years, blacks continued to pressure for the reestablishment of their voting rights. In August 1841 they convened the State Convention of Colored Freemen of Pennsylvania in the hopes of coordinating statewide efforts for the restoration of the vote. The all-black convention worried some of the city's fathers. Rumors spread that the blacks were gathering to defy whites and there were threats of attacks. The Reverend Lewis Woodson, in a politically astute and forceful public declaration, forestalled any attacks by whites. Blacks, he said, had no intentions of parading, for that sort of public demonstration was outmoded, but they did intend to meet to discuss their particular problems. "The participation of others is not rejected out of any disrespect to them," he observed, "but because it is natural and right. Every man knows his own affairs best, and naturally feels a deeper interest in them than anyone else, and therefore on that account ought to attend to them."[8] The meeting was held, and the convention once again condemned the exclusion of blacks from the electoral rolls.

Between the year 1831—when young Martin Delany arrived in the "Smoky City" (or as a contemporary called it, "Hell without the lid on")—to the founding of Delany's newspaper *The Mystery* in 1843, blacks continued to develop a cohesive and supportive community. Their numbers were augmented by newcomers from Virginia, Maryland, Washington, D.C., and eastern Pennsylvania seeking a niche in the rapidly developing industrial city. A significant sector of the community also consisted of fugitive slaves, mainly from Virginia and Maryland, who soon married into and were protected by the community. By 1840, blacks were mainly employed in menial services, on the rivers and canals, and in the large city hotels. Toward the middle of the decade, they were investing extensively in real estate and establishing small businesses. In Allegheny City they organized the Moral Lever Association as the vehicle for procuring real estate. By the end of the decade, the "Allegheny Institute and Mission Church" was founded on the North Side with funds donated mainly by the Reverend Charles Avery and supported by a grant from the Pennsylvania legislature.[9] The institute, which in 1858 changed its name to the Avery Institute, continued to provide education for local black youths for the rest of the century.

To a large extent, the cohesiveness of the black community was forged from determined efforts to defend fugitive slaves from possible recapture and, where necessary, to aid them on their journey farther north. Their efforts were boosted by the passage of an 1847 state law which prohibited the kidnapping of free blacks. The law prohibited justices of the peace and aldermen from acting in support of the 1793 fugitive slave law. It also protected fugitives from unlawful seizure, gave judges the power to issue writs of habeas corpus in fugitive cases, and, more important, banned the use of state jails for the detention of fugitives.[10] To Pittsburgh's commercial and industrial interests, this law was particularly alarming, for it could seriously affect the city's important contacts with the South. Pittsburgh lay at the head of the rising internal trade along the Ohio and Mississippi rivers, and by the late 1840s its industrial goods were in great demand in New Orleans, Memphis, and Natchez. In 1848, Delany observed that antislavery activity in the city was being seriously undermined by this contact, "The Mississippi valley and its connecting rivers, are but the train of communication, or the great telegraphic medium which binds Pittsburgh, New Orleans and St. Louis together in interest; merchants here, being interested in trade, vessels and shipping houses there, families there, until they have . . . become one." The *Pittsburgh Post,* Delany warned, was the watchdog of southern interests in the city and "the Judges of Pennsylvania Courts, with a few honorable exceptions, are but the *pledged* minions of the slave power in this country."[11]

Notwithstanding Delany's views, blacks and white abolitionists continued to use the courts to undermine the efforts of slave catchers. One month after the passage of the 1847 act, Pittsburgh's abolitionists tested its application in the famed Lockhart case. Daniel Lockhart was born a slave in Virginia and sometime in the 1840s escaped to Pittsburgh, where he worked as a casual laborer in the city. In April 1847 he was approached by a stranger and employed to take a trunk from the Monongahela House. When Lockhart arrived at the hotel, he was seized by his owner and two constables from Virginia. He put up a fierce struggle, all the time shouting that he was being murdered. Many of the blacks working at the hotel ran to his aid, but his captors resisted. Word quickly spread throughout the community that a fugitive had been cap-

The Fugitive Negro.

Pittsburgh was the destination of Virginia and Maryland fugitive slaves because it had many agents for the Underground Railroad. Life under the Fugitive Slave Law of 1850 was terrifying for Pennsylvania blacks; not only fugitive slaves but also free blacks were in danger of being captured in broad daylight and taken to the South. This cartoon by an unknown artist was printed in a postbellum era newspaper. (Courtesy of Ruth Hodge) tured, and a large crowd of blacks greeted Lockhart and his captors when they left the hotel. The crowd converged on the slave catchers, seized Lockhart, and took him into hiding. He was subsequently sent to Canada.

But the slave catchers' troubles were not over, for they were soon charged, under Section 4 of the 1847 act, with the tumultuous and riotous arrest of a slave. Logan, Lockhart's owner, and his companions filed a writ of habeas corpus before Judge Lowrie, a prominent supporter of the American Colonization Society. In his opinion Lowrie argued that the return of a slave was not only recognized by federal law, but was also an important guarantee for the survival of the Union: "We must not at least, while claiming the benefits of union, refuse the performance of the duties arising from it. While union exists we must honestly perform the covenant of union; and let us not dishonestly begin our nullification by claiming the blessings and rejecting the burdens belonging to the relation." Lowrie dismissed the charges brought against Logan and his companions.[12] Even if Pittsburgh's blacks and their abolitionist supporters failed to win a verdict against Logan, they sent out a warning to slave catchers and their local supporters that it was exceedingly difficult and expensive to kidnap a fugitive from the area.

Western Pennsylvania had few famous fugitive cases to compare with the Latimer, Crafts, and Shadrach cases in Boston, or the Jerry case in Syracuse, either before or after the passage of the Fugitive Slave Law. This in large measure was the result of the well-organized system devised by blacks and white abolitionists for protecting fugitives in their community. Only the Anthony Hollingsworth case in Indiana, Pennsylvania, gained any national prominence. In 1845, Hollingsworth and two other fugitives from Virginia found a sanctuary and employment at Dr. Robert Mitchell's farm just outside Indiana. Their master, Garrett Van Metre, and two assistants followed them to Mitchell's farm, where after a struggle Hollingsworth was taken prisoner. Mitchell immediately filed for a writ of habeas corpus for Hollingsworth's release, on the grounds that no evidence had been submitted to prove that slavery did exist in Virginia. Hollingsworth was released and returned to his job on Mitchell's farm. Two years later, another attempt was made to take Hollingsworth, and after a bloody struggle he fled to Canada and settled in Windsor. Frustrated by Hollingsworth's successful resistance and determined to destroy the small pocket of abolitionists in Indiana, Van Metre brought suits against Mitchell, the first of which was heard by Judge Grier in United States Circuit Court in Pittsburgh in November 1847.[13]

Judge Grier was no friend of the "extremist" and "fanatical" abolitionists. He insisted on a strict interpretation of both the 1793 and, later, the 1850 fugitive slave laws, and he dismissed peremptorily any attempts by abolitionists to employ the niceties of state laws designed to subvert the efforts of slave catchers. In the 1853 Wilkes-Barre slave case, Grier warned abolitionists who had three local officers arrested for "riotous behavior" and who used undue force to capture a fugitive (who later escaped) that "If this man Gildersleeve [an abolitionist] fails to make out the facts set forth in the warrant of arrest, I will request the Prosecuting Attorney of Luzerne county to prosecute him for perjury. . . . If any two-penny magistrate, or any unprincipled interloper can come in and cause to be arrested the officers of the United States whenever they please, it is a sad state of affairs." A successful prosecution of this kind, in his view, would only make those who celebrated the "Syracuse riot" and "the Christiana murder" rejoice. At the opening of the U.S. Circuit Court in Pittsburgh in November 1849, Grier observed that the time had come for the country to put pad to the actions of the abolitionists and their black supporters, "when their railings and vituperations were becoming successful as means of intimidation against the honest and sane portion of the community; when mobs of Negroes were urged on to madness, and counseled to arm themselves for the purpose of rebellion against the laws, and were hounded on to murder its officers, such diseased members of the body politic could no longer be treated with contempt or indifference."[14] It is no surprise that blacks and their abolitionist supporters put little faith in men like Grier.

Van Metre's cases against Mitchell were not finally resolved until 1853. In the series of cases, Van Metre won an award for $500 plus costs in November 1851 and subsequently sued for action of debt for penalty under the 1850 act. Under the act, a slaveholder was entitled to $500, plus "saving moreover to the person claiming such labor of service his right to action of the said injuries, or either of them." In his charge to the jury, Grier observed that no Pennsylvania law aimed at restricting the slave master's right to recapture his slave could supersede federal law. Moreover, he said, "illegal harboring is not to be measured by the religious or political notions of the accused, or the correctness or perversion of his moral perceptions. Some men of disordered misunderstanding or perverted conscience may conceive it a religious duty to break the law, but the law will not tolerate their excuse." The jury found in favor of Van Metre, and, according to Christy, Mitchell had to sell a large part of his pine forest to defray the expense of the $10,000 suit.[15]

But while the series of suits by Van Metre followed a tortuous course through the federal courts, blacks continued to protect fugitives in their community. In January 1847, three men from western Virginia attempted to capture a fugitive named Briscoe in Allegheny City. In this case, it appears that the police supported the efforts of the blacks who rescued Briscoe and sent him north.[16] Three months later, a slaveholder from Mississippi arrived with four slaves at the Monongahela wharf on his way to Maryland. A large crowd of blacks soon gathered and tried to persuade the slaves to leave their master, but only one accepted. When it appeared that their efforts would fail to win the freedom of all the slaves, they attempted to rush the boat, but the Mayor's Police intervened and prevented a successful rescue of all the slaves.[17] A pattern of action is discernible in both these attempts to rescue fugitives and slaves from their masters. It appears that blacks had a carefully organized system of communications that quickly transmitted news of any danger and that, when necessary, they had the ability to bring together a large crowd to attempt rescues of slaves traveling with their masters. A similar pattern was followed in the rescue of Lockhart. We will discuss this issue more extensively later.

The 1850s dawned with ominous rumblings of southern nullification. This threat had been made before, but now the South seemed determined to fulfill its dire warnings on the future of the Union if the North continued to ignore its demands for extension of slavery territory. During the debate on the Wilmot Proviso, there were from the South many reports of movements calling for a cessation of trading with northern firms. Unless northern merchants recognized the seriousness of the South's intentions, one pamphleteer warned, "they might very soon discover, to their dismay, that the valuable Southern trade had passed into the hands of foreign merchants."[18] Pittsburgh's business interests kept a close watch on developments in Congress. The *Gazette*'s New York correspondent reported on the efforts of New York merchants to win support for Henry Clay's Compromise Bill, which conceded to the South the need for a more stringent and enforced fugitive slave law. Moses Hampton, a congressman from Allegheny County, observed that "To the question of the reclamation of fugitive slaves, we all acknowledge the obligation imposed by the Constitution, and all are willing to fulfill those obligations." But Hampton raised the specter of sectional interests when he concluded that the North had also lost considerable revenue following the repeal of the tariff in 1842. What was necessary, therefore, was "proper legislation for the protection of property."[19]

Unlike other northern communities, Pittsburgh remained relatively quiet throughout the long debate leading up to the passage of the bill. Blacks, however, were adamant in their opposition to any increased concessions to the South. At a mass meeting held in June at the Wylie Street AME Church, resolutions were passed condemning the proposed fugitive bill and calling on blacks to consolidate their associations to ensure their protection. A memorial issued by the meeting and sent to Congress stated in part: "We the colored people of Allegheny County, in the State of Pennsylvania, do most respectfully and solemnly remonstrate and Petition against the provisions of the Act of Congress, 1793, relative to the recapture of Fugitive Slaves, and against all and every Act, Bill, or Provision now in existence or that may hereafter be introduced into either Houses of Congress of the United States, in any way or manner infringing upon our liberties as American citizens."[20]

In spite of similar appeals from other northern communities, the Compromise Bill was signed into law in September 1850. Of all its sections, the Fugitive Slave Law met with the most sustained opposition from blacks and white abolitionists. The law was composed of ten sections. It created commissioners to supervise the execution of the law who were to receive $10 if fugitives were remanded to their owners and $5 if they were not. Owners of fugitive slaves, or their agents, were empowered to pursue and reclaim fugitives either by procuring a warrant from a judge or commissioner or by simply seizing the suspected fugitive. The fugitive could then be taken before a judge or commissioner, and if his identity was established a certificate was to be issued authorizing his removal to the slave state from which he escaped. The right of habeas corpus did not extend to fugitives, for under no circumstances was their testimony to be accepted as evidence. Molestation of slave catchers in their attempts to return fugitives south by courts, judges, magistrates, or any other person was strictly prohibited. If a slave catcher suspected that an attempt would be made to rescue a fugitive, the officer who made the arrest was authorized to employ as many persons as necessary to prevent the rescue. The expenses for such an effort were to be paid out of the federal treasury.[21]

Northern black communities were thrown into a panic by the passage of the bill. In Boston, New York, Syracuse, Philadelphia, Cleveland, Detroit, and Pittsburgh, blacks left in large numbers for Canada. By September 25, some 100 fugitives had already left Pittsburgh for Canada. On the 24th, forty fugitives living in the upper part of Allegheny City had joined the exodus. *The Liberator,* in a report of the flight from Pittsburgh, observed that all the waiters in one hotel had fled. By October almost 300 fugitives had departed the community in which they had established firm roots. The *Pittsburgh Gazette* reported that, since their escape, these fugitives had "intermarried with free persons of color but they are thus once more compelled to sever all the family ties." They left in small parties, armed with rifles, revolvers, and bowie knives, all pledged to defend one another to the death. The *Gazette* was relieved that so many had decided to leave for the safety of communities farther north, "since there would most assuredly have been bloodshed had their masters endeavored to recapture them."[22] When the Reverend William King and a Dr. Burns visited Pittsburgh in November to raise money for the black community of Buxton, Canada West, they found "a large number of well-to-do colored people living in Pittsburgh who wished to come to Canada and buy themselves a home in what was really a free country." Blacks continued to leave the area throughout the decade, and by 1860 the census reported a loss of 800 blacks from Pittsburgh and 706 from Allegheny. Many joined the estimated 15,000–20,000 blacks entering Canada from the United States between 1850 and 1860.[23]

Meetings were called throughout southwestern Pennsylvania to protest the Fugitive Slave Law. The "citizens of Allegheny" met at the Diamond on September 28 to voice their opposition to the law. The Reverend Avery condemned the act as unconstitutional for its suspension of habeas corpus and the right to trial by jury. It would force ministers, he said, "whose duty it was to proclaim peace in the world, and let the captive go free, . . . to aid and assist the bloodhounds of slavery, and trample under foot all Devine [sic] Authority, to join in this work of infamy and crime." He argued that Pennsylvania congressmen should be pressured to repeal the law and that anyone who accepted a commission under the law should be "shunned as though he were a leper." All the candidates in the November congressional election, with the exception of Salisbury, the Democratic Workingman candidate, attended and spoke against the law. Howe, the Whig candidate, promised to fight for repeal if elected to Congress, and the crowd shouted "We'll send you." The meeting pledged to work for repeal of the law by "all lawful means" and not to vote for candidates who did not commit themselves to work for repeal, called on editors to publish the names of those who accepted positions as commissioners, and condemned all the Pennsylvania congressmen who voted for the bill.[24]

The second meeting in the Allegheny markethouse followed a similar pattern. The crowd condemned Salisbury for not participating in the first meeting, where they had pledged their support for Howe, and Salisbury was therefore forced to explain his absence. He condemned the law because it made slave catchers out of the free men of Pennsylvania. He was in favor not only of the emancipation of the black slave "but also for the freedom of the white slaves in the Northern workshops." When he commented on child labor in the cotton factories of the city, there were shouts of "stick to the questions." The meeting then degenerated into a heated debate over larger issues—the repeal of the tariff and the failure of the National Bank—as politicians jostled for position and votes. But Delany soon brought the meeting back to the issue of the Fugitive Slave Law with a rousing speech of defiance:

> Under the operation of this Bill . . . no colored person is safe. . . . Who is there to swear that I was not born a slave? . . . Here I am a freeman, liable at any time to be taken away and kept forever in bondage. . . . Honorable Mayor, whatever ideas of liberty I may have, have

been received from reading the lives of your revolutionary fathers. No, my course is determined should the slave pursuer enter my dwelling, one of us must perish. I have treasures there: there are a wife and children to protect; I will give the tyrant timely warning; but if the sanctuary of my home is violated, if I don't defend it, may the grave be to my body no resting place, and the vaunted heavens refuse my spirit.

The meeting reaffirmed its pledge to oppose the law.[25]

But while blacks and white abolitionists were seeking ways to stymie the law's operation, men like Howe and his supporters sought political capital. Howe was elected to Congress in November, at a time when the fortunes of the Whigs were exceedingly low in Allegheny County. It is quite reasonable, therefore, to assume that his public commitment to oppose the law may have won him significant support. Yet, soon after his election, he wrote General William Robinson: "It is well known, to the citizens of this District, that I regarded its [the slave law's] provisions, under the most favorable construction of which they seem susceptible, as exceedingly severe, difficult of execution, and eminently calculated to inflame the Northern mind. . . . They have, however, received all the necessary sanctions required by the Constitution, and are the law of the land and as such, must be respected and obeyed." He condemned those who were committed to oppose the law, for the Union, in his view, "is obedience to the laws."[26] Indeed, Howe was articulating the views of the city's prominent citizens. The *Gazette* called for a modification of the law to reflect the public's regard for "the personal rights and liberties of their own citizens," for it wished to see the provisions of the Constitution regarding fugitive slaves carried out to their fullest.

While the *Gazette* was taking a middle ground, the *Washington (Pennsylvania) Examiner* would brook no opposition from "the whole body of Northern *niggerdom,* embracing the colored and their white advisers and accomplices, [who] have banded together and established a precedent which, if sanctioned and observed, would eventuate in the utter destruction of all law and drench . . . the whole land in blood." Of all the local newspapers, only the *Saturday Visitor,* an abolitionist weekly edited by Jane Grey Swisshelm, uncompromisingly opposed the Fugitive Slave Law and called for total resistance to its implementation.[27] Attempts by the Church of Unity to win approval from the annual meeting of the Pittsburgh Presbyterian (Old School) Synod in October resulted in the most amazing display of intellectual gymnastics. Replete with non sequiturs, the meeting's resolution stated: "While strictly, for conscience sake, rendering all due honor to civil government, as the obedience of God, and yielding all due obedience to the civil rulers as the minister of God to men for good, yet on no account yield compliance with any enactments or commands, if such compliance involve any violation of principle or duty."[28]

In the face of the new law and the calls for obedience to the Constitution, blacks and their white supporters harnessed their energies and employed their associations for the protection of the fugitive and the black community from the slave catchers. In fact, these men and women had a particularly formidable record, for few fugitives were returned from western Pennsylvania in the 1850s. The Underground Railroad, composed of whites and blacks, was one of the amorphous associations employed to subvert the enforcement of the slave law in the area. Two of its lines met at Uniontown, bringing fugitives from Virginia and Maryland. From Uniontown, two lines led north to Pittsburgh and a third to Indiana. From Pittsburgh they traveled by rail to the Western Reserve and Cleveland or followed the Allegheny River and its tributaries north. Another line followed the Wheeling Creek to West Alexandria and then to West Middletown, from where fugitives were sent north.[29]

But the major burden of support for the fugitive was shouldered by the black community. As we have seen, they had developed a well-organized system long before the enactment of the Fugitive Slave Law. After 1850 they employed an array of methods against the law: quiet or forceful abductions; organization of large crowds to resist returns; and, where these failed, utilizing the full range of legal devices to prevent the kidnapping of fugitives. In this, their methods reflected those employed by other northern black communities. Through the Philanthropic Society and an extensive network of communications centered on the city hotels, they brought together large crowds of blacks to resist the return of fugitives or to abduct and send suspected slaves north. Slaveholders and slave catchers were always amazed by the speed with which news of their presence in the area spread and by the determination of the crowds to resist their efforts. As soon as a suspected slave arrived at a hotel, blacks employed in the establishment quickly met to plan the slave's capture and to inform the Philanthropic Society of his presence.

Thomas A. Brown, one of the employees at the Monongahela House, left a vivid account of their efforts to capture a slave from the hotel: "Half a dozen determined men held a brief but decisive consultation. Mrs. Crossan [the proprietor's wife] and the chamber maid on the third floor were taken into our confidence. Watches were stationed in the several halls and on the stairways; a special one was placed to observe the movements of the planter. The headwaiter was instructed to delay serving the courses at dinner. With all speed messages were dispatched to friends in the city. The word soon came that a closed carriage would be at the door at 9 p.m."[30]

The effort was successful. Blacks were not reluctant to use force when necessary. In capturing the suspected slave of a Mr. Slaymaker in March 1855, a large number of blacks stormed into the City Hotel's dining room and removed the slave. A report of the incident stated: "Several individuals who were breakfasting at the same time state that the whole affair was so sudden and precipitate, that it was difficult to tell how many colored persons were present or who positively laid hands on the woman."[31]

Sometimes even free blacks accompanying whites were abducted. The suspected slave of Slaymaker, Caroline Cooper, turned out to be a free black. After she was captured, the crowd hurried her through a private alley to Third Street and then to the barbershop of Mr. Davis, from where she was taken to a safer hiding place in another part of the city. Slaymaker subsequently proved to the mayor that Cooper was free, and Delany was brought in to inspect the evidence. Once Delany was convinced that Cooper was free, he agreed to have her returned. Accompanied by an officer, he went to Webster Street, where a small group of blacks were meeting to plan her escape north. They agreed that Cooper was free and returned her from a house "somewhere near the intersection of Cherry Alley and Strawberry Alley" to the City Hotel. In order to ensure Cooper's safe passage, Delany issued Slaymaker with a letter addressed to "The Friends of the Liberty."[32]

The abduction network also extended beyond Allegheny County. In May 1853, Pittsburgh's blacks and abolitionists received a letter from J. Lindley of the Pennsylvania Abolition Society in Philadelphia informing them that Thomas Adams of Nashville was traveling to Pittsburgh with a black youth named Alexander Hendrchkure and requesting them "to have the matter investigated, and we will pay all expenses." A large crowd met the train, and Hendrchkure was taken. A writ of habeas corpus was filed, and Adams was taken into custody and only released when he promised to give up the youth, who was then handed over to Delany. As it turned out, Adams had persuaded Hendrchkure, a Jamaican, to accompany him to America with promises of opening riches to him in California. It appears that his intention was to sell the youth into slavery in Kentucky.[33] Three months later, blacks were informed by telegram that a white man from Missouri traveling from Crestline, Ohio, with a black woman and her three children. When the man left the station in Allegheny City to go in search of a hack, the woman and her children were taken and driven to the mayor's office. When he returned, blacks threatened to tar and feather him or dunk him in the canal. Pleading that he was the father of the three children, he fled across the river to Pittsburgh and quickly left the city when a warrant for his arrest on charges of kidnapping was issued. According to the *Evening Chronicle* the man was on his way to Baltimore, where he intended to sell the woman and her children into slavery.[34]

Where necessary, the courts were used to protect fugitives. In March 1850, two slave catchers from Louisville arrived in Pittsburgh intent on taking a fugitive named Woodson, who had made his home in Beaver. A warrant for Woodson's arrest was issued by Commissioner Sweitzer, and the fugitive was arrested. Fearing an abduction attempt, the slave catchers called for and got protection from Mayor Joseph Barker. At the trial before Judge Irwin, blacks testified that they had known Woodson, or Paul Gardner as they called him, since the spring of 1848. The slave catchers argued that Woodson had escaped from his mistress in 1848. They described him as a very black person, which did not tally with Woodson's obvious mulatto complexion. Irwin, ignoring this blatant discrepancy, decided in favor of the slave catchers. Again fearing that blacks might attempt to prevent Woodson's return, he was slipped out of the city jail and taken to a steamer. But before Woodson and his guard of police could reach the wharf, a large crowd gathered. The strength of the police prevented any capture, and the *Gazette* thankfully commented: "Thus terminated the first fugitive slave case in Pittsburgh, not the slightest riot or confusion having been excited by it." Immediately plans were drawn up to raise money to purchase Woodson's freedom. The $600 was soon raised, and Woodson returned in triumph to Pittsburgh in April, less than one month after his capture.[35] Two years later, Calvin Jones, a waiter in the city, was arrested as a fugitive from Memphis. David Reed, J. M. Kirkpatrick, and other leading white lawyers defended Jones. There were so many glaring holes in the slave catchers' testimony that Jones was released.[36]

All these efforts met with a large measure of success. The feeling of defeat over the Woodson case was quickly alleviated by his purchase and return. Blacks and their supporters suffered only one major defeat in the 1850s—the failure to capture the Boyd slave. Lloyd Boyd of Kentucky, former Speaker of the House, arrived at the St. Charles Hotel with his family and a female slave in March 1855. As in the Slaymaker incident, which took place two days earlier, the black employees of the hotel attempted to capture the slave. But their attempt was foiled by a group of whites in the hotel. Fearing another attempt, Boyd decided to leave Pittsburgh immediately. News of their presence spread throughout the community, and a large crowd of blacks gathered at the wharf to attempt a rescue. Boyd eluded his pursuers and got on board the steamer before the crowd could get to him. Frustrated by their failure, the crowd threatened to storm the steamer if the slave was not handed over. But they were forced to allow Boyd to leave with his slave when the captain threatened to shoot anyone who attempted to cross the gangway.[37]

This failure was particularly galling. Following the passage of the Kansas-Nebraska Act in 1854, which annulled the Missouri Compromise of 1820 prohibiting slavery above the thirty-sixth parallel, blacks and their abolitionist supporters had redoubled their efforts and determination to abduct slaves from their masters. As occurred in other northern communities, the new act met with a rising chorus of protest against further northern acquiescence to southern interests. The Allegheny County Whig convention adopted a strong antislavery platform at its annual meeting in 1854. Condemning slavery as a sin, the Whigs called for the total abolition of slavery, open opposition to the Fugitive Slave Law, and demanded that there should be "no more slave states, no slave territory, no nationalized slaver, [and] no national legislation for extradition of slaves."[38] Efforts were already being made by a small group of local businessmen—concerned that the expansion of slavery and the growth of southern political power was affecting business in the city and posing a threat of competition between slave and free labor—to form a local political party known as the Pittsburgh Republicans. They took issue, as Leland Baldwin points out, "with the extension of slavery more because they were seeking the welfare of industry than because they were concerned about farmers and free laborers."[39] But others were afraid that rising sectional antagonism and increasingly bold attempts to capture slaves from their masters would do inestimable damage to the city's business future. The *Post,* in a bitter denunciation of blacks and abolitionists following the Boyd case, commented:

> Millions of dollars have been invested in our railroads and canals; and it is proposed to invest millions more in the improvement of the Ohio River. The aim of this outlay is to bring through out the city and State a large share of the travel and trade of the South and West. These efforts to increase our prosperity will be useless if travelers are to be assailed by lawless mobs, and forced to fly from the city to escape personal violence, and prevent the kidnapping of what they hold as their property under the laws of their States. . . . Shall our prosperity and reputation as a community be given over to the control of an irresponsible mob of Negroes, who do little for the prosperity of the city themselves.

The *Post* concluded with the hope that similar actions in the future would "be suppressed by the strong arm of the law; or met with plenty of well charged revolvers in ready and resolute hands."[40]

But even the *Post*'s blustering could not deter the joint efforts of blacks and abolitionists. Throughout the decade, blacks continued to abduct slaves passing through the area and to assist fugitives on their way north. "The wind blows from the South today" was the warning informing them of the presence of slaves and fugitives in the area. Immediately the black secret society, which so tormented the *Post,* and the Underground Railroad were put into action, and very rarely did they fail. Following the Drennen case in July 1850, McD. Crossan, proprietor of the Monongahela House, warned southern slaveholders against bringing their slaves to Pittsburgh, where there is "a secret and powerful organization of free Negroes to promote escapes."[41] By the middle of the 1850s, it had become increasingly expensive for slave catchers to recapture fugitives from the area, and foolhardy for slave masters to travel through Pittsburgh and Allegheny with their slaves. In fact, after 1855 there were no instances of attempted rescues, simply because masters left their slaves at home. At the same time, the Underground Railroad continued to aid escaping slaves north.

The study of blacks' and abolitionists' aid for fugitives and the abduction of slaves is a study of resistance to southern interests and political power. Unlike New York and Philadelphia, there was no organized vigilance committee in Pittsburgh. Nonetheless, the Philanthropic Society, operating as a small but very active secret society and working as part of the Underground Railroad, had the same effect as its New York and Philadelphia counterparts. It formed part of a larger, albeit uncoordinated, national network of associations organized by blacks and white abolitionists to resist slavery. In spite of the dire warnings that their activities threatened the stability of the area's economy, the society and its white supporters continued to oppose the notion that slaveholders had a right to hold other men as property. Their activities, like those of other northern urban communities, particularly in the early 1850s, heightened the sectional conflicts between the North and the South that led finally to the abolition of slavery.

Notes

1. Clarence Rollo Turner, "Black Pittsburgh: A Social History, 1790–1840. A Census Compilation" (paper prepared for the Urban Historians' Group, University of Pittsburgh, March 1974), 2, 5, 13.

2. *The Liberator,* February 25, 1832.

3. William Lloyd Garrison, *Thoughts on African Colonization,* part 2 (1832; reprint, New York, 1968), 34–35.

4. Erasmus Wilson, *Standard History of Pittsburg Pennsylvania* (Chicago, 1898), 816–17. See also Robert Wallace Brewster, "The Rise of the Antislavery Movement in Southwestern Pennsylvania," *Western Pennsylvania Historical Magazine* 22 (March 1939): 1–18 (hereafter *WPHM*).

5. Victor Ullman, *Martin R. Delany: The Beginnings of Black Nationalism* (Boston, 1971), 24.

6. Ibid., 27; Frank A. Rollin, *Life and Public Services of Martin R. Delany* (1883; reprint, New York, 1969), 43.

7. *Memorial of the Free Citizens of Colour in Pittsburgh and Its Vicinity Relative to the Rights of Suffrage Read in Convention, July 8, 1837* (Harrisburg, Pa., 1837).

8. *Pittsburgh Gazette,* n.d., quoted in Ullman, *Martin R. Delany,* 41–43.

9. Martin Delany to Frederick Douglass, reprinted in *The North Star,* July 6, 1849.

10. *Laws of the General Assembly of the Commonwealth of Pennsylvania Passed at the Session of 1847* (Harrisburg, Pa., 1847), 206–8. Section 6 of the law, banning the use of state jails to hold fugitives, was repealed during the Democratic administration of Governor William Bigler as a sop to "national interests." See also *Laws of the General Assembly of the Commonwealth of Pennsylvania Passed at the Session of 1852* (Harrisburg, Pa., 1852), 295; Mary Florence Durkin, "William Bigler, A Pennsylvania Democrat" (M.A. thesis, University of Pittsburgh, 1937), 11; and *Journal of the Senate of the Commonwealth of Pennsylvania* (Harrisburg, Pa., 1852), 1:71.

11. *The North Star,* February 11 and 18, 1848; Catherine E. Reiser, "Pittsburgh, the Hub of Western Commerce, 1800–1850," *WPHM* 25 (September–December 1942): 121–34.

12. *Pittsburgh Daily Morning Post,* April 17, 19, and 20, 1847. See also Benjamin Drew, *A Northside View of Slavery* (New York, 1968), 45–50, for Lockhart's account of his experiences as a slave and fugitive in Pittsburgh.

13. For an account of the incidents, see Sarah R. Christy, "Fugitive Slaves in Indiana County," *WPHM* 18 (December 1935): 255–66.

14. *Pittsburgh Gazette,* November 21, 1850; Frederick Douglass Paper, October 28 and November 11, 1853; *Pittsburgh Evening Chronicle,* October 8, 1853.

15. Christy, "Fugitive Slaves," 285. For *Van Metre v. Mitchell* cases, see *Federal Cases: Circuit and District Courts, 1789–1880* (St. Paul, Minn., 1896), 1036–44.

16. *Pittsburgh Daily Morning Post,* January 28, 1847.

17. Ibid., April 21, 22, 1847. For another instance of blacks preventing slave catchers from recapturing their slaves, see *Pittsburgh Daily Commercial Journal,* July 7, 1848, and *Pittsburgh Gazette,* July 8, 1848.

18. Philip S. Foner, *Business and Slavery: The New York Merchants and the Irrepressible Conflict* (Chapel Hill, N.C., 1941), 22–23.

19. *Pittsburgh Gazette,* June 6, 1850.

20. *The North Star,* July 11, 1850; U.S. Congress, Senate, *Congressional Globe,* 31st Cong., 1st sess., 1850, 21, pt. 2: 1390.

21. Stanley W. Campbell, *The Slave Catchers: Enforcement of the Fugitive Slave Law, 1850–1860* (Chapel Hill, N.C., 1970), 23–25.

22. *Pittsburgh Gazette,* September 24, 25, and 26, 1850; *The Liberator,* October 4, 1850.

23. Fred Landon, "The Negro Migration to Canada After the Passing of the Fugitive Slave Act," *Journal of Negro History* 5 (January 1920): 22; Robin W. Winks, *The Blacks in Canada: A History* (New Haven, Conn., 1971), 235, has questioned Landon's estimate of the number of blacks entering Canada in the 1850s. By 1857, however, blacks constituted about two-thirds of the population of Chatham, Canada West. *Chatham Tri-Weekly Planet,* December 11, 1857; Turner, "Black Pittsburgh," 2; Rev. William King, "Autobiography" (unpublished ms.), 112, National Archives, Ottawa, Canada; Victor Ullman, *Look to the North Star: A Life of William King* (Boston, 1969), 169–74.

24. *Pittsburgh Gazette,* September 30, 1850; *Pittsburgh Daily Morning Post,* September 30, 1850.

25. For Delany's speech, see J. Ernest Wright's unpublished manuscript "The Negro in

Pittsburgh," 65–66. For a different version of Delany's speech, see Rollin, *Life and Services of Martin Delany,* 76; *Pittsburgh Gazette,* October 1, 1850; *Pittsburgh Daily Morning Post,* October 1, 1850.

26. *Pittsburgh Commercial Journal,* December 2, 1850.

27. *Pittsburgh Saturday Visitor,* November 16, 1850; *Washington Examiner,* October 26, 1850; *Pittsburgh Gazette,* October 17, 1850.

28. *Pittsburgh Gazette,* October 30, 1850; *Presbyterian Advocate,* October 30, 1850.

29. Earle R. Forrest, *History of Washington County Pennsylvania,* 3 vols. (Chicago, 1926), 1:424; Boyd Crumrine, *History of Washington County, Pennsylvania* (Philadelphia, 1882), 261–62; Wilbert H. Seibert, *The Underground Railroad from Slavery to Freedom* (1892; reprint 1967), 122–23; Irene Williams, "The Operation of the Fugitive Slave Law in Western Pennsylvania," *WPHM* 4 (July 1921): 151; Christy, "Fugitive Slaves," 279.

30. Hallie Q. Brown, *Tales My Father Told and Other Stories* (Wilberforce, Ohio, n.d.), 6.

31. *Pittsburgh Gazette,* March 8, 1855.

32. Ibid.

33. *Anti-Slavery Bugle,* June 11, 1853; *Pittsburgh Gazette,* May 30, 1853; *Pittsburgh Daily Morning Post,* May 31, 1853; *Pittsburgh Commercial Journal,* May 31, 1853.

34. *Pittsburgh Evening Chronicle,* August 12, 1853; *Pittsburgh Gazette,* August 12, 1853.

35. For accounts of the Woodson case, see the *Pittsburgh Gazette* for March and April 1851; and *Pittsburgh Saturday Visitor,* March 22 and 29, 1851.

36. *Pittsburgh Gazette,* May 14, 1853.

37. *Pittsburgh Daily Morning Post,* March 12, 1855.

38. *Pittsburgh Gazette,* June 2, 1854; *Pittsburgh Evening Chronicle,* January 31, 1854.

39. Leland D. Baldwin, *Pittsburgh: The Story of a City* (Pittsburgh, 1937), 308.

40. *Pittsburgh Daily Morning Post,* March 14, 1854.

41. *Pittsburgh Gazette,* July 11, 1850.

CHAPTER SIX

The Forten-Purvis Women of Philadelphia and the American Antislavery Crusade

Janice Sumler-Lewis

Nineteenth-century reform movements in the United States have received much scholarly attention. While historians have acknowledged the contributions of black men to the antislavery, temperance, civil rights, and women's rights crusades, they largely ignored the participation of black women. Except for a recent publication by historians Sharon Harley and Rosalyn Terborg-Penn, we possess little research on the black females who labored in the reform movements with their white counterparts, like Lucretia Mott and Susan B. Anthony.[1]

We cannot hope to know the complete story of reform in this nation until the role of black women also comes to light. Investigations of antebellum era diaries, letters, organizational records, and periodicals reveal that many black women activists made a profound impact upon the struggles for liberty and for social justice in America. As black females in a racist-sexist society, they brought a unique perspective to their work. Because of a sharpened awareness and because of daily experiences in a biased America, black women activists guided female reform groups toward a more straightforward liberal posture.

This chapter was first published in the *Journal of Negro History* 66 (Winter 1981–82): 281–87. Reprinted by permission.

In this way, the combined activism and insightful perspective of black women reformers contributed in important ways to the directions of change in the country.

Such was the case with the Forten-Purvis women of nineteenth-century Philadelphia. In a generational study of this Afro-American family, I detailed how the affluent and cohesive domestic environment produced male abolitionists, like the family patriarch, James Forten Sr., his two oldest sons, James Jr. and Robert, and his son-in-law Robert Purvis; the same environment afforded female family members an opportunity to oppose slavery. While the Forten and Purvis men labored beside such friends of emancipation as William Lloyd Garrison and Wendell Phillips, the Forten-Purvis women brought a black perspective to the reform movement in their native Philadelphia and the surrounding areas.[2] The extent and magnitude of their participation rivaled that of their more famous white female contemporaries.

How did their involvement become possible? Transcending the traditional roles of wife and mother to enter the broader spheres of public life was an uncommon occurrence during the Victorian era. Scorn and even ostracism often greeted a woman who dared to venture outside what many considered to be her God-given realm. Beginning in the 1830s and 1840s, however, many women defied these social pressures and became both public and private individuals.[3]

The Forten-Purvis women joined the ranks of this new breed of nineteenth-century women. They successfully combined the role of reformer with the traditional responsibilities related to marriage and child-rearing. James Forten Sr.'s outlook did much to determine the activist roles of his wife, daughters, and later his granddaughters. As a Revolutionary War veteran, a reformer, and a feminist, Forten had incorporated the American ideals of liberty and equality into his personal philosophy. Though he was a free black and a wealthy businessman, he sustained a keen racial consciousness as well as an empathy with the plight of his enslaved brethren and with that of all women. Moreover, Forten Sr. shared this enlightened philosophy with his son-in-law Robert Purvis, who adopted it wholeheartedly. As a result, both the male members and the female members of the Forten and Purvis households received an education and were encouraged to take an interest in public affairs.[4]

A constant exposure to the reform careers of their parents facilitated the emergence of the Forten-Purvis women as activists. As the young people emulated these role models, humanitarianism became a family affair. During the antebellum era, James and Charlotte Forten accompanied their sons and daughters to numerous antislavery and moral reform meetings in and around Philadelphia, and even as far away as New York City. In subsequent years,

Women like Charlotte Forten Grimke struggled against
both sexism and racism in their society. Moreover, unlike
their brothers after 1870, they could not vote and were
excluded from most occupations. Thus their idealism,
political activism, and lack of empowerment put black
women in a paradoxical situation. (Courtesy of the
Schomburg Center for Research in Black Culture)

the second-generation Fortens and Forten son-in-law Robert Purvis also encouraged emancipation and civil rights activities in their respective offspring.[5]

The Forten-Purvis women's reform involvement became extensive. Collectively, Mrs. Charlotte Forten, her three oldest daughters, and two granddaughters participated in numerous aspects of the emancipation crusade.
Major areas of their activities included acting as hostesses for important anti-
slavery gatherings, writing for reformist publications, and lobbying for
the black abolitionist perspective in organizations with which they were
affiliated.

Gracious hospitality was a tradition in the Forten and Purvis households. During the second decade of the nineteenth century, Harriet, Margaretta, and Sarah Forten were youngsters. They joined in greeting and conversing with Pan-Africanist Paul Cuffe; Philadelphia ministers Richard Allen and Absalom Jones; and other prominent persons who frequented the Forten home. As the antislavery crusade gained momentum during the 1830s, scores of reformers found support and a restful haven with the Fortens and with newlyweds Robert and Harriet Purvis. Their guests included Bostonians William Lloyd Garrison and Samuel May, British abolitionists George Thompson and Harriet Martineau, New York businessmen Arthur and Lewis Tappan, and numerous others; indeed, the Forten-Purvis family cultivated activist friendships.[6]

The New England poet John Greenleaf Whittier once became so enchanted with his Forten hosts that he wrote a poem entitled "To the Daughters of James Forten." Following a May 1832 visit to Philadelphia, where he was the guest of Robert and Harriet Purvis, William Lloyd Garrison even felt it pertinent to extol the moral character of his black hosts. Garrison described his visit in a letter to a friend:

> I wish you had been with me in Philadelphia to see what I saw, to hear what I heard, and to experience what I felt in associating with many colored families. There are colored men and women, young men and young ladies, in that city, who have few superiors in refinement, in moral worth, in all that makes the human character worthy of admiration and praise.

Such favorable association offered the Forten-Purvis family members an opportunity to influence the thinking of their guests. For the white reformers, positive contacts with this black family gave them exposure to the black middle class while adding further proof of the acceptability of blacks in American life and the righteousness of the struggle to achieve human freedom.[7]

Complementing their role as hostesses, the Forten-Purvis women carried their antislavery involvement outside the home—they entered the broader sphere of public life through affiliations with various organizations. Four of the twenty-one women who met at Catherine McDurmot's schoolroom on the evening of December 9, 1833, to coordinate their abolitionist activities were Forten women. Mrs. Charlotte Forten, her three oldest daughters, and her prospective daughter-in-law Mary Woods, all signed the Philadelphia Female Anti-Slavery Society's charter, which daughter Margaretta Forten had helped to draft. These women declared their intent to put all the resources at their disposal toward removing the stain of slavery from the nation and elevating the status of black Americans. Recognizing Margaretta's leadership qualities, the members of the new Society elected her recording secretary. In time, two Forten granddaughters, Charlotte L. Forten and her cousin Hattie Purvis, joined this group. Throughout the organization's forty years of emancipation and civil rights efforts, three generations of Forten-Purvis women remained active members and financial contributors.[8]

The Forten-Purvis women's involvement in the Philadelphia Female Anti-Slavery Society extended well beyond the life of their membership. Through key offices they held and through lobbying efforts, they influenced the group's activities and its philosophical direction. Working in conjunction with other black members, like Grace Douglass and her daughter Sarah, and with liberal whites, like Lucretia Mott, the Forten-Purvis women often enabled this predominantly white organization to reflect a black abolitionist perspective, a perspective equally dedicated to the abolition of slavery and to the triumph of racial justice in America, but a perspective usually more militant. Consequently, with the Forten-Purvis women's assistance, their female Society went far beyond reflecting the views of well-meaning ladies; it emerged as an aggressive, persistent force for change in the Philadelphia area.[9]

An awareness of both the importance of educational opportunities for blacks and the problems resulting from a segregated school system were two areas toward which the Philadelphia Female Anti-Slavery Society reflected a black abolitionist perspective. Margaretta Forten, a teacher, served on her female Society's educational committee; it dedicated itself to improving the quantity and the quality of local black schools. In accordance with this objective, the committee quickly acted upon an 1838 request for financial assistance from their abolitionist colleague Sarah Douglass, the black coordinator of a Philadelphia primary school. Acknowledging Douglass's fine work, the Society voted to assume responsibility for the school's financial obligations. This arrangement lasted for two years, then the school became self-sustaining. The Society's minutes reveal how the two Forten women played key roles in this instance. Sarah sat on the Society's governing board of managers while, as a member of the educational committee, Margaretta supervised specific financial details. By their involvement, the two Forten sisters helped to serve the educational needs of Philadelphia's black community.[10]

During Sarah Forten's three consecutive terms on the Philadelphia Female Anti-Slavery Society's board of managers, this governing body involved itself in many projects and made important decisions, a great number of which reflected an aggressive abolitionist perspective. One such project was an extensive petition campaign conducted in Philadelphia and the surrounding counties. Sarah Forten actively led this endeavor. From 1835 to 1838, she assisted in drafting and circulating petitions which appealed to the U.S. Congress to abolish the slave trade in the District of Columbia and to abandon further moves toward annexing Texas. According to the Society's minutes, Sarah and other members of the petition committee gratefully acknowledged a March 9, 1837, letter from Pennsylvania Senator Samuel McKean; he had delivered their lists of signatures to his congressional colleagues.[11]

Realizing the difficulty abolitionists often met in securing a meeting house, Sarah Forten, Lucretia Mott, and six other members of the Society formed a special committee on December 8, 1836. This committee launched a community-wide effort to sell shares in the cost of building Pennsylvania Hall, erected two years later on Delaware, Sixth, and Haines Streets in Philadelphia.[12]

While the Forten-Purvis women and other members of the Philadelphia Female Anti-Slavery Society publicly professed their adherence to moral suasion as the only acceptable abolition tactic, these women frequently employed a more vigorous action against the "peculiar institution" of slavery. These apparently quiet, law-abiding, reserved women donated hundreds of dollars to harbor fugitives from slavery. Between 1839 and 1842, an effective partnership existed between this Society and the Philadelphia Vigilant Committee; it was one link in the fugitive assistance network under the leadership of Robert Purvis, Charles W. Gardiner, and other local blacks. The Philadelphia women responded generously to requests for aid from the Vigilant Committee. They answered a $15 request with a gift of $50 during January 1841. On that occasion, their money relocated several fugitives in Canada. The following winter, when icy river conditions prevented travel north, the Society's funds boarded runaways in the city. The women collected garments for the often destitute bondsmen. For their efforts, they received frequent reports on the Vigilant Committee's progress. The committee reported on January 9, 1842, that it had recently sent forty-six fugitives to Canada.[13]

It is not difficult to explain the Philadelphia Female Society's financial and philosophical support for this predominantly black Vigilant Committee. First, Robert Purvis had proven his friendship to female reformers. Beyond giving frequent and encouraging lectures at the women's meetings and bazaars, he consistently defended their rights as citizens and as abolitionists. Second, because four members of the Forten-Purvis family were members and officers of the Society, Vigilant Committee chairman Robert Purvis had his own lobbying elements within the organization. For example, Purvis's sister-in-law Sarah Forten sat on the board of managers, which authorized the release of treasury funds. Another Purvis sister-in-law, Margaretta Forten, was selected to audit her Society's financial accounts of 1840.[14]

The Philadelphia Female Anti-Slavery Society's members fully realized that financial aid to the Vigilant Committee and the implementation of an aggressive abolitionist perspective required a large treasury. Consequently, following the example of the Boston Female Anti-Slavery Society, the Philadelphia women organized annual fund-raising fairs and bazaars. The Forten-Purvis women contributed considerable time and talent toward this effort. From 1841 through 1869, the three sisters—Margaretta and Sarah, and Harriet—worked diligently to make these annual events successful. Beginning in 1866 and for the next three years, Hattie Purvis, the teenage daughter of Robert and Harriet Purvis, also joined this effort. The labors of these Philadelphia women were rewarded: the fairs realized substantial profits. By one estimate between 1840 and the start of the Civil War, the Philadelphia Female Society raised over $32,000.[15]

As the wife of prominent abolitionist Robert Purvis and the mother of their five children, Harriet Purvis maintained a busy schedule. Aside from her domestic responsibilities and her work with the annual bazaars, as hostess for antislavery events, and occasionally lecturing on the evils of racial segregation in the North, Harriet still found time to extend her abolitionist activities beyond the local Philadelphia area. Harriet and her sisters journeyed to New York in 1837, where they attended the Anti-Slavery Convention of American Women. Two years later, in an effort to curtail the profits resulting from slave labor, Harriet became a member of the regionally based Free Produce Society. While visiting the New England area during May 1854, Harriet accompanied her niece Charlotte Forten to a fugitive slave protest meeting.[16]

In all of her reform activities, Harriet Purvis received full support and encouragement from her husband. And Robert Purvis did not stop with approving Harriet's activist role; he worked closely with his wife, so that the two formed an effective abolitionist team. During May 1840, the couple attended antislavery conventions, first in Harrisburg, Pennsylvania, then a week later in New York City. Harriet and Robert continued their reform efforts at the close of the Civil War. They joined the American Equal Rights Association and entered the struggle to enfranchise black men and all women. The Purvises' egalitarian marriage and activist partnership presented a unique phenomenon. Few such relationships existed during the Victorian era. Their marriage demonstrated one man's commitment to the concepts of equality and freedom of expression. Further, it revealed one woman's ability to transcend contemporary mores to share in both the private and the public spheres of her husband's life and work.[17]

Beyond their organizational affiliations, the Forten-Purvis women's abolitionist activities found expression in written form. The publication of their insightful poems, essays, and letters provided these black women with yet another opportunity to share their views with the American public. Beginning in 1831, Sarah Forten's poetry frequently appeared in the *Liberator.* Only 17 years old at that time, this creative young woman condemned America's hypocritical commitment to liberty and equality. In "The Slave," she urged Americans to remember their struggles for freedom against the British and to liberate the bondsmen. In the same year, she denounced in an essay, "The Abuse of Liberty," the northern practices of racial segregation and the denial of civil rights to blacks. Appealing to the professed religious nature of Americans, she reminded her readers that in time slavery would provoke God's wrath:

> I say, cry unto Him for aid; for can you think He, the Great Spirit, who created all men free and equal—He, who, made the sun to shine on the black man as well as on the white, will always allow you to rest tranquil on your downy couches? No,—He is just, and his anger will not always slumber. He will wipe the tears from Ethiopia's eyes, he will shake the tree of liberty, and its blossoms shall spread over the earth.[18]

Through the years, Sarah Forten remained dedicated to poetic expression. As the Anti-Slavery Convention of American Women assembled in New York City in 1837, she wrote a poem for the gathering; it was read during the proceedings. Her verse poignantly articulated one black woman's desire to eliminate racial animosity and strife within abolitionist ranks. She also called for a bond of universal sisterhood and cooperation to transcend race.[19]

Like her Aunt Sarah, Charlotte Forten, daughter of Robert and Mary Forten, showed poetic talent. While she was studying, and later while she was teaching in Salem, Massachusetts, in the 1850s, Charlotte Forten's pieces appeared in the *Liberator,* in the *National Anti-Slavery Standard,* and in Bishop Daniel Payne's *Anglo African Magazine.* Although this young scholar-activist wrote verses on a variety of subjects, reform and racial pride were favorite themes. In 1855 she demonstrated her respect for William Lloyd Garrison and dedicated a poem to him. Three years later she wrote a song for the public commemoration of the Boston Massacre and black hero Crispus Attucks.[20]

Charlotte Forten's experience as a teenage abolitionist and an author proved invaluable, and in 1862 she traveled as a teacher to the Sea Islands of South Carolina. The Philadelphia Port Royal Relief Commission had selected Charlotte, who was then 25, as one of the first northern blacks to be involved with the experimental reconstruction project. Charlotte also represented her activist family in the final phase of the emancipation struggle.[21]

Besides serving as teacher for the native black population, Charlotte Forten assumed the role of propagandist for the reconstruction plan. Like many Sea Island volunteers, she believed that the former bondsman could bridge the gap from slave to productive citizen. A very skeptical and largely racist American public remained unconvinced of this fact, but Charlotte accepted the challenge. Through her letters and articles published in the *Liberator* and in the *Atlantic Monthly,* she described the rapid gains and accomplishments of the Sea Island residents. Because of her insight, her empathetic nature, and her eagerness to help her race, Charlotte Forten brought a unique perspective to the Port Royal project. Several of her colleagues acknowledged this, among them Laura Towne, a white teacher from Philadelphia, who praised the accuracy and the sensitivity of Charlotte's account of their Sea Island labors. In a journal entry, Towne wrote: "Lottie Forten's article in the *Atlantic,* sent [to] me by Mr. Pierce is very good indeed. They are her letters to Whittier revised and tell more of our life than anything yet published."[22]

After the two years at Port Royal and after the conclusion of Civil War hostilities, Charlotte accepted a position as secretary of the Freedmen's Aid Society in Boston. Part of her assignment was to select teachers and missionaries for work among the southern blacks. On June 8, 1867, recalling her work on the Sea Islands, Charlotte encouraged Lucy Chase, a freedmen's teacher. While she recognized the many self-sacrificing efforts and the disappointments that Chase encountered, she assured her friend that the rewards of her work would far outweigh the problems. Charlotte could suggest no nobler work than dedicating one's life to "the regeneration of a down trodden and long suffering people."[23]

With those words, Charlotte Forten expressed the philosophy which had sustained her family's nearly century-long commitment to reform in America. Working for three generations with their men, the Forten-Purvis women brought a unique black female perspective and spirit to the crusades for freedom and for equality of opportunity. The legacy of their contributions offers inspiration to those who would follow their footsteps.

Notes

1. Sharon Harley and Rosalyn Terborg-Penn, eds., *The Afro-American Women: Struggles and Images* (Port Washington, N.Y., 1978). The following only briefly mention the black female reformer: Benjamin Quarles, *Black Abolitionists* (New York, 1969); Jane H. Pease and William

H. Pease, *They Who Would Be Free: Blacks Search for Freedom, 1830–1861* (New York, 1974); Blanche Glassman Hersh, *The Slavery of Sex: Feminist-Abolitionists in America* (Urbana, Ill., 1978).

2. Janice Sumler-Lewis, "The Fortens of Philadelphia: An Afro-American Family and Nineteenth-Century Reform" (Ph.D. diss., Georgetown University, 1978); "Constitution of the Philadelphia Female Anti-Slavery Society," December 14, 1833, Historical Society of Pennsylvania (hereafter HSP).

3. Hersh, *The Slavery of Sex,* 1, 4, 18–21; Gilbert H. Barnes and Dwight L. Dumond, eds., *Letters of Theodore D. Weld and Angelina Grimké Weld and Sarah Grimké* (New York, 1934), 472.

4. Robert Purvis, *Remarks on the Life and Character of James Forten Delivered at Bethel Church on March 30, 1842* (Philadelphia, 1842), 16, 17.

5. "Minutes of the Philadelphia Female Anti-Slavery Society," December 9, 1833; December 14, 1833, HSP: *Proceedings of the American Moral Reform Society Held at Philadelphia in the Presbyterian Church on Seventh Street Below Shippen from the 14th to the 19th of August 1837* (Philadelphia, 1837); *Proceedings of the Third Avenue Meeting of the American Anti-Slavery Society in 1836* (New York, 1836). See the following entries in the "Charlotte Forten Diary," I, Howard University Manuscripts, May 27, 1854; June 1, 1854; October 29, 1854; August 19, 1855; July 4, 1856.

6. See the following letters contained in the Paul Cuffe Collection, Free Public Library, New Bedford, Massachusetts: Paul Cuffe to James Forten, May 29, 1816; Paul Cuffe to James Forten, January 18, 1817; James Forten to Paul Cuffe, July 25, 1816, "Paul Cuffe Journal," entries for May 11, 1812, and May 12, 1812. From 1806 to 1860, the Fortens lived at 92 Lombard Street. See the *Philadelphia Directory.* Barnes and Dumond, *Weld-Grimké Letters,* 351; James Forten to William Lloyd Garrison, December 30, 1830, and May 6, 1832, both contained in the Rare Books and Manuscripts Department, Boston Public Library (hereafter BPL); Lewis Tappan, *The Life of Arthur Tappan* (Cambridge, 1870), 360; Samuel J. May, *Some Recollections of Our Anti-Slavery Conflict* (Boston, 1869), 81–88.

7. Garrison's letter describing his Philadelphia visit contained in Archibald H. Grimké, *William Lloyd Garrison: The Abolitionist* (New York, 1891), 162; *William Lloyd Garrison to Robert Purvis,* May 30, 1832, BPL; Whittier's poem contained in Anna Julia Cooper, *The Life and Writing of the Grimké Family* (Washington, D.C., 1951), 2:13.

8. "Minutes of the Philadelphia Female Anti-Slavery Society," December 9, 1833; December 14, 1833; December 13, 1866; June 11, 1868; March 21, 1870; Esther M. Douty, *Charlotte Forten, Free Black Teacher* (Champaign, Ill., 1971), 31–33.

9. Besides Grace and Sarah M. Douglass, other black women who joined the Philadelphia Female Anti-Slavery Society included Sarah McCrummel, Mary Woods, Anna Woods, Debrah Coates, Hannah Coates, and Amy Matalida Cassey. See Quarles, *Black Abolitionists,* 225, 230–31, 234–35.

10. Margaretta Forten was listed as a private grammar school teacher in Benjamin C. Bacon, *Statistics of Colored People of Philadelphia* (Philadelphia, 1859), 8. For information concerning the Philadelphia Female Society and the Sarah Douglass school, see "Minutes of the Philadelphia Female Anti-Slavery Society," March 8, 1838, and April 9, 1840.

11. "Minutes of the Philadelphia Female Anti-Slavery Society," June 10, 1835; September 13, 1835; March 9, 1837; May 18, 1837; August 10, 1837.

12. "Minutes of the Philadelphia Female Anti-Slavery Society," December 1834; December 16, 1835; May 14, 1835; June 13, 1835; December 8, 1836; January 12, 1837; May 18, 1837. For information on the burning of Pennsylvania Hall, see *The History of Pennsylvania Hall, Which Was Destroyed by a Mob on the 17 of May 1838* (Philadelphia, 1838).

13. "Minutes of the Philadelphia Female Anti-Slavery Society," January 13, 1841; February 10, 1842; March 10, 1842; April 13, 1842; January 9, 1842. See also the "Vigilant Committee of Philadelphia Minutes Book, 1839–1844," HSP.

14. Richard C. Smedley, *History of the Underground Railroad in Chester and the Neighboring Counties of Pennsylvania* (1883; reprint, New York, 1968); "Minutes of the Philadelphia Female Anti-Slavery Society," January 9, 1840; Quarles, *Black Abolitionists,* 154–55, 158.

15. Occasionally the Forten-Purvis women chaired the fair committees. See "Minutes of the Philadelphia Female Anti-Slavery Society," February 4, 1856, and February 10, 1859. Young Hattie Purvis joined the Society on February 8, 1866, and she worked with the fair committees through 1868.

16. "Minutes of the Philadelphia Female Anti-Slavery Society," April 12, 1838; October 10, 1839; September 13, 1866; *Proceedings of the Anti-Slavery Convention of American Women, Held in New York City* (New York, 1837); "Charlotte Forten Diary," I, May 27, 1854.

17. "Minutes of the Philadelphia Female Anti-Slavery Society," May 6, 1840, and May 7, 1840; "Broadside of the Philadelphia Female Anti-Slavery Society's Festival of Friends," January 17, 1868, HSP; *National Anti-Slavery Standard,* June 1, 1867; Ida Husted Harper, *The Life and Work of Susan B. Anthony* (1898; reprint, New York, 1969), 259–66.

18. In a letter to Garrison, James Forten Sr. identified the pieces in *The Liberator* under the pen names "A" and "Ada" as the work of his daughter Sarah. See James Forten Sr. to William Lloyd Garrison, February 23, 1831, BPL. Sarah also used the pen name "Magawisca." For examples of Sarah's poetry and articles, see *The Liberator,* January 29, 1831; March 26, 1831; April 16, 1831.

19. Barnes and Dumond, *Weld-Grimké Letters,* 381–82; Quarles, *Black Abolitionists,* 23; Edward T. James, *Notable American Women, 1607–1950* (Cambridge, Mass., 1971), 194.

20. Annual Report for the School Committee of Salem, Massachusetts, February 1854, 29–30; "Charlotte Forten Diary," I, August 10, 1854; December 31, 1854; March 13, 1855; June 18, 1856; "Charlotte Forten Diary," III, June 18, 1858, and July 26, 1858; *The Liberator,* March 16, 1855; May 27, 1857; February 26, 1858. A copy of Charlotte's song has not survived, but Benjamin Quarles refers to it in *Black Abolitionists,* 233.

21. Charlotte arrived at Hilton Head, South Carolina, on October 28, 1862. See "Charlotte Forten Diary," III, October 27, 1862, written at sea, and October 29, 1862.

22. "Laura Towne Diary," November 4, 1862, and May 18, 1864, James Dabbs Papers, Southern Historical Collection, University of North Carolina, Chapel Hill; *The Liberator,* December 19, 1862; Charlotte Forten, "Life on the Sea Islands," *Atlantic Monthly* 13 (May and June 1864).

23. Charlotte Forten to Lucy Chase, June 8, 1967, American Antiquarian Society Manuscripts, Boston.

CHAPTER SEVEN

No Balm in Gilead:
Lancaster's African American Population and the Civil War Era

Leroy T. Hopkins

As a result of the television miniseries *The Civil War,* and especially the feature film *Glory,* public awareness of the role played by African Americans in the nation's most destructive war has been greatly increased. It is a sad commentary on the state of race relations that the entertainment industry must provide information that is lacking in the school history curriculum. Locally as well as nationally, recognition of service to the Union cause has been largely one-sided and ignores the valor, sacrifice, and altruism of almost 200,000 men of color who fought on land and sea to defend a country and a constitution that had denied them the basic right of citizenship just four years before the outbreak of the war. In the following we shall examine the experience of local men of color in the Civil War and attempt to understand that experience in the context of the decades preceding and following the war.

To date, about 300 men of color associated with Lancaster County have been identified as having served sometime between 1862 and 1867 in all eleven of the USCT regiments mustered in Pennsylvania, as well as the Massachusetts Fifth and the famous Fifty-fourth and Fifty-fifth Volunteers. In

This chapter was first published in the *Journal of the Lancaster County Historical Society* 95, no. 2 (1991): 20–31. Reprinted by permission.

addition, some of these men were not native to Pennsylvania, but were part of the huge northward migration caused by the war and were mustered into a regiment from Lancaster. Muster rolls on deposit in the State Archives in Harrisburg indicate that men from as far away as Mississippi and England were accepted into Pennsylvania regiments. When one considers the status of African Americans in Lancaster County and the Commonwealth in general before 1860, it is obvious that this enthusiastic response was rooted in a vision of the war being a final barrier to full integration into American society. Unfortunately, this hope found no justification in the events preceding, during, and after the war.

The antebellum era in Pennsylvania was a period of crisis for persons of color. In his pioneer study of African American communities in southeastern Pennsylvania between 1780 and 1860, Carl Oblinger characterizes economic life in rural Pennsylvania in the following terms.[1]

> By mid-century, the new, and depressing, structure of racial relations, the pattern of employment in day labor and menial service, and the pattern of endogamous marriages had been set. As industrial capitalism transformed the economy, new employment opportunities hardly touched black labor; nearly all, especially the elite, remained in preindustrial patterns of work including domestic service. As late as the 1830s blacks in southeastern Pennsylvania were in the mainstream of town life, by 1860 they were on the periphery.

The prewar period was punctuated by repressive laws, such as Lancaster's registration law,[2] and by antiblack mob violence, such as the infamous "Columbia race riots" of 1834–35. Although the Underground Railroad and the "Christiana Riot" exemplify local resistance to slavery, it would be a mistake to think that the majority of Lancaster Countians were abolitionists or advocated the cause of the people of color. This is clear from the testimony of one of the principals involved in the operation of the semimythical railroad.

William Whipper (1803–76)—intellectual, civil rights and temperance advocate, and successful entrepreneur—resided in Columbia from the 1830s until after the Civil War. A partner of Stephen Smith, Whipper was a leader of the antebellum African American community, as documented by his presence at various "Negro National Conventions" between 1830 and 1860 and his editorship of the first African American magazine. After the war, William Still, chairman of the Vigilance Committee of the Pennsylvania Anti-Slavery Society, compiled a history of his involvement in the Underground Railroad.

An interesting letter from Whipper recounted the latter's efforts in Columbia between 1847 and 1861. Looking back on the decades preceding the war, Whipper summarized:

> It would have been fortunate for us if Columbia, being port of entry for the flying fugitives, had been also the seat of great capitalists and freedom-loving inhabitants; but such was not the case. There was but little Anti-slavery sentiment among whites, yet there were many strong and valiant friends among them who contributed freely.[3]

Whipper's perspective was neither unique nor idiosyncratic. The principal goal of the riots in Columbia in 1834–35 had been to eliminate African Americans as serious economic competitors. The principal target of the violence was Stephen Smith (1795–1873), whose meteoric career as a businessman epitomized for some Columbians the dangers of black competition. Although the riots did not achieve their purpose, life was certainly difficult for Smith and others. A letter written by Smith to State Senator John Strohm just one year after the race riots exemplifies not only the precarious status of local blacks but also a rare altruism that enabled Smith to place this situation in a broader sociopolitical context.

Smith requested action from Strohm even though he realized that such action might be denied him because "an overruling policy not founded in justice has assigned me with thousands of others a place without the pale and influence of your political Judicature."[4] Smith's words were to be prophetic. Although here he was only referring to the common practice of excluding African Americans, in 1838 Pennsylvania adopted a new state constitution that specifically restricted the right to vote to free white men. Smith could therefore not rely on custom or tradition to obtain help from Strohm, but he did hope that their friendship would make the legislator receptive to his request.

Considering the damage done to his office during the riot, and the public threats made against him should he continue to conduct business in Columbia, one would expect Smith to ask for a law to protect individuals such as himself from mob violence. Instead, he pleads eloquently for protection of the freedom of speech. This rather strange request has a clear motivation:

> The many appeals that will doubtless be made by Southern Governors, and Legislatures to the Executive of our State and through him to your honorable body (i.e., the Senate), praying for the passage of such laws shall inflict heavy penalties on such of your fellow citizens, as shall dare to think, speak, or write on any subject that conflicts with

the interest of slaveholding or the perpetuity of American slavery, will doubtless rouse indignation in the bosom of every freeman in this commonwealth.[5]

Clearly Smith sees his situation in Columbia as part of the general struggle against slavery; by placing his and his race's situation within the context of freedom of speech, a basic constitutional right of all Americans, Smith apparently assumes that the constitutional guarantees automatically applied to the African American. Denial of that fact verified that the promise of America was flawed by inequality. Above all, this letter documents Smith's and a large portion of the African American elite's belief in the system. This belief was put to the test by the continued violence and oppression of the 1840s and 1850s.

The 1850s created a psychologically oppressive atmosphere which quickened earlier interest shown by African Americans in leaving America for a supposedly friendlier country, such as Canada. The passage of the Fugitive Slave Act in 1850, and its opportunistic exploitation by groups such as the notorious Gap Gang, posed daily threats to fugitive and free black alike. Two events at the end of the decade underscored the precariousness of everyday life for African Americans in the North.

On March 6, 1857, the U.S. Supreme Court declared that blacks were not and had never been intended to be citizens by the framers of the Constitution. The enormity of that decision, and the bleak promise it represented to all persons of African descent, was lost on local commentators. The *Daily Evening Express* reported the decision without commentary. The *Lancaster Intelligencer,* the organ of Lancaster Democrats and a supporter of the recently inaugurated James Buchanan, exulted:

Thus has the last prop of Black Republicanism been knocked from under it by the highest judicial tribunal of the land. These agitators may make wry faces and say all manner of bad things against the majority of the Court, but it will not avail. There is no appeal from the decision. It stands, and will continue to stand, as the law of the land, decided in accordance with the Constitution, and will, as a matter of course, *settle the whole slavery question for all time to come* [italics added].[6]

To the editor, the Dred Scott decision had no human face. It was vindication by the judiciary of a political platform. By declaring the unconstitutionality of the Missouri Compromise, the Supreme Court belatedly approved the

Kansas-Nebraska Act. A point of law was settled, but what about the human element—especially in Lancaster?

Just nine months after the Dred Scott decision, an event occurred which exposed the ugly undercurrent of racism and dehumanization that informed race relations in the nineteenth century. Although triggered by a brutal criminal act, public reaction seems to have been incommensurate with the magnitude of the crime. On December 15, 1857, two itinerant black chimney-sweeps and occasional thieves, Henry Richards and William Anderson, in the course of the attempted robbery of a farmhouse in Manheim Township, raped and brutally murdered two German women. The outcry created in this "Manheim tragedy" inflamed racial animosities and shocked local sensibilities. So violent was public reaction to the murders that at one point an attempt was reportedly contemplated to secure permission to burn the murderers alive. Anderson appealed to the officers of Lancaster's African Methodist Episcopal church to accept his body for burial. The request was denied, allegedly on moral grounds; more likely, the deprecations visited on the county's black community after the Christiana Riot were still fresh in memory.

Public executions had been banned in the Commonwealth since the 1830s, but when the convicted were executed inside the walls of the jail an enterprising individual rented spaces on a scaffold erected on a neighboring lot for $1 apiece to the curious onlookers of this public amusement. The descriptions of the executions published in the local press and in the special edition of Anderson's confession were both graphic and exact in their detail.

Given the indignities and injuries suffered by local blacks before the Civil War, it is almost incomprehensible that, when Fort Sumter fell and a call was issued for volunteers, a company of black volunteers was formed.[7] Their offer was, of course, refused since blacks were prohibited by state law from joining militias. It was not until 1862 that the arming of African Americans was seriously considered on the state and federal level. Given the comments on the possible unworthiness of African Americans for battle—all the achievements in previous American wars were conveniently forgotten—the call for black volunteers was answered.

Lancaster County's response compares favorably with the response elsewhere in the state and in the nation. Nationally, men of color served in 135 infantry regiments, six cavalry regiments, twelve regiments of heavy artillery, and ten batteries of the light artillery.[8] Pennsylvanians accounted for 5 percent of all blacks recruited for the war and thus ranked sixth overall, and first in the North.[9] In Pennsylvania, eleven regiments were raised between July 1863 and February 1865[10]; prior to that time, however, Massachusetts' call for volunteers had attracted 500 Pennsylvanians. The June 13, 1863, edition of the *Columbia Spy* listed twenty-three men from that area who were leaving to join the Massachusetts Fifty-fifth:

George Sweeney	James T. Ricks	Isaac Coats
Edward Miller	Isaac Cain	John Price
Jacob Lee	Frank Isar	William J. Stedem
Henry Way	Robert J. Smith	Isaiah Jackson
Charles Righly	Sam'l Wilson	Robert Davis
Jackson Griffin	John H. Diggs	Gabriel Shadd
Nicholas Berry	Edward Parker	Robert Last
Thomas Watson	Charles Brown	

Twenty-six Lancaster Countians served in the Massachusetts Fifty-fourth Volunteers, and perhaps the most famous of these was Stephen Swails, a native of Columbia who was enrolled in Elmira, New York, and because of bravery in battle was recommended for two promotions. Racial prejudice delayed his promotions to first lieutenant almost to the end of the war.

The effects of prejudice are dramatically portrayed in the film *Glory,* which underscores the inequity of the pay which black soldiers were offered. Although the government had reneged on its promise of equal pay, the men of the Fifty-fourth did not allow their anger to affect their devotion to duty. The regiment entered battle and acquitted itself quite well at the disastrous attack on Fort Wagner, which claimed the life of their commander, Colonel Shaw. Subsequent engagements turned skeptical observers into reluctant admirers of the colored troops' bravery under fire. The mood on the home front was, however, unchanged.

In June 1863 when the men were departing Lancaster to join their regiment, the *Examiner & Herald* reported:[11]

> as they passed by the different stations, they loudly cheered (themselves) but, with few exceptions, received no response; but instead thereof, insulting and scurrilous remarks respecting "nigger soldiers." Even the remarks of good Union men were, in the highest degree, unfeeling, such as—"That's the right way to get rid of the darkies," "I would rather see them sent off to be killed than white men."

Verbal abuse was the lesser of the abuse heaped on black recruits. On July 11, 1863, just a short time after the Gettysburg battle, a notice appeared in the *Daily Evening Express:*

TO MEN OF COLOR!
A Mass Meeting
of the able-bodied men of color will be held on
Wednesday at 8 o'clock, Fulton Hall,
Lancaster City,
to promote recruiting for
United States Colored Troops
For the War
Frederick Douglass
and other distinguished speakers will address the
meeting, and a detachment of the Third Regiment
U.S. Colored Troops will be present.

Frederick Douglass did not, however, have an opportunity to address a Lancaster audience on this occasion, for rather interesting reasons:

July marked the beginning of mass conscription for the war effort, and the results of the draft were published in area newspapers. In the county, 12,948 whites and 491 blacks were enrolled in various subdivisions. Only 10,409 were eligible, and of that number 3,030 were in military service on March 3, 1863. The whole draft process disturbed a segment of the local German population, and they displayed their objections quite forcefully on July 16. A crowd of Germans assembled outside the Lancaster courthouse and attempted to storm the draft office housed there. Thwarted in their efforts, the mob lay siege to the building, and even the appearance of the marshal and Mayor Sanderson did not restore law and order. According to newspaper accounts, the mob was led by a group of German women who shouted curses and brandished clubs.

The *Examiner & Herald,* which was decidedly unsympathetic to the Germans, described the rioters as "German men and women, principally of the lowest class," noted that many had given "leg bail" to avoid arrest and expressed the hope that "if these would be followed by several score of like chaps the community would be rid of a great nuisance, and the Howard Association during the coming winter have fewer noisy but unworthy claimants upon its relief fund."

To the *Examiner,* the incident was a semi-humorous semi-irksome occurrence involving the German underclass. This view was especially evident in the account of the Reverend Anthony Schwartz, of the German Catholic church, scolding the rioters from the pulpit on the Sunday following the "riot." The title of the report was "Pouring Hot Shot into the 'Riotous' Dutch Women."

The *Intelligencer,* Mayor Sanderson's paper, did not share the *Examiner*'s

Stephen Swails of Columbia, Lancaster County, was first
sergeant and later first lieutenant in Company F of the Fifty-
fourth Massachusetts Infantry regiment. He was the first
African American commissioned officer in the Massachusetts
regiments and was honored for his bravery in the Battle of
Olustee, February 20, 1864. (Courtesy of the U.S. Military
History Institute)

levity. Instead, sympathy was expressed with the motives of the rioters,
whom the editorialist described as "a few poor women who could not bear
the idea of having their husbands conscripted." Contributing to the excitement of the moment, according to the *Intelligencer,* was

> the unwise and unjustifiable attempt made by certain leading Aboli-
> tionists in Philadelphia to have the somewhat notorious and foul-
> mouthed Negro orator, Fred Douglass, deliver a lecture on the evening
> previous in Fulton Hall, and by the marching of a squad of armed

Negro soldiers from Philadelphia through our streets during the afternoon.[12]

The Democratic *Intelligencer* continues here the antiabolitionist politics which since the 1830s had pitted the ethnic underclass against blacks and portrayed the abolition crusade initiated by William L. Garrison as a thinly veiled attempt to promote amalgamation or interracial mixing.

Douglass did not appear in Lancaster. The reason given in a cancellation notice published on July 15 in the *Daily Evening Express* was that the organizers had been unaware that most of the able-bodied men of the city and county had already been recruited. This motive seems a bit suspect since the bulk of Lancaster Countians who served in a USCT regiment were enrolled after July 1863. Whether planned or not, the cancellation was fortuitous since, according to the *Express,* about fifty or sixty men, "principally Germans from the Northwest and Southeast wards, congregated in front of Fulton Hall, the object apparently being to disturb the meeting which was advertised to be held at that place by Fred Douglass."

Finding the meeting canceled, the men soon dispersed and were allowed to drift homeward unmolested by the police. The reporter for the *Express* mused: "Perhaps if they had been anywhere interfered with they would have endeavored to get up a miniature New York row." The reference is, of course, to the infamous Draft Riot. Either by happenstance or shrewd speculation, a serious racial incident was narrowly avoided. All was certainly neither quiet nor supportive for Lancaster's black soldiers on the homefront, but the latent and overt hostility did not seem to deter or dissuade them.

Without giving a litany of the engagements, battles, and skirmishes in which local blacks were involved, suffice it to say that the men served in the 3rd, 6th, 22nd, 24th, 25th, 32nd, 41st, 45th, and 127th USCT, as well as several regiments not organized in Pennsylvania. The war carried them to South Carolina, Virginia, Florida, and after the war six of the regiments served in Texas during the excitement over Maximilian. Instead of recounting martial accomplishments let us look at the human side of the war.*

The manuscript collection of the Lancaster County Historical Society contains two very rare letters. These letters were most probably sent to a Mr. and Mrs. Martin D. Hess from a soldier of the Forty-fifth USCT and contain fragmentary glimpses of the war written in a matter-of-fact and sometimes fractured English orthography and syntax. A soldier's simple faith is manifest

---

*EDITORS' NOTE: Short excerpts of a document entitled "Volunteer Enlistment" appeared in this section. Because we were unable to duplicate the item for this volume, we refer readers to the original essay for details.

in the statement "We have been in three or four batels and the Lord has spared me to come out." References are also made to a Samuel Harris, who, according to Ellis and Evans's *History of Lancaster County* joined the Third USCT but may have later joined the Forty-fifth. The letters contain the eternal complaint of anyone far from home: no letters received recently. The March 8, 1864, letter summarizes the soldier's war experiences quite succinctly: "Wish yaw would pleas tell George Foster & [illegible] to come down hear and take me out of this damd dirty hole."

The end of the war brought the veterans back to a cool reception. At home, the high hopes that most certainly inspired the early enthusiasm for the war were cooled in the postwar reality. Very little had changed. Slavery had ended, but black Pennsylvanians did not regain the right to vote until the Fifteenth Amendment was ratified in 1870. Education was still segregated and limited; the first black youth to graduate from high school did not do so until the 1880s, and as recently as the 1920s, black high school graduates were listed separately in high school yearbooks. Even though school segregation was outlawed in the 1880s, it lived on de facto well beyond that date, reinforced by the increasing ghettoization of the African American population. The veterans themselves kept alive the memory of their sacrifice, which the nation slowly and reluctantly honored only to question again in subsequent wars.

The 1890 Census of Soldiers, Sailors, Marines, and Widows presents an interesting mosaic of the war's aftermath. Seventy-six individuals living in Lancaster City, in twenty-one locations outside of the city, and in the county jail were identified. Interestingly enough, only ten widows were listed. One, Lucinda Moore, the widow of James Moore and a resident of 316 Middle Street in Lancaster, knew little about her late husband's military career, which moved the census taker to note in the margin: "This negro wench knows nothing." Abraham Wanner (a.k.a. Warner), my great-grandmother's brother, could not find his discharge papers, and therefore there is nothing in census about his exploits with the Twenty-second USCT. Afterward he was assigned to the Army of the James in January 1864 and participated in the battle of Petersburg. After the war, Wanner was present at Lincoln's funeral, participated in the capture of John Wilkes Booth, and was stationed for five months along the Mexican border in Texas.

Certainly not forgotten by their own community, some veterans formally organized their own GAR chapter on January 18, 1892, and named it Sergeant Benn Post No. 607 in honor of Job Benn, who had recruited men from the Christiana area for the First Pennsylvania Colored Volunteers. These men were then enrolled in the Third USCT. This GAR post first appeared in Polk's directory of Lancaster City for 1897 where we find: "Sergeant Benn Post,

607 (colored)—Meets every Friday evening, third floor in Reynolds Hall, 42½ N. Queen, Edward Wilson, Adjutant."[13] This Edward Wilson had been among the group of incorporators that included:[14]

William Proctor	David Molson
Jonathan Sweeney	John M. Book
Simon Molson	John Johnson
John H. H. Butler	Henry Barber
George Hall	Jacob Moore
Edward B. Harris	Steven Duban
Edward Wilson	David Offord
George Richardson	James Thomas
Anthony Maxwell	Zachariah Snively
Samuel Jackson	John Stotts
Bernard Sweeney	John M. Lebar
George Turner	Charles Green
Levi Anderson	Wesley Green

Although the post was named in honor of an individual associated with the Third USCT, the incorporators were representative of the entire spectrum of regiments connected to Lancaster County.

Men from the 3rd, 8th, 24th, 25th, 41st, 43rd, and 45th USCT were among the incorporators. And John Stotts, who in 1890 resided in Columbia, was a veteran of the Massachusetts Fifty-fourth. Sergeant Benn Post was therefore an institution with close ties to the African American community. Mrs. Maude Wilson Ball, the oldest living member of Lancaster's Bethel AME Church, recalls in her oral history of Bethel these veterans and the section of Bethel's cemetery reserved for their earthly remains.[15] The veterans' relationship to Bethel is especially evident from the 1898 entry in the city directory.

The post had moved and no longer met on North Queen Street; instead, it now convened at Bethel's hall, located at 525 Chester Street. Bethel had acquired the property just two years after an act of arson destroyed the historic sanctuary and meeting hall on Strawberry Street. Known first as "Love & Charity Hall" and then as "Odd Fellows Hall," this building housed many black social organizations. Sergeant Benn Post, Hod Carriers' Union No. 8020, and Mt. Horeb Lodge No. 14 F&AM met there until 1900. In that year, the GAR post relocated to 503 North Street and presumably remained there until 1909, when it moved again, this time to Columbia to the Odd Fellows Hall on Concord near Fifth Street. By the end of 1909, however, the post was disbanded, due probably to natural attrition.

Not all of Lancaster County's African American veterans were obliged to enroll in a segregated post. There is an intriguing photograph of the Lt. D. H. Nissley Post 478 (Mount Joy) which shows a group scene that includes William Jackson and Thomas Yellets. Jackson (1838–1913) served in Company F, 127th USCT, and Yellets, a descendant of a local family that can trace its roots to the Revolutionary War era, served in Company K of the 127th. It is not entirely clear whether the appearance of these men in a white GAR post was accidental or typical of other posts throughout the county. More research is needed.

The year 1993 is the 130th anniversary of the enlistment of men of color from Lancaster and throughout the Commonwealth to defend the United States Constitution and the sanctity of the Union. After the war, these men returned to a social status essentially unchanged from the prewar period. Despite what must have been the bitter disappointment of the Reconstruction era, local veterans remained patriotic and loyal to a nation only casually interested in their welfare. The measure of their devotion to their country is that, despite their war experiences and the segregation and discrimination they found upon their return to civilian life, many of the men lived to see the younger generation—brothers, sons, and nephews—enter the service of the nation to fight in the Spanish-American War and World War I. This remarkable sacrifice and dedication is deserving of our respect.

Notes

1. Carl D. Oblinger, *New Freedoms, Old Miseries: The Emergence and Disruption of Black Communities in Southeastern Pennsylvania, 1780–1860* (diss., Lehigh University, 1988), 235.

2. See "The Negro Entry Book: A Document of Lancaster City's Antebellum Afro-American," *Journal of the Lancaster County Historical Society* 88 (1984).

3. William Still, *The Underground Railroad: A Record of Facts, Authentic Narratives, Letters, etc.* (Philadelphia, 1872), 739.

4. Stephen Smith, Columbia, to the Hon. John Strohm, Harrisburg, January 15, 1836, Pennsylvania State Archives, Harrisburg.

5. Ibid.

6. *Lancaster Intelligencer,* March 17, 1857.

7. See *Daily Evening Express,* July 11, 1863.

8. William A. Gladstone, *United States Colored Troops, 1863–67* (Gettysburg, Pa., 1990), 11.

9. John B. Trussell, "So Loud Yon Bugles Blow" (manuscript), 522.

10. Ibid., 523.

11. *Examiner & Herald,* June 6, 1863.

12. *Lancaster Intelligencer,* July 1863 [date unknown].

13. *Polk's Lancaster City Directory, 1897.*

14. Charter of the Sergeant Benn Post No. 607 of Lancaster Pennsylvania State Archives.

The post was organized on January 18, 1892, in Philadelphia; it disbanded on December 31, 1909.

15. For some of the names of those buried at Bethel, see "Bethel African Methodist Church (Lancaster): Prolegomenon to a Social History," *Journal of the Lancaster County Historical Society* 90, no. 4 (205–36); see also my "Freedom's Second Generation," *Journal of the Lancaster County Historical Society.*

Appendix I to Chapter 7

This appendix represents information garnered from many sources, including regimental histories of the Massachusetts Fifty-fourth and Fifty-fifth Voluntary Troops, Colonel John Trussell's soon-to-be-published manuscript, and, most notably, the payment records of Lancaster County for indigent veterans and the WPA survey of veterans' graves. The compilation is not complete and needs augmentation. This represents a necessary first step. [*Editors' note:* Reprinted here exactly as it first appeared.]

Name	Rank	Regiment	Unit	Interred	Death
Aaron, Levi D.		22nd USCol. Inf.	Co. C	Hilltown, Colerain	Jun. 30, 1902
Anderson, John		54th USCT	Co. D		
Anderson, Levi		3rd USCT	Co. H	Mt. Bethel (PF)	1934
Archer, Franklin		3rd USCT	Co. A	Stevens Greenland	
Armstrong, Wesley		54th Mass. Vol.	Co. F	Marietta Borough	Jan. 1892
Atley, George		3rd USCT			
Barber, Henry C.	Private	45th USCT	Co. F	Stevens Greenland	1916
Ben, Jerome		3rd USCT			
Benson, John		3rd USCT			
Berry, Elijah		54th Mass. Vol.	Co. D		des. 5/20/6?
Berry, Nicholas		55th Mass. Vol.			
Bingle, William		3rd USCT			
Body, Charles W.		54th Mass. Vol.	Co. G		missing Ft. Wa
Bond, Joshua		3rd USCT			
Book, George	Private	6th Reg. Col. Tps	Co. E	St. Peters, Salisbury	
Boots, Arthur	Corporal	22nd USCol. Inf.	Co. K	St. Peters, Springvl.	Mar. 28, 1899
Boyer, Abraham		6th Col. Pa. Reg.	Co. B	St. Peters, Springvl.	
Brown, Franklin		32nd USCI	Co. B	Potters Field (PF)	1876
Brown, George		US NAVY		AME Church, Lanc.	
Brown, Joseph H.		41st Penna Col.	Co. E	Hilltown E. Drunmore	1894
Bucks, William		3rd USCT			
Burrell, Sylvester		54th Mass. Vol.	Co. D	Mt. Bethel (PF)	
Butler, J. H. H.	Corporal	24th USCol. Inf.	Co. I	AME, Lancaster	Sept. 28, 1899
Cain, Isaac		55th Mass. Vol.			
Carter, Lewis	Private	127th Col. Inf.	Co. A	Bird-In-Hand, ME	
Chew, Samuel M.		3rd			
Clark, Daniel	1st Sgt.	8th USCol. Reg.	Co. E	AME, Lancaster	
Clark, James	Corporal	41st Col. Inf.	Co. D	Stevens Greenland	
Coats, Isaac		55th Mass. Vol.			
Collins, James A.	Private	10th US Cavalry	Trp. M	Stevens Greenland	1917
Cook, George	Private	3rd USCT	Co. C.	Mt. Bethel (PF	
Cook, Reuben		3rd USCT			
Cooper, John W.	1st Sgt.	3rd Reg. USCT	Co. D	Columbia	Mar. 21, 1886

Name	Rank	Regiment	Unit	Interred	Death
Cowell, George	Private	127th Penn. Vol.	Co. B	Lincoln AME Mt. Joy	
Craig, Alexander		3rd USCT			
Craig, David	Private	25th USCol. Inf.	Co. A	Stevens Greenland	1921
Craig, William		3rd USCT			
Davis, James		54th Mass. Vol.	Co. D		
Davis, Robert	Sergeant	55th Mass. Vol.			
Dellam, Michael	Private	22nd USCol. Tr.	Co. K	Mt. Bethel (PF)	Feb. 9, 1897
Diggs, Henry	Private	25th USCol. Vol.	Co. F	Mt. Bethel (PF)	May 11, 1898
Drummore, George	Private	3rd USCT	Co. H	Mt. Bethel (PF)	1870
Eadens, Joseph		3rd USCT			
Edgerly, William		54th Mass. Vol.	Co. D		KIA Ft. Wayne
Edmond, John		32nd USCI	Co. I	Marietta, (PF)	Oct. 6, 1889
Erving, Joshua		55th Mass. Vol.			
Evillers, Fisher		3rd USCT			
Fairfax, Richard	Private	3rd Penna. Col.	Co. G	Zion Meth. Marietta	
Ferguson, George W.	Private	3rd Col. Reg.	Co. F	Union Presb.	
Fields, Isaac	Private	?	?	Penn Hill Fulton Tw	1888
Ford, Samuel		54th Mass. Vol.	Co. G		KIA Ft Wayne
Frey, David		3rd USCT			
Gails, Benjamin	Sergeant	3rd USCT			
Gibson, Madison		41st USC Troop	Co. B	Colored Cemetery	July 27, 1887
Green, Abe	Corporal	127th Col. Vols.	Co. K	Walton Farm Martic	
Green, Benjamin	Private	25th USCol. Inf.	Co. F	African Holtwood Rd	
Green, John	Private	22nd USCI	Co. K	Asbury, Gap	May 29, 1887
Gregg, Wm. Andrew		8th USCT	Co. D	Mt. Zion AME Sadsb	May 15, 1896
Griffin, Jackson		55th Mass. Vol.	Co. I	Mt. Bethel (PF)	
Hailstock, Charles A.	1st Sgt.	22nd USCol. Inf.	Co. H	Lancaster	Mar. 14, 1897
Hall, George	Sergeant	3rd USCol. Inf.	Co. G	Lanc. Cemetery	Oct. 1, 1894
Hallagher, David	Private	127th Penn. Co.	Co. C	Mennonite River	1916
Harris, Abraham	Private	8th USC Inf	Co. D	Old Asbury, Gap	1904
Harris, Edward B.	Corporal	43rd USVol. Inf.	Co. A	AME, Lancaster	1904
Harris, George J.	1st. Lt.	12th Penna. Col.	Co. E?		
Harris, Moses		54th Mass. Vol.	Co. G		
Harris, Samuel		3rd USCT			
Harris, Thomas	Private	32nd USCI	Co. F	Mt. Bethel (PF)	1906
Henry, Andrew	Private	127th Col. Inf.	Co. C	Mt. Bethel (PF)	1909
Henry, Benjamin	Corporal	41st USCI	Co. B	AME, Lancaster	1900
Henry, George	Private	127th Col. Inf.	Co. B	Mt. Bethel	1913
Henry, Thaddeus S.	Private	12th Penna. Col.	Co. M	Stevens Greenland	1929
Henson, John		127th Col. Vols.	Co. A&I	Watsons, Salisbury	Apr. 19, 1896

Name	Rank	Regiment	Unit	Interred	Death
Hill, John	Private	25th USCol. Inf.	Co.G	AME, Lancaster	1900
Hill, John	Private	25th USCol. Inf.	Co. D	AME Conestoga Tw	Oct. 10, 1900
Hillery, William E.		127th Col. Vols.	Co. E	Zion AME Sadsbury	Feb. 14, 1893
Hilton, William		3rd USCT			
Hoffmann, C. B.		? USCI		Lanc., Lancaster	1893
Holsinger, Uriah	Corporal	3rd USCo. Inf.	Co. A	Mt. Bethel (PF)	Dec. 27, 1894
Jackson, Abraham	Private	127th USCol. Inf.	Co. K	Lincoln AME Mt. Joy	1898
Jackson, Edward	Private	41st USCI	Co. D	AME, Lancaster	1906
Jackson, Isaac	Private	3rd USCol. Inf.	Co. E	Penn HIll (Fulton)	7/8/63absent
Jackson, William	Private	127th USCI	Co. F	Lincoln AME Mt. Joy	1913
James, Henry	Sgt Maj.	3rd USCT	Co. B	Mt. Zion AME	
Janes, James		3rd USCT			
Johnson, Charles	Private	3rd USCol. Inf.	Co. B	Old Asbury (Gap)	
Johnson, David	Private	25th USCI	Co. B	Mt. Bethel (PF)	
Johnson, John	Private	3rd USCol. Inf.	Co. F	AME, Lancaster	
Johnson, Lewis		3rd USCT			
Johnson, Samuel	Private	3rd USCol. Inf.	Co. A	AME, Lancaster	
Johnson, Thomas W.	Trooper	6th US Col. Tps	Co. B.	Mt. Hope ME, E.D.	Mar. 5, 1900
Jones, Robert	Musician	54th Mass. Vol.	Co. D		5/10/1865
Jones, William	Private	22nd USCol. Inf.	Co. K	Lancaster Cemm.	May 11, 1887
Kane, Robert	Corporal	54th Mass. Vol.	Co. D		
Kennard, William H.		54th Mass. Vol.	Co. D		
Kennedy, R.	Cook	US NAVY (1 yr.)		Hilltown, Colerain	1892
King, Hiram	Sergeant	127th Col. Inf.	Co. E	Asbury	1908
Landon, John		3rd USCT			
Laurrel, George		25th USCT	Co. K	Columbia Cemetery	Oct. 23, 1887
Loney, James A.	Private	127th Col. Inf.	Co. B	Mt. Bethel (PF)	April 1891
Looney, R.	Private	32nd USCI	Co. E	Columbia (PF)	1869
Lust, Robert		55th Mass. Vol.			
Magee, Daniel	Private	127th Col. Inf.	Co. I	Greenwood, Lanc.	1912
Martin, Jacob		3rd USCT			
Martin, Jessie	Private	23rd Pa. Col. Tr.	Co. F	Mt. Bethel (PF)	1916
Martin, Theodore	Private	24th USCol. Inf.	Co. E	St. Mary's Lanc.	1891
Martin, W.		22nd US Col. Tr.			1926
Maxwell, Abraham	Sergeant	25th USCI	Co. F	Stevens Greenland	1912
Maxwell, Anthony	Private	24th USCol. Inf.	Co. A	AME, Lancaster	
Mayhew, Henry	Private	32nd USCI	Co. B	Mt. Hope ME (PF)	Jan 6, 1887
McClintook, Lorenzo	Private	127th US Col. Inf.	Co. K	Eastland Friends	1928
McGill, Bruster		3rd USCT			
McGill, William	Private	3rd USCInf.	Co. C	Mt. Bethel (PF)	1872

Name	Rank	Regiment	Unit	Interred	Death
McKinney, Allen	Corporal	127th Reg. USCI	Co. H	Strasburg Preby.	Nov. 16, 1908
Meade, Andrew		54th Mass. Vol.		Mt. Bethel (PF)	
Middleton, Samuel		54th Mass. Vol.	Co. C		
Milford, Elias R.		3rd USCT			
Milford, Emory		3rd USCT			
Miller, Edward	Corporal	55th Mass. Vol.			
Mills, Stephen	Private	25th USCT	Co. H	Zion(col)Columbia	1869
Molson, David	Private	41st USCI	Co. B	Mt. Bethel (PF)	Nov. 27, 1898
Molson, James	Sergeant	41st USCI	Co. B	Mt. Bethel (PF)	
Molson, Simon	Corporal	25th USCI	Co. I	Mt. Bethel (PF)	
Molton, Charles	Private	24th USCol. Inf.	Co. A	Stevens Greenland	1925
Moore, Jacob J.	Private	32nd USCI	Co. H	Stevens Greenland	1936
Moore, James		2nd US Col. Cav	Co. L	Columbia Cemetery	May 12, 1889
Morris, Moses	Corporal	54th Mass. Vol.	Co. D		
Mouten, W.	Private	15th US Col. Vol.	Co. H	Columbia (PF)	
Nelson, George		32nd USCT	Co. K	Mt. Zion AME	July 7, 1895
O'Neal, John	Private	22nd USCol. Inf.	Co. K.	Lancaster	Aug. 25, 1892
Oaky, John		54th Mass. Vol.	Co. G		
Parker, Henry		54th Mass. Vol.	Co. D		Oct. 5, 1863
Parker, Isaac		3rd USCT			
Pierce, George	Private	32nd Penna. Inf.	Co. C	AME Marietta	1902
Pierce, Henry	Private	32nd Penna. Inf.	Co. C	AME Marietta	
Pinn, Walter Samuel		54th Mass. Vol.	Co. D		
Plesant, S.	Private	23rd USC inf.	Co. I	Columbia (PF)	
Presberry, William	Private	25th USCI	Co. A	Drumore Friends	
Proctor, William	Private	8th USCol. Inf.	Co. H	Greenwood, Lanc.	1906
Prosser, George T.		54th Mass Vol.	Co. D		
Quomany, Abraham J.	Corporal	24th US Col. Inf.	Co. E	Stevens Greenland	1912
Randolph, John	Private	32nd Penna. Inf.	Co. I	Mt. Bethel (PF)	1890
Reynolds, James	Private	24th USCol. Inf.	Co. E	Mt. Bethel (PF)	
Rice, Daniel A.	Private	32nd Col. Vols.	Co. C	Mt. Bethel (PF)	1910
Richards, John		32nd	Co. C		
Richardson, G. W.	Private	24th USCol. Inf.	Co. D	Greenwood Mifflin G.	1905
Richardson, Sanderson	Private	45th USCI	Co. K	Stevens Greenland	1911
Richardson, William	Private	3rd USCol. Inf.	Co. I	Lincoln AME, Mt. Joy	
Richfield, Melchia	Private	127th Penna. Co.	Co. G	Mt. Zion AME	1918
Ridgley, Charles		55th Mass. Vol.			
Ring, Thomas C.		3rd USCT			
Roberts, John		3rd USCT			
Roberts, William G.		3rd USCT			
Robinson, Lewis		54th Mass. Vol.	Co. A		
Sebastian, P. G.		5th Mass. Cav.	Co. H	Beth, AME Marietta	
Shadd, C. J.		55th Mass. Vol.	Co. I	Mt. Bethel (PF)	

Name	Rank	Regiment	Unit	Interred	Death
Shadd, Charles		55th Mass. Vol.			
Shively, Zacharias	Private	3rd USCol. Inf.	Co. H.	Mt. Bethel	
Singelton, C. H.	Sergeant	24th USCol. Inf.	Co. C	Lancaster Cem.	Oct. 28, 1893
Smith, James	Private	32nd USCI	Co. K	St. Johns UB	1907
Smith, Levi		3rd USCT			
Smith, Robert		55th Mass. Vol.			
Smith, Samuel	Private	25th USCI	Co. F	Mt. Bethel	Mar. 4, 1894
Stedman, William J.	Sergeant	55th Mass. Vol.			
Stotts, John H.		54th Mass. Vol.	Co. D	Mt. Bethel	Jun 22, 1893
Swailes, Stephen Atkins	1st Lt.	54th Mass. Vol.			
Swayne, Stephen		3rd USCT			
Sweeney, George W.		55th Mass. Vol.			
Sweeny, Samuel	Fifer	3rd USCT	Co. H	Lancaster County	Mar. 10, 1901
Sweeny, Stephen		3rd USCT	Co. J		
Taylor, Joseph		6th Regiment			
Thomas, William		32nd USCT	Co. I		
Thompson, Miller		3rd USCT			
Thompson, Nathan		3rd USCT			
Thomson, Abram		3rd USCT			
Thomson, John		3rd USCT			
Tillson, Isaac		41st USCT	Co. B		
Turner, George		24th USCT	Co. G	Harford Co., MD	Sep. 28, 1893
Turner, John J.		54th Mass. Vol.	Co. D		
Turner, John		3rd USCT			
Turner, Solomon		54th Mass. Vol.	Co. D		
Turner, William		3rd USCT	Co. H	Family Graveyard	May 6, 1900
Warner, Abraham		22nd USCT	Co. E	AME Conestoga	1896 in Hbg.
Waters, John	1st Sgt.	22nd USCT	Co. K	AME, Lancaster	Nov. 23, 1897
Webster, Alfred	Sergeant	6th USCol. Inf.	Co. F		
Webster, Jeremiah	Sergeant	25th USCT	Co. A		
Wesley, John		25th USCT	Co. A	Columbia Colored	Mar. 27, 1888
Wesley, John H.		25th USCT	Co. A		
West, Lewis		54th Mass. Vol.	Co. D		
White, Jonathan		3rd USCT			
Williams, Dorsey		127th Col. Inf.	Co. I		
Williams, Lewis				Strasburg Presby.	Aug. 1913
Wilson, Isaac		3rd USCT			
Wilson, Stephen		?USCI	Co. H		
Wilson, Thomas		3rd USCT			
Woodborn, George/ John		24th USCT	Co. G	Compass, Ches Co.	Apr. 21, 1899
Wright, Lorenzo		3rd USCT			
Young, John W.		54th Mass. Vol.	Co. D		
Young, Robert		3rd USCT			

Appendix II

This table is drawn from the 1890 census of widows and veterans.

Name	Rank	Unit	Service	Location
Alford, Daniel	Private	E, 21st Cav.	3/13/65–2/15/66	Columbia
Anderson, Levi	Private	H, 3rd		Columbia
Archer, Jacob	Private	K, 45th		Drumore
Benson/Green,				
Chas.	Private	A, 25th	6/4/64–12/6/65	Lancaster
Boddy, Harriet	Private	G, 54th Mass.		528 Middle St.
Boyer, Theodore	Private	E, 25th		Wakefield
Brown, Frances	Private	B, 32nd		Marietta
Brown, Stephen	Private	K, 24th	11/3/65–1/10/65	210 Middle St.
Butcher, Julia	Private	K, 127th		McSparran
Butler, John H.	Private	I, 24th		Lancaster
Cook, Reuben A.	Private	K, 3rd		Furnis
Cook, Robert	Private	E, 33rd		Lititz
Craig, David	Private	A, 25th		Edwin
Craig, Irwin	Private	I, 3rd		Nine Points
Devals, Solomon	Private	F, 22nd		Columbia
Diggs, Henry	Private	F, 25th		Prison
Dorsey, Phillip	Private	I, 127th		Columbia
Elder, Lydia	Private	K, 22nd		Columbia
Fells, Isaac	Private	I, 25th	2/9/64–10/6/65	Lancaster
Forward, Filena	Private			McSparran
Green, Henry	Private	41st		Green Bank
Harris, Christian	Private	B, 43rd		Lancaster
Harris, Edward	Corporal	A, 43rd	3/4/64–10/20/65	Lancaster
Harris, George	Private	6th		Ephrata
Harris, Thomas	Private	F, 32nd	2/26/64–8/22/66	Columbia
Henry, Andrew	Private	G, 127th		Prison
Henry, Benjamin	Corporal	B, 41st		Lancaster
Henry, George	Private	D, 127th		Columbia
Henry, Thaddeus S.	Private	M, 2nd US Cav.	2/18/64–2/12/66	Lancaster
Hopkins, Samuel	Private	E, 32nd	2/24/64–3/14/65	Quarryville
Johnson, John	Private	F, 3rd		Lancaster

Name	Rank	Unit	Service	Location
Johnson, Thomas	Private	B, 6th		Quarryville
Johnson, Samuel	Private	A, 3rd		346 N. Christian
Jones, Albert	Private	C, 25th		Prison
Lake, Charles W.	Private	D, 4th	8/26/63–5/4/66	Lancaster
Landsdale, Richard	Private	A, 127th	8/22/64–10/20/65	Christiana
Lebar, John M.	Corporal	I, 24th	3/17/65–10/1/65	Lancaster
Lefever, George	Private	G, 122nd		Quarryville
Lewis, James H.	Private	K, 127th		Colerain
Loney, Benjamin	Private	C/E, 25th		Columbia
Loney, James	Private	E, 127th		Columbia
Lyons, John	Private	C, 45th		Collins
Magee, Daniel	Private	I, 47th	9/6/64–9/8/65	Lancaster
Malson, David	Private	B, 41st		
Malson, James	Private	B, 41st		Columbia
Malson, Simon	Private			Columbia
Martin, Theodore	Private	E, 24th	2/18/65–10/10/65	Lancaster
Maxwell, Anthony	Private	A, 24th	1/18/65–10/1/65	Lancaster
Mayhew, William	Private	I, 8th		Bartville
McKinney, Allen	Private	H, 127th		Strasburg
Moore, Lucinda	Private			316 Middle St.
Nelson, George	Private	K, 32nd		Christiana
Pierce, George W.	Private	C, 32nd		Marietta
Proctor, William	Private	H, 3rd		Lancaster
Rice, Daniel	Private	C, 32nd		Columbia
Richfield, Malach	Private	G, 127th		Wakefield
Robinson, Amelia	Private	K, 22nd		Columbia
Smith, John	Private	H, 40th	1/17/67–8/26/68	Columbia
Smith, Samuel	Private	K, 22nd		Columbia
Snively, Zachary	Private	H, 3rd		
Steele, James A.	Private	C, 25th		Gap
Stotts, John	Private	D, 54th Mass		Columbia
Stout, Jonathan	Private	G, 32nd		Peters Creek
Sweeney, Barnard	Private	F, 21st		Columbia
Sweeney, Cather	Private	I, 55th Mass		Columbia
Sweeney, Steven	Private	3rd USCT	7/21/63–10/31/65	416 N. Market

Name	Rank	Unit	Service	Location
Swift, Edward E.	Private	A, 4th	3 yrs.	Fulton House
Turner, George	Private	G, 24th		Columbia
Walker, Glenn	Musician	B, 32nd		Marietta
Wanner, Abraham	Private	E, 22nd	12/25/63–(3 yrs)	Lancaster
Wilson, Sarah J.	Private	I, 3rd		Lancaster
Wilson, Susanna	Private	B, 32nd	2/7/62?–7/24/62	Lancaster
Woods, Jacob	Private	E, 22nd		316 Middle St.
Woods, Peter	Sergeant	K, 32nd		Prison
Yellets, Thomas	Private	K, 127th		Florin

CHAPTER EIGHT

Nineteenth-Century Philadelphia Black Militant:
Octavius V. Catto (1839–1871)

Harry C. Silcox

One of the least mentioned figures in Pennsylvania's struggle for human rights during the Reconstruction Era is black teacher Octavius Valentine Catto. He was the one leader around whom Philadelphia blacks rallied and the one that the state's Radical Republicans most consulted. Possessor of a combative and aggressive nature, Catto was linked with every important black movement of the day. His assassination in the election riots of 1871 only served to enhance his popularity and make him a martyr still remembered with pride by black Philadelphians. No less a figure than W. E. B. Du Bois was taken by Catto's youthfulness, militancy, and courage on behalf of black causes. To him, Catto's death was a tragedy for urban northern blacks.[1] Although documentation concerning Catto's birth is unavailable, his family heritage indicates that he was in all likelihood born free. When Octavius was five years old, the Presbyterian church called his father to Philadelphia, and eventually to the ministry of the First African Presbyterian Church.[2]

Catto's father, William T. Catto, advocated an articulate black ministry and spoke for Philadelphia blacks who favored higher education. To him, "the church has its aim and its end, it is an intelligent intellectual body . . .

This chapter was first published in *Pennsylvania History* 44 (January 1977): 53–76. Reprinted by permission.

ever growing, enlightening, civilizing and Christianizing." The history of the First African Presbyterian Church written by Catto in 1857 remains today an expression of these beliefs and a valuable historical record of the black churches in antebellum Philadelphia.[3]

William's intellectual curiosity and emphasis on scholarly pursuits provided a model for Octavius to pursue in later life. This, coupled with William's belief in individual responsibility and a life anchored by deep religious convictions, formed the basic principles by which Octavius would live. Every individual had a responsibility to contribute to the progress of mankind, never to be pushed aside by the will of the masses. As William Catto often told his audiences, "Every man, more or less, has some part to perform in the drama of life. . . . As individuals we must go forward and contribute our something toward the press of interest that impels forward; who moves not will be pushed aside; or irresistibly borne forward, uncared for and unhonored."[4] Aware that governments might stand in the way of the individual and his advancement, William Catto cautioned that "no man in the great world of life and action can be idle and indifferent to the callings and claims of government."[5] Individual responsibility as advocated by William included a life based on Christian morality and virtuous behavior. Octavius "must be the salt of the earth; [his] example in life and practice must show to me that [he has] been with Christ and [has] been taught by him; this [he] must evidence by [his] life." Clearly, the values learned at his father's knee by Octavius were the necessity to strive for an education, the responsibility of each individual to improve mankind, the adoption of a Christian way of life, and a concern for government.

In addition to this home training, Octavius Catto gained the rudiments of his education at the local public schools. He attended the segregated Vaux Primary School, held in a church near his home. So primitive were the facilities that school had to be closed on days of funerals since the services took place in the school hall and the burial in the schoolyard.[6] Later Catto attended the more elaborate but also segregated Lombard Grammar School taught by Quaker James Bird. The emphasis at Lombard was upon systematic drill and repetition as then in use under the Lancaterian system of instruction.[7] In 1853 the family moved to Allentown, New Jersey, where, by the influence of former Governor William A. Newell, Octavius gained admission to that city's white academy. The next year he returned to Philadelphia ready to attend the newly opened black high school, the Institute for Colored Youth.[8]

Begun by a group of Quakers as a farm school in 1842, the institute moved to the city in 1852 at the urging of a group of black ministers led by William Catto.[9] As might be expected, Catto and his supporters prevailed upon the Quakers to change the curriculum from farming and trade preparation to

Octavius Catto taught at the Institute for Colored Youth, a
forerunner of today's Cheyney University. Cheyney and Lincoln
University of Pennsylvania are institutions of higher education
with a long history of service to the Commonwealth's African
American community. (Courtesy of the Pennsylvania State
Archives)

courses in higher mathematics, Greek, and Latin. Haitian-born Charles L.
Reason, a professor of mathematics at New York Central College, was hired
to be in charge of implementing this new curriculum. Reason never neglected
his primary goal of establishing an academic atmosphere at the institute. As
soon as the institute opened, he ordered that a school library be established.
By the end of the school's second year there were 1,300 volumes on hand for
the use of students. Lectures were held nightly in the library, enabling the
institute to become the intellectual center of the black community.[10]

Clearly the blacks, led by Catto, had created a high school for their children similar to the newly established Central High School attended by whites only. The Quakers were to maintain control over the financial aspects of the school, the hiring of a faculty, and the admission and dismissal of students, but Reason was given responsibility for what was to be taught and for the day-to-day operation of the school. Given his Haitian background and nurtured in the revolutionary fires of an earlier generation and his beliefs in equality, Reason offered black students more than academic training. His stories of Haiti and its free people encouraged black students to seek more forcefully their own goals of freedom and equal rights.[11]

During Octavius's stay at the institute, Jacob C. White Jr., son of the director of Catto's father's Sunday school, became his closest friend, a relationship which would last for the remainder of their lives.[12] Both joined the Banneker Debating Society, a group which met during evening hours in the institute building to discuss scholarly matters and the events of the day. Catto often presented papers at these weekly meetings. Undoubtedly, the Debating Society provided an oratorical training ground for the young scholar.[13]

In 1855, to the disappointment of Catto and the other students, Reason resigned his post, and black teacher Ebenezer Don Carlos Bassett succeeded him. A graduate with high honors from the Birmingham Academy and the Connecticut Normal School, Bassett had taught in the public grammar schools of New Haven and taken graduate courses at Yale University. The students found their new principal capable and prepared to continue the academic courses instituted by Reason.[14]

Bassett came to recognize the scholarly Catto as one of the his best students. In 1858, Octavius became the fourth graduate of the institute and won high praise from Bassett at the graduation ceremonies for "outstanding scholarly work, great energy, and perseverance in school matters."[15] Still, Catto was not satisfied with his ability to speak and use the classical languages. After leaving the institute, he went to Washington, D.C., for an additional year of study. Private tutoring in the Latin and Greek languages by Professor Caruthers followed. Feeling himself completely qualified and versed in the language arts, Catto now returned to his old teacher, Ebenezer Bassett, seeking a position at the institute. Bassett agreed to support Catto, and the Quaker board of managers made the appointment effective in September 1859.[16]

During the next twelve years, Catto became one of the most respected blacks in the state. His wide circle of friends and supporters encompassed most of the young blacks in the cities along the East Coast. His rapport with white leaders, especially politicians, made him one of the most renowned local blacks of his day. In addition, his teaching career at the institute brought him recognition among blacks and whites, for despite time spent in organizations outside the classroom, he was always prepared with scholarly lectures.[17]

His address to the graduating class on May 10, 1864, entitled "Our Alma Mater," was so well received that it was printed for distribution. In this pamphlet, Catto advocated a new building for the institute to be located on Bainbridge Street above Ninth. He complimented the Quaker board: "We may readily perceive the intention of the Board to make this a first class institution among the best of our Normal Schools. For this noble determination on their part, . . . the colored people themselves should be grateful and their friends well pleased." To Catto's credit, the new building was completed and opened for classes in 1866.[18]

Octavius's position at the institute and his growing reputation made him one of the most eligible bachelors in the city. Always preferring to wear well-made expensive clothing, he dressed immaculately. His light brown skin and black hair and mustache and his intellectually based charm made him popular with the opposite sex. Catto's charm and literary style are apparent from a note that accompanied a gift to his girlfriend Cordelia Sanders in 1860:

> And if, perchance one pleasing ray,
> Of true poetic fevor beams,
> Along my unambitious way
> Thyself hath been th' inspiring theme.
> Accept it then and believe me
> Yours Always and always yours.
>
> O. V. Catto[19]

By 1867, Catto had settled on the girl he wished to marry. She was Caroline V. LeCount, a graduate of the Institute for Colored Youth and a teacher in the public schools of the city. Octavius came to center his attentions on Caroline because of their similar interest and background. Both were to be important contributors to black education and to the fight for equal rights in the city of brotherly love during their lifetimes.[20]

Given these circumstances, Octavius Catto could have married and lived in middle-class respectability, a financially comfortable existence, but he did not choose to do so. Remembering the earlier advice of his father, Catto increasingly directed his energies and talents toward the progress of blacks in a prejudiced white world. Early in his teaching career he came to realize that it was folly to rely upon schools alone to solve the problems facing blacks. The real issues, as his father had warned years before, were traceable to formal and informal laws supported by government. Catto came to see that the solutions to educational issues rested on the ability of blacks to change racially restricting laws. In order to accomplish this, Catto joined numerous organizations and groups in the private sector of the community. These activities outside the classroom shaped his destiny.

It was during the Civil War that Catto first began to attract public attention. In June of 1863, General Robert E. Lee's army moved northward toward an eventual showdown with the Union army at Gettysburg. The Philadelphia newspapers were filled daily with the events of the northward movement. Governor Andrew Curtin and Mayor Alexander Henry issued proclamations calling for new recruits to bolster the state militia. Ignored by most Philadelphians, the call to arms caused great excitement in the black community. Meetings were held in the black churches of the city, fifers and drummers paraded in the streets, and orations of patriotism occurred throughout the day. Headquarters were opened at the Institute for Colored Youth at 715–717 Lombard Street for the expressed purpose of recruiting a black company. The students at the institute were in the center of the recruiting activity. Catto was among the first to volunteer and immediately was selected to lead the newly formed company. The institute students followed Catto almost en masse— Lombard L. Nickens, William T. Jones, Martin M. and Joseph White, Joseph B. Adger, Andrew Glasgow, Henry Boyer Jr., Joseph G. Anderson Jr., and Jacob R. Ballard leaving school to go off to fight Lee's army.[21]

The newly organized company, with Catto leading the way, marched to the West Philadelphia train station, where a large number of blacks had gathered to say their farewells. Upon reaching Harrisburg, they were fully mustered in and issued equipment, but Major General Darius N. Couch, of the Department of the Army in the Susquehanna area, refused to allow them to be inducted. His excuse was that Congress provided for the enlistment of blacks for not less than three years. Since this company was an emergency militia unit enlisted for limited services of a few months, they could not serve. Considering the dire state of the nation, Couch's view indicates his prejudice.

Reading of Couch's decision in the June 18, 1863, *North American and U.S. Gazette,* Secretary of the Army Edwin M. Stanton telegraphed Couch: "You are authorized to receive into the service any volunteer troops that may be offered, without regard to color." But it came too late. The damage was done, since the Catto-led black company had returned to Philadelphia.[22]

The black community and various segments of the white community became indignant when told of the treatment of the black troops. Scarcely a week elapsed after Catto's return from Harrisburg before he attended a mass meeting at Franklin Hall to protest Couch's actions. Speeches by blacks and whites decried the treatment of Catto's recruits. Major George Stearns, one of the few whites in favor of enlisting the black regiment sent to Harrisburg; William D. Kelley, the Republican congressman; Ebenezer D. Bassett, the principal of the institute; and black David E. Gipson spoke out for the necessity of enlisting black troops. The rally produced resolutions in which Philadelphia blacks offered to throw "aside unpleasant memories of the past," to look to the future, and to ask only the same guarantees and fair play received by whites. They also reiterated their "willingness and readiness to defend the union."[23]

This meeting led to rumors in Philadelphia that a proscribed list of blacks, Catto included, were being singled out for hostile treatment by white groups. For this reason, blacks deemed it wise to move "cautiously" on the streets and to go home early at night.[24]

George Stearns turned to the Union League and appealed to patriotic Philadelphians to help. Finally, a group of seventy-five Philadelphians organized themselves as the Supervisory Committee for Recruiting Colored Regiments. Cooperating with Stearns, this committee raised eleven regiments of U.S. troops for Pennsylvania and established the Free Military School at 1210 Chestnut Street for white officer candidates who were to become leaders of black regiments. Camp William Penn, the training ground of black soldiers located in Chelten Hills, also became part of the committee's responsibility. Events now occurred with such rapidity that by the end of 1863 Philadelphia blacks were wearing the uniform of the Union Army.[25]

Octavius V. Catto became active in the first division of the Pennsylvania National Guard. Commander General Louis Wagner, recognizing his abilities, approved his appointment as a major and inspector for the Fifth Brigade. Undoubtedly Catto gained increased military status because of his continued close association with members of the Republican party and his membership in the newly formed Equal Rights League. Wagner found Catto to be a "conscientious and faithful officer . . . [who] labored effectively in the organization of this command . . . [an] honored and respected soldier of the Commonwealth." Army records and what is known of Catto's life during the war years indicate that he never saw action but remained in the Philadelphia area, where he continued his service as a teacher at the institute.[26]

Catto's military experience made him an ardent and confirmed Republican. He saw the principles of republicanism as the hope for American blacks. The formation of a state Equal Rights League was welcomed by Catto, since it was begun by Republicans with the expressed purpose of helping blacks to gain the right to vote. In October 1864 he met with black leaders from all over the country at the National Convention of Colored Men in Syracuse, New York. At the opening session, Convention President Frederick Douglass declared: "We are here to promote the freedom, progress, elevation, and perfect enfranchisement of the entire people of the United States."[27] To Douglass, the cause of acquiring equal rights demanded national organization.

Organization of a National Equal Rights League supported by state leagues followed, with Douglass as president.

In November of 1864, Pennsylvania's blacks met in Philadelphia to found the Pennsylvania State Equal Rights League. Catto was elected to the position of corresponding secretary; Jacob C. White Jr., recording secretary; and William Nesbitt of Altoona, president. The league's objectives consisted of encouraging "morality, education, temperance, frugality, industry, and prompt[ing] everything that pertains to a well ordered and dignified life and to obtain by appeals to the mind and conscience of the American people or by legal process a recognition of the rights of the colored people."[28] Leaders Nesbitt and Catto urged the systematic arrangement of auxiliary leagues in every city and town of the state. By the time of the first statewide convention in Harrisburg in February 1865, the Pennsylvania Equal Rights League had organizations in sixteen of the larger cities. The Philadelphia delegation of twenty-four men, headed by Catto and Joseph Bustill, constituted the largest bloc of voters.

After electing Reverend John Peck of Pittsburgh president, the league proceeded to the business of discussing the specific demands of the state's black population. What occurred next displayed Catto's ability to crystallize the thinking of blacks into specific demands. It all began on the second day of the convention, when James J. Wright of Wilkes-Barre presented what he hoped would be the convention's stand on education.

> Inasmuch as the School Law of Pennsylvania provides that where there are twenty children of African descent, a separate school shall be established for them; and as we know by experimental knowledge, that colored children make greater advancement under the charge of colored teachers than they do under white teachers, therefore we consider it . . . incumbent . . . , as lovers of the advancement of our race, to see to it, that our schools are under the charge of colored teachers.[29]

John Quincy Allen, the first black teacher in Philadelphia's public schools and at the time a teacher at the Institute for Colored Youth, took the floor and spoke against passage of the resolution. Allen argued for an amendment that "no discrimination on account of color ought to be made in the appointment of teachers for colored schools," since this convention by its very declaration was for equal rights for all men.[30] Reverend William J. Alston, of the Sanitary Commission at Philadelphia's St. Thomas Presbyterian Church, disagreed with Allen, noting that the abilities of black teachers to teach black students "had been made evident to him by the experience of twelve years, and instanced [in] the difference in appearance between the schools under white and those under colored teachers."[31]

Wright, loath to accept Allen's amendment, advocated passage of his original resolution. He told Allen: "There [is] no use of our making provision about literary qualifications, for white teachers sufficiently qualified could not be induced to take charge of colored schools." He was "surprised to hear gentlemen of intelligence discussing this amendment favorably." Alfred Green thought it disgraceful for colored men, particularly those of the Philadelphia delegation, to argue against Wright's resolution, since they knew better than anyone the poor treatment "which colored persons had received at the hands of that city's Board of Controllers." Green believed that any black Philadelphian at the convention who voted for Allen's amendment would "be ashamed to meet their constituents."[32]

Allen's amendment was voted down by the convention. Catto then asked to address the convention. He agreed with the black-teachers-in-black-schools argument, but he disagreed with the phraseology, since such a resolution might be quoted as a statement based on preference for certain teachers merely on account of color. Catto "did not wish to turn his back on the fact that the colored man was the best teacher for colored children [since] he had long been of the belief that no white man could so well instruct colored children as could a colored teacher." He credited the latter's success to a clear recognition by all blacks that black teachers "had the welfare of the race more at heart, knowing that they rose or fell together."[33] Catto's amendment read: "In the appointment of teachers for these schools, colored persons, their literary qualifications being sufficient, should receive the preference, not by reason of their complection, but because they are better qualified by conventional circumstances outside of the school-house."[34] With this addendum, Wright's motion passed unanimously and served as a plank in the platform of the State Equal Rights League.

This educational platform became the credo for Catto's fellow teachers at the Institute for Colored Youth. Motivated partly by their own need for employment and partly by their feeling that they were fitted best to educate black children, institute members advocated Catto's stand for the next thirty years. Complaints in the black newspaper *The Christian Recorder* also advanced Catto's position and illustrated his ability to speak for his people in racial matters:

> It constrains us more than ever to adhere to our motto of "Colored teachers for colored schools," and further that those white teachers take no real interest in their work nor of the scholars but teach and

tolerate them only in order to enable them to draw the money they receive at the end of each month.[35]

Now, if white people of this country are so bitterly opposed to sending their children to school with the colored, why is it that they are so anxious to teach us? . . . It must be the dollars and cents they are after and not the moral interest of our children. . . . We are tired of white overseers, we got enough of them during the days of slavery.[36]

Catto's role in reconciling the opposing elements at the Equal Rights Convention, while still proposing a platform which had the support of the black community, demonstrates his leadership qualities among his people. However, his position on black teachers for black schools make him a greater threat to whites who were coming more and more to the view that the institute was the center for black malcontents. Rumors of teachings about Haiti, the enlistment of blacks for military service, and the news that Catto had become a moving force in the Equal Rights League all tended to arouse whites against schools with an all-black teaching staff. As Catto was demonstrating at the institute, black teachers in black schools meant a loss of control over black students by whites and increased opportunities for the development of militant black leadership. What Catto did next attracted these growing antagonisms to him personally.[37]

Continuing his interest in the Equal Rights League during the Reconstruction era, Catto used the weight of that organization to fight for the desegregation of Philadelphia streetcars in 1866. While some blacks tried to force the local streetcar companies to change their policies, Catto took another approach.[38] Appointed to lead a three-man committee from the Equal Rights League, he went to Harrisburg to solicit the support of legislators in ruling against the segregation of streetcars throughout the state. There he solicited the support of national representatives Thaddeus Stevens and William D. Kelley and state representative Morrow B. Lowry to influence state legislators to support black claims. Also helpful in publicizing events surrounding the controversy was Colonel John W. Forney, owner of the *Philadelphia Press*.[39] Catto's tactics won the day, for despite local foot-dragging by city officials, the state legislature, under pressure from Radical Republicans, passed on March 22, 1867, a bill that desegregated the streetcars of the state.

Just three days after passage of the law, Catto's fiancée, Caroline LeCount, was refused entry to a streetcar at Ninth and Lombard Streets. Adding insult to the injustice, the conductor shouted: "We don't allow niggers to ride." How influential Catto was in what transpired next is uncertain, but Caroline went to a local magistrate, who would not act since he had not received official notification of the law and would not rely on newspaper reports. Not to be discouraged, Caroline went to the Pennsylvania secretary of state, who was then in the city, obtained a copy of the bill, and returned to the magistrate. The conductor was arrested and fined $100. With this, the rights of the blacks to ride streetcars in Philadelphia were ensured.[40]

The streetcar victory served to increase the respect and admiration of local blacks toward Catto, but it was his athletic ability that broadened his popular appeal to include blacks from the various urban centers of the North. Despite his medium size and a tendency to be stout, Catto was an agile baseball player. While still a student at the institute, Catto learned the English game of cricket in games played against Lombard School. In 1865 Catto, like many Union soldiers, began to play the American version of the same game: baseball.[41]

The first black baseball team to leap into prominence was the Monitor Club of Jamaica, Long Island (1865). Then came the Bachelors of Albany, New York (1865), followed by the Excelsiors of Philadelphia (1866). Other teams forming at the same time were the Mutual and Alert Clubs of Washington, D.C.; the Blue Sky Club of Camden, New Jersey; the Monrovia Club of Harrisburg; and the Unique Club of Chicago.[42]

Philadelphia became the center of interest for black baseball in the late 1860s, when a second local team was formed. The Pythians, as they came to be called, were captained by Catto, who was also the team's star player. During these early years, there was keen competition between the two Philadelphia teams for players, prompting some black families and friends to feud over which team to support.[43]

More than just a game, baseball provided the Philadelphia black community with a social event which, in some cases, lasted over an entire week. There were picnics, dances, and lunches showered upon the players. Black women planned nightly entertainment and dinners that caused great excitement within the community. This was particularly true in September 1867, when the first black team to visit the city, the Bachelors from Albany, came to play a series against Catto's Pythians. A field was equipped with stands at Eleventh and Wharton Streets, and the beginning of a black baseball dynasty had begun.[44]

Later the same month, the Mutual and Alert baseball clubs of Washington visited Philadelphia. The Mutual team listed among its players two young prominent blacks of the day: Major Charles R. Douglass, son of Frederick Douglass, and Hugh M. Brown, later principal of the Cheyney Training School. By the end of the 1867 season, Catto's Pythians had compiled a record of nine wins and one loss—that to the Bachelors.[45]

That winter, meetings of the Pythian Club were held in a second-floor room at Liberty Hall, Seventh and Lombard Streets, to determine means for strengthening the team. Catto and Jacob C. White Jr. formulated plans to improve the team. Hard practice during the spring and a few new players seemed the best approach. That spring, Catto enticed two outstanding players to join the Pythians. The first, John Cannon, was "considered by whites a baseball wonder," even in those early days of the sport. Of equal ability was George Brown of West Chester, "a pitcher, the best amateur of his day." The result of the training by Catto, and the addition of these two players, was an undefeated season in 1867. All of this served to increase Catto's popularity with lower-class blacks, who were spectators and participants in baseball.[46]

Baseball had provided Catto with a vehicle for gaining contacts with blacks from other sections of the country. Games with black teams from Chicago, Brooklyn, Albany, and Washington had permitted social intercourse and discussions of the major issues of the day. Communication between the various black communities of the North had been enhanced, and Catto's leadership among young blacks was becoming more evident.

In 1868 a group of white teams met in Harrisburg to form the Pennsylvania Convention of Baseball Clubs. As might be expected, Catto's undefeated Pythian Club attempted to join the league and integrate baseball. Although they were supported by Representatives Hayhurst and Ellis of the Philadelphia Athletics, the majority of white teams opposed the black team's membership. Again, even in his leisure time, Catto became a central figure in efforts to remove discriminatory barriers facing blacks. His aggressive nature and strivings for equality had again exceeded the role that whites expected of blacks. In this case, he offended the lower classes of white society that enjoyed baseball. They intended to keep their teams and league white, and they did.[47]

Catto's dealings with the Quaker board of managers at the Institute for Colored Youth reflected a similar discontent on his part with the status quo. He had always demanded fair and equal treatment from the board. As a new, underpaid teacher in 1862, Catto threatened to leave the institute for a higher-paying position at a Brooklyn public school. He submitted a "Declaration on the Subject of Leaving the Institute," which was answered by an increase of $100 a year in salary. Catto's reply at the time was simply "I . . . [am] satisfied and . . . [will] continue with the institute."[48]

When Ebenezer D. Bassett left the principalship in 1868 to become ambassador to Haiti, Catto wrote Alfred Cope, chairman of the board of managers, and requested the position. In his favor Catto could cite service to the school, an unqualified position as a leader among Philadelphia blacks, and efforts on behalf of civil rights. Catto wanted the position, and Cope knew it. In a polite reply, Cope carefully avoided any commitment to the black leader. He wrote on April 4, 1869:

> My Esteemed Friend O. V. Catto . . . we all have a high appreciation of thy services to the Institute and shall be glad to do whatever we can to promote thy welfare . . . [but] to necessity we must yield and no one could complain of us for that.[49]

A month later, Catto learned of the board's appointment of Fanny Jackson (Coppin), an Oberlin graduate and head of the institute's female department, to the position he had sought. Catto considered resigning from the school, and applied for the principalship of the Brooklyn Colored School on May 11, 1869.[50] Whether rejection of his application followed is not clear, but the board saw fit to reduce his teaching load and make him head of the boys' department. These concessions convinced Catto to continue as a teacher at the institute.[51]

The reason for the board's rejection of Catto is not spelled out clearly in the rather bland and self-patronizing minutes of the institute. Still, when viewed in historical perspective, there were some characteristics of a man like Catto that rankled the sensitivities of Quakers and made his candidacy for leadership of their institute repugnant to them.

Catto always believed in his right to act independently and to forcefully push for improvement of the conditions of blacks in the world outside the classroom, but this was not an approach which endeared him to Quakers, with their ideas of loyalty to the group and a nonmilitant, peaceful pursuit of desired goals. In what appeared to some whites as arrogance, Catto always contended that the blacks could and would eventually be leaders in the nation. There were times when the institute was drawn into civil rights campaigns and war-recruiting activities, and this did not fit the nonviolent nature of Quakerism. Catto, of course, was the leader in these efforts. To the Quaker, the fight of the black man for political and social equality was a matter which should be kept outside the school. The classroom was for learning subject matter, not for proselytizing black hopes and dreams.

Catto's charismatic leadership and his ability to sway groups at public forums made him a threat to the board of managers. The Quakers wanted to continue to make the major decisions affecting the institute. Clearly, if Catto became principal he could use his influence with the black community to undermine that power. It was Catto's position with Philadelphia blacks that had forced the board to grant him raises in salary so that he would not leave the institute. How embarrassing it would have been for the Quakers to lose the services of a black leader and educator like Catto. Despite their need to keep him at the institute, the managers could not risk his promotion.

The appointment of Fanny Jackson (Coppin) was much safer. She was a well-educated and respected black who owed the managers a favor. They had given her numerous loans to relieve her indebtedness, for which she was always appreciative. How comforting for the managers to have someone that relied upon them for help as their educational leader. The fact that Jackson was a woman also presented much less of a threat to their control of the school. Ironically, once she became principal, Jackson became an aggressive and outspoken leader. On numerous occasions, she disobeyed her superiors and did what she thought was best for the students.[52] Despite these later disagreements, the implication remains that in O. V. Catto the managers saw a greater threat to their control of the school, and for that reason he was passed over for the principalship.

In spite of these undercurrents, the record of the Institute for Colored Youth board of managers in promoting black advanced education during this period cannot be disparaged. A plaque on the present Cheyney State Library building expresses these sentiments:

> This tablet is set up to express the lasting gratitude of Alumni, students and teachers for the pioneer service rendered by the Society of Friends to the cause and education of the American Negro, first in the Institute for Colored Youth in Philadelphia then in the Cheyney Training School for Teachers in Cheyney. From 1837 to 1920 Friends built up and supported a private school for the professional training of Negro teachers. They maintained the highest standards, visioning ever the highest humanity. It was a venture of faith in dark days of our national life requiring foresight, Christian courage, patience, self-sacrifice and the giving of their material substance. In 1920 this Institution became the fourteenth state normal school in this Commonwealth of Pennsylvania.[53]

Still, the board's relationship with Catto in 1859 illustrates the dilemma which its policies and attitudes forced upon black educational leaders. Rather than encouraging black independence and prompting black efforts to change the views of a prejudiced society, they continued to demand black compliance with their views. While Quakers did provide educational opportunities for blacks, they did not support nineteenth-century activities by blacks in political and social matters.

Although disappointed with his treatment at the hands of the Quaker managers, Catto never let these feelings interfere with his relentless campaign aimed at equal treatment for blacks. In the summer of 1869, at the request of Republican leaders, Catto went south to speak in the state of Virginia on behalf of the Fourteenth Amendment. The next year he was granted a leave of absence to go to Washington, D.C., to organize the black schools of that city to accommodate the freedman. Clearly, Catto was now beginning to emerge as a national black figure. His intimate friend, William H. V. Wormley, encouraged him to stay in Washington as director of these schools, but Catto could not obtain a release from his teaching duties at the institute.[54]

The passage of the Fifteenth Amendment in 1870 set off celebrations among the blacks of Philadelphia on April 26. Church services began the festivities early in the day. Bunting and decorations were seen everywhere in the city's black districts. Scores of halls had parties scheduled to mark the occasion. One celebration at Horticulture Hall featured music and speeches by abolitionists Frederick Douglass and Robert Purvis, while another ceremony at the Union League focused upon the presentation of a banner commemorating the event to Octavius V. Catto and other black leaders. Catto pledged to his Republican friends that "the black man knows which side of the line to vote." Despite the merriment and excitement of the day, there was a foreboding shadow cast upon the event when some shots were fired into the crowd of marchers on their way home.[55] Threatening letters to Catto after the incident indicated the extent to which his enemies would go to keep him from organizing the black vote. Reassured by a friend to pay little attention to "their authors or contents," Catto continued his efforts to organize blacks for voting.[56]

In the fall of 1870, Catto's name again came before the public's eye. He was the central character in a racial dispute at the Franklin Institute. Guest lecturer B. Howard Rand, M.D., refused to lecture at the institute because Catto had recently been admitted as a member. While many city whites supported Rand and agreed that Catto should be ousted, the institute did not. The lecture was canceled, and Catto retained his membership. Still, the event only sharpened white Philadelphia's growing concern over the young militant's behavior.[57]

Even more alarming to most whites were the elections that were taking place at the time of the institute dispute. For the first time, blacks, enfranchised by the Fifteenth Amendment, appeared in large numbers to vote. To avoid trouble, Democrats and Republicans agreed that blacks would vote after whites. However, when blacks were formed into separate polling lines, rumors spread concerning possible violence. Under the provisions of the 1870 Force Act, General E. M. Gregory, U.S. Marshal for the Eastern District of Pennsylvania, sent a company of marines to keep order. No violence ensued, but Mayor Daniel M. Fox, a Democrat, protested the action, and Governor

John W. Geary expressed doubt before the General Assembly that the action was necessary.[58]

In the summer of 1871, Catto returned to Washington to aid in the administration of the freedman schools. His travels to the nation's capital increased his interest in politics. Praise came from his Republican friends that "he was prominent in politics, being looked up to and confided in by his people as a man of earnest convictions and judgments beyond his years." To a Philadelphian, "he was the pride of his race in this city, . . . being the ablest and best educated among the colored men of this city."[59]

Catto returned to Philadelphia in early October 1871 to continue his teaching at the Institute for Colored Youth. On Election Day October 10, a fight broke out between black and white voters two blocks away and in the vicinity of Sixth and Lombard Streets. Mass violence erupted throughout these black sections, and local police, rather than federal troops, were called to intervene. They did little to stop the racial rioting that continued throughout the day.[60]

At the institute, the students had been dismissed at the first signs of disorder so that they might arrive at home before the situation became more serious. Catto used his free time in the school to write up some military reports, and then told a fellow teacher that he would go to vote. Warned of the dangers, Catto replied that he had no chance to vote earlier and that he intended to exercise his right as a citizen. He left the school building unarmed. After a confrontation with some whites a block away from the school, Catto headed for the mayor's office to seek help. On Chestnut Street he was again accosted by some white ruffians who pointed a pistol at him, threatening his life if he went to vote. Catto went to a nearby store and purchased a pistol. When a friend reminded him that he had no cartridges, he replied that he had some at home.

Catto now proceeded down Ninth Street onto South Street, where a white man with a bandage on his head came up from behind and called out to him. Catto moved away from the man, later identified as Frank Kelly, cognizant of the gun held in his hand. Whether Catto pulled his gun or not is unclear, but Kelly fired three shots into Catto, killing him instantly. Kelly ran from the scene while numerous citizens stood staring at the bleeding body lying in the streets.[61] The body was moved to a nearby police station, where in a heartrending scene Caroline LeCount identified her fiancé's body. Two other blacks met death, and many whites and blacks were wounded before the melée subsided.

At a mass meeting on Friday, October 21, 1871, black and white citizens passed resolutions deploring the bloodshed and censuring city officials for not having maintained order. Investigations of the riot showed more police abuses than mob violence. A Lieutenant Haggerty actually had encouraged his men to keep blacks from voting, and for this Judge of Elections Joseph Allison placed him under $10,000 bail.[62] A slain black man, Levi Bolden, had been shot in the back, and a warrant was issued for a policeman following Dr. Elisha Shapleigh's postmortem.[63] All of this led Robert Purvis to comment that "in the death of Mr. Catto liberty has been strengthened."[64] Unfortunately for blacks, Purvis had spoken too quickly, for further court hearings produced no convictions.[65]

In a full military funeral led by Major Catto's Fifth Brigade, the cortege left the city armory at Broad and Race Streets in an hour-long procession down Broad Street. A contingent of grief-stricken students from the institute joined the funeral march. Thousands of whites and blacks lined the route of march to honor the fallen leader. Newspaper reports the next day judged the funeral to be the most elaborate ever held for a black person in America.

At the institute, the pupils spent the next two weeks in solemn meditation in remembrance of their former teacher, but the Quaker managers avoided taking a position which would uphold justice. In a special meeting, the managers appointed a committee of two to obtain legal counsel and attend the coroner's inquest into Catto's death. Three days later, they reported that the proper authorities were at work on the case and that the committee's services were not necessary. However, the eventual report by the coroner amounted to nothing more than a whitewash, and although the managers had declared that they learned "not only to highly estimate his [Catto's] service as an instructor which his faithfulness made more valuable every year . . . [and] that a life which promised to be one of much more than ordinary usefulness, had been lost and this loss would be especially felt by the school," there is no evidence of further committee activity.[66]

Even more disturbing was the rapid retreat of most blacks from politics. The Republican-sponsored Equal Rights League moved its headquarters from Philadelphia to Reading in 1872.[67] Isaiah C. Wears assumed the leadership of local black Republicans but lacked the charismatic leadership quality of Catto. Important issues such as school desegregation and increased political activities were left virtually untouched by black politicians like Wears. Catto's death brought to an end black militant behavior in nineteenth-century Philadelphia.[68]

Using the assassination of Octavius V. Catto as a barometer of racial attitudes among northern whites, the outlook for urban northern blacks was bleak. Assessing the situation, a white contemporary spokesman cited racial reasons. "Catto did not die because the murderer was his natural enemy. He died because a poor demented wretch was taught that the black man had no right the white man should respect."[69] Obviously, the feeling of prejudice against blacks was as strong in the North as in the South during the Reconstruction period. The northern urban-dweller never really wanted equality for blacks, even one as reputable as Catto. Ironically, it was the quality of his intelligence, his upright character, and his charismatic leadership that increased fears among whites. How uncomfortable, even dangerous, for urban whites to have such a man in their midst. Black minister J. Walker Jackson made this point clear when he asked, "Could it have been because of his erudition and eloquence that his life was taken?" Apparently those present agreed, shouting "That's it!" and "That's Right!"[70]

Clearly, Catto did not fit the white stereotype of what a black man should be. To most Philadelphia whites, his entrance into Republican politics only served to increase racial tensions within the community. As an outspoken supporter of the Republican party, he laid himself open to the scorn and animosity of local Democrats. It was precisely this political involvement which motivated those who killed Catto. Never before had the black community of Philadelphia produced a leader who saw so clearly the necessity for blacks to increase their participation in government and politics. In actuality, Catto's death served as a warning for Philadelphia blacks to stay out of politics.

Catto's fanatical insistence on equality for all men further exacerbated the situation. His success in integrating the local militia units, the Franklin Institute, and the local streetcars had made him a symbol of black militancy in the city. In the end, Catto died because he chose to act on an equal basis with whites, even to the point of exercising his political rights at a time when most whites considered him to be inferior and entitled to no rights. This widespread black prejudice did not even allow the trial of Catto's known assassin, Frank Kelly—proof that a white man in Philadelphia could not be convicted of killing a black man any more than a white man in the South could be held for a similar crime.

Clearly, the racial atmosphere in Philadelphia did not permit the growth of local black leadership. In all likelihood a similar atmosphere existed throughout the North.[71] Is it any wonder that black leadership for the next thirty years, until the emergence of W. E. B. Du Bois, would come from the black schools of the South? Could the mentality of submission, as symbolized by Booker T. Washington, have had its beginnings in the violence and suppression of the urban North and not in the rural South? Octavius V. Catto's life and death give credence to just such a hypothesis.

Notes

1. W. E. B. Du Bois, *The Philadelphia Negro* (Philadelphia, 1899), 40–41. Despite this acclaim, few historians of the Reconstruction era besides Du Bois have ever mentioned Catto in their writings. This oversight can be traced to a number of factors. Catto, at the time of his

death, was a local figure just emerging on the national scene, thus appearing at first glance to be a rather unimportant black leader. Ignoring men like Catto, historians chose to devote most of their attention to events taking place in the South. This view of Reconstruction history tended to minimize the importance of events taking place in the North. Catto's rise to power in an urban black community of the North offers another view of blacks previously hidden by the mass of writings on Reconstruction in the South.

Octavius V. Catto was born in Charleston, South Carolina, on February 22, 1839. His father, William T. Catto, was a Presbyterian minister; his mother, Sarah Isabella Cain, was a descendant of one of the most distinguished mulatto families in that city—the DeReefs.

2. *Philadelphia Press,* October 14, 1871. R. E. DeReef and Joseph DeReef, relatives of Catto's mother, were free blacks whose wealth ranged from $15,000 to $125,000. See C. W. Birnie, "Education of the Negro in Charleston, South Carolina, Prior to the Civil War," *Journal of Negro History* (hereafter *JNH*) 12 (1926):17.

3. William T. Catto, *A Semi-Centenary Discourse, . . . May, 1857* (Philadelphia, 1857), 10.

4. Ibid., 7.

5. Ibid.

6. James M. Truman Jr., Vaux School Committee, to the Board of Public Education, May 8, 1862; October 9, 1862; November 13, 1862. Abolition Society Papers, Box 45, Historical Society of Pennsylvania (hereafter HSP).

7. William C. Bacon, *Colored School Statistics, 1853* (Philadelphia, 1853), 1.

8. The Institute for Colored Youth is now Cheyney State College, located at Cheyney, Pennsylvania. *Philadelphia Press,* October 14, 1871; Charline F. H. Conyers, "A History of the Cheyney State Teachers College, 1837–1851" (diss., New York University, 1960), 51.

9. Conyers, "History of Cheyney State," 100. A full list of the blacks who formed the "Board of Education Auxiliary to the guardianship of the Estate of R. Humphies [*sic*]" included Stephen H. Gloucester, James M. Bustill, John P. Burr, Morris Brown, Nathaniel M. Dupree, Peter Lester, and William T. Douglass.

10. Ibid., 1–50; *The Liberator,* September 29, 1853; *Pennsylvania Freeman,* April 7, 1853.

11. The connection between the Institute staff members and Haiti cannot be denied. First, Principal Reason was in Haiti, Ebenezer Bassett became the first U.S. ambassador to Haiti in 1869, and Jacob C. White Jr. was a local agent who provided transportation for blacks wishing to migrate to Haiti. Institute student James H. Smythe was also recommended for the Haitian ambassadorship in the 1880s. See William J. Simmons, *Men of Mark* (Cleveland, 1887), 872; George Laurence Jr. to Henry J. Lombard, Esq., Pennsylvania Railroad Company, 1861, 1862, and 1898, Jacob C. White Papers, HSP.

12. Catto, *Discourse,* 102.

13. Banneker Institute Minutes, 1855–59, Gardiner Collection, HSP. For the list of activities conducted by the institute, see Negro Activities, Gardiner Collection, Box 13G, HSP.

14. Conyers, "History of Cheyney State," 130–60.

15. *Pennsylvania Freeman,* April 7, 1853.

16. *Philadelphia Press,* October 14, 1871.

17. *Philadelphia Tribune,* "Pencil Pusher Points," November 16, June 8, and March 30, 1912. Written by black historian William Carl Bolivar, a graduate of the institute, these columns contain a history of nineteenth-century Philadelphia from the black point of view. Bolivar's obituary appears in the *Philadelphia Tribune,* December 19, 1914.

18. Octavius V. Catto, "Our Alma Mater," *An Address Delivered at Concert Hall on the Occasion of the Twelfth Annual Commencement of the Institute for Colored Youth* (Philadelphia, 1864), 17. The speech was printed by Jacob C. White Jr., president of the Alumni Associa-

tion "in a slightly modified form." See Conyers, "History of Cheyney State," 138. A public examination of the institute was held in May 1863 and published in *The Christian Recorder,* May 16, 1863.

19. O. V. Catto to Cordelia Sanders, Philadelphia, May 28, 1860; Wanamaker store bills for coat, gloves, and suit, Catto Papers, Gardiner Collection, HSP.

20. *Philadelphia Press,* October 14, 1871.

21. *Philadelphia Tribune,* August 30, 1913; January 2, 1914; Frederick M. Binder, "Pennsylvania Negro Regiments in the Civil War," *JNH* 37 (October 1952): 383–417.

22. *The War of the Rebellion: A Compilation of the Official Records of the Union and Confederate Armies,* ser. 1, 27, part 3:203. This statement stands in marked contrast to earlier rejections of black efforts to join the service. In 1853, "Colored gentlemen" asked Thomas Firth, inspector general of the Pennsylvania Militia, if they could join the army. His reply was: "My opinion is it would produce a devil of a riot and some of the lawyers might indict me for 'inciting a riot.' But joking aside—My own mind is made up. If the Adgt. Genl. [General George Cadwalader] desires this done he has got to find another Inspector in my place—for I hope to go to—. . . if I ever put on My uniform to inspect any set of Niggers. . . . I don't believe the almighty ever intended a Nigger to be put a par with the whites and I won't be a party to such matters. . . ." See Thomas Firth to General Cadwalader, Philadelphia, April 13, 1853, Cadwalader Collection, HSP.

23. *Philadelphia Press,* and *U.S. Gazette,* June 25, 1863.

24. Jacob A. White [*sic*] to Joseph C. Bustill, August 19, 1862, *Journal of Negro History* 11 (January 1926): 83.

25. Binder, "Pa. Negro Regiments," 389–90.

26. *Philadelphia Press,* October 1, 1871. Louis Wagner had been the commander of Camp William Penn, the training area for black troops during the Civil War. It was located in suburban Philadelphia from 1863 to 1865.

27. *Proceedings of the National Convention of Colored Men, Held in the City of Syracuse, New York, October 4, 5, 6, and 7, 1864, with the Bill of Wrongs and Rights and the Address to the American People* (Philadelphia, 1969), 11. Catto's activities in Philadelphia on behalf of the Rights League were numerous. For one such meeting, see *Christian Recorder,* September 1, 1866.

28. Minutes of the Pennsylvania State Equal Rights League, 1864–72, October 10, 1864, 11, Gardiner Papers, HSP.

29. *Proceedings of the State Equal Rights Convention of the Colored People of Pennsylvania Held in the City of Harrisburg, February 8th, 9th, 10th, 1865* (Philadelphia, 1863), 19.

30. Ibid., 19–20.

31. Ibid., 20.

32. Ibid.

33. Ibid.

34. Ibid., 21.

35. *Christian Recorder,* February 2, 1881.

36. *Christian Recorder,* November 1882 [exact date unknown].

37. In 1866 the *Age* raised the issue of Haiti-like rule in Philadelphia if blacks received the vote. See *Philadelphia Age,* September 4, and 29 and October 2, 3, and 4, 1866. White reaction to the institute was generally negative. Simon Gratz, a member of the Board of Education, noted: "They [blacks] send their children to what is known as 'The Colored High School' which is about the same grade as one of our grammar schools. The number of colored people who have high aspirations in this direction is comparatively small." Catto's abilities indicate

that Gratz underestimated the curriculum at the institute. Simon Gratz Scrapbook, 1880–92; *Philadelphia Times,* July 7, 1881, Gratz Collection, HSP.

38. Minutes of the State Equal Rights League, passim. For a recent study of the streetcar issue, read Philip S. Foner, "The Battle to End Discrimination Against Negroes on Philadelphia Streetcars," *Pennsylvania History* 40 (April and October 1973): 261–92, 355–79.

39. *Philadelphia Tribune,* December 7, 1912. The *Press* was a Republican paper and generally gave the blacks of the city greater coverage than any of the other white daily papers. Catto lauded John W. Forney at a serenade on May 26, 1867, on the occasion of the Grand Reunion Festival. See the *Christian Recorder,* May 4, 1867.

40. Foner, "Battle to End Discrimination," 373.

41. "Pencil Pusher Points," *Philadelphia Tribune,* May 3, 1913.

42. "Pencil Pusher Points," *Philadelphia Tribune,* January 2, 1913.

43. Ibid. For a complete description of the Pythian Baseball Club activities, read MS Pythian Baseball Club Papers, Gardiner Collection, HSP.

44. "Pencil Pusher Points," *Philadelphia Tribune,* January 2, 1913.

45. "Pencil Pusher Points," *Philadelphia Tribune,* May 3, 1913.

46. Ibid.

47. "Pencil Pusher Points," *Philadelphia Tribune,* May 3, 1913; January 2, 1913.

48. O. V. Catto to H. H. Pierson, Philadelphia, October 10, 1862; and private paper preserved in the Catto Papers entitled "Declaration on the Subject of Leaving the Institute," Gardiner Collection, HSP.

49. Alfred Cope to O. V. Catto, Philadelphia, April 4, 1869, Catto Papers, Gardiner Collection, HSP.

50. O. V. Catto to William Buckley, Philadelphia, May 11, 1869, Catto Papers, Gardiner Collection, HSP; Levi Coppin, *Unwritten History* (Philadelphia, 1919), 352. Coppin states that Catto would "not teach under a woman." This explanation does not consider the relationship of Catto to the managers.

51. Conyers, "History of Cheyney State," 163–64.

52. Fanny Jackson Coppin introduced the study of German without the consent of the managers, for which she was reprimanded. Later she fought for industrial education as a new curriculum at the institute even though the managers would not endorse the project. See ibid., 174, 182–90.

53. The plaque is currently located to the left of the main entrance to the library at Cheyney College.

54. *Philadelphia Press,* October 14, 1871; Conyers, "History of Cheyney State," 165. The friendship of Wormley is expressed in a letter to Catto. See William H. V. Wormley to Catto, Washington, D.C., September 17, 1860, Catto Papers; and O. V. Catto to Jacob C. White Jr., Washington, D.C., October 2, 1871, White Papers, Gardiner Collection, HSP.

55. Ira V. Brown, *The Negro in Pennsylvania History* (University Park, Pa., 1970), 53. See also "Pencil Pusher Points," *Philadelphia Tribune,* April 19, 1913.

56. John Thomas Johnson to O. V. Catto, Washington, D.C., August 14, 1870, Catto Papers, Gardiner Collection, HSP.

57. *Philadelphia Press,* October 14, 1871.

58. Brown, *The Negro in Pennsylvania History,* 52–55.

59. *Philadelphia Press,* October 14, 1871.

60. Ibid.; *Philadelphia Tribune,* July 27, 1912.

61. *Philadelphia Public Ledger,* October 13, 1871.

62. *Philadelphia Public Ledger,* October 25, 1871.

63. *Philadelphia Public Ledger,* October 13, 1871.

64. Ibid.

65. *Philadelphia Press,* October 14, 1871; Conyers, "History of Cheyney State," 167–68.

66. MS Report of the Institute for Colored Youth, Yearly Report of the Managers, May 21, 1872, Quaker Book Store, Third and Arch Streets, Philadelphia.

67. Minutes, Equal Rights League, 1872.

68. Isaiah C. Wears Papers, Gardiner Collection, HSP.

69. *Philadelphia Press,* October 14, 1871.

70. Ibid.

71. Leon F. Litwack, *North of Slavery* (Chicago, 1961). Litwack shows the antebellum North to have the same racial prejudices as the South. Undoubtedly these attitudes continued and grew more intense during the Reconstruction period.

CHAPTER NINE

"Two Steps Forward, a Step and a Half Back":
Harrisburg's African American Community in the Nineteenth Century

Gerald G. Eggert

Those who lived at the bottom of the socioeconomic ladder in nineteenth-century American cities did most of the "totin'," "liftin'," and "choppin'." They were the casual laborers and servants who regularly shifted from job to job, doing housework, waiting tables, carting goods, cleaning streets, cutting hair, chopping wood, hauling trash, running errands, and doing most of the community's other necessary but low-paying chores. At Harrisburg, recent immigrants and children of the poor performed part of this work. The bulk fell to its African American residents.

Although Harrisburg was a middle-sized rather than a major urban center after mid-century, its black community was one of the largest in the state. The city ranked sixth among Pennsylvania cities in population from 1850 to 1880, then drifted to eighth by 1900; its black population, which numbered second in 1860, was third in 1850, 1870, 1880, and 1890, and was fourth in 1900. Until the dawn of the new century, the proportion of its black to white residents hovered near 10 percent or a little above, greater than that of any other major city in Pennsylvania, including Philadelphia and Pittsburgh. Although nearly 9 percent of the seaport metropolis' residents were blacks in

This chapter was first published in *Pennsylvania History* 58 (January 1991): 1–36. Reprinted by permission.

1850, that figure fell to less than 5 percent through 1900; Pittsburgh's blacks throughout stood at 5 percent or less.[1]

As elsewhere, the interactions of three principal forces shaped the black urban experience at Harrisburg: external pressures such as white attitudes and behavior toward blacks, the internal response of blacks to their environment, and such nonracial forces as changes in the economic structure.[2] In common with others of their race, Harrisburg blacks suffered under the dual disabilities of their slave heritage and what has been called the "privatization" of the American economy. White Pennsylvanians, not unlike their countrymen at large, held ambivalent attitudes toward blacks and slavery, alternately displaying sympathy and hostility to both. Economic matters they saw as essentially individual rather than community concerns.[3] Such advances as Harrisburg's African Americans made came chiefly from their own persistence and the grudging concessions of whites. With few exceptions, African Americans held the lowest-paying jobs, owned little real estate, and made relatively slight economic and social gains by the end of the century. Industrialization, which so considerably altered the lives of whites, largely passed blacks by before 1900. Progress for blacks on all fronts was slow; every two steps forward were followed by a step and a half back.

During the Revolution, for example, Pennsylvania had been the first state to free its slaves by legislation. The gain of freedom, however, was offset by the provision in the Act of 1780 for gradual rather than immediate manumission. As a result, the Commonwealth was among the last of the northern states still holding a few slaves as late as 1840.[4] Similarly Philadelphia, some of whose Quakers were leaders in the abolition movement, host city for the founding meeting of the American Antislavery Society in 1833, five years later witnessed the firing of Pennsylvania Hall by a hostile mob bent on preventing the meeting of a women's antislavery convention. That same year, 1838, Pennsylvania adopted a new constitution depriving free blacks of the right to vote. Apparently few had voted under the previous constitution, and only in a few counties, but it was a privilege that could be exercised. Now persons of color were officially relegated to separate and inferior citizenship.[5] Although the Civil War and the Thirteenth Amendment finally ended involuntary servitude, the mixed attitudes of white Pennsylvanians toward blacks persisted. Whites in Harrisburg reflected that ambivalence.

The earliest residents, including John Harris, the first settler at Harrisburg, brought slaves with them. Once the frontier passed and agricultural pursuits became the chief livelihood of the region, the number of slaves increased. When the act freeing slaves took effect in 1780, most slaveholders in the community kept their property by simply registering them as the law provided. Children born to slaves after 1780 were free, but remained indentured

Table 9.1. Harrisburg blacks, 1790–1900

Year	Population	Blacks		Slaves		Free in White HHs		Free in Black HHs	
		No.	%	No.	%	No.	%	No.	%
1790	875	26	3.0	25	96.2	1	4	0	0
1800	1,472	60	4.1	16	26.7	44	73	0	0
1810	2,287	59	2.6	2	3.4	18	31	39	66
1820	2,990	177	5.9	1	0.6	47	27	129	73
1830	4,312	493	11.4	2	0.4	107	22	384	78
1840	5,980	646	10.8			168	26	478	74
1850	7,834	886	11.3			114	13	778	87
1860	13,405	1,326	9.9						
1870	23,104	2,271	9.8						
1880	30,762	2,906	9.4						
1890	39,385	3,612	9.2						
1900	50,167	4,123	8.2						

SOURCES: Except for data on blacks for 1790–1870, the data are from published census records. The data on blacks are from manuscript census schedules (1790–1840) and Computerized Manuscript Census Data (1850–70). These figures differ slightly from published data, apparently because of careless addition by early census takers.

servants of their former masters until the age of 28.[6] According to the first federal census in 1790, Harrisburg had twenty-six black residents: twenty-five slaves and Mathias Hootman, who was free. The Harrises were among the community's more persistent slaveholders. The younger John Harris, founder of the town, with six slaves was the borough's largest slaveholder in the first census. A decade later his son Robert listed five blacks in his household. Four were free (but probably indentured servants), and one was a slave. Robert's sister Mary, widow of Congressman John Hanna, owned a slave woman as late as 1820.[7]

Although most Harrisburg blacks were freed soon after 1790, one or two were listed as slaves in each census through 1830. The freedom they enjoyed was relative at best. Only gradually were they able to set up households apart from their masters and employers. In 1800 they all lived in white households, as if still slaves. So long as they remained indentured servants, their masters controlled where they lived and kept them close at hand, the better to utilize them. Even those who were completely free usually lacked the means to purchase or rent homes and were therefore obliged to accept room and board from their employers as part of their pay. They strove, nonetheless, to live separately, and by 1810 two-thirds did. After 1820 the proportion was three-fourths or more.

Pennsylvania's blacks became more mobile with emancipation, for the most part moving from rural areas to towns and cities. Philadelphia drew large numbers, but a larger proportion located in middle-sized or smaller communities. As the metropolis blacks swelled in number from 6,354 in 1810 to 10,507 by 1840, its share of the state's total African American population declined from 47 percent to 41 percent. Only 5 percent fewer lived in the eleven counties of southeastern Pennsylvania. Harrisburg seems to have attracted many of its blacks from farms in nearby Dauphin County. Each decade, its share of the county's blacks increased: by a third in 1800, by more than half by 1830, by two-thirds by 1850, and by three-fourths by 1860. Joining this flow were migrants from the nearby states of Maryland and Virginia: freeborn blacks, manumitted slaves, and fugitives from bondage.[8]

White reactions to the growing black enclave in their midst ranged from sympathy to suspicion to hostility. Sympathetic whites (including Mary Harris Hanna, who still owned her slave) organized and financed churches and schools for blacks, including a "Negro Sunday School" for adults and a "sabbath school" that had separate classes for young whites and blacks. In May 1817, Daniel Coker, a black Methodist clergyman from Baltimore, helped organize an African Methodist Episcopal (AME) Society in Harrisburg. With fewer than 200 blacks in the area, whites assisted in raising funds by subscription for an "African Church." Dr. Samuel Agnew chaired the drive, and George Lochman, pastor of Zion Lutheran Church, was treasurer. Agnew and Lochman were white, but a black man, Thomas Dorsey, served as secretary. In this period, whites controlled the boards of most such institutions, assisted by selected blacks.[9]

Once Harrisburg's African Americans became numerous enough, acquired some funds, and developed the necessary self-confidence, they increasingly built up and managed their own institutions and community. Lacking the numbers and resources of Philadelphia's blacks, those at Harrisburg lagged a decade or more in similar developments.[10] Blacks in the larger city, for instance, launched schools of their own between 1800 and 1803. Not until 1817 did Thomas Dorsey open his school for "coloured children . . . both bound and free" at Harrisburg.[11] In 1829 a group connected with the town's original AME Society withdrew and formed Wesley Union Church, which affiliated with the AME members (a quarter of Harrisburg's black population); it was the second largest congregation in the conference. Beginning worship in a log building at Third and Mulberry Streets, the congregation had by 1839 built a new brick church with a small subsidy from Dauphin County and opened a school for black children. It closed three years later, when the county commissioners stopped all aid and suggested that blacks send their children to public schools.[12]

Only a few Harrisburg whites supported abolitionism. A small group organized the Harrisburg Anti-Slavery Society in 1836, and when the founding session of the Pennsylvania Anti-Slavery Society met in the borough the next year, thirteen residents attended as delegates. Nationally prominent abolitionists Frederick Douglass and William Lloyd Garrison jointly addressed a public meeting at the courthouse in 1847, probably under the sponsorship of the society. However, if still functioning after 1848, its meetings attracted no notice in any of Harrisburg's six newspapers. In the elections of 1848 and 1852, Free Soil presidential candidates who opposed the spread of slavery drew but 11 and 15 votes respectively in the borough. Such antislavery sentiment as persisted took the form of secret support for the Underground Railroad.[13]

At the other extreme were whites who preferred being rid of blacks altogether. For example, Robert Harris joined with other prominent citizens to form a local chapter of the American Colonization Society in 1819. This group believed, as they said in an address to the community, that blacks could "never be identified with our national character—nor rise to all the amenities of respected and respectable citizens" and so should be removed to Africa. A rash of suspicious fires in 1820 led to the scapegoating of blacks. In a move against them, the borough council supplemented the nightwatch that was authorized to "apprehend all suspicious and disorderly persons." A local newspaper hailed the measure as a success when a number of blacks promptly left town. A second ordinance required "all free persons of color" to register with the chief burgess. Strangers of that race who lacked certificates of registration were subject to arrest and punishment.[14] Throughout, gangs of white boys added to the burdens of African Americans by teasing and harassing them on the streets and on occasion disrupting their church services by such acts as tossing red pepper into the stove, forcing evacuation of the building. The 1847 visit of Douglass and Garrison attracted spirited rowdies who showered "brickbacks, fire-crackers, and other missiles" on the speaker.[15]

The economic progress of blacks in this period was slow. Those who continued to live in white households or white institutions such as hotels and boardinghouses all worked as servants of one sort or another. Even the great majority of those fortunate enough to live in homes of their own had essentially the same employment. Black males served white families as gardeners, servants, coachmen, and the like. Their wives and daughters cooked for white families, tended their children, washed and ironed their clothes, cleaned their houses, and performed dozens of other such tasks before returning to do the same work for their own families.

In 1850, federal census-takers for the first time gathered data that provided insights into the status of the African Americans beyond number, age category, and whether they were free. In Harrisburg they identified 886 blacks and mulattoes.[16] More than three-quarters lived in 174 family units, housed in 151 separate residences. The other one-quarter consisted of "singles" who roomed in black households or with their employers, regardless of race. Except for crowding more families into fewer residences, the percentages of blacks living in family units and as singles persisted with little change for the next two decades.[17]

Item	1850	%	1860	%	1870	%
Total blacks	886		1,326		2,271	
No. of family units	174		233		497	
No. in family units	681	76.7	1,028	77.5	1,791	78.9
No. of singles	205	23.3	298	22.5	480	21.2
Avg. no. per family unit	3.9		4.4		3.6	
No. of residences	151		179		364	
Families w/sep. res.		86.8		76.8		73.2

The census' inclusion of the occupations of males over the age of 15 gives some indication of the extent to which blacks had risen above household service by the eve of industrialization. The 195 black males with occupations held only sixteen different jobs. Since most were designated as "laborer," the exact nature of their work is not known. A few (4 clergymen, 2 "doctors," and a schoolteacher) were professionals and semiprofessionals. In an era when white professionals were as likely to have acquired their status by apprenticeship as by formal education, it is improbable that the blacks had specialized schooling of any sort. The clergymen were probably charismatic preachers, the doctors were probably practitioners who healed with folk remedies and herbs, and the teachers were probably persons who were literate.[18]

Seventeen blacks apparently operated small businesses of their own. Ten had barbershops, and of these, 6 worked alone and the others each had from 1 to 3 employees. Five ran oyster houses and 2 were teamsters, each with a horse and cart, who transported goods on demand. Seven blacks were skilled craftsmen: 4 shoemakers, 2 coopers, and 1 butcher. Two were boatmen working on the canal. The remaining 54 filled serving positions: 34 waiters, 15 servants, 3 hostlers, 1 groom. Although the 1850 census made no provision for listing the occupations of females, it showed 9 black women with jobs: 5 cooks, 2 servants, 1 washwoman, and 1 laborer. It seems safe to assume that 77 other blacks (9 men and 68 women) who lived in white households and had no listed occupations were also servants. Blacks monopolized or dominated a few occupations, providing all 34 of the town's waiters, 18 of its 20 barbers, 17 of 20 servants, and 5 of the 9 cooks listed in the census.

In sum, slightly more than half were unspecified "laborers," more than one-quarter were servants, and not more than 16 percent held other occupa-

Table 9.2. Occupational classification of Harrisburg blacks, 1850–1870

Occupational Class	1850	1860	1870
Males	N = 195	N = 263	N = 605
Professionals	3.6%	3.4%	1.8%
Self-employed	8.7	11.0	9.4
Craft workers	3.6	4.6	2.0
Industrial workers	0	2.3	3.8
Servants	27.7	35.4	23.6
"Laborers"	51.8	34.6	56.9
Other employees	4.6	8.7	2.1
Miscellaneous	0	1.5	0.3
Females	N = 9	N = 120	N = 174
Craft workers	0	3.3	2.9
Industrial workers	0	0	0.6
Servants	88.9	93.3	95.4
"Laborers"	11.1	2.5	1.1
Miscellaneous	0	0.8	0

SOURCE: Computerized Manuscript Census Data, 1850, 1860, 1870.

tions (see Table 9.2). Harrisburg in 1850 offered its blacks fewer opportunities for higher-level jobs than did larger northern cities. At the same time, it gave them a better chance at owning real estate, probably because land was less expensive than in larger cities.[19]

Harrisburg tax records in 1825 listed only 6 black property holders. The richest, James McClintock, owned three houses, two half-lots, and a stable.[20] By 1850, local tax records showed 28 blacks (5 of whom were women) holding real estate and horses and carriages for hire valued at a total of $13,300. The federal census for the same year listed 30 black property holders (including 3 women) with a total of $20,100 worth of real estate (see Table 9.4).[21] Those owning land valued at $1,000 or more included a barber ($1,800), a waiter ($1,500), a servant and a hairdresser ($1,200 each), and a waiter, a doctor, and a laborer ($1,000 each).

These gains did not prevent whites from continuing to regard blacks as inferior. Local newspapers that did not simply ignore them alternately mimicked, ridiculed, patronized, and insulted blacks. In contrast to a later era, the tone was indulgent rather than bitter, and terms such as "nigger" appeared infrequently. The *Telegraph,* a Whig paper generally sympathetic during the early 1850s, nonetheless sought to brighten its columns with squibs about them. With tongue in cheek, it denied a rumor that the odd taste of drinking water one summer was due to the presence of a black corpse in the town reservoir. A bit of ice would remove the alleged "extract de Africano" taste,

Harrisburg blacks traditionally lived in two areas: "Verbeketown," or the Sixth Ward (north of the Capitol), and the Eighth Ward, a racially mixed neighborhood east of the Capitol. Here a black streetcleaner works in the Eighth Ward district on the west side of Filbert Street looking north from Walnut Street in 1910. (Courtesy of the Dauphin County Historical Society)

it added. Stereotypes abounded. A report on a "colored camp meeting" noted that from the "loads of water-melons" headed in that direction it was apparent that physical as well as spiritual needs were receiving attention. A burial rite conducted by the black Odd Fellows Lodge was described as "imposing in appearance, and well conducted." The editor observed: "The colored gentlemen possess a peculiar faculty in imitating the refined ceremonies of civilized life."[22]

Traveling troupes of black entertainers and whites in blackface frequently played in Harrisburg. Papers carried notices of such events as the "Ethiopian Serenaders," a group of "negro melodists," and Kendall and Dickinson's "Ethiopian Minstrels," whose "delineation's of Negro character" were "perfect."[23] Watching blacks in their churches and at social events provided whites with additional entertainment. "It is rich—so unique and so peculiar to hear a genuine sable divine hold forth and give out his notions of things,

Table 9.3. Number and percentage of blacks in specific occupations, 1850–1870

Occupation	1850		1860		1870	
	No.	%	No.	%	No.	%
Barber	17	89	23	92	25	52
Carter	0		13	42	15	65
Coachman, driver	0		6	30	11	55
Cook	5	56	6	75	16	30
Domestic, male/female	0		3	6	109	24
Hostler	4	27	1	10	18	55
Laborer	102	21	94	17	346	25
Oysterman/restaurateur	5	56	4	25	3	14
Porter	0		10	83	24	92
Servant, male/female	17	85	131	31	54	29
Teamster, trucker	2	67	1	6	18	35
Waiter	34	100	27	87	52	87
Washwoman, laundress	1	33	14	25	9	60

SOURCE: Computerized Manuscript Census Data, 1850, 1860, 1870.

Table 9.4. Real estate held by Harrisburg blacks, 1850–1870

Item	1850	1860	1870
Blacks holding real estate	30	106	69
Black adults with real estate (%)	6.1	15.1	5.3
Value of black-held real estate	$20,100	$97,300	$104,800
Percent of increase		384.1	7.7
Average black holding	$670	$918	$1,518
Percent of increase		37.0	64.5
Median black holding	$600	$800	$1,000
Percent of increase		33.3	25.0
Size of real-estate holdings			
Real-estate value	N = 30	N = 106	N = 69
$5,000–$9,999 (%)		0.9	4.3
$2,000–$4,999 (%)		6.6	23.2
$1,500–$1,999 (%)	6.7	5.7	14.5
$1,000–$1,499 (%)	16.7	26.4	30.4
$500–$999 (%)	40.0	35.8	21.7
$100–$499 (%)	36.7	24.5	5.8

SOURCE: Computerized Manuscript Census Data, 1850, 1860, 1870.

temporal and spiritual," the *Telegraph* observed.[24] Their religious encampments across the river in New Cumberland often drew crowds of whites who reportedly "went over to see how the camp meeting was going on." When Harrisburg's "ladies and gentlemen of color" had a "grand supper" at Shakespeare's Hall, "quite a number of white ladies and gentlemen of respectability were present, and entertained at a separate table." The behavior of blacks who attended mixed social gatherings was commented on as if they were children: "The colored folks present were of a most respectable caste and appearance, and their deportment was very exemplary. A proper line of demarcation was recognized and a proper decorum observed."[25] On the other hand, overfamiliarity between the races was discouraged. Young white men, for example, drew criticism for frequenting oyster bars and dance houses run by blacks.[26]

More troubling to African Americans than the newspaper slights, which most probably did not read, was their inability to escape completely the curse of slavery. Even the nearly 90 percent born in Pennsylvania were not exempt. Although by 1850 few of this group had themselves been slaves or indentured servants, most if not all were the children or grandchildren of slaves or bond servants. The older ones could remember seeing slaves in Harrisburg as late as 1830 and could tell stories of forebears who were slaves. The 10 percent born in slave states, chiefly Maryland or Virginia, were at greatest risk. Those born free or manumitted could lawfully live where they chose; those who were runaway slaves, if discovered, could be seized and returned to bondage at any time. Few knew for certain who were which.

The size of Harrisburg's black community and the importance of its North-South transportation routes regularly attracted fugitives to the community, where a small number of individuals of both races provided these travelers with food and lodging before hurrying them along toward freedom in Canada. Although most continued northward, a few remained, thinking they were safe. On at least two occasions, local blacks mobilized to free captured runaways. In 1828 a party of slaveholders took a captive before a county judge for authorization to return him to bondage. Even as the hearing took place, town blacks armed with "clubs and cudgels" gathered outside. When the slave owners emerged victorious, the blacks fell upon them, hoping to free the captive. Alarmed at such behavior, Harrisburg authorities arrested twenty of the rioters. Eight subsequently went free, but the remaining twelve were found guilty of rioting. Six were sentenced to six months at hard labor, the others to a year. When a group of whites later petitioned the borough council to pardon the prisoners, the council voted only to allow them "leave to withdraw their petition." Before the trial, a black who had lived in town for at least eighteen years, owned real estate, and ran a business of his own offered bail for one of the accused. His addressing the judge as "Massa" indicated how narrow he gauged the gap between slavery and freedom at that time.[27]

A remarkably similar affair occurred in 1850. Again, runaways were captured in Harrisburg and brought into court on a charge of stealing their master's horses. "Doctor" William M. Jones, a leader in the black community, testified that the prisoners had lived in town for some time and were not the runaways being pursued. Although the judge disregarded Jones's testimony, he ruled that the charge of horse theft was a ruse for preventing the men from escaping and accordingly ordered their release. At the same time, he intimated that they were fugitives and as such could be reclaimed by their master so long as no undue violence was used. A party of armed southerners waited outside the courtroom to seize the runaways as they emerged. Meanwhile, an even larger party of local blacks surrounded the courthouse, intent on preventing the master from carrying off his property. A short, sharp struggle ensued. Thanks to a 31-year-old black laborer named Joseph Poeple who rushed into the fray, one slave escaped. Overpowered by the slaveholders, Poeple, "bloody as a butcher," could not free the others. Because of the turmoil in the near presence of his court, the judge ordered all involved parties arrested for contempt.[28] In the end, the southerners were allowed to take their slaves home. Local blacks made bail for the rioters, and the judge, responding to a petition of prominent Harrisburg whites, dismissed all charges against them.[29]

Enactment of a new and stronger federal fugitive slave law in September 1850 soon divided Harrisburg whites as never before over slavery and terrified the town's African American community. The new measure provided that slaveholders had only to bring alleged runaways before a special U.S. commissioner, not a court of law, and swear that the captives were their property. The accused could not testify, and unless some white person gave convincing contrary evidence or the commissioner doubted the claimant, the accused were remanded south.[30]

Richard McAllister, a local attorney who sought to advance himself politically as a Democrat by catering to the pro-South wing of the party, sought and won appointment as slave commissioner for the area. During his two-and-a-half-year tenure, McAllister remanded nearly every black brought before him as a runaway slave. He also turned the measure into a racket for collecting fees and receiving rewards from grateful owners by engaging the town's elected constables to track down recent runaways and by hiring spies of both races to uncover longtime residents who were escaped slaves.[31]

Harrisburg, a Democratic party stronghold at the time, initially seemed indifferent to or even supportive of the law. By March 1853, the inherent evils of the measure, as well as McAllister's abuses of it, changed public opinion. Some people were offended that the law deprived free blacks accused of being runaways of the right to testify in their own defense. It separated parents from a child because they were escaped slaves who had to be returned while the child was free because born in Pennsylvania. McAllister's agents seized some blacks known to be free, and had not excited crowds come to their rescue they might well have been taken south. A small black boy who mysteriously disappeared from Harrisburg was found somehow to have reached Baltimore, where he had been sold into servitude; he was returned to his family. A Maryland police officer shot and killed an alleged fugitive while he and one of McAllister's agents were holding the captive between them.[32]

The turning point came when a respected black teamster, James Phillips, a married man with children who had lived in Harrisburg as if free for fifteen years, was picked off the streets as a fugitive slave. McAllister, whose men had detected Phillips's status, remanded him to his master. The master in turn sold Phillips to a slave dealer for a sale farther south. Angry Harrisburgers hired a lawyer to trace the victim's whereabouts and redeemed him by public subscription.[33]

Several newspapers that once supported the law or accepted it as a necessary evil turned against it. They pointedly criticized McAllister and the local constables for going beyond the requirements of the law to ferret out and remand fugitives in order to collect fees and rewards. Persons unknown attempted to set fire to McAllister's home while he and his family were on vacation, and when he sought election as a delegate to the Democratic State Convention he lost in every ward. At the borough elections in March 1853, 20 percent more voters than usual turned out to defeat for reelection those constables who ran slaves for McAllister. When the commissioner resigned in May 1853 and moved to Kansas, no one was appointed in his place. Two years later, one of his agents and a black accomplice were found guilty of kidnapping blacks and spent three years in prison.[34] Clearly the white community had developed some concern for justice, whatever their views on blacks and slavery.

Even before McAllister's campaign, fugitives living in Harrisburg apparently attempted to disguise their status by lying to federal census takers about their place of birth. Phillips, for example, had given Pennsylvania as his birthplace in 1850. Ten years later, after being remanded to slavery and redeemed, he admitted to being born in Virginia. That he was not alone is indicated by the changes that some Harrisburg blacks made in their birthplaces in the censuses between 1850 and 1870. Of 58 such changes between 1850 and 1860, when it was dangerous to be from a slave state, 39 who previously claimed birth in the South now gave a free state as their place of birth. Nineteen shifted from free to slave state. A decade later, when the crisis was over and it was safe to tell the truth, 48 changed their birthplaces: 36 from free to slave state, 12 from slave to free state. Had the changes been mistakes or corrections of previous errors rather than deliberate, the number changed in each direction should have been approximately equal. Instead, by a margin of two to one in 1860 the shifts favored safety, and in 1870 they shifted in the direction of candor by a margin of three to one.[35] Those who could be traced through two or more censuses, of course, were probably only part of the whole number of runaway slaves living in Harrisburg. Some may have consistently listed themselves as freeborn in all three censuses even when no longer necessary. Also, the number of fugitive slaves who moved to Harrisburg and lived there too short a time to be recorded in a census cannot be known.

A series of public debates in February 1853 revealed the growing frustration of many African Americans. Over the course of a month, they listened to local blacks argue the relative merits of America and Africa as homelands for their race. The affair marked the debut of Thomas Morris Chester, the 19-year-old son of a local oysterman and his wife who had escaped from slavery in Maryland several years before and not been detected. Young Chester, encouraged by one of Harrisburg's white antislave lawyers, had decided on a career in law. He attended Allegheny (later Avery) College, an institution established to educate blacks in the sciences, literature, and languages. There, near Pittsburgh, he fell under the influence of Martin Delany, a black nationalist calling for the return of his people to Africa. Back in Harrisburg in time for the debates, Chester spoke in favor of an African homeland with an "eloquence" that reportedly rivaled "some of the great guns on the hill [white politicians at the capitol]." Not long after, he left for Liberia.[36]

The closing of the slave commissioner's office in 1853 considerably eased tensions in the black community. Local newspaper bias against them also lessened. As the Know-Nothing nativist crusade gained momentum, a new editor at the *Telegraph* focused on "Americanism," prohibition, and the need to curb immigration. Going by the columns of that paper, it appeared that only Irish papists engaged in petty crimes, drank to excess, brawled, and in other ways disturbed the peace. For the moment, the Irish drew the heaviest fire and replaced blacks as the butt of newspaper humor.[37]

The emergence of the new Republican party by 1856 soon subsumed nativism in the greater effort to halt the spread of slavery. The Civil War, in turn, gave African Americans new hope that the South's "peculiar institution" would soon be ended and fuller freedom achieved in the North. Wartime incidents in Harrisburg demonstrated that blacks still faced daily prejudice. For example, soldiers stationed at Camp Curtin, north of the city, often battled with blacks during their off-duty hours. Whether the soldiers blamed the blacks for the war with all its sacrifices and discomforts or were simply giving vent to deep-seated racial prejudice is not known. In any event, a number of clashes resulted in damages to the homes and property of blacks.[38]

One of the uglier incidents occurred in May 1863. Soldiers drinking at a beer parlor were asked by the black owner to pay when served. They threw him out of the building for asking and left, carrying off several tumblers and other objects. A policeman who witnessed the incident arrested the ringleaders, but the magistrate who heard the case released them for lack of sufficient evidence. Not long after, friends of the soldiers went to the black's home, where they "destroyed all the furniture in the house" and stole clothing, a lady's gold watch, and $25 in cash, "the hard savings of the family." After breaking out the windows and doors of the nearby black Masonic Hall, they vandalized five or six homes of blacks, forcing open shutters, breaking sashes, and carrying off anything of value. White troublemakers "piloted" the soldiers, indicating properties that belonged to blacks. The next day, whites in uniform attacked several black men, leaving them "unmercifully beaten." That evening, police in another part of town prevented further assaults on black families. Finally, on Wednesday, the sheriff who had been absent returned to town and enrolled a large enough force to prevent any further disturbances. Although the *Telegraph* faulted the mayor for not acting promptly, no one was punished.[39] Lesser affairs continued until the end of the war, with the *Telegraph,* now a Republican paper, usually taking the side of the victims and castigating soldiers and officials who did little about the episodes.

Despite such abuses, blacks were eager to participate in the war. As early as March 1863, Harrisburg blacks made their way north to enlist in a new Massachusetts Fifty-fourth Regiment. Although officered by whites, its ranks were reserved for African Americans. On June 9, only a week after the beer-parlor riot, a party of twenty-five to thirty recruits left to enlist in a second such regiment, the Fifty-fifth, also forming in Massachusetts. The next day, under the leadership of Chester, now designated as "a leading colored citizen," yet another 135 blacks, some 45 of whom came from Harrisburg, entrained for Boston. This happened after a "War Meeting" in Tanner's Alley, where Chester and several black clergymen addressed the assemblage.[40] "From barber shops and hotels, from Tanner's Alley and South streets, from 'Bull Run's' classic ground, from suburban settlements and subterranean 'dives' and rookeries, their beauty and their chivalry had flocked," reported the *Patriot* sarcastically. Even so, the paper admitted that Chester's talk was "sensible and patriotic, and was interspersed with passages of genuine eloquence." When the meeting ended with the entire audience singing "the 'John Brown' song . . . , the chorus fairly lift[ed] the roof."[41]

Those who enlisted with such enthusiasm encountered disappointment in the months ahead. Some were rejected from service for medical reasons. Even those who were sworn in faced betrayal. Originally promised pay equal to that of white regulars, they were in fact offered only what the army paid slaves in the South who attached themselves to army units as cooks, servants, and common laborers. Too proud to soldier for the pay of menials, they declined compensation even when the Commonwealth of Massachusetts offered to supplement the army's offer to make it equal with the pay of regulars. Not until October 1864 did a reluctant Congress relent and grant the wages due the men.[42]

Within days of the departure of the second group of black enlistees from Harrisburg, rebel armies approached Gettysburg. Their outriders reached as far as the hills opposite Harrisburg, where they scouted the bridges into the city. Newspapers reported a flood of refugees of both races pouring into the city from the Cumberland Valley. On June 24, blacks met in their Masonic Hall in Tanner's Alley to organize and offer their services to the governor. Many were refugees anxious to do what they could in the emergency. The next day, fifty-four volunteers organized into two companies officered by Captains Chester and Henry Bradley, a local barber and a major black landowner. Although Pennsylvania ordinarily accepted blacks only if they enlisted for three years, an exception appears to have been made for the emergency. The city armed the units over the mayor's objections, to help ward off the nearing enemy. Since no attack came, they were praised for the good cheer and zeal with which they cleaned and polished equipment. Meanwhile, other blacks, both locals and refugees, were pressed into filling barrels with water and digging entrenchments on the shore opposite the city.[43]

Local officials who had been glad enough to use blacks during the crisis, sought to disarm them and get them out of the city as soon as the danger passed. On July 8, Mayor A. L. Roumfort rehearsed before the city council his objections to arming them in the first place and allowing them to take the weapons home afterward. Turning to the refugees, he complained that they were receiving rations from the city and asked that steps be taken to remove them from the community. To support his request, he presented a petition from thirty-three citizens "praying for the removal of the Colored people" in and about Tanner's Alley and South and Short Streets. Their concern was the number of blacks and their "filthy condition"—which might lead to an epidemic, "there having been already several cases of smallpox among them."[44] The council adopted a resolution to have the refugees removed, and the next morning the police collected more than 300 of them near the mayor's office. That evening they were "sent up the valley . . . in an extra train."[45]

In November 1865, following the end of hostilities, the "Black boys in blue" were honored at a parade in Harrisburg, followed by a "grand dinner."

Because Governor Andrew Curtin was ill, former Secretary of War Simon Cameron reviewed the soldiers from his home on Front Street and made a short address. Chester served as Chief Marshal. A recruiter of black soldiers early in the war, he himself had declined to serve in the United States Army, because blacks could rise no higher than sergeant. Instead he became the war's only black news reporter, working for the *Philadelphia Press.*[46] William Howard Day, of whom much would be heard later in Harrisburg, gave the principal address. Among other things, these leaders hoped to use the occasion to build support for extending the suffrage once more to blacks. According to the local Democratic organ, the *Patriot,* the goal of the "Darkies Jubilee" was to promote "niggers" holding office, intermarrying with whites, and ruling America.[47] The vote was denied Pennsylvania blacks until adoption of the Fifteenth Amendment to the federal Constitution in 1870.

Coverage of African Americans by Harrisburg newspapers soon became reminiscent of the prewar years, but with a difference. By 1867, bitter, racist invective appeared as blacks became pawns in the politics of Reconstruction. The Democratic *Patriot* turned increasingly negrophobic. It frequently referred to blacks as "nigs," "coons," "smokes," "darkies," and "the culled population" and made much of variations in complexion: "tan colored street walker," "ebony-colored scoundrel," "a Yaller gal," "wenches of every conceivable hue, from liver color to a dirty, light yellow." Even the *Telegraph,* controlled from behind the scenes by Simon Cameron and seeking to secure the vote for blacks, sometimes strayed from "colored person" or "Negro." Both papers, for instance, referred to the black section of town as "Buzzard's Glory."[48] Intermarriage of blacks and whites drew especially strong denunciations from the press. The *Patriot,* for example, described a drunken white woman who had a black husband as "mean and groveling enough to be married to a nigger." Such marriages were rare, however, and whites kept their objections vocal rather than turning to physical violence.[49]

Meanwhile, the *Patriot* filled its local column with reports of blacks involved in rapes, attempted rapes, brawls, and drunken sprees. It even blamed them for unsolved crimes, such as a rash of chicken thefts in the Sixth Ward in the autumn of 1867. "Depredations of this kind occur very frequently in that section of the city," it noted, "and the supposition is that they are committed by Negroes who have no ostensible means of livelihood, but nevertheless manage to subsist very comfortably." The ward's "large and worthless Negro population . . . huddled together promiscuously in small filthy shanties, many of them without occupations or employment, and too lazy to work if they had an opportunity." It was from that district that "juvenile beggars" came daily to beg for food at the homes of whites. With winter nearing, the *Patriot* warned, the "condition of these wretches will become still worse, and their depredations more numerous."[50] Quite unintentionally the item spoke volumes about how blacks fared in post–Civil War Harrisburg.

The real concerns of the *Patriot* were political; its appeals to defeat Radical Republicans in Pennsylvania were racist. It warned that, if elected, the Radicals would soon be "breaking down the barriers of race" and elevating blacks to positions as voters, jurymen, office holders and "controllers of legislation." They would compel school directors to admit blacks "upon perfect equality with the white children." Their proposal for equal access to transportation would require railroad officials to admit any black male, however "dirty and unkempt, possibly drunk and a blackguard, but at any rate odoriferous," to cars set aside for women. There he would be free to take a seat by the side of "whichever lady best pleases his fancy." Yet another measure would be to force industries to admit blacks to apprenticeships. Although their work would be inferior, they would compete with whites for jobs and drive down wages.[51]

The *Patriot*'s concern that Republicans were trying to use blacks to advance their political ends was justified. Reelected to the Senate in 1866, Simon Cameron was constructing the archetypal Gilded Age state political machine with himself as boss. His chagrin at his machine being able to dominate the state but regularly failing to carry the city where he lived can be imagined. To offset the Democratic party's alleged manipulation of the Irish vote to carry communities such as Harrisburg, the Cameron machine sought to enfranchise blacks, who, it assumed, would vote Republican.

Given the limited social and political gains of Harrisburg's African Americans in the 1850s and 1860s, how did they fare economically? Although industrialization came to the city later than to other comparable communities in the Northeast, it proceeded rapidly after 1849. That year the Pennsylvania Railroad reached town, and soon connected the capital city with Philadelphia to the east and Pittsburgh and Chicago to the west. Within five years, a cotton factory, a large anthracite blast furnace, iron rolling mills, a railroad car manufacturing plant, and a firm specializing in machinery sprang up. The war helped by transforming Harrisburg into a major railroad center. There, enormous quantities of supplies and men from the Midwest were transferred from east-bound trains of the Pennsylvania Railroad to south-bound trains of the Northern Central headed for Washington, D.C., and the eastern front. The conflict also stimulated the expansion of all Harrisburg's major industries except the cotton mill.[52]

Although managers in the city rarely hired blacks to work in the new factories, industrialization nonetheless benefited blacks indirectly during the 1850s. The building of shops and mills, hundreds of new homes for a swelling workforce, and schools, stores, and other structures created a need for people to haul materials, clear worksites, and clean up after construction. Many of those jobs went to blacks, raised their incomes, and increased the number able to acquire real estate. But the progress of the blacks that decade appeared to be short-lived, seeming largely to evaporate during the decade of the 1860s.

Although African Americans increased significantly in number during the two decades, they did not quite maintain their proportion of the city's total population (see Table 9.1).[53] Until the 1860s, their community had been relatively stable. Contentment, inertia, or perhaps lack of alternatives kept a considerable number of the same people living in Harrisburg for ten, twenty, or even thirty years.[54] Of 101 heads of black households in 1840, for example, one-third reappeared in the 1850 census, one-fifth were still there in 1860, and one-eighth after thirty years. The 183 heads of black households in the 1850 census had even higher persistence rates; nearly half remained at least ten years, and one-quarter for twenty. With the war and its aftermath, however, persistence declined noticeably. Only a little more than one-quarter of the heads of household in the 1860 census (72 of 261) were in Harrisburg ten years later. Persistence trends for all blacks, as opposed to just heads of household, were essentially similar. One-fifth of all residents in the 1850 census were there a decade later, and one-eighth twenty years later. On the other hand, of all 1860 blacks, the rate was half what it had been a decade earlier; that is, one-tenth rather than one-fifth persisted.[55] Why this was so is not clear. Certainly the drive to capture runaway slaves in the 1850s would seem sufficiently disruptive to produce an outflow. But whatever the motivations during that decade, only half as many left Harrisburg as would during the next.

Industrialization was accompanied both by more jobs and by a greater variety of occupations for blacks. In 1850, some 191 black males were employed at only sixteen different occupations. By 1860 that had grown to 254 in 35 different job classifications, and a decade later to 559 in 40 occupations. Inasmuch as the 1850 census did not call for listing female occupations, the nine black women shown with jobs had been at the whim of the census taker. In 1860, one-fifth of the city's black women above the age of 15 (115) filled fifteen different occupations. Although the number expanded to 153 (only 18 percent of black women over 15) in 1870, the number of different jobs they held declined by one.[56]

The kinds of work performed also changed. Between 1850 and 1860, for example, a higher percentage of males moved into occupations other than unspecified laborer or one of the varieties of servant. Despite the general practice, at least half a dozen held factory jobs, and others listed as laborers in the census may in fact have performed menial tasks in industry. Although the percentage of professionals declined slightly that same decade, both self-employed persons and craftsmen increased. Where fewer than one-sixth had been in those categories in 1850, by 1860 they totaled more than one-fifth of all employed males.

These encouraging developments for blacks did not continue in the following decade. The percentages of professionals, self-employed persons, and craftsmen all declined. Only persons employed in factories increased. Put another way, the percentage employed as laborers or servants reached a peak in 1870. That represented a substantial setback from 1860 and was slightly worse than 1850. The types of work open to women remained dismal throughout the period. Because census takers reported the jobs of so few women in 1850, it is impossible to measure with any precision whether their situation improved. Inasmuch as 112 of 120 in 1860 were cooks, domestics, servants, and washerwomen, precision would seem to make little difference. By 1870, matters were worse; only 6 out of 174 were not servants or laborers.

By 1870, black males no longer dominated such relatively desirable jobs as barbering or running oyster bars and small restaurants, nor were black women any longer the majority of hired cooks. Those jobs were now shared with immigrants and their children. On the other hand, black men increased their holds on such occupations as carters, coachmen, hostlers, and porters, and black women held on to laundering and other domestic service occupations.

Persistence in the city, combined with slightly higher percentages of blacks holding better-paying jobs, resulted in increased ownership of real estate by 1860. Landowners more than tripled in number, the percentage of adult blacks owning real estate increased, and the value of their combined holdings advanced nearly fivefold. The average value of land holdings also rose by $250 during the 1850s. Where merely a third of landholders in 1850 owned plots valued at less than $500, only one-fifth owned plots so low in value a decade later. The wealthiest real-estate holder in 1850, a barber named John Williams, had property worth $1,800. Eight blacks owned land valued above that figure in 1860—the wealthiest, a retired clergyman named Albert Bennett, holding land worth $7,000.

As with jobs, gains in the property ownership during the 1850s reversed during the war decade. The number of landowners dropped more than one-third, leaving only about one adult in twenty holding real estate; even so, the combined value of their holdings increased nearly 7 percent. The value of the average holding increased some 65 percent, but much of that gain may have been wartime inflation.

Among African American real-estate holders, those who remained in Harrisburg from one census to another saw the value of their land rise. Half of the landowners in the 1850 census reappeared a decade later with average

Table 9.5. New and continuing black real-estate holders, Harrisburg, 1850–1870

1850			1860			1870		
No.	Value	Aver.	No.	Value	Aver.	No.	Value	Aver.
30	$20,100	$670	15	$26,000	$1,733	7	$16,000	$2,286
			new 91	71,300	784	17	27,400	1,612
			106	97,300	918			
						new 45	61,400	1,364
From 1850 to 1860:			*From 1860 to 1870:*			69	104,800	1,519
15 (50%) persist			24 (23%) persist					
15 (50%) lost			82 (77%) lost					

Source: Computerized Manuscript Census Data, 1850, 1860, 1870.

holdings one-and-a-half times greater in value. Nearly half of those, in turn, remained another decade and saw the value of their holdings, on average, increase another third. Similarly, new real-estate holders in 1860 who remained through 1870 enjoyed a doubling in value of their average holding. But did land ownership serve to keep owners in the community? In contrast to 1850, only one-fifth of new property owners in 1860 remained a full decade. An additional fifteen landowners in 1860 remained in the community through 1870 but had lost their property. At least in the period under consideration, persistence favored increased value of real-estate holdings. Ownership of land, however, did not of itself determine whether people remained in the community.

Until 1860, economic conditions improved for Harrisburg's blacks, and their community enjoyed relative stability. Even if all who later admitted birth in a slave state are excluded, between 85 and 88 percent were born in Pennsylvania, and many, regardless of birthplace, appeared in two or more consecutive censuses as residents of the city. Job prospects were improving, and land ownership, though restricted to a small minority, was on the increase.[57] After 1860 these trends all shifted direction. Fewer blacks remained between 1860 and 1870, the percentages in jobs other than unspecified laborer or servant declined, and considerably fewer owned real estate.

These generalizations about the 1860s, accurate enough for the whole African American community of Harrisburg, can be misleading. Although the total percentage of blacks remained steady, the composition of the black community changed markedly in that decade. By 1870, only slightly more than half gave Pennsylvania as their birthplace. The others were natives chiefly of Maryland and Virginia. Obviously a large number, probably newly emancipated slaves for the most part, migrated into Harrisburg during and immediately after the war. Equally important is that a significant number of Pennsylvanian-born blacks, including property owners, left the city.

Why these simultaneous migrations took place is not clear. The treatment of blacks in the city during and immediately after the war, and the near approach of Confederate armies on two occasions, may have induced blacks to leave. But could they have expected better treatment, or perhaps better occupational opportunities, in other northern communities? And were the threats of enemy occupation sufficient to induce permanent moves rather than temporary flights to safety? Until these questions can be answered, the motivations of those who left will remain a mystery.

Similarly, why former slaves from Maryland and Virginia came to Harrisburg in such large numbers is not known.[58] Possibly some had relatives living there and came to be near them. Some refugees may have come during the war and avoided expulsion when the city purged itself of such groups following the battle of Gettysburg. The *Patriot* in August 1867 offered another explanation. For the past two years the Freedmen's Bureau had been quietly shipping small groups of blacks to northern cities to ease the refugee burden in Washington. No less than 50,000 had been scattered throughout the eastern and middle states, "generally as hotel and house servants." As usual, the *Patriot* sniffed political conspiracy. The goal was to add to the number of potential Republican voters in the North.[59]

Certainly the Bureau provided transportation for refugees to northern communities where jobs were offered. It sent the great majority south, however, where field hands were in demand, and altogether transported only about 30,000 freedmen to all places.[60] Bureau records for the District of Columbia (where many of the moves originated) show that only 48 refugees were sent to Harrisburg. They traveled alone or in parties not exceeding 5, almost all at the request of persons wanting household servants. The names of the migrants were listed in twenty-eight instances, all coming to Harrisburg between April 1866 and July 1867.[61] Of that number, only four appeared in the manuscript census of 1870. The impact of the Bureau's policy on Harrisburg appears to have been slight: few blacks were shipped in, and fewer remained long.

Setting aside why they moved, the two migrations in effect produced two subgroups within the black community by 1870. The first were used to life as free persons. They were born either in Pennsylvania or in some other northern state, or if born in the South had resided in the North for at least a decade. The other group, only slightly smaller, was made up of the newcomers from Virginia and Maryland who either had been slaves or had spent their lives in a slaveholding community and migrated to Harrisburg after the close of the war.

The latter group differed in several ways from those who had spent much

Table 9.6. Illiteracy and real-estate holding among Harrisburg blacks, 1870, by length of residence and place of birth

| | | Illiterates | | Real Estate | | | |
| | Total | | | Holders | | Value | |
Group	No.	No.	%	No.	%	Total	Avg.
All blacks age 20+	1,299	561	43.2	69	5.3	$104,800	1,519
Free state residents:							
Persister birthplace free state[a]	128	14	10.9	20	15.6	43,000	2,150
Persister birthplace slave state	54	19	35.2	14	25.9	22,100	1,579
Newcomer birthplace free state[b]	365	70	19.2	11	3.0	13,400	1,218
Newcomer birthplace S1,							
Pennsylvania 10+ years	48	28	58.3	3	6.7	2,700	900
Total	595	131	22.0	48	8.1	$81,200	$1,692
Slave state resident to 1865; newcomer birthplace slave state	704	430	61.1	21	3.0	$23,600	$1,124
All persisters, 10 yrs +	182	33	18.1	34	18.7	65,100	1,915
All newcomers, −10 yrs	1,117	528	47.3	35	3.1	39,700	1,134
All birthplace free state	493	84	17.0	31	6.3	56,400	1,819
All birthplace slave state	806	477	59.2	38	4.8	48,400	1,274

SOURCE: Computerized Manuscript Census Data.

[a]Persister = listed in Harrisburg in census of 1850, 1860, or both.

[b]Newcomer = not listed in Harrisburg in previous census.

or all of their lives in relative freedom. For example, more than 60 percent of the adults could not read or write, raising illiteracy among all black adults in Harrisburg, which had been 23.5 percent in 1850, to 43.2 percent in 1870 (Table 9.6). Adults born in slave states, regardless of how long they subsequently lived in the North, were far less likely to learn to read and write than those born in the North. Well over half of those who had lived in the North (but not in Harrisburg) for at least ten years, and more than one-third of those who had lived in Harrisburg for a decade or more, remained illiterate. By contrast, less than one-fifth of the newcomers from free states were illiterate, while the illiteracy rate of northern-born blacks who had lived in Harrisburg at least a decade was little more than one in ten.

Only 3 percent of black newcomers moving to Harrisburg between 1860 and 1870, whether southern- or northern-born, held real estate, compared with nearly 19 percent of those who had lived in the community for more than a decade. Though place of birth did not much affect the percentage of newcomers holding land, the average value of the holdings of those born in the South was 8 percent lower on average than of northern-born newcomers.

Over time, if the previous experience of Harrisburg blacks held, the recently freed men [and women] from the South were more apt than their northern counterparts to acquire real estate. The average value of those holdings, however, would be less. One-quarter of southern-born blacks in 1870 who had persisted in Harrisburg for ten or more years held real estate, compared with fewer than 16 percent of northern-born persisters, but the value of their holdings averaged 40 percent less.

In part, the differences in land ownership were related to occupational opportunities. The southern-born newcomers, because of their previous experience as slaves, found employment chiefly as laborers and servants. None in Harrisburg became professionals, only a handful set up in business for themselves, a few were craftsmen. Among the better-paying jobs of barbering and waiting table in hotels, the southern-born were either poorly represented or completely absent. Instead, they found work at lower-paying jobs, including more than 70 percent of the blacks listed as "laborers" and the great majority of black carters, hostlers, porters, servants, and teamsters. To the limited extent that blacks found factory jobs, 80 percent were southern-born newcomers.

Clearly, Harrisburg's black community as a whole suffered economic setbacks during the 1860s. However, those losses were at least partially the result of the dual migrations that deprived the group of many of its more prosperous residents and replaced them with persons only recently liberated from bondage. The latter group, however hardworking and ambitious, could hardly be expected to adjust to life as free persons, move from a rural to an urban setting, fit into a new community, find good jobs, and become landowners, all in less than ten years. The fact that some two dozen did acquire land by 1870 was remarkable in itself and testified to their desire to improve.[62]

It could be done, as the career of Turner Cooper illustrated. Newly freed and illiterate, Cooper came from Alexandria, Virginia, in 1868 with his wife and seven children. The census of 1870 found him working as a brickyard employee. No doubt with the assistance of his two older sons, who were laborers, he had acquired real estate worth $1,500. A religious man, Cooper hated living in Harrisburg's "Bloody Eight" Ward and so sought a location in the Allison Hill district several blocks east of the capitol beyond the transportation corridor. There he not only built himself a home, but with the help of a white carpenter and five blacks, at least two of whom were also illiterate natives of Virginia, began the Springdale neighborhood. By 1890 it was a "thriving, populous community of blacks and whites."[63]

During the final three decades of the century, Harrisburg's African Americans improved their condition. As had been true from the beginning, churches were central in the social life of their community. Not counting storefront

Table 9.7. Selected occupations of various Harrisburg blacks, 1870

Occupation	Total Blacks	Persisters	Northern Newcomers	Southern Newcomers
Laborer	344	39	58	247
Barber	25	15	10	0
Carter	15	1	0	14
Hostler	18	3	5	10
Porter	24	6	3	15
Servant	20	0	6	14
Teamster	18	2	4	12
Waiter	52	15	16	21

SOURCE: Computerized Manuscript Census Data.

congregations, Harrisburg blacks supported six churches. The oldest, largest, and most prestigious was Wesley Union AME. Newer churches included Bethel AME (founded in 1835) and a Presbyterian congregation. A southern influence was reflected in two Baptist churches and a Church of God. By 1890 the Roman Catholic diocese was supporting a mission for blacks. These groups offered not only regular worship services, and the rites usually associated with Christian family living (weddings, baptisms, and funerals), but also a wide range of social functions as well. They sponsored concerts and musical programs, staged plays, and raised funds for charity. They also brought distinguished black lecturers to the community, including Frederick Douglass (whose 1847 visit had been disturbed by white troublemakers), Booker T. Washington, and William E. B. Du Bois.[64]

As was true of the white community in the same period, lodges became popular. There were two Odd Fellows groups in the 1880s, and a third by the turn of the century. More than 100 belonged to five Masonic lodges during the 1890s, and there was a black chapter of the Elks. Those who had fought in the Civil War formed a unit of the Grand Army of the Republic. Other social groups included bands, choirs, and an orchestra. Blacks organized and supported charitable organizations for their own poor, and insurance and mutual aid societies similar to those that were common among immigrant groups in those same years. During the 1880s, they also launched a number of weekly newspapers: *The Times* (1880–94), the *Home Journal* (1882), which merged in 1883 with the *State Journal* (1883–85), and the *Advocate Verdict* (1887–1920).[65]

Although blacks encountered both discrimination and segregation, neither was absolute or rigid. Churches and lodges were segregated, and blacks had their own labor unions and cemetery. On the other hand, blacks were admitted to the public library, the city hospital, and the trolley lines without discrimination. They also served on both petit and grand juries and sued and were sued in the courts with apparent fairness. After 1870, the local Republican machine protected their right to vote and later to run for and hold some public offices.[66]

Encouraging blacks to vote had started as a device for shifting Harrisburg from a Democratic to a Republican party stronghold. The impact on city politics was almost immediate following black enfranchisement in 1870. The Eighth Ward, where the largest number of blacks lived in 1869, had elected a Democrat as councilman with 63 percent of the vote. One year later, with blacks voting for the first time, the Republican candidate for mayor, though unsuccessful in the city at large, carried the ward with more than 53 percent of the vote. Thereafter, the ward regularly elected Republicans to the city council with majorities ranging from 52 to 70 percent and contributed 81, 53, 11, and 34 percent of the margins of victory for Republican mayors elected in 1872, 1874, 1876, and 1879.[67]

In time, blacks came to expect more from enfranchisement than merely being allowed to support the Cameron machine and its local candidates. In 1882, a revolt broke out in the Eighth Ward. There blacks complained that a Republican mayor whom they had helped elect failed to give them any recognition in his appointments to the police force. Even the *Telegraph* supported their claim, complaining that blacks were "an integral part of our city, pay taxes, support public institutions and by their votes keep in power in this city the party which gave Mayor [John C.] Herman his office." Philadelphia blacks, the Democratic *Patriot* pointed out, had helped elect a Democratic mayor of that city when its Republican mayor refused to appoint black police officers. Meeting a few days before the election, aggrieved blacks adopted resolutions threatening that, if not given some appointments, they would "pursue our own respect and protection." In the voting a week later, the Sixth and Eighth Wards, both heavily black and usually solidly Republican, each elected one Democratic councilman with the help of black voters. Thereafter, blacks began holding a few public offices, among others, that of alderman in the Eighth Ward in 1884.[68]

The situation in housing and schools was more complex. From very early in the century, Harrisburg's housing for blacks followed the southern pattern of being located in alleys to the rear of the homes of the wealthier whites who gave them employment. Eventually the district immediately east of the Capitol, which became the heart of the Eighth Ward, emerged as the principal enclave for blacks. In 1857, William K. Verbeke, a wealthy real-estate developer, purchased a block there that contained some twenty to thirty "huts" occupied by blacks. To provide for them, he bought ten acres in Susquehanna Township "some distance" above the borough line, an area that would be annexed to the city in 1860. There he sold lots to such of the displaced blacks as wanted to relocate, moved their houses for them, and allowed them to repay him at the rate of one dollar a week. "Verbeketown," as blacks called the area, became the nucleus of their second major location, the Sixth Ward, north of the Capitol.[69] Although blacks lived in all nine wards of the city, more than one-third lived in the Eighth Ward, nearly as many in the Sixth Ward, and all but 8 percent in six wards. Few lived along the river or in the newer developments in the outer districts of the city.[70]

Despite state law to the contrary, neighborhood grammar schools generally were segregated in practice. The black schools were staffed by teachers and administered by principals of the same race. The city's two high schools, which were segregated by gender, remained completely white until 1879. The entry of blacks that year produced open hostility in the white community. Four years later, two blacks graduated from Boys High School in a class of thirty-six. White resentment flared again when it was learned that one of the blacks ranked first in the class. Six or seven other blacks failed to graduate that same year from Girls High School, allegedly because of "teacher prejudice." The next year, two blacks graduated from each of the schools without incident.[71]

A sample study of 235 couples from the two central black wards in 1880 provides further insights into the improving situations of that race. Those born in the South still constituted about half the population; well over half of the heads of family and 45 percent of their spouses were born in Virginia or Maryland. Both partners were natives of Pennsylvania in only 27 percent of the instances, while 31 percent included one partner born out of state. The postwar newcomers and more recent migrants from the South were marrying into established local families, thereby hurrying reunification of the divided black community.[72]

Meanwhile, the occupational status of males improved. Although two-thirds were still unspecified laborers and servants, that was 12 percentage points lower than a decade before. Jobs were available for them at a tar works, at quarries and tanneries, and of course as haulers of goods, among other things. Industrial workers stood at 19 percent, a gain of 15 points since 1870. Factory jobs were chiefly in iron and steel, with some blacks traveling five miles to Steelton, south of the city, each day. It may safely be assumed that their jobs were the least skilled and lowest paid. Even so, these jobs provided steadier work, and perhaps higher incomes than could be earned as casual laborers. Skilled craftsmen, such as Turner Cooper, made up one-tenth of the sample, compared with only 2 percent of all black males in 1870.

The percentage of professionals, after dropping to 1.8 percent in 1870, had climbed to 3.4 percent in 1880, the same as in 1860 and the same as for all residents of the city in 1880.[73] One of this group, Dr. William H. Day, emerged as a leader not only of the black community but also of Harrisburg as a whole. Born in New York City and holding both a bachelor's and a master's degree from Oberlin College and an honorary doctorate of divinity from Livingston College, he had moved to Harrisburg in 1872. For several years a teacher and administrator in the public schools, he became the first black elected to the city school board in 1878 and served fifteen years. Elected by his twenty-five white colleagues to preside over the board between 1891 and 1893, he was one of the earliest blacks in America to be so honored.[74]

The majority of scholars who studied northern urban blacks from Du Bois in 1899 to the present agree that the conditions of African Americans generally deteriorated economically, socially, and politically between the Civil War and the end of the century. The benefits of the industrial revolution passed them by, because white owners usually refused to hire them for any but the most menial factory jobs. European immigrants encroached on the better-paying occupations traditionally held by blacks (barbering, carting, waiting table, catering food). Northern labor barred blacks from union membership and apprenticeships; and northern whites, by refusing to engage either black professionals or black artisans, in effect limited their clientele to members of their own race, who paid poorly. As white business firms grew larger and undersold them, the number of black enterprises and entrepreneurs declined. Meanwhile, de facto segregation in northern cities forced them into increasingly black enclaves, barred them from equal educational opportunities, sometimes restricted their right to vote, and usually kept them from holding any but the least important public offices.[75]

Most of these studies involved much larger cities than Harrisburg: Boston, Cleveland, Detroit, Milwaukee, Philadelphia, and Pittsburgh, to name only six. At the same time, but especially before 1900, blacks did not constitute as great a part of the populations of these centers as they did in Harrisburg. From 9.8 percent in 1870, Harrisburg's proportion of blacks slowly declined to 8.2 percent by 1900. By contrast, these larger cities had black communities ranging from less than 1 percent throughout, as at Milwaukee, to 5 percent by 1900 at Pittsburgh. It was after 1914, when World War I and postwar restrictions halted European immigration, that the Great Migration of southern blacks to northern cities and factory jobs began. Although the roots of ghettoization and the rise of a black industrial proletariat could be traced to the post–Civil War decades, the greatest deterioration in black conditions came in the new century.[76]

Harrisburg's experience differed from the others. The newly freed blacks who came immediately after the Civil War were the last great wave of that race to come prior to World War II. Moreover, between 1870 and 1920 they were a shrinking portion of the city's population. Although highly concentrated in the Sixth and Eighth Wards, they were not restricted to a black ghetto. Similarly, although one-fifth of married males among them found factory jobs by the end of the century, Harrisburg developed no large black industrial proletariat.

The African American community at Harrisburg also faced a much smaller proportion of immigrants, especially of the "new immigrants" who flooded in from southern and eastern Europe between 1890 and 1914. This was important because the two groups of outsiders were often antagonistic and frequently competed for the same housing and jobs. In the larger cities already cited, and at nearby Steelton, immigrants constituted between one-fifth and one-third of the population throughout the period from 1870 to 1920. By contrast, Harrisburg's foreign-born never exceeded one-eighth of the total population, and the New Immigration after 1890 was negligible. Through most of its history, the city's proportions of blacks and immigrants were roughly equal. From a high of 12.1 percent in 1870, the proportion of immigrants gradually fell to 4.9 percent by 1900. By 1920, blacks constituted 6.9 percent while the foreign-born were 5.5 percent.[77]

The primary reason that neither the New Immigration nor the Great Migration caused more than demographic ripples at Harrisburg was that there was a major change in the city's economic structure after 1880. Its highest rate of population growth, more than 70 percent each for two decades, occurred between 1850 and 1870, when the community industrialized. Between 1880 and 1910 that rate slowed to between 25 and 33 percent, then dropped sharply, and eventually turned negative. By 1880, industry had peaked in the city. After that date, few new mills or factories arose and the economy gradually shifted from an industrial base to one resting on governmental and administrative functions. Meanwhile, at the larger cities, industrialization went on apace, attracting first southeastern Europeans and then southern blacks.[78]

In the absence of repeated large waves or even a steady flow of newcomers from the South after 1870, Harrisburg's whites had little reason to fear inundation by blacks or to feel a need to repress those already there. No large foreign-born group vied with them for jobs. As a consequence, blacks enjoyed a relatively calm period not unlike that between 1820 and 1850, during which they rebuilt their community and institutions and resumed the fight for the modest gains here described. Too small a group to be independent of the white economy, blacks pushed for improvements but also sought accommodation.[79] Race relations, if not especially good, also were not antagonistic or marked by violence. In characterizing the degree of progress achieved by 1900, much depends on the scale used. Measured against their original servitude, the gains made by Harrisburg's African American community were significant. Measured against the goal of complete freedom and equality, they were painfully small and left much undone.

Notes

1. *Census of the United States: 1870*, 1:243–57; *1880*, 18:733–902; *1890*, 50:570–74; *1900*, 1:637–41. In 1850, Harrisburg also had fewer residents and blacks, but a larger proportion of blacks, than such northern cities as Albany, Boston, Brooklyn, Buffalo, Cincinnati, New York, Providence, and St. Louis. Closest was St. Louis, with 5.21 percent blacks. See Leonard Curry, *The Free Black in Urban America, 1800–1850* (Chicago, 1981), 246.

2. Kenneth L. Kusmer, "The Black Urban Experience in American History," in Darlene Clark Hine, ed., *The State of Afro-American History* (Baton Rouge, La., 1986), 91–122, esp. 105–8.

3. Sam Bass Warner, *The Private City* (Philadelphia, 1968). Alternating waves of Negrophobia and sympathy for blacks is a prominent theme of Gary B. Nash, *Forging Freedom: The Formation of Philadelphia's Black Community, 1720–1840* (Cambridge, Mass., 1988).

4. Arthur Zilversmit, *The First Emancipation: The Abolition of Slavery in the North* (Chicago, 1967). Thirty-six percent of Pennsylvania's blacks were slaves in 1790, 10 percent in 1800, a little more than 3 percent in 1810, and thereafter 1 percent or fewer through the Census of 1840. Edward R. Turner, *The Negro in Pennsylvania* (1911; reprint, New York, 1969), 253.

5. Ira V. Brown, "Pennsylvania and the Rights of the Negro, 1865–1887," *Pennsylvania History* 28 (January 1961): 45–46. According to Turner, *The Negro in Pennsylvania*, 184–85, blacks voted in at least seven counties, including Dauphin, before 1838.

6. William Henry Egle, *History of the Counties of Dauphin and Lebanon, Pennsylvania* (Philadelphia, 1883) (hereafter *History of Dauphin County*), 20–21; *Statutes at Large of Pennsylvania, 1780*, 67–73.

7. U.S. Census, manuscript schedules for Harrisburg (on microfilm), 1790–1840.

8. Computations based on data from the *Ninth Census of the United States* (Washington, D.C., 1878), 1:58–59, 243–57. The eleven counties were Adams, Berks, Bucks, Chester, Cumberland, Dauphin, Delaware, Franklin, Lancaster, Montgomery, and York. Curry, *The Free Black*, 239–40, suggests that urban areas were attractive because they concentrated demand for unskilled labor, offered greater educational and social opportunities, and contained larger pools of potential marriage partners. Urban areas also provided anonymity, which allowed free blacks some escape from the personal hostility of whites and fugitive slaves reduced likelihood of detection.

9. Mary D. Houts, "Black Harrisburg's Resistance to Slavery," *Pennsylvania Heritage* 4 (December 1977): 10; Rev. Jeanne B. Williams to author, July 5, 1989. Williams, a student of AME history in Pennsylvania, has generously shared her research with me.

10. Nash, *Forging Freedom*, 66–133.

11. Ibid., 204; Houts, "Black Harrisburg's Resistance," 11, quoting from an advertisement in the *Dauphin Oracle*.

12. Williams to Eggert, July 5, 1989; Egle, *History of Dauphin County*, 348–49, 367.

13. Statement of Principles and Membership List, Historical Society of Dauphin County (HSDC); Garrison to his wife, August 9, 1847, in *Letters of William Lloyd Garrison* (Cam-

bridge, Mass. 1973), 3:506–9; *Pennsylvania Freeman,* August 19, 1847. For election returns, see *Harrisburg Keystone,* November 14, 1848; *Pa. Telegraph,* November 11, 1852. For underground railroad activities, see Egle, *History of Dauphin County,* 557.

14. Houts, "Black Harrisburg's Resistance," 10–11, quoting a newspaper report and borough ordinances.

15. Harrisburg newspapers, 1849–50, passim; Garrison to his wife, August 9, 1847, *Letters of Garrison* 3:507.

16. For my forthcoming book on Harrisburg's industrialization after 1850 [*Harrisburg Industrializes* (University Park: The Pennsylvania State University Press, 1993)], I put the entire manuscript census schedules for the city in 1850, 1860, and 1870 on computer and have produced a number of listings and computations (hereafter cited as Computerized Manuscript Census Data). Whether a person of color was designated as black or mulatto was left to the discretion of the census takers. Sometimes parents in a given family were listed as black, while one or more of their children were listed as mulattoes, or vice versa. For some persons they changed from one census to the next. Given such unreliability, I classified both mulattoes and blacks as black.

17. Persons with the same surname who lived in the same household were classified as family members. Those with different surnames, including some who may have been family members, were classified as "singles."

18. Two black doctors were variously listed in the manuscript censuses between 1850 and 1870 as "doctor," "I. Doctor" (probably meaning Indian Doctor), and "druggist."

19. Curry, *The Free Black,* 258–61, 268.

20. Houts, "Black Harrisburg's Resistance," 11.

21. Fourteen people in the federal manuscript census were not listed in the county tax records, ten in the county records were not in the census, and five listed in the county rolls were shown in the census but without property. Since the local assessment included items not included in the census, and the census listed real estate wherever located, it is not surprising that the two did not agree on the value of holdings in a single instance. "County Assessment, Real Estate, Horses, and Carriages Used for Hire," Dauphin County Courthouse, Harrisburg.

22. *Pa. Telegraph,* August 14, 1850; September 4, 1850; March 24, 1852. The *Democrat Keystone* almost never mentioned local blacks; the *Democratic Union*'s comments were unsympathetic.

23. *Democratic Union,* September 12, 1849; *Telegraph,* October 20, 1852.

24. *Telegraph,* April 3, 1852.

25. *Telegraph,* August 20, 1851; March 12, 1851; September 8, 1852.

26. *Morning Herald,* May 22 and 23, 1855.

27. Houts, "Black Harrisburg's Resistance," 9, 11.

28. *Telegraph,* August 28, 1850.

29. For a fuller account of this incident, see Gerald Eggert, "The Impact of the Fugitive Slave Law on Harrisburg: A Case Study," *Pennsylvania Magazine of History and Biography (PMHB)* 109 (October 1985): 541–45.

30. *U.S. Statutes at Large,* 9:462–65; Stanley W. Campbell, *The Slave Catchers: Enforcement of the Fugitive Slave Law, 1850–1860* (Chapel Hill, N.C., 1968), 3–25.

31. For McAllister's motivation, see his letter to Simon Cameron, July 25, 1853, Cameron Papers, HSDC; for his conduct in office, see Eggert, "Impact of the Fugitive Slave Law on Harrisburg," 547–50.

32. Eggert, "Impact of the Fugitive Slave Law," 546–47, 550–52.

33. Ibid., 552–53.

34. Ibid., 553–67.

35. The changes were determined by comparing place of birth for the same person in Computerized Manuscript Census Schedules, 1850 through 1870.

36. *Telegraph,* February 5; *Borough Item,* February 23, 1853; interview with Chester in the *Patriot,* September 13, 1892. For Delaney's ideas, see Cyril E. Griffith, *The African Dream: Martin R. Delany and the Emergence of Pan-African Thought* (University Park, Pa., 1975), 18–29. After eighteen months in Africa, Chester returned to Thetford Academy in Vermont for two years. Between 1857 and 1862, he alternated three stints of teaching, newspaper editing, and dabbling in politics in Liberia, with fund-seeking and promotion of Liberia in the United States. See Allison Blakely, *Dictionary of American Negro Biography* (New York, 1982), 107; biographical essay in Thomas Morris Chester, *Black Civil War Correspondent* [hereafter T. M. Chester], ed. R. J. M. Blackett (Baton Rouge, La., 1989), 14–34. For Chester's later visits and speaking engagements in Harrisburg, see *Morning Herald,* October 31 and November 1 and 8, 1854; *Telegraph,* December 28, 1854; January 3, 1855.

37. The *Telegraph* fell into the hands of Stephen Miller, a Methodist lay-preacher and prohibitionist, who turned it and the *Morning Herald,* which he founded, into Know-Nothing organs. Gerald Eggert, " 'Seeing Sam': The Know Nothing Episode in Harrisburg," *PMHB* 109 (October 1985): 308–14.

38. Janet Mae Book, *Northern Rendezvous, Harrisburg During the Civil War* (Harrisburg, Pa., 1951), 64, 65, 84–85.

39. *Patriot,* May 27; *Telegraph,* June 1, 1863.

40. *Telegraph,* June 9, 1863. A check of published rosters of the regiments turned up only forty men from Harrisburg, see Luis F. Emilio, *History of the Fifty-fourth Regiment of Massachusetts Volunteer Infantry, 1863–1865* (Boston, 1891), 327–90; Charles B. Fox, *Record of the Service of the Fifty-fifth Regiment of Massachusetts Volunteer Infantry* (Cambridge, Mass., 1868), 90–144. That many who signed up were subsequently rejected for medical reasons may explain the difference in numbers.

41. *Patriot,* June 10, 1863.

42. Fox, *Record of the Fifty-fourth,* 17–18, 37.

43. *Telegraph,* June 25 and 26; Robert G. Crist, *Confederate Invasion, 1863* (Camp Hill, Pa., 1963), 8, 27.

44. Minutes of City Council, July 8, 1863, Office of the Clerk, Martin Luther King Jr. Municipal Center, Harrisburg; reports in the *Patriot* and the *Telegraph,* July 9, 1863.

45. *Telegraph,* July 10, 1863.

46. Ibid., November 13, 1865. After the war, Chester returned to England, studied law, and in 1870 became the first American black admitted to the British bar. Moving to Louisiana, he was active in Reconstruction politics from 1871 to 1877. Afterward he served as U.S. Commissioner of Courts in New Orleans and as special assistant to the U.S. Attorney for the Eastern District of Texas. Chester was admitted to the bars of Louisiana (1871), the District of Columbia (1879), and Pennsylvania (1881). He returned to his boyhood home, ill, in April 1892 and died there September 30. Biographical essay, *T. M. Morris,* 50–91; Blakely, *Dictionary of American Negro Biography,* 107–8.

47. *T. M. Morris,* 48; *Patriot,* November 13, 1865.

48. *Telegraph* and *Patriot* for 1867, passim.

49. *Patriot,* July 27, 1867; Michael J. Nestleroth, unpublished paper, "The Black Community of Harrisburg, 1860–1910: A Study of the Black Community of a Small Northern City" (copy on file, HSDC), 11, found eight interracial marriages in the city during the 1880s but no instances of white violence against them. He also reported that a black professional baseball player in Harrisburg who married a white woman was jeered but not removed from the team.

50. *Patriot,* October 1, 1867.

51. *Patriot,* September 7, 25, and 28, 1867.

52. Based on research for my book on the industrialization of Harrisburg, 1850–1900, *Harrisburg Industrializes* [see note 16].

53. The trend would continue into the twentieth century, with the percentage of blacks declining to 7.1 by 1910 and 6.9 by 1920, then rising to 8.0 by 1930, 8.7 by 1940, 11.3 by 1950, 18.0 by 1960, 30.7 by 1970, and 43.6 by 1980.

54. To determine persistence among blacks, I had the computer separate out black families and put them in alphabetical order by head of household for the censuses of 1850, 1860, and 1870. This facilitated checking by hand. Using families rather than individuals resulted in greater accuracy, because from one census to next the names of individuals were spelled differently, sometimes initials rather than given names were used, age did not always increase ten years, and place of birth changed. Only by careful examination of names, ages, and other characteristics of all family members was it possible to be reasonably sure of identification. Another benefit was that this system allowed a more certain identification of persons with common family names. Persons not living in family units were listed separately and counted as persisters only if their names, ages, and other characteristics were very close from one census to the next. Attempting to program a computer to make such judgments, in my opinion, would be too complex to be practicable. Unfortunately, persisting women were probably undercounted. Because they adopted the family name of their husbands, those who married between censuses were lost. Even so, slightly more women than men persisted in each census, suggesting that among blacks, at least, males rather than females tended to be more mobile geographically.

55. Computerized Manuscript Census Data, 1850, 1860, 1870.

56. Ibid.

57. Literature on urban blacks is slight for the decade of the 1850s. Most pre–Civil War studies (for example, Nash's *Forging Freedom* and Curry's *The Free Black in Urban America*) end in 1840 or 1850. Studies of the postwar period, such as Howard N. Rabinowitz, *Race Relations in the Urban South, 1865–1890* (New York, 1978); Elizabeth Hafkin Pleck, *Black Migration and Poverty, Boston, 1865–1900* (New York, 1979); George C. Wright, *Life Behind a Veil: Blacks in Louisville, Kentucky, 1865–1930* (Baton Rouge, La., 1985); and Roger Lane, *Roots of Violence in Black Philadelphia, 1860–1900* (Cambridge, Mass., 1986), for the most part begin in 1860 or later. The absence of comparable materials makes uncertain whether the gains of Harrisburg's blacks in that decade were common in urban centers, restricted to smaller cities, or unique.

58. Apparently the greatest block of former slaves to leave the South at the end of the war went west rather than north. See Herbert G. Gutman, *The Black Family in Slavery and Freedom, 1750–1925* (New York, 1976), 433. Harrisburg seems to have been an exception, adding at least 704 blacks who moved to Harrisburg after 1865 and remained through the census of 1870.

59. *Patriot,* August 19 and 28, 1867.

60. George R. Bentley, *A History of the Freedmen's Bureau* (Philadelphia, 1955), 124–25; John Alcott Carpenter, *Sword and Olive Branch: Oliver Otis Howard* (Pittsburgh, 1964), 114–15; Paul S. Pierce, *The Freedmen's Bureau: A Chapter in the History of Reconstruction* (Iowa City, 1984), 100.

61. Records Relating to the Transportation of Freemen and Bureau Personnel, July 1865–68; Records of the Assistant Commissioner for the District of Columbia, Record Group 105 (on microfilm, M1055, reel 17), National Archives. Neither former Secretary of War Cameron, who at the time was opening his Lochiel Iron Works in Harrisburg, nor any other Harrisburg

entrepreneur contacted the Bureau for refugees to serve as cheap factory labor between 1865 and 1872. As Pleck, *Black Migration and Poverty,* 27, found for Boston, the Bureau served chiefly as "an employment bureau for domestic servants."

62. W. E. Burghardt Du Bois, *The Philadelphia Negro* (New York, 1899), 269, argued that emancipation and pauperism went hand in hand in postwar Philadelphia. Pleck, *Black Migration and Poverty,* 44–67, questioned whether postwar migrants from the South accounted for the general decline of conditions for Boston's blacks. She found many newcomers from Virginia who already had acquired urban habits and skills, having first lived in Richmond or some other urban center, and had an adult literacy rate of 32 percent. She also cited Theodore Hershberg's finding that Virginia blacks migrating to Philadelphia had an adult literacy rate of 35 percent (p. 53). I believe that the adult illiteracy rate of more than 61 percent for black newcomers from the south to Harrisburg by 1870 indicates a much larger number of recent fieldhands without urban experience there.

63. Pauline Allen, newspaper article entitled "Freed Slave Began Hill Development," *Patriot,* February 9, 1982.

64. Nestleroth, "Black Community of Harrisburg," 20–22.

65. Ibid., 23–25; Glenora E. Rossell, *Pennsylvania Newspapers: A Bibliography and Union List,* 2nd ed. (Pittsburgh, 1978), 83–87.

66. Nestleroth, "Black Community of Harrisburg," 5, 18, 32–33.

67. Election returns as reported in the *Patriot,* October 14, 1869; October 12, 1870; October 14, 1872; February 17, 1874; February 16, 1876; and February 20, 1879.

68. *Telegraph,* February 7; *Patriot,* February 8, 16, and 22, 1882; and February 20, 1884.

69. Egle, *History of Dauphin County,* 323.

70. Nestleroth, "Black Community of Harrisburg," 13.

71. Ibid., 30–31. For the law and practice regarding blacks in schools in Pennsylvania, see Ira V. Brown, *The Negro in Pennsylvania History* (University Park, Pa., 1970), 52–54.

72. Nestleroth, "Black Community of Harrisburg," 6–8.

73. Ibid., 16–17.

74. Ibid., 28–29; item prepared at the office of the Harrisburg School Board, Genealogical File, State Library, Harrisburg; obituaries; *Telegraph,* December 3, 1900; *Patriot,* December 4, 1900.

75. In addition to Du Bois, *The Philadelphia Negro,* see, for example, Peter Gottlieb, *Making Their Own Way: Southern Blacks' Migration to Pittsburgh, 1916–1930* (Urbana, Ill. 1987); David M. Katzman, *Before the Ghetto: Black Detroit in the Nineteenth Century* (Urbana, Ill., 1973); Kenneth L. Kusmer, *A Ghetto Takes Shape: Black Cleveland, 1870–1930* (Urbana, Ill., 1976); Lane, *Roots of Violence;* Pleck, *Black Migration and Poverty;* and Joe William Trotter Jr., *Black Milwaukee: The Making of an Industrial Proletariat, 1915–1945* (Urbana, Ill., 1985). For a southern border city, see Wright, *Life Behind a Veil.*

76. The principal thrust of Kusmer's study was after the Great Migration, while Gottlieb's and Trotter's deal with the era after 1915. For the proportions of blacks in Harrisburg, see note 53 above; for the other cities, see the studies cited or the published census for appropriate years.

77. The percentage of foreign-born at Harrisburg were: in 1880, 7.5 percent; in 1890, 6.6; in 1910, 6.4; in 1920, 6.9; in 1930, 4.6; and since 1940, between 3.9 and 2.5 percent. Calculated from published census figures, 1860–80. The data on the other cities are from the studies cited or from the published census. For Steelton, see John Bodnar, *Immigration and Industrialization: Ethnicity in an American Mill Town, 1870–1940* (Pittsburgh, 1977), 15.

78. The data on population are from published census figures. I trace the gradual shift in

Harrisburg's economic structure in my forthcoming book on industrialization at Harrisburg [see note 16].

79. Wright, *Life Behind a Veil,* argues that the gains made at Louisville, Kentucky (in some respects more impressive that those at Harrisburg) were essentially token devices of whites to co-opt black leaders and placate the rest of the race to keep them "in their place." Kusmer, "The Black Urban Experience in American History," 106–8, points out that blacks in northern cities shifted to an accommodationist stance before World War I, as segregation and hostility to blacks increased. Once the size of their communities grew, after World War I, and professionals became less dependent on a white clientele, black militance increased.

PART THREE

THE INDUSTRIAL ERA
New Patterns of Class, Race, and Ethnicity, 1870–1945

Working in steel mills was hot, noisy, and dangerous work. It was not uncommon for workers to work a ten- or twelve-hour shift regularly. Yet the promise of relatively high wages continued to draw migrants from the South to Pittsburgh steel mills. Here an African American taps a blast furnace in the Pittsburgh area in 1938. (Photo by Arthur Rothstein; Courtesy of Library of Congress)

As elsewhere in the urban North, African American life in Pennsylvania unfolded within two distinct but overlapping phases of industrial change: (1) the high point of growth and expansion from about 1870 to the 1920s, and (2) the gradual, long-term decline during and following the Great Depression and World War II. Although African Americans gradually moved into industrial centers like Philadelphia, Pittsburgh, Harrisburg, and Steelton during the late nineteenth and early twentieth centuries, only during World War I did they find increasing opportunities in the industrial sector. Wartime labor demands, declining conditions in southern agriculture, immigration restriction legislation, and a new resolve on the part of African Americans themselves all fueled the movement of blacks into the state's industrial economy. In Philadelphia, Midvale Steel, Atlantic Refining, Franklin Sugar, and Hog Island Shipyard recruited thousands of African Americans. In the Pittsburgh district, Carnegie Steel, Jones and Laughlin Steel, and Crucible Steel, among others, also hired black workers. In Johnstown and elsewhere also, employers turned to southern blacks to fill their labor needs.

As southern blacks migrated to Pennsylvania in rising numbers, racial violence broke out, racially segregated neighborhoods expanded, and new forms of economic discrimination emerged. The mass migration of European immigrants to the state, the expansion of the predominantly white labor movement, and the persistence of discriminatory employment practices hampered the progress of black workers. The 1911 lynching of black worker Zachariah Walker in Coatesville was followed by destructive race-rioting in Chester in 1917, in Philadelphia in 1918, and in Johnstown in 1923. Such conflicts underscored changing race and class relations in Pennsylvania.

Intraracial conflict also increased in the wake of the Great Migration. Such conflict gained expression in recurring tensions between old residents and newcomers, on the one hand, and between workers, business, and professional people. Still, despite such friction, Pennsylvania's African American population found common ground, built new institutions, and launched new movements to combat racial discrimination and inequality. Such political and social activism included the expansion of the NAACP, the Urban League, and the Garvey Movement during the 1920s; participation in the New Deal coalition and the Congress of Industrial Organizations during the 1930s; and the March on Washington movement during World War II. In Pennsylvania, as elsewhere, the March on Washington movement also signaled the rise of the state's modern civil rights movement.

Taken together, the chapters in this section demonstrate the impact of the Great Migration, the Depression, and World War II on blacks in Pennsylvania. Community studies by John E. Bodnar, Peter Gottlieb, and Frederic Miller provide insight into Steelton, Pittsburgh, and Philadelphia. Carolyn Leonard Carson's investigation of black migrant women, and Dennis Dickerson's study of the black church, complement Gottlieb's chapter on Pittsburgh; finally, Merl E. Reed illuminates the impact the March on Washington movement had on the economic position of blacks in the Keystone State.

CHAPTER TEN

The Impact of the "New Immigration" on the Black Worker:

Steelton, Pennsylvania, 1880–1920

John E. Bodnar

Northern industrial centers and large urban areas had been acquiring sizable Negro populations in the three decades before 1900. The black population of Pittsburgh, for instance, more than tripled between 1880 and 1900. Buffalo doubled its Negro community in the same period, while Cleveland's grew from 2,000 to nearly 6,000. In smaller industrial centers the pattern was the same. In Pennsylvania steel towns such as Johnstown, the Negro community tripled in the last two decades of the nineteenth century. McKeesport, which had a mere 15 blacks in 1880, counted more than 700 by 1900.[1]

This rising tide of blacks, however, began to slow considerably in the first decade of this century. Pittsburgh, whose black population had increased by 100 percent between 1890 and 1900, saw its Negro community grow by 25 percent in the decade after 1900. Industrial centers such as Lorain, Ohio, gained only 73 blacks in the ten years after 1900, after gaining more than 700 Negroes in the previous decade. Similar trends were evident in larger and smaller urban areas. McKeesport, which had gained 600 blacks in the 1890s, gained only 50 between 1900 and 1910. Between 1890 and 1900 the Negro population of Homestead, Pennsylvania, grew by more than 500. In

This chapter was first published in *The Pennsylvania Magazine of History and Biography* 97 (April 1973): 199–209. Reprinted by permission.

the subsequent decade, Homestead gained only 150 blacks. The black population of Buffalo, which had increased by more than 700 in the 1890s, grew by only 73 in the ten years before 1910. The Negro population of Erie did not grow at all between 1900 and 1910. Wilkes-Barre had fewer blacks in 1910 than it had in 1900.[2]

What was salient in the experience of Pittsburgh, Buffalo, Erie, Wilkes-Barre, McKeesport, Lorain, Johnstown, and similar cities was that they were all industrial centers attracting a vast influx of Slavic and Italian immigrant labor, especially during the first decade of this century. The newcomers were largely unskilled workers and peasants, some with previous industrial experience. These immigrant workers, consequently, challenged the Negro worker for semiskilled and unskilled occupational opportunities. To date, however, except for some impressionistic accounts, the impact of Slavic and Italian immigrant labor upon the Negro worker has been relatively neglected by historical scholarship.[3] By concentrating on the impact immigrants had on Negro workers in a typical Pennsylvania steel town, I hope to suggest the complexity of factors which were tending to slow the growth of black communities in numerous northern industrial centers immediately after 1900.

Steelton, Pennsylvania, lying just south of Harrisburg on the east bank of the Susquehanna River, was a good example of a northern industrial town where "new immigrants" and southern blacks met in direct competition for lower level jobs. Communities such as Steelton, in fact, were attracting black laborers even before they began employing Slavic and Italian newcomers. Steelton grew up around the works of the Pennsylvania Steel Company which began erecting its mills in 1866. Within the next four decades, the community had attained a population of more than 12,000. Included in the population were some 1,200 Afro-Americans and more than 3,000 immigrants, mostly southern Slavs and a few Italians.[4] The black population numbered about 1,270 in 1900. Indeed, a Negro community with three churches was flourishing in Steelton by 1890, before the influx of Slavs and Italians began. The first Slavic group did not organize until 1893, when Croatians and Slovenes formed a fraternal lodge. The bulk of the Slavic immigration, however, arrived after 1900. Thus, a Serbian Orthodox church was begun in 1903, and Bulgarians erected a church in 1909.[5]

The character of the immigrant population in Steelton had changed markedly between 1880 and 1905. While the trickle of Irish and English, and to a lesser extent Catholic Germans, slowed considerably, large numbers of Italians and Slavs entered the mill town. These "new immigrants," however, found it difficult to achieve occupations above the low, unskilled strata. Of 403 Slavic and Italian immigrants studied in 1905, some 79 percent were in

During the Great Migration in 1916, Bethlehem Steel took over the Pennsylvania Steel Company plant in Steelton and brought in African American workers to meet the wartime labor shortage. This view of the western end of the steel company in 1985 looks toward the south. The city of Steelton is in the background; Conrail railroad tracks and the Susquehanna River can be seen on the right. (Courtesy of Bethlehem Steel Company and the Historical Society of Dauphin County)

unskilled occupations; this was 9 percent higher than the figure for "old immigrants" in 1880. Slavic and Italian newcomers, moreover, had fewer of their members in semiskilled ranks in 1905 (13 percent to 8 percent) and skilled ranks (9 percent to 0 percent), than the German, Irish, and English immigrants had in 1880 (see Tables 10.1a and 1b).[6]

By 1915, some two decades after the first Croatians and Slovenes had settled in Steelton, more than three-fourths of the immigrants were still in unskilled endeavors. This was nearly three times the percentage for native whites and a slight increase from 1905. While the number of Slavs and Italians moving into semiskilled and skilled positions from 1905 to 1915 increased, the figure was small. The 8 percent of the immigrants who were classed as semiskilled in 1905 became 10 percent in 1915. Where no immigrants could be found in skilled trades in 1905, some 3 percent were skilled workers ten years later.

Table 10.1a. Occupational distribution, immigrants, Steelton, 1880–1915

	(English, Irish, German) 1880	(Slavic & Italian) 1905	(Slavic & Italian) 1915
Unskilled	70%	79%	76%
Semiskilled	13%	8%	10%
Skilled	9%	0%	3%
Low nonmanual	0%	12%	11%
High nonmanual	8%	4%	1%
N =	58	403	616

SOURCES: The list of German, English, and Irish immigrants for 1880 was compiled from the *Tenth Census* (1880) for Steelton. The list of Slavic and Italian immigrants for 1905 and 1915 was compiled from the volumes of *Naturalization Service: Petition and Record, Prothonotary's Office.* Dauphin County Court House: *Records of Interment for St. Mary's Croatian Church and St. Nicholas Serbian Orthodox Church* and lists of immigrants in the *Golden Jubilee of St. Ann's [Italian] Catholic Church* (Steelton, 1953), *Consecration and Sixtieth Anniversary, Holy Annunciation and Macedonian-Bulgarian Orthodox Church* (Steelton, 1970), and *30th Anniversary of the Founding of St. Peter's Church [Slovenian]* (Steelton, 1939). The most complete listing of immigrants in Steelton, however, is to be found in the "Alien Lists" of the *Annual Enumeration and Assessment of All Persons, Property, and Things* for Steelton in 1903 and 1905, located at the Dauphin County Court House, Harrisburg. These lists were special surveys of the immigrant population by assessors, so that aliens could be properly enumerated and taxed. Once immigrants were identified, they were traced in *Boyd's Directory of Harrisburg and Steelton* (1905, 1915, and 1925). The total of 403 Slavs and Italians appearing in 1905 in the city directory, moreover, represented only about 25 percent of more than 1,600 Slavs and Italians appearing in the Alien Lists. Unfortunately the Alien Lists did not indicate an immigrant's occupation while, of course, the city directories did. City directories tended to be less accurate in the coverage of unskilled and lower-class workers. In fact, the number of unskilled immigrants and blacks used here was probably a conservative figure. See Peter Knights, "A Method for Estimating Census Under-Enumeration," *Historical Methods Newsletter* 3 (December 1969):5–8; and Charles M. Dollar and Richard Jensen, *Historian's Guide to Statistics* (New York, 1971), 12. The classification of unskilled, semiskilled, and skilled was derived from published wage figures. A lawyer, doctor, or large merchant, for instance, would be put into a high nonmanual category since he was self-employed. The low, nonmanual ranks consisted of clerks who worked for someone else. Highly skilled machinists or patternmakers would be classed as skilled workers, while semiskilled occupations included a heater, a melter, a molder, a blacksmith, or a crane operator. Common laborers formed the bulk of the unskilled. The occupation ranking in Table 10.1b was drawn from much more extensive wage data provided in the *Reports of the Immigration Commission, Immigrants in Industry: Iron and Steel* (Washington, D.C., 1911), 1:612–25.

If immigrants experienced little advancement occupationally before World War I in Steelton, they could find a parallel in the experience of black migrants from the southern United States. From the inception of steel production in 1866, Negroes had come or were in some instances brought to Steelton. They came largely from Maryland and Virginia in the decades before 1910 and from the Deep South afterward.[7]

In 1880, some 95 percent of all black workers in Steelton were unskilled. This ratio was substantially larger than for any other group. It compared poorly with the 60 percent of German, English, and Irish steelworkers who

Table 10.1b. Wage scale of Steelton plant for selected occupations, 1910

Skilled	
Machinist	$3.98/day (salary)
Patternmaker	3.00/day
Carpenter	.32/hr
Heater	.29/hr
Semiskilled	
Molder	.26/hr
Melter	.25/hr
First Class Electrician	.24/hr
Second Class	.22/hr
Blacksmith	.22/hr
Crane Operator	.20/hr
Foreman (Labor gang)	.17½/hr
Blower	.17/hr
Engineer	.16/hr
Keeper	.16/hr
Charger	.16/hr
Unskilled	
Ladleman	.13½/hr
Helper	.13/hr
Fireman	.13/hr
Laborer	.11/hr

SOURCE: *Reports of the Immigration Commission, Immigrants in Industry: Iron and Steel* (Washington, D.C., 1911), 1:612–25.

NOTE: For a more extensive discussion of categories in this study, see Clyde Griffen, "Occupational Mobility in Nineteenth-Century America: Problems and Possibilities," *Journal of Social History* 5 (Spring 1972):310–30.

Table 10.2. Occupational distribution of blacks, Steelton, 1880–1915

	1880	1905	1915
Unskilled	95%	61%	70%
Semiskilled	3%	33%	26%
Skilled	0%	0%	0%
Low Nonmanual	0%	4%	3%
High Nonmanual	2%	3%	1%
N =	87	300	323

SOURCES: A group of blacks was compiled by taking all black males from Steelton who appeared in the Dauphin County Marriage License Dockets from 1890 to 1915 and in *Twelfth Census, 1900*. Moreover, there were lists of black members of the African Methodist Episcopal Church in the AME church. The 1880 group was drawn from the *Tenth Census, 1880*.

were unskilled and the 60 percent of native-born whites. No Negroes at all were found among the skilled positions in 1880, a situation which Slavic immigrants encountered in 1905. Only 3 percent of all Afro-Americans were in semiskilled positions, and only 2 percent of nonmanual ones. The latter category consisted of two Negro barbers.

By 1905, however, blacks had considerably improved their lot in Steelton's work force. The number of Negroes employed in unskilled tasks had dropped more than 30 percent in the generation before 1905. Only 61 percent of all blacks were now unskilled. Indeed, the percentage of Negroes in semiskilled jobs increased some ten times in the generation before 1905. Moreover, while blacks failed to make any incursions into the skilled ranks, 5 percent more were lodged in nonmanual positions in 1905 than in 1880 (see Table 10.2).

What is peculiar and perhaps crucial to the black immigrant experience, however, is that the percentage of the former in unskilled positions was at its lowest point in 1905. The ratio of Negroes in semiskilled positions and nonmanual positions reached its peak in 1905 and declined thereafter. Blacks never entered the skilled trades, such as the machinists.

The 32 percent of black workers in semiskilled endeavors in 1905 had dwindled to 26 percent in 1915 and remained at that level past 1920 and 1930. In addition, the 61 percent of black workers categorized as unskilled had never been lower before 1905 and would not be as low afterward. These facts are even more striking when one considers that the growing Negro population of Steelton tapered off after 1890 and actually declined between the turn of the century, when Slavic and Italian immigrants began to arrive in substantial numbers, and World War I, which largely terminated the immigration of Italians, Serbs, Croats, Slovenes, and Bulgarians.[8] The wave of Slavs and Italians sweeping into Steelton after 1895 halted the steady growth of the black community, which was five times larger in 1890 than it had been a decade earlier.[9]

Blacks had made significant advances in Steelton before 1900. They had established three churches and a newspaper, *The Steelton Press*. Peter Blackwell, a Negro, was elected to the town council in 1904, and several black constables were employed during the 1890s. While 94 percent of black laborers had been unskilled in 1880, as indicated above, only 61 percent were so engaged by 1905. Although their movements upward were only into semiskilled blue-collar jobs, Afro-Americans were advancing.[10]

At the height of European immigration in 1905, blacks actually held a stronger position in the labor force than did Croats, Slovenes, and Serbs. Only six out of every ten Negroes were classified as unskilled in 1905. In comparison, 75 percent of Slavic and Italian workers were in low-level occu-

Table 10.3. Earnings of laborers in Steelton plant, 1910

	No.	% Earnings over $1.50/day	% Earnings under $1.50/day
Natives	1,450	79.4	20.6
Negro	149	59.1	40.9
Slovenian	57	47.4	52.6
Croatian	676	34.3	65.7
Serbian	273	14.3	85.7
Bulgarian	61	8.2	91.8

Immigrants in industry 1,707

pations. Afro-Americans enjoyed a higher proportion of semiskilled work-ers—32 percent—than did the "new immigrant," at 8 percent. The federal immigration commission, which studied Steelton in 1910, discovered that the average earnings of Negro laborers were higher than those for any other eth-nic group except the native-born whites (see Table 10.3).[11]

In 1915 the differences between immigrants and blacks had changed some-what. The difference between the proportion of Negroes and immigrants in unskilled endeavors had narrowed. Afro-Americans, however, continued to have fewer of their numbers in unskilled categories than did immigrants. Moreover, more blacks, 26 percent, held semiskilled positions than Slavs, 10 percent. Immigrants did hold more nonmanual positions than blacks in 1905 and 1915, due primarily to a greater proliferation of neighborhood ethnic stores among Croats, Slovenes, and Bulgarians than among blacks. Neither Negroes nor immigrants made significant incursions into the skilled trades. No blacks appeared at all in 1905 or 1915. Immigrants, however, finally made some inroads by 1915, but the skilled trades still included only 3 percent of their ranks.

In a comparison of black and immigrant workers after 1920, the stronger position Afro-Americans held over Slavs and Italians before 1920 was com-pletely reversed. Whereas blacks had a smaller proportion of their workers listed as unskilled in 1905 and 1915 than immigrants, only 33 percent of all immigrants were unskilled between 1920 and 1939, as compared with 67 percent of the blacks. The early dominance that Negroes enjoyed in semi-skilled jobs had given way to immigrant superiority—47 percent to 27 per-cent. Blacks, however, continued to be left out of skilled occupations. The relative preponderance of immigrants over blacks in nonmanual fields contin-ued at about the same rate (see Table 10.4).

The marked improvement of the Slav and Italian in relation to the Negro

Table 10.4. Occupational distribution of Steelton work force, 1920–1939

	NBNP[a] (White)	FBFP[b] (Slavic & Italian)	Blacks	NBFP[c] (Slavic & Italian)	NBFP[c] English, Irish, German	Total
Unskilled	12%	33%	67%	16%	20%	30%
Semiskilled	50%	47%	27%	60%	45%	46%
Skilled	11%	9%	5%	4%	15%	6%
High Nonmanual	7%	3%	1%	7%	8%	6%
Low Nonmanual	20%	8%	2%	3%	12%	12%
N =	514	293	372	379	78	1,655

SOURCE: Data compiled from all males applying for marriage licenses from Steelton between 1930 and 1939. The 1,655 men represent every Steelton male listed in the Dauphin County Marriage License Dockets between 1920 and 1939. These records, after 1920, gave the age, place of birth, and occupation of the applicant as well as the place of birth and occupation of the applicant's father.

[a]Native born with both parents natives.

[b]Foreign born with foreign parents.

[c]Native born with foreign parents.

was modest in many respects. While the ratio of immigrants in unskilled jobs declined from 78 percent in 1915 to only 33 percent after 1920, eight out of ten immigrants were still in a blue-collar job after 1920, exactly as they had been in 1905 and 1915. Immigrants shifted from unskilled to semiskilled positions, but they were unable to escape blue-collar positions. Tom Benkovic, a Croat, moved from the brutal heat of the open hearth to a position as a crane operator in a career that spanned more than forty years.[12] Immigrants enjoyed upward mobility, but on a limited and modest basis.

Although blacks were surpassed by Slavs and Italians after 1920, both groups remained largely in unskilled and semiskilled positions throughout the first four decades of this century. As the semiskilled segment of the work force expanded, these positions were assumed at a more rapid rate by new immigrants rather than Negroes. Yet, neither blacks nor immigrants ever escaped blue-collar work in any large numbers. More than eight out of every ten immigrants worked in blue-collar positions throughout their lifetimes. Blacks, while occupying lower positions at a higher rate, constantly found more than nine out of every ten of their ranks in low-level jobs (see Table 10.5).

In addition to studying the occupational distribution of Steelton's ethnic groups, two other indicators reveal the impact immigration had upon the black worker: occupational and geographical mobility rates. Between 1905 and 1915, only 5 percent of the Slavic and Italian immigrants were able to rise occupationally, largely from unskilled to semiskilled positions. In the

Table 10.5. Immigrants and blacks in unskilled and semiskilled jobs, Steelton, 1905–1939

	1905	1915	1920–39	Average
Immigrants (Slavic and Italian)	83%	88%	80%	84%
Blacks	93	96	94	94

Table 10.6. Blacks and new immigrants: upward mobility from unskilled positions, Steelton, 1905–1925

	Immigrants (Slavic & Italian)				Blacks		
Year and No.	No Change	Up	Down	No.	No Change	Up	Down
1905 group:							
1915: 95	91%	5%	—	67	71%	25%	—
1925: 46	71	29	—	(too small to compute)			
1915 group:							
1925: 214	76	22	—	35	87	13	—

next decade, the rate of upward mobility did increase substantially for Slavs and Italians, from 5 percent to 29 percent. Yet, the most common experience by far remained no mobility at all for Slavs and Italians. An average of eight out of ten new immigrants remained immobile between 1905 and 1915 (see Table 10.6).

Blacks showed considerably more upward mobility between 1905 and 1915 than immigrants from southern Europe, although out of seventeen blacks who advanced in the decade after 1905, all moved from unskilled to only a semiskilled position. While the rate of Negro advancement was faster than that of the "new immigrant" before 1915, the pattern was reversed during the decade after 1915 and 1925. During those years, black mobility slowed from 25 percent to 13 percent.[13]

Persistence rates, which have been defined as the proportion (usually expressed in a percentage) of a population remaining in a delimited area after a given time interval, provided another indication of the impact Slavs and Italians were having on the black.[14]

Members of the "old immigration"—English, Irish, and German—were exceptionally stable in their persistence patterns. Where only half the entire population remained in Steelton from 1880 to 1888, an incredible nine out of every ten English, Irish, and German immigrants did so. Moreover, these rates continued through the next seventeen years and ran more than 20 percent higher than those for the population as a whole. In fact, among the

Table 10.7. Persistence rates of immigrants, Steelton, 1880–1925

	No.	1880	1896	1905
1880 Group (English, German, Irish)				
Unskilled	42	90%	86%	100%
Semiskilled	8	90	100	100
Skilled	4	100	100	100
Nonmanual	4	100	100	75
Total	58	90	90	96

1905 Group (Slavic & Italian)			
	No.	1915	1925
Unskilled	303	27%	40%
Semiskilled	30	43	46
Skilled	0	0	0
Nonmanual	70	44	45
Total	403	32	47

1915 Group (Slavic & Italian)		
	No.	1925
Unskilled	479	37%
Semiskilled	61	59
Skilled	20	30
Nonmanual	76	53
Total	616	42

SOURCE: Persistence rates were obtained by tracing immigrants and blacks through *Boyd's Directory of Harrisburg and Steelton* (1888, 1896, 1905, 1915, 1925).

semiskilled and skilled "old immigrants," all eleven persisted from 1888 to 1905. While the persistence rate was lower for the unskilled among these immigrants, it was still considerably higher than the rates for the rest of the population (see Table 10.7).

The pattern for the Slavs and Italians of the "new immigration" differed significantly from that of the newcomers from northern Europe. Whereas 90 percent of "old immigrants" stayed in Steelton during the 1880s, only 32 percent of the Slavs and Italians persisted there from 1905 to 1915. As usual, the longer an immigrant remained in the town, the less were his chances of leaving. Yet, even among the newcomers who had lived in Steelton from 1905 to 1915, more than half still decided to seek other homes in the decade

Table 10.8. Persistence rates for blacks, Steelton, 1880–1925

	No.	1888	1896	1915	1925
1880 Group					
Unskilled	82	45%	90%		
Semiskilled	3	33	10		
Skilled	0	0	0		
Nonmanual	2	100	10		
Total	87	47	85		
1905 Group					
Unskilled	183			33%	
Semiskilled	96			10	
Skilled	0			0	
Nonmanual	21			10	
Total	300			23	
1915 Group					
Unskilled	220				28%
Semiskilled	84				7
Skilled	0				0
Nonmanual	19				0
Total	323				21

SOURCE: Persistence rates were obtained by tracing immigrants and blacks through *Boyd's Directory of Harrisburg and Steelton* (1888, 1896, 1905, 1915, and 1925).

after 1915. The unskilled, newly arrived immigrant showed the greatest tendency to leave the borough from 1905 to 1915. Only 27 percent of the unskilled immigrants who were in Steelton in 1905 could be found there ten years later. This compared unfavorably with the 44 percent of nonmanual immigrants from the 1905 group who persisted throughout the ten-year period (see Table 10.8).

It is interesting that, after immigrants remained in Steelton for at least a decade, the persistence rates among the various skill categories were nearly the same. However, it should be emphasized that more than half the immigrant population left Steelton during a given decade.

The immigrants who appeared in Steelton in 1915 were slightly more stable in the subsequent decade than Slavs and Italians from the 1905 group. Yet, only four out of every ten could still be found after a decade, compared with three in ten for the 1905–15 group. Again, persistence rates were considerably higher for nonmanual workers than for the unskilled immigrant.

While blacks compared poorly in persistence rates with the English, Irish, and Germans in Steelton during the 1880s, their rates were only slightly lower than that for the population as a whole. Forty-seven percent of the Negroes appearing in 1880 could still be found in Steelton eight years later. Characteristically, of those blacks who remained in Steelton for most of the 1880s, the chances were greater than eight in ten that they would remain throughout the 1890s (see Table 10.8).

What was salient was the tremendous decrease in the black persistence rates during the years of the heavy Slavic immigration into Steelton. Croats, Slovenes, Serbs, and Bulgarians were slowly replacing Afro-Americans in semiskilled occupations. This disruption of the black position in Steelton was also indicated in persistence rates. From a persistence rate of 42 percent between 1880 and 1888, rates fell to 23 percent between 1905 and 1915 and to 21 percent between 1915 and 1925. This was lower than the 32 percent (1905–15) and 42 percent (1915–25) displayed by "new immigrants." Moreover, the downward trend in black persistence rates compared poorly with Slavic and Italian rates, which were slowly rising. It should be remembered, however, that among both groups the turnover in population remained substantially high (see Table 10.8).

Even more striking in comparing the extent of geographical mobility between blacks and Slavs and Italians were the greater persistence rates among immigrants after 1905. This is not to minimize the tremendous turnover in the immigrant population itself, but immigrant persistence rates did substantially exceed those of the Afro-Americans. At a time when new immigrants were replacing blacks in the semiskilled job categories, from 1905 to 1939, they were also causing a greater degree of outward migration among blacks.[15]

The influx of Croats, Serbs, Slovenes, Bulgarians, and Italians into Steelton, especially after 1900, had a devastating impact upon the town's black work force. Black upward mobility rates, which had been rising before 1915, began to slip after World War I. Of all the town's ethnic groups, only the black group witnessed a decline in population between 1890 and 1910. And the rising persistence rates displayed by Afro-Americans before 1905 began to erode when they were faced with immigrant competition. The moderation of Negro population rates in numerous northern industrial areas immediately after 1900 can be linked to the rising influx of Slavic and Italian labor. If Steelton is any indication, Negro workers were not only losing semiskilled occupations to Slavs and Italians but also, consequently, being forced to leave their northern homes, presumably in search of work, at an increasing rate. World War I would terminate European immigration and increase Negro migration northward *again*. The years just before the war, however, had assured the Negro worker that he would have to start his economic climb over again— from the bottom.[16]

Notes

1. The population figures are computed from 47th Cong., 2nd sess., H.R. Dec. 42; *Statistics of the Population of the United States at the Tenth Census* (Washington, D.C., 1883), 423–24; U.S. Census Bureau, *Eleventh Census, 1890, Part I; Twelfth Census, 1900, Population, Part I.*

2. See note 1 and U.S. Census Bureau, *Thirteenth Census, 1910.*

3. For a discussion of occupational background of immigrants in Europe, see Jozo Thomasevich, *Peasants, Politics, and Economic Change in Yugoslavia* (Stanford, Calif., 1955), 160–80; Philip Taylor, *The Distant Magnet* (New York, 1971), 48–64; Josef John Barton, "Immigrants and Social Mobility in an American City: Studies of Three Ethnic Groups in Cleveland, 1890–1950" (Ph.D. diss., University of Michigan, 1972), 306–33. Scholarship dealing with a comparison of the immigrant and black experience includes Joseph S. Roucek and Francis J. Brown, "The Problem of the Negro and European Immigrant Minorities: Some Comparisons and Contrast," *Journal of Negro Education* 18 (1939): 299–312. Roucek and Brown, in dealing with lower-class aspirations, claimed that since Negroes could not escape their status so easily they have less hope of climbing up the ladder of social mobility than the average immigrant. See also John J. Appel, "American Negro and Immigrant Experience: Similarities and Differences," *American Quarterly* 18 (1966): 95–102; Edward McDounagh and Eugene S. Richards, *Ethnic Relations in the United States* (New York, 1953), 295–96; and Charles H. Wesley, *Negro Labor in the United States, 1850–1925* (New York, 1967), 75–76, 199. Some valuable insights can be gained from Judith R. Kramer, *The American Minority Community* (New York, 1970), 213; Timothy Smith, "Native Blacks and Foreign Whites: Varying Responses to Education Opportunity in America, 1880–1950," in *Perspectives in American History* 6 (1972): 309–11; John R. Commons, *Races and Immigrants in America* (New York, 1907), 147–52. The animosity of Irish immigrants toward blacks, their chief rivals for unskilled jobs, has been discussed. See Oscar Handlin, *Boston's Immigrants: A Study in Acculturation* (Cambridge, Mass., 1959), 133, 205, 216. See especially Niles Carpenter, *Nationality, Color, and Economic Opportunity in the City of Buffalo* (Buffalo, N.Y., 1927), 190–91; Carpenter declared that immigrants rose faster than blacks. J. Iverne Dowie, "The American Negro: An Old Immigrant on a New Frontier," in O. Fritof Ander, ed., *In the Trek of the Immigrants* (Rock Island, 1964), 241–60, has called Negroes "America's oldest immigrants" and felt that they were held down until they moved northward. See David Brody, *Steelworkers in America* (Cambridge, Mass., 1960), 185–267; and Gilbert Osofsky, *Harlem: The Making of a Ghetto* (New York, 1969), 34–40.

4. William H. Egle, *History of Dauphin and Lebanon Counties* (Philadelphia, 1883), 400–404; George P. Donehoo, *Harrisburg and Dauphin County* (Dayton, 1925), 210–11; "A History of the Steelton Plant: Bethlehem Steel Corporation, Steelton, Pennsylvania," unpublished manuscript Charles Schwab Memorial Library, Bethlehem, Pennsylvania.

5. African Methodist Episcopal Church, *Historical Record* (Steelton, Pa., 1905); *Spomen-Knijiga 25 Godisnjica Hrvatsko-Ridnicko Podporno Drústvo Sv. Louro, 1895–1920* (Steelton, Pa., 1920), 6–9. See my essay "The Formation of Ethnic Consciousness: Slavic Immigrants in Steelton," in John Bodnar, ed., *The Ethnic Experience in Pennsylvania* (Lewisburg, Pa., 1973).

6. In addition to sources listed in Table 10.1a, see Paul Worthman, "Working Class Mobility in Birmingham, Alabama, 1880–1914," in T. K. Hareven, ed., *Anonymous Americans* (Englewood Cliffs, N.J., 1971), 192.

7. The origins of Steelton's early Negro population can be seen in the U.S. Census Bureau, *Tenth Census, 1880;* for Steelton, Marriage License Dockets for Dauphin County reveal arrivals from the deeper South after 1910. See also *Eleventh Census, 1890,* 1:53; *Twelfth Census,*

1900, 1:679. In studying another steel town in the first decade of this century, Margaret Byington noted that the break between Slavic immigrants and the rest of the community was more absolute than between whites and Negroes. See Byington, *Homestead: The Households of a Mill Town* (New York, 1910), 14–15.

8. The black population of Steelton was 202 in 1880. It reached 1,273 in 1890, and in 1910 it had declined to 1,234. It did climb steadily after immigration was restricted, and it amounted to more than 2,500 by 1930.

9. See Appel, "American Negro and Immigrant Experience," 95–103; Roucek and Brown, "Problem of the Negro and European Immigrant Minorities," 299–312. Competition between Irish, Italian, Negro, and Jewish workers is treated briefly in Carolyn Golab, "The Polish Communities of Philadelphia, 1870–1920: Immigrant Distribution and Adaptation in Urban America" (Ph.D. diss., University of Pennsylvania, 1971), chap. 1. See also Stephan Thernstrom and Elizabeth Pleck, "The Last of the Immigrants? A Comparative Analysis of Immigrant and Black Social Mobility in the Nineteenth Century Boston," paper presented at the 1970 meeting of the Organization of American Historians; Thernstrom, "Immigrants and WASPS: Ethnic Differences in Occupational Mobility in Boston, 1890–1940," in Thernstrom and Richard Sennett, eds., *Nineteenth-Century Cities* (New Haven, 1969), 125–64; Clyde Griffen, "Making It in America: Social Mobility in Mid-Nineteenth Century Poughkeepsie," *New York History* 50, no. 1 (1970): 479–99. Griffen (485) argues that ethnic origin may be critical in explaining differences in social mobility. See also Richard J. Hopkins, "Occupational and Geographical Mobility in Atlanta, 1870–1896," *Journal of Southern History* 34 (1968): 208; Hopkins found fewer unskilled workers in the ranks of immigrants than blacks in 1870. Carl Oblinger has found blacks being forced from certain building trades by Irish and German newcomers between 1840 and 1860; see his "Arms for Oblivion: The Making of a Black Underclass in Southeastern Pennsylvania, 1780–1860," in Bodnar, *Ethnic Experience in Pennsylvania.*

10. See John Bodnar, "Peter C. Blackwell and the Negro Community of Steelton," *Pennsylvania Magazine of History and Biography* 97 (1973): 199–209.

11. Blacks in Steelton even had a lower rate of illiteracy (11 percent) than the foreign-born (28 percent), according to the U.S. Census Bureau, *Fourteenth Census, 1920,* 3:872.

12. Taped interview with Thomas Benkovic, Steelton, July 11, 1971.

13. Paul Worthman's study of working-class mobility in Birmingham, Alabama, shows also that in the early twentieth century the large influx of white migrants—some of them Russians, "Hungarians," and Italians brought into Birmingham mills from the North—helped erode black domination of some trades (Worthman, "Working Class Mobility," 185). Worthman also states (179) that unfortunately he was not able to provide systematic examination of immigrant patterns of mobility since he could not find information about the birthplace of workers in 1890 and 1899. See also Thernstrom and Pleck, "Last of the Immigrants?" 18–20, who found native-born sons of Irish immigrants were much more successful in climbing to middle-class positions. However, "Boston's [Irish] immigrants resembled Negroes in their occupational distribution rather more than they did old-stock Americans, though somewhat ahead of the Blacks; the least favored immigrants, the Irish, were virtually indistinguishable from Blacks, ranking a shade *behind* them in white-collar positions in 1880 and a shade ahead of them in 1890." The quotation is reproduced courtesy of Professor Thernstrom.

14. Peter R. Knights, "Population Turnover, Persistence, and Residential Mobility in Boston, 1830–1860," in Thernstrom and Sennett, *Nineteenth-Century Cities,* 258.

15. The Marriage License Dockets for Steelton between 1920 and 1939 show that of 332 Slavic immigrant sons applying for marriage licenses, 87 percent were born in Steelton. On the

other hand, of 372 blacks applying for licenses during the 1920s and 1930s, only 11 percent were natives of Steelton. The data suggested, of course, that immigrant children were tending to settle within the same community at a much larger rate than black children. The blacks who were marrying in Steelton between 1920 and 1939 were not the children of blacks who lived in the community in the first two decades of the century, yet the immigrant children were largely the sons of those who persisted in Steelton.

16. Lloyd Warner and Leo Scrole, *The Social System of American Ethnic Groups* (New Haven, Conn., 1945), 2, argue that an ethnic group's low socioeconomic position stemmed from the fact that it had only recently arrived in an urban-industrial area. Inevitably, however, a group would climb through several generations and be replaced at the bottom of the social heap by newer arrivals. However, blacks in Steelton were pushed down and out, rather than upward by immigrants who followed them.

CHAPTER ELEVEN

Migration and Jobs:
The New Black Workers in Pittsburgh, 1916–1930

Peter Gottlieb

Beginning in 1916 and continuing until the depression of the 1930s, Pittsburgh received thousands of southern black migrants who were participants in the Great Migration, which carried a million and a half black men and women from the South to the North. Most of those new arrivals in Pittsburgh left the states of Virginia, North Carolina, South Carolina, Georgia, and Alabama. They moved north basically for the same reason the southern and eastern European immigrants had come to America: to seek jobs in the iron and steel mills. Between 1910 and 1930, the black population of Pittsburgh grew 115 percent—from 25,623 to 54,983. The number of black iron and steel workers in Pittsburgh in this period increased from 786 to 2,853, or 626 percent.[1]

The experience of southern black migrants to Pittsburgh represents a chapter in the epic story of rural people lured from their homelands by the possibilities of higher wages in the industrial city. The pattern of life among rural blacks in the South after Reconstruction, the particular aspirations they brought with them to the North, and their opinions of Pittsburgh as a new

A version of this chapter was originally presented at the California State College History Forum on May 1, 1976, and subsequently published in *Western Pennsylvania Historical Magazine* (now called *Pittsburgh History*) 61 (January 1978): 1–15. Reprinted by permission.

home and as a place to work produced a unique variation on the country-to-city theme. In this experience, it was the life-sustaining jobs—both those which southern blacks left to come north and those they sought in Pittsburgh—that provided the key elements in the migrants' decision to leave, in the organization of their movement, and in their encounters with urban life.

In this article, oral histories of Pittsburgh migrants allow the voices of southern blacks to be heard in the recounting of their northward movement. Not since the migration period itself have students brought the migrants' own views of their experience into analyses of this transition from rural to urban worlds. Aside from the remarkable migrant letters collected by Carter G. Woodson and edited by Emmett J. Scott,[2] investigators have had to use mainly secondary sources. Much of the material presented in the article comes from twenty-eight tape-recorded interviews with southern-born men and women who came to Pittsburgh.[3] The migrants' spoken accounts reveal aspects of their geographic movement that are not easily obtainable by other means. Nowhere is this more true than in the social and economic dynamics of southern rural life from which the migration sprang.

Southern blacks had been on the move long before the Great Migration began in 1916. After winning their freedom in the Civil War, blacks gained a greater ability to seek work wherever they could find it. Two clear directions of movement among southern rural blacks developed between 1865 and 1890. One was the continuation of the shift of black population toward the southwestern area of cotton cultivation, which had begun when white planters settled new territory inland from the Atlantic Coast and took their slaves with them. This southwestward movement continued after 1865, as black agricultural laborers and tenant farmers sought the newer cotton lands and the higher wages paid to day laborers in Oklahoma, Texas, and Arkansas.[4] The second direction was from rural areas toward the cities of the South. In the decades following the end of the Civil War, many ex-slaves moved to the burgeoning centers of manufacture such as Atlanta, Birmingham, Memphis, Richmond, and New Orleans. Between 1870 and 1890, the average increase in black population in nine major southern cities was 74 percent.[5]

Blacks had also moved north before 1916. In fact, the decade of the 1890s witnessed an average increase in the black population of eight northern cities of almost 75 percent.[6] This sudden spurt in the number of southern blacks living in the northern cities was to be dwarfed by the growth during the Great Migration, yet it demonstrates in the same way as the population movement within the South that the first large, sustained black migration northward had its precedents, the importance of which will be noted later.

One of the reasons southern blacks became more geographically mobile in the last decades of the nineteenth century, one can hypothesize, was their resort to seasonal migration between rural and urban areas and between farm and nonfarm work. For the 85 percent of the southern black population which resided in rural areas in 1890, the attachment to the land in the wake of Emancipation had assumed the form of tenancy. Under various sharecropping and renting arrangements, rural southern blacks mortgaged part of a cash crop in return for use of a landowner's acreage, tools, animals, fertilizer, and in some cases provisions to support the tenant family between harvests. Because the ability of black tenants to save money and to buy or improve land was obstructed on many sides, movement from one rented farm to another, or off the land altogether, naturally presented itself to the black rural population as one of the easiest solutions to their problems. But many also resorted to seasonal migration from their farms to places where they could work temporarily in domestic service, laundries, lumber, mining, dockside labor, or other lines of nonagricultural work.[7] Money earned during forays into nonfarm labor markets might tide over the rural family which had ended a crop year in debt to its landlord. While the leading black educators and reformers advocated land ownership as the ultimate solution to the problems of blacks in the South, the increasing mobility of rural families suggested that other answers were being sought.

Seasonal migration in the South might have worked this way: a young male or female member of the black rural family would leave the rented farm and travel to the nearest town or city where a job could be found. Women probably were limited to the choices of domestic work or laundering. Men, however, had options of working in primary industries like lumbering or mining, of street work in towns or cities, unskilled labor in manufacturing, section-gang work on the railroads, or agricultural day labor. Short absences from the farm were not detrimental to the family's agricultural fortunes if they occurred during a season when the crops had been "laid by" and needed little care. Consequently, though, jobs were held only briefly until work on the family's land demanded the presence of all hands.[8]

Seasonal migration entailed important economic consequences for southern blacks. As a device to overcome the precarious marginal position of tenant families, migration readjusted the family resources. Just as family members in their prime working years became seasonal nonfarm employees, they also became only part-time residents on the family's rented land. Only by keeping well attuned to labor demand in southern industries could rural black families continue to maintain themselves as farming units. Southern tenant farming by the late nineteenth century seemed to have been approaching the point where, in Marx's phases, "part of the agricultural population is . . . on the point of passing over into an urban or manufacturing proletariat, and on the look-out for circumstances favorable to this transformation."[9]

If seasonal migration had been intended to provide greater stability on the land for rural southern blacks, the irony of its adoption by tenant farm families was that it seemed to commit family members to continual movement over longer and longer distances, thereby prohibiting extended periods of residence on the farm. The tendency for seasonal migration to become routine might have been the consequence of knowledge of regional or even national labor markets becoming more widely diffused among southern rural blacks as the twentieth century approached. A young man who had traveled no farther from home than the nearest population center the preceding year might risk going on to the state capital the next year, if by chance jobs were harder to come by the second time around. His own experience in finding work, added to the knowledge of other work situations gained through conversations with relatives and friends who had ranged still farther afield, enabled the migrant to extend the territory covered in his search for employment. Thus, major cities in the border states could become his next destination.

In this fashion, the resort to seasonal migration by increasing numbers of rural southern blacks broke ground for the southern blacks' sudden and massive response to the wartime labor demand of northern industry. The ability of hundreds of thousands of blacks to move to northern cities in a period of twenty-four to thirty months (April 1916 to December 1918) was made possible in part by the preceding decades of seasonal migration.[10] If this was in fact the case, the Great Migration was more continuous with the overall migratory experience of southern blacks than has previously been recognized, for the large northward population movement which began in 1916 was also characterized by brief periods of residence and seasonal fluctuations in the migrants' destinations, suggesting that what happened was in part little more than an extension of the geographical scope of earlier seasonal migration.

Evidence of a transient character in the southern black migrant population in Pittsburgh emerges from their age, marital status, and residences. Abraham Epstein, who surveyed the black migrants in Pittsburgh in 1917, found that about half were in their prime work years (ages 18 to 30), that the vast majority resided in boardinghouses for unmarried men, and that more than two-thirds had been in the city for less than six months.[11] A preliminary analysis of a sample of personnel records from the A. M. Byers Company in Pittsburgh, a wrought-iron manufacturer, yields a migrant profile very similar to Epstein's. Of black workers at Byers who arrived in Pittsburgh between 1916 and 1930, some 51 percent were between the ages of 21 and 30 and 52 percent lived in boardinghouses. Single men had come to the city in almost equal proportions to married men (single, 47 percent; married, 52 percent).[12] Although the fact that the majority of the migrant group in Pittsburgh was married indicates that heads of families as well as single family members were seeking jobs in northern industry, the data from both Epstein's survey and the Byers records show that the more recently a married individual had come to Pittsburgh, the more likely it was that he had left his spouse and children in the South.[13]

By sharpening the focus on the migrants in Pittsburgh, traces of seasonal movements become more distinct. The Byers records allow us to determine the months of the year when southern blacks arrived in the city. May and June were the months of heaviest in-migration to Pittsburgh; more than one-third of the migrants working at the Byers plant who started when they arrived came to the city during those months; nearly half came to Pittsburgh in April and May. Arrivals fluctuated over the other seasons of the year but were lowest in August and October, increasing somewhat in the early winter then decreasing again until April. Migrants who quit their jobs—indicating that they were leaving the city—most often chose the months of October, November, and June; departures decreased throughout the winter and early spring. Thus, over a fourteen-year period of migration to Pittsburgh, entrances to and exits from the city were not evenly spaced over a twelve-month span, but rose and fell with changes of the seasons.

Were the springtime migrants to Pittsburgh the same as the autumnal departures? The very brief period which black migrants worked at the Byers firm suggest that often the two were the same. In a sample of migrants at Byers, 28 percent worked no more than thirty-one days, while 83 percent were employed no longer than six months. By Christmas, most of those who had come in the spring or early summer would have left the city, perhaps to return again the next April or May.[14]

The vast majority of all southern blacks who were hired at the A. M. Byers Company clearly were not putting down roots in the black communities of Pittsburgh. It seems that, in most cases, the migrants, on arrival in Pittsburgh, did not expect to remain permanently, but came with initial plans to work only briefly before going elsewhere. Of ten people the author has interviewed who grew up on farms in the South and who migrated to the North after 1916, all had engaged in seasonal migration away from their homes. They worked for a short period in Pittsburgh, left, returned to work again, departed once more, and eventually came back to settle in the city.

The work histories of former migrants who have been interviewed show how the tides of seasonal migration carried them to Pittsburgh. H.G. left his father's farm in Georgia when he was 16, abandoning his goal to farm a larger piece of land than his father's. He traveled to many cities seeking work and a suitable place to live. In 1916, he got a job at the Oliver Iron and Steel Company on Pittsburgh's South Side, but he frequently traveled back

The Homestead Grays, a famous Negro League baseball team, was started by African American steelworkers from Homestead, Pennsylvania. African American workers also were team members and fans of another local Negro League team: the Pittsburgh Crawfords. In this photograph dated 1913, the Grays are shown with their manager-owner, Cum Posey (third from the left). (Courtesy of the Carnegie Library of Pittsburgh)

to Georgia. Often the purpose of the visits back home was to see a woman he was courting. In 1922, he married her and returned to Pittsburgh to settle permanently and raise a family.[15]

J.G. had a similar experience. His first wage-earning job was at a sawmill near his parents' farm in South Carolina. He decided to work there after the boll weevil devoured his family's income and made money from other sources necessary. After he turned 21, J.G., continuing to support his parents and younger brother, moved with a group of friends from South Carolina to Wilmington, North Carolina, where they worked for two months in a fertilizer factory. He then went to Richmond, Virginia, where blacks were being recruited as laborers in the Carnegie mills at Homestead, Pennsylvania. From Homestead, J.G. sent back part of each pay he earned to his South Carolina home. He also kept money for his own travels ready at the post office, for he did not intend to stay indefinitely in Homestead.

The pattern of movement emerges in J.G.'s words:

> I was a rambler. Comin' near Christmas we jacked up, got all our
> money, and went home, wonderin' whether we would come back—we
> didn't know. But the boss and all of them would tell us, "Leave one
> pay in the mill, so when you come back you won't lose no time."
> Stay thirty days, come back and you still wouldn't lose no time. But
> we couldn't see it . . . We got our money. When you did that, when
> you come back you had lost that service. . . . Every year I would get
> my money and go home. . . . I was a rambling man. . . . In 1928 I
> came back and stayed.[16]

The migrant itineraries could be still more complex. W.H. grew up on a
farm in New Kent County, Virginia, just east of Richmond. He worked at the
age of 16 at a sawmill, and during World War I he went to Richmond to work
in a munitions plant. His father, meanwhile, had left the family on the farm
and had moved to Coatesville, Pennsylvania, to get a steel-mill job. W.H.
followed him there in September 1917. The moves he made from Coatesville,
and the time he spent in each place before his return to Homestead, were:
Philadelphia (two years); Cleveland–Akron (two months); Philadelphia (three
months); New Kent County (two years); Homestead (six months); and Cleveland–Erie–Buffalo (two months).[17]

If these work histories are representative of the black migrants as a group,
then one can assume the migrants were rural mainly in their southern geographical origins, but not in their work backgrounds and residence just before
moving north. It would seem more appropriate to regard men like H.G., J.G.,
and W.H. as unskilled itinerant laborers, accustomed to different kinds of
work, both industrial and agricultural, rather than as direct farm-to-city migrants. Their movements within the South preceding migration to the North
may have functioned to transform them gradually from agricultural to industrial workers.

Testimony on the degree to which some of the migrants were already initiated into the urban labor markets when they moved north can be found in the
letters from prospective migrants in the South to northern newspapers and
employment agencies collected by Emmett J. Scott. Many letters open with
a statement of intent and continue with the writers' job experiences and pref-
erences for work in the North. Most often, though, the southerners expressed
a willingness to try their hand at any kind of remunerative work, and they
hoped to continue in the trade or occupation most familiar to them. These
correspondents demonstrated a firm grasp of the labor market situation in
1916–17 and the expenses of travel, lodging, and basic necessities in northern

cities.[18] Taken together, the letters of inquiry contradict a popular portrayal of the migrants as an excited, jubilant crowd of rural blacks whooping their way to the Promised Land with little understanding of, or care for, the industrial work conditions they would encounter.[19]

The work histories of southern black migrants, and their behavior in northern cities, also call into question one widely accepted rendition of the northward movement in which the southerners vow never to return to Dixie. "Many migrants must have been homesick for the South, but few went back," claims Florette Henri.[20] However, through the work histories recounted above runs the theme of the southern home the migrant left behind. Now fading into the background as the migrant shifts from place to place in the North, now coming strongly to the fore with the advent of a holiday season or with the sudden and unexpected illness of a parent, the place of origin seldom relinquished all claims on the migrants until long after they had departed. The migrants' families could for many years remain financially dependent on them, and regular contributions from the North were often vital even after the migrants had come to rest in a particular place. Or, in order to help out with work on the family's rented land, migrants returned home when parents and siblings could not manage.

Sentimental bonds to the childhood home were no less strong than material ones. The comparatively well-paid jobs in a northern city might justify working there, but the black migrant went back home to find a bride and a helpmate. Revivals held in the church in which the migrant had been brought up called him back too, and all occasions when old friends and relatives—many of whom probably also had left their southern homes—might gather were times that those who had gone north could not bear to miss; birthdays, graduations, and funerals were especially important.

Attachment to the southern home assumed many forms. Seasonal migration within the South and between the North and the South, brief periods of work in northern industry, and frequent trips home all expressed this commitment. Whatever the particular circumstances surrounding their departure from the South and their travels to northern cities, the migrants did not often completely spurn their birthplaces for the new places of employment, no matter how happy their experience in the freer air of the North might have been. An important question bearing on the nature of black migration in this period (but one very difficult to answer) is: how many southern blacks came north, worked for a short period of time, and then returned south to stay? The least which can be said with a large measure of certainty is that many black migrants were only intermittent residents in northern industrial cities, and that their work there was only one phase of a year's labor.

Because of the objectives the migrants sought by their seasonal movements, work in northern cities could only be temporary. Before long, the southerners would be traveling to another northern city where a different industry or employer might offer higher wages, or they would turn their backs on the North to return home. In any case, the job itself was not, and was not expected to be, an anchor for the migrants in the North, nor was it to provide over a period of years steady income with which to raise a family, educate children, buy a home, or to join a church, fraternal society, or other community organization. Instead, jobs in northern cities were entered by many migrants primarily to gain only a limited amount of money. The new black workers intended to spend at least part of their earnings from industrial work in the areas from which they have moved.

Let us review briefly the length of time southern black migrants worked at the A. M. Byers plant in Pittsburgh. Of those who quit their jobs at Byers and left Pittsburgh, 11.3 percent worked from one to fourteen days. Seventeen percent worked from fifteen to thirty-one days. Thirty-two percent kept their jobs from one to three months; 22.6 percent from three to six months; and 13 percent for twelve months or more. That is, about one-quarter of the southern blacks who quit work and left town labored one month or less, and three-fifths of them (60.4 percent) stayed no longer than three months.

Employers and supervisors were quick to misinterpret the high turnover rates among black migrants in northern industries. The tendencies to lay off frequently and to make many trips out of the northern city were ascribed to "racial characteristics" of laziness, intemperance, lack of perseverance, and other reasons. Comparing black workers with other ethnic working-class groups in Chicago, one employment manager commented, "The colored are indolent; they go to sleep waiting for a job. They spend their money on railroad fare; I think they would go home if a [pet] dog died."[21] But it was precisely because industrial work was temporary that it was highly valued by the migrants. Jobs paying relatively high wages were the vital link in the process of seasonal migrations, providing *in the short term* the needed increment to the migrant family's income.

The crucial phase in the migration of any particular southern black, therefore, was the search for work in the northern city. If successful in finding a job relatively quickly, the migrant would have exhausted less of his resources, would be earning money sooner, and would be saving more of his pay. Thus, whenever possible, southern blacks moved where they believed work could be most easily secured. We have already seen how some sent letters of inquiry to northern employment agencies and industrial firms, trying to ascertain their chances for success before leaving the South. Relatives or friends already residing in a particular city might have been able to aid migrants in finding a job, but even for those without organizational or family resources to help them, a knowledge of where men were being hired and which employers had good reputations was not hard to come by. The boardinghouses, poolrooms, taverns, and streetcorners became informal clearinghouses for employment information during the periods of heavy in-migration to northern manufacturing centers. Actually getting hired, on the other hand, remained the task of the individual migrant. It was at the employment office that seasonal migrants placed their stakes.

The following is, in its outlines, a typical migrant experience in finding work. The storyteller, unlike many migrants, was a devout Christian; his efforts to get a job probably have been related many times over and have in the process taken on a quality of drama and suspense only the master narrator can bestow. But such a confrontation between the southern migrant on one side, single-mindedly set on finding work, and the scrutinizing employment agent at the factory gates, on the other side, must have been altogether commonplace in the experiences of many southern blacks during the migration period.

> I had $2.50 left—that's all I had . . . I got on that #55 car and went as straight to the Westinghouse as I ever did, [to] the employment office. Me and him went in there, and there was eighty-some men standing in line. Me and him was the only colored in the line. Well, we were in the rear. And they turned them down like that . . . hired one white fellow, a machinist. Didn't need no help. All right. When I got close to the man by the door, he looked and saw me. "Stand aside," [he said]. I stepped aside. Man, I'd been standing up there and I'd seen them turning them folks down like *that!* I knowed there was no chance for me, and how I prayed. I just *believed* I was going to work. So I walked up to the desk. He look at me, says, "What do you want?" I said, "I want to go work this morning." That man sat there pecking on his desk [with a pencil] four or five minutes, says, "I don't need no laborers." "I'm not particular about laboring." "Can you write?" I told him, "Yeah, I can write." He kept tapping on his desk. . . . Man, I was praying all the time, "Lord, don't let him say no." He said, "I'm going to give you a *good* job. If you're good at it, and stick with it, you can make good."[22]

This story illustrates several important aspects of the migrants' attitudes and perceptions of work in the North. First, the cardinal importance of the job itself to the migrant comes through in every line. In this case, the southerner was nearly broke and faced the prospect of having to borrow money simply to get through the next day. But just as evident is the fate of this individual's more fundamental motive in migration—to prepare himself for the ministry. In the comparatively well-paid work of the northern industries was the key to all the broader objectives in coming north: increasing family income; buying land in the South; supporting projects of self-improvement. With jobs as the modus vivendi in the migrant's plans, a vaunted estimation of industrial work in the North quickly became one common element in the new black worker's outlook.

To judge by other work-search stories, success in finding a job seemed to depend on a combination of the migrant's own aggressiveness, an understanding personnel officer, and some intangible factor, whether it was the migrant's intuition, providential intervention, or simple luck. In the following story, the intangible factor is absent but the job seeker's own actions and the personnel officer's responses are the keys to the happy ending:

> I came to the J&L employment office . . . and when I walked into the office there, the man was saying [to the job applicants], "That's all." And I said one word. I said, "Well, everywhere I go that's what I've heard someone say—'that's all.'" And I'll never forget this fellow as long as I live. . . . His name was Jack. And he said to me, "Hey, come here!" He said, "Can you stand heat?" And I said, "I can stand heat and most anything about doing a job." He said, "Can you come back to work tonight?" I said, "I sure can."[23]

At times even greater assertiveness by the southern black migrant was needed. The next story shows how the new workers could push their chances of getting hired almost to the limit.

> I started back to work. Saturday morning I think it was. And I got up to this [street corner] there, and something just spoke to me: "Go to J&L." I just turned and went down a little side street. When I got over there men were lined up a mile, from 25th to 26th Street. A ton of men. I just kept walking. Got up to the employment office; I was turning to go in, and you could hear them guys hollerin' over here: "Stop him! Stop him!" The old beathouse cop on the inside said I had to wait. "Hell, I don't get in line for pay day!" He looked at me. "That's the rule." I said, "Well, I wouldn't get in line no how, and I don't have time. If I want this job here, I'm goin' on to work anyhow, I mean it. I'm not going to get in line for pay day. I'm going to be the first or second man." I believed in goin' about my business. Never late, no time. So, the employment manager was looking over his glasses. He said to the other fellow, "Bring that fellow over here." I

went over there. He said, "This guy is comin' to work. He's the kind of man we want . . . I'm going to sign this kid up. He's going to be a man 'round J&L." This old cop was saying, "Breaking the rules." He [the employment manager] said, "Rules is made to break."[24]

These work-search stories offer another clue to migrants' perceptions of the industrial world they are entering. The experiences related above emphasize the general hostility the southern blacks felt in Pittsburgh. Black residents of the city seemed to them unfriendly and uncaring. Temptations of urban life beckoned to the migrant whose plans centered not on amusement but on work. The atmosphere of the employment office itself, with men standing in line, all anxious for the few jobs opening that day, apparently etched itself deeply in some migrants' memories. The difficulties of finding work, and the perceived hostility, may have discouraged many, convincing them that fairer prospects lay elsewhere, but for others the obstacles to getting jobs became hurdles for them to clear. That they felt opposition to their attempts to find work made the jobs all the more important to the ambitious migrants. Although thousands of recent arrivals from the South might be getting hired, to the individual migrant finding a position in Pittsburgh was a personal victory over antagonistic forces.

Taken as a whole, the circumstances surrounding the migration of southern blacks and their search for work imbued the jobs opened to them during World War I with a transcendent importance. Some observers of the movement of southern blacks to the North believed that the accompanying talk of freedom and justice concerned a changing attitude toward migration and work in the minds of the migrants. "There was created in the minds of the Negro rural peasants and urban wage-earners a new consciousness of the fact that they have the liberty and the opportunity to move freely from place to place. The migration . . . gave the rank and file the belief that they could move to another part of the country and succeed in gaining a foothold in its industrial life and activity."[25]

This much, however, might have been said of the consciousness of southern blacks even before 1916. Seasonal migration within the South had been altering traditional attitudes toward work opportunities for some time before the really large out-migration got under way.

The Great Migration earned its reputation not because southern blacks moved north and found jobs but because they did so in unprecedented numbers, because the jobs they entered were ones by and large closed to them before, and because the timing and dimensions of the migration created intense excitement in the southern black communities. That which had been routine was given a new cast by the conditions surrounding northward movement of southern blacks from 1916 on.

The spirit which was created by the Great Migration imparted to the new black workers the sense that they had a right to the jobs opening to them in northern industry and that they were as well able to perform the work as the next man. "He [the employment agent] looked at me and said, 'Boy, you're pretty young. Do you know how to work?' I said, 'I can do anything you can do.' Just like that. That was my strategy. You ask me can I do something, I ask you can you do it. . . . I still believe I can do anything another man can do, if I want to."[26] The brief periods they intended to work in mills and factories and the perceived hostility of their new environment notwithstanding, black migrants understood that their restricted occupational position in northern cities was breaking down, and they approached the new positions in the work force with an almost militant attitude.

One consequence of the new black worker's perception of his changing role in the work force was a refusal to accept working conditions he felt were unnecessarily dangerous or undesirable. The reason migrants quit their jobs at the Byers mill in at least two cases out of every ten concerned working conditions, foremen, or other workers. Another 20 percent of the southern blacks who quit went to other jobs which they considered better than those assigned to them at the Byers company. Migrants who labored in the galvanizing shop complained about the acid in which finished products were immersed; those in departments where iron pipe was tested quit because the work was "too wet"; others left the plant because they found conditions too hot, too hard, or too heavy.

The reasons black migrants gave for leaving their jobs at Byers undoubtedly reflected objectionable conditions under which they had to work. But the complaints lodged against the firm also suggest that migrants had come to Pittsburgh with expectations higher than could be met by industrial work in the city. In the search not for any job but for a job with decent working conditions, the Great Migration became much more than a net redistribution of black people in the United States. It was more fundamentally a rapid elevation in the southern black migrants' aspirations and expectations. Because they brought with them from the South their own standards for industrial jobs and working conditions, the new black workers were probably not, as some authorities have claimed, the prime material for employers' paternalistic labor relations schemes.[27] We need to reexamine with care the migrants' own ways of gauging their work experience in northern cities in order to discover the basis on which they, as a group, gradually became a permanent part of the industrial working class in America.

The manifold changes that grew out of southern black migration to Pittsburgh defy any effort to summarize them in a few sentences. On one level, we can see that northward movement expanded blacks' educational, occupational, and cultural resources, but on a deeper level the meaning of the migration of blacks' advancement remained ambiguous. The introduction to northern industrial labor, which was the cutting edge of the migrants' transformation from a rural to an urban group, produced diverse reactions among the new black workers. Some found Pittsburgh jobs adequate to their needs for permanent homes, many others discovered that urban labor and living conditions were not better in every respect than the way of life that they had known in the South. One migrant to Pittsburgh wrote to the pastor of his home church in words that expressed the ambivalent feelings of thousands of southern blacks in the city: "I like the money O.K. but I like the South betterm [*sic*] for my Pleasure. this city is too fast for me they give you big money for what you do but they charge you big things for what you get . . . its [*sic*] largest city I ever saw . . . smoky city . . . some places look like torment or how they say it look and some places look like Paradise."[28] .

Notes

1. U.S. Census Bureau, *Negroes in the United States, 1920–1932* (Washington, D.C., 1935), 55; *Thirteenth Census of the United States, 1910* (Washington, D.C., 1913), 4:590–91; and *Fifteenth Census of the United States, 1930* (Washington, D.C., 1932), 4:1416.

2. Emmett J. Scott, comp., "Letters of Negro Migrants of 1916-1918," *Journal of Negro History* 4 (July 1919): 290–330; Emmett J. Scott, comp., "Additional Letters of Negro Migrants, 1916–1918," ibid., 4 (October 1919): 412–65.

3. I conducted the oral history interviews for this study over an eleven-month period, from October 1973 to August 1974. Sixteen interviews were collected for the Pennsylvania Historical and Museum Commission's Pittsburgh Oral History Project, June–August 1974.

4. Louise V. Kennedy, *The Negro Peasant Turns Cityward* (New York, 1932), 27–28; H. H. Donald, "The Negro Migration of 1916–1918," *Journal of Negro History* 6 (October 1921): 394.

5. U.S. Census Bureau, *Compendium of the Eleventh U.S. Census, 1890* (Washington, D.C., 1892), 540–73. The nine southern cities were Richmond, Virginia; Washington, D.C.; Louisville, Kentucky; Memphis, Tennessee; Atlanta, Georgia; New Orleans, Louisiana; Charleston, South Carolina; Houston, Texas; Birmingham, Alabama.

6. Ibid. The northern cities were New York (excluding Brooklyn), Philadelphia, Pittsburgh, Cleveland, Detroit, Chicago, Baltimore, and St. Louis.

7. T. J. Woofter Jr., *Negro Migration* (New York, 1920), 126–27; Clyde V. Kiser, *From Sea Island to City* (New York, 1932), 149–50.

8. This outline of seasonal migration dynamics is derived from Kiser, *Sea Island to City*, 149–50, and from the personal histories of several former black migrants, gained through interviews will be cited only by the respondent's initials and the date of the interview, J.G.,

November 26, 1973; W.H., October 25 and 30, 1973; C.M., August 5, 1974; C.C., February 21, and March 1, 1976; J.B., March 8 and 10, 1976.

9. Karl Marx, *Capital* (1867; reprint, London, 1970), 1:642.

10. Estimates of the number of southern blacks who moved north between 1916 and 1918 vary widely. See Florette Henri, *Black Migration* (Garden City, N.Y., 1975), 51.

11. Abraham Epstein, *The Negro Migrant in Pittsburgh* (Pittsburgh, 1918), 11–12, 18.

12. A. M. Byers Collection, Archives of Industrial Society, Univeristy of Pittsburgh (hereafter Byers Collection).

13. Epstein, *Negro Migrant in Pittsburgh,* 10.

14. Byers Collection.

15. H.G., August 23, 1974.

16. J.G., November 26, 1973.

17. W.H., October 25, 1973.

18. Scott, "Letters of Negro Migrants of 1916–1918," 290–328.

19. Richard Wright, *Twelve Million Black Voices* (New York, 1941), 86–88, 92–93.

20. Henri, *Black Migration,* 130.

21. Paul S. Taylor, *Mexican Labor in the United States: Chicago the Calumet Region,* University of California Publications in Economics, 7, no. 2 (Berkeley and Los Angeles, 1932), 88.

22. J.T., November 1 and 23, 1973.

23. C.M., August 5, 1974.

24. H.G., August 23, 1974.

25. George E. Hayes, "Effect of War Conditions on Negro Labor," *Academy of Political Science Proceedings, 1918,* 171.

26. H.G., August 23, 1974.

27. S. D. Spero and A. L. Harris, *The Black Worker* (Port Washington, N.Y., 1966), 130.

28. Scott, "Additional Letters of Negro Migrants," 459–60.

CHAPTER TWELVE

The Black Migration to Philadelphia:
A 1924 Profile

Frederic Miller

"The city Negro is only now in evolution."
—Charles S. Johnson

As a prominent black sociologist, Charles Johnson was well aware that there had been blacks living in American cities since the seventeenth century. Yet his proclamation in *Survey*'s famous issue on Harlem and the "New Negro" of the 1920s remains accurate, for he was referring to the emergence of large, sophisticated, and cosmopolitan communities of people fully committed to city life.[1] The massive racial transformation of urban America through black migration was concentrated in the half-century framed by World War I and the riots of the late 1960s. Perhaps because of the racial unrest which soon followed, the exceptional circumstances surrounding the start of the mass movement from the South around 1916 have been fairly well chronicled. The post–World War II movements are more exhaustively documented. But the crucial years of the early 1920s—the real onset of a self-sustaining migration—have been relatively unexplored. This chapter analyzes responses to an unusually comprehensive survey conducted in Philadelphia in 1924 of more than 500 recently arrived black migrants.[2] At the time, Philadelphia still had the nation's second largest urban black population. Thus, the survey illumi-

This chapter was first published in *The Pennsylvania Magazine of History and Biography* 108 (July 1984): 315–50. Reprinted by permission.

nates an important part of the process which changed not just Philadelphia but most of America's great industrial cities.

The picture which emerges is richly textured, providing us with extraordinary detail about the experiences of people too often lost to history. This chapter will examine the migrants in the South, before they came to Philadelphia, and study who they were, where and how they lived, and what kinds of jobs they held. It shall then investigate the process of migration, including the reasons people gave for coming North and which families came together. In Philadelphia itself, the survey allows us to study the migrants' housing conditions, neighborhoods, occupations, individual and family incomes, church membership, and attitudes toward life in the northern city. A statistical analysis will also reveal a number of intriguing patterns, both within the black migrant community and in comparison with the community development of contemporary European immigrants.

The Philadelphia survey recorded one of the most striking developments in America's modern social history. In 1915, the nation's black people were overwhelmingly rural and southern. The 1910 census had shown that 73 percent lived in rural areas and, more strikingly, that 89 percent (down little from 91.5 percent in 1870) still lived in the South.[3] There had been considerably greater black migration in those four decades to the trans-Mississippi South and West than to the Midwest and the Northeast. That pattern was reversed abruptly by the northern demand for labor during World War I and the simultaneous boll weevil epidemic in southern cotton fields. Northward migration then continued as a result of the postwar industrial boom of the 1920s, the virtual end of immigration from southern and eastern Europe, and the southern agricultural constrictions. Both blacks and poor whites streamed out of the South, with the black migration proportionately larger. Between 1910 and 1920, the net out-migration of blacks from the eleven states of the Southeast was about 554,000, nearly 7 percent of the area's total black population. In the 1920s, the net out-migration rose to about 902,000, a little over 10 percent of the remaining blacks, and three times the white rate.[4] While the 1916–18 migration was primarily a response to World War I, the renewed migration after 1921, concentrated in the early 1920s, clearly grew out of long-term trends in both the southern and northern economies. According to the Department of Labor, during the height of the migration between September 1922 and September 1923, nearly half a million blacks left the South.[5] By 1930, the proportion of America's 12 million black people in the South had fallen to 78.7 percent, and there were more than 2 million blacks in the metropolitan areas of the Northeast and the Midwest.[6]

Though Philadelphia had previously had a large black population, this new "Great Migration" affected the city profoundly. As of 1910 the 84,459 black

Philadelphians comprised 5.5 percent of the population. This was more than the slightly under 4 percent, which had prevailed from the 1860s to the 1890s, but it was below the range of 7.4–9.5 percent found in the first half of the nineteenth century. Between 1910 and 1920 the black population rose to 134,224, or 7.4 percent of the city's total, with most of the increase coming between 1916 and 1919.[7] The rise of the 1920s was considerably greater, with migration peaking between 1922 and 1924 at more than 10,000 per year.[8] A net increase of just over 85,000 raised the city's black population to 219,599, or 11.3 percent, by 1930. Thus, it was only in the 1920s that a new level was reached by Philadelphia's black community in terms of both absolute numbers and proportions of the city's population. In fact, the growth rate for the 1920s was 63.5 percent, compared with 58.9 percent on a much smaller base for the 1910s. By 1930, only 30 percent of the city's black people were Pennsylvania-born; while Virginia, the traditional leader in out-of-state origin, had 18.9 percent, South Carolina 13 percent, and Georgia 10.6 percent.[9] Migrants from these three southern states made up most of the respondents in the 1924 survey.

There had been several earlier surveys of black migrants to Philadelphia in the twentieth century. The Philadelphia Housing Association, the Armstrong Association (local affiliate of the Urban League), and the Traveler's Aid Society investigated the World War I migration, primarily in terms of housing and overcrowding.[10] In 1921, Sadie T. Mossell (later Alexander) of the University of Pennsylvania became the first black woman in America to earn a doctorate for her survey of the living standards of 100 migrant families.[11] Contemporary surveys were also taken of black migrants to other cities, and in 1930 Louise Venable Kennedy based her classic *The Negro Peasant Turns Cityward* on nineteen surveys done since 1917 of urban social and economic conditions.[12]

Yet there are several unique features of the 1924 Philadelphia survey. First, the original worksheets have survived, whereas for almost all the other surveys only the summaries remain. The individual answers to the dozens of questions asked in 1924 can be studied, analyzed, and compared in detail. Second, the survey covered a very wide range of issues about migration and about life in both the South and Philadelphia. Few studies of black migration deal with the particulars of either the southern background or the migration itself, usually because the data have been unavailable. Many of the surveys used by Kennedy described northern housing and employment in detail but discussed an almost undifferentiated "South." Third, modern scholars have given relatively little attention to the 1920s in comparison with the World War I migration, perhaps assuming that by 1920 the foundations of the northern ghettos were firmly in place. The 1924 survey therefore offers a detailed profile of the whole process of migration at a crucial yet underreported moment in time.

The origins of the survey were complex. As migration to Pennsylvania increased sharply in 1922 and 1923, various public and private agencies began to conduct research and to hold discussions as they had during the war. In August 1923 the Philadelphia Housing Association, a fourteen-year-old private reform group, issued a report on "Housing Negro Migrants" which grew out of the work of an interagency Committee on Negro Migration. That fall, work began on a statewide plan, and on January 3, 1924, the state convened a "Conference of the Needs of the Negro Population in Pennsylvania" with Governor Gifford Pinchot as the keynote speaker. Pinchot appointed a Statewide Interracial Committee and ordered a survey as the first order of business. The Housing Association, still a classic Progressive-era organization in its faith in the value of detailed social research, offered to develop and test the survey instrument. William D. Fuller, a Wharton School sociology student assigned as a researcher to the Association, directed the survey in the spring and finished his report on June 1, 1924.[13] We do not know whether Fuller, who was white, worked with any black assistants from cooperating organizations like the Armstrong Association or Mercy Hospital, although a check of handwriting reveals that the survey was a group effort.

But was all their work worthwhile? Is the survey a valid, useful, and representative picture of the migrant community? The Housing Association and Fuller were aware of potential pitfalls and, specifically, of the need to get honest answers from a representative sample. Addresses of recent migrants were culled from the files of the Housing and Armstrong Associations, the Traveler's Aid Society, and the all-black Mercy Hospital. A total of 435 addresses were visited, and usable information was obtained from 87. The response rate of only 20 percent was not encouraging to Fuller; further, it raises questions about the usefulness of the survey today. But the explanations provided in Fuller's report restore some confidence in the findings. Aside from unusable and largely uncompleted forms, the nonrespondents were explained primarily as people who had moved or returned South (118 addresses), were "alleged not known" (101), "did not respond" (37) or were away at the time of the visit (26).[14] The last category probably explains the underrepresentation of single people, especially males, in the survey. The numbers having moved or returned South are consistent with findings elsewhere. Fuller explained the 138 "not known" or "did not respond" answers by the fear of money collectors or, even more immediately, of vaccination. The 1923 migration had been followed by a smallpox outbreak, accompanied by 28,000 vaccinations and the quarantining of 303 predominantly black

Table 12.1. Household structure and Philadelphia income

Household Type	No.	Head's Age	Family Size	Head's Daily Income	Family's Daily Income
All households	142	32.8	3.59	$3.55	$4.72
Male headed—All	113	32.9	4.01	3.91	5.26
Families	104	33.2	4.28	3.94	5.39
Singles	9	30.1	—	3.56	—
Female headed—All	29	32.6	1.93	1.97	2.62
Families	11	41.4	3.45	2.04	3.65
Singles	18	27.2	—	1.94	—
Unskilled male laborers' families	74	33.8	4.36	3.90	5.49
Families with single earner	53	31.0	4.00	3.87	—
Working spouses	36	28.4[a]	3.47	1.90[a]	5.95

[a]Refers to spouse, not household head.

blocks.[15] Some of those surveyed might easily have suspected that Fuller's survey might be the prelude to another series of vaccinations and quarantines.

The central issue remains whether these factors skew the survey to the extent that it does not represent an accurate sample of the migrant population. Fuller's careful explanations give no indication of a major systematic bias. More crucial is that summarized data from the survey about family composition, age, income, time of migration, occupation, rent, and other indicators repeatedly coincide with quantifiable information from such sources as the U.S. Census and similar surveys in other cities. The results also generally coincide with reliable qualitative testimony about the "respectable," hardworking, family-oriented character of the migrants of the 1920s. Ironically, one of the most persuasive pieces of evidence in favor of the survey's accuracy would not seem to reflect that image. Asked if they had yet joined a church in Philadelphia, 105 of 141 household heads replied they had not. That is hardly the answer that would come from a group that was excessively privileged, hopelessly subservient, or plain dishonest. Instead, it adds credence to the total survey results.

Unfortunately, it is not easy to determine precisely how many different households were surveyed. There were several related families living together, and single individuals staying with families. We will use here the figure of 142 households, including 27 single person households, with a total of 510 members. A breakdown of the major types, with average size and age of household head, appears in Table 12.1. The most striking fact is the dominance of the core nuclear family—a man and wife, with or without children.

Since only one of the male-headed families was without a spouse, a total of 103 or 142 households, with 445 of the 510 people (87.3 percent) conforms to that pattern. Correcting for the probable underrepresentation of single men would have only a marginal impact on these figures. They clearly conform to Herbert Gutman's finding that between 1880 and 1925 the "typical Afro-American family was headed by two parents." Gutman found 83 percent of New York black households in 1925 to be kin-related with a nuclear core; the 1924 Philadelphia survey shows 72.5 percent to be nuclear, although other relatives perhaps were living nearby.[16] Attached to the 103 husband-wife-centered households were only seven other relatives, including four grandparents, scattered among seven households.

Louise Kennedy's picture of a northern black population containing a "preponderance of young adults and a small number of children, and older people" is also confirmed.[17] In the male-headed families in Philadelphia, the husband's average age was 33.2, the wife's 28.5, and there were an average of 2.4 children. Thirty of the 103 couples had no children at all. This small family size is not unusual. Stanley Lieberson noted in *A Piece of the Pie: Blacks and White Immigrants Since 1880* that "fertility rates for the first generation black women in the North remained considerably lower than those of new European immigrant groups as recently as 1940." In that year southern-born black women aged 45–54 who lived in the North reported having had an average of 2.2 children, compared with 4.6 for Italian-born women of the same age and 3.1 for Russian-born women.[18] The group that does appear unusual in our survey is the female-headed families, in which the average age of the head of household was 41, with a very small number of children and with no family exceeding three.

While the overall demographic features may not be surprising, the southern backgrounds of the migrants are more complex than is sometimes assumed. As the figures in Table 12.2 demonstrate, the migrants cannot simply be classified as tenant farmers driven off the land or as displaced unskilled workers already adapted to city life. Instead, tenant farmers and unskilled workers formed the largest groups, and a whole spectrum of intermediate and tangential individuals and families existed as well. Since time of residence of those coming from southern cities is unavailable, we cannot investigate the issue of gradual adaptation to urban life. Origin was more concentrated by state than by size of place or occupation and showed the clear shift of the Upper to the Deep South as the source of Philadelphia's black migrants. Georgia (59) and South Carolina (45) accounted for more than 100 households, with Virginia (11), North Carolina (10), and Maryland (8) providing almost the rest. A significant proportion of Georgia's migrants (26 of 59) came from large cities, and that state also provided more than half of all the single people

Table 12.2. Occupation and residence in the South

| | Size of Southern Residence | | | |
Head's Occupation[a] in South (No.)	Under 2,500	2,500- 10,000	10,000- 50,000	Over 50,000
Farmer owner (6)	2	1	2	1
Tenant farmer (44)	24	16	4	0
Farm laborer (3)	1	0	2	0
Unskilled worker (40)	13	7	2	18
Domestic (12)	2	3	2	5
Services (10)	2	1	1	6
Skilled work (12)	4	1	2	5
Business owner (1)	0	0	0	1
Total (128)	48	29	15	36

| | Home Tenure in South | | | |
Head's Occupation[a] in South (No.)	Own House	Rent in Cash	Rent in Crops	Rent Apartment
Farmer owner (6)	6	0	0	0
Tenant farmer (43)	8	6	29	0
Farm laborer (3)	1	1	0	1
Unskilled worker (40)	7	26	2	4
Domestic (12)	4	6	0	1
Services (10)	6	3	0	0
Skilled work (12)	5	6	1	0
Business owner (1)	0	1	0	0
Total (128)	37	49	32	6

[a]For purposes of putting people in occupational categories, "domestics" are considered those strictly in personal service (cleaning and washing; butlers and maids), while "services" includes nonpersonal positions like waitress, building janitor, fireman, driver, and restaurant worker. "Skilled work" includes foremen, mechanics, carpenters, teachers, plasterers, and paperhangers. This analysis was used for Philadelphia as well as for the South. Most unskilled labor is described simply as "day" or "general" labor, although occasionally plants are named. The pay rate usually makes the level of skill apparent.

surveyed (14 of 27). South Carolina's migrants, in contrast, came overwhelmingly from communities with less than 10,000 inhabitants (36 of 45).

The occupational diversity of the rural and small-town South was reflected in the northward migration. All occupational categories were represented among the people from those areas. Even considering only the communities with less than 2,500 people, nonagricultural work accounted for 21 of the 48 employed household heads. Most of these rural workers were drivers, carpenters and other craftsmen, and general laborers who worked at least sometimes in the fields as well as the towns and villages. To the extent that they all depended on agricultural conditions, they were caught up in the crisis that had shaken the South since the advent of the boll weevil around the turn of the century. Between 1920 and 1925, with the boll weevil ravaging Georgia and South Carolina and with soil erosion taking an added toll, the number of black-owned farms declined from 218,000 to 195,000.[19] City workers were subject to different economic cycles, but one pattern prevailed in both the rural and the urban south. In most cases, all the family's adult members worked at least part of the time. This was naturally true on the farm, where "sharecropping was in essence a family based system."[20] But even figures from married male laborers in the South show that 28 of 35 had working wives, all but one of whom were domestics.

As a result of the multiple incomes, the average family income of those having cash wages was not very low by the minimal standards of the early 1920s. The 47 male-headed families averaged $3.60 per day. More detailed analysis reveals that 52 male household heads, including singles, made $2.55 per day, while 38 working spouses averaged only $1.18, a few cents less than single women. These figures remind us that "the basic southern unskilled wage did not differ greatly between black and white workers."[21] For example, in Virginia in 1928, daily laborers' wages were found to be about $3.49 for whites and $3.07 for blacks.[22] In terms of agricultural income, Georgia and South Carolina figures for the 1920s indicate a day farm labor wage of about $1.00 for all workers.[23] Per capita tenant farm income was about $150 per year in cash crops, to which must be added home-grown produce.[24] While southern blacks were certainly poor, they were not very much poorer than the immense number of whites in similar occupations.

The migrants' southern housing conditions reflected their range of incomes and occupations. Of 134 reporting households, 43 owned houses and 85 rented them, paying in either cash (51) or crops (34). Table 12.2 outlines the relationship between house tenure and southern occupation. The 50 reported rents average exactly $10 per month, considerably lower than in Philadelphia. Overcrowding was also less of a problem than in the North, with 4.24 rooms per household and just under one person per room. Of course, most of the rural houses, even if fairly large, were primitive shacks or cabins without indoor water or adequate toilet facilities, so that meaningful comparisons beyond simple room-counting are difficult to make.

The living standards, occupations, and incomes of the migrants in the South indicate that they should be described as the working poor, rather than the destitute. The group's respectability is reflected in the fact that 85 percent of household heads were church members, a statistic valuable for illustrating social attitudes—100 percent membership existed among the 12 skilled workers. While the attitude of the northern black elite was probably summarized in Mossell's assertion that "the migration retarded the steady progress of the colored people of Philadelphia,"[25] more optimistic views came from white observers. The Housing Association reported that the 1921–24 migrants "seemed well supplied with funds" and were "of a better grade" than their wartime predecessors.[26] Lieberson concludes that available data "indicate a high degree of positive self-selection from those living in the South."[27]

But why did these people "self-select" to migrate? Since the 1920s, most writers have agreed that the primary motives were economic, and that, as Howard University economist Edward Lewis wrote in 1932, "both the 'push' of agricultural disorganization and the 'pull' of industry were important influences in the movement of the Negro."[28] The push out of cotton-dominated states like Georgia and South Carolina resulted from the boll weevil epidemic, which made the debt-based crop system unworkable, and from the associated diversification away from the labor-intensive cotton production. The pull was the well-publicized lure of regular and relatively high wages paid by northern industries, faced in 1922 and 1923 with a booming economy and the collapse of European immigration. The number of immigrants fell from 652,000 in 1921 to 216,000 in 1922; the number of incoming Italians, a major source of unskilled labor, fell from 222,000 to 40,000.[29] Southern blacks were so aware of and eager to meet the resulting demand that a return to the 1916–18 labor agent recruiting system was unnecessary. Fuller noted that there was "not a single case in which the Negro had a job in Philadelphia before his coming," because migrants felt they could choose among jobs after their arrival.[30]

The primacy of economic motives does not mean that social oppression in the South was unimportant. But as early as 1923, Charles Johnson noted that there was no correlation between migration and oppression when specific counties were examined.[31] Kennedy stated in 1930 that social conditions were "secondary and contributing causes" of the migration, and Vickery's elaborate statistical analysis four decades later found that the migration was "just too rational economically" to be explained any other way.[32] Nevertheless, it is also true that the racial situation formed the context in which the economic forces quickly led to the mass migration. As Fuller put it, blacks may have had a longing to escape the South, but "the cotton crop is the one thing which has exerted pressure upon the Negro to fulfill this desire."[33]

The primary reason for migration offered by the surveyed group both confirms and modifies the common interpretations. Philip Taylor wrote in *The Distant Magnet* that the motives of European immigrants were "a delicate balance between several forms of persuasion." The point applies to black migrants as well.[34] The migration occurred not as a simple push/pull process. Some migrants were mainly pushed; others, mainly pulled. But a third group

Table 12.3. Migration: Motivation and process

| Head's Occupation in South (No.) | Reason for Migrating | | | |
	Boll Weevil	"Took a Notion"	Lack of Work	Contacts in Phila.
Farmer owner (6)	5	0	0	0
Tenant farmer (42)	23	8	2	4
Farm laborer (3)	1	0	0	1
Unskilled worker (38)	2	12	9	9
Domestic (11)	0	6	0	4
Services (9)	0	1	3	4
Skilled work (12)	0	4	5	2
Business owner (1)	0	0	0	0
Total (122)	31	31	19	24

| Head's Occupation in South (No.) | Reason for Migrating | | Family Came Together? | |
	More Money	Social Conditions	Yes	No
Farmer owner (6)	0	1	3	3
Tenant farmer (42)	1	4	14	30
Farm laborer (3)	1	0	1	2
Unskilled worker (38)	6	0	27	13
Domestic (11)	1	0	8	4
Services (9)	1	0	7	3
Skilled work (12)	0	1	6	6
Business owner (1)	1	0	1	0
Total (122)	11	6	67	61

was directed by several forces. Occupation was the best predictor of motivation; 30 of the 53 farmers and farm laborers cited the boll weevil as their reason for coming North. Social conditions, another "push" factor, were also cited as a reason by the agricultural sector, which provided five of the six household heads who advanced that reason for migrating. The nonagricultural migrants, more inclined to "pull" factors, had a wider range of motivations. A quarter of all migrants reporting cited a vague wanderlust or alienation which appears on the survey form as "Took a Notion," "See the North," and similar statements.

Various demographic and locational factors not illustrated in Table 12.3 further illuminate migrant motivation. Almost half of the single people (13 of 27) indicated a sense of wanderlust or alienation while a similar proportion of female family heads (5 of 11) referred to contacts in Philadelphia. Conversely, among 104 male-headed families, the boll weevil (30) and lack of work (17) were disproportionately important. There were also distinctions by age. Those looking for more money (30.6) or citing reasons like a "notion" (29.5) were younger, on the average, than those who left because of lack of work (34.0) or the boll weevil (36.4). This predictable correlation of the "push" factors with older respondents incidentally helps confirm the validity of the answers given in the survey. More unexpected is that for those with cash wages the average family incomes of migrants citing a lack of work ($3.54) or the desire to make more money ($3.37) were higher than those who mentioned northern contacts ($2.71) or the wanderlust/alienation reasons ($2.96). Thus, those who already had higher incomes were most conscious of wanting even more. Finally, there were some variations by location aside from the rural emphasis on the boll weevil and social conditions. Most notably, contacts with people in Philadelphia were offered as the prime motivation by only 5 of the 52 residents of areas with less than 2,500 residents, but by 11 of the 38 from cities having over 50,000. Larger populations apparently generated a self-sustaining network of people moving North to the same city, as most studies of migration have shown.

The importance of contacts reminds us that the process of migration is as complex as the motivation. As in the national pattern, almost all of the household heads surveyed arrived in Philadelphia between spring 1922 and fall 1923. There were two main waves, peaking in the fall of 1922 and, more prominently, the spring of 1923, when half of all the migrants arrived. Migrants from rural and urban areas showed the same seasonal pattern. But a key question is whether whole families came together, as with most Russian Jews, or whether the household head came first to get work, as with most Italians and Slavs. While four-fifths of all migrants—and 88 percent of all farmers—had acquaintances in Philadelphia before their migration, there were important variations in the way families migrated. As with motivation, occupation is the most reliable determinant. The relationship is clear in Table 12.3. However, two variations by population should be noted. In contrast to tenant farmers, fourteen unskilled laborers' families came north together from places with under 50,000 population; only five families did not. But for families from big cities, the division was equal, eight to eight. One explanation might be that people with weak economic and psychic attachments to the local social pattern—like rural laborers, and domestic and service workers—would be more willing to make an abrupt break than tenant farmers, urban laborers, or skilled workers.

Another common pattern of migration is several families moving together to a new location. An analysis of households from the same place in the South living at the same address in Philadelphia indicates that even after at least nine months in the North 54 of the 142 households can be so linked to one or two others. Of these, 21 were from cities of more than 50,000 and 33 from smaller places. Only ten families in five groups—four from rural areas—were obviously related by blood, though the likelihood of undetected cousinhood is high. The length of time since migration, the unreported addresses, and the lack of data on the 1916–19 migration make it virtually certain that a large majority of households, not just the 54 obvious cases, were closely linked to other families that had migrated to Philadelphia. The identified linked households do not differ significantly from the entire surveyed population in terms of location or occupation in either the South or Philadelphia. However, there was a notable demographic difference. More than half the single women (8 of 15), compared with 36 percent of the rest of the group, were part of a group of households which came from the same place in the South and settled together in Philadelphia.

The overall settlement pattern of the migrants in Philadelphia challenges some common beliefs about both the distribution and the concentration of urban blacks. Many writers have maintained that migrants concentrated in already established black neighborhoods and that the more prosperous blacks sought newer areas.[35] Certainly this model could have fit Philadelphia, which already had one of the North's few ghettos before World War I. Fortunately, unpublished Philadelphia data available from the 1920 and 1930 census enable us to test this theory. The 1920 figures give population by race for each of more than 1,500 Enumeration Districts (EDs) while the 1930 data are at the much larger Census Tract (CT) level still in use. For each household, the black percentage of its 1920 ED or 1930 CT was calculated, resulting in what Lieberson called an "isolation index."[36] These averages appear in Table 12.4 and mean, for example, that the average surveyed family in North Philadelphia was living, *in 1924* in a 1920 ED which had been 20.5 percent black and a 1930 CT which was to be 27.3 percent black.

The four-district division used here provides a sense of the overall settlement pattern. The "Ghetto" refers to the heavily black area on either side of South Street, including all of the Seventh and Thirtieth Wards and the northern fringes of the Twenty-Sixth and Thirty-sixth Wards, an area in which all the EDs were at least 35 percent black in 1920. The vast majority of black migrants in South Philadelphia, outside the "ghetto," lived in the poor Italian, Jewish, and Polish neighborhoods east of the main black concentration. Thus, the "South Philadelphia" defined here was overwhelmingly white, but also quite poor. In more prosperous North and West Philadelphia the migrants generally lived in the same area as the rest of the black population. But there are several differences between the migrants' citywide distribution and that of the black population as a whole. For both groups, only about 29 percent lived in the Ghetto. North Philadelphia had about 43 percent of the overall

Table 12.4. Philadelphia districts

| District (No.) | Head's Occupation in Philadelphia | | | | |
	Unskilled Labor	Domestic	Service	Skilled Labor	Owner
Ghetto (42)	21	10	1	4	2
South Phila. (41)	26	6	2	3	0
North Phila. (41)	24	7	7	3	0
West Phila. (18)	12	2	2	1	1
Total (134)[a]	83	25	12	11	3

District (No.)	Head's Income	Family Income	Family Size	1920 Black (%) (EDs)	1930 Black (%) (CTs)
Ghetto (42)	$3.36	$4.24	2.9	64.1	61.1
South Phila. (41)	3.63	4.57	3.7	2.9	13.5
North Phila. (41)	3.73	4.86	3.5	20.5	27.3
West Phila. (18)	3.34	5.83	5.3	27.7	30.3
Total (134)[a]	3.55	4.72	3.6	29.2	33.7

[a]Eight household heads reported no occupation in Philadelphia.

black population but 29 percent of the migrants and, similarly, West Philadelphia had 20 percent of all blacks but only 13 percent of the survey group. In contrast, South Philadelphia held 29 percent of the migrants and only 8 percent of all black Philadelphians. As observers like Thomas Woofter noted at the time, blacks took over as Jews and Italians left their worst neighborhoods.[37] But that black vanguard apparently consisted of migrants, not of long-standing residents dispersed out of the nearby Ghetto. One result of these realignments was that by 1930 blacks were more concentrated together—segregated from others—than Russian Jews or Italians. This had not been true in 1920, but the white immigrant groups were able to move to some degree into nonimmigrant white areas, an option closed to blacks because of discrimination. [EDITORS' NOTE: See original essay for map.]

The geographic distribution also produces an unexpectedly low overall isolation index for the migrants. Of the 142 households, 60 (42.3 percent) lived in 1920 EDs less than 10 percent black, 40 of which were in South Philadelphia. Only 36 (25.4 percent) were in EDs over half black, while 46 (32.4 percent) were in areas 10 to 50 percent black. Remarkably, the 1930 census figures indicate that the surveyed migrants were probably less segregated than the whole black population. In 1930 the average black Philadelphian lived in a tract that was 34.7 percent black, little different from the surveyed migrants who in 1924 were in tracts that would be 33.7 percent black in the next census. So Lieberson's calculated 6.5 percent increase in the ward level isolation index in the 1920s was probably not due primarily to the migration but to broader black-white interaction, in particular to the effects of racism as manifested in restricted housing choice for blacks.[38]

Outside the Ghetto, the surveyed migrants were in areas experiencing marked increases in the 1920s over previously low black populations. While not everywhere part of the vanguard, as in South Philadelphia, neither did the migrants lag behind the citywide black movement. Because two different units are used, it is impossible to compare 1920 ED figures directly with 1930 CT figures. However, the pattern of increased concentration is clear, especially in South and West Philadelphia. Despite the larger area and consequent dilution of ethnic concentrations, 36 of 41 South Philadelphia households were in CTs that were to be 10 to 25 percent black in 1930, as compared with 40 of 41 in the 0 to 9 percent category in 1920 terms. For West Philadelphia, a range of low figures in 1920 terms translates into 16 of 18 households living in CTs 26 to 50 percent black in 1930.

Few variations in concentration and distribution can be explained in terms of demography, southern origins, or the migration process. Both single people (in 1920 EDs 31.1 percent black) and female-headed families (32.9 percent) lived in more heavily black areas than did male-headed families (28.3 percent). The most prominent variations by district were in West Philadelphia where 17 of 18 households were male headed, with 13 of those 17 headed by former tenant farmers. West Philadelphia had significantly older male family heads, averaging 39.8 years of age compared with 33.1 for the rest of the city. The widest range of southern occupations was found in the Ghetto, but that district also contained an unusually low number of tenant farmers (7) and a high number of former domestics (8) among the 38 reporting households.

The size of the southern place of origin did have some effect on settlement patterns, with migrants from smaller communities tending to settle in areas with high white populations. Of 52 households from places with under 2,500 residents, 30 settled in 1920 EDs less than 10 percent black, primarily in South and lower North Philadelphia. Migrants from cities with over 50,000 population were concentrated in the Ghetto and adjacent South Philadelphia, with none in West Philadelphia. Those from cities between 10,000 and 50,000 settled mainly in North and West Philadelphia (10 of 17). Their 1920 isolation index was 27.4 percent, compared with 24.7 percent for rural migrants and 34.7 percent for those from large cities. Some aspects of the way people came north also affected place of settlement in Philadelphia. Only 28 household heads reported having no friends in Philadelphia, and 22 of them lived

The Great Migration brought into Philadelphia an influx of African Americans, who competed with whites for limited housing and jobs. This was a major cause of civil disturbances, such as the Philadelphia Riot of 1918. In this photograph, African Americans are working in the shipyard at Philadelphia's Hog Island in 1917. (Courtesy of the Atwater Kent Museum)

in the Ghetto (12) or North Philadelphia (10), the two largest black communities. Blacks without contacts stayed away from mostly white South and West Philadelphia. The ghetto was also the only district in which a majority of male-headed families had migrated together, another indication of its function as the preferred sanctuary of the uprooted and the friendless.

The occupational breakdown of the migrant group was strikingly simple compared with this complex settlement pattern. Regardless of family structure, age, southern origin, or Philadelphia residence, the overwhelming majority of males were unskilled laborers, and almost all the working females were domestics. Figures for the household heads and for all working family members are given in Tables 12.4 and 12.5. Other breakdowns reinforce the basic picture. Of 104 male family heads, 74 were unskilled laborers, as were 8 of 9 single men; of 11 female family heads, 8 were domestics. Of 36 working wives, 34 were also domestics, 27 of whose husbands were unskilled laborers. However, in Philadelphia only 20 out of 73 married mothers worked, a number 10 fewer than those having wage income in the South, and not counting those who worked in the fields. The total of 36 spouses working out of 103 coincides with the 39 percent of black homemakers employed citywide in 1930. As Lieberson found, "black women were more likely to be employed away from the home than women from the new European ethnic groups," continuing the southern work pattern.[39] The occupational distribution for working children, who averaged 18.5 years of age, was the same as for adults. Of 22 males, 16 were in unskilled labor, and 14 of 16 females were in domestic service.

While remarkable in its homogeneity, the migrant occupational breakdown was not very different from that of all Philadelphia blacks or from black migrants elsewhere. For male workers, World War I had marked a decisive advance from services into industrial employment. But in the 1920s they could not advance further and break through the "job ceiling" keeping blacks in unskilled work. Kennedy concluded in 1930 that blacks were "still largely confined to unskilled labor and positions which are closely allied to domestic and personal service." She added that this was especially true in the Northeast.[40] In Philadelphia, the largest groups of unskilled black workers were employed in iron and steel mills, machine shops, shipyards, car works, and general construction. Certain major companies were known as willing employers of blacks, including the Pennsylvania and Reading Railroads, United Gas, Baldwin Locomotive, Philadelphia Rapid Transit, Midvale Steel, Cramps Shipyard, Westinghouse, Atlantic-Refining, and Lukens Steel. A 1923 Migration Committee report found that these ten companies employed 7,313 blacks or 14.6 percent of their workforce, and that 5,641 (77.1 percent) were classified as unskilled.[41]

Occupational variations by district were small, as indicated in Table 12.4. The Ghetto contained an overrepresentation of domestics and some underrepresentation of unskilled laborers with families (17 of 74) and working spouses (7 of 36). In turn, unskilled laborers lived in 1920 EDs averaging 25.9 percent black as opposed to 32.0 percent for domestics and 35.9 percent for skilled workers. Many of the latter were in trades like carpentry, which depended for work on a large black population. The unskilled laborers needed no such base, and 42 of them, out of 83, lived in 1920 EDs less than 10 percent black compared with only 15 of 51 of the other occupational groups.

These unskilled laborers came from a diverse southern background described in Table 12.5. The overall picture is one of social compression and de-skilling. Whatever the poverty and other difficulties faced by tenant farmers in the South, their work did involve a variety of responsibilities and skills. But only six became skilled workers in Philadelphia, three of them carpenters, while twenty-seven became unskilled laborers. Previous occupa-

Table 12.5. Philadelphia occupations

Head's Occupation in North (No.)	Head's Occupation in the South					
	Farm Owner	Tenant Farmer	Farm Labor	Unskilled Labor	Domestic	Service
Unskilled labor (83)	6	27	1	35	0	6
Domestic (25)	0	4	1	0	11	0
Services (12)	0	5	1	2	0	3
Skilled labor (10)	0	6	0	2	0	0
Owner (2)	0	1	0	0	0	0
Total (124)[a]	6	43	3	39	11	9

Head's Occupation in North (No.)	Head's Occupation in South		Head's Daily Income	Family Daily Income	Total Family Members	
	Skilled	Owner			Male	Female
Unskilled labor (83)	6	0	$3.88	$5.29	98	3
Domestic (25)	2	0	$2.01	$2.73	5	70
Services (12)	1	0	$2.96	$4.07	14	3
Skilled labor (10)	3	0	$5.21	$6.24	11	3
Owner (2)	0	1	—	—	3	1
Total (124)[a]	12	1	3.55	4.72	131	77

[a]Eight employed household heads reported no southern occupation.

tions—as well as places of origin—had little impact on the pattern of male unskilled labor and female domestic service. However, two groups involving twelve cases of occupational mobility—the six tenant farmers who became skilled workers and the six southern skilled workers who became laborers—provide exceptions to the general experience. The first group, former tenant farmers, came north mainly because of the boll weevil, and none of their fairly large families (averaging 5.16 persons) came all together. Four of the six came from places with 2,500 to 10,000 residents, where they may have done odd jobs in addition to farming. None settled in the Ghetto. Despite their high individual ($5.15 per day) and family ($6.40 per day) incomes, five of the six families were either considering or definitely planning to return South.

The six southern skilled workers, including two carpenters and two mechanics, who became laborers in Philadelphia present a very different picture. They were older than the fellow laborers, averaging 37.8 years of age, and five of the six heads initially came north without their families, unlike most southern unskilled workers. Three of the six came from cities over 50,000 population. As a group their 1920 isolation index was a low 20.8 percent, meaning that they lived in poor white neighborhoods. But we should pause before lamenting their new condition. For their individual daily incomes rose from an average of $3.08 in the South to $3.75 in Philadelphia. Because more family members had worked in the South the increase in family income was less, from $4.24 to $4.65. Nevertheless, four of the six household heads indicated they would definitely not return South. Thus, while the economically upwardly mobile families were planning to return, the apparently proleterianized were planning to stay North. Within the limits imposed by the small numbers, we might suspect that culture and upbringing drew farmers back to the land and that those remaining in Philadelphia were accustomed to making decisions on a more strictly economic basis.

The search for work reveals some statistically significant variations. Although the demand for migrant labor was high in 1924, the question of whether household heads found it difficult to find work elicited a pattern of responses which suggests the possibility that some of the unskilled workers formed part of a floating proletariat, especially in construction. In terms of occupation, 41 percent of the unskilled workers (a total of 34) and 44.6 percent of unskilled family men reported some difficulty finding work, as opposed to 29 percent (10) of the domestic and service workers and 20 percent (2) of the skilled workers. Further, there was a clear relationship between the ability to find a job and to keep it. Of the 40 heads who had held four or more jobs in Philadelphia, 21 (52.5 percent) had difficulty finding work. In contrast, such difficulty was reported by 22 of 50 (44 percent) with two or three jobs, and only 8 of 43 (19 percent) who had never changed their jobs. These findings are paralleled by data for residential change. Among the 63 households which had never moved, 45 heads reported no difficulty finding work. Among the remaining 67 households, only 35 reported having no difficulty. Clearly, there was a group of people who had difficulty finding work, keeping jobs, and establishing a permanent residence. But location was also a factor in job seeking. In both South and West Philadelphia half of the respondents reported difficulty finding work, compared with 30 percent in both North Philadelphia and the Ghetto. In other words, migrants found work somewhat more easily in the well-established, predominantly black neighborhoods than in heavily white parts of the city.

As with occupation, the pattern of individual and family income was also dominated by male unskilled labor and female domestic service. Other factors which helped determine household income were family size and the number of family members working. Tables 12.1, 12.4, and 12.5 break down household head and family income by household structure, location, and occupation. Probably the best means for understanding migrants' income are the figures for the 74 families headed by a male unskilled laborer—$3.90 per day for the head and $5.49 for the survey's 510 people. Most observers agree that there was little racial wage differential for nonunion unskilled work in the North as in the South.[42] The National Conference Board estimated that daily wage rates in 1924 averaged the equivalent of about $4.16 for unskilled labor nationwide, while Paul Douglas calculated about $4.03 for a five-and-a-half-day week.[43] In these terms, the surveyed migrants were doing reasonably well for recent black arrivals.

In terms of family income, there were actually two very different patterns among male-headed families. As Sadie Mossell had found with the wartime migrants, the crucial factor was still the number of working family members.[44] The incomes of the unskilled laborers' families were fairly typical for mid-1920s working-class America, mainly because only 32 of 74 unskilled workers' families relied solely on the incomes of the household head. The average daily income of working wives and children was $1.90 and $2.41 respectively. As a result, there was a statistically significant correlation between male unskilled workers' family incomes and family size (.35), while the correlation between family incomes and head's income was insignificant.[45] In sharp contrast, 8 of 11 male skilled workers were sole earners in their families, as were 8 of 11 service workers, despite their low wages.

The income of female-headed households formed another distinct pattern. Most striking was the persistence of the male-female income gap from South to North. For the 67 households with cash wages in both regions, the daily income of male heads was twice as high as that of female heads in Philadelphia ($3.91 to $1.97), just as it had been in the South ($2.54 to $1.29). In terms of family income, the gap narrowed in proportion but widened in size, from $3.52 for males and $1.46 for females to $5.26 and $2.62 respectively. But female income in Philadelphia had two other peculiarities. There was a consistent negative correlation of age with the income of single women $(-.36)$, spouses $(-.41)$, and female family heads $(-.12)$. This was not the case for women in the South or men in either region. For the eleven female family heads, there was also a strong negative correlation between family and individual head's income $(-.38)$, but a strong positive correlation between family income and number of children (.49). Both resulted primarily from the fact that only four female domestics were the sole support of their families.

In determining income, as with occupation, the influence of the South was minimal. The main factor was a general increase in cash income experienced by 45 of the 60 families with cash incomes in both the South and Philadelphia and by almost all the ex-tenant farmers. Comparable household head cash income increased an average of 54.4 percent from $2.26 per day to $3.49 per day, while family income rose 39.3 percent, from $3.05 to $4.25 per day. In terms of southern origin, the 49 reporting households from places under 2,500 in population had higher daily incomes in Philadelphia ($4.84) than the 32 from cities with more than 50,000 ($4.57). This was the result of more ex-rural family members working, since individual heads' income were actually a little higher for those from the big cities ($3.47 versus $3.35 per day). Sex and household type reflect only a slight correlation between family cash income in the South and Philadelphia. This surprising result is caused by a combination of chance, the narrow bounds of unskilled wage rates, and the limited overlap of spouses working in both the North and South.

Family size seems the decisive factor in creating the difference in income by district displayed in Table 12.4. The income figures show the impact of the gap between the Ghetto's 2.9 persons per family and West Philadelphia's 5.3. For male-headed families, the difference was 6.2 and $6.57 per day in West Philadelphia, compared with 3.5 and $5.07 per day in the Ghetto; the variation due to a slightly higher spouses' income in the latter area. North and South Philadelphia had intermediate male-headed family sizes of a little over four. However, the daily income of North Philadelphia's average male-headed family was $5.71, compared with South Philadelphia's $4.89, because of the former's high individual daily incomes. These figures may reflect the broader industrial and manufacturing opportunities available in North Philadelphia. The total result is that the pattern of migrants' family incomes—though not individual heads' incomes—conforms to the traditional pattern of black Philadelphia as a whole. West Philadelphia is at the top, followed by North Philadelphia, while the Ghetto and South Philadelphia trail behind. Of the six families earning more than $9 per day, three each lived in North and West Philadelphia, with none south of Market Street.

The fairly logical arrangement of family income by district does not carry over to black concentration. Neither the 1920 nor the 1930 figures yield clear patterns or meaningful correlations for either family or individual income. For example, the highest household incomes ($4.84 per day) are in the 1920 EDs 0 to 9 percent and 51 to 75 percent black. Incomes were not significantly lower in the predominantly black areas than in the heavily white area settled by migrants, notably South Philadelphia.

Income levels were also related to job turnover and residential mobility, both of which are summarized in Table 12.6. Ericksen and Yancey found that black residential mobility by ward was about the same in the 1920s as for foreign-born Irish and Italians, and less than that of Russian Jews.[46] The average migrant household reported .99 moves in the 8 to 20 months that most had been in Philadelphia, with single people having a much lower average (.44) than families (1.08). For a newly arrived family to move once or twice in its first few years in Philadelphia does not indicate any serious insta-

Table 12.6. Philadelphia mobility and housing conditions

District (No.)	No. of Jobs (Household Head)			No. of Moves			
	1	2–3	4+	0	1	2	3+
Ghetto (42)	24	12	6	23	4	12	3
South Phila. (41)	10	14	17	12	7	17	5
North Phila. (41)	12	17	12	25	4	10	2
West Phila. (18)	6	7	5	9	5	3	1
Total (142)	52	50	40	69	20	42	11

District (No.)	Toilet Facilities			Persons per Room	Monthly Rent
	Inside	Outside	Both		
Ghetto (42)	5	18	19	1.74	$15.83
South Phila. (41)	4	29	8	1.67	12.45
North Phila. (41)	9	12	18	2.07	14.63
West Phila. (18)	9	5	4	2.09	7.94
Total (142)	27	64	49	1.86	13.51

bility. The level of job turnover was higher, reflecting the presence of many Philadelphia blacks in fields like building and construction, shipping and other waterfront industries, where each job customarily lasted only for a limited period. Thus the surveyed migrants fit the pattern summarized by Kennedy in 1930 when she wrote that "according to most recent national surveys, Negroes still have a higher rate of turnover than whites."[47]

The impact on income of job turnover and residential mobility varied. For the unskilled laborers, the largest group, income was independent of both. But for skilled workers, individual income tended to increase with number of jobs held, a result of the craftsman's independent work pattern. Of the 11 skilled workers, 5 had held 4 or more jobs since arriving north, compared with only twenty-two of eighty-three unskilled laborers. Domestics, on the other hand, had a strong positive correlation between individual income and the number of residential changes (.60), but no significant correlation between income and number of jobs. Relocation for them may reflect increased or at least stable income, starting from a very low base. Service workers, many of whom were drivers and porters, had strong negative correlations between individual income and number of jobs ($-.44$) and between number of moves and both individual ($-.60$) and family income ($-.56$). In this group, the highest incomes tended to be earned by those who had held only one or two jobs and had never moved once initially settled.

Such interactions between job and residential change are more helpful in distinguishing between different parts of the city than in explaining income variation. For the city as a whole, a linkage between the two processes is evident, but it is far from an exact correlation. Of the 52 household heads who had not changed jobs, 33 had not moved. But 15 who had held 4 or more jobs also had not moved. Similarly, while 17 heads with 4 or more jobs had moved at least twice, 16 others who had moved twice had not changed their jobs. Clearer distinctions emerge on the district level. The contrasts between the stability of the Ghetto, the volatility of South Philadelphia, and the intermediate situations of North and West Philadelphia are evident from Table 12.6. Figures for male-headed families parallel those for the entire survey group. The high job turnover in South Philadelphia is the major factor leading to a negative correlation between the number of jobs and the 1920 black ED population for the whole surveyed group ($-.25$) and, even more strongly, for unskilled laboring men's families (-37). These figures hold even when controlling for such factors as age, family size, household structure, and residential mobility. They contrast with the lack of such correlations between residential change and black concentration.

Interactions between changes in jobs and residence further illustrate the differences between districts. More than a third of Ghetto households (15) had changed neither job nor residence since their arrival in Philadelphia, while nearly a third of South Philadelphia households (13) had changed both at least twice. North and West Philadelphia had less uniform combinations. In the latter, though the totals are quite small, the number of heads who had not moved or changed jobs (5, or 27.8%) accords with the type of older, extenant farmer with a large family attracted to that area. By far the largest group of household heads in North Philadelphia—18, or 44 percent of the total—also had not moved but had held two or more jobs. As with the district's relatively high wages, the figure probably represents job availability in this heavily industrial part of the city.

This data about mobility, like that about migration, occupation, and income, was incidental to the main object of the survey—the investigation of living conditions, especially housing. The contemporary view was that residential segregation led to slum overcrowding, considered the main social problem growing out of the black migration. The *Public Ledger* summarized this view in a July 1923 editorial which warned that while the city's economy was "absorbing the influx of Negro labor, which is of an excellent grade . . . their character cannot hope to be maintained under living conditions that are degrading to the self-respect of the newcomers."[48] Philadelphia was not unique, and Kennedy reported that housing was the most intensively investigated aspect of the migration nationally.[49] On both the local and national levels, it also dominates published reports; here only a few of the many issues addressed in the 1924 questionnaire can be highlighted. In most cases, the responses support the thesis that black urban housing in the 1920s was neither better nor worse than the housing of recent European immigrants and other poor whites.

Philadelphia's rowhouse pattern of course dominated black as well as white housing. Thus 82 of the 87 buildings housing migrants were three stories or less, and the average house held only 2.58 households, including nonmigrants. Survey investigators reported overcrowding in 38 of the 87 buildings, the worst problems being the 50 households in one-room apartments. The average household rented 2.06 rooms, with male-headed families renting 2.34, and the average room size was about 125 square feet. As Table 12.6 indicates, slightly higher densities of people per room prevailed in North and West Philadelphia than south of Market Street, probably because multiple occupancy was more common in the slightly larger rowhouses of the two newer districts. But on the whole overcrowding had not reached crisis proportions. As A. L. Manly wrote in an article on Philadelphia in *Opportunity* in 1923, the probable explanation was the relatively small size of the young migrant families.[50] In fact, the number of rooms correlates well with family size for the whole population (.67) and for male-headed families (.59), an indication that larger families were usually able to find larger living quarters.

Apart from gross size, there was often only a tenuous relationship between rent and housing conditions. One of the best gauges of those conditions in the mid-1920s was whether the toilet facilities were indoors or outdoors. The situation is summarized in Table 12.6. On the district level, the breakdown is similar to that of family income, with West and North Philadelphia clearly better than the other two districts. But that neat pattern does not carry over to specific family incomes. Among 20 households earning less than $3 per day, 5 had indoor toilets and 10 outdoor, while among the 39 making between $5 and $7 per day, 10 had indoor toilets, but 18 still had outdoor facilities. This anomaly persisted in terms of rent. The average rent in a building with indoor plumbing exclusively was $11.62 per month, but it was $13.23 in those with outdoor toilets only, and $15.20 for building with both.

The whole rent situation is filled with such apparent contradictions. Rent was only weakly correlated with number of rooms, with an average rent of $11.83 for one room and $15.96 for three rooms, which often was an entire small rowhouse. There was also little correlation between rent and household income, even controlling for family size, and between rent and family size itself. For male-headed families, there was a slight, and statistically insignificant, negative correlation between rent and family size. Overall, the Housing Association concluded in 1924 that blacks were "paying a slightly higher rent" than whites and that the migration was widening the gap. In 1922–23, rents increased 27.5 percent for blacks but only 17.8 percent for whites.[51] Since less than 12 percent of Philadelphia blacks (as opposed to almost 45 percent of whites) owned their own homes, these rent increases had a significant impact on the black community.[52] Migrant rents were no higher than the average black rents. The 1926 average of $13.51, which Thomas Woofter calculated, was 35 percent above the 1922–23 average cash rent paid by migrants in the South.[53] This is still less than their average increase in family income in Philadelphia over the South. The district breakdown in Table 12.6 indicates higher rents in the two major black areas, the Ghetto and North Philadelphia. The abnormally lower rents in West Philadelphia are difficult to explain, unless they resulted from the common crowding of several families in one building and/or the rent-depressing effect of racial transition.

Two other surveyed aspects of the social context of rent were lodging and house owners' nationality. Though the survey phrasing is somewhat confusing, it appears that about 30 of the 142 households took in lodgers and that about 30 were themselves lodging. This is consistent with other figures reported in the 1920s for both Philadelphia and Chicago.[54] Of the 27 single people, 19 were lodgers, so that probably less than a dozen families were lodging. Lodging was a factor in 27 of the 42 Ghetto households, but only 5 of the 41 in South Philadelphia, where there were few established black families. In both North and West Philadelphia, the number divided equally. The lodgers' rent went to black families, who were in turn paying house owners, and the survey found that 14 of the owners were themselves black. The largest number, 51, were Jewish, while 11 were European ethnics and 39 were described as "American." Nine of the black owners were in the Ghetto and none in South Philadelphia, while 20 Jewish owners and 9 of the 11 ethnics were in the latter area.

Such ethnic complexities remind us that the social environment the migrants encountered in Philadelphia differed greatly from what they had left behind in the South. The survey clearly showed that their hopes for increased educational opportunities for their children in the North were apparently being fulfilled. Of 96 school-age children in the surveyed families, 90 were enrolled in the public schools. Citywide black enrollment rose from 19,859 in 1922 to 24,702 in 1924, demonstrating the immediate impact of the migration.[55] As Lieberson found, in terms of education, blacks were "not doing too badly" in the 1920s compared with European immigrants.[56] Black migrants were often assumed to fare somewhat worse than immigrants in terms of health. Nevertheless, the survey found none of the predicted effect of the cool, damp northern climate. Its investigators conscientiously recorded the many complaints of grippe, colds, and other minor ailments, but uncovered no major health problems.

There was, however, an evident crisis in one key area of black social life—church membership. The figures contradict the notion that immigrants easily continued church activity after moving north.[57] Instead, church membership was demonstrably affected by such factors as previous urban experience, occupation, and Philadelphia residence. A clear majority of household heads, 83 of 142 (58.5 percent), reported that they had belonged to a church in the South but did not yet belong to one in Philadelphia. Only a quarter (35) reported church membership in both regions, while 15.5 percent (22) belonged in neither. The general pattern was most pronounced among migrants from places in the South of between 2,500 and 10,000 inhabitants, with 26 of 33 household heads reporting church membership in the South but not in Philadelphia. Church membership was most prevalent in the South in cities above 50,000 in population (35 of 38), and these people remained more inclined to church membership in Philadelphia (13 of 38) than those from smaller communities (23 to 103).

The decline in church membership in the North cut across all occupational lines, except for the skilled workers. As in the South, skilled workers tended to be church members, though a 12 to 0 division in the South became a bare 6 to 5 majority in Philadelphia, with all 6 having been church members in the South. In contrast, more than three-quarters of all unskilled laborers (64 of 83) and 84 percent of domestics (21 of 25) were nonmembers in Philadelphia, though in each case more than three-quarters of these people had belonged to a church in the South. There were also limited variations by district. In each of the two poorer sections, the Ghetto and South Philadelphia, 83 percent of household heads were not yet church members. North Philadelphia (58.5 percent) and West Philadelphia (66.7 percent) had significantly lower proportions of nonmembers, which accords with their established aura of relative propriety and respectability in terms of the citywide black community.

Reviewing the whole social and economic experience of the migrants, William Fuller concluded his survey report on an optimistic note.[58] Though prices and rents were higher in Philadelphia than in the South, the migrants seemed pleased with the relative freedom of the North and satisfied with the increase in their standard of living. A sharp reduction in discrimination had evidently occurred, with greatly expanded cultural and economic opportunities. His finding supports Kenneth Kusmer's conclusion that "the black masses in the northern ghettoes in the 1920s could view their status as representing both an absolute and a relative advance over their former condition."[59]

Yet this picture of prosperity and satisfaction is not the entire story, for more than half of the surveyed household heads were either definitely planning to return South or were considering it. Among all household heads, 64

had decided to stay in Philadelphia; 31 to return South; and 45 were unde-
cided. With only a tenth of the single people and female family heads definitely planning to return South, the figures for the male-headed families show
considerable ambiguity about the North. Only 44 out of 103 were definitely
staying in Philadelphia, while 27 had decided to return South and 32 were
considering returning. Such breakdowns were by no means unique to blacks.
Taylor estimated that between 1908 and 1924 about a third as many Europeans returned home as immigrated to America, with the proportion rising to
about half as many for Italians and Slavs.[60] As in their migration process
and socioeconomic conditions, so in re-migration there was initially a strong
similarity between black migrants and contemporary European immigrants.

Various aspects of life in the South and in Philadelphia seem to have affected attitudes toward remigration. The tenant farmers' reluctant migration
is echoed in their attitudes toward staying North. Former tenant farmers were
more likely to have decided to return (29.5 percent) than former unskilled
laborers (20 percent) or farm owners (0 of 6). Conversely, a very large proportion of both the former service workers (7, or 70 percent) and skilled
workers (8, or 66.7 percent) were definitely staying in Philadelphia, compared
with between 34 percent and 38.5 percent of the ex-tenant farmers, unskilled
laborers, and domestics. More than half (16 of 28) of male family heads from
large southern cities were definitely staying North, compared with 37 percent
of the migrants from places under 50,000 inhabitants (28 of 75), to whom
Philadelphia must have seemed far more intimidating.

In Philadelphia, the only occupational group deviating significantly from
the norm was again the skilled workers, five of whom (45.5 percent), had
decided to return south, with only 2 of 12 committed to Philadelphia. Their
division parallels other unusual patterns in the city. The proportion of male
family heads planning to return South was higher in North Philadelphia (29.0
percent) and West Philadelphia (33.3 percent) than in relatively poorer South
Philadelphia (20.7 percent) or the Ghetto (21.4 percent). More surprising is
that for male-headed families both individual and family incomes were higher
among those planning to return South than those planning to stay North. The
former had an average individual income of $4.40 per day and a family in-
come of $5.68 per day in Philadelphia, while the figures for the latter were
only $3.78 and $5.31 respectively. Of course, the different southern experiences of the tenant farmers and the unskilled laborers, who certainly saw
higher cash wages in Philadelphia, would have affected these decisions. Nevertheless, in terms of occupation, income, and desirable residence, there was
a persistent inverse relationship between economic success and the decision
to stay in Philadelphia.

Such unexpected results remind us to be cautious in generalizing from the

1924 survey. Black migration in the 1920s was a complex process in which broad social and economic forces interacted with personal and family situations. Few surveyed households were "average," and the latitude for individual decision-making was considerable. As in most historical research based on the chance survival of records, conclusions based on only 510 people in 142 households have no claim to "scientific" validity. Nevertheless, this does seem to have been a fairly typical group of people, whose experience was probably shared by most of Philadelphia's contemporary black migrants.

What conclusions can be derived from the 1924 survey? The surveyed migrants were predominantly in husband-and-wife families with few children. They came from a variety of southern backgrounds, rural and urban, agricultural and nonagricultural. Both their motives and their methods of migrating varied according to their background. Some were forced to come North by agricultural failure; others were lured from southern cities by high wages. Some family heads came with their families; others explored Philadelphia initially on their own. The migrants settled in several areas of the city and like the overall black population were less segregated from whites than Philadelphia blacks later became. Migrant life varied by neighborhood, ranging from residential mobility and job turnover in white immigrant South Philadelphia to relative stability, or stagnation, in the traditional ghetto around South Street. In contrast to job and residential variations, the occupations of the migrants were everywhere and overwhelmingly unskilled labor for the men and domestic service for the women. But with multiple wage-earning common, total family incomes and general living conditions were similar to those of contemporary European immigrants, and certainly marked a distinct improvement over the South. Vastly improved educational opportunities and race relations also seemed evident in comparison with the South. However, many migrants had ambiguous feelings about Philadelphia, and the survey revealed that a majority were either planning or seriously considering returning south. This ambiguity was prescient, for the subsequent history of the city's black community, suffering from the effects of racial discrimination, social dislocation, and regional economic decline, was very different from the generally hopeful scene sketched by the survey. Yet that crucial divergence makes the experience of the "Great Migration" all the more important in understanding the history of Philadelphia since the 1920s.

Notes

1. Charles S. Johnson, "Black Workers and the City," *The Survey* 53 (March 1, 1925): 642.

2. The ten original worksheets onto which the data from individual houses were transcribed

came to Temple University's Urban Archives in 1969 as part of the records of the Housing Association of Delaware Valley, formerly the Philadelphia Housing Association. Related correspondence and minutes, and a typescript of the final survey report, were also deposited.

3. Marcus Jones, *Black Migration in the United States with Special Emphasis on Selected Central Cities* (Saratoga, Calif., 1980), 137; Reynolds Farley, "The Urbanization of Negroes in the United States," *Journal of Social History* 1 (Spring 1968): 250.

4. William Vickery, "The Economics of the Negro Migration, 1900–1960" (Ph.D. diss., University of Chicago, 1969), 15.

5. Louise Venable Kennedy, *The Negro Peasant Turns Cityward* (New York, 1930), 35.

6. Jones, *Black Migration,* 50.

7. Vincent P. Franklin, *The Education of Black Philadelphia: The Social and Educational History of a Minority Community, 1900–1950* (Philadelphia, 1979), 8.

8. Committee on Negro Migration, July 1923 report, in the Negro Migration Study Collection, Urban Archives, Temple University.

9. U.S. Census Bureau, *Fifteenth Census of the United States,* vol. 2: *Population,* 219.

10. Records of the wartime activities are in the Housing Association Collection, series 2 (1917–20), folders 120–26.

11. Sadie T. Mossell, "The Standard of Living Among 100 Negro Migrant Families in Philadelphia," *Annals of the American Academy of Political and Social Science* 98 (November 1921): 173–222.

12. Kennedy, *Negro Peasant,* 60–67.

13. Housing Association Collection, ser. 3 (1921–50), folder 259; Negro Migration Study Collection, folders 1–3.

14. William Fuller, "The Negro Migrant in Philadelphia" (unpublished manuscript), 27–30, in Negro Migration Study Collection.

15. *Philadelphia Housing Association Annual Report for 1923* (Philadelphia, 1924), 19.

16. Herbert Gutman, *The Black Family in Slavery and Freedom, 1750–1925* (New York, 1976), xix, 445–46.

17. Kennedy, *Negro Peasant,* 142.

18. Stanley Lieberson, *A Piece of the Pie: Blacks and White Immigrants Since 1880* (Berkeley and Los Angeles, 1980), 194.

19. Horace Hamilton, "The Negro Leaves the South," *Demography* 1 (1964): 283.

20. Gavin Wright, "The Strange Career of the New Southern Economic History," *Reviews in American History* 10 (December 1982): 173.

21. Ibid., 175.

22. Arnold Taylor, *Travail and Triumph: Black Life and Culture in the South Since the Civil War* (Westport, Conn., 1976), 97.

23. Kenneth Kusmer, *A Ghetto Takes Shape: Black Cleveland, 1870–1930* (Urbana, Ill., 1976), 223; Carter Goodrich et al., *Migration and Economic Opportunity: The Report of the Survey of Population Redistribution* (Philadelphia, 1936), 130.

24. Goodrich et al., *Migration and Economic Opportunity,* 131,

25. Mossell, "Standard of Living," 216.

26. Housing Association Collection, ser. 2, folder 259; *Philadelphia Housing Association, Annual Report for 1923,* 17.

27. Lieberson, *A Piece of the Pie,* 220.

28. Edward Lewis, "The Southern Negro and the American Labor Supply," *Political Science Quarterly* 48 (June 1933): 182.

29. Philip Taylor, *The Distant Magnet: European Emigration to the U.S.A.* (New York, 1971), 254.

30. Fuller, "Negro Migrant," 66.

31. Charles S. Johnson, "How Much Is the Migration a Flight from Persecution?" *Opportunity,* September 1923, 274.

32. Kennedy, *Negro Peasant,* 52; Vickery, *Economics of Negro Migration,* 137.

33. Fuller, "Negro Migrant," 15.

34. Taylor, *Distant Magnet,* 59–60.

35. See, for example, Thomas J. Woofter Jr., *Negro Problems in Cities* (Garden City, N.Y., 1928), 39; Franklin, *Education of Black Philadelphia,* 1920.

36. Lieberson, *A Piece of the Pie,* 254–57.

37. Thomas J. Woofter Jr., *Negro Housing in Philadelphia* (Philadelphia, 1927), 5; Fuller, "Negro Migrant," 23.

38. Lieberson, *A Piece of the Pie,* 288.

39. Ibid., 178.

40. Kennedy, *Negro Peasant,* 74–75, 80–81.

41. George Haynes, "Negro Migration," *Opportunity* 2 (September 1924): 274; Migrant Committee Industrial Report, Negro Migrant Study Collection, folder 2.

42. Kennedy, *Negro Peasant,* 42; Sterling Spero and Abram Harris, *The Black Worker: The Negro and the Labor Movement* (New York, 1931), 194.

43. National Industrial Conference Board, *Wages, Hours, and Employment in the United States, 1914–1936* (New York, 1936), 53; Paul Douglas, *Real Wages in the United States, 1890–1926* (Boston, 1930), 182.

44. Mossell, "Standard of Living," 184–85.

45. Correlation is the relationship, or association, between two or more quantifiable characteristics, like unemployment rate and Democratic percentage of the vote. The correlation measurement used here (Pearson's r) ranges from +1.00 when two characteristics always go up or down together, to −1.00 when they always move in opposite directions. The first is positive correlation, the second is negative correlation. A correlation figure close to 0.00 indicates that there is no real relationship between the characteristics. All the correlation figures used here are at least 95 percent certain *not* to signify merely random relationship.

46. Eugene Ericksen and William Yancey, "The Industrial Causes of Ethnic Segregation: Philadelphia, 1910–1970" (unpublished paper), table 3.

47. Kennedy, *Negro Peasant,* 121.

48. *Philadelphia Public Ledger,* July 10, 1923.

49. Kennedy, *Negro Peasant,* 143.

50. A. L. Manly, "Where Negroes Live in Philadelphia," *Opportunity* 1 (May 1923): 12–13.

51. Housing Association Collection, series 3, folder, 258.

52. Woofter, *Negro Problems,* 137.

53. Woofter, *Negro Housing,* 22.

54. Kennedy, *Negro Peasant,* 165; Woofter, *Negro Problems,* 87.

55. Franklin, *Education of Black Philadelphia,* 50.

56. Lieberson, *A Piece of the Pie,* 128.

57. Kennedy, *Negro Peasant,* 202.

58. Fuller, "Negro Migrant," 80–82.

59. Kusmer, *A Ghetto Takes Shape,* 233.

60. Taylor, *Distant Magnet,* 105.

CHAPTER THIRTEEN

The Philadelphia Race Riot of 1918

V. P. Franklin

With the entrance of the United States into World War I in April 1917, many Americans, especially blacks, hoped for a cessation or at least a decrease in mob violence throughout the nation. It is a common phenomenon for domestic hostilities and conflicts to subside and a "united front" to be created when a foreign foe threatens the further existence of the entire society. However, the mobilization of America for war against Germany did not seem to provide sufficient cause to end large-scale violence by whites against black Americans. Although there was a decrease in the number of lynchings between 1916 and 1917 from 54 to 38, racial violence flared up in several places, including Houston, Texas; Chester, Pennsylvania; and, most notably, East St. Louis, Missouri.[1] By 1918 the number of lynchings rose dramatically to 68; mob violence increased throughout the nation and waxed even greater in the immediate postwar period (1919).[2]

These domestic hostilities were utilized by the Germans for propaganda purposes, both in the United States and abroad. And, as a result, pressure was exerted on President Woodrow Wilson by domestic and foreign journalists and diplomats to make a public statement condemning the violence.[3] It is

This chapter was first published in *The Pennsylvania Magazine of History and Biography* 99 (July 1975): 336–50. Reprinted by permission.

ironic that on the very day that President Wilson issued his statement violence broke out in Philadelphia which eventuated in one of the city's most serious racial conflagrations.

America's mobilization for the war necessitated an increase in the supply of labor at a time when immigration from Europe had virtually ceased and thousands of American workers had been conscripted into the army. In order to fill this gap, employers turned to women and blacks.[4] In the period 1914–17, hundreds of thousands of blacks migrated to many northern industrial centers and gained jobs in railroad maintenance, steel production, meat packing, and automobile production. Migrants to Philadelphia throughout the war period were employed in some industries, but, most important, in the new shipbuilding facility in Hog Island Yard, located in the southern section of the city.[5]

The influx of newcomers into Philadelphia placed an additional strain on the already overcrowded housing available to blacks. According to the census of 1910 there were 84,459 blacks in the city. By 1920 this figure had jumped to 134,229, a 58 percent increase, with the largest numbers arriving in the period 1915–20. According to Emmett Scott, adviser to the Department of Labor on "negro problems," "Housing facilities [in Philadelphia] being inadequate, temporary structures were quickly built and when these did not suffice, in the case of railroads, ordinary tents and box cars were used to shelter the new laborers."[6] Attempts were made to improve these conditions. Committees of concerned citizens, black and white, worked to assist the migrants in gaining suitable housing. The Armstrong Association, the National Urban League affiliate in the city, not only involved itself in finding employment for the recent migrants, but also joined in the search for suitable shelters. In December 1917, the Association coordinated a meeting between the various social agencies serving the black community, and several of the corporations employing Negro labor. At this conference it was agreed that renewed efforts would be made by both groups to improve the housing situation for black workers.[7] However, it was difficult to get around the real problem of migrants being forced to settle in the "colored" sections, which were already overcrowded. Eventually, blacks began to move out of the "ghetto" and into all-white or mostly all-white areas, and another dimension was added to the problem of housing. The potentiality for racial friction existed throughout the period, with violence finally breaking out during the summer of 1918.[8]

The first widely reported racial incidents occurred on June 29 and 30, in the 2500 block of Pine Street in South Philadelphia. These incidents involved attacks upon two black families by white neighbors and the burning of the household furnishings of one of the families. Although personal injuries suffered were minimal, the incidents provoked an acerbic editorial by the city

Blacks arriving in Philadelphia during the Great Migration worked mainly at general labor or domestic work. Discrimination by labor unions and companies kept blacks out of the skilled trades. A typical occupation of blacks was that of hod carrier or carrying bricks at construction sites. These Philadelphia men were photographed in 1924. (Courtesy of the Urban Archives, Temple University)

editor, G. Grant Williams, of the *Philadelphia Tribune,* the leading black newspaper in the city. In the editorial, entitled "Dixie Methods in Philadelphia," Williams discussed several of the attacks upon blacks by whites since the fall of 1917 and described the situation as "smoldering." He then went on to give some advice to blacks who might become victims of attack:

> We favor peace but we say to the colored people of the Pine Street war-zone, stand your ground like men. This is a free city in a free country and if you are law-abiding you need not fear. Be quiet, be decent, maintain clean wholesome surroundings and if you are attacked defend yourselves like American citizens. A man's home is his castle, defend it if you have to kill some of the dirty foul-mouthed, thieving crew of Schuylkill rats that infest the district. They have ever been a menace to the peace and decency of the district and many of the police either feared or worked in collusion with them.

You are not down in Dixie now and you need not fear the ragged rumcrazed hellion crew, prototypes of your old cracker enemies. They are enemies of all decent law-abiding citizens and the time has come to clean out this nest of dirty curs. . . . They may burn some of the property, but you burn their hides with any weapon that comes handy while they are engaged in that illegal pastime. We stand for law and order, decency and cleanliness, but knowing as we do the facts, that our people are driven from pillar to post looking for houses to rent and that they pay more rent than whites for the same shacks, our patience runs out.

Be at peace with all men at all times is our motto, if they will let you be; but when they tread upon your rights, fight them to the bitter end. While the world is being made safe for Democracy, Philadelphia must be made a safe city, wherein to dwell and if the law is insufficient we'll meet the rowdies of the town and give them shot and shell. These skunks are shouters for home rule but they represent the scum of Erin's sod.[9]

On July 26, 1918, just three weeks after this editorial appeared, racial violence erupted.

The precipitating incident involved Mrs. Adella Bond, a probation officer in the municipal court, who purchased and moved into her new home in the 2900 block of Ellsworth Street on July 24. On Friday evening, July 26, a large crowd of whites gathered outside her home. Finally, someone in the mob hurled a large rock through Mrs. Bond's parlor window. According to Mrs. Bond, "I didn't know what the mob would do next, and I fired my revolver from my upper window to call the police. A policeman came, but wouldn't try to cope with the mob alone, so he turned in a riot call."[10] During the commotion, a white man named Joseph Kelly was shot in the leg. Kelly and several other men were arrested and later held by Magistrate Carl Baker for rioting.[11]

The only major incident reported for Saturday, July 27, involved William Box, a Negro who was accused of thievery and chased by a group of white men. At Second and Bainbridge Streets, Louis Sacks, a clerk in the Bureau of Police, attempted to stop Box, who then allegedly pulled a knife and cut Sacks on the arm. Several policemen arrived on the scene but were unable to curb the mob of whites, and "the negro was struck many times by persons in the crowd. Cries of 'Lynch him' caused the police to send for help, and a squad of reserves arrived in time to prevent the mob doing serious injury to the negro." Box was arrested and taken to the hospital.[12]

Early Sunday morning, hostilities broke out again between blacks and whites, this time near the corner of Twenty-sixth and Oakford Streets. A mob of whites began chasing Jesse Butler as he returned home from a party. While running, Butler fired a shot into the mob of pursuers, and it was alleged that it hit Hugh Lavery, a white man who was in the midst of the action. In a short time, police arrived and found that Butler had also been wounded in the melee. They took both wounded men to Polyclinic Hospital, but Lavery died before arriving.[13]

Violent clashes between groups of whites and blacks continued throughout the day. At about three o'clock on Sunday afternoon, a mob of whites encountered Henry Huff, a black, in the vicinity of Twenty-seventh and Titan Streets. Huff was said to have dared the crowd to attack him and brandished a pistol, before running into a house on Titan Street. When Thomas McVay, a patrolman in civilian clothes, followed Huff and attempted to take the gun away, he was shot and killed. Another policeman, Detective Thomas Myers, received a bullet in the thigh. Frank Donohue, a civilian, was shot in the groin as he approached the house into which Huff had fled. Police finally rushed the house and captured Huff as he was reloading his revolver. He was beaten and arrested and finally dragged from the building.[14]

The news of the shootings spread, and a general outbreak of hostilities followed. Groups of whites attacked blacks as they alighted from trolley cars or walked through the streets. Policemen from all over the city were ordered into the riot zone to bolster the police of the area.[15] The Home Defense Reserves, made up of civilians who were used in emergencies during the wartime shortage in police manpower, were mobilized and assisted the police in their activities. By nightfall Sunday, approximately 250 police and Home Defense Reservists were patrolling the section, but violent flare-ups continued.[16]

On Monday, July 29, rioting was renewed and attacks on blacks became more frequent. A large mob attacked the home of Henry Huff, allegedly to avenge the slaying of Patrolman Thomas McVay. Although the family was able to escape unharmed, the mob wrecked the interior of the house on Titan Street, hurled out the furniture, and set it on fire. According to one account, "Policemen arrived only after the damage had been done, although nearly one hundred men took part in the raid upon the house, and the houses of half a dozen other colored families living in the same neighborhood were destroyed."[17]

Saloons in the riot area were ordered closed on Monday by Captain William Mills, Acting Superintendent of Police. This occurred, however, only after F. M. Holden, depot quartermaster of the Federal Arsenal, threatened to close them. Holden was reacting to the shooting of William Black, a Negro employee at the Arsenal, in one of the saloons near the government installation.[18] Superintendent Mills also decided to accept the assistance of the local armed forces and allowed sixty-five sailors and fifteen marines to aid the police in patrolling the riot zone.[19]

The killing of the one black who was to die in the racial disturbance took place that Monday morning. Patrolmen Roy Ramsey and John Schneider encountered Riley Bullock on Point Breeze Avenue. The policemen stopped Bullock, searched him, and, finding a pocket knife, decided to beat and arrest him. According to early accounts, after the patrolmen were able to "subdue" Bullock, they brought him to the rear entrance of the Twenty-first and Federal Streets Station. While taking him into the station, Bullock was shot by "a negro, who was seen making his escape. The police gave chase, but the alleged assailant managed to escape."[20] It was later revealed, however, that Bullock was killed by a bullet from the gun of Patrolman Roy Ramsey. The officer later claimed that he slipped on the steps and the gun "went off" as he was taking Bullock into the station. This incident was to form the basis upon which black citizens would enter into extended litigation to determine whether or not the killing was really an "accident."[21]

One of the most controversial and brutal incidents of the race riot also involved Officers Ramsey and Schneider. This incident was not reported in the daily newspapers. In the arresting of Preston Lewis by Ramsey and Schneider on Monday morning, it was alleged that Lewis was beaten so badly that he had to be taken to Polyclinic Hospital. While under the care of several doctors and nurses of the hospital, it was reported that Schneider began striking Lewis as he lay on the operating table. White officers present did nothing to stop him, and the hospital attendants became frightened and rushed from the room. Finally, a black policeman intervened, whereupon an altercation began between the two officers. At that point, several white officers grabbed Schneider and carried him from the room.[22] This incident also became the subject of litigation involving many members of the black community.

Frequent arrests were made throughout the four days of rioting, but most of those arrested were black, although many observers agreed that whites were the instigators of the vast majority of the riotous situations.[23] After receiving reports of sniping, Acting Superintendent Mills ordered the search of homes of blacks for weapons. On Sunday and Monday, attempts were also made to keep nonresidents from entering the riot zone after it was reported that Negroes from other sections were bringing "reinforcements by the automobile-load into the riot torn area." Rain on Monday evening kept incidents to a minimum as police and reservists patrolled riot sections.[24]

On Tuesday, July 30, only a few flare-ups were reported, the most noteworthy being the attempted lynching of Harold Freeman for allegedly stealing a watermelon from the store of Julius Swisky at 518 South Lombard Street.[25]

Thus, after four days of disturbances, three persons were dead, one lay dying of wounds received during the rioting, and several hundred persons were recovering from injuries sustained.

To protest these events, a meeting was scheduled by B. G. Collier, head of the Knights of Pythias, for Monday evening, July 29, in order to plan an organized black response to the rioting. Representatives were chosen at that meeting, and on Tuesday morning two delegations of prominent black Philadelphians called on city officials. One delegation led by Collier represented the lay organizations; the other, led by the Rev. R. R. Wright Jr., represented the black Methodist ministers of the city. Unable to meet with Mayor Thomas Smith, the delegations spoke with the director of public safety, William H. Wilson, and left a letter stating the position of some members of the black community on the causes and consequences of the riot. Subsequently reprinted in several newspapers, the letter expressed the disgust of blacks over the lack of protection they had received from mob violence. With respect to the rioting, the letter stated:

> We put the whole blame upon your incompetent police force. But for the sympathy of the police, their hobnobbing with the mob, what had now become the disgrace of Philadelphia would have been nothing more than a petty row. Your police have for a long time winked at disorder, such as the beating up of Negroes, the stoning of their homes and the attacking of their churches.

The letter went on to deplore the wholesale arrests of Negroes, while allowing "white hoodlums to roam free to do damage." It ended by suggesting that the riot would not have been as bloody if black policemen had been allowed to patrol the riot zone.[26] G. Grant Williams of the *Tribune* wrote to the mayor and asked:

> Is it not lawful Mr. Mayor, for a man to protect his home if anyone attempts to damage it? Why then do your police arrest a colored man or woman for protecting their home? . . . The colored people of Philadelphia are law-abiding citizens and ask your protection, and if you don't protect them, they shall and will defend themselves.[27]

After the initial arrests on Sunday, July 29, black lawyers led by G. Edward Dickerson were in the courts defending blacks who were arrested during the rioting. However, this was just one of the many problems blacks faced in Philadelphia in the immediate aftermath of the riot. Many persons felt that as a group they needed to insure the future protection of their civil rights through an organized effort. Thus, during the week of August 10, several leading ministers and representatives of many black lay organizations met and formed the Colored Protective Association. Under the leadership of the Rev. R. R. Wright Jr., the Association was to serve several purposes. It was to work "to protect colored people who have been arrested unjustly and who are sent to prison often because they have no friends to speak for them. The Association will speak for the friendless Negro in the courts. . . . In a year thousands of Negroes are sent to prison, not because they are guilty, but because they have no one to represent them." At the same time, the Colored Protective Association was going to involve itself with the ongoing problems of the Philadelphia black community. It was to support the right of blacks to live anywhere in the city. The Association would provide counsel in cases of discrimination involving not only housing but also the schools, places of amusement, and employment. It had as its ultimate goal "to reach the last Negro in the city of Philadelphia, to bring all colored people into one organization for the purpose of having a permanent organization of protection."[28]

In its early days, the Colored Protective Association was quite successful in securing contributions for its efforts from the black community. Hundreds of dollars were raised at rallies sponsored by black churches. Many of the most important members of the black community were listed among its officers, directors, and membership.[29] The Association virtually took upon itself the prosecution of Patrolman Roy Ramsey for the killing of Riley Bullock, and Patrolman John Schneider for the assault on Preston Lewis. It also spearheaded an investigation of the practices of the police in the Seventeenth District. In all three instances, it met with some degree of success.

One of the main reasons for the organization of the Colored Protective Association was the lack of activity of the Philadelphia branch of the National Association for the Advancement of Colored People (NAACP) on behalf of the blacks who were victims of racial discrimination and police brutality in the city. The NAACP from its beginning in 1911 remained highly centralized, and the main office maintained close contact with and control over its branches. However, within this centralized structure, local branches were not only supposed to supply information about the activities of the Association and hold mass meetings to raise funds, but they were also supposed to work to lessen race discrimination and "to secure full civil rights and political rights to colored citizens and others."[30] Whereas the Philadelphia branch was fairly successful in the former obligations, it was sadly lacking in the latter.

Early in July 1918, John Shillady, national secretary for the NAACP, received two letters from white Philadelphians mentioning racial incidents that had occurred in Philadelphia, which the writers felt should be investigated. The first, from a Mrs. Helen Marshall, provided the National Office with detailed information on the attacks on the black families in Philadelphia at the end of June 1918.[31] The second letter came from a Mr. Edward C. Gumby, who described the discrimination leveled against black soldiers who stopped to eat at the Normandie Hotel, located at Thirty-Sixth and Chestnut Streets in Philadelphia. Mrs. Marshall stated that the reason she had not brought her matter to the attention of the Philadelphia branch of the Association was that she had been told by two people that "the local branch would not consider the matter, and that the matter would be referred to a certain lawyer, who would do nothing but would be sure to secure a good fee."[32] Walter White, the assistant secretary of the Association, was sent to Philadelphia to investigate the riot and was informed by Shillady of the charges in the letter.[33]

In the numerous accounts of the riot that appeared in the daily white press and the weekly black press, no mention was made of the Philadelphia branch of the NAACP. However, in the account of the riot written by Walter White and published by the Philadelphia branch of the Association, one of the largest sections of the report was devoted to a discussion of "Action Taken by the Philadelphia Branch of the NAACP." In that section, White pointed out that the Association was represented at the protest meeting called by B. G. Collier on Monday evening, July 29, and that J. Max Barber, president of the Philadelphia branch, was a member of the delegation that called on Mayor Smith on Tuesday, July 30, 1918.[34] This was followed by an appeal to Philadelphians to support the Association in the fight for civil rights in the city, rather than "many duplicating organizations with overlapping purposes." In concluding, White, speaking for the Philadelphia branch, pointed out: "We wish to express to disclaim the slightest hostility of purpose or intent to any movement heretofore or hereafter to be organized. Our appeal is not for prestige or preferment but for a united Philadelphia that we may better serve the common cause to which our organization is dedicated."[35] It was too late, however, and the Colored Protective Association, which had early taken the initiative to support and protect the black victims of mob violence and police brutality, had become identified with the legal struggle to redress the grievances of black Philadelphians in the aftermath of the July riot.

The most notable success of the newly mobilized black community following the riot was the transfer of the commander, and all of the police officers in the Seventeenth District, to other districts throughout the city. The accusations of lack of protection of black citizens and close association with the white criminal element in the district finally resulted in the removal of the entire force by the director of public safety. The event was hailed as a major victory for the Philadelphia black community.[36]

The Colored Protective Association involved itself very closely in the two cases of alleged police brutality. Its representatives were present with witnesses at the various inquests into the death of Riley Bullock, and in the subsequent court hearings the Association worked to bring about the conviction of Officers Roy Ramsey and John Schneider. The most disappointing aspect of the entire affair, and one of the main reasons that both Ramsey and Schneider were not convicted, was the poor performance in court of the black policemen who were present at the killing of Bullock and the assault on Preston Lewis. In court, the colored policeman, who was supposed to have kept Officer Schneider from killing Lewis as he lay on the hospital bed, claimed that he "saw nothing." The two colored policemen who were supposed to have been in the station at the time of the shooting of Bullock went so far as to claim in court that they "never saw Officer Ramsey before."[37]

Nevertheless, the Colored Protective Association did succeed in mobilizing the black community and in informing blacks of their civil rights under the law and of the alternatives to gross racial discrimination. Speeches were given in numerous churches by representatives of the organization to inform black citizens of its existence and activities. Legal assistance was provided for those blacks who were arrested or victims of assaults by whites.[38] In the months following the riot, attacks on blacks were given wide coverage in the *Philadelphia Tribune*. Protests were made to government officials when white sailors stationed in the city were involved in attacks on black citizens. These complaints eventually led to an official investigation of the situation by the commander of the Fourth Naval District. Black Philadelphians received guarantees from as high as the secretary of the navy, Josephus Daniels, that these incidents would be investigated and steps would be taken to see that they would not recur.[39] These were the more significant and graphic results of the organized efforts of blacks to improve their situation in the City of Brotherly Love in the aftermath of the July 1918 riot.

This race riot fits very closely into several of the patterns of racial violence suggested by Allen Grimshaw.[40] As in other "northern-style riots," the causes of the riot were primarily "secular"—that is, the competition for limited housing between blacks and whites generated the racial friction. The precipitating event—the attack on the home of Mrs. Bond—can also be considered a "secular" event, although several newspapers did report the rumor that the riot started because two white girls had been insulted by a group of black men.[41] A second characteristic of northern-style riots, also found in the Philadelphia situation, was the fact that white aggression and violence were met with black aggression and violence. A third characteristic—the failure to restore the earlier accommodative pattern of race relations—also occurred in Philadelphia. Whereas in "southern-style riots" no major disturbances usually occurred after the riot, in northern riots, such as those in Philadelphia and Chicago, minor violence continued to erupt sporadically in the following months and years.[42]

At the same time, however, the Philadelphia riot took place primarily in what can be described as an "ecologically contested area," and only second-arily in the "Negro slum" area of the city. This was contrary to the pattern identified by Grimshaw, who found that "violence in time of major race riots has been concentrated in Negro slums, which in many cities were served largely by white businesses. Casualties and fatalities occurred most often in slums or along their fringes, and destruction of property, particularly looting, was greatest there."[43] As was mentioned above, the riot in Philadelphia began when blacks began to move into areas that were previously all or mostly white—that is, a contested area.

The accounts of the riot in the Philadelphia white press fit into the "general pattern of misreporting" suggested by Terry Ann Knopf.[44] Most of the news-papers were guilty of "rumor-mongering," that is disseminating unverified reports which reflect "the gamut of rumors about blacks circulating in the white community." One newspaper went so far as to suggest that blacks were amassing weapons to drive the whites out of South Philadelphia.[45] Some papers used loaded language in describing blacks who were merely defending themselves, such as "hoodlum" or "vicious brute." And many times the papers published stories that might excite the white community without checking these accounts for their accuracy.[46]

William M. Tuttle Jr., in the preface to his lengthy study of the Chicago race riot of 1919, castigated white liberal and black scholars who have fo-cused on the negative aspects of the black experience in America—"on the failure, not the success; on group statistics, not on individual human beings; on passive recipients of injustice, not on people capable of adjusting to and ordering their own lives within a caste society." But Tuttle felt that because his was a study of race riot it "has little to say about the healthy or positive aspects of life in the nation's black communities. To most observers, of course, urban riots represent the ultimate failure in a city's race relations."[47] Though this may have been the case with respect to the Chicago riot, it does not characterize the consequences of the Philadelphia race riot of 1918. The riot had the effect of mobilizing the black community. Black victims of po-lice brutality became the "rallying points" around which the community gathered its resources and began to challenge anew the dominant white estab-lishment. The citizens' committees, and especially the Colored Protective Association, were well aware of the connection between the overt brutality of the mob, and the more subtle discriminations to which blacks were subjected in the schools, theaters, and other public places. And though many of the committees and associations were short-lived, they did have the effect of

pushing the lethargic NAACP branch in Philadelphia into action on behalf of
civil rights for blacks.[48] These Philadelphia Negroes were not victorious in
all of the legal and political battles in which they became involved in the
years following the riot, but they did win a few. And those few victories
could set a formidable precedent for any future challenges to the dominant
political establishment in the city.

Notes

1. Jessie P. Guzman, "Lynching," in Allen D. Grimshaw, ed., *Racial Violence in the United States* (Chicago, 1969), 58–59; Edgar Schuyler, "The Houston Race Riot, 1917," *Journal of Negro History* 29 (1944): 301–38. There has been no study of the Chester riot of 1917, but for an account of the riot see *Philadelphia Tribune,* July 28, 1917, 1, 4; August 4, 1917, 1. See also Elliott M. Rudwick, *Race Riot at East St. Louis, July 2, 1917* (Carbondale, Ill., 1964).

2. Guzman, "Lynching," 58–59.

3. The statement of President Wilson on mob violence was printed in most newspapers on July 26 or 27, 1918; see, for example, *Philadelphia Evening Bulletin,* July 26, 1918, 1; *North American,* July 27, 1918, 14. For a discussion of the NAACP protests to Wilson against mob violence, see Charles F. Kellogg, *A History of the National Association for the Advancement of Colored People* (Baltimore, 1967), 1:227–30.

4. John Hope Franklin, *From Slavery to Freedom: A History of Negro Americans* (New York, 1956), 466–67; Frank Friedel, *America in the Twentieth Century* (New York, 1960), 183–85.

5. Friedel, *America in the Twentieth Century,* 185–86.

6. For an excellent short discussion of the changes in the African American population in Philadelphia in the period 1900–1960, see E. Digby Baltzell, "Introduction to the 1967 Edition," *The Philadelphia Negro: A Social Study* (New York, 1967), ix–xiv; and Emmett Scott, *Negro Migration During the War* (New York, 1920), 134–35.

7. Scott, *Negro Migration,* 138–39. See also Philadelphia Housing Authority, "Negro Migration Study, 1917" (copy), Philadelphia Housing Authority Papers, Urban Archives, Temple University, Philadelphia.

8. Louise V. Kennedy, "Race Relations," *The Negro Peasant Turns Cityward* (1930; reprint, New York, 1968), 212–20.

9. Editorial, *Tribune,* July 6, 1918, 4.

10. This statement of Mrs. Bond was reprinted in the *Philadelphia Inquirer,* July 31, 1918, 15; and the *Tribune,* August 3, 1918.

11. *Inquirer,* July 28, 1918, 8; *North American,* July 28, 1918, 18.

12. *Inquirer,* July 28, 1918, 8; *North American,* July 28, 1918, 1.

13. Variations of the story appeared in the following Philadelphia papers on July 29, 1918: *Public Ledger, Record, Press, North American, Evening Bulletin, Inquirer.* See also Walter White, *Philadelphia Race Riots of July 26 to July 31, 1918* (published by the NAACP and the Philadelphia branch, November 1918), 4.

14. See the same newspapers listed in note 13. See also White, *Philadelphia Race Riots,* 3–4.

15. For pictures of whites attacking blacks, see *Public Ledger,* July 29, 1918, 2; *Inquirer,* July 29, 1918, 2. See also *North American,* July 29, 1918, 1, 4.

16. *North American,* July 29, 1918, 4; *Inquirer,* July 29, 1918, 4.

17. Quoted in the *Inquirer,* July 30, 1918, 1. See also *Evening Bulletin,* July 30, 1918, 1.

18. *Inquirer,* July 30, 1918, 3; *North American,* July 30, 1918, 1, 4.

19. The incident that led to the decision to use local servicemen was the reported shooting of Mrs. Sarah Abrams, a white woman, in the arm by a Negro man, and the shooting of Rosanna Hill, a 9-year-old white girl, in the leg on Monday afternoon. See *Evening Bulletin,* July 30, 1918, 1; *Philadelphia Press,* July 30, 1918, 7; *North American,* July 30, 1918, 4.

20. Most of the daily newspapers carried the unconfirmed story that Bullock was shot by a "negro" on July 30, 1918. The papers reported that he was killed by a bullet from the gun of Officer Ramsey on July 31, 1918.

21. White, *Philadelphia Race Riots,* 3–5.

22. Ibid., 4–6. Depositions of eye-witness accounts of the attack on Preston Lewis may be found in NAACP Records, Administrative Files, Subject Files, "Lynching, Philadelphia, Pa. (Race Riots)," July–November 1918, Box C364, Library of Congress, Washington, D.C.

23. In the four days of rioting, approximately sixty blacks and three whites were arrested. See White, *Philadelphia Race Riots,* 6.

24. Quoted from *Philadelphia Record,* July 29, 1918, 1; *Press,* July 30, 1918, 7.

25. *North American,* July 31, 1918, 2; *Record,* July 31, 1918, 10.

26. White, *Philadelphia Race Riots,* 6–7; *Tribune,* August 3, 1918, 1; *Inquirer,* July 31, 1918, 1; *Evening Bulletin,* July 30, 1918, 1.

27. Editorial (G. Grant Williams), *Tribune,* August 3, 1918, 4.

28. Extended reports on the activities of the Colored Protective Association are found in the *Tribune,* August 17, 1918, 1; September 28, 1918, 1.

29. *Colored Protective Association officers:* President, R. R. Wright Jr. *Vice-presidents:* R. J. Williams, A. R. Robinson, C. A. Tindley, A. Hanum, Secretary, J. C. Beckett. *Assistant Secretary:* F. H. Butler. Treasurer: F. W. Graham. Advisory Board: Bishop Levi J. Coppin, Bishop J. A. Johnson, Bishop J. S. Caldwell, Bishop G. L. Blackwell, Bishop W. H. Heard, Bishop E. Tyree, Bishop P. A. Boulden, Bishop B. Ramsey, the Hon. J. C. Dancy, the Revs. J. A. Whitted, W. G. Parks, E. W. Johnson, L. J. Jordan, S. C. Jackson, H. L. Philips, and P. Scott. Among the directors were W. A. Harrod, I. H. Ringgold, W. A. Creditt, E. C. Brown, C. L. Knox, H. M. Minton, W. H. Moses, W. H. Barnes, C. D. Atkins, and others. See *Tribune,* August 17, 1918, 1.

30. Kellogg, *History of the NAACP,* 120.

31. Mrs. Helen R. Marshall to NAACP, July 18, 1918, NAACP Records, Box C364 (see note 22 above).

32. Ibid.; Edwin C. Gumby to Editor of *The Crisis,* July 16, 1918, NAACP Records, Box C364.

33. John R. Shillady to Walter White, July 31, 1918, NAACP Records, Box C364.

34. Statement of J. Max Barber, November 6, 1918, NAACP Records, Box C364. It is interesting that in the three earlier drafts of the report of White's investigation there was also no mention of the action of the local NAACP branch. However, much of the information presented by Barber in the statement of November 6 appears in the final published pamphlet.

35. White, *Philadelphia Race Riots,* 6–7.

36. *Tribune,* August 31, 1918, 1.

37. *Tribune,* September 28, 1918, 1.

38. Ibid. For the list of churches that sponsored rallies for the Colored Protective Association, see also the *Tribune,* August 17, 1918, 1.

39. Josephus Daniels to G. Grant Williams, September 23, 1918; Commander F. W. Hoffman to G. Grant Williams, September 30, 1918. Letters were reprinted in the *Tribune,* October 5, 1918, 1.

40. Allen D. Grimshaw, "Three Cases of Racial Violence in the United States," in *Racial Violence in the United States* (note 1 above), 105–15.

41. Ibid., 107. Grimshaw contrasts "secular" incidents, those involving "assaults (by blacks) upon the accommodative pattern related to secular spheres," with "sacred" incidents, those that challenge the sacred doctrines of white supremacy, in differentiating causes of racial violence.

42. Ibid., 113–15.

43. Grimshaw, "Urban Racial Violence in the United States: Changing Ecological Considerations," in *Racial Violence in the United States,* 290.

44. Terry Ann Knopf, "Race, Riots, and Reporting," *Journal of Black Studies* 4 (March 1974): 303–27.

45. *Record,* July 30, 1918, 2, reported erroneously that "a dozen or more loaded revolvers, four modern repeating rifles, one of them loaded with dum dum bullets, and a shotgun were displayed in the hearing room to show that the Negroes had prepared to 'clean up' the white population of the section in which the rioting occurred."

46. The most widely reported example of "misinformation" appeared in white dailies on July 29, 1918. These papers reported that upon hearing that her husband had been killed, Mrs. Lavery, who was pregnant, dropped dead. The newspapers also reported that her baby did not survive. This information was completely wrong, and retractions appeared on the following day. *Philadelphia Inquirer,* July 29, 1918, 1; July 30, 1918, 1; *North American,* July 29, 1918, 1; July 30, 1918, 4.

47. William M. Tuttle Jr., *Race Riot: Chicago in the Red Summer of 1919* (New York, 1970), vi–vii.

48. The author has read the *Philadelphia Tribune* for the period 1918–30 and found no further mention of the activities of the Colored Protective Association after 1920. During the 1920s, however, the Philadelphia branch of the NAACP became more active in the protection of rights in Philadelphia. NAACP Records: NAACP Branch Correspondence, Philadelphia Branch, 1920–30, Boxes G186 and G187.

CHAPTER FOURTEEN

And the Results Showed Promise . . . Physicians, Childbirth, and Southern Black Migrant Women, 1916–1930:

Pittsburgh as a Case Study

Carolyn Leonard Carson

African American women who migrated from the South to northern cities during the Great Migration period chose to shun familiar childbirth traditions and utilized available medical services due to the influence of the Urban League. Black northern urban women's childbirth experiences differed markedly from those of southern women, although research suggests that changes which occurred in the North possibly already had begun in the South, but the transition to medical childbirth there took much longer. At the same time, and possibly as a result of the development of new medical services and the utilization of those services by black women, infant and maternal mortality rates showed a slight decline in the urban North. In addition, this research suggests that African American women and white women may not necessarily have received the same medical care. This study emphasizes how historical inquiry can serve to inform current policy debate. The establishment and widespread utilization of medical services for childbirth suggested some promise of improved health in the 1920s. This topic, therefore, deserves additional study to determine how these various factions may relate to current issues.

This chapter was first published in the *Journal of American Ethnic History* 14 (Fall 1994): 32–64. Reprinted by permission Transaction Publishers. Copyright © 1994. All rights reserved. Used by permission.

Between 1916 and 1930, approximately half a million blacks, or 5 percent of the total southern black population, migrated from the South to northern cities, seeking a better way of life. They were lured by the anticipation of better educational opportunities for their children and sought higher wages and employment opportunities brought on, initially, by the high labor demand of wartime. Poverty, an oppressive sharecropping system, Jim Crow laws, a plague of boll weevils, and the sexual harassment of women were other factors that motivated them to head north.[1] Between 1900 and 1920, the black population of Pittsburgh increased by 85 percent.[2] By 1928, some 7.7 percent of the population of Pittsburgh was African American.[3] Blacks poured into the community and settled just at the time when immigration from Europe declined.

In spite of the horrible living conditions blacks encountered, medically speaking it was to the black woman's benefit that she arrived in the North when she did. Coincidentally, certain services for the poor expanded dramatically during the early years of migration.[4] Pittsburgh's black pregnant women were brought into the mainstream of medical care before they had a chance to settle into another system—unlike their European counterparts, who had arrived earlier, before the advent of numerous programs to assist indigent parturient women. In other words, immigrant women, in order to benefit from new services, would have had to change the patterns of health care, such as the use of midwives, they had previously established when they arrived in the city and adapted to the American context. Blacks, however, were offered the new services immediately upon their arrival. When they settled in the city, the new programs were just beginning to develop. Northern African American women, in contrast to southern black women, utilized medical services for obstetrical care. The Urban League, devoted to helping southern migrants adjust, played the key role in linking new arrivals with available health-care facilities.

Two major trends occurring simultaneously explain the creation of new programs offering medical and obstetrical care to the indigent. First, obstetricians were beginning to professionalize and raise their status in the medical community by improving their medical education. Second, social reformers were advocating services in an attempt to reduce the alarmingly high rates of infant and maternal mortality.

The northward migration of blacks occurred at the same time that childbirth practices were changing from a social to a medical phenomenon.[5] Increasing numbers of women were choosing physicians over midwives as attendants and were selecting the hospital as the site for their confinements. In Pittsburgh, in 1915, some 12.9 percent of all births took place in the hospital, but by 1931 that figure had risen to 54.6 percent. During the same period, the number of black women giving birth also grew. In 1915, only 3.6 percent of the infants born in the city were black; by 1931, some 10.4 percent of all resident births were to black women.[6]

Judith Leavitt has argued that middle- and upper-class women, primarily those of urban areas, were the agents of change in moving childbirth from the home to the hospital.[7] This focus might be redefined, for agents of change were urban women more generally, including elements of the poorer classes and the black race. Residence, not class, may have been critical. Nancy Schrom Dye has suggested that poor and working-class women were central to the transformation of birth from a social to a medical phenomenon since they were the first to experience the new scientific obstetrics. It was those patients who were the first to restructure the doctor-patient relationship.[8] Dye has argued that the patterns of medical authority that evolved in those relationships served as the social basis for medical management of childbirth throughout the twentieth century.[9] It is now clear that African American women, whether from the rural or urban South, played a key role in the process of medical childbirth as they migrated northward and utilized similar services.

It is not yet clear whether or not this Pittsburgh study is representative of a national pattern. However, so little work has been done in this area that a case study can at least raise important possibilities. Pittsburgh is representative of the urban northern areas to which southern blacks migrated, so it is worth examining, if only as a stepping-stone to further research.

Migrant Families

Black families came from the Deep South as well as the border states, and Pittsburgh attracted married women more than single women because of the job market. Although the city offered industrial jobs to men, it had few job opportunities for black women outside of domestic service.[10] It has been estimated that 75 percent of the migrants were between 18 and 40 years of age.[11] This figure is not surprising since the incentive to migrate was often employment. The significance of this was that many women of childbearing age were arriving in Pittsburgh during this period. Of the entire black population in Allegheny County by 1930, some 49.9 percent were between the ages of 20 and 44.[12] Further, 66.3 percent of the black population were born outside the state of Pennsylvania, and 62.1 percent of the total black population were born in the South.[13] Blacks were predominantly migrants.[14] By 1930, for every 100 black males, there were 97.1 females in the city.[15] The potential need for obstetrical services was obvious.

Better education as well as employment opportunities attracted migrants. They felt the school systems in the North would serve their children better than those in the South.[16] Urban blacks were much more likely to send their children to schools than were either the Poles or Italians.[17] In addition, the entire self-selective nature of the migration process meant that migrating women were likely to be better educated than black southern women who remained.[18] This information suggests that the newly arrived black women may have been much more receptive to the health education campaigns to which they were exposed.

Migrant families in Pittsburgh followed common patterns in living arrangements. Women generally married at a much younger age than white women or first- or second-generation foreign women. The average age of marriage for black women was before age 20.[19] Newly married couples usually lived alone, apart from their parents, who encouraged their children to be self-sufficient.[20] This emphasis on self-sufficiency may have discouraged the supportive female networks so necessary to the social childbirth which Leavitt has described whereby women gathered together to support a friend or relative in labor.

It was common for black women to be employed. Men usually entered the industrial work force at the bottom and had little success in moving up due to discriminatory attitudes of employers. Furthermore, the advent of labor-saving devices in the factories resulted in a decrease in the number of unskilled jobs available for men. Employers' labor demands tended to peak and fall, leading to obvious job insecurity.[21] Parents could not rely on income from older adult children, who tended to live independently from their parents.[22] For these reasons, mothers were forced to seek employment in order to support their families. Although his study was not quantitative, Abraham Epstein, surveying black migrants in 1918, formed the impression that "practically all of the mothers are doing some work outside the home." Another study suggested that approximately one-third of the black women were working in 1930 and, of those, 90 percent were in domestic service.[23] Women lived separate and apart from one another, and it was found that women living next door to each other, though often having come from the same state or even the same city, hardly knew one another.[24] This family pattern further reduced the likelihood of establishing a significant female network or support system.

Black families were not part of a large, cohesive group in Pittsburgh, because they were divided along class and geographic lines. Peter Gottlieb identified three socioeconomic levels for blacks. The first group were the old elites, middle-class blacks who had resided in the city for several decades; the second group comprised economically stable skilled and unskilled workers; and in the third group was a lower class of transients. The last two groups—the darker-skinned migrants from the South, often the Deep South—were primarily industrial laborers. According to Gottlieb, these three groups did not associate with one another.[25] The middle-class physicians and lawyers, for example, seldom offered aid to those less fortunate members of their own race.[26] Due to the hilly topography, the residential neighborhoods of the black community further discouraged any kind of black cohesiveness. None of the ghettos was all black, as blacks and immigrants frequently lived in the same areas. Further, blacks were not concentrated in one area of the city. This lack of cohesiveness within the race and within the family may have been one of the key factors that compelled black women to curtail the use of midwives and seek medical obstetrical care.[27]

Infant and Maternal Mortality

Infant and maternal mortality rates were higher among blacks than whites in the United States. In 1916, there were 185 black infant deaths per 1,000 live births, compared with 99 white infant deaths. By 1921, the death rate declined, but at approximately the same rate for both races, so that the black infant death rate continued to exceed that for whites. The rate that year was 108 black deaths per 1,000 live births and 72 white infant deaths. The black infant death rate continued to exceed that for whites in the following decade. In the period 1933–35, the rate per 1,000 live births in Pennsylvania was 84.3 for blacks and 51.4 for whites.[28]

It is, however, vital to note the differences between infant death rates among blacks in urban and rural areas. The urban infant death rate for black infants exceeded the rural rate in the United States as a whole, but not within the northern states alone. In the northern states, in 1933–35, the rural death rate for black infants was 100.9, compared with an urban rate of 81.0. In Pennsylvania in 1933–35, the urban infant death rate per 1,000 live births for blacks was 81.0, compared with a rural rate of 109.6. In the South the rates were reversed (rural, 80.2; urban, 109.3). These statistics offer a stimulus to research in order to determine what caused the distinctive pattern in the urban North.[29] Elizabeth Tandy, senior statistician for the Children's Bureau, suggested that the living conditions in the northern as well as the southern cities were characterized by crowded housing, "with inadequate facilities for care of their health and recreation." She surmised that the high infant mortality rates in urban areas in the southern states were due to the lack of child-health activities in southern cities.[30] The existence of various health reform programs in the northern urban regions undoubtedly helps to explain this urban-rural difference.

In 1920, Pittsburgh lost more babies in proportion to its births than any other of the large American cities for which reliable records were available. Half of those deaths occurred within the first month of life, reflecting a national pattern (48 per 1,000 live births in 1920).[31] The overall infant death rate in Pittsburgh in 1920 was 110 per 1,000 live births, but for blacks the rate was 164. In 1926, the infant death rate per 1,000 live births was 81.5 for white residents and 111.8 for blacks. Although the rates continued to drop, as they did nationally, they still remained much higher among the black population than among the white population of Pittsburgh. In 1934, the white infant death rate was 51.5 and the rate for blacks was 77.8.[32]

Stillbirths in Pittsburgh, following the pattern of the national rates, were considerably higher for blacks, with a rate of 7.4 per 100 live births for blacks and 3.5 for whites in 1923.[33] In 1931, although the stillbirth rates had declined, they were still considerably higher for the black population, at 6.1 per 100 live births, compared to 3.4 for the white population.[34]

Maternal mortality rates were also higher among blacks than whites. During the period 1933–35 in the United States, the rate for black women was 96.1 per 10,000 live births, compared with 54.6 for white women.[35] The statistics for Pittsburgh in 1935 show an even greater gap between maternal death rates for white and black mothers. The rate for white mothers was 37.0 per 10,000 live births, compared with 91.0 for black mothers.[36] The most frequent causes of maternal mortality among blacks in the 1933–35 period were puerperal sepsis and toxemia, both of which were recognized as preventable. Combined, those two causes accounted for 68 percent of the deaths of black mothers in the United States. The other deaths were due largely to puerperal hemorrhages and accidents of pregnancy or labor.[37]

During the migration period, and shortly thereafter, there were a number of theories regarding the causes of the high maternal and infant death rates among blacks. Members of the National Urban League suggested that the habits and conditions of the mother's living before childbirth, as well as her physical condition, contributed to these high death rates. "These deaths have been found to be most common among mothers who are forced to work and where proper medical care cannot be secured."[38] The Urban League in 1923 further contended that infant mortality, especially during the neonatal period, or first month of life, was largely caused by diseases classified as "developmental." These included congenital malformations, prematurity, and congenital debility which resulted, it was thought, from the lowered physical condition and habits of the mother's living before childbirth.[39] Rates of tuberculosis and syphilis, often results of poor, overcrowded, unsanitary housing, were also higher among blacks, which suggests that black women were in poorer health than their white counterparts which could have affected the outcome of their confinements.[40] Grace Abbott, director of the Urban League in 1923, also noted the higher incidence of death among working women whose husbands' wages were low and who lived in rear houses or houses in the alleys.[41] These socioeconomic factors undoubtedly adversely affected the maternal and infant death rates among blacks.

Professionals of the period also recognized the prevalence of rickets among blacks.[42] Grace Abbott noted the disproportionate rate of rickets among black children. In the early 1920s the Children's Bureau made a study of rickets in the Washington, D.C., area, with the hope of finding a method to decrease the rate of the disease.[43] Dr. John Whitridge Williams, professor of obstetrics at Johns Hopkins University, also noted the "prevalence of rickets among blacks," which led to the increased incidence of contracted pelvises among black mothers, a condition which had the potential of adversely affecting labor. An analysis of Baltimore women in 1911 revealed that 7.7 percent of all white patients had contracted pelvises, compared to 33.2 percent of the African American mothers.[44]

Current studies have noted the role of poor nutrition in the high maternal and infant death rates among blacks in the early part of this century. Phillip Cutright and Edward Shorter found that puerperal fever was the largest single cause of maternal death in childbirth, though there was also an increased incidence of deaths due to toxemia and other causes. They suggested that blacks' obstetrical mortality was due largely to infection and that this susceptibility was probably due to a poor diet that had a chronic lack of protein. They also noted the increased incidence of rickets among blacks that led to contracted pelvises and prolonged labor which increased the risk of infection.[45]

Other studies of the period suggest that the comparatively high death rates were due partially to the lack of adequate medical and nursing care. The Urban League recognized the high death rates among women who did not receive adequate medical care. "The most effective method by which the community can cut the high ratio of these losses is by providing care and instruction for the mother before her baby's birth and skilled attendance during her confinement."[46] Here was a link between the disproportionate health problems of maternal and infant mortality during the black migration period, the resultant attempted solutions, and changes in traditional health-care patterns.

Progressive reformers had been taking an interest in infant health for over four decades prior to World War I, but at that time their focus began to change. After 1914 there was an increasing awareness of the value of improving the health of gestative and parturient women. Earlier attention had been given to reducing the neonatal death rate by dealing with postnatal threats to infant life by improving the domestic sanitary environment and the quality of infant care. In 1911, the New York Milk Committee conducted an experiment that suggested prenatal care reduced stillbirth and neonatal death rates. This information prompted welfare workers in other cities to institute prenatal care in their programs. In 1910 the American Association for the Study and Prevention of Infant Mortality (AASPIM) was founded by physicians and public health officials who were disturbed about the infant mortality rate.[47] They were partially responsible for the founding of the United States Children's Bureau in 1912, within the Department of Labor, which worked to decrease infant and maternal mortality rates.

In 1917 the Children's Bureau conducted a landmark study entitled "Maternal Mortality from All Conditions Connected with Childbirth in the United States and Certain Other Countries." This study revealed that childbirth caused more deaths among women age 15 to 44 than any diseases other than tuberculosis. Only two of fifteen countries surveyed had maternal death rates higher than the United States for 1900–1910.

Social reformers responded to these studies on a wide scale. Often with the aid of the federal Children's Bureau, cities and states in the United States established special bureaus to deal specifically with improving the health of infants and children. Most of these agencies, which included prenatal care in their services, were created between 1919 and 1921, the period when southern migration was growing and white immigration was on the decline.[48]

Physicians also responded to the high infant and maternal mortality rates. At the request of the AASPIM, John Whitridge Williams conducted a study in 1911 which revealed that medical schools were "inadequately equipped for teaching obstetrics properly." He referred to the degraded position of obstetrics in this country. He urged that people "be taught that a well conducted hospital is the ideal place for delivery, especially in the case of those with limited incomes."[49] As physicians sought to improve the training of obstetrics, they also sought a patient population from which they could learn. Crucial to their professionalization was the elimination of the practicing midwife, for "she had charge of fifty percent of all obstetrics material of the country without contributing anything to our knowledge of the subject; a large percentage of the cases are indispensable to the proper training of physicians and nurses." Dr. Charles Edward Ziegler, professor of obstetrics at the University of Pittsburgh and medical director of the Elizabeth Steel Magee Hospital, felt that students of medicine should be trained under careful supervision and by recent graduates who had themselves been trained in well-equipped and properly conducted maternity hospitals. Ziegler not only sought adequate obstetrical education, but also argued that every woman had a right as a citizen and as a mother to proper care during and following childbirth. Dr. Ziegler's plan, which would allow for adequate training of students and proper care of patients, was implemented in Pittsburgh with admirable results.[50]

Influential Factors

Even with its limitations, the new medical experience entailed significant change, a real human transition. Black women arriving from the South had been familiar with midwives' services, and yet evidence suggests that they made no attempt to continue the tradition in the North. Their experience is unlike that of white immigrant women, who appeared to be far more reluctant to accept medical care. Why did the change occur? The most elusive factor involves African American women's own attitudes, expectations, and motivations regarding medical care. There is no evidence to suggest why women sought medical care or how they felt about it. It is not clear whether they perceived physician care as better than the traditional care of a midwife or whether it was just more available.[51]

The fact remains that black women in large numbers began utilizing the services of nurses, white physicians, and integrated hospitals for maternity care fairly early in the migration period. Several organizations were influential in informing women of available services and encouraging women to take advantage of them. The major difficulty was not in getting women to use the services but in making them aware of their existence. "When the Negro mother is made acquainted with the existence of a prenatal clinic it is not difficult to get her to attend. The problem is to acquaint the ignorant Negro mother with the opportunity."[52]

Black women were brought into the medical system largely due to the efforts of the Urban League. There is no way to determine the numbers of women the League influenced, but their influence was spread throughout the city. All of the black neighborhoods were exposed to the health programs the League offered. The League had established a network between numerous hospitals, clinics, physicians, and social agencies which provided obstetrical care.

Blacks and whites first launched the Urban League in 1915 as the Council for Social Services Among Negroes, which was organized within the Associated Charities to aid migrants seeking employment. On January 14, 1918, the council became the Urban League, part of a national organization whose chief activities were educational, promotional, or interpretive. Health was one of the major issues that it addressed. The Pittsburgh facility opened at 505 Wylie Avenue on March 1, 1918. The League's chief instruments were research, education, and publicity.[53]

Immediately following the organization of the Urban League, its agents began their campaign for better health. They launched a Negro Health Education Campaign the last week of April 1918. The pastors of thirty-one churches cooperated by preaching on the seriousness of health conditions. More than 20,000 pieces of literature supplied by the government, the city, and the Metropolitan Life Insurance Company were distributed. In one week noted white and black doctors and educators conducted fifteen meetings to explain how to better preserve health. Two famous black physicians were brought in from New York and Chicago to speak at two mass meetings.[54]

The Urban League later sponsored a program for the local celebration of National Negro Health Week. Booker T. Washington started this educational movement in 1914 through the National Negro Business League, and soon thereafter won the cooperation of the National Urban League, the Surgeon General's Office, and other organizations.[55] During this celebration in Pittsburgh, physicians and dentists gave at least fifty health lectures and talks.[56] Eugene Kinkle Jones cited this particular educational movement as "possibly the most effective educational movement for improving health among Negroes generally."[57]

Within the first few years of the Urban League's existence it had established a widespread health-care network for poor blacks of which it was the center. Mutually beneficial relationships existed between several city hospitals, clinics, dispensaries, social agencies, and the Public Health Nursing Association. John T. Clark, executive director of the Urban League of Pittsburgh, stated that the cooperation of the Negro Medical Society, the City Department of Public Health, the Public Health Nursing Association, hospitals, physicians, and social workers in presenting health education campaigns caused growing attention to be paid to health problems in congested black sections. The result was that the proportionate black death rate gradually declined between 1918 and 1923, even though the population increased.[58] David McBride has suggested that black doctors and nurses in New York City played a key role in "effectively usurping working-class blacks' health beliefs and resistance to medical institutions."[59] In Pittsburgh, it seems that they were also instrumental, but only within the network of which the Urban League was the center.

Little is known of the African American doctors and nurses who worked to improve the health of members of their own race. Clearly, many leaders associated with the League felt that black women may have been more receptive to black medical practitioners. Speakers brought in from other cities were often black. The Public Health Nursing Association hired two black nurses to work in the community, upon the recommendation of the Urban League.[60] The African American physician and nurse "being accustomed to reckon with the personal idiosyncrasies of Negroes and to treat the patient as well as the disease is, therefore, best fitted to handle such cases, because those of the white race in quite a number of cases look upon Negroes as mere subjects for observation."[61] Although this may have been the ideal situation—and the Urban League certainly made every attempt to utilize black medical practitioners—there were limitations because of discriminatory policies in the local hospitals. Clearly, the Urban League's primary concern was that of providing medical care for black women, even in spite of those policies. The black practitioners were influential outside the hospital setting by providing information and primary and preventive care. They advised patients to utilize hospitals and white physicians. Although little is known of these individuals and their activities, their roles should not be minimized.

A black migrant's first contact with the Urban League in Pittsburgh may have been with the Traveler's Aid worker who met blacks at the railroad stations upon their arrival. During the last twenty days of March 1923, some 1,165 migrants, 532 of which were women, arrived in Union Station (the largest of five railroad stations in the city). Within six months, the Traveler's Aid worker rendered service to more than 1,100 black travelers.[62]

The Urban League had two departments which were particularly instrumental in establishing and utilizing this informal network of services. One of the first departments to be established within the League was the Department of Information and Advice. Individuals as well as organizations sought numerous types of assistance from this agency, which either responded directly or referred the problem elsewhere. Blacks sought advice concerning employment and housing, for example. Of importance here is the fact that individuals also sought health-care advice. A man in April 1920 brought his 16-year-old pregnant daughter to the League, seeking a home for her until her confinement. She was referred to the Bethesda Home, a home for unwed mothers. Another man sought information regarding a hospital that treated diseases of the eyes and ears and was directed properly. One patient, ill in a boardinghouse, was unable to pay a private physician. The physician refused to treat him, but did refer him to the Urban League, which obtained a bed for him at West Penn Hospital. According to the executive secretary's report of

1920, there were a number of requests from individuals needing help getting into hospitals.[63]

The Home Economics Department workers, employed by the Urban League as early as 1919, were key figures in acquainting black migrants with available medical facilities. John T. Clark described the workers as having "been valuable in overcoming their prejudices against hospitals . . . as well as in teaching economy and thrift in household management."[64] Workers visited the homes of migrants as early upon their arrival as possible and found that they were welcomed with open arms with very few exceptions. Cards were distributed, which listed ten points of advice "For the Negro in Pittsburgh." Point number five suggested that one "send for a doctor when sick, don't use patent medicines." Upon arrival, then, the migrant was introduced to an organization and to individuals who emphasized orthodox medical care.[65]

Home economics workers not only visited new migrants but other blacks in the communities as well and regularly made referrals to health-care facilities, described as cooperating agencies, within the city. As many as 260 homes of poor blacks were visited in one month alone. Patients requiring medical care were referred to the nurses at the settlement house, the University Maternity Dispensary, or the Public Health Nursing Association. The workers also "secured the services" of West Penn, Mercy, Homeopathic, Allegheny General, St. Francis, St. Margaret's, Passavant, and Magee hospitals.[66] The migrant's health problems were varied, but maternity patients were included in those in need of care. One woman who had recently arrived from Virginia was pregnant, suffering from regular "nervous fits," and in need of immediate hospital care, which was secured for her at once.[67]

The relationship that the Urban League forged with the cooperating health agencies was reciprocal. Saint Francis and Mercy Hospital each requested that someone from the League visit several patients who had been receiving treatment at the hospitals. West Penn's social service department asked that follow-up care be provided for several "cases of unfortunate girls that had received attention at the hospital." Magee Hospital needed a place where a young mother and her 15-day-old infant could go to convalesce together, as the hospital did not want them to be separated. The League found a Mrs. Washington on Wylie Avenue who agreed to take the mother and baby into her home. Magee Hospital and the Public Health Nursing Association each sought help in placing babies.[68]

Local hospitals, as part of the network that provided care, directly sought the assistance of the Urban League in soliciting patients. The Western Pennsylvania Hospital wrote asking for the League's cooperation in promoting their outpatient obstetrical service. The service, available in several adjacent neighborhoods, provided standard prenatal care in the dispensary, and a doctor and nurse in attendance at confinement in the patient's own home, as well as postnatal care of mother and baby. Only women unable to pay a private physician were eligible.[69]

The League divided the city into districts where the home economics workers organized neighborhood meetings or clubs for African American women, largely from the rural south. The purpose of the regular meetings, held in churches and settlement houses, was to acquaint each woman with proper nutrition, canning techniques, sewing skills, and other methods which would allow her to raise her family in a healthy environment with limited funds. Women also received instruction about good health habits and were encouraged to use public facilities such as clinics and dispensaries.[70] Clubs sometimes brought in speakers, such as the public health nurses or Dr. Sarah Brown of Washington, D.C., who spoke on sex hygiene in February 1920.[71] Subcommittees were sometimes organized to study problems of child care or to report cases of sickness or need within the community to the home economics worker.[72]

The Urban League sponsored "Better Baby Shows," sometimes organized by the neighborhood groups, on a regular basis. These shows capitalized on mothers' pride by encouraging them to show off their youngsters. The primary purpose, however, was to provide health screenings, which were conducted by Jeanette Washington, the first black public health nurse in Pittsburgh, and Dr. Marie Kinner, a black physician. Within one year, the attendance at these "clinics" tripled.[73] During the shows, literature from the local health bureau and the Metropolitan Life Insurance Company was distributed. Dr. Kinner lectured to groups of women on baby hygiene and other subjects as well during the baby shows. Organizers showed motion pictures on proper health care. The result, according to a 1921 publicity letter, was that "hundreds of mothers [are] now registering their babies in various health centers and clinics."[74] As noted earlier, reformers recognized by this time the value of prenatal care in ensuring the health of a new infant. It is likely that this was also emphasized at the better baby shows. Further, the same individual providing assistance to the mother usually cared for infants during the first six postpartum weeks. Infant care and the health of the pregnant mother were interrelated.

The Urban League's publication, *Opportunity,* also served to inform and educate African American women. By 1930, northern urban black women under the age of 44 were as literate as northern white women. The illiteracy rates for southern African American women were five times higher than those of northern urban blacks.[75] It is, therefore, reasonable to assume that periodi-

Baby show, Morgan Community Center, Pittsburgh. Standing at right is Jeanette Washington, R.N., the first black public health nurse in the city. Following World War I, professional medical services slowly supplanted earlier dependence on midwives. (Courtesy of the Archives of Industrial Society, University of Pittsburgh)

cals such as *Opportunity* may have been fairly influential for the southern migrants in Pittsburgh.

The Urban League was very much aware of the high rates of infant and maternal mortality among African Americans and perceived that education regarding prenatal and infant care and medical obstetrical services would help to reduce the appalling rates. Furthermore, they published articles regarding these issues. Readers were informed that the handicaps of poverty, which were blamed for the high mortality rates, could be overcome by providing black mothers with information regarding the care of herself during pregnancy and childbirth and care of her infant.[76] For example, diarrheal diseases accounted for 28.3 percent of infant deaths in 1916–20 and were considered to be due to bad feeding habits and inadequate instruction of black mothers.[77] Maternal deaths were believed to be most common among mothers who had not secured "proper medical care."[78] In 1924, although black infant mortality rates were still high, they were decreasing. It was believed that they would steadily improve "as more Negroes migrate to the larger cities of the North and West where prenatal and obstetrical work is well organized and is open to all regardless of race."[79] Clearly, the Urban League was well aware of appalling high infant and maternal mortality rates among African Americans. Furthermore, they saw education and medical care as a solution to the problem. Black women were not directed by the Urban League workers, but they may have read these materials that implied that medical care was superior to folk medicine, midwifery, and other traditional practices in coping with high death rates among infants and parturient women.

Settlement houses also played a role in bringing services to black women, by making space available to other agencies. Although the Irene Kaufmann settlement, located in the Hill District, was primarily for the Jews, "invaluable service has been rendered to Negroes through the personal service work of the Settlement. Negroes are constantly in attendance at the various clinics held there; they are clients of the social agencies quartered there."[80] The Kaufmann settlement also housed a substation for the Public Health Nursing Association. There were nine nurses employed there, including two black nurses and two black student nurses.[81]

Churches played a vital role in educating blacks regarding proper health care. They provided space for Urban League meetings and activities and, as noted, the ministers assisted by preaching about health-related issues. Within the Third and Fifth Wards there were forty-five churches, eighteen of which were storefronts; some of them reached less-educated blacks, to whom the Urban League by itself had limited access.[82]

Migration and the imposing network of medical and service agencies did not transform all health habits. Many Pittsburgh blacks continued to practice folk medicine, sometimes because they had neither the money nor the inclination to seek formal medical care. Jacqueline Jones suggests that discrimination by northern urban hospitals influenced these practices. Pittsburgh blacks sought the help of spiritualists, crystal-gazers, voodoo, or herb doctors. Many believed in amulets, assorted superstitions, or other devices that were designed to protect them from danger. Dream books sold for 10 to 25 cents and sold by the thousands.[83] Yet two points are worth noting. The first is that these types of beliefs and the belief in the efficacy of scientific medical practice are not necessarily mutually exclusive. Women undoubtedly sought the help of medical practitioners while still retaining some of their superstitious beliefs. Dr. Paul Titus, director of the dispensary at West Penn Hospital, noted that blacks believed that intercourse at the beginning of labor would result in a light labor.[84] He cited numerous other superstitious practices followed by whites as well as blacks, even as they engaged a physician's care. Second, when medical care was available, the black women may have been willing to abandon some of their old practices. It is clear that blacks did indeed utilize available medical facilities, from the 1920s onward, in spite of the existence of assorted faith healers. It is possible, given the concentration of educational efforts, if nothing else, that this evolution occurred particularly rapidly where childbirth was concerned.

From Southern Midwife to Northern Physician

When black women, who were frequently in poor health, arrived in the urban North, they faced inadequate living conditions and discriminatory practices in an unfamiliar environment. It would not have been surprising if they had sought familiar types of medical practitioners who had been prevalent in the South. In fact, however, urban black migrants utilized the care of hospitals, dispensaries, and clinics in order to have safe deliveries and healthy infants. They did so willingly upon the advice of the more experienced women with whom they had contact. There is no evidence to suggest that they utilized the services of midwives or other healers, although this remains possible in some cases. What is clear is that the maternity care they received was totally unlike that which they were accustomed to in the South.

It is well documented that southern black women had midwives attend them during delivery.[85] As late at 1940, midwives attended more than 75 percent of the births of black women in Mississippi, South Carolina, Arkansas, Georgia, Florida, Alabama, and Louisiana.[86] Several studies of midwives have treated immigrants and blacks as one group. Frances Kobrin has stated that primarily blacks and the foreign-born employed midwives and that midwives themselves usually shared race with their customers.[87] Judy Barrett Litoff noted that immigrants and blacks were attracted to midwives because of lower fees and a wider variety of services provided. For example, a midwife functioned as birth attendant, nurse, housekeeper, cook, and babysitter. Further, a study of blacks in Texas in 1924 revealed that blacks preferred midwives because of their accessibility. Immigrants and blacks alike, it was argued, opposed male attendants.[88] Against these generalizations, the evidence strongly suggests that southern black women who had migrated to the North did not use midwives on a large scale—an important change that accompanied urban adaptation in this region.

It is difficult to ascertain the actual feelings of the African American mothers, in the North or South, who sought assistance with childbirth. It is not certain whether they made choices or accepted whatever care was available. Evidence seems to suggest, however, that African American women in certain regions of the South had little choice regarding birth attendants. Midwives were not necessarily preferred or chosen, but may have been the only attendants obtainable. Studies have, in fact, pointed out that in some regions of the South midwives were hired because they were more accessible in regions where doctors were virtually unavailable. Litoff noted that southern physicians usually lived in towns and cities, often quite far from black rural women's homes. Doctors, in fact, reluctantly supported the existence of midwives because the distances between homes of patients and doctors were too great. In Georgia, in 1927, midwives attended 31.4 percent of all births. Doctors themselves felt it would have been impossible for them to perform all those deliveries.[89] In addition, impoverished women had to consider fees charged by birth attendants. Poor southern women could not afford a doctor's care, and physicians were not interested in caring for them because of the low fee they would receive.[90] The assumption that southern African American women preferred midwives is, therefore, somewhat debatable.

If southern African American women could not afford physicians, or if they lived in a region where the only physician was miles away, then they had no choice but to create their own birth attendants. Other studies seem to suggest that midwives were established in communities where there was need. Midwives clearly did not enter their profession for financial reward. They were seldom paid, or sometimes received animal products, vegetables, or some service in return for delivering an infant.[91] They established themselves as midwives sometimes because they were "called by the Lord" or because of community pressure.[92] They learned their craft from observation, experience working with friends or relatives who were midwives, or occasionally, from physicians.[93] Debra Anne Susie has suggested that a hospital birth was preferable to replacing a long-standing midwife who was no longer practicing.[94] Perhaps southern African American women were beginning to desire physician-attended childbirths, if available, during this period but generally were unable to make that choice. Perhaps the tradition of midwife-attended childbirth among southern black women was not culturally defined but was in fact merely rooted in necessity.

Jacqueline Jones has stated that due to the discriminatory practices of northern urban hospitals and the fact that many migrants had neither the money nor the inclination to seek formal medical care, black women relied on elderly women skilled in the ways of healing, including granny midwives.[95] Evidence, however, suggests, that if there were black midwives in Pittsburgh, or if immigrant midwives assisted the black women, few African American mothers were assisted by them during childbirth. As previously noted, studies of southern midwives imply that, where there was a need, black midwives were established. It seems reasonable to assume that if the southern black women who migrated to northern cities had wanted midwives, they would have pressured women into filling that role the same way they did in the South. Litoff claims that the preference of immigrants for midwives was reinforced by the fact that it was a long-standing European tradition to have them serve as attendants at birth. When immigrant women arrived in America, they continued to employ midwives.[96] It has long been known that southern black women practiced the same "tradition," and yet they did not continue the practice in the North, certainly not on a large scale.

Some of the factors cited for the demise of the midwife include women's attitudes. As the fertility rates declined, women began to believe that delivery was rare and therefore necessitated increased concern and expense.[97] It is noteworthy that the fertility rates of northern urban African American women were lower than those of southern women, black or white, urban or rural.[98] Black women in Pittsburgh were bombarded with information suggesting that medical care was the best obstetrical care. Perhaps black women too were becoming increasingly self-conscious about their own welfare and perceived that medical care was better. They were already well aware that midwives called physicians in situations which were dangerous to either the mother or child. The transition to physician-attended childbirth, in light of these new attitudes, is not so surprising. African American women, possibly, were agents of change along with their white native-born counterparts in the North.

General statistics, to be sure, suggest that white women in the United States went to hospitals for delivery sooner than black women. By 1935, only 17 percent of all black births occurred in hospitals, compared with 40 percent of all white births. Further, only 43 percent of black births were attended by physicians, compared with 94 percent of the white births.[99] Infants which were not delivered by physicians were delivered primarily by midwives, who, overall, attended the births of more than half of the black infants in the United States at that time.[100] Northern urban black women, however, had different experiences in childbirth than their southern counterparts. These women normally chose the hospital as a birthplace and chose a physician as the birth attendant, regardless of where the delivery occurred. They largely, if not completely, abandoned the southern midwifery tradition. Elizabeth Tandy's study in 1937 showed that 97.9 percent of all black births in northern cities were attended by physicians and that 61.8 percent of those occurred in the hospital. Findings for New York City were similar: 98.3 percent of the black births occurring between 1917 and 1923 took place in the hospital or within the home under the care of hospital personnel.[101] This was marked contrast to the rural districts of the South, where physicians attended only 20 percent of all the black births and only 0.6 percent occurred in hospitals. In southern cities, however, physicians attended 61.8 percent of all births, and 38.5 percent of the babies were born in hospitals.[102] This information suggests that African American women in the South made a transition to medical childbirth when it was feasible. The transition moved much more quickly in the urban North. A rural-urban distinction existed in the South, but even the urban South differed from migrant behavior in the North.

The city of Pittsburgh exemplifies the northern cities cited in the other noted studies. Midwife use among whites and blacks dropped in Pittsburgh from 16.4 percent of all deliveries in 1920 to 1.6 percent by 1935.[103] Other statistics suggest that this was true for whites as well as African Americans. In 1938, some 77.2 percent of white births occurred in the hospitals, compared with 79.3 percent of black births. And whole 0.9 percent of the white home births were attended by midwives, there is no evidence to suggest that midwives attended any of the black home births.[104] Another study done in 1936 of unmarried black mothers noted that of 159 mothers, 125, or 79 percent, delivered at home, 10 were attended by a physician, and 1 had no medical care. The details regarding delivery were unknown for 15 of the women.[105] A black woman, born in 1903, who spent her entire life living in the Hill District and who also worked as a social service worker at Magee Women's Hospital, has no recollection at all of black midwives.[106]

Notable differences between the black southern migrant woman and her white immigrant counterpart have already been cited. Whereas immigrants, in a combination of tradition and necessity, might develop a pattern of childbirth based on the services of a midwife who was present in an already established community when they arrived, black women reaching the northern city were eager to shake off southern ways—and at precisely the time when other facilities became available and accessible.

Medical Maternity Care and Black Women

Black women in Pittsburgh had several options for prenatal care. In addition to six hospitals known to have accepted black women as patients in their outpatient obstetrical clinics, the Public Health Nursing Association (PHNA) provided prenatal care in the home.[107] This private agency, which was organized in July 1919, was supported by subscriptions from the Red Cross, individuals, clubs, and societies, plus industrial affiliations, patient fees, insurance payments.[108] Patients were referred by private physicians, the University Medical Dispensary (UMD), hospital clinics and other social agencies, including the Urban League. Individuals could also request nursing care by phoning or visiting one of the substations located at Saint Peter's Parish House in Oakland, the Kaufmann settlement on Center Avenue, or other stations located in Lawrenceville, Homewood, South Side, North Side, McKees Rocks, or Braddock.

Care was provided by a nurse in the home, but under a physician's direction. Trained registered nurses visited patients' homes regularly (once a month for the first seven months and twice a month for the last two) to teach the hygiene of pregnancy, delivery preparation, and proper diet. Special emphasis was placed on early medical supervision. Patients were also instructed about the proper layette for the baby. Symptoms and complications were reported to the attending physician. Postpartum care was also provided for several weeks following delivery. The infant was referred to a PHNA Well Baby Conference Station after five weeks.

This service brought care to many of the indigent in Pittsburgh. During 1933, the association claimed to have made 20,480 home visits to 5,660 pregnant residents of the city. During that same year, the City Bureau of Health recorded a total of 9,308 resident births.[109] Not all of the prenatal patients delivered in 1933, but the large percentage of patients receiving home prenatal care is noteworthy.

Most of the care provided was free to the patient. Patients who could afford to pay provided $1.00 per visit, or $1.50 for mother and baby.[110] Patients with more limited funds paid on a sliding scale, but the majority of patients received care free of charge. In 1929, some 55 percent of the patients did not pay anything, 3 percent paid a part of the fee, and only 2 percent paid the full fee. The other 40 percent were patients on service contracts.[111] The John Hancock Life Insurance and Metropolitan Life Insurance companies, for example, had contracts with the association whereby they paid the organization directly for nursing care for their policy holders.[112]

Black southern migrant women were choosing physicians as birth attendants, and the hospital as well as the home for a birthplace, when they became residents of Pittsburgh. One of the services utilized by parturient black women was the Pittsburgh Maternity Dispensary (later known as the University Maternity Dispensary, or UMD), a home birthing service established by Dr. Charles Ziegler in 1912.[113] Seven different clinic substations were located in the poor neighborhoods of the city by 1920, and served only women unable to pay a private physician. Several of them were housed in settlement houses, including the Kaufmann settlement and the Kingsley House. Women frequently referred each other to the UMD. Newspaper articles about settlement house activities also served to inform women of the availability of these services.[114] A salaried full-time obstetrician was in charge of the dispensary, which also employed graduate nurses and a social worker. The dispensary provided clinical experience for students of the University of Pittsburgh School of Medicine and nursing students from the Magee Hospital School of Nursing.[115]

Patients were urged to register with the dispensary as early in their pregnancy as possible so that pelvic measurements, routine examinations, a Wassermann test, and urinalysis could be performed. The importance of proper care during pregnancy was impressed upon each woman at that time. When a woman was in labor, a medical student, a physician in charge, and a nurse, sometimes a student nurse, drove to the woman's home, where the delivery occurred under sterile conditions. If the patient had complications, she was taken to the hospital.[116] During the postpartum period, a physician visited the patient five times. The nursing care was turned over to the Public Health Nursing Association under the supervision of the doctor in charge of the dispensary. Ten calls were made by a nurse, more if the physician deemed it necessary. At the end of five to six weeks a final examination of both mother and baby were made and instructions were given to the mother regarding her personal care and that of her baby.[117] During the first six years of the Pittsburgh Maternity Dispensary (1912–18), 16 percent (of 3,384 total home deliveries) of the mothers were African American.[118]

Many southern black migrant women also chose to have their babies in the hospital. In 1921, some 19 percent of the deliveries which occurred in the Elizabeth Steel Magee Hospital were to black mothers and, notably, 66.9 percent of those births were to southern-born women. The 175 black births at the Magee Hospital represented 17 percent of the 1,026 black births which occurred in the city that year.[119] A local general hospital responsible for the second higher number of deliveries in the city delivered 41 black infants in that year.[120] Those two hospitals combined delivered 21 percent of all black babies born in Pittsburgh. At least six other hospitals were known to have accepted black maternity patients as well, so that the percentage of hospital births was almost certainly higher than 21 percent.[121] Yet in the same year, only 27 percent of all births, white and black, occurred in city hospitals; black rates, in other words, already approximated the city average.[122] In 1932, there were 1,081 black resident births in the city and 521 black births at Magee Hospital alone.[123] These numbers are fairly significant when considering that there were other hospitals which accepted black maternity patients.

It is important to point out that black patients who chose to have hospital deliveries did so in spite of discriminatory policies and in spite of the existence of midwives (forty-five of whom were listed in the city directory in 1919).[124] Women who chose hospital delivery chose white doctors because black doctors were denied hospital privileges.[125] Hospitals also discriminated against the admission of black patients in terms of the types of beds that they made available. Institutions provided only ward accommodations for them, forbidding access to private rooms.[126] In some of the hospitals, the wards were racially integrated, but in at least two hospitals separate wards were provided for black patients.[127] In other words, black women chose white doctors and discriminatory facilities over a midwife.

The care that black mothers received as patients in integrated hospitals was somewhat different from that of white private patients, which qualified the impact of the new medical settings. Records from the general hospital that delivered the second highest number of babies per year in Pittsburgh were examined during two different time periods: the summer of 1919 and the winter of 1920–21.[128] Each sample comprised 130 patients. Although the samples are small, some generalizations regarding the care of black women can be ventured. The records suggest some differences in the interference on the part of a physician during delivery, and differences between white and black groups regarding the use of anesthesia during delivery. By examining only patients whose care was supervised by one physician (the supervisor of the clinic population), the issue of variations in skill levels and judgments of physicians was alleviated though not entirely eliminated, because this was a teaching hospital and it is likely that residents and medical students were caring for the charity patients. It is reasonable to assume, then, that the white and black clinic patients, however, should have received similar care. Three groups of patients were identified: private white patients were those admitted to private or semi-private rooms, while white clinic patients and black patients were admitted to the ward.

The most notable trends during the eighteen-month span were the increase in the use of forceps for the white and black clinic patients and the increase in the use of anesthesia for all three groups. It is important to note that the use of forceps almost always requires some form of anesthesia and, in addition, the use of ether or nitrous oxide occasionally forces the physician to utilize forceps for delivery. It is not clear from the records which decision, to use forceps or anesthesia, was made first. The differences in care which whites and blacks received, however, remained similar for both sample groups, so the groups were combined for further analysis.

White private patients were far more apt to suffer interference from the physician than nonpaying clinic patients, whether white or black (see Table 14.1). Some 34 percent of all private patients had forceps-assisted deliveries, compared with 8 percent of the white clinic patients and 11 percent of the black patients. John Whitridge Williams, a leader in obstetrics and gynecology at Johns Hopkins, noted that black women suffered contracted pelvis several times more often than white women, due to "the prevalence of rickets

Table 14.1. Patients in sample who had forceps delivery, by race

	Total Patients	No. of Forceps Deliveries	%
Private	115	39	34
White—clinic	100	8	8
Black	45	5	11
TOTAL	260	52	—

SOURCE: Data compiled from birth records of a local general hospital which requests that its name not be used in any publication.

Table 14.2. Uncomplicated patients in sample who received anesthesia, by race

	No. Uncomplicated Patients	Anesthesia	%
Private	50	44	88
White—clinic	81	34	42
Black	37	8	22
TOTAL	168	86	—

SOURCE: Statistics compiled from birth records of a local general hospital which requests that its name not be used in any publication.

among blacks and the general physical degeneration which seems to overtake members of that race who live long in large cities." "That labor is not more disastrous to them is due to the fact that their children are smaller and have softer heads than white children." Williams also noted that in spite of pelvic deformities among blacks, operative delivery was required far more frequently among white women. According to him, the small size of black babies and their compressible heads compensated for the smaller size of the pelvis.[129] This does not explain, however, why operative delivery was less common among white clinic patients than among white paying patients. Rosemary Stevens has noted that forceps-assisted deliveries rose with the patient's income, signifying a higher level of technology for those who could afford it.[130] Joyce Antler and Daniel Fox also noted that the percentage of Caesarean sections performed in municipal hospitals was lower than in obstetric or voluntary hospitals, also signifying that paying patients were either demanding the use of new technology or that private physicians were more willing to offer it to them.[131]

What is more interesting still is the difference between the three patient groups regarding the administration of anesthesia during labor and delivery (see Table 14.2), for here race as well as wealth showed up clearly. Of all of the white private patients who did not have complications or who did not have operative deliveries (C-sections or forceps-assisted deliveries), 88 percent still received ether or nitrous oxide. Of the white nonpaying patients who were uncomplicated, 42 percent received anesthesia, but only 22 percent of the uncomplicated black patients were given an anesthetic agent. Stevens has suggested that patients with higher incomes enjoyed the benefits of medical technology, but that does not explain the difference between the two classes of indigent patients, especially when considering that some of the black ward patients may have been of the middle class and able to afford anesthesia. It simply is not clear whether African American patients were more reluctant to accept anesthesia or whether physicians were less willing to offer it to them, but the differential treatment stands out, whatever the explanation.[132]

Results of Medical Care

Many cities had evidence that increased prenatal services and medical care for confinement seemed to result in a lower infant and maternal mortality. Grace Abbott claimed that wherever communities had undertaken through well-baby clinics or child health centers to provide information to mothers, the death rate was promptly reduced. In 1924, she noted that the infant death rates in urban areas for the preceding five years decreased more rapidly than the rural rate, because the organization of education work among urban mothers was so much easier, with the same expenditure of time and money, than among rural mothers.[133] Ziegler noted that, at the New York Maternity Dispensary, intensive prenatal care was responsible for a 50 percent reduction in the number of still births and infant deaths. Glenn Steele, of the Children's Bureau, cited studies of other cities that had similar results. In Cleveland, in 1919, the death rate for infants under one month (in a district where the infant death rate had been much higher than the overall city level), dropped to 24.8 per 1,000; the city rate was 31.4. In Boston, in 1920, the city death rate for infants under two weeks was 37 per 1,000. This dropped to 13 per 1,000 in an area where over 4,000 mothers received prenatal care by the district nursing association.[134]

The facilities which were available and utilized in Pittsburgh by poor black women also offered a solution, albeit of limited proportions, to the problem of high infant and maternal deaths. In Pittsburgh, during the University Maternity Dispensary's first six years (3,384 confinements, 1912–1918) the maternal death rate was 1.7 per 1,000, compared with the city's 1920 rate of 9.6 per 1,000.[135] Glenn Steele noted a reduction of infant mortality in 1920 in the Third Ward of the Hill District, which had a rate of 94 deaths per 1,000 births (rate for the entire city that year was 110). The wards on either side of the Third Ward, which were otherwise not dissimilar, had rates of 156 and 143. Steele attributed this to the existence in the Third Ward of two free maternity clinics, two city milk stations, a Public Health Nursing Association substation, and the only well-baby clinic in Pittsburgh housed at the Kaufmann settlement. The rate in the Fifth Ward in 1920 was 105 infant deaths per 1,000 live births.[136] What is interesting is that the Third and Fifth Wards—the Hill District—housed 45 percent of the city's black population by 1933.[137] In 1920, the Fifth Ward was 54 percent black.[138] Not only did these two wards have infant death rates lower than the 1920 national black rate of 164 per 1,000, but they had rates lower than the overall city rate. As a result, there were some individuals at the time who perceived that the health of African Americans was improving. Eugene Kinckle Jones, an executive officer of the National Urban League, delivered a speech before the National Conference of Social Work in May 1923 in which he cited various statistics regarding the health of urban blacks to "show conclusively" that the "Negro has actually improved in health."[139]

Conclusion

White immigrant women and black migrant women arrived in the urban North with different expectations and aspirations, which may help to explain the migrants' willingness to adapt to medical childbirth. African Americans optimistically strived for social and economic improvement by pursuing specific occupational goals and by encouraging their children to attend school. They were also more likely than Poles or Italians to engage in small entrepreneurial opportunities.[140] Given this, it is not surprising that black women's obstetrical choices also differed from that of the white immigrants. Their apparently willing transition to medical childbirth provides another example of the distinctive attitudes of African Americans, compared to various white groups during the decades of the Great Migration. Medical childbirth may well have represented one aspect of the advancement in their lives blacks so readily sought when they left the South.

Unfortunately, current mortality statistics suggest that all expectations were not met. This study, therefore, serves also to highlight the complexity of the historical dimension behind familiar current problems. Maternal and infant mortality rates in the 1980s remain at least twice as high for blacks as for whites. By 1986, infant mortality rates had been reduced to 8.9 per 1,000 live births for whites and 18.0 for blacks.[141] In 1986, the maternal mortality rate was 5.1 per 100,000 live births for white women and 16.6 for black women.[142] Infant mortality rates in Pittsburgh continue to be high as well. The black infant mortality rate in the city for 1989 was the highest it had been since 1972, three times above the white rate. The rate for whites was 9.9 per 1,000 live births, compared with 34.8 per 1,000 black births.[143]

Numerous causes for the current high infant and maternal mortality rates and racial gap have been suggested. Adequate prenatal care seems to be the one factor which would reduce these causes, such as low birth weight for example, the incidence of which had decreased in whites but increased in blacks.[144] In addition, studies have suggested that maternal deaths could be prevented with adequate prenatal care.[145] Research has shown that blacks are not seeking adequate prenatal care on as wide a scale as whites, and socioeconomic factors have been cited as the cause.[146] A 1988 report stated: "Outreach efforts are no match for the pervasive barriers faced by low income women in trying to secure adequate prenatal and maternity care services." These studies have identified the barriers to care as money and the fact that the system is not "user friendly."[147]

Yet the ready historical explanation that African Americans long resisted medicalization for whatever reason is clearly inaccurate. Despite discrimination, black women in the 1920s who utilized the new services, including available prenatal care, received some benefits in terms of reductions in infant and maternal mortality. To be sure, these services may not yet have attracted the majority of black women, and their impact should not be exaggerated. But some of the results can serve to inform current policy debate regarding the improvement of infant and maternal health, especially among blacks and minorities. They also emphasize the importance of continuing historical inquiry to trace the relationship between the initially prompt transition and current explanations for the serious mortality gap.

Urban black women during the migration period showed a remarkable ability to adapt to the new scientific obstetrics by utilizing available hospitals and physicians. As an increasing number of women, white as well as black, were drawn into mainstream medical care for obstetrics, an eventual reduction in the racial gap in mortality rates would have been expected. Within the past seventy years, mortality rates have declined, due to improvements in medical care and wider use of medical facilities for childbirth. The initial enthusiasm shown on the part of black women, and the educational programs designed to assist them did not, however, generate the widespread use of medical care characteristic of white parturient women today. The experience of the 1920s

suggested not only that black maternal and infant health would improve, but
that the racial gap would narrow further. Yet the anticipated trajectory was
not realized, due possibly to racial differences in medical care, subsequent
shifts in attitudes that might relate to medical discrimination, or broader characteristics of the black community and its relationship to the city at large.
African Americans were unable to overcome wider results of racial discrimination in cities like Pittsburgh. In addition to exploring possible medical
reasons for the higher black rates, issues of discriminatory policies and other
socioeconomic barriers to adequate care need to be addressed in greater
depth, in linking, historically, the striking adaptation of the 1920s to the
dilemma of the present day.

Notes

1. This time period was identified by Peter Gottlieb, *Making Their Own Way* (Chicago,
1987), 1–9. For this reason, the study was confined to this period; however, some statistics
cited from the mid- to late 1930s are applicable to the migrants who arrived only several years
earlier. Jacqueline Jones, *Labor of Love, Labor of Sorrow: Black Women, Work, and the Family
from Slavery to the Present* (New York, 1985), 151, 153, 156, 157.

2. John Bodnar, Roger Simon, and Michael P. Weber, *Lives of Their Own: Blacks, Italians,
and Poles in Pittsburgh, 1900–1960* (Urbana, Ill., 1982), 29.

3. Ira De A. Reid, "Social Conditions of the Negro in the Hill District of Pittsburgh,"
General Committee on the Hill Survey (Pittsburgh, 1930), 20–21.

4. Laurence Glasco, "Double Burden: The Black Experience in Pittsburgh," in Samuel P.
Hays, ed., *City at the Point: Essays on the Social History of Pittsburgh* (Pittsburgh, 1989), 79.
Glasco states, for example: "Health conditions and crime rates reached scandalous levels."
Crowding, high rates of tuberculosis, whooping cough, flu, scarlet fever, and venereal disease
were additional problems.

5. The term "social childbirth" was first used by Richard and Dorothy Wertz in *Lying-In:
A History of Childbirth in America* (New Haven, Conn., 1977), chap. 1, according to Nancy
Schrom Dye, "Modern Obstetrics and Working-Class Women: The New York Midwifery Dis-
pensary, 1890–1920," *Journal of Social History* 20 (Spring 1987).

6. Statistics compiled from Report of the City Department of Public Health, City of Pittsburgh. U.S. Census Bureau, *Birth Statistics for the Registration Area of the United States 1915*
and *1931* (Washington, D.C., 1917, 1933).

7. Judith Walzer Leavitt, *Brought to Bed: Childbearing in America, 1750–1950* (New York,
1986), 8.

8. Dye, "Modern Obstetrics and Working-Class Women," 550.

9. Ibid., 560.

10. Jones, *Labor of Love,* 159. It is not that domestic service attracted married women, but
that it did not attract single women, who performed other types of work and were therefore
attracted to other cities.

11. A. G. Moron and F. F. Stephan, "The Negro Population and Negro Families in Pittsburgh

and Allegheny County," *Social Research Bulletin*, April 20, 1933, 2; Abraham Epstein, *A Study in Social Economics: The Negro Migrant in Pittsburgh* (Pittsburgh, 1918), 18.

12. Philip Klein, *A Social Study of Pittsburgh: Community Problems and Social Services of Allegheny County* (New York, 1938), 271.

13. Moron and Stephan, "Negro Population," 2.

14. Miriam Rosenbloom, "An Outline of the History of the Negro in the Pittsburgh Area" (master's thesis, University of Pittsburgh, 1945), 23.

15. Alonzo G. Moron, "Distribution of the Negro Population in Pittsburgh, 1910–1930" (master's thesis, University of Pittsburgh, 1933), 38.

16. Bodnar, Simon, and Weber, *Lives of Their Own,* 36.

17. Nora Faires, "Immigrants and Industry," in Hayes, *City at the Point,* 11.

18. Jones, *Labor of Love,* 155.

19. Anne Rylance Smith, *Study of Girls in Pittsburgh* (Pittsburgh, 1925), 82.

20. Jones, *Labor of Love,* 189.

21. Glasco, "Double Burden," 76–77; Bodnar, Simon, and Weber, *Lives of Their Own,* 117; Gottlieb, *Making Their Own Way,* 55–56, 89, 99.

22. Jones, *Labor of Love,* 189.

23. Bodnar, Simon, and Weber, *Lives of Their Own,* 92, 99, 101, 106, 108.

24. Epstein, *Study in Social Economics,* 61–62.

25. Gottlieb, *Making Their Own Way,* 185; Glasco, "Double Burden," 80.

26. Ralph L. Hill, "A View of the Hill: A Study of Experiences and Attitudes in the Hill District of Pittsburgh, Pa., 1900–1973" (Ph.D. diss., University of Pittsburgh, 1973), 130.

27. Glasco, "Double Burden," 79.

28. Elizabeth C. Tandy, "Infant and Maternal Mortality Among Negroes," *Journal of Negro Education* 6 (1937): 329–34.

29. Ibid., 331.

30. Ibid., 332, 343.

31. Glenn Steele, *Infant Mortality in Pittsburgh,* U.S. Department of Labor Children's Bureau Publication 86 (Washington, D.C., 1921), 5.

32. Report of the City Department of Health, Pittsburgh, 1926–35.

33. Reid, "Social Conditions of the Negro," 43.

34. U.S. Census Bureau, *Birth Statistics for the Registration Area of the United States, 1931* (Washington, D.C., 1932). Tandy, "Infant and Maternal Mortality," 329–34; the national rate in 1933–35 per 1,000 live births was 72 for blacks and 32 for whites.

35. Tandy, "Infant and Maternal Mortality," 337.

36. Report of the City Department of Health, Pittsburgh, 1926–35.

37. Tandy, "Infant and Maternal Mortality," 337.

38. "Mortality of Negro Mothers," *Opportunity* 3 (April 1925): 99.

39. "Why Negro Babies Die," *Opportunity* 1 (July 1923): 195–96.

40. Tandy, "Infant and Maternal Mortality," 337.

41. Grace Abbott, "Methods by Which Children's Health May Be Improved," *Opportunity* 2 (January 1924): 10–11.

42. Rickets is a disease caused by a deficiency of Vitamin D in the diet, which results in bone deformities.

43. Abbott, "Methods," 11.

44. John Whitridge Williams, *Obstetrics: A Text-Book for the Use of Students and Practitioners,* 5th ed. (New York, 1926), 783. Contemporary medical literature did address causes of high maternal and infant mortality rates, but of concern here are the opinions of medical and social reformers who were influential in the development of programs to combat the problem.

45. Phillip Cutright and Edward Shorter, "The Effects of Health on the Completed Fertility of Nonwhite and White U.S. Women Born Between 1867 and 1935," *Journal of Social History* 13 (1979): 196. The authors also noted that a New York City study of the period found that 90 percent of black infants had rickets.

46. Steele, *Infant Mortality in Pittsburgh,* 16.

47. Judy Barrett Litoff, *American Midwives 1860 to the Present* (Westport, Conn., 1978), 57.

48. Ibid., 50–55.

49. J. Whitridge Williams, "The Midwife Problems and Medical Education in the United States," *Transactions of the American Association for Study and Prevention of Infant Mortality* 2 (1911), a condensed version of which was printed in *Journal of the American Medical Association (JAMA)* in January 1912.

50. Charles Ziegler, "The Elimination of the Midwife," *JAMA* 60 (January 4, 1913): 32–38. Opposition to midwives was based on other factors as well, including an anti-immigrant and antiblack sentiment prevalent during the period. Midwives were also viewed as an economic threat to the medical profession. See Litoff, *American Midwives,* 64–83, for a thorough discussion of midwifery opposition.

51. Records reflecting patient attitudes were sought in several hospitals and the Urban League but were not found.

52. *Negro Survey of Pennsylvania* (Harrisburg, 1927), 48.

53. Klein, *Social Study of Pittsburgh,* 403, 405; Antoinette Hutchings Westmoreland, "A Study of Requests for Specialized Services Directed to the Urban League of Pittsburgh" (master's thesis, University of Pittsburgh, 1938), 7; Urban League of Pittsburgh Records, FF235, report, 1918, Archives of Industrial Society, University of Pittsburgh (hereafter AIS).

54. Urban League of Pittsburgh Records, FF235, office files, report 1918, AIS.

55. Eugene Kinckle Jones, "The Negro's Struggle for Health," *Opportunity* 1 (June 1923): 4–8.

56. Klein, *Social Study of Pittsburgh,* 836.

57. Jones, "The Negro's Struggle for Health," 4–8.

58. John T. Clark, "The Migrant in Pittsburgh," *Opportunity* 1 (October 1923): 303–7.

59. David McBride, "God Is the Doctor: Medicine and the Black Working Class in New York City, 1900–1950" (paper presented at the Annual Conference of the American Historical Association, December 1990), 3.

60. Clark, "Migrant in Pittsburgh," 304.

61. Charles H. Garvin, "Negro Health," *Opportunity,* November 1924, 342.

62. Clark, "Migrant in Pittsburgh," 303–4.

63. Urban League of Pittsburgh Records, FF82, reports of Department of Information and Advice, April 1920 and February 13, 1920; FF215, reports of the executive secretary, April 1920, AIS.

64. Clark, "Migrant in Pittsburgh," 305.

65. Urban League of Pittsburgh Records, FF80, Reports of Home Economics Worker, February 1919, AIS.

66. Urban League of Pittsburgh Records, FF80, Reports of Home Economics Workers, 1919–23.

67. Urban League of Pittsburgh Records, FF80, Home Economics Reports, case work report, February 1925, AIS.

68. Urban League of Pittsburgh Records, FF80, monthly reports, April 1921, August 1921, August 1922; FF212, report, April 30, 1925, AIS.

69. Urban League of Pittsburgh Records, document c. 1919; this service probably was the Pittsburgh Maternity Dispensary, which was taken over by West Penn Hospital when Magee Hospital closed temporarily in 1918 to care for soldiers suffering from influenza. Pittsburgh at this time had no hospitals that were specifically for the care of the African American population.

70. Urban League of Pittsburgh Records, FF240, brochure, vol. 7, no. 1, March 15, 1924, AIS.

71. Urban League of Pittsburgh Records, FF215, reports of executive secretary, February 1920, AIS.

72. Urban League of Pittsburgh Records, FF80, report, February 1925, AIS.

73. Arthur J. Edmunds, *Daybreakers: The Story of the Urban League of Pittsburgh* (Pittsburgh, 1983), 61.

74. Urban League of Pittsburgh Records, FF244, publicity letter, 1921; FF240, bulletin, vol. 4, no. 2, March–May 1921, AIS.

75. Jones, *Labor of Love,* 193.

76. Frederick L. Hoffman, "The Negro Health Problem," *Opportunity,* April 1926, 120; Grace Abbott, "Methods by Which Children's Health May Be Improved," *Opportunity,* January 1924.

77. "Why Negro Babies Die," *Opportunity,* c. 1921.

78. "Mortality of Negro Mothers," *Opportunity,* April 1925.

79. Charles H. Garvin, "Negro Health," *Opportunity,* November 1924, 341.

80. Reid, "Social Conditions of the Negro," 75.

81. Ibid., 111. This is curious, as there were no nursing schools at that time in Pittsburgh that accepted black students, but they may have been affiliated with a school outside of the city. It was not unusual for nurses affiliated with a school to benefit from clinical experience elsewhere.

82. Ibid., 99; Alonzo G. Moron, "Distribution of the Negro Population in Pittsburgh, 1910–1930" (master's thesis, University of Pittsburgh, 1933); Andrew Buni, *Robert L. Vann of the "Pittsburgh Courier"* (Pittsburgh, 1974), 56. Reid noted in his study a distinct apathy toward the church on the part of approximately half of the black population, whereas Moron described the black church as being more intimately part of the black community than the white church. These statements may not be as contradictory as they seem. Buni noted that blacks, especially those who were better educated, looked elsewhere for answers to the rampant problems in their community, such as to the Urban League. Spiritual needs may not have been met, so perhaps the church's greatest function was in providing space and educational opportunities. Buni's comment also suggests a willingness on the part of the blacks to respond to the directives of the Urban League.

83. Jones, *Labor of Love,* 192; "The Negro in Pittsburgh" (Works Project Administration, Pennsylvania Ethnic Survey, 1938–41), 59.

84. Paul Titus, "Obstetrical Superstitions," *Pennsylvania Medical Journal,* April 1918, 478–79.

85. Edward H. Beardsley, "Race as a Factor in Health," in Rima Apple, ed., *Women, Health, and Medicine in America* (New York, 1990), 125; Debra Anne Susie, *In the Way of Our Grandmothers: A Cultural View of Twentieth-Century Midwifery in Florida* (Athens, Ga., 1988); Jane B. Donegan, "Safe Delivered, But by Whom? Midwives and Men-Midwives in Early America," in Judith Walzer, ed., *Women and Health in America* (Madison, Wis., 1984), 313; Sharon Robinson, "A Historical Development of Midwifery in the Black Community, 1600–1940," *Journal of Nurse-Midwifery* 29 (July–August 1984): 247.

86. Robinson, "Historical Development of Midwifery," 247.

87. Frances E. Kobrin, "The American Midwife Controversy: A Crisis of Professionalization," in Judith Walzer Leavitt and Ronald L. Numbers, eds., *Sickness and Health in America* (Madison, Wis., 1985), 197.

88. Litoff, *American Midwives,* 28–30.

89. Ibid., 30, 75, 105.

90. Ibid., 75, 105; Marie Campbell, *Folks Do Get Born* (New York, 1946), 8–9.

91. Campbell, *Folks,* 25, 44–50; Susie, *In the Way,* 28–29.

92. Susie, *In the Way,* 12; Litoff, *American Midwives,* 32; Campbell, *Folks,* 7.

93. Litoff, *American Midwives,* 32.

94. Susie, *In the Way,* 17.

95. Jones, *Labor of Love,* 192.

96. Litoff, *American Midwives,* 29.

97. Kobrin, "American Midwife," 324–25.

98. Jones, *Labor of Love,* 189.

99. Tandy, "Infant and Maternal Mortality," 327. Although these statistics refer to a period later than the migration period, it is reasonable to assume that they refer to the same generation of women who arrived in the North from 1916 to 1930.

100. Katherine F. Lenroot, "The Health-Education Program of the Children's Bureau, with Particular Reference to Negroes," *Journal of Negro Education* 6 (1937): 509.

101. McBride, "God Is the Doctor," 13.

102. Tandy, "Infant and Maternal Mortality," 327.

103. City Bureau of Health Records, 1935.

104. Ivan G. Hosack, *Public Health in Pittsburgh: Analysis–Progress–Recommendation, 1930–1933 . . . with additional comments for 1939–1940* (Pittsburgh, 1941), 84–85.

105. *Services for Negro Unmarried Mothers in Allegheny County,* study sponsored by a special committee of the Child Welfare Division of the Federation of Social Agencies of Pittsburgh and Allegheny County (Pittsburgh, 1938), 4.

106. Telephone interview with Mrs. Orlean Ricco, January 1991.

107. Reid, "Social Conditions of the Negro," 44–48; Marian H. Ewalt and Ira V. Hiscock, *The Appraisal of Public Health Activities in Pittsburgh, Pennsylvania, 1930 and 1933* (Pittsburgh, 1933), 50, 54.

108. Ewalt and Hiscock, *Appraisal of Public Health Activities in Pittsburgh,* 54; Margaret Chappell, "Public Health," ca. 1925. School of Nursing Archives, Magee Women's Hospital; Public Health Nursing Association brochure, 1923, 2–5, AIS.

109. Ewalt and Hiscock, *Appraisal of Public Health Acitivities in Pittsburgh,* 54; unpublished report of the City Bureau of Health, Pittsburgh, 1935.

110. Public Health Nursing Association files, document, ca. 1920, AIS.

111. Public Health Nursing Association files, brochure, 1932, AIS.

112. Public Health Nursing Association files, document, ca. 1920, AIS.

113. When the University of Pittsburgh took over the service it was known as the University Maternity Dispensary. The dispensaries were operational until 1957.

114. K. Emmerling, home delivery reports, 1925, School of Nursing Archives, Magee Women's Hospital; *Pittsburgh Press,* March 15, 1929; *Sun-Telegraph,* November 11, 1928; *Chronicle Telegraph,* January 18, 1923.

115. *Pittsburgh Dispatch,* November 9, 1911; Barbara Paull, *A Century of Medical Excellence: The History of the University of Pittsburgh School of Medicine* (Pittsburgh, 1986), 108.

116. Paul Titus, "Dispensary Care of Obstetric Patients in Pittsburgh," *The Weekly Bulletin* (Allegheny County Medical Society), June 1919.

117. Charles J. Barone, "Report of the Kingsley House Sub-Station of the University Maternity Dispensary," *Annual Report of the Kingsley Settlement House,* April 1919–April 1920.

118. Charles Edward Ziegler, "How Can We Best Solve the Midwifery Problem," *American Journal of Public Health* 12 (1922): 410.

119. Statistics compiled from birth records, Elizabeth Steel Magee Hospital; U.S. Census Bureau, *Birth Statistics for the Birth Registration Area of the United States, 1921* (Washington, D.C., 1923), 143.

120. Statistics compiled from birth records of a local general hospital which requests that its name not be used in any publication.

121. Reid, "Social Conditions of the Negro," 44–48.

122. Report of the City Department of Health, Pittsburgh, 1926–35.

123. Report of the City Department of Health, Pittsburgh, 1926–35; Mabel Ammon Barron, "A Study of Births at the Elizabeth Steel Magee Hospital, 1932–1944" (master's thesis, University of Pittsburgh, 1944), 11; comparisons of census records with Department of Health Records suggest that approximately 95 percent of black births within the city registration area were to resident mothers.

124. The race of these women is unknown, but most of the women's last names suggested southern and eastern European origins.

125. "The Negro in Pittsburgh," *Works Project Administration (WPA) Pennsylvania Ethnic Survey, 1938–41,* Microfilm F35, reel 2.

126. Epstein, *Study in Social Economics,* 58; Reid, "Social Conditions of the Negro," 12; *Pittsburgh Press,* February 19, 1922.

127. Ibid.

128. The large local general hospital that recorded the second highest number of deliveries in the city per year at that time agreed to open its records for research purposes, with the stipulation that the hospital's name not be used in any publication.

129. Williams, *Obstetrics,* 16, 783.

130. Rosemary Stevens, *In Sickness and in Wealth: American Hospitals in the Twentieth Century* (New York, 1989), 174. The iatrogenesis factor and resultant implications for the patients who received anesthesia or had forceps-assisted deliveries may be significant but is not relevant to this study.

131. Joyce Antler and Daniel M. Fox, "The Movement Toward a Safe Maternity: Physician Accountability in New York City, 1915–1940," in Leavitt and Numbers, *Sickness and Health in America* (note 87 above), 496.

132. Although the sample is small, a more extensive study involving other aspects of obstetrical care would be warranted if similar results can be obtained in other cities.

133. Abbott, "Methods" (note 76 above), 10.

134. Steele, *Infant Mortality,* 14–16.

135. Ziegler, "How Can We Best Solve the Midwifery Problem," (note 118 above), 409.

136. Steele, *Infant Mortality,* 11.

137. Moron and Stephan, "Negro Population" (note 11 above), 4.

138. Gottlieb, *Making Their Own Way,* 66.

139. Eugene Kinckle Jones, "The Negro's Struggle for Health" (note 55 above), 4–8.

140. Bodnar, Simon, Weber, *Lives of Their Own* (note 2 above), 36, 42, 130, 264.

141. "From the Assistant Secretary for Health," *JAMA* 262 (October 27, 1989): 2202.

142. Hani K. Atrash et al., "Maternal Mortality in the United States, 1979–1986," *Obstetrics and Gynecology* 76 (December 1990): 1055.

143. Roger Stuart and Mary Kane, "City's Black Infant Death Rate Jumps," *Pittsburgh Press,* March 26, 1991.

144. "Infant Mortality Receiving Increasing Attention," *JAMA* 263 (May 16, 1990): 2604.

145. Atrash et al., "Maternal Mortality," 1057.

146. "From the Assistant Secretary for Health," *JAMA,* 2202. In 1987, it was reported that only 4 percent of white non-Hispanic mothers received inadequate prenatal care, compared with 12 percent of blacks.

147. Jody W. Zylke, "Maternal Child Health Needs Noted by Two Major National Study Groups," *JAMA* 261 (March 24 and 31, 1989): 1687.

CHAPTER FIFTEEN

Black Workers, Defense Industries, and Federal Agencies in Pennsylvania, 1941–1945

Merl E. Reed

On June 25, 1941, President Franklin D. Roosevelt issued Executive Order 8802, which established the Committee on Fair Employment Practices (COFEP). The Committee was empowered to receive and investigate complaints, to issue findings and directives, and to hold hearings on job discrimination. Employers and unions in defense industries, as well as government departments and agencies handling training programs and defense contracts, were ordered to avoid using race, creed, color, or national origin as an excuse for denying "equitable participation" in the workplace. The President issued his order reluctantly, and only after black leaders such as A. Philip Randolph threatened to lead a march on the nation's capital to protest job discrimination. At Randolph's insistence, two blacks served on the Committee, which began meeting in July.[1]

Subsequently, COFEP announced that it would hold hearings across the nation to publicize the existence of discrimination against all minority groups. Hearings in Los Angeles, Chicago, and New York took place without incident, but when the Committee ventured into the Deep South (Birmingham, Alabama) on June 18, 1942, it touched off a wave of hostility that

This chapter was first published in *Labor History* 27 (June 1986): 356–84. Reprinted by permission.

eventually led to the virtual destruction of COFEP. On May 26, 1943, the President issued Executive Order 9346, which created a somewhat stronger body—the Fair Employment Practices Committee (FEPC)—increased its budget, and placed the Committee directly under the President. The FEPC immediately began establishing regional offices in twelve of the nation's cities, including Philadelphia. In February 1945 a suboffice in Pittsburgh began to deal directly with employment problems of minorities in the western part of the state.[2]

At first glance, Pennsylvania might seem like an unlikely candidate for the Committee's attention. As an industrial mecca, the state was a magnet for thousands of immigrants foreign and domestic, white and black. It had no 2Jim Crow laws or other obvious symbols of race prejudice, and most of its white citizens would probably have denied or professed ignorance of any job discrimination. But Pennsylvania blacks knew better, as the work of the FEPC revealed.[3] A few examples illustrate the nature of the Committee's task.

1. In May 1941, as the nation's defense effort quickened and unemployment declined, a personnel officer at the Philadelphia Navy Yard wrote to an acquaintance in the private sector on behalf of a young man named Louis P. Clark. At age 27, Clark had a bachelor's degree from Fisk University and a master's in physics from the University of Michigan. "We don't often get a man with better references," the officer wrote, but "he is unfortunately a negro and I can find no place for him in our department. Our men are required to go out into the Navy Yards and boss a gang of sailors. . . . Naturally, a negro would not be able to boss a crew of this kind." The writer hoped Clark could be placed as a "research physicist or mathematician who could work by himself and not be humiliated by fellow workers."[4] Clark's employment difficulties illustrated the problem faced by black professionals in the "City of Brotherly Love" and elsewhere in Pennsylvania during World War II.

2. Twenty-year-old Matthew M. Culler, another Afro-American, had a different experience at the Philadelphia Navy Yard. Culler found no difficulty getting hired in a semiskilled position during 1943, but he was discharged with prejudice before his six-month trial period ended. Under Civil Service rules, a federal employee could be dismissed without cause during this trial period. Culler's superiors gave a reason: improper conduct toward white women workers. One woman reported that "the colored man called 'Mac' " was "skylarking" and "matching pennies with a Jewish girl." The relevance of the girl's ethnic origin is not clear. Another female employee reported that Culler "held the hands of white women when they passed work to him" and that he "tried to put his arms around me." Apparently, no investigation of

the charges followed, nor was the "Jewish girl" asked her opinion of Culler's behavior. However, FEPC officials in Philadelphia suspected that Navy Yard appointing officers, who dared not refuse to hire blacks, used the trial period to get rid of them.[5]

3. Afro-Americans also faced discrimination in the post offices, where they had found employment since Reconstruction under Republican administrations. In 1942 the National Alliance of Postal Employees listed six major complaints against Philadelphia post offices: (1) blacks could not get permanent positions in several departments; (2) they were not permitted to work as Civil Service monitors; (3) only two blacks served on a supervisory force of 250; Afro-Americans were also denied preferred window jobs except at Station D, "the Negro station"; (4) black carriers were not upgraded; (5) Civil Service positions were not properly posted for blacks to see, while white employees received information verbally about job openings; and (6) in the custodial force of 450 there were no black supervisors. One Arthur Woody, who served as an acting supervisor for several years, applied for a labor foremanship numerous times, but whites junior to him in service always received the promotions.[6]

The FEPC contacted Philadelphia Postmaster Joseph Gallagher about the complaints in April 1944. According to Gallagher, the charges were untrue; almost every department employed blacks on a temporary basis. When FEPC investigators told the postmaster that Afro-Americans wanted permanent jobs, Gallagher made several points: discrimination existed long before he became postmaster, so he did not originate it; he sympathized with the idea of equal opportunity but felt blacks were taking advantage of the war emergency to press their claims; and overall, blacks "had done very well in the seventy-five years." Noting that post office employees advanced on the basis of their records, Gallagher did not see how anything could be done about the problem, implying that black workers did not merit upgrading. In this situation, the FEPC succeeded in changing Gallagher's policies only by appealing to the Postmaster General of the United States. By spring 1945, eight blacks served as supervisors and five had window jobs, one in the general office building. A new seniority system also went into effect.[7]

4. Employers in the private sector also discriminated. Blacks seeking white-collar positions usually found a closed job market. In 1944, Earl Williams of Philadelphia interviewed with the Ward Baking Company for a position as driver-salesman. If hired, Williams was ready to post a security bond, but Ward never called him back. Inquiries by the U.S. Employment Service brought the following reply from a company spokesman: "There is not a Negro in Philadelphia . . . or in the whole northern United States, who had

such a job," and Ward would not inaugurate the practice. The policy of Ward, one of the largest baking companies in the country, was typical of the private business sector.[8]

5. The Bell Telephone Company of Pennsylvania was another reluctant employer of Afro-Americans. Few could be found among the company's 6,000 employees when a group in Pittsburgh, the Housewives Cooperative Guild, began seeking work late in 1942 for black operators and stenographers. The Housewives wanted jobs for only three people, but Bell's Pittsburgh office, with more than 1,200 employees, refused. In 1940, a company spokesman explained, Pennsylvania Bell "of [its] own volition . . . to be a good citizen and in an attempt to aid the negro race," opened up jobs in house service work. Immediately the company faced union demands for separate locker and washroom facilities. As a result, Bell's management decided against hiring blacks. In 1943, however, the company did promise the FEPC that some black clerks and typists would be considered, but they must enter employment as messengers and elevator operators, the same job route all Bell employees allegedly had to take. By March, Bell had employed eleven black women, but the FEPC believed the company's efforts represented only tokenism. Bell submitted no plan in writing for hiring minorities, and only vague and generally evasive statements came from company officials about the future.[9]

Meanwhile, Bell's Pittsburgh concessions had no immediate effect on its policies elsewhere in the state. In Philadelphia, blacks continued to operate the elevators in the firm's executive office building as they always had. Convinced it would be futile, few Afro-Americans bothered to apply for white-collar work. Their pessimism was well founded. During three years of negotiations, the Housewives Guild, the Urban League, and the FEPC made little progress. By November 1945, Pennsylvania Bell employed only 126 black workers. Eighty of these were elevator operators, and 17 held clerical jobs in the vice-president's office, but none became telephone operators, despite the fact that sister companies in New York and New Jersey integrated that coveted position during the war without incident. In Pennsylvania, Bell officials worried about getting a reputation as "the Negro company." Consequently they refused to move faster than other businesses in hiring blacks for white-collar jobs. Even the reminder that Bell was a monopoly and a public utility made little impression on the company's leadership.[10]

Complaints like those of the fired trainee, the post office employees, the would-be bakery worker, and the Pittsburgh Housewives would probably have gone unnoticed under normal circumstances. But the creation of the President's Committee on Fair Employment Practices introduced a new element: for the first time in history, blacks could take their appeals to a federal agency and command attention. Just as significant was the fact that blacks constituted an important part of that agency's personnel. At FEPC headquarters in Washington, besides two of the seven committee members, Afro-Americans constituted at least half of the staff. In Pennsylvania, G. James Fleming, of a prominent local black family, headed the FEPC's Philadelphia office, and Milo Manly, a black industrial relations expert, worked with Fleming until Manly took charge of the FEPC's Pittsburgh suboffice. These and other dedicated field representatives—with patience, tact, and considerable negotiating skills—sought remedies to problems of discrimination. But the FEPC could not have functioned well without the support of black organizations like the Pittsburgh Housewives, the Urban League, the National Association for the Advancement of Colored People (NAACP), and many others.

Black Pennsylvanians and the FEPC fought most battles against discrimination in the state's two major cities, Philadelphia and Pittsburgh. In 1940, Afro-Americans in the Philadelphia area numbered 315,041, more than 10.8 percent of the area's 2,898,644 people. In Pittsburgh they were less numerous (115,020) and a smaller percentage of the area's total population (5.7 percent out of 1,994,060). Philadelphia became the center of Pennsylvania's wartime activity, ranking sixth among the nation's twenty industrial cities in the size of its war contracts. Pittsburgh was important because of its historical position in the iron and steel industry. Housing shortages, crowding, and racial friction troubled both cities, but Philadelphia's problems became more acute. By late 1943 that city was placed on a national list of tension areas. Nevertheless, during the war, Philadelphia had only two major strikes growing out of racial conflict. One occurred in November 1943 when white workers at the Chase Bag Company walked out to protest the referral of three blacks by the U.S. Employment Service. The other was a weeklong transit strike in 1944.[11]

The public transportation systems in both cities relied heavily on black patrons but offered them limited job opportunities. Philadelphia's transit strike developed directly out of the jobs issue. The Philadelphia Transportation Company (PTC) employed more than 11,000, of whom fewer than 5 percent were Afro-Americans. The Pittsburgh Railway Company had a worse record. Only 2 percent of its 3,200 employees were black. In both systems, Afro-Americans performed the least desirable menial tasks. Platform jobs—that is, positions as motormen and conductors—went to whites only. In August 1941, as labor shortages created platform vacancies, black Philadelphia transit workers unsuccessfully requested upgrading and promotions. Repeatedly rebuffed by the company and its independent union, the Philadelphia Rapid Transit Employees Union (PRTEU), blacks by the fall of 1943 sought the intervention of the FEPC, which by that time had opened its regional office in Philadelphia. An FEPC directive issued in November ordered the company and the union to cease discrimination against black employees and job applicants. The PRTEU, whose members violently opposed admitting blacks to platform jobs, responded by seeking aid from the powerful Congressman Howard Smith of Virginia. In January 1944, Smith held hearings in Washington to embarrass the FEPC or possibly to destroy it. Meanwhile, the Transport Workers Union (TWU-CIO) challenged the PRTEU and in an April election won support of a majority of PTC workers for union recognition. In this campaign, the TWU opposed all discrimination and insisted that blacks should be given jobs for which they were qualified. At that time, transportation service in Philadelphia had been curtailed because of shortages of white motormen and conductors.

Meanwhile, under pressure from the FEPC and the War Manpower Commission, the company agreed to hire and upgrade blacks for platform jobs. The PTC accepted their applications and began training toward the end of July. Shortly, however, more than a hundred workers from the defeated independent union organization formed an ad hoc steering committee and led most of the PTC motormen and conductors in a weeklong strike. It was broken after federal seizure of the company, army intervention, and Justice Department arrest of several strike leaders for violating the Smith-Connally Act, which outlawed wartime strikes against a government-possessed facility. There was little violence, but Philadelphians went without public transportation for the entire week and war production suffered. After the strike ended, the training of blacks for platform jobs resumed without incident. With the Philadelphia crisis over, blacks in Pittsburgh renewed efforts for upgrading on the Pittsburgh Railway. By April 1945 both the company and the AFL's Amalgamated Association of Street and Electric Railway and Motor Coach Employees union agreed that blacks in that city would also receive platform jobs.[12]

Larger numbers of black Pennsylvanians found employment in the shipbuilding and the iron and steel industries clustered around the state's two major cities. Two of the principal shipbuilders were the Sun Shipbuilding Company, located six miles south of Philadelphia on the Delaware River near Chester, and the Dravo Corporation, on Neville Island in the Ohio River near Pittsburgh. The Sun facility, owned by the Pew family of the Sun Oil Company, particularly attracted blacks. In mid-1941, Sun began a massive building program. In this expansion the company, in response to a request from the federal government, promised to end discrimination in hiring. At the time, 10 percent of Sun Ship's employees were Afro-Americans. Traditionally they worked only as helpers and in maintenance, but with the defense effort under way 750 black workers held both skilled and unskilled jobs, including forge and blacksmith work, pipefitting, bolting and riveting, bending, and garage

During World War II, new federal laws against racial discrimination, pressure from civil rights groups, and an increased need for labor created opportunities for African American men and women that had not existed before. Here welders at Sun Ship's Negro Yard in Chester, Pennsylvania, in 1943 are seen going home from work. From left, Arnold Bamble, Clarence Thoms, James Madison, James Ryan, and Emory Glass. (Courtesy of the Historical Society of Pennsylvania)

and janitorial services. Early in 1942, Sun Ship received a large contract from the Maritime Commission to build eighty-seven tankers costing more than $235 million. This new order required additional plant construction, and the company searched the Philadelphia area for scarce workers.[13]

By that time the manpower situation was critical. In March, Sun Ship's top officers, John G. Pew and his son, John G. Jr., apparently decided to explore the possibility of using more black workers in their expanding shipyards. They sought advice from Emmett J. Scott, the aging protégé of Booker T. Washington and a columnist for the *Pittsburgh Courier*. Scott's columns had often expressed concern about discrimination in defense industries. That very week, he reported the results of a Bureau of Employment Security survey in which respondents admitted their unwillingness to hire blacks in more than half of the estimated 282,245 available jobs. Whether Scott discussed this subject with the Pews is unknown, but the three men, arch-conservatives in their respective activities, apparently got along very well. On March 4, 1942, the Pews commissioned Scott to begin his own survey, although the *Courier* never revealed what Scott was supposed to survey or what his findings were. By May, however, Scott began recruiting black workers for Sun Ship, and in July he became director of employment for an all-new Number 4 Yard to be manned solely by blacks, from supervisors and electric welders to janitors. The men would be trained by a cadre of thirty instructors each with at least six years of experience in shipbuilding.[14]

The *Pittsburgh Courier,* which claimed to have "fathered" the Sun Ship venture, reported the story with superlatives. It would be "an industrial utopia wherein 9,000 race workers are to hold every job and execute every task," said the *Courier,* with a $21,000,000 payroll for the race alone. The two Pews were "spending unnamed millions—probably fifty or more—to build from the ground up, its No. 4 yard, a brand new and model shipyard, the most advanced, modern and best equipped in the world," boasted the *Courier.* By June 1942, more than 2,000 blacks were already at work, either building ships or constructing the yards. But there was serious opposition to the plan from "certain racial sources" because "the new plant" would be segregated. The *Courier* deplored such negative reaction. There were "two kinds of segregation," the paper explained, "one wilful and harmful, the other the opposite." Under good segregation, black skilled workers "will be free of the new subterfuge and chicanery [that occurs] in big plants." Criticism from the *Courier*'s sister newspaper, the *Philadelphia Tribune,* must have rankled. The Pews' belief that segregation was necessary, wrote *Tribune* columnist Arthur Huff Fauset, was "nonsense, and we as Negroes can in no way countenance" such views. Blacks must resist this invasion of the North by Jim Crowism. The Pews, Fauset wrote, should be made to organize the Number 4 Yard democratically. Anything less was like siding with Hitler. Meanwhile, another *Tribune* reporter surveyed the man in the street and found strong opposition to the segregated yard. Men should be hired on the basis of fitness, interviewers told the reporter.[15]

But the *Pittsburgh Courier* spent most of its time attacking critics other than the *Tribune.* Condemnation of the segregated yard came mainly from three sources, according to the *Courier.* One, Dr. Frederick D. Patterson of Tuskegee Institute in Alabama, the *Courier* named as the ring leader. Another, Walter White of the NAACP, wanted an integrated work force. Segregation, White charged in a letter to Sun Ship, led to inequities, misunderstandings, antagonism, and frequently to differentiation in working conditions. White and the NAACP, believing segregation violated Executive Order 8802, filed a complaint with the President's Committee on Fair Employment

Practices. The Pew plan, White charged, implied that Negroes could not work in harmony with other people. Even worse, when reductions in force came at the end of the war, the black worker would be the first to go. The *Courier* attacked White's position vigorously and wondered sarcastically whether the NAACP, with its policy of a "whole loaf or none," worked for the Negro or against him. The third group opposing the segregated yard comprised the followers of Dr. Robert Weaver in the federal government. These people the *Courier* dismissed as mere public relations experts who held jobs before the war emergency. They had absolutely no authority and could make no policy, but as professional officeholders they cared only about their own jobs. Although all three groups of critics had been active recently in Negro affairs, they disagreed among themselves on most other issues. To Patterson, White was an "obstructionist," while White allegedly believed Patterson to be an "Uncle Tom." All envied Emmett Scott and his job with Sun Ship, which each group coveted for one of its own lesser assistants. When Scott got the position, they all began screaming "segregation." Their attacks were "vicious and destructive," the *Courier* avowed, "with a flavor of personal greed."[16]

Meanwhile, the President's Committee having received the NAACP complaint against Sun Ship, discussed the matter on June 9, 1942. Earl B. Dickerson—an attorney, Chicago alderman, and one of two black appointees—concluded reluctantly that employing all black workers in one section of a plant did not violate the President's executive order, which dealt only with discrimination, not segregation, in defense industries. Indeed, segregation was legal in the southern states. The Committee could attack segregation only when it resulted in discrimination, such as the denial of employment or advancement. Dickerson believed segregation to be contrary to the things the Committee was trying to accomplish, but it was not illegal. Nevertheless, the Committee had to formulate a policy because of many requests about segregated workplaces from all over the country. For example, an ammunition plant in St. Louis was in the process of creating a segregated plant.[17]

Committee member David Sarnoff, president of the Radio Corporation of America, also opposed segregation and favored an FEPC policy discouraging it. Tell those making inquiries that segregation violated the spirit of the executive order, Sarnoff suggested. At the same time, however, he worried that Committee condemnation of segregation would result in less employment for blacks and thus harm the war effort. In his own company, before Sarnoff's appointment to the FEPC, he turned down a recommendation to construct a separate building and take on a black work force there, "but frankness compels me to tell you that had I approved [the plan] there would be more Negroes employed by RCA than there are today." If the Committee enforced the executive order without segregation, Sarnoff feared, employers might hire a few token blacks so they could say they did not discriminate. But if the Committee did not condemn segregation, an employer might hire 2,000.

It was a difficult question for Dickerson and Milton Webster, the other black committee member. Both men believed segregation to be both discriminatory and a violation of the Constitution. After careful consideration, Dickerson concluded: "I would rather see 10,000 Negroes out of work in Philadelphia . . . walking the streets . . . rather than to have those 10,000 work in a separate place" when Pennsylvania's industrial establishment is not separated. The state's blacks "have gotten along reasonably well working around certain spots" while living in a mixed society, Dickerson noted. But if separate industries were set up, "everyone . . . in Pennsylvania will be thinking in terms of separateness." Mark Ethridge, editor of the *Louisville Courier-Journal* and a so-called liberal on the race issue, urged his fellow Committee members to come up with some kind of policy statement. However, to condemn segregation outright, Ethridge warned, would be the worst mistake possible. Instead, he proposed a policy based upon regional and local custom. To the NAACP, Ethridge would say that there is nothing in the executive order empowering the President's Committee to deal with segregation. At Sun Ship, the Committee should condemn the building of a plant for blacks because it was contrary to the local practice in Philadelphia. In the end the Committee did nothing, and merely agreed to defer a decision on this troublesome issue.[18]

Meanwhile, the Sun Shipbuilding Company went on with the plans for a segregated yard. In November 1942, Emmett Scott, director of Employment and Personnel Relations in Yard 4, announced the beginning of a paid training program involving four hours of work per day, seven days a week, in one of the labor departments. The remaining four hours each day would be spent in the classroom without pay. Although no time limit existed for completion of the course, most applicants could finish in three to four weeks. Yard 4 opened early in 1943. At peak employment, about 6,200 blacks worked there, according to an FEPC investigator; another 2,800 were scattered among the remaining yards, which were integrated. By May, Yard 4 launched the *Marine Eagle* built entirely by black workers.[19]

Unfortunately, Yard 4 failed to become the "utopia" envisioned by the *Pittsburgh Courier*. Initially, many problems grew out of attempts by rival unions to organize the yard. The protagonists were the International Union of Marine and Shipbuilding Workers of America (IUMSWA-CIO) and the independent Sun Ship Employees Association (SSEA), a company union formed in 1936, the IUMSWA charged, to keep out the Congress of Industrial

Organizations (CIO). The independent union won an election in 1937, but as the war emergency expanded the work force and changed its composition, the Marine and Shipbuilding Workers in 1943 renewed their efforts to organize Sun Ship. An NLRB election was scheduled for the end of June. However, trouble began in May, when Herman J. Smith, a CIO shop steward, received a one-week layoff. Upon protesting, he was beaten by seven company guards and jailed for eight hours. The incident led 600 workers to walk out. They ended the work stoppage after selecting a committee of sixteen to ask President Pew for a hearing.[20]

The IUMSWA tried to make gains among blacks by attacking Yard 4's segregated setup, but the union was handicapped by embarrassing racial incidents involving CIO locals elsewhere. Late in May, white IUMSWA members in Mobile rioted when the Alabama Dry Dock and Shipbuilding Company, under the FEPC and War Manpower Commission orders, hired black welders and assigned them to the night shift with whites. In addition, white CIO workers at the Packard Motor Company in Detroit during the spring of 1943 renewed racial hate strikes that had begun earlier. The Sun Ship Employees Association exploited these incidents to the fullest. "Colored Workers Injured in Strike by CIO Members" at Packard and Mobile, screamed a large SSEA advertisement in the *Philadelphia Tribune*. "Don't Allow Yourselves to Be Robbed." Another SSEA appeal charged: "Negroes are not permitted to do skilled work in any CIO-controlled plants in this vicinity." The ad cited as examples the Cramp and New York Shipbuilding companies, both in the Philadelphia area. The IUMSWA made headway despite such charges. At a mass meeting in June at the White Rock Baptist Church, 300 workers voted their support after an IUMSWA spokesman reported that the union was trying to advance interracial understanding. An additional boost came from the *Philadelphia Tribune,* which editorialized in favor of the CIO union. "Colored Americans are at a crossroads," the paper noted, and they must decide whether to support organized labor or the employers. Although both labor and capital shared the guilt of discrimination, the "colored" worker could not remain neutral, the *Tribune* argued. Since most blacks were "toilers," they should "cast their lot" with labor. In the NLRB election on June 30, blacks in Yard 4 apparently gave strong support to the CIO, although in the shipyards as a whole the contest was close. With more than 25,000 workers participating, the Marine and Shipbuilding workers won by only 61 votes—less than a majority because 864 voted for no union. The NLRB certified the IUMSWA, despite challenges from both the company and the SSEA. A subsequent suit by the SSEA in federal court failed to overturn the certification decision.[21]

In the midst of the contest between the rival unions, an ugly incident in

Yard 4 led to the shooting of five workers by black company guards. As reported in the *Tribune* on June 19, the altercation started in the cafeteria after William Smith, one of the victims, talked back to a guard who ordered Smith to "get a move on" after the first whistle had blown. Four of the wounded were innocent bystanders, one man later died. "Men with easy trigger fingers, regardless of their color, should not be permitted to possess firearms," editorialized the *Tribune*. The shootings were unnecessary. Although this incident was unrelated to the upcoming NLRB election, company guards arrested a CIO shop steward, Eddie Abrams, and charged him with inciting a riot even though witnesses said Abrams was trying to calm the crowd. Meanwhile, the company withheld the names of the guards, refused interviews with the wounded men, and blamed CIO organizers for the shooting incident.[22]

Yet the IUMSWA election victory did not end tensions at Sun Ship. In Yard 4, unrest continued over alleged discrimination in hiring, upgrading, the administration of the bonus system, and punishment for rules infractions. Another issue which agitated black workers and the union was the existence of a cleaning unit called Department 67, which serviced the entire shipyard. Only blacks could work in that unit; unskilled whites who were fit only for cleaning duties got higher positions elsewhere, as helpers or laborers. Blacks with better qualifications often began in Department 67 at the lowest step: cleaner.[23] By March 1944 there was an unauthorized work stoppage. With the appointment of a special arbitrator to hear grievances, tensions abated somewhat.

Sun Ship's curious experiment with one segregated and three integrated yards, and an all-black cleaning crew, was probably unique outside the South. The success of Sun Ship's integrated units disproved the Pews' assumption that blacks would not be accepted by white workers. On the other hand, blacks insulated in Yard 4 were scarcely happy workers. Company policies still affected all blacks in a discriminatory way. For example, Sun Ship's white superintendent of welding required Afro-American job applicants to take a special aptitude test, from which whites were generally exempted. Black leading men in Yard 4 had to deal with a white supervisor who "does not treat Negroes as men." Yet FEPC Regional Director G. James Fleming, in a May 1944 report to superiors in Washington, found Yard 4 to be unexceptional. The grievances that existed there, he wrote, were no different from any number of problems in the nonsegregated sections of Sun Ship or in any large industry. Nearly a year later, another FEPC investigator, Samuel Risk, suggested that conditions in Yard 4 were worse than in other parts of the shipyard. Risk found Sun Ship discriminating against blacks in order to fit them into the segregated setup. He recommended that Yard 4 be closed. To some extent, Yard 4 undoubtedly assuaged black pride with its output of fifteen ships and thirty-five car floats by March of 1945. Because of Yard 4, a few workers received rapid upgrading as the company developed black leadership. Yet there is no evidence that segregation created more jobs for blacks at Sun Ship. Black unhappiness in Yard 4 was a constant problem to the union and a source of irritation to Philadelphia civil rights organizations. Although the yard provided blacks with training and new skills, so did Sun Ship's integrated yards. Worker segregation was not the wave of the future in America, even in the South. Thus, Yard 4 denied several thousand blacks and whites a valuable work experience that could help prepare them for the inevitable integration that came in the postwar years.[24]

Dravo Shipbuilding Company at Pittsburgh apparently never seriously considered segregation. It began hiring black workers in March 1942 at the Neville Island facility, following pressure from the Pittsburgh Urban League. By early 1944, Dravo employed about 13,000, including 1,700 nonwhites and 2,184 women. Like Sun Ship, Dravo operated a training program for the unskilled and ostensibly maintained a policy of open hiring, training, and upgrading. But an FEPC examiner early in 1944 found that certain shops had no black workers, and Dravo emphatically refused to employ black women above the level of cleaner or laborer. Many blacks believed there was racial prejudice at Dravo, and the IUMSWA early in 1944 filed a complaint with the FEPC about the "intolerable Jim Crow discrimination existing at the shipyards." A strike of about fifty black power-brush operators on January 18 highlighted Dravo as a tension area and brought a speedy federal response. The power-brush crew worked in the holds and compartments of the ships brushing off rust and scale from the steel before painting. It was the dirtiest job in the yards. The brushing process raised thick dust injurious to health, and as far as the workers were concerned the goggles and masks provided by the company were inadequate. They wanted better equipment and higher wages. There were also charges of discrimination in the issuance of bonus checks. Their wage rates had to be approved by the War Labor Board, and the company agreed to recommend an increase. However, the equipment had been recommended by the Mine Safety Division of the Department of Labor and was allegedly the best available. Dravo fired the strikers but agreed to settle the dispute by arbitration.[25]

Nevertheless, fearing that the power-brush strike might spread, Dravo invited Milo Manly, a small, light-complexioned, black FEPC field examiner in his early forties, to investigate conditions at the yard. Working out of the newly established Philadelphia office, Manly had earlier been instrumental in settling racial confrontation at the Jones & Laughlin steel plant at Aliquippa, Pennsylvania. This accomplishment made him one of the most respected racial crisis negotiators in the state. Dravo gave Manly a free pass to visit the shipyard at will, and he immediately began studying race relations there. Manly interviewed community leaders as well as black workers and made several recommendations. First, he suggested that the company news magazine, *Dravo Slant,* which over the period of a year had printed only one item about black workers, explain yard activity and give more attention to Afro-Americans. Manly believed the company should have a black in its Industrial Relations Department, and he urged that Robert Patience, an expert at Dravo's Delaware yard in Wilmington, spend part of his time at Neville Island because there was no one with whom Afro-American workers could discuss their problems. Manly also recommended full integration of the work force: recruiting and training black women along with white women, mixing painting crews in place of separate gangs of whites and blacks, integrating the power-brush crews, and opening up all jobs to black trainees. Finally, Manly opposed the earlier agreement between the company and union to arbitrate the power-brush strike. He believed it would produce friction because the workers did not understand arbitration. Furthermore, since the power-brush walkout violated the contract, any arbitrator would have to give the decision to the company, yet a company victory would be pointless and would cost it the goodwill of the men. Better for management and the union to work out a settlement without arbitration, Manly thought. Both parties agreed. Manly later reported that all recommendations were accepted and had actually been put into operation—including the appointment of Robert Patience, not just as "the Negro representative" in Dravo's Industrial Relations Department, but as an assistant to the director with duties that involved the whole operation.[26]

The tensions at Dravo in many ways mirrored the racial and labor relations in the larger Pittsburgh area, in which iron and steel, not shipbuilding, dominated. Like most northeastern cities during the war, Pittsburgh's population declined. Although the number of blacks remained stable, more than 138,000 fewer inhabitants resided there in 1943 than in 1940. There were serious labor shortages in the massive steel mills—huge complexes stretching for fifteen miles—as people seemingly ignored unattractive local jobs and went elsewhere. Most of the job openings in the mills were unskilled; the plants filled the better positions through upgrading and in-plant training. Meanwhile, the government kept increasing the war orders. By September 1944, the demand for labor in the Pittsburgh area officially exceeded supply by about 4,000, although there were many more jobs than that available in the steel mills. For example, at one Jones & Laughlin plant 9,000 men did the work of 14,000 by "doubling out." Under such conditions, the work force received big pay envelopes but remained tired, disgruntled, and high-strung. Added to this tension were housing problems that had not been alleviated by Pittsburgh's population decline. The situation became particularly acute for blacks. In the city, every apartment project was filled except one, although outside Pittsburgh two privately owned apartment complexes had more than 400 vacancies, none apparently available to blacks. In the one biracial housing project, black families claimed discrimination by school and recreational personnel, while nearby white residents became alarmed at the increasing number of Afro-Americans moving into the area. To deal with some of these problems, one interracial organization was set up by black, Jewish, and Northside Unitarian religious groups, and several black organizations formed a separate Citizens Coordinating Committee. Despite tensions, however, community social patterns basically remained open. There was no segregation in schools, in federal housing, or in other community services such as theaters or public carriers. In the large department stores and other places, increasing numbers of blacks could be seen clerking where they had never before been hired.[27]

When World War II began, blacks were not strangers to the Pittsburgh area or to the steel mills. Thousands were recruited during World War I, and thousands more migrated in the 1920s—some to take seasonal jobs and return south, others to stay permanently. In the mills, blacks usually got the least desirable jobs—tending blast furnaces and coke ovens. In 1938, as the defense effort got under way, nearly half of the Afro-Americans in the nation's steel mills were unskilled. The Pittsburgh district did not vary from the pattern. The steel producer most closely associated with blacks in the city—the Jones & Laughlin Steel Corporation—had two mills, the Southside (or Hazelwood) Works and the Northside Works; northwest of Pittsburgh, Jones & Laughlin operated another mill at Aliquippa. Several miles south of Pittsburgh at Clairton on the Monongahela River, Carnegie-Illinois, a subsidiary of the United States Steel Corporation, operated a huge complex. There was trouble at all of these mills, growing out of racial problems and bad labor relations. Company policy had traditionally been discriminatory, but overbearing foremen and superintendents were particular sources of friction. Some of the old-line steel men were gruff, tyrannical, and prejudiced, while others who were rapidly promoted during the war emergency lacked qualifications. Top management policy changes did not always seep down to the foremen, who, according to one report, were resented by black and white workers alike. Unions also were reluctant to accept blacks on the basis of their qualifications, although the CIO policy of nondiscrimination had a salutary influence on the locals of the Steel Workers Organizing Committee (SWOC), later United Steel Workers (USW), in the area.[28]

In August 1941, black workers at both Jones & Laughlin's mills—Hazelwood and Northside—filed identical grievances with their respective unions, charging discrimination. Blacks performed only the dirtiest, hottest, and most dangerous tasks, they claimed, were denied better jobs, such as riggers, and were discouraged from applying for work in the new strip mill. They believed that discrimination originated with the superintendents and sometimes with the small bosses. At the Hazelwood mill, Superintendent Robert Campbell told a black in the salt house that "colored" workers would do only manual labor as long as he was in charge. These conditions had existed for years, but black resentment peaked in 1941 when whites with little training and seniority moved into better jobs for which blacks with longer service were qualified. Investigation revealed that the problem at Hazelwood, at least, involved both supervisor prejudice and company policy. Jones & Laughlin, which employed 20,000 at the Hazelwood facility, including 2,000 blacks, remained determined to keep a 10 percent ratio in all hiring for the new strip mill. But in other departments, blacks worked in the most skilled areas and could be upgraded.[29]

Conditions at Jones & Laughlin's Aliquippa mills appeared to be worse than at Hazelwood. The company kept blacks out of higher-skilled jobs in the Fourteen Inch Mill and excluded them from the Seamless Tube Mill. Black females could not get production jobs. Afro-Americans could attend plant safety meetings but were excused early, while white employees stayed on for private sessions. The management, while adamantly insisting there was no discrimination, installed separate restrooms. The thorniest issue at Aliquippa involved promotions. One man, Dave Walker, worked in the Fourteen Inch Mill for fifteen years but could not get an inspector's job. Another, Louis Causby, a straightener-helper for ten years, had been told since 1938 there were no openings for the job of straightener. However, during that period four white men had been trained and promoted to the position Causby wanted, the last one being Carl Hague, whom Causby helped train. In addition, some Aliquippa superintendents were brazenly insulting and crude in dealing with black employees. When William H. Snow Jr. told Superintendent Welch he wanted an inspector's job in the Fourteen Inch Mill, Welch replied, "My God-dam mouth was too big . . . you have gone as high as you can. [There are] certain jobs here for colored boys and certain jobs . . . for whites." Floyd Parham, another black worker, asked for a stockman's job and received even worse abuse from Welch: the job was

> not for the "nigger" it was for the white boys, and so long as he was there I would never get the God-dam job. . . . He was going to kick my God-dam black ass to hell out of here you black son-of-a-bitch. I am sick of you. I hate your God-dam guts, you are the worst enemy I have on earth. . . . He runs this god-dam 14 Mill and not them birds across the tracks.[30]

Beginning in February 1942 efforts to resolve the Aliquippa grievances by the SWOC, the Office of Production Management, and the War Manpower Commission failed in the face of company intransigence. Finally, after a hearing in August 1943 still produced no change in the company attitude, 450 blacks from the Fourteen Inch Mill walked out. Local representatives of the War Production Board and the U.S. Employment Service got the men back to work and promised to try to adjust their grievances, but the effort proved fruitless and another work stoppage threatened. On September 18, the company called the FEPC's Milo Manly and asked him to try to persuade the workers not to walk out again. For a full week in late September, Manly worked twelve- and fourteen-hour days creating a plan of progression and then selling it to the black workers in the Fourteen Inch Mill. There is no evidence of company opposition to the plan, which established the method of worker promotion up the line from one job to another. First implemented on a ninety-day basis, the plan eventually became permanent. That one of the largest employers in the Pittsburgh district accepted in writing the principle that competent blacks must be promoted as a matter of course was precedent-setting.[31]

For the next two years, Milo Manly played a role in most disputes involving discrimination in the Pittsburgh area. Most of the problems resulted from breakdowns in communications and a lack of imagination by management and union leaders alike. Speaking to a mixed-race group of several hundred at Local 1211 in Aliquippa, Manly found the men ignorant of the grievance procedure, the line of progression, and even the reasons for double shifts and the hiring of women workers. In addition to union leaders, foremen and superintendents also had difficulty communicating with the workers. Manly persuaded Jones & Laughlin to hire professionals who would begin educating management people about industrial and job relations.[32]

Manly's greatest challenge came in 1944 when blacks left their jobs at the coke ovens in the by-products plants at Carnegie-Illinois in February and at Jones & Laughlin–Hazelwood in April. Both by-products facilities provided fuel for their respective mills, and when left unattended the ovens melted down. At Carnegie-Illinois, six miles of plants and buildings would have been idled for three to four weeks. In both by-products plants, qualified black workers demanded upgrading. At Hazelwood, for example, Superintendent Campbell precipitated the walkout by bringing in a white man from another department and placing him in a job several blacks were qualified to fill. More than fifty walked out, but Campbell persuaded them to return by temporarily upgrading one black employee. The next night, Campbell tempted fate by bull-headedly bringing in another white man. This time when the men walked out, they refused to return or to be pacified by union, company, or

U.S. Conciliation Service representatives. Only a telephone call from the FEPC in Philadelphia persuaded the men to stay on and save the equipment. Meanwhile, Manly hurried from Philadelphia to deal with the crisis.[33]

When Manly arrived in Pittsburgh, the rolling mill and blast furnaces were shut down, with Jones & Laughlin closing the entire Hazelwood works. Manly went immediately to the union hall, which was packed with workmen from all three shifts. He convinced the men that the trouble should be worked out by the conference method: a committee representing the men would meet with union and company officials and make frequent progress reports. The men agreed to return to work. The dispute involved not only upgrading but also the difficult issue of seniority, which pitted white unionist against striking black workers. A company proposal, if adopted, would have upgraded every white employee in the by-products plant ahead of the blacks. After a detailed study of the plant, Manly developed a complex progression chart for promotions that was readily accepted by all the participants. In subsequent compliance checks, the FEPC verified that Manly's plan was working. Earlier Manly settled the Carnegie-Illinois dispute by using equally direct tactics— talking to groups of striking men, asking each to appoint a representative to meet with him, and promising to investigate valid complaints. At Carnegie, Manly found in the contract a line of progression that had never been clearly explained to the union members. At a large meeting of Clairton Local 1557, Manly drew visual aids on the walls as the union president read the line of progression from the contract so that all the members, many of whom were illiterate or poorly educated, clearly understood what it said.[34]

While other issues arose during the remainder of the war emergency, none was as serious as the 1944 walkouts in the two by-products plants. Explaining the causes for such confrontations, Manly cited weaknesses both in company management and in union leadership. Many work stoppages, Manly felt, could have been avoided by less-dictatorial superintendents and more alert company labor relations people. Nevertheless, by mid-1945 the FEPC examiners could report that at Jones & Laughlin, at least, the policy toward blacks had changed for the better. Working conditions improved, and the company several times accepted grievances directly from black workers, who took matters into their own hands after the union refused to process their complaints. While some of this company flexibility undoubtedly came as a ploy to embarrass the union, Local 1843 at that time had weak leadership and gave insufficient consideration to the problems of black workers. One FEPC examiner reported that, throughout the Pittsburgh area, the rank and file in the mills knew little about the meaning of unionism and that the United Steel Workers had no educational program to correct this situation. In many locals, it was reported, only contract requirements, such as maintenance-of-membership and the dues checkoff sustained the unions, certainly not the loyalty of the membership.

Continuous challenges by rival union organizers from the United Mine Workers and the American Federation of Labor increased the USW's problems. A new contract signed in 1945 included several FEPC suggestions for improvements in the grievance procedure, yet the USW issued no copies to its members. The result was skepticism toward the grievance procedure, particularly among blacks. In the entire field of labor-management relations in the Pittsburgh area, the FEPC examiner concluded, the rank and file had insufficient knowledge of union structure, contracts, and general procedure. Misunderstandings about procedures were the cause of most minor work stoppages.[35]

In addition, most steelworkers labored under incredible wartime pressures. At Aliquippa, where 9,000 "doubled out," men sometimes worked straight eight-hour turns (sixteen hours a day), seven days a week because the plant operated continuously. As Milo Manly reported, nerves were ragged, tempers were short, the men existed near to physical exhaustion, and there were no recreation facilities. At Carnegie-Illinois in Clairton, the workers had additional problems. The company recruited many blacks through the U.S. Employment Service in Washington, D.C. Recruits were promised adequate housing, good recreational facilities, and moral conditions of excellent quality. Instead, they found gambling and prostitution to be the chief recreational pursuits at Clairton. Prices for lodgings were exorbitant, as were grocery bills, and eating facilities remained inadequate. Some migrants from the Deep South with farming backgrounds were unfamiliar with steelmaking and plant operations. Recruiters allegedly promised excellent working conditions, the opportunity to learn a trade, good pay, and rapid advancement. After arriving, many could barely tolerate the heat and gases in the steel plants and coke ovens. Turnover rates were high, necessitating additional recruiting in distant places with probable misrepresentations of the working conditions. To cut down on worker turnover, the War Production Board made several proposals—a war housing project in Clairton, in-plant feeding, a community center, and stricter OPA supervision of prices and rents. That these amenities and controls did not exist by the end of 1944 provides some measure of the degradation and desperation of the migrants, particularly blacks, in steel towns like Clairton.[36]

From Pittsburgh's steel mills to the shipyards of Philadelphia and between, economic racism pervaded Pennsylvania's boardrooms, unions, industrial plants, and federal installations as World War II began. Indeed, recent studies of Detroit's black automobile workers and San Francisco's shipyard workers note similar patterns of discrimination.[37] Thus Pennsylvania's wartime industrial race relations in varying degrees seemed typical of the Northeast and probably of the nation, outside the segregated South. Blacks challenged economic racism with a militancy that embarrassed the Roosevelt administration and led to more direct though limited federal action. In the ensuing efforts to get better jobs for the minority workers, both the FEPC and black organizations possessed little real power. Consequently, their tactics stressed cooperation with each other and investigation, negotiation, publicity, and moral indignation in regard to job discrimination. Nevertheless, federal involvement, though anemic, was important because it made opposition to discrimination official government policy. In addition, the FEPC carefully documented thousands of cases of discrimination providing evidence that federal agencies and war contractors could scarcely ignore. Also significant was the emphasis on equal participation. Blacks and the FEPC in Pennsylvania demanded for minorities the same opportunities that the majority of Americans took for granted: hiring at the highest level of competency, training, upgrading, promotions, and the accompanying economic rewards.

As the war progressed, so did black worker protest. Individuals on the job resisted tyrannical and prejudiced foremen and superintendents. Groups of workers staged spontaneous strikes over working conditions, upgrading and pay. They also challenged unions that were unresponsive to their grievances. Within some unions there was racial polarization over the lines of progression, which exposed the explosive problem of job seniority. All of these issues became extremely relevant in the postwar years. Thus, although a messianic leader had not yet appeared to organize and focus the efforts of a civil rights movement, scores of individuals and organizations dealing with job discrimination in wartime Pennsylvania were already engaged in such activity. If a Congress hamstrung by southerners and their sympathizers could not pass civil rights legislation, a federal agency, weak though the FEPC was, worked for equal participation and, aided by wartime conditions, made progress with federal agencies and in the public transportation, iron and steel, and shipbuilding industries. While the future for shipbuilding would be bleak in the postwar world, the other industries and the agencies were areas with stable or growing employment, viable unions, and larger numbers of blacks, skilled and unskilled, than ever before. Although the federal effort faltered temporarily with the demise of the FEPC in 1946, change had come to some of Pennsylvania's industries and to many black workers.

Notes

1. The earliest accounts of the COFEP, particularly its internal organization and relations with other government agencies, came from two men who served on the Committee's staff: John A. Davis and Cornelius A. Golightly. See John A. Davis, "Non-Discrimination in the

Federal Services," *Annals of the American Academy of Political and Social Science* 244 (March 1946): 65–74; John A. Davis and Cornelius A. Golightly, "Negro Employment in the Federal Government," *Phylon,* 1945, 337–46. Three book-length works deal with certain aspects of the organization: Louis G. Kesselman, *The Social Politics of FEPC: A Study in Reform Pressure Movements* (Chapel Hill, N.C., 1948); Louis Ruchames, *Race, Jobs, and Politics: The Story of FEPC* (New York, 1953); and Herbert Garfinkel, *When Negroes March: The March on Washington Movement in the Organizational Policies for FEPC* (New York, 1969).

2. During the first two years of the Committee's existence, its official title was "Committee on Fair Employment Practices," although a few black newspapers referred to the "Fair Employment Practices" or "FEP" Committee almost from its beginning. By late 1942, occasional reference was made at the White House and the Justice Department to the "Fair Employment Practices Committee." The agency officially assumed that name in May 1943 under a new authorization, Executive Order 9346. See Memorandum, Jonathan Daniels to Marvin McIntyre, December 14, 1942, OF 4246-G, Box 9, U.S. Department of Justice, Franklin D. Roosevelt Library (hereafter FDRL), and Fair Employment Practices Committee (typescript, n.d.), Box 45, FEPC, Hass Papers, Catholic University, Washington, D.C.

Space limitations prohibit the complete listing of the numerous works which have dealt with COFEP/FEPC as part of the New Deal and/or the larger civil rights movement during the war years. However, a few of these accounts are of special interest. By the mid-1960s, some writers began to view the President's Committee as important because the federal government bowed to the pressure of Negro mass action and for the first time since Reconstruction took the side of black citizens. Indeed, one historian referred to the Committee's creation as "the greatest achievement in American history for organized Negro action." Barton J. Bernstein, "America in War and Peace: The Test of Liberalism," in Barton J. Bernstein, ed., *Toward a New Past: Dissenting Essays in American History* (New York, 1968), 297–98. See also Charles Silberman, *Crisis in Black and White* (New York, 1964), 65; Lerone Bennett, *Confrontation, Black and White* (Chicago, 1965); Arthur M. Ross and Herbert Hill, eds., *Employment, Race, and Poverty* (New York, 1967), 184–85. Another writer referred to World War II as "Forgotten Years" and suggested that the war represented a "turning point" or "watershed" in the civil rights movement when blacks would no longer accept discrimination without protest. However, by establishing the Committee, the President, not the leaders of the March on Washington Movement, was the victor, because Roosevelt weakened black opposition to his handling of racial matters and the war. Richard Dalfiume, "The Forgotten Years of the Negro Revolution," *Journal of American History* 55 (1968): 90; Dalfiume, *Desegregation of the United States Armed Forces: Fighting on Two Fronts, 1939–1953* (Columbia, Mo., 1969), 120–22. Whether a victory for blacks or for the administration, the Committee's work was diminished, according to a later writer, because black leaders retreated from the kind of militancy that forced the Committee's creation and because the White House, in the face of stiff southern protest, began giving the Committee a "runaround." Yet to the black community as a whole the Committee came to symbolize what could be achieved by the use of protest and militant tactics. The President's attempts to keep it under tight rein brought forth even more black militancy, which served as a warning to the more conservative black leaders to join in the struggle or face ostracism. Harvard Sitkoff, "Racial Militancy and Interracial Violence in the Second World War," *Journal of American History* 58 (1971): 661, 678; Sitkoff, *A New Deal for Blacks: The Emergence of Civil Rights as a National Issue,* vol. 1: *The Depression Decade* (New York, 1978), 322–25. As far as the Committee's work was concerned, however, one of the latest assessments has been less than enthusiastic. Although the President's "boldest move in behalf of civil rights," the Committee record overall was one of failure because of its weaknesses. Black employment gains during the war resulted primarily from manpower shortages, not Committee activity, according to this account. Richard Polenberg, *One Nation Divisible: Class, Race, and Ethnicity in the United States Since 1938* (New York, 1980), 33, 117, 121–23.

3. Certain ethnic workers faced job discrimination in some of Pennsylvania's steel centers as late as the 1940s. See John E. Bodnar, *Immigration and Industrialization: Ethnicity in an American Mill Town* (Pittsburgh, 1977). In regard to black workers during the war, one book by a contemporary is virtually a reference item. See Robert O. Weaver, *Negro Labor, a National Problem* (New York, 1946). Two other works on black and white worker attitudes and relationships in two West Coast industries, a shipyard and an aircraft plant, were published shortly after the war and have almost a documentary flavor. Katherine Archibald, *Wartime Shipyard: A Study in Social Disunity* (Berkeley and Los Angeles, 1947); Bernice Anita Reed, "Accommodation Between Negro and White Employees in a West Coast Aircraft Industry, 1942–1944," *Social Forces* 26 (1947): 76–84. Another writer, Herbert Northrup, whose scholarly career began during World War II and who served as an adviser to the FEPC, has written numerous books and articles on the black workers: "Negroes in a War Industry: The Case of Shipbuilding," *Journal of Business* 16 (1943): 160–72; "Organized Labor and Negro Workers," *Journal of Political Economy* 11 (1943): 206–21; "Unions and Negro Employment," *Annals of the American Academy of Political and Social Sciences* 244 (1946): 42–47; *Organized Labor and the Negro in the Rubber Tire Industry* (Philadelphia, 1969). Two works that deal extensively with black workers in federal employment are William Bradbury Jr., "Racial Discrimination in the Federal Service" (Ph.D. diss., Columbia University, 1952); and Samuel Krislov, *The Negro in Federal Employment* (Minneapolis, 1967). Others who have written studies of black workers that covered material during the war period include Herbert Hill, *Black Labor and the American Legal System: I, Race, Work, and the Law* (Washington, 1977); Philip Foner, *Organized Labor and the Black Worker, 1619–1973* (New York, 1982). An indispensable work for anyone studying blacks during World War II is Neil A. Wynn, *The Afro-American and the Second World War* (New York, 1976). Finally, a few historians have utilized the case records of the President's Committee, especially those from the field offices, to better understand the role of black organizations and workers and their relationships to unions and various federal agencies. See August Meier and Elliott Rudwick, *Black Detroit and the Rise of the UAW* (New York, 1979); William H. Harris, "Federal Intervention in Union Discrimination: FEPC and West Coast Shipyards During World War II," *Labor History* 22 (1981): 325–47; Merl E. Reed, "FEPC, the Black Worker, and the Southern Shipyards," *South Atlantic Quarterly* 74 (1975): 446–67, and "FEPC and the Federal Agencies in the South," *Journal of Negro History* 55 (1980): 43–56; Allan Winkler, "The Philadelphia Transit Strike of 1944," *Journal of American History* 59 (1972): 75–89; and Alexa B. Henderson, "FEPC and the Southern Railway Case: An Investigation into Discriminatory Practices of Railroads During World War II," *Journal of Negro History* 61 (1976): 173–87.

4. A. Springer Jr. to Walter Pritz, May 15, 1941, Region 3, Philadelphia Navy Yard, Records of the FEPC, Record Group 228, National Archives and Records Service, available on microfilm as Field Records, reel 36 (hereafter reel no. followed by FR). Michigan Congressman Rudolph Tenerowicz eventually helped Clark get employment in his area of expertise at a naval aircraft factory.

5. G. James Fleming to George M. Johnson, June 24, 1943, Region 3, Philadelphia Navy Yard, 36FR. Fleming was director of the FEPC's Region 3, which included Pennsylvania, New Jersey, and West Virginia. Fleming observed that most complaints of discrimination involving government agencies came from people discharged during the trial period. He recommended a study of trial period discharges as a basis for submitting recommendations to the Civil Service Commission.

6. Departments in which blacks did not have permanent positions included Bookkeeping, Cashier, Drafting, Inquiry, Money Order, Personnel, Printing and Supplies, Registry, Safeguarding, Revenue Service, Classification, Scheme Examiner, and Section Examiner. Although a few blacks worked in the Money Order section, they held only temporary positions and feared the jobs would become all white when the war ended. In all the postal stations except D, whites with less seniority than blacks always got appointed. Memorandum, Charlence Mitchell to Malcolm Ross, December 7, 1944; Fleming to Mitchell, June 13, 1945, Philadelphia Post Office, 3 GR 673, 37FR.

7. W. T. Grinnage, field visit, April 5, 1944, K. P. Aldrich to Mitchell, March 3, 1945, Philadelphia Post Office 3 GR 673, 37FR. There were also complaints about discrimination in the post offices at Pittsburgh and New Castle. U.S. Post Office, New Castle, 3 GR 1867, 28FR, U.S. Post Office, Pittsburgh, 3 GR 1844, 27FR.

8. Ward Baking Company, 3 BR, 403, 40FR.

9. George M. Johnson to Bell Telephone Company of Pennsylvania, December 4, 1942; E. W. Clark to Lawrence W. Cramer, January 19, 1943; Clark to Johnson, March 3, 1943, Bell Telephone of Pennsylvania, active-unarranged, 28FR.

10. Fleming to Pennsylvania Bell, November 30, 1944; Fleming to Mitchell, November 11, 1945, 3 BR 851, 28FR.

11. U.S. Census Bureau, *Sixteenth Census of the United States, 1940: Population,* I (Washington, D.C., 1942), 936–37; *Population,* II, part 6 (Washington, D.C., 1943), 258, 263. Population statistics as reported by the FEPC's Office of Review and Analysis (R&A) must be used with considerable care. For Philadelphia, the R&A office used census data for city population (1,931,334) rather than the area population (2,898,644). Thus, the city's 251,000 blacks constituted 13 percent of its population. For Pittsburgh, R&A office documents apparently used an area base even greater than the Census Bureau's. For 1940, R&A office documents included 88,000 more people in Pittsburgh area than the census takers did. The R&A office also compiled data on population growth during the war. There is little reason to doubt its conclusions that 21,000 additional Afro-Americans migrated to Philadelphia between the 1940 census and October 1943. Indeed, Philadelphia, with its extensive war contracts, saw a modest increase in its total population during the war years, while other northeastern cities, including Pittsburgh, experienced population declines. Office Files of John A. Davis, Migration–Negro, 4, Records of the FEPC, Record Group 228, National Archives and Record Service, available on microfilm as Headquarters Records, reel 68 (hereafter, reel no. followed by HR). Office Files of Marjorie Lawson, Leland Tension Area Study, 69HR; Tension File, Pennsylvania, Focal Issues–Philadelphia, 76HR; Walter L. Simmons to John A. Davis, March 22, 1944; Joy P. Davis to John A. Davis, May 31, 1944, Tension Area Reports, 63HR.

12. *Pittsburgh Courier,* January 15, July 15, and August 12, 1944; April 14, 1945; Progress Report, August 28, 1944, Pittsburgh Railway Company, active–unarranged, 27FR; Report by the Greater Pittsburgh Citizens Coordinating Committee, February 10, 1945; Milo A. Manly to Patrick T. Fagan, April 5, 1945, active–unarranged, 28FR; Allen M. Winkler, "The Philadelphia Transit Strike of 1944," 73–89; Ruchames, *Race, Jobs, and Politics,* 100–120. August Meier and Elliott Rudwick, "Communist Unions and the Black Community: The Case of the Transport Workers Union, 1934–1944," *Labor History* 23 (1982): 182–97.

13. *Philadelphia Tribune,* July 3, 1941, 1; April 25, 1942, 1, 5; *Pittsburgh Courier,* July 12, 1941, 4; June 6, 1942, 5.

14. *Pittsburgh Courier,* March 7, 1942, 14; May 9, 1942, 24; June 6, 1942, 5; *Philadelphia Tribune,* April 25, 1942, 1, 5; May 30, 1942, 2.

15. *Pittsburgh Courier,* June 6, 1942, 5; *Philadelphia Tribune,* June 6, 1942, 4.

16. *Pittsburgh Courier,* June 6, 1942, 5; June 13, 1942, 4; July 11, 1942, 3; August 1, 1942, 12. *Philadelphia Tribune,* June 6, 1942, 1, 4; June 13, 1942, 4. According to one FEPC report, the number of black workers employed by Sun Ship reached 8,322 out of the 25,860 employees. The blacks worked at nearly all skills. Office Files of John A. Davis, Studies 2, 68HR.

17. Verbatim transcript, Committee meeting, June 9, 1942, P.M., 82–89, 63HR.

18. Ibid.

19. Samuel Risk to G. James Fleming, March 10, 1945, 3 BR 2060, 28FR; *Philadelphia Tribune,* November 14, 1942, 20; May 15, 1943, 1.

20. *Philadelphia Tribune,* May 15, 1943, 1; June 12, 1943, 3.

21. *Philadelphia Tribune,* June 26, 1943, 20; July 10, 1943, 1; July 24, 1943, 4; July 31, 1943, August 14, 1943, 2; August 21, 1943, 1; Meier and Rudwick, *Black Detroit,* 162–65, 166, 167, 168; Reed, "Southern Shipyards," 446–67.

22. *Pittsburgh Courier,* June 26, 1943, 1, 8; January 8, 1944, 10. *Philadelphia Tribune,* June 19, 1943, 1; June 26, 1943, 4; July 3, 1943, 1; July 24, 1943, 2.

23. Office Files of Cornelius Golightly, Strike Summaries, 72HR; Samuel Risk to G. James Fleming, March 10, 1945, Sun Shipbuilding Company, 3 BR 2060, 28FR.

24. Final Disposition Report, June 29, 1945, 3 BR 906, 39FR; Risk to Fleming, March 10, 1945, 3 BR 2020, 28FR.

25. George E. De Mar to Robert Weaver, August 25, 1942; Milo Manly to G. James Fleming, February 9, 1944, 3 BR 566, 32FR.

26. Milo Manly to G. James Fleming, February 9 and November 27, 1944, Dravo Shipbuilding Company 3 BR 566, 32FR; Joy P. Davis to John A. Davis, March 25, 1944, Region 2, Tension Area Reports, 63 HR; Dravo Corporation, Neville Island, Pennsylvania, active–unarranged, Pittsburgh Railway, 27FR. Manly, of West Indian origin, had previously worked at the Pennsylvania Department of Public Assistance. Telephone interview with Clarence Mitchell, July 12, 1982; Will Maslow to Father Hass, August 17, 1943, Office Files of George M. Johnson, Personnel, 4HR.

27. The War Manpower Commission reported that 77 percent of the total manpower needs was concentrated in three industries, iron and steel (41 percent); transportation, including shipbuilding (30 percent); and ordnance and accessories (6 percent). Joy P. Davis to John A. Davis, May 31, 1944; Telegram to John R. Steelman, September 28, 1943, Region 3, Tension Area Reports, 63HR.

28. Aliquippa and Clairton were each about twenty-five miles from downtown Pittsburgh. In 1938, some 49.2 percent of the nation's black steelworkers were unskilled, 38.3 percent were semi-skilled, and 12.5 percent were skilled. For whites, the proportions were about reversed. Northrup, *Organized Labor and the Negro,* 175. For a brief study of the black worker in Pittsburgh before 1930, see Peter Gottlieb, "Migration and Jobs: The New Black Workers in Pittsburgh, 1916–1930," *Western Pennsylvania Historical Magazine* 61 (1978): 1–15. For material on steelworkers in another Pennsylvania city, see Bodnar, *Immigration and Industrialization.* In the mid-1930s, blacks constituted 7 percent of the wage earners in the steel mills of the Pittsburgh district. Richard L. Brown, *The Negro in the Steel Industry* (Philadelphia, 1968), 27. Jones & Laughlin, with about 5 percent of the nation's output, was the largest of several small independents competing with the "Big Three": United States Steel, Bethlehem, and Republic. Gertrude S. Schroeder, *The Growth of Major Steel Companies, 1900–1930* (Baltimore, 1953), 16, 197–98. The Carnegie-Illinois Clairton plant had 16,000 workers, 17 percent of whom were black. Carnegie-Illinois Steel, 3 BR 734, 31 FR. Jones & Laughlin's Aliquippa plant had 14,000 employees, 11 percent black. Jones & Laughlin, 3 BR 209, 29FR. Joy P. Davis to John A. Davis, March 31, 1944, Region 3, Tension Area Reports, 64HR.

29. The grievance was sent to SWOC Locals 1272 (Hazelwood) and 1843 (Northside). Memorandum, August 27, 1941, Jones & Laughlin Steel, active–unarranged, 27FR. Report of Reginald A. Johnson, October 21, 1941, Jones & Laughlin, active–unarranged, 28FR.

30. The Aliquippa grievances were reported by Local 1211–SWOC to the Labor Division of the Office of Production Management early in 1942, and an investigator confirmed all of the complaints. Steel Workers Organizing Committee to Reginald A. Johnson, February 22, 1943; Johnson to W. H. Harvey, March 16, 1943; Harvey to Johnson, April 12, 1943, Jones & Laughlin, active–unarranged, 28FR, statements of Louis Causby, William H. Snow Jr., and Floyd Parham, Jones & Laughlin, 3 BR 209, 29FR.

31. *Philadelphia Tribune,* September 4, 1943, 1. Clarence Mitchell to George M. Johnson and Will Maslow, September 4, 1943, Reports, 1–2, a–j, 48HR; Frank L. McNamee to G. James Fleming, September 18, 1943, Jones & Laughlin, Aliquippa, 3 BR 209, 29FR; telegram to John R. Steelman, September 28, 1943; Fleming to Maslow, October 7, 1943, Region III, Tension Area Reports, 63HR; *Pittsburgh Courier,* October 30, 1943.

32. Manly to Fleming, February 6, 1944, Jones & Laughlin, 3 BR 209, 29FR.

33. Manly to Fleming, March 7, 1944, Carnegie-Illinois, 3 BR 477, 31FR; Manly to Fleming, March 7, 1944, Carnegie-Illinois, 3 BR 477, 31FR; Manly to Fleming, May 3, 1944, Jones & Laughlin–Hazelwood, 3 BR 645, 29FR.

34. Manly to Fleming, May 3, 1944; Final Disposition Report, May 24, 1944; Compliance Report, December 14, 1944, Jones & Laughlin–Hazelwood, 3 BR 645, 29FR; Manly to Fleming, March 7, 1944, Carnegie-Illinois, 3 BR 477, 31FR.

35. Report on Work Stoppages, February 26, and June 11, 1945, Office Files of Emanuel Bloch, Miscellaneous, 6HR.

36. Manly to Fleming, March 6, 1944, Jones & Laughlin, 3 BR 209, 29FR; Manly to Fleming, October 6, 1944, Carnegie-Illinois, 3 BR 822, 32FR.

37. Meier and Rudwick, *Black Detroit,* 125–26, 156–57; Harris, "West Coast Shipyards," 225–47.

CHAPTER SIXTEEN

The Black Church in Industrializing Western Pennsylvania, 1870–1950

Dennis C. Dickerson

The growth of corporate business in the United States during the nineteenth and early twentieth centuries caused employers to recognize the importance of regulating large groups of previously undisciplined industrial laborers. In an attempt to develop a dependable and efficient force of employees, industrialists supported churches that espoused the work ethic and preached thrift and sobriety to industrial workers.[1] Employers in the Pittsburgh area developed a particularly close relationship with black churches in Western Pennsylvania. Black industrial workers who played important roles in religious affairs impressed businessmen and convinced them that employment stability was tied to church membership. Both before and after World War I, employers believed that black churches preaching the work ethic deserved their support and encouragement. As a result they gave money and property to struggling black congregations, and they hired black welfare workers who actively participated in church affairs. Once these ties were established, an intricate and deferential relationship evolved between black churches and big business in the Pittsburgh vicinity. Black clergymen believed the numerical growth of their congregations resulted from increased employment opportunities in

This chapter was first published in *Western Pennsylvania Historical Magazine* (now called *Pittsburgh History*) 64 (October 1981): 329–44. Reprinted by permission.

local industries, and some black preachers who ministered to small churches took jobs in industrial facilities throughout the Pittsburgh area. Since they and their churches benefited from industrial philanthropy, few among the black clergy protested against racial discrimination in hiring, promotion, and job assignments. Not until labor unions developed in the mass production industries during the 1930s did black clergymen support organized labor and openly denounce unfair employment practices against black workers.

Pittsburgh possessed the largest concentration of blacks in Western Pennsylvania. Between 1870 and 1880 the black population dramatically grew from 1,996 to 6,136. A slow, but steady migration of blacks, principally from Virginia and Maryland, quadrupled the black population to 25,623 in 1910. The black migration from the South also affected several outlying communities, mainly along the Ohio, Monongahela, and Allegheny rivers. In 1910, blacks were most numerous in Homestead, Braddock, McKeesport, and Washington, where their numbers ranged from 500 to 1,400 people. Other towns with more than 200 blacks included Rankin, Johnstown, Monessen, New Castle, Duquesne, and Coraopolis.[2]

In Pittsburgh, 2,859 black men were engaged in manufacturing and mechanical jobs in 1910, and they constituted nearly one-third of the city's 9,940 gainfully employed black males. These industrial workers were scattered in scores of occupations, but the largest single groups were general laborers, who numbered 1,226, and iron and steel workers, who came next with 789. The same pattern prevailed in industrial communities in other parts of Western Pennsylvania. General laborers predominated, but blacks also worked as iron and steel employees, coal miners, coke laborers, and tin plate workers.[3]

The first black congregations in Western Pennsylvania were the African Methodist Episcopal (AME) and the African Methodist Episcopal Zion denominations in Pittsburgh. A traveling denominational missionary started Bethel AME Church in 1822. Several years later, in 1836, a series of prayer meetings and preaching services culminated in the founding of John Wesley AME Zion Church. In the late 1830s, Avery AME Zion Church and Brown Chapel AME Church developed independently out of another series of religious gatherings among black residents in Allegheny City, now Pittsburgh's North Side. The "mother" church among black Presbyterians was Grace Memorial Presbyterian Church, founded in the Hill District in 1868. In 1914 and 1917 the Reverend Charles H. Trusty, pastor of Grace Memorial, nurtured two additional congregations in other sections of Pittsburgh. Bidwell Street Presbyterian Church started in the East Liberty area. Black Episcopalians gained a congregation in 1904 when the Reverend Scott Wood organized the St. Augustine Mission. St. Philip's Church, a branch congregation also established by Wood, merged with St. Augustine in 1917 under the Reverend Shelton Hale Bishop and formed the Church of the Holy Cross. Despite the denominational diversity, the Baptists claimed the most congregations among Pittsburgh blacks. Before World War I, they had at least thirty churches in the Smoky City. Metropolitan and Ebenezer, the leading congregations, founded in 1868 and 1875 respectively, each counted more than 1,000 members during the early 1910s.[4]

Usually two or three congregations served as the center of religious life for black migrants in nearby industrial communities. One Methodist congregation affiliated either with the African Methodist Episcopal or the African Methodist Episcopal Zion denominations existed with one or two Baptist churches. In 1882, fourteen Homestead blacks organized Park Place AME Church. Between 1883 and 1900, it was a part of a preaching circuit and was variously attached to AME congregations in Braddock, Duquesne, and Pittsburgh's South Side. Its membership reached 100 in 1905, and shortly before the wartime migration, it was dropped from a circuit that it shared with Duquesne and was given a full-time minister. The other congregation, Clark Memorial Baptist Church, was organized as Clark's Chapel during the 1890s. At the turn of the century, Coraopolis had three black congregations: Mount Olive Baptist Church started in 1889; St. Paul AME Zion Church began in 1900; and in 1904 several members of Mount Olive withdrew to form New Hope Baptist Church.[5]

In most cases these congregations owed their existence to black migrants who came to Western Pennsylvania to work in its burgeoning industries. Blacks moved to the region to improve their economic condition, and they sought familiar religious institutions to help them adapt to their new surroundings. These factors motivated James Claggett, a migrant from Mount Zion, Maryland, who became an employee at the Duquesne steel plant in 1888. In 1891 he became a charter member of Payne Chapel African Methodist Episcopal Church. Similarly, Samuel Marshall of Halifax, Virginia, secured a job at the National Tube Company in 1892 and helped to organize Bethlehem Baptist Church in McKeesport in 1889. Another migrant from the Old Dominion, Oliver Douglass, worked as a machinist in the steel industry and was an employee of the Carbohydrogen Company. He also viewed the black church as an important part of his new life in Western Pennsylvania and helped to establish New Hope Baptist Church in Coraopolis in 1904.[6]

Before World War I, a few industrial employers expressed an interest in these new and struggling congregations. They believed their support of black churches would help their employees adapt to the industrial environs of Western Pennsylvania and remind them of the importance of the work ethic and the value of thrift and sobriety. During the 1870s, William H. Rosensteel,

Ebenezer Baptist Church, 2001 Wylie Avenue, Pittsburgh. Organized in 1875, Ebenezer built its first edifice in 1882 at Cowell and Miller Streets. As the membership expanded, the church moved to the current site in 1914 and built the above structure in 1930–31. Ebenezer was the first black Baptist congregation in Western Pennsylvania to own its own building. (Courtesy of the Pittsburgh History and Landmarks Foundation)

proprietor of the Rosensteel Tannery in Woodvale, Pennsylvania, played an important role in the development of Cambria Chapel AME Zion Church in Johnstown. In 1873 he went to Maryland to recruit blacks to work in his newly established tannery. Charles W. Cook, a black Civil War veteran, responded to Rosensteel's offer, came to Johnstown with a few others, and organized an AME Zion congregation. Rosensteel helped the struggling Zionites by allowing them to worship in his tannery loft and later by helping them to secure a lot on which to build a church. The Cambria Iron Company cooperated in 1875 by selling some land to the congregation for the nominal sum of one dollar.[7]

When World War I inaugurated a massive migration of black southerners to Western Pennsylvania, industrial employers formalized their relationship with black churches. Black welfare workers whom they hired to recruit black laborers and to facilitate their adjustment to northern life participated actively in religious affairs. Moreover, industrial officials provided black congregations with verbal encouragement, financial assistance, and help in locating and acquiring property. Since black churches promoted work discipline and provided migrants with familiar social and religious institutions, they attracted substantial support from mill, mine, and factory officials.

The wartime migration brought more than 8,000 blacks to Pittsburgh between 1915 and 1917. They increased the city's black population from 25,623 in 1910 to 37,725 in 1920 and raised the percentage of blacks in the total population from 4.8 percent to 6.4 percent. John T. Clark of the Pittsburgh Urban League estimated that another 25,000 blacks settled in the Smoky City during a second wave of migration in 1922 and 1923. In 1930, Pittsburgh's black population was 54,983, or 8.2 percent of all city residents. Similar increases occurred in numerous industrial communities throughout Western Pennsylvania. In Homestead, for example, the black population rose from 867 in 1910 to 1,814 in 1920, and to 3,367 in 1930; the percentage of blacks in Homestead's total population rose from 4.6 percent to 8.8 percent between 1910 and 1920, and then to 16.2 percent in 1930. Immediately before World War I, black industrial laborers in the Pittsburgh area numbered 2,550. The wartime migration swelled their numbers to 7,897 in 1916 and to 14,610 in 1919. The number of black steelworkers in the Pittsburgh vicinity rose from 820, or 2.2 percent of the industrial work force to at least 7,000 during the peak of the war, making up 13 percent of all steel employees in the region. The postwar influx of blacks to Western Pennsylvania pushed their numbers up further—to 16,900 by 1923, or 21 percent of all industry laborers. During the 1910s and 1920s, coal mines in Western Pennsylvania drew substantial numbers of migrants to Uniontown, Westland, Washington, Canonsburg, Midland, and other towns in the region. In 1927 the importation of black strikebreakers dramatically increased the number of black coal miners in the area. Before the strike, the Pittsburgh Coal Company employed fewer than 350 blacks, or 7 percent of the work force. By 1928 the company had 3,516 black miners, who made up 38.9 percent of all its employees. Similarly, the number of black employees at the Pittsburgh Terminal Coal Company rose from 100, or 2 percent of the work force, to 962, or 42 percent of all company laborers.[8]

The task of acclimating these recent migrants to the work regimen of industry and to life in local mill and mining communities fell to black welfare workers. Beginning in 1918, employers hired these social service employees to reduce the high turnover among black laborers, to supervise community centers, and to provide migrants with a variety of social and recreational activities. The involvement of these welfare officials in black religious affairs extended the influence of their employers and symbolized the importance industrialists attached to black churches. Cyrus T. Greene, the black welfare worker at the Westinghouse Electric and Manufacturing Company in East Pittsburgh, enthusiastically endorsed black churches. He boasted that black Westinghouse employees helped to raise $75,000 in a 1920 fund drive for one of the local congregations. He noted that their contributions "were as large, if not larger, than a majority of the members," and that in one church black Westinghouse workers comprised the majority of the deacon board.[9]

Black welfare workers developed close ties with black pastors and their congregations. Because they carefully cultivated close relationships with black preachers and black churches, industrialists were certain to have a positive public image within this important segment of the black population. Macon Lennon of the Duquesne steel works encouraged the Workingmen's Bible class in 1920 by allowing the pastor of Fourth Street Baptist Church in Rankin to preach at a company-run boardinghouse. One of his successors, Charles Broadfield, belonged to Payne Chapel AME Church, where in later years he served as a trustee and choir director. When the congregation outgrew its building in the 1920s, Broadfield offered the mill's community center to the Reverend P. A. Rose for use during the summer. Like Broadfield, George Foster Jones of the Clairton steel works served First AME Church as its choir director. In 1921 he organized a "colored community chorus" which benefited from the support of First AME Church and Mount Olive Baptist Church. Jones also brought black preachers to the mill's community room to speak to black workers each Sunday. At least twice he invited the Reverend C. Y. Trigg, pastor of Warren Methodist Episcopal Church in Pittsburgh, who in 1920 participated in a conference on blacks in northern industry.

Grover Nelson of the Homestead steel works was similarly involved in black religious affairs. Like his colleague Jones in Clairton, Nelson had an interest in music. In 1921, Jerusalem Baptist Church in Duquesne invited him to play his saxophone at a special musical program. Nelson became acquainted with the Reverend J. A. Terry Sr., pastor of Homestead's newly founded Blackwell AME Zion Church. In 1925, when the denomination's Allegheny Annual Conference convened at Terry's church, Nelson came to the gathering to represent his employers. He also belonged to Rodman Street Baptist Church in Pittsburgh, and during the 1920s he decided to enter the ministry. Homestead steel officials adjusted his schedule to allow him to attend the Western Theological Seminary in Pittsburgh. After briefly serving at a church established for black workers by the Pittsburgh Plate Glass Company in Ford City, Nelson agreed to become the pastor of another congregation formed in Homestead in 1930. In subsequent years, while still employed at the Homestead steel works, Nelson pastored Mount Olive Baptist Church in Rankin and Victory Baptist Church in Pittsburgh. In 1937 he served as supervisor of the Western District of the Pennsylvania Baptist Convention.[10]

Industry officials supplemented the efforts of black welfare workers by extending direct encouragement and financial assistance to area black churches. Samuel G. Worton, assistant superintendent of the Duquesne steel works, spoke at Jerusalem Baptist Church in 1919 during a cornerstone-laying ceremony. He commended the Reverend John M. Clay for undertaking this major project, and he praised his black employees for belonging to Jerusalem Church and helping the pastor to acquire a new edifice. In the early 1920s, Clark Memorial Baptist Church in Homestead erected a new building at a cost exceeding $100,000. In less than three years, the congregation raised about $90,000 to pay on its debt. In 1924, during a mortgage liquidation drive, the Carnegie Steel Company offered the church a $5,000 contribution if the congregation agreed to raise a comparable sum to match it. In the late 1920s officials at the Aliquippa Works of Jones & Laughlin Steel gave an annual gift of $150 to each of the town's black congregations. They included Bethel Baptist Church, Tried Stone Baptist Church, Jones Chapel Methodist Episcopal Church, Emmanuel AME Zion Church, and the Church of God in Christ. In 1928, Wright Chapel AME Zion Church in Washington benefited from a "financial campaign" that local white businessmen conducted for the congregation. On other occasions, industry officials in Western Pennsylvania preferred to help black churches by allowing them to worship on company-owned property. In 1917 in Johnstown, the Reverend J. H. Flagg organized Bethel AME Church, and the Reverend W. Sloan started Mount Sinai Baptist Church. Since the Cambria Steel Company owned a building previously occupied by a white congregation, local mill managers permitted the two black groups to share the building. The same year, black migrants from Clayton, Alabama, organized Shiloh Baptist Church. Cambria Steel responded by donating another company-owned structure for Shiloh to use. In the early 1920s, the Lockhart Iron and Steel Company in McKees Rocks sponsored a Baptist church for black employees and allowed them to use a chapel located in a company-owned recreation center. Similarly, in 1931, a coal firm in the mining town of Brownsville allowed a Colored Methodist Episcopal congregation to worship in one of its buildings.[11]

Black ministers and denominational leaders recognized that increased employment prospects for blacks in the Pittsburgh vicinity meant greater opportunities to found new congregations and add to the membership of existing churches. The Colored Methodist Episcopal (CME) Church, a southern-based denomination, had no congregations in Western Pennsylvania before the World War I black migration. At the 1916 session of the Washington–Philadelphia Annual Conference, Bishop Lucius H. Holsey and the delegates approved the creation of a new Pittsburgh district. Bishop Randall A. Carter, who was assigned to the Pittsburgh area, believed "that thousands of our CMEs would be coming to the city for employment." In May 1917 the denomination gave Carter $2,000 to purchase property for a new CME congregation in Pittsburgh. His episcopal colleagues also raised money in their respective districts for "the Pittsburgh work." As a result of this national support, three Colored Methodist Episcopal congregations—Carter Chapel, Cleaves Temple, and Beebe—were organized in Pittsburgh by 1926. The CME church also spread to Monessen, Donora, Ford City, Johnstown, Vandergrift, Brownsville, and Washington and to the steel town of Farrell, "where our people are coming by the hundreds."[12]

Bishop George Lincoln Blackwell of the AME Zion Church observed similar opportunities in the industrial areas of Western Pennsylvania. In 1924 he divided the Allegheny Annual Conference into two presiding elder districts and directed his subordinates to expand the denomination into several coal-mining communities. In 1927 the Reverend William A. Blackwell, presiding elder of the Pittsburgh district which included the Kiski coal region, hoped "to enter Leechburg [since] many of our people have gone there to work and will stay for some time." Also during the late 1920s, the Zion congregation in Leisenring No. 1 in Westmoreland County gained "many new members from Alabama" because of job opportunities in the town's coke-making facilities.[13]

As a result of the black migration to Western Pennsylvania, the membership of area black churches increased dramatically. Leading black congregations in Pittsburgh grew even larger because of employment opportunities in local industrial plants. Euclid Avenue AME Church reported 305 members in 1905 but grew to 1,500 in 1926. The membership of Ebenezer Baptist Church increased from 1,500 to 3,000 between 1915 and 1926. Central Baptist Church gained 544 new parishioners during 1917 and early 1918, bringing its total membership to 1,752, while John Wesley AME Zion Church attracted 1,200 new members between 1920 and 1926. The Reverend Elijah L. Madison, pastor, established a branch congregation, Wesley Center AME Zion Church, in 1927, and it grew to 2,500 members in 1948. Similar, but less dramatic increases occurred in outlying industrial communities. Jerusalem Baptist Church in the steel town of Duquesne, for example, had 40 members in 1915 but expanded to 200 members in 1919. In Homestead, site of another important steel facility, Park Place AME Church grew from 90 members in 1916 to more than 400 members in 1924.[14]

Aspiring black clergymen also settled in Western Pennsylvania during the black migration of World War I and the 1920s. Like other migrants, they came to the area primarily to find industrial jobs, but they continued their deep involvement in church affairs. Two migrants, the Reverends J. H. Flagg and Isaac S. Freeman, belonged to the AME church. Flagg, a blacksmith in Enterprise, Alabama, migrated to Johnstown in 1916 to work in the Cambria steel mills. Freeman, a migrant from Blakely, Georgia, moved to Philadelphia in 1923 and to Aliquippa in 1924, where he became an employee in the nail mill at Jones & Laughlin Steel. African Methodist Episcopal congregations existed in neither Johnstown nor Aliquippa when Flagg and Freeman moved to Western Pennsylvania. In 1917, Flagg organized Bethel AME Church in Johnstown, and during the 1920s Freeman started Ebenezer AME Church in Aliquippa. Some black migrants with ministerial aspirations chose to serve their churches as assistant pastors. William Hall, a Virginian, and William Thomas, a South Carolinian, came to Duquesne in 1921 and 1923 respectively. Each became an employee at the Carnegie steel works. Moreover, Hall served Jerusalem Baptist Church as an assistant pastor, and Thomas held the same position at Payne Chapel AME Church.[15]

Black clergymen who doubled as industrial employees, and preachers whose congregations consisted primarily of steelworkers, coal miners, and factory laborers, depended upon local industrialists for employment and for occasional philanthropy to their struggling congregations. As a result of this relationship between clergymen and industrialists, black preachers emphasized the importance of the work ethic and avoided trenchant criticism of discriminatory practices in black hiring, promotions, and job assignments.

Numerous black clergymen who pastored small congregations were not inclined to criticize their employers. Their churches had limited resources, which compelled their ministers to find jobs in local industries. In most cases these preachers served congregations in outlying mill and mining communities, where black churches tended to have fewer members than most black congregations in Pittsburgh. Theodore Roosevelt Snowden, a migrant from

Portsmouth, Virginia, and an alumnus of Lincoln University in Pennsylvania, became an employee at the Jones & Laughlin Steel plant in Aliquippa in 1933. While he worked in the blast furnace department, Snowden pastored First Missionary Baptist Church, a small congregation in Leetsdale. J. A. Terry Jr. started preaching in the Allegheny Annual Conference of the AME Zion Church in 1931. In 1939 he became the pastor of AME Zion congregations in Bedford and Walker's Mill. During the early 1940s, while serving the Braddock Park AME Zion Church in Braddock Hills, Terry secured a job at the Blaw-Knox Company in Pittsburgh. Although his bishop later assigned him to Zion congregations in the mining towns of McDonald and Blairsville, Terry continued to work as a crane man at his plant's Pittsburgh mill. African Love Hope Baptist Church and Trinity AME Church, two black congregations in Ellwood City, each had less than fifty members. In 1950 the pastors of both congregations worked for the National Tube Company, a subsidiary of the United States Steel Corporation.[16]

Black clergymen espoused the work ethic and encouraged blacks to value their jobs and obey their employers. Although these preachers were not industrial stooges, they shared similar views with employers on the importance of hard work and sobriety. In 1911 the Reverend J. E. Morris of Corey Avenue AME Church in Braddock wrote the *Pittsburgh Courier* about William Darwin, a black worker who lost his eye while laboring at the American Steel and Wire Company in Rankin. Morris congratulated Darwin for engaging "in the honest pursuits of life" rather than "loafing around some saloon or pool room (like) many of our young men." In 1923 the Reverend Henry P. Jones of Euclid Avenue AME Church in Pittsburgh eulogized W. A. Clay, a molder and boss rougher at the Carnegie steel mills since the 1890s. When "a high company official" came to pay his respects to his deceased employee, Jones praised Clay and other black workers who valued "their positions of trust." Also in 1923, the Pennsylvania Baptist Convention met in Pittsburgh and discussed the issue of "shiftlessness" among black industrial workers. Before the meeting ended, the clergymen decided to appoint "special representatives" to speak with local employers about ways to improve the attitudes of their black employees. In 1928 three black speakers, including the Reverend A. L. Walker of Moon Run, told a crowd of black miners that the Pittsburgh Coal Company had a policy of standing by its black employees. They encouraged blacks to be "upright and industrious" and to appreciate "the excellent opportunities" that the company provided.[17]

Some courageous black preachers criticized industrial employers for their discriminatory treatment of black workers and for their hostility toward organized labor. In 1928 the Reverend I. H. Hawkins, pastor of Mount Lebanon Baptist Church in Brownsville, supported his coal-mining parishioners in their efforts to improve working conditions, and he backed his son, Isaiah Hawkins, in his attempt to reform the United Mine Workers of America. When the Reverend J. A. Terry Sr. became the pastor of an AME Zion congregation in Meyersdale during the 1930s, he assisted a local union of coal miners by serving as their secretary. As trade unions gained increased support from the Roosevelt administration through the passage of Section 7a of the National Industrial Recovery Act in 1933 and later through the Wagner Act of 1935, more black clergymen endorsed the labor movement and abandoned their deferential relationship to industrial employers. Since the CIO declared its opposition to racial discrimination and promised to promote the interests of black workers, several black organizations, including the NAACP, the National Urban League, and the National Negro Congress, became allies of its affiliate unions. When the National Negro Congress and the CIO convened a conference in Pittsburgh in 1937 to discuss strategies for bringing black steelworkers into the union, they won the cooperation of the Reverend T. J. King of Ebenezer Baptist Church in Pittsburgh and Bishop William J. Walls of the Allegheny Annual Conference of the AME Zion Church. Several other black churches in Pittsburgh also supported the effort.[18]

Some steelworker-preachers played an important role in advancing unionism in the Pittsburgh vicinity. The Reverend Fletcher Williamson, a black minister and a chipper at the Duquesne steel works, for example, helped to organize a local lodge of the Amalgamated Association of Iron and Steelworkers in 1933. When the Steelworkers Organizing Committee absorbed the Amalgamated Association in 1936, Williamson preached unionism among black workers and was eventually elected an officer of Local No. 1256. During the organizing drives of the late 1930s, Williamson testified in Pittsburgh at a hearing of the National Steel Labor Relations Board. Under heated questioning by the attorney for his employer, the United States Steel Corporation, the nervous Duquesne preacher defended the steelworkers union and its efforts to unionize both black and white employees.[19]

Although other steelworker-preachers possessed firsthand knowledge of the racial problems that they and other blacks encountered in local industries, they did not publicly promote unionism in Western Pennsylvania. Charles W. Torrey, an Alabama migrant who pastored Macedonia Baptist Church in Duquesne and worked at the Edgar Thomson steel plant in Braddock, personally endorsed the CIO and became a member. Unlike Fletcher Williamson, however, Torrey gave steel unionism no public support, and he used his considerable oratorical and organizational skills exclusively in the church on religious matters. J. L. Simmons, an employee at Lockhart Iron and Steel in McKees Rocks and a Baptist pastor in Carnegie and Pittsburgh's West End, personally embraced steel unionism to free himself and others from the arbitrary will of plant bosses. However, four black organizers assumed the task of acquainting fellow black Lockhart employees with the Steelworkers Organizing Committee, while Simmons, the Georgia-born preacher, stood on the sidelines.[20]

The growth of influential labor unions in several mass production industries and the involvement of federal, state, and local fair employment practices commissions in black worker affairs, however, reduced the dependence of black clergymen and black churches on the goodwill of employers. During the 1940s, blacks in such important industries as steel, coal mining, auto making, and rubber manufacturing belonged to CIO unions. Because of this development, Horace Cayton, a black sociologist and a columnist for the *Pittsburgh Courier,* wrote in 1946 that "few Negro preachers" dared to oppose the United Steelworkers of America and other such unions since it would mean the sure loss of their congregations.[21]

The unionization of black workers allowed their ministers to speak out against industry's discriminatory treatment of black employees and facilitated the occupational advancement of several black steelworker-preachers. During World War II, the Reverend Benjamin M. McLinn of St. Paul AME Church in Washington, and a fellow black clergyman, the Reverend Rucker, made successful attempts to eliminate discriminatory hiring practices at Jessop Steel, the American Can Company, and a few other industrial plants. In 1943 they began to cooperate with the local U.S. Employment Service in making periodic reviews of the Washington labor market in order to spot employment opportunities for black workers. The Reverend Theodore Roosevelt Snowden, a Jones & Laughlin Steel employee and Baptist pastor in Leetsdale, was proud of his long affiliation with Local No. 1211 of the United Steelworkers of America. He contended, "My union has helped me and my people in the field of civil rights and in the mills where we can hold any job for which we can qualify by experience and seniority."[22]

Strong industrial unions and government involvement in black worker affairs reduced the importance of industrial philanthropy to black clergymen and black churches in Western Pennsylvania. In the past, financial contributions to struggling black congregations and gifts of property and buildings facilitated the growth of black religious institutions. Black preachers with small congregations found jobs in area industries and supplemented their meager salaries. Black denominational leaders welcomed employment opportunities in area mills, mines, and factories because they drew black migrants to the Pittsburgh vicinity and provided new members for churches in Western Pennsylvania. The unionization of black workers during the 1930s, however, loosened ties that bound the black church to big business in the Pittsburgh area. The involvement of black workers in labor organizations which challenged the power of industrial employers freed black ministers to extend their racial protests to the crucial occupational concerns of black clergymen and laymen in the mines, mills, and factories of Western Pennsylvania.

Notes

1. Paul E. Johnson, *A Shopkeeper's Millennium: Society and Revivals in Rochester, New York, 1815–1837* (New York, 1978), 116–18; Anthony F. C. Wallace, *Rockdale: The Growth of an American Village in the Early Industrial Revolution* (New York, 1978), 296–397; David Brody, *Steelworkers in America* (Cambridge, Mass., 1960), 116–17; August Meier and Elliott Rudwick, *Black Detroit and the Rise of the U.A.W.* (New York, 1979), 9–10, 17–18.

2. Ann G. Wilmoth, "Toward Freedom: Pittsburgh Blacks, 1800–1870," *Pennsylvania Heritage* 4 (December 1977): 15; U.S. Census Bureau, *Thirteenth Census of the United States, 1910: Population,* 1:212; U.S. Census Bureau, *Negro Population in the United States, 1790–1915,* 102–3.

3. U.S. Census Bureau, *Thirteenth Census of the United States, 1910: Population, Occupation Statistics,* 4:590–91; Richard R. Wright Jr., *The Negro in Pennsylvania: A Study in Economic History* (Philadelphia, 1912), 222–32. See also microfilm rolls of the 1900 census for such towns as Duquesne, McKeesport, Connellsville, Homestead, and Braddock.

4. J. Ernest Wright, "The Negro in Pittsburgh," WPA Survey, American Guide Services, Ethnic Survey, 1940, unpublished manuscript in the State Archives, Pennsylvania Historical and Museum Commission, Harrisburg, Pennsylvania, 3–5, 8–9; "A Brief Historical Statement Concerning Grace Memorial Presbyterian Church, Pittsburgh, Pa.," Afro-American Council Program, 1959, manuscript, Presbyterian Historical Society, Philadelphia; souvenir program, *29th Anniversary of Bidwell Street Presbyterian Church, Pittsburgh, Pa.,* October 24–November 1, 1943 (courtesy of the late Dr. Samuel G. Stevens, Lincoln University, Pennsylvania); Bethesda UP Church, *Golden Anniversary, 1917–1967, and Silver Ordination Anniversary of Rev. Leroy Patrick, 1942–1967,* manuscript, Presbyterian Historical Society; *New York Age,* September 30, 1909; January 20, 1910; *Holy Cross Episcopal Church Bulletin,* Pittsburgh, Pa. (n.d.) (courtesy of Wendell L. Wray, University of Pittsburgh); *Pittsburgh Courier,* January 27, 1912; Randall K. Burkett, *Black Redemption: Churchmen Speak for the Garvey Movement* (Philadelphia, 1978), 114.

5. Wallace G. Smeltzer, *Homestead Methodism, 1830–1933* (Pittsburgh, 1933), 154, 157 (Carnegie Free Library, Munhall, Pennsylvania); *98th Annual Session, Pittsburgh Annual Conference of the African Methodist Episcopal Church,* September 21–26, 1965; Park Place AME Church, Homestead, Pennsylvania, *Souvenir Program Booklet* (courtesy of Mr. and Mrs. Louis Wheeler, West Mifflin, Pennsylvania); *Minutes of the 38th Session of the Pittsburgh Annual Conference of the AME Church, meeting in Bethel AME Church, Wilkes-Barre, Pennsylvania* (1905), 313–14, 339–40 (courtesy of Dr. Edna McKenzie, Allegheny County Community College, Pittsburgh); Edward Maurey, *Where the West Began: A Story of Coraopolis and the Ohio Valley* (1930), Archives of Industrial Society, University of Pittsburgh, Pittsburgh, Pennsylvania.

6. *Duquesne Times,* May 1, 1952; *Pittsburgh Courier,* September 18, 1926; March 17, 1928.

7. "Heritage: A Black History of Johnstown," *Tribune-Democrat,* February 12, 1980, 3; Florence M. Hornback, *Survey of the Negro Population of Metropolitan Johnstown, Pennsylvania* (1941), 15, University of Pittsburgh Libraries, Pittsburgh, Pennsylvania.

8. The author discusses these black population and employment increases in his "Black Steelworkers in Western Pennsylvania, 1915–1950" (Ph.D. diss., Washington University, 1978), 18–22, 25–27, 32–33. See also *Pittsburgh Courier,* October 24, 1925, and Leonard Allen, interviewed by Dennis C. Dickerson, Westland, Pennsylvania, September 9, 1975. Readers will also benefit from the following articles, which explore the issues of black migration to Pittsburgh: Peter Gottlieb, "Migration and Jobs: The New Black Workers in Pittsburgh, 1916–1930," *Western Pennsylvania Historical Magazine* 61 (January 1978): 1–15; and John Bodnar, Michael Weber, and Roger Simon, "Migration, Kinship, and Urban Adjustment: Blacks and Poles in Pittsburgh, 1900–1930," *Journal of American History* 66 (December 1979): 548–65.

9. Cyrus T. Greene, "The Negro Workman at the Westinghouse," *Competitor,* October–November 1920, 181.

10. *Duquesne Times,* July 20, 1920, April 8, 1921; *Homestead Messenger,* July 8, 1925; *Clairton Tattler,* March 18, 1921, April 22, 1921, January 13, 1922; *Pittsburgh Courier,* August 21, 1937; "Industrial Conference Meets," *Competitor,* March 1920, 75; Mrs. Mattie Christian, interviewed by Dennis C. Dickerson, Duquesne, Pennsylvania, April 22, 1975; Mrs. Colesta Long, interviewed by Dennis C. Dickerson, Philadelphia, March 27, 1979; Paul L. Payne, interviewed by Dennis C. Dickerson, Clairton, Pennsylvania, March 15, 1975; the Reverend J. A. Terry Jr., interviewed by Dennis C. Dickerson, Pittsburgh, March 3, 1980; Mrs. Irma Baskerville, interviewed by Dennis C. Dickerson, Pittsburgh, March 4, 1980.

11. *Duquesne Times,* August 8, 1919; *Pittsburgh Courier,* August 23, 1924; *The Star of Zion,* July 26, 1928; *The Christian Index,* June 11, 1931; Bartow Tipper, interviewed by Dennis C. Dickerson, Aliquippa, Pennsylvania, March 4, 1980; Hornback, *Survey of the Negro Population,* 190–91; "Heritage," *Tribune-Democrat,* February 2, 1980, 7; "Golden Anniversary Souvenir Booklet of Shiloh Baptist Church, 1917–1967, Johnstown Pa.," Pennsylvania Historical and Museum Commission, Harrisburg, Pennsylvania; William P. Young, "The First Hundred Negro Workers," *Opportunity,* January 1924, 18; "National Association of Corporation Training, Pittsburgh Chapter, Minutes of Meeting, Unskilled Labor and Americanization Section, Feb. 2, 1922," 4, Industrial Relations Department, Affiliates File, Box 34, Series 4, Records of the National Urban League, Library of Congress, Manuscript Division, Washington, D.C.

12. *The Christian Index,* July 20, 1916; January 31, 1918; February 28, 1918; May 3, 1923; November 8, 1923; July 14, 1927; June 11, 1931; U.S. Census Bureau, *Religious Bodies: Summary and Detailed Tables* 1 (1926): 511; *Yearbook of the 21st Session of the Ohio Annual Conference, CME Church, 1954,* 25, 35, 51.

13. William J. Walls, *The African Methodist Episcopal Zion Church: Reality of the Black Church* (Charlotte, N.C., 1974), 262; *The Star of Zion,* February 18, 1926; March 24, 1927.

14. Pennsylvania Department of Welfare, *Negro Survey of Pennsylvania* (Harrisburg, 1927), 63; *Minutes of the 38th Session of the Pittsburgh Annual Conference of the AME Church, 1905;* Burkett, *Black Redemption,* 114; *The Crisis,* April 1918; *Pittsburgh Courier,* October 9, 1926; April 30, 1927; Walls, *African Methodist Episcopal Zion Church,* 602; *Duquesne Times,* April 25, 1919; *Homestead Messenger,* November 1, 1924.

15. "Heritage," *Tribune-Democrat,* February 12, 1980, 4; *AME Christian Recorder,* December 25, 1978; Tipper interview; *Duquesne Times,* September 12, 1941; October 16, 1956.

16. *Steel Labor,* December 1960; Terry interview; Charles R. Walker, *Steeltown* (New York, 1950), 225–74.

17. *Pittsburgh Courier,* March 25, 1911; January 20, 1923; October 27, 1923; September 15, 1928.

18. *Pittsburgh Courier,* May 12, 1928; Terry interview; Wright, "The Negro in Pittsburgh," 19–20; Lawrence S. Wittner, "The National Negro Congress: A Reassessment," *American Quarterly* 22 (Winter 1970): 893.

19. George Powers, *Cradle of Steel Unionism: Monongahela Valley, Pa.* (East Chicago, Ind., 1972), 42; *Pittsburgh Courier,* June 4, 1960. Roger Payne and Carl O. Dickerson, interviewed by Dennis C. Dickerson, Philadelphia, April 13, 1976.

20. The Reverend Charles W. Torrey, interviewed by Dennis C. Dickerson, Duquesne, Pennsylvania, 1975; the Reverend J. L. Simmons, interviewed by Peter Gottlieb, Pittsburgh, June 13, 1974, Pittsburgh Oral History Project, Pennsylvania Historical and Museum Commission, Harrisburg.

21. *Pittsburgh Courier,* February 16, 1946. For a discussion of these issues of black involvement in industrial unions and federal involvement in black workers' affairs see my dissertation "Black Steelworkers in Western Pennsylvania, 1915–1950," chaps. 5 and 6.

22. Milo A. Manly to G. James Fleming, November 15, 1944, Records of the FEPC, Region 3, R G. 288, Box 610, National Archives, Washington, D.C.; G. James Fleming to Will Maslow, October 30, 1944, ibid.; "Rev. Benjamin M. McLinn," in Richard R. Wright Jr., ed., *Encyclopedia of African Methodism* (Philadelphia, 1947), 191–92; *Steel Labor,* December 1960.

PART FOUR

THE TRANSFORMATION OF THE BLACK COMMUNITY

Toward the Postindustrial Era, 1945–1985

The national crusade for civil rights reached its peak during the 1960s. In Pennsylvania, the Girard College protest mobilized the Philadelphia black community. Eventually the U.S. Supreme Court ruled that Girard College must admit blacks. Here Philadelphia NAACP President Cecil B. Moore is seen addressing a protest rally at Girard College. (Photo by Jack T. Franklin; courtesy of Jack T. Franklin and the Afro-American Historical and Cultural Museum, Philadelphia)

The African American experience in Pennsylvania during the postindustrial era has been one of stark changes anchored in the industrial decline of the state since 1945. Industries that once had attracted southern black migrants to Pennsylvania, such as steel, curtailed production in response to foreign competition or closed plants altogether. The postwar shift of service and high-technology jobs from the central city to the suburbs, and racial tension during the civil rights era, were some of the factors that transformed the African American community. In some areas the demographic change was dramatic. The Homewood-Brushton district of Pittsburgh went from 22 percent black in 1950 to 62 percent in 1960. Similar demographic changes occurred in Philadelphia, Harrisburg, Erie, Reading, and Williamsport.

Unfortunately, under the impact of these new demographic and economic changes, once-vibrant centers of black life, such as Wylie Avenue in Pittsburgh and North Broad Street in Philadelphia, experienced urban decline. As Pennsylvania moved into the 1970s, the term "black underclass" was used frequently to describe the "have-nots" in economically depressed communities across the state. There is a significant gap in income not only between whites and blacks but also between African American men and women. Clearly, the postindustrial era, which continues to unfold, poses a tremendous challenge to those dedicated to revitalizing Pennsylvania's communities.

The postindustrial era is a period that historians have only begun to research. Here we have chapters that suggest the persistence of old patterns of class and race relations, as well as the emergence of new ones: Laurence Glasco on black Pittsburgh; John Bauman, Norman P. Hummon, and Edward K. Muller on urban poverty and public housing in Philadelphia; and Elijah Anderson's ethnographic perspective on contemporary urban life.

CHAPTER SEVENTEEN

Double Burden:
The Black Experience in Pittsburgh

Laurence Glasco

Scholarly studies of black Pittsburgh are numerous but uneven in their coverage. In the 1930s the Works Progress Administration (WPA) assembled a rich body of material on the social life, politics, and even folklore of the city's blacks. But the projected general history was never completed, and its unedited pages until recently lay forgotten in the state archives.[1] The gap left by the lack of a general history, moreover, is not filled by specialized studies because these are uneven in their coverage. The nineteenth century, for example, has been especially neglected: the scholarly literature on that period consists of one article, one dissertation, and one undergraduate thesis, all of which focus on the antislavery movement of the Civil War era.

The twentieth century, in contrast, has received considerable attention, and the period between World War I and World War II has been especially well covered. More than 100 specialized studies—including 56 master's theses and dissertations—describe the adjustment problems of black migrants and the emergence of the Hill district as a predominantly black ghetto. The years following World War II also have interested scholars; more than 50 studies—

This chapter was previously published in *City at the Point: Essays on the Social History of Pittsburgh,* ed. Samuel P. Hays. Copyright © 1989 by the University of Pittsburgh Press. Reprinted by permission of the University of Pittsburgh Press.

primarily doctoral dissertations—examine the racial dimensions of poverty, segregation, and government efforts to alleviate those conditions. Finally, black Pittsburgh from approximately 1930 to 1980 has been visually well documented in the collection of Teenie Harris, a photographer for the *Pittsburgh Courier* whose 50,000 to 100,000 photographs rival those of New York's Vander Zee collection in portraying the texture of black urban life.[2] At least for the twentieth century, then, the scholarly sources on black Pittsburgh are quite extensive—more so than for any of the city's other ethnic groups—and are sufficient to highlight the broad contours of black history in Pittsburgh.

Taken together, the historical material indicates that, in addition to suffering the same racial discrimination as their counterparts elsewhere, blacks in Pittsburgh have borne two additional burdens. The first was economic. The stagnation and decline of Pittsburgh's steel industry began just after World War I—well before that of most northern cities—and very early closed off opportunities for black economic progress. The second burden was geographic. Whereas the flat terrain of most northern cities concentrated blacks into one or two large, homogeneous communities, Pittsburgh's hilly topography isolated them in six or seven neighborhoods, undermining their political and organizational strength.

The record also shows that, despite these two extra burdens, black Pittsburghers accomplished much. They created a distinguished newspaper, owned two outstanding baseball teams, maintained a lively cultural life, and nurtured musicians and writers of national prominence. However, economically and politically, the community stagnated. It was unable to develop a stable working class, its middle class remained small, and its geographic fragmentation into several neighborhoods severely diluted its political and institutional strength. As a result, by the 1980s Pittsburgh blacks lagged behind their counterparts in most other cities in terms of economic and political development.

The Black Community Before World War I

The burdens of economic and racial discrimination can be traced to the earliest years of black settlement. Before the Civil War, Pittsburgh's black community was typical of those found in most northern cities—small, impoverished, and victimized by racial discrimination. Although blacks arrived with the very earliest colonial settlers—as trappers, pioneers, soldiers, and slaves—the population grew slowly. In 1850 they comprised only 2,000 people, less than 5 percent of the city's population, and were centered in "Little Hayti," an area just off Wylie Avenue in the lower Hill district where housing was cheap and close to downtown.

The black community was poor because racial discrimination excluded its men from the industrial and commercial mainstream of the city's economy. Barbering was the most prestigious occupation open to blacks, and they operated most of the downtown barberships that catered to the city's elite. (To cut the hair of other blacks would have cost them their white customers.) Most, however, could find work only as day laborers, whitewashers, janitors, porters, coachmen, waiters, and stewards. The men's low earnings forced their wives to seek work outside the home, typically in low-paying and demeaning jobs as servants, domestics, and washerwomen.[3]

Despite their exclusion from the city's industry and commerce, some blacks prospered. As early as 1800 Ben Richards, a black butcher, had accumulated a fortune by provisioning nearby military posts. At mid-century John B. Vashon operated a barbershop and a fashionable bath house, while John Peck was a wigmaker and barber. Most members of the black elite, however, were men of modest holdings: by 1860 Richards's fortune had been dissipated and the manuscript census listed only twelve blacks—three barbers, three stewards, a musician, a porter, a waiter, a pattern finisher, a grocer, and a "banker"—with property worth $2,000 or more.[4]

Pittsburgh's pre–Civil War black community supported a remarkable number of institutions. These included an AME (African Methodist Episcopal) church, an AME Zion church, four benevolent societies, a private school, a cemetery, a militia company, a newspaper, and a temperance society. The community also contained an impressive set of leaders, such as Vashon, Peck, and Lewis Woodson, all barbers and all active in civic affairs. The best-known leader was Martin R. Delany who, after publishing *The Mystery,* a newspaper in Pittsburgh, co-edited *The North Star,* Frederick Douglass's paper, and authored an important nationalist tract: *The Condition, Elevation, Emigration, and Destiny of the Colored People of the United States.* The race pride of Delany is indicated in a comment by Frederick Douglass that he thanked God for simply making him a man, "but Delany always thanks him for making him a black man."[5]

The community and its leaders placed great emphasis on education. They maintained their own school—the existence of which had originally attracted Delany to Pittsburgh—and avidly pursued higher education. Delany went on to become one of the first blacks to study medicine at Harvard University; Vashon's son became the first black to graduate from Oberlin College; Peck's son became one of the nation's first blacks to obtain a medical degree; and Lewis Woodson, in addition to his duties as barber and minister, taught in the community's own school.

The community stressed both cultural attainments and gentility. The accomplishments of two of its children reflect those emphases. Henry O. Tanner became an award-winning painter based in Paris, and Hallie Q. Brown became a leading elocutionist who performed throughout the United States and Europe.

Culture and gentility also became social stratifiers, often in combination with pride in place of origin. A. B. Hall, a nineteenth-century resident, recalled that the pre–Civil War community was dominated by an aristocracy of genteel families and cliques: "The Virginians, District of Columbia and Maryland folk, consorted together; the North Carolina people, thought themselves made in a special mould; those from Kentucky, just knew they were what the doctor ordered; while the free Negroes, who drifted in from Ohio and New York, didn't take a back seat for anybody."[6]

Despite their stress on culture, gentility, and education, black Pittsburghers faced daily indignities and threats to their personal and civil rights. They were excluded from, or confined to separate sections of, the city's theaters, restaurants, and hotels. Occasionally they were attacked by white mobs, although they were spared the major riots that convulsed black communities in New York, Philadelphia, and Cincinnati.

They also faced continual efforts to deny them an education. Protests by Harvard students forced Delany to leave that institution before getting his M.D. degree. Fear of student protests at the University of Pittsburgh (then the Western University of Pennsylvania) prompted professors to ask John C. Gilmer, the school's first black student, to sit in the hallway outside the lecture room.[7] And in 1834 Pittsburgh excluded black children entirely from the city's new public school system, to which blacks responded by establishing their own school and vigorously protesting their exclusion from the public system. Three years later the city provided blacks with a segregated school system on Miller Street, but its wretched condition disappointed and angered black residents.

In addition to being deprived of an equal education, blacks were denied even basic rights of citizenship. In 1837 Pennsylvania disfranchised its black residents, causing enraged black communities throughout the state to hold numerous protest meetings and rallies. Even more trauma was in store when, in 1850, the federal government passed the Fugitive Slave Act. This act, which was designed to help slave catchers apprehend runaway slaves, was the most terrifying law passed in the pre–Civil War era. It made lawbreakers of Pittsburghers—black and white—who had been working to help runaway slaves, and facilitated the recapture of Pittsburgh blacks who themselves were runaway slaves. The act terrified so many that during the 1850s the city's black population dropped from 1,974 to 1,149. Those who did not flee were galvanized into action, establishing an elaborate network of spies, harassing slave catchers, and even kidnapping slaves passing through the city with their owners. The pessimism of that decade caused Martin Delany to give up hope in America and urged blacks to emigrate. Delany himself traveled to Nigeria and negotiated with Yoruba chiefs for a settlement near Abeokuta, whence his later reputation as the "Father of Black Nationalism."[8]

In resisting slavery and racial discrimination, Pittsburgh's blacks were not without white supporters. In the 1850s the city had several antislavery societies which worked to frustrate the fugitive slave law. Two local physicians who were abolitionists as well as supporters of black progress, Joseph Gazzam and Julius LeMoyne, trained Martin Delany and sponsored his entry into Harvard Medical School; another wealthy abolitionist, Charles Avery, acknowledged the social and biological equality of blacks—something rarely done even by the most ardent abolitionists. In 1849 he established the all-black Allegheny Institute (later Avery College) for their education.[9]

Following the Civil War, legislation designed to ensure the rights of southern freedmen helped northern blacks—including those in Pittsburgh—to secure their own civil rights. Thus the Fifteenth Amendment to the Constitution, ratified in 1870 to secure the black vote in the South, forced Pennsylvania finally to grant the vote to all its male citizens.[10]

The fight for a desegregated school system also was won during the postbellum years. Blacks continued to protest their inferior school system until, in 1875, enrollment in the Miller Street School was so low that the Board of Education abolished it and desegregated the entire system. From that point on, Pittsburgh was one of the few large cities with a desegregated system. The victory, however, was bittersweet: cities with segregated systems provided jobs for the black teachers, but because it was unacceptable for whites to study under a black, black teachers were not employed in Pittsburgh.[11]

Despite gains in education and voting rights, most other forms of racial restriction persisted throughout the post–Civil War era. In 1872 the Democratic *Pittsburgh Post* lampooned Republican hypocrisy in posing as friends of Negroes when blacks in Republican Allegheny County "could not be admitted to the orchestra, dress or family circle of the opera house, could not purchase a sleeping berth on any of the railroads that leave the city, could not take dinner at the Monongahela House, Hare's Hotel, or any A No. 1 restaurant," and could not even enter the Lincoln Club "except as a waiter."[12]

The *Post* failed to mention something even more serious: blacks could not find work—except as temporary strikebreakers—in the region's mines, mills, factories, and offices. By the turn of the century, Pittsburgh was the nation's sixth largest city, annually attracting thousands of European immigrants to its busy industries, while still confining blacks to jobs that white workers, including immigrants, did not want. As a consequence, most blacks still worked as teamsters, refuse collectors, janitors, and laundresses, while the "lucky" worked as waiters, barbers, railroad porters, butlers, maids, coachmen, and gardeners.[13]

Although we know relatively little about the black community between 1875 and World War I, there are several indications that this was an important period in its development. First, it was a period of rapid growth. Between 1870 and 1900 the rate of population growth for black Pittsburgh was greater than during any other period, increasing from 1,162 to 20,355, and making the Pittsburgh black community the sixth largest in the nation.[14]

During this period blacks made notable economic strides. Although the great majority worked as maids, laundresses, coachmen, and janitors, a surprising number operated successful businesses. In 1909 an investigator counted eighty-five black-run businesses, including owners of pool rooms and print shops, plasterers, cement finishers, pharmacists, paper hangers, and haulers—even a savings and loan. Some businesses were quite large, such as the Diamond Coke & Coal Company of Homestead, with 1,000 employees, and two contractors employed more than 100 men each. In addition, a caterer (Spriggs and Writt) and a wigmaker (Proctor) served a predominantly white clientele, as did several grocers, restaurant owners, and barbers.[15]

By the end of the nineteenth century, Pittsburgh blacks had developed a set of social distinctions more elaborate than those at mid-century. According to a contemporary observer, social lines hardened after the Civil War as longer-term residents and property owners held themselves aloof from southern migrants, cultivated genteel manners, and "accepted into their 'social set' only those who could point to parents and grandparents and say they were 'old families' with 'character.' "[16]

By 1900 black Pittsburghers supported an impressive range of clubs dedicated to social, cultural, and community uplift. The most prestigious— Loendi, Aurora Reading Club, Goldenrod Social Club, and White Rose Club—emphasized social and cultural activities. Blacks were excluded from white fraternal lodges, but established all-black chapters of their own, many of which, such as the Elks, Masons, Odd Fellows, Knights of Pythias, and True Reformers, emphasized community improvement. They erected a Home for the Aged and Infirm Colored Women, a Working Girls' Home, and a Colored Orphans' Home. Churches which catered to the district elite— Ebenezer Baptist, Grace Memorial Presbyterian, Bethel AME, Warren ME, and St. Benedict the Moor Roman Catholic—also were active in community activities, while more than twenty-five women's clubs devoted themselves to both charitable activities and social affairs.[17]

A number of groups—including the Aurora Reading Club, the Frances Harper League, the Wylie Avenue Literary Society, the Homewood Social and Literary Club, the Emma J. Moore Literary and Art Circle, and the Booker T. Washington Literary Society—promoted the cultural life of the community through reading and discussing literature. In addition, the prestigious Loendi Club, established in 1897, invited outstanding speakers to address their members and the black community. Community interest in classical music was reflected in the creation of three black concert and symphony orchestras, one by William A. Kelly, a coal miner and graduate of Oberlin, a second by Dr. C. A. Taylor, who had played in the Toronto Civic Orchestra, and a third by David Peeler, a local contractor and builder.[18]

In sum, against all odds and in ways not yet understood, the black community before World War I managed to grow substantially and to develop an impressive set of social, economic, and cultural institutions. This promising foundation, combined with the breakthrough of blacks into the city's mills and factories during World War I, should have led to a flowering of black society. As we will see, the breakthrough did energize and transform the community's social and cultural life, but economically and politically its full promise was not realized.

Between the Wars:
Migration Amid Economic Stagnation

World War I stands as a watershed in black history, both nationally and locally. Economic expansion and the war-related cutoff of European immigration forced northern industries to open up factory jobs for the first time to black Americans. This touched off a migratory wave from the South that, between 1910 and 1930, increased the northern black population by more than 500,000. Newly opened jobs at places like Jones & Laughlin Steel enlarged Pittsburgh's black population from 25,000 to 55,000, while hiring by Carnegie Steel plants in Aliquippa, Homestead, Rankin, Braddock, Duquesne, McKeesport, and Clairton raised the black population in those neighboring towns from 5,000 to 23,000.[19]

The migrants gave the community a new energy and creativity that quickly attracted attention. Wylie Avenue, Centre Avenue, and side streets in the Hill district "jumped" as blacks and whites flocked to its bars and night spots.

Wylie Avenue, seen in the 1940s, was the major artery of Pittsburgh's Hill District, which boasted of black Pittsburgh's businesses and entertainment establishments. On the left is the first Crawford Grill. It opened in 1931 and quickly attracted an interracial crowd that came to hear black musicians like Walt Harper, Billy Eckstein, and Johnny Mathis. It closed in 1952, after a fire. (Courtesy of the Historical Society of Western Pennsylvania)

The Collins Inn, the Humming Bird, the Leader House, upstairs over the Crawford Grill, as well as Derby Dan's, the Harlem Bar, the Musician's Club, the Sawdust Trail, the Ritz, the Fullerton Inn, the Paradise Inn, and the Bailey Hotel attracted some of the nation's finest jazz musicians. Marie's and Lola's, small and stuffy clubs, provided spots for late night jam sessions and helped make Pittsburgh a center for nurturing internationally known musicians. Jazz notables born, reared, or nurtured in the Pittsburgh area between the wars include Lena Horne, Billy Strayhorn, Kenny Clarke, Art Blakey, Earl "Fatha" Hines, Roy Eldridge, and Leroy Brown, in addition to such notable female musicians as Mary Lou Williams, Louise Mann, and Maxine Sullivan. As the district's fame spread nationwide, Claude McKay, leading poet of the Harlem Renaissance, labeled the intersection of Wylie and Fullerton Avenues—in the heart of the Hill—"Crossroads of the World."[20]

In addition to energizing the social and musical scene of Pittsburgh, the migrants helped create a wide range of neighborhood sports—baseball, basketball, and football—which have been beautifully described in *Sandlot Seasons* by Rob Ruck. The most famous of such teams, the Pittsburgh Crawfords, emerged from integrated neighborhood clubs in the Hill district. Organized originally for pick-up games by Bill and Teenie Harris, they later were bankrolled by Gus Greenlee, black numbers czar and owner of the Crawford Grill. The 1936 Crawfords boasted five eventual Hall of Famers—Satchel Paige, Josh Gibson, "Cool Papa" Bell, Oscar Charleston, and Judy Johnson—and, according to Ruck, were "possibly the best baseball team [white or black] ever assembled for regular season play." The Homestead Grays, financed by "Cum" Posey, son of a prominent black businessman, was also filled with premiere players. Organized around the turn of the century as an amateur sporting outlet for black steelworkers, by the 1930s the Grays were tough competitors of the Crawfords and, after Greenlee resurrected the Negro National League, helped make Pittsburgh the national center of black baseball.[21]

The Burden of Economic Stagnation

Signs of vitality in music and sports, however, masked serious economic problems. Black migrants entered the industrial work force at the bottom and had almost no success in moving up. Abraham Epstein's 1918 study, "The Negro Migrant in Pittsburgh," found that 95 percent of black industrial workers were in unskilled positions, and investigations five years later by two black graduate students, Abram Harris and Ira Reid, found blacks still mired at the bottom of the job ladder and experiencing difficulty holding on to even those lowly jobs. In 1923, for example, some 17,224 blacks were employed in seven major industries in the Pittsburgh area, but in 1924 recession reduced their number to just 7,636. Moreover, the building trades offered no escape; blacks were excluded entirely from more than half the trades, and the few to which they belonged confined them to positions as hod carriers and common laborers and insisted that they be paid less than union scale. A situation that was bleak during the 1920s turned disastrous during the Great Depression, when 33 to 40 percent of black adults were unemployed. A study of 2,700 black families found 41 percent destitute and another one-third living in poverty.[22]

Black economic problems were caused by more than white prejudice. Blacks had entered the city just as its heavy industry had stopped growing. Two economists writing in the 1930s noted that the expansion of Pittsburgh's iron and steel industry "began to slow up" as early as 1900, and "by 1910 the era of rapid population and growth was completed." Moreover, as John Bodnar, Roger Simon, and Michael P. Weber show, the steel industry was eliminating common laborers. Unskilled workers declined from 32 to 22 percent of the work force between 1900 and 1930. As a result, blacks and other unskilled workers found "increasing competition for work at the lowest levels of the occupational scale."[23]

Many white workers responded to the retrenchment in steel by leaving the city. During the 1920s the city's white population grew by only 12 percent, and it declined absolutely from 1930 to the 1980s. Blacks, with fewer options, elsewhere, saw their population grow by 46 percent during the 1920s and increase in each subsequent decade. Although their numbers continued to grow, the stagnant job situation prevented blacks from establishing occupational beach-heads, which had been important to white ethnics in finding employment and job mobility. Thus, even without racial discrimination—which certainly was pervasive—black migrants would have been more likely to be laid off in an economic downturn and to suffer greater occupational instability than their immigrant predecessors.[24]

As a result, work conditions for blacks remained deplorable, with few opportunities to escape into better jobs in the mines and mills. Former workers, when interviewed by Dennis Dickerson, told how they had been brought in by the trainload, housed in hastily constructed dormitories, confined to the hottest, dirtiest, and most physically demanding jobs, paid inadequate wages, harassed by prejudiced foremen and police, and excluded from most public accommodations. They became sick from the acid fumes, fainted from the intense heat, caught pneumonia in the drafty housing, and suffered accidents at a much higher rate than white workers. They were seldom promoted: some even trained white workers, only to suffer the humiliation of seeing the latter promoted over them. Alienated by the prejudice and harassment of white steel workers, they refused to join the strike of 1919, which embittered whites but persuaded mill owners to see blacks as a valuable and permanent part of the labor force.[25]

Racism also pervaded the region's coal fields. The United Mine Workers of America (UMWA), led by John L. Lewis, systematically restricted the entry of black miners and made sure that the few who did work were assigned only jobs that whites did not want. In 1925 this practice enabled the Mellons to destroy the union at its Pittsburgh Coal Company by creating a labor force that was half black and assigning blacks to all jobs in the mines, including those formerly reserved for whites. The benefits proved elusive, however, and blacks were quickly disillusioned. With the union broken, pay was cut drastically, the number of hours increased, mine safety deteriorated, and the mine police became more vicious than ever.[26]

That blacks were not hostile to union activity per se is indicated by their enthusiastic response to nonracist unions. They shunned the UMW, but were attracted to the Communist-led National Miners' Union (NMU), which backed up its commitment to interracial unionism by electing a black, William Boyce, as vice-president. During the Depression of the 1930s, however, things deteriorated for black miners, as the NMU was replaced by the UMWA, now somewhat less racist, but still an organization in which blacks had to fight for fair treatment.[27]

Racism and economic stagnation in coal and steel were not the only factors complicating the economic adjustment of migrants. Peter Gottlieb, in his *Making their Own Way: Southern Blacks' Migration to Pittsburgh* (1987), argues that their unfortunate work experience was also caused by their attitudes toward industrial labor. Using records of the Byers specialty steel company, supplemented by interviews with ex-steelworkers (not from the Byers company), Gottlieb found a conundrum: most migrants had already experienced some industrial work in the South, and their work performance was rated "good" by two-thirds of the Byers foremen—but they had an astronomical turnover rate. To maintain 223 black workers in 1923, the company had to make 1,408 separate hires! Gottlieb believes that migrants still regarded industrial labor in the same way they had regarded it in the South: as temporary work to be done between planting and harvesting season. Consequently, many approached the Pittsburgh mills looking for temporary work; once they had made some money they were prepared to return home. Others quit their jobs in the mill in order to return home for a visit, but planned to return later and find another job. Finally, most were prepared to quit should the work prove unsatisfactory—which often it did.[28]

Consequences of Economic Stagnation

The effects of economic stagnation and racial discrimination were visible in the deplorable living conditions of the migrants. As they poured into Pittsburgh during and after World War I, the migrants settled mainly in the lower Hill district, the most densely inhabited section of the city and characterized by a housing stock already old and dilapidated. Doubling up—with men on night shifts sleeping in beds vacated by day workers—caused an unsatisfactory situation to deteriorate even further. Health conditions and crime rates reached scandalous levels. Tuberculosis, influenza, whooping cough, scarlet fever, and venereal disease plagued the community, the death rate soared from 23.4 to 31.3 per 1,000, and crime rose 200 percent.[29]

More serious, perhaps, than the physical consequences were the social and psychological consequences. The migrants were financially unable to buy homes; by 1930 only 1 percent of the residents of the lower Hill were home-owners, compared with 24 percent of residents of heavily Slavic Polish Hill and 47 percent of those in Bloomfield, which was heavily Italian. Lack of homeownership increased residential instability and undermined possibilities for the emergence of a stable working-class community.[30]

The Burden of Geographic Dispersal

An additional burden borne by Pittsburgh blacks was that of geographic dispersal. Pittsburgh's hilly topography created neighborhoods of small ethnic pockets. The Hill district contained the largest single group of blacks in the city, but was never the only important place of black settlement. Indeed, during World War I, only 41 percent of the city's blacks lived there, while another 17 percent lived four miles away in East Liberty, and others lived even farther away—across the Allegheny River in the North Side, south of the Monongahela River in Beltzhoover, and east of the city in Homewood.[31]

The city's terrain encouraged this process of spatial differentiation and meant that, unlike other northern cities, growth of the black population resulted in several neighborhoods rather than in one compact ghetto. This splintering did not reduce the amount of racial segregation in Pittsburgh. Joe Darden, in his doctoral dissertation, calculated that, in 1930, 72 percent of blacks in Pittsburgh would have to move to another census tract to fully desegregate residential patterns, and that 74 percent would have to do so in 1940. This would put Pittsburgh among the least segregated of northern cities in that year. However, Karl and Alma Taeuber calculated Pittsburgh's percentage as 82, which would make it average for the North. Whichever figure one accepts, the fact is that Pittsburgh remained a very segregated city.[32]

These numerous "mini-ghettoes," however, did have several negative consequences. First, they delayed the time when blacks would dominate their own "turf." By 1930 the Hill housed less than half the city's black residents—43 percent—and, as a result, the district was barely majority black by 1930. Between 1910 and 1930, the district changed from 25 percent black to 53 percent black—a majority, to be sure, but not the solid majority that would ensure political and economic dominance.[33]

Second, neighborhood dispersal caused the separation of the black middle class from the masses. Financially stable residents—both black and white—tended to move away from the lower Hill and its deteriorating conditions and settle in other neighborhoods, especially East Liberty, Homewood-Brushton, Beltzhoover, and the upper Hill (Schenley Heights or "Sugar Top"). The result was that the lower Hill became increasingly black and poor; by the 1930s one researcher termed it the residence of "the most disadvantaged of the disadvantaged" in the city.[34]

Homewood is the only middle-class black neighborhood for which we have more than fragmentary information. In that eastern community, former residents of the Hill augmented a nucleus of proud descendants of servants to wealthy families dating back to the Civil War era. By 1930 these residents—described as "respectable, working people desirous of making their homes and neighborhoods as attractive as possible"—had a clear sense of their special residence and identity.[35]

Class Divisions in the Black Community

More than residence separated working-class migrants from the middle class. Most migrants came from the Deep South—especially Georgia and Alabama—and were overwhelmingly industrial laborers. The city's more established, long-term residents, by contrast, were born in the North or the upper South—especially Virginia and Maryland—and worked as barbers, waiters, janitors, and (for the lucky) postal clerks, railroad clerks, chauffeurs, and butlers. The groups did not even share skin color: older residents tended to be lighter skinned than the migrants.

The few blacks who attended area universities came from the middle class. Jean Hamilton Walls, the first black woman to enroll at the University of Pittsburgh, was one of those students. Her 1938 doctoral dissertation, which examined black students at Pitt, found that most had a middle-class background. Their fathers tended to be employed either in personal service, the professions, or public service; their mothers were usually housewives; and the parents of one-fourth had themselves attended college.[36]

Class differences were reflected in such institutions as the church. By 1930 the Hill district contained some forty-five churches, many of which were "storefront" institutions created by the migrants as part of their adjustment to urban life. These new churches isolated migrants from older residents and divided the community along lines of class and even color. Such divisions, moreover, could exist even within a given church: dark-skinned worshipers in one of the community's most prestigious churches reportedly sat or were seated toward the back.[37]

A church's degree of community involvement and style of service also reflected class and status differences. The more established churches tended to be involved in broader community activities. In Homestead, for example, Clark Memorial Baptist, located on the Hilltop, was organized in the 1890s by families from Virginia. The church had new buildings, educational and social programs, auxiliaries, clubs, and a foreign mission. Its ministers often had degrees from colleges or theological seminaries and gave sermons on political as well as religious topics. Physically, and probably socially as well, Clark looked down on Second Baptist Church, which began around 1905 as a storefront church located among the poorer migrants in the lower "Ward." Not until the 1940s did the latter have its own building. It had few clubs and auxiliaries, no community recreation center, a membership drawn primarily from the Deep South, and pastors who stuck closely to orthodox religious worship.[38]

In Pittsburgh, as in other northern cities, one response of middle-class blacks to the influx of newcomers was to withdraw into exclusive clubs. A clear example of this is provided by the Frogs, the community's most prestigious club of the time. Organized in 1910, membership in the Frogs was limited to about twenty-five, making it a smaller and more exclusive subset of the prestigious Loendi Club. With few exceptions, the Frogs were OPs, or Old Pittsburghers, residents proud of having been in the city before the Great Migration. The occupations of these club members—postal worker, railroad clerk, chauffeur, lawyer, funeral director, laundry owner—indicate how constricted was the range of jobs then open to the blacks.

Because income and occupation were not convenient stratifiers, one's social life became all the more important. The Frogs were a determinedly social organization; one officer termed it a "haven for those who wish to escape from . . . noble crusades." Invitations to its social events were highly coveted, and the numerous parties and galas of its annual "Frog Week" attracted upper-class revelers from around the country.[39]

The social life of this middle class filled the "Local News" section of the *Pittsburgh Courier,* the creation of Robert L. Vann, a handsome, talented, and industrious migrant from the South. Born in North Carolina, Vann earned his undergraduate degree at Virginia Union University in Richmond. He then attended law school at the University of Pittsburgh, attracted by the availability of an Avery Scholarship for black students. The scholarship—one of several legacies of the nineteenth-century philanthropist and abolitionist Charles Avery—was only for $100, so Vann basically worked his way through law school and in 1909 became its first black graduate. He quickly gained the acceptance of Old Pittsburghers and, by 1910, had married, established his law practice, and become editor and part owner of a weekly newspaper, the *Courier.*[40] The paper covered the activities of black upper- and middle-class clubs like the Frogs, the Loendi, the Arnett Literary Society, the Aurora Society, and the Girl Friends; it chronicled the social life of elite families, such as the Stantons, Joneses, Monroes, Googins, Morrisons, Douglasses, Buchannons, Pooles, Leftridges, Marshalls, Byrds, Allens, and Andersons; and it informed readers about who had gone on vacation, married, and had parties.[41]

The *Courier*'s masthead—"Work, Integrity, Tact, Temperance, Prudence, Courage, Faith"—reflected the values of Pittsburgh's black middle class and their faith in the American Dream. The paper endorsed the philosophy of Booker T. Washington: "Concentrate your earnings, and make capital. Hire yourselves, produce for yourselves, and sell something for yourselves." As an ultrapatriotic journal, it supported World War I, opposed socialism, had no sympathy for unions, and applauded restrictive quotas on immigrants.[42]

Although many have criticized the black bourgeoisie for endless social affairs, Pittsburgh's black elite also pursued cultural and intellectual activities. The Centre Avenue YMCA regularly invited lecturers such as George Washington Carver, W. E. B. Du Bois, Alain Locke, Walter White, and Mary McLeod Bethune. Blacks turned out to hear artists like Jessie Fauset, Countee Cullen, Langston Hughes, James W. Johnson, Marian Anderson, Roland Hayes, and Paul Robeson. They attended performances by numerous theater groups, one of which the Olympians in 1939 won first-place honors in the Pittsburgh Drama League's annual competition. (The league had long banned black theater groups.) The community also supported classical music. Between 1915 and 1927, the Peeler Symphony Orchestra gave regular performances; in 1937 Dr. A. R. Taylor's symphony orchestra presented concerts at the Centre Avenue YMCA; and Aubrey Pankey, a baritone in the choir of Holy Cross Church, toured the United States and Europe giving recitals of lieder, opera arias, and other songs.[43]

The Black Middle Class and the Burden of Racism

Despite their loyalty and 100 percent Americanism, middle-class blacks bore the same burden of racism that confronted their working-class counterparts. The only position open to them in industry was that of social worker, assigned to recruit and help in the adjustment of black migrants. Even independent professionals faced difficulties: black lawyers had credibility problems with white juries, and not until 1948 was the first black physician permitted to practice at a local hospital.

Opportunities for stable work, in fact, may have declined over this period. In 1900 blacks operated most of the city's prestigious downtown barbershops; by 1930 they operated almost none. In 1900 they had driven most of the city's taxis, hacks, buses, and trucks; by 1930 they drove mainly garbage trucks. Middle-class women fared even worse. They maintained their position as domestic servants to wealthy whites but could not clerk in "white" stores even in the Hill district. Sheer desperation drove some who could "pass" for white to do so, often with feelings of guilt that lasted a lifetime. Writing of her experiences during the 1920s and 1930s, one light-skinned woman, Martha Moore, recalled how, frustrated in not being able to find employment, she took her mother's advice and "for twenty-five working years, as a medical secretary, salesgirl, office manager, governess, and Draft Board clerk in World War II, was any race they wanted, or designated, me to be."[44]

Especially frustrating was the continued refusal by the Board of Education to hire black teachers. Ralph Proctor shows that prior to 1937 blacks who graduated from the University of Pittsburgh's School of Education had to go elsewhere if they wanted to teach. The Board of Education often would help them find jobs in the South and in northern cities like Philadelphia and Indianapolis. Rather than leave the city, Frank Bolden—who was light enough to pass for white—went to work for the *Courier* after being told by the board's director of personnel: "It's too bad you're not white. I'd hire you immediately."[45]

Nor were opportunities much better for other college graduates. Walls's study of black graduates of the University of Pittsburgh between 1926 and 1936 found that half of the men and 60 percent of the women lived outside the state, largely because of lack of job opportunities. Walls concluded: "Pittsburgh has suffered the loss of many of its Negro college graduates because it offered them so few opportunities to use their training in earning a livelihood."[46]

Middle-class blacks also suffered a wide range of social discrimination. In 1936 a black student at the University of Pittsburgh complained that "admission to major sports and clubs was not impossible but unbearable and often embarrassing," while another reported that his application to a student law club had been rejected because of the objection of several southern club members.[47] The Ku Klux Klan in the Pittsburgh region boasted 17,000 members in the 1920s, and the police tolerated crime as long as it was black on black. In "white" restaurants, blacks found salt in their coffee, pepper in their milk, and overcharges on their bills; in department stores they received impolite service; in downtown theaters they were either refused admission or were segregated in the balcony. Forbes Field, where the Pirates played baseball, confined blacks to certain sections of the stands, and visiting blacks— even those as prominent as W. E. B. Du Bois and A. Philip Randolph—could not stay in the city's hotels.[48]

Middle-class blacks had difficulty finding integrated housing. In 1911, Robert Vann (who was often mistaken for an Indian) and his wife (who looked white) bought a pleasant house in Homewood, where they got along well with the neighbors and with the other black family on the street. In 1917, after Vann bought the house next door and rented it to another black family, his neighbors began what Vann called the "Battle of Monticello Street": handbills, meetings, and unending talk about "undesirables" continued. Within ten years Vann's block was almost solidly black.[49]

Some businesses refused to sell to blacks. Vann wanted to buy a new Cadillac in 1926 and, although he could pay cash, he had to buy it in Altoona because the Pittsburgh dealer would not sell to him for fear that Cadillacs might become labeled "a nigger car." Nor were local business associations willing to accept black members, even those who were prominent business-men and staunch advocates of capitalism. In 1925 Vann applied for admission to the Chamber of Commerce and, despite his obvious credentials, was turned down.[50]

Efforts at Community-Building

Because middle-class blacks faced many of the same problems of racism as did poorer and more recent arrivals, they championed race causes in any way they could—through the pages of the *Pittsburgh Courier,* through political activity, and through organizations like the Urban League and the National Association for the Advancement of Colored People (NAACP). The institu-tion most clearly committed to creating a sense of community and promoting black interests was the *Pittsburgh Courier,* which by the 1920s was the na-tion's largest and most influential black paper. Vann made it a voice of pro-test, crusading on the issues of housing, education, job opportunities, political awareness, crime, and Jim Crow.[51]

In 1928 a close student of the black press rated the *Courier* as America's best black weekly. Its four editions—local, northern, eastern and southern—were distributed in all forty-eight states plus Europe, Africa, Canada, the Philippines, and the West Indies. By 1938 its circulation reached 250,000, making it the largest of all black weeklies in the United States.

Vann hired excellent writers, including George Schuyler, sometimes re-ferred to as the "black H. L. Mencken," and Joel A. Rogers, the historian. Schuyler traveled around America reporting on blacks; Rogers traveled to Africa and Europe, researching and reporting on ancient black kingdoms and heroes. During World War II, *Courier* reporters stationed in Ethiopia covered the efforts of Emperor Haile Selassie to fight off the invading Italian troops. Sports also got extensive coverage, with writers like W. Rollo Wilson, Chester "Ches" Washington, Wendell Smith, Cum Posey Jr. (manager of the Homestead Grays), and William G. Nunn Sr.

Political and Economic Weaknesses

Despite the urgings of its politically conscious newspaper, the black community failed to develop political power commensurate with its potential. Even before the migration of World War I, black politics was characterized by voter apathy and by short-lived ineffective organizations. Neither party offered blacks much—the Republicans because of blacks' guaranteed loyalty to the "Party of Lincoln"; the Democrats because of sensitivity to southern white prejudices. Blacks supported the openly corrupt and prejudiced Magee-Flinn machine because it provided them with a few patronage jobs and because its opponents, the reform forces, were even more prejudiced.[52]

Despite their increased numbers following the Great Migration, the political situation remained virtually unchanged. In 1919 Robert H. Logan made a promising start toward political empowerment when he became the city's black alderman. Logan, however, was not reelected and, despite increasing numbers of potential voters, blacks suffered a string of electoral losses throughout the 1920s and 1930s. Sickened at the defeat of one especially capable candidate (Homer S. Brown) in 1932, the *Courier* editor attributed the loss to voter apathy and disunity. The *Courier* excoriated Pittsburgh blacks as "the most backward of Negroes to be found in any large city" and considered them "absolutely in a class by [themselves] when it comes to the question of civic and political advancement."[53]

The Great Depression broke the Republican grip on the black electorate but had little effect on the political fortunes of Pittsburgh blacks. By 1932 Vann had formally switched to the Democratic party and in that year issued his famous statement urging blacks to turn "Lincoln's picture to the wall." For several reasons, however, blacks made few advances as a result of the switch. First, local whites also voted solidly Democratic in 1932, so that the party did not need the black vote to win. Also, the state's Democrats paid more attention to Philadelphia's 280,000 blacks than to Pittsburgh's 70,000.[54]

White prejudice was not the only reason for black political weakness. Two others—apathy and geographic dispersal—were examined in a thesis by Ruth Simmons. Simmons noted that by 1945 blacks had only three elected officials—Homer Brown in the state legislature, plus one alderman and one constable in the Hill district—and did not control the Democratic party organization even in wards where they formed a clear majority. Simmons believed that apathy partly explained this dismal situation: "Only those persons who hold office or jobs under the patronage of a political party exhibit any political interest," she noted, and "many of the rank and file" fail to vote. A second explanation was geographic: "If Negro voters were not so widely scattered throughout the city, they might obtain a few more elective offices."[55]

Other community institutions also were ineffective as voices of black protest. The NAACP, after an enthusiastic founding in 1915, soon declined in membership and spirit. A later director, the Reverend J. C. Austin, spoke of finding the organization "just about as Christ found Lazarus after the fourth day of his death, not only dead but buried," and national headquarters informed the Pittsburgh branch that it was "weaker than any other unit we have in a city of the same size." By the late 1920s Homer Brown and Daisy Lampkin had revived the organization, and through the late 1930s membership stabilized at about 1,000. But by the late 1930s, with Brown in the state assembly, the branch once again became dormant.[56]

The Urban League was more active, but was oriented toward social welfare rather than political protest. Created in 1918 as the outgrowth of the interracial Pittsburgh Council of Social Services Among Negroes, the officers and employees of the league were drawing from the elite of the black community. To fulfill their primary goal of promoting the welfare of black migrants and industrial workers, they established a travelers' aid booth, provided homemakers to advise on nutrition and family matters, placed welfare workers in some of the larger mills, and commissioned an important study by Abraham Epstein on the plight of black migrants in the Hill district. The league had less to offer middle-class job seekers, but did provide jobs for some of them as social workers in its own offices, helped train young women in secretarial skills, raised scholarship money for college expenses, and urged the employment of black teachers by the public schools.[57]

Inexplicably, although the black community had little political or institutional strength at the local level, it elected a politician of influence at the state level. Constance Cunningham has described the career of Pittsburgh's most famous black politician, Homer S. Brown. Born in West Virginia, in 1923 Brown became the third black to graduate from the University of Pittsburgh's law school. After establishing a law practice with Richard F. Jones, one of his classmates, Brown became president of the local NAACP, a position he held until 1949. In 1934—two years after the loss so greatly lamented by Robert L. Vann—Brown was elected to the state legislature. Why Brown succeeded at the state level, while he and others regularly failed at the local level, is not clear, although Simmons attributes his subsequent reelections to the respect and popularity he enjoyed among white as well as black voters.[58]

Brown had a distinguished legislative career. Respected for his knowledge of constitutional law, he helped David Lawrence and Richard King Mellon craft legislation to launch the "Pittsburgh Renaissance." He also was applauded by *Time* magazine for astuteness and integrity and achieved international recognition as a member of the U.S. National Commission to UNESCO when he helped draw up the Covenant on the International Rights of Man.

Brown's most dramatic achievement during the 1930s was the convening of a state legislative hearing on the refusal of the Pittsburgh Board of Education to hire black teachers. After the schools were desegregated in the 1870s, the board adamantly refused to hire black teachers because of objections to having them teach white students. As more schools became predominantly black, pressure to hire black teachers increased—if only for the purpose of controlling the students. Leadership to change board policy, however, had to come primarily from the state level because black Pittsburgh lacked the political activism to force a change. Moreover, the community was divided on which unpleasant choice to campaign for—integrated schools with white teachers or segregated schools with black. Faced with that dilemma, the community fell silent. However, the board, in response to the legislature's finding of discrimination, promised to promote its one black professional, Lawrence Peeler, a part-time teacher hired in 1933 to teach music in the Hill. However, the board did not begin hiring black teachers in more than token numbers until the late 1940s.[59]

In sum, racism, economic decline, and geographic dispersal frustrated the benefits promised by blacks' entry into the city's industries during World War I. By World War II, black Pittsburgh was socially and culturally vibrant, but was politically and economically stagnant. Moreover, as we will see, the continuing decline of Pittsburgh's industrial base devastated the black working class, while a continuation of the neighborhood divisions and apathy prevented blacks from attaining the political influence that their numbers would permit. On the other hand, the shift to a service economy, combined with the lowering of racial barriers to employment and public accommodations, opened up new opportunities to the middle class.[60]

After World War II: Middle-Class Gains and Working-Class Frustrations

Diminished Opportunities for the Working Class

Because the period following World War II witnessed a number of important developments, it is unfortunate that it has not received much scholarly attention from historians. One of the most notable trends was a bifurcation of the black experience along class lines, caused by the deindustrialization of the region. Between the end of World War I and the early 1980s, Pittsburgh's share of national steel production fell from 25 percent to 14 percent, and its manufacturing employment declined from 338,000 to 240,000, a loss that proportionally was larger than in all but one of the nation's major manufacturing centers.[61]

The consequences of this decline were serious for most Pittsburghers, but were devastating for working-class blacks. By the 1980s black families lived on an income that was only 57 percent that of local whites and suffered an unemployment rate of 35 percent, 3.5 times the white rate. Pittsburgh blacks also lost ground relative to blacks elsewhere: in 1987 a national consultant ranked Pittsburgh forty-first out of forty-eight metropolitan areas in terms of the comparative economic status of local blacks and whites. These dismaying economic developments were reflected in other areas of black life. A 1987 study by the University of Pittsburgh's Institute for the Black Family documented the disintegration of many local families. As was true in black communities throughout the nation, the black marriage rate was falling while rates of teenage motherhood and the proportion of female-headed households were rising.[62]

Compounding this economic disaster were a series of other setbacks. The first was the destruction of the lower Hill—home to thousands of residents—for the sake of "urban renewal." Surprisingly, this was accomplished with the cooperation of the community's leading politician, Homer Brown, who, like other Pittsburghers, apparently regarded the area as a slum not worth saving. While in the state assembly in the late 1940s, Brown worked with Lawrence, Mellon, and other business leaders to pass legislation permitting the condemnation of the area and its renewal as part of an expanded central business district. After helping to pass such legislation in the late 1940s, Brown, as the first black judge on the Allegheny County Court, authorized its demolition in the early 1950s. What urban historian Roy Lubove has called "bulldozer renewal" uprooted 1,500 black families in order to make way for a domed Civic Arena and luxury apartments. That it was accomplished without protest is simply another sign of the community's passivity. Not until the mid-1950s, when developers began to eye the middle and upper-Hill—the residence of middle-class blacks—was a protest mounted and the process halted.[63]

Because the uprooting was sudden and no provision was made for their resettlement, the scattering of these families did not produce better housing for them. They simply crowded into integrated neighborhoods such as East Liberty and Homewood-Brushton, beginning the abandonment of those areas by the middle class, both black and white.[64]

A second setback for the local black poor was their inability to get government agencies to respond effectively to their needs. The federal War on Poverty of the 1960s often failed because of poor management, politics, and insufficient funds, but Pittsburgh's agency, CAP (Community Action Pittsburgh), won praise from the local press and was cited by the federal government as a model agency. A study of CAP argues that it failed because of the geographic dispersal of its clients into seven neighborhoods. Competing leaders, priorities, and strengths of those neighborhoods deprived them of the unity needed to force the bureaucracy to respond.[65]

The failure of the War on Poverty led to the riots of the late 1960s, which some saw as a "political" statement by the poor to call attention to their continuing plight. A further effort was made in 1969, the year after the riots, when Nate Smith and the Black Construction Coalition halted work on ten building projects, put 800 marchers on the North Side, and, after two weeks of demonstrations, produced the Pittsburgh Plan, which was hailed as a national model to train blacks for construction jobs but was only marginally effective.[66]

Nor were opportunities opening up for black children to escape the poverty of their parents. Throughout the postwar period, Pittsburgh's school became increasingly segregated because of housing patterns. The percentage of black pupils in the Pittsburgh school system rose from 19 percent in 1945 to 37 percent in 1965; over approximately the same years, the percentage of black pupils in schools with overwhelmingly black enrollments rose from 45 percent to 67 percent in the elementary grades, and from 23 percent to 58 percent in the secondary grades. Even more serious, academic performance in the segregated schools was substandard, with elementary students in predominantly black schools reading as much as three grade levels below their counterparts in predominantly white schools.[67]

Part of the failure to force federal agencies and the local school board to effectively address black needs stemmed from continued political weakness. Following the war, tentative steps toward political power were only partially successful. In 1954 blacks elected City Council Member Paul Jones and in succeeding years maintained at least one member on the council. In 1958 they elected K. Leroy Irvis to the Pennsylvania legislature, and over the next three decades of a distinguished career, Irvis served as minority whip, majority whip, and Speaker of the House. Black political presence probably peaked in 1970, with the rise of Lou Mason to council president. But its fragility was revealed in 1985 when, due largely to political in-fighting among black ward leaders and low voter turnout, blacks wound up with no representation on city council. Some blamed the at-large electoral system, without explaining how during the previous three decades blacks had consistently elected one, sometimes two, councilmen. The Reverend Junius Carter, an Episcopal priest in Pittsburgh, echoed the lament of Robert L. Vann fifty years earlier when he complained, "Pittsburgh is lagging behind every other city in the nation in terms of the political power of blacks."[68]

Unable to change the system, blacks were forced simply to cope. Melvin Williams provides an ethnographic study of that adjustment in Belmar, a neighborhood of middle-class blacks located near Homewood that was "invaded" by lower-class persons displaced from the lower Hill. Williams documents three major lifestyles by which residents adapted to the stresses of ghetto life. One he labels "mainstream" because it is pursued by the few who have both the values and the economic means of the majority population, and whose behavior is "difficult to distinguish . . . from their white counterparts anywhere in America." Another style, which he labels as "spurious," characterizes those with mainstream values who lack the income, networks, and "stylistic codes" needed to live a mainstream life. Resentful of the mainstreamers and contemptuous of the "no-good" among whom they are forced to live, they lead an isolated, bitter life, "in but not of the ghetto." Finally, there is the group called "no-good" by the spurious but, curiously, labeled "genuine" by Williams. Proud of their flamboyant lifestyle and contemptuous of the values of mainstream society, they live by their wits—the women on welfare and the men by hustling and various illegal and semilegal activities.[69]

There is perhaps a fourth adaptive lifestyle, pursued by a group which one might label the "churched." Williams, in another study, describes people whose entire lives revolve around church activities and who have as little as possible to do with this world, which they regard as "irredeemably wicked." Although his Zion Holiness Church (not a real name) is located in the lower Hill, its counterparts exist throughout the ghetto, as poor blacks attempt to create a community of morality and order amid a society characterized by immorality and disorder.[70]

Expanding Opportunities for the Middle Class

If opportunities were closing off for the black working class, they were opening up for the middle class. The latter had long suffered from occupational exclusion. During the 1920s, when black workers were finding jobs in the city's factories and mills, middle-class blacks were still excluded from offices, stores, schools, corporations, and most professions. The postwar period was to be their period of opportunity.

A major breakthrough occurred in the late 1940s, when the Board of Education increased its hiring of black teachers. As late as 1948 only fifteen black teachers had been hired, but as schools became increasingly black, the board finally changed its policy. Hiring increased steadily in the 1950s and accelerated in the 1960s, so that by 1970 more than 400 black teachers were employed in the Pittsburgh school system, and blacks made up more than 10 percent of the system's professional staff (although 37 percent of the student population). As Pittsburgh closed the hiring gap with other cities, blacks overcame barrier after barrier to equal employment in the schools. With pressure, protest, and demonstrated competence, they moved from being elementary teachers in the Hill (1937), to secondary teachers in the Hill (late 1940s), to elementary teachers outside the Hill (mid-1950s), to secondary teachers outside the Hill (mid-1960s). A similar progression occurred for principals, who were hired first in the Hill (1955) and then outside the Hill (1968), until by 1970 the system employed forty-eight black principals and assistant principals. One argument for hiring black teachers and administrators was that they could help raise the academic performance of their students. And, indeed, Doris Brevard of Vann, Janet Bell of Westwood, Vivian Williams of Madison, and Louis Venson of Beltzhoover—all principals of elementary schools composed primarily of students from "deprived" backgrounds—created what one researcher has termed "an abashing anomaly" by raising their schools' reading and mathematics scores consistently above the national norms.[71]

Occupational breakthroughs in other fields were aided by the city's shift to a service economy. Indeed, the massiveness of that shift was emphasized by two economists, who noted that by the 1980s Pittsburgh's industrial mix had become more heavily oriented toward nonmanufacturing activity than in the United States as a whole. As steel production shrank, medicine, business services, education, and banking increasingly became the engines of Pittsburgh's employment growth. Success in making this transition to a service economy was partly responsible for the rating of Pittsburgh as the nation's "most livable city" in the 1985 *Rand McNally Atlas*.[72]

Most black Pittsburghers would have disputed the city's livability ranking, but some middle-class blacks enjoyed expanding job opportunities. Gladys McNairy was appointed to the Board of Education and in 1971 was elected board president. At the University of Pittsburgh, a sit-in by black students at the computer center produced a Black Studies Department, with Jack Daniel (then a graduate student) as chairman and Curtiss Porter as associate chairman. This was followed by a program to increase the number of minority students and faculty, such that by 1980 there were 2,233 black students and

103 black faculty on the Oakland campus, comprising, respectively, 7.6 percent of the students and 4.9 percent of the faculty. As moderate as those figures may seem, by one calculation the University of Pittsburgh had become "the institution with the largest degree of overrepresentation" of black undergraduates among the nation's major research universities. In addition, during the 1970s, blacks at the University of Pittsburgh were promoted to several positions of responsibility: Lawrence Howard became dean of the School of Public and International Affairs, David Epperson dean of the School of Social Work, and James Kelly dean of the School of Education.[73]

Opportunities also opened up in the private sector. The city's Urban League, which in the 1920s had been involved in finding employment primarily for working-class blacks, now was negotiating to place blacks in clerical, managerial, and professional positions. In the 1940s the league's "young firebrand" staff member, K. Leroy Irvis, led the picketing of downtown stores that resulted in the hiring of black salesclerks—the first such incident in the nation. In the 1950s, under the leadership of Joe Allen, the league pressed for increased black hiring, especially in the public sector. In the 1960s, under the leadership of Arthur Edmunds, it worked with a handful of black leaders and enlightened corporate executives—notably Fletcher Byrom of Koppers—to get the city's many corporations to hire blacks for more than janitorial duty. They began by hiring secretaries and, to provide a pool of future black managers, supported NEED, a scholarship fund for black college students.[74]

In the 1980s, expanded corporate hiring, affirmative action requirements, and an enlarged pool of black college graduates led to occupational breakthroughs of blacks into middle-management positions. A few of those hired gained professional recognition and moved into upper management, including William Bates, 1987 president of the Pittsburgh chapter of the American Institute of Architects; Darwin Davis, senior vice-president of Equitable Life Insurance Company; Jack Burley, vice-president of finance at Heinz Corporation; and Lawrence Moncrief, vice-president and general counsel of the H. K. Porter Company.

The postwar period also saw the fall of Jim Crow patterns of segregation that had humiliated blacks for over a century. After the war, blacks—and their white allies—mounted attacks on segregated public facilities, including hotels, parks, pools, restaurants, and theaters. Typical of these efforts was the protracted campaign in the 1950s, led by the Urban League's executive secretary, Joseph Allen, to desegregate city swimming pools. During the 1950s and 1960s the barriers continued to fall, until by the 1980s even the city's most prestigious clubs opened to blacks: Darwin Davis, for example, integrated the exclusive Duquesne Club; Milton Washington the Pittsburgh Athletic Association; and Eric Springer, David Epperson, and James Kelly the University Club.

The fall of such barriers, ironically, undermined some black institutions. Following the integration of major league baseball, professional black teams withered away, including the Pittsburgh Crawfords and the Homestead Grays. The *Pittsburgh Courier* followed a similar trajectory: as white papers included more news about blacks, the *Courier*'s circulation dropped until it was bought by Chicago interests in the mid-1960s. However, new businesses that benefited from the improved racial climate opened. These included Beacon, a construction firm owned by Milton Washington with more than 100 employees; Sheradan Broadcasting, owned by Ronald Davenport, which in the 1970s was one of the few black-owned stations in America; and ALBA Travel, created by Audrey Alpern and Gladys Baynes Edmunds, one of the larger female-owned businesses in Pittsburgh.[75]

Black Pittsburgh also witnessed a minor flowering of cultural life. August Wilson, a playwright born and reared in the Hill district, won the New York Drama Critics award in 1985 for *Ma Rainey's Black Bottom,* and *Fences,* based on life in the Hill district in the 1950s, won the Pulitzer Prize in 1987. John Wideman, a basketball star and Rhodes Scholar reared in Homewood-Brushton, authored a well-received trilogy of novels set in the neighborhood of his youth—*Damballah, Hiding Place,* and *Sent for You Yesterday,* the last of which won the PEN/Faulkner Award in 1984. Another work, *Brothers and Keepers,* published in 1984, was featured on the television show *60 Minutes,* and a subsequent novel, *Reuben,* also received national attention. In 1964, Patricia Prattis Jennings, daughter of *Pittsburgh Courier* Editor P. L. Prattis, broke the color barrier at the Pittsburgh Symphony when she became the orchestra's pianist.[76] One year later Paul Ross became one of the symphony's violinists. In jazz, Pittsburgh continued its prewar creativity, producing such international stars as Billy Eckstine, Erroll Garner, and Mary Lou Williams in the 1940s; Ahmad Jamal, Stanley Turrentine, Dakota Staton, and George Benson in the 1950s and 1960s; and (though not from Pittsburgh) Nathan Davis in the 1970s and 1980s.

In addition, the University of Pittsburgh's Kuntu Repertory Theater, directed by Rob Penny and Vernell Lillie, and Bob Johnson's Black Theater Dance Ensemble brought excellent theater and dance to the area, while Roger Humphries and Walt Harper continued the city's notable jazz tradition. Local artists such as Harold Neal and Thad Mosely continued to receive local and occasionally national recognition. In 1987 Bill Strickland's Manchester Craftsmen's guild opened on the North Side, a multimillion-dollar building which quickly became a showplace for black and white photographers, artists, and musicians.

Conclusion

This survey has shown that, like their counterparts elsewhere, blacks in Pittsburgh have borne a heavy burden of racial discrimination. Disfranchised in 1837, they regained the vote only after the Civil War. Long barred from the city's economic mainstream, they entered local industry only after World War I, and until World War II they were even excluded from most forms of public accommodation.

The study also suggests that, in addition to racial discrimination, blacks here have borne two further burdens. The first burden was economic. As blue-collar workers in a city whose industrial base declined earlier than most, they had fewer opportunities for economic mobility, and fewer resources with which to support a middle class. The second burden was geographic. As members of a community dispersed across seven or more neighborhoods, they faced unusual difficulties developing community-wide social, economic, and political institutions.

Although the literature on black Pittsburgh is surprisingly rich, there remain important gaps in our knowledge. We especially need investigations of black neighborhoods. Although the existence of several black residential areas inhibited black unity and delayed black economic and political progress, the precise ways in which this operated remain unclear and need to be specified. Furthermore, many people derived a great degree of satisfaction from living in smaller areas, where they knew each other and interacted on a regular basis. Many older black residents remember friendly interactions with their white neighbors and maintain a strong sense of identification with their old neighborhoods.

The role and position of black women in Pittsburgh also needs to be explored. Despite the numerous studies of the black community, none specifically addresses the experience and contribution of black women to the community. In Pittsburgh, as elsewhere in America, black women have been instrumental in the development and sustenance of numerous community organizations, the church in particular. They maintained an active club life and engaged in numerous activities of benefit to the community. Sororities and clubs such as the Business and Professional Women's Organization would be excellent topics for research. Moreover, Pittsburgh had a surprisingly large number of women-owned businesses, and the entrepreneurial role of these women would be a fascinating and important area of study.

We also need an examination of the pre–World War I community, in order to understand how a people with so few job opportunities managed to create such vibrant social, cultural, and economic institutions by the turn of the century. We especially need an investigation of the leading members of the early community, the Old Pittsburghers, in order to understand the failure of them (and their children) to maintain their entrepreneurial beginnings and to develop political leadership after World War I. In addition to understanding the black elite, we need studies of the black middle class of Pittsburgh, particularly of their neighborhoods, such as Homewood, East Liberty, and Beltzhoover—the destination of many "migrants" who were local and middle class rather than southern and blue collar. Moreover, we need studies of race relations. Rob Ruck's study of black sports documents a remarkable amount of informal integration among neighborhood sandlot teams, and there may have been other areas of interracial cooperation, such as schools and family visiting. The presence of so much "high culture" within the community also needs to be investigated, particularly the active theater life and the symphony orchestras.

For the period following World War II, virtually all aspects of community life need to be examined. We have no studies of community leaders or achievers during this period. In particular, we need a study of K. Leroy Irvis to place alongside that of Homer Brown, explaining how both those men continued to be reelected to an important statewide post despite relative political weakness at the local level. We need a study of the remarkable dislocation of thousands of blacks, without protest, from the lower Hill district during the early 1950s. Finally, we need studies of such community institutions as the leading churches and the NAACP. The research agenda is set far into the future.

The big question that needs to be explored regarding the history of black Pittsburgh is why so much political passivity prevailed here even following the dramatic increase of black numbers during and after the 1920s. The hypothesis of special double burden invites comparative research, both to test its validity and to give it broader significance. First, we need comparative histories of black political development in order to locate the political development of black Pittsburgh somewhere along a continuum. Second, we need a comparative economic history of American cities in order to assess how special the economic burden of Pittsburgh's blacks was. A comparison with Detroit, whose economy declined some forty years after Pittsburgh's, would help establish whether racism or overall economic opportunities were more important in blocking the development of a stable black working class. Third, we need comparative studies of the social development of black communities nationally in order to assess the institutional strengths and weaknesses of black Pittsburgh. A comparison with Cincinnati, another hilly, industrial city with dispersed black communities, would tell us whether geographic dispersal inevitably undermines the entrepreneurial, institutional, and political development of a community. Finally, a comparison with cities that had segregated school systems but employed black teachers would clarify the trade-offs between segregation and jobs for the middle class.

Through such comparative studies, the experience of black Pittsburghers can take on more than local significance. Whether the Pittsburgh experience was unique—or an advanced stage of a natural experience—their lives and experiences can provide a message for blacks throughout the nation.

Notes

1. The WPA project was part of the Federal Writers Project Ethnic Survey, ca. 1940, microfilmed by the Pennsylvania State Archives in Harrisburg (reel 2). The typescript was discovered in the early 1970s by Professor Rollo Turner of the Black Studies Department of the University of Pittsburgh.

2. Harris's photographs are being identified and cataloged by Dennis Morgan and Professor Rollo Turner of the University of Pittsburgh's Department of Black Community Education, Research and Development (Black Studies). See Rollo Turner, "The Teenie Harris Photographic Collection," *Pennsylvania Ethnic Studies Newsletter* (University of Pittsburgh, University Center for International Studies), Winter 1987. Turner's article estimates that the collection contains 50,000 items; Morgan, in a personal communication with the author, reports having located perhaps another 50,000 items in Harris's possession, plus photographs taken by other *Courier* photographers.

3. There were also black communities on the north side of the Allegheny River in Allegheny, as well as in Minersville (today Schenley Heights), a few miles east of the Hill. The pre–Civil War black community is described in Ann G. Wilmoth, "Pittsburgh and the Blacks: A Short History, 1780–1875" (Ph.D. diss., Pennsylvania State University, 1975); Ernest J. Wright, "The Negro in Pittsburgh," unpublished typescript for the WPA; and Janet L. Bishop, "In the Shadow of the Dream: The Black Pittsburgh Community, 1850–1870" (undergraduate paper, Department of History, Princeton University, 1982). Regarding Minersville, see Bradley W. Hall, "Elites and Spatial Change in Pittsburgh: Minersville as a Case Study," *Pennsylvania History* 48 (October 1981): 311–34.

4. Wilmoth, "Pittsburgh and the Blacks," 9–16, table 27.

5. Wright, "The Negro in Pittsburgh," chap. 3, pp. 29ff.

6. Ibid., chap. 12, pp. 2–7, 14–20; Rayford Logan and Michael Winston, eds., *Dictionary of American Negro Biography* (New York, 1982), 67–68, 577–80. The genteel lifestyle of Pittsburgh's black community in the 1850s is recalled by Brown in *Tales My Father Told and Other Stories* (Wilberforce, Ohio, 1925). In the 1890s, two Tanner descendants, Parthenia Tanner and Mary Tanner Miller, were the first blacks to be hired as switchboard operators by the Bell Telephone Company in Pittsburgh.

7. Wright, "The Negro in Pittsburgh," 52ff.; Wilmoth, "Pittsburgh and the Blacks," 19; *University Times* (University of Pittsburgh), February 19, 1987.

8. Wilmoth, "Pittsburgh and the Blacks," chaps. 5 and 6. It was always exceptional for free blacks in southern cities to be able to vote. Even in the North, however, free blacks were increasingly restricted in their access to the franchise. Boston was the only major city in which, during the first half of the nineteenth century, they were allowed to vote on equal terms with whites. See Leonard P. Curry, *The Free Black in Urban America, 1800–1850: The Shadow of the Dream* (Chicago, 1981), 88; Wright, "The Negro in Pittsburgh," chap. 4; Richard J. M. Blackett, "Freedom, or the Martyr's Grave: Black Pittsburgh's Aid to the Fugitive Slave," *Western Pennsylvania Historical Magazine* 61 (January 1978): 117–34; Wilmoth, "Pittsburgh and the Blacks," chap. 4 and pp. 52ff. The phrase "Father of Black Nationalism" was used by Theodore Draper in *The Rediscovery of Black Nationalism* (New York, 1969), x.

9. Wilmoth, "Pittsburgh and the Blacks," chap. 3.

10. Ibid., chap. 5.

11. Ibid., chap. 6.

12. Wright, "The Negro in Pittsburgh," chap. 5; pp. 1–67; the quotation is from pp. 65–66.

13. However, the few who were employed in steel apparently were promoted and reasonably well treated. See R. R. Wright's "One Hundred Negro Steel Workers," in Paul U. Kellogg, ed., *Wage-Earning Pittsburgh: The Pittsburgh Survey,* vol. 6 (New York, 1914), 97–110. See also Wright, "The Negro in Pittsburgh," chap. 12.

14. This simply reflected overall growth of the city's population, which by 1900 was the seventh largest city in the nation. Not until 1920 did blacks make up more than 5 percent of the city's population.

15. These businesses were not confined to the Hill district, but were dispersed in several sections of the city—the Strip, the Hill district, the North Side, and Lawrenceville. Helen A. Tucker, "The Negroes of Pittsburgh," *Charities and the Commons,* January 2, 1909, reprinted in Kellogg, *Wage-Earning Pittsburgh,* 424–36.

16. Wright, "The Negro in Pittsburgh," chap. 12, pp. 2–7, 14–20, 28–49.

17. Andrew Buni, *Robert L. Vann of the Pittsburgh Courier: Politics and Black Journalism* (Pittsburgh, 1974), 26. Of necessity they also had their own cemeteries. See Joe T. Darden, "The Cemeteries of Pittsburgh: A Study in Historical Geography" (master's thesis, Department of Geography, University of Pittsburgh, 1967). Between 1896 and 1924, community activities were listed in "Afro-American Notes," which appeared each Sunday in the *Pittsburgh Press.*

18. Wright, "The Negro in Pittsburgh," chap. 12, pp. 28–49; chap. 13, esp. pp. 5–7.

19. For an overview of black migration during World War I, see Florette Henri, *Black Migration: Movement North, 1900–1920* (New York, 1976). Frank Bolden, former reporter for the *Pittsburgh Courier,* feels that the earlier migrants were a more sober family- and church-oriented group, whereas those who came during the 1920s were more likely to be single and "problem-prone." Moreoever, he argues, this party reflected the type of recruiter. The Reverend Nelson of East Liberty, for example, recruited the former type, whereas "Reverend" Van Harty of the North Side was much less selective. For an overview of the evolution of the Hill district, see Ralph L. Hill, "A View of the Hill: A Study of Experiences and Attitudes in the Hill District of Pittsburgh, Pa., from 1900 to 1973" (Ph.D. diss., University of Pittsburgh, 1973).

20. Wright, "The Negro in Pittsburgh," 75. The McKay quote is from Ishmael Reed, "In Search of August Wilson," *Connoisseur,* March 1987, 95. See also William Y. Bell Jr., "Commercial Recreation Facilities Among Negroes in the Hill District of Pittsburgh" (M.A. thesis, Department of Social Work, University of Pittsburgh, 1938).

21. Rob Ruck, *Sandlot Seasons: Sport in Black Pittsburgh* (Urbana, Ill., 1987), 61, 114, 154–55. See also Ruck's "Soaring Above the Sandlots: The Garfield Eagles," *Pennsylvania Heritage* 8 (Summer 1982): 13–18, for an examination of a neighborhood football team during the same period; and David K. Wiggins, "Wendell Smith, the *Pittsburgh Courier-Journal* and the Campaign to Include Blacks in Organized Baseball, 1933–1945, *Journal of Sport History* 10 (Summer 1983): 5–29.

22. Published as Abraham Epstein, *The Negro Migrant in Pittsburgh* (Pittsburgh: National Urban League, 1918), 32. See Abram Harris, "The New Negro Worker in Pittsburgh" (M.A. thesis, Department of Economics, University of Pittsburgh, 1924); Ira DeA. Reid, "The Negro in Major Industries and Building Trades of Pittsburgh" (M.A. thesis, Department of Economics, University of Pittsburgh, 1925), 10, 35ff.; Ira Reid, *Social Conditions of the Negro in the Hill District of Pittsburgh* (Pittsburgh, 1930); James H. Baker, "Procedure in Personnel Administration with Reference to Negro Labor" (M.A. thesis, Department of Economics, University of Pittsburgh, 1925); Alonzo G. Moron and F. F. Stephan, "The Negro Population and Negro Families in Pittsburgh and Allegheny County," *Social Research Bulletin,* April 20, 1933; John T. Clark, "The Migrant in Pittsburgh," *Opportunity* 1 (October 1923): 303–7; Clark's "The Negro in Steel," *Opportunity* 4 (March 1926): 87–88; and W. P. Young, "The First Hundred Negro Workers," *Opportunity* 2 (January 1924): 15–19.

See also John N. Rathmell, "Status of Pittsburgh Negroes in Regard to Origin, Length of Residence, and Economic Aspects of Their Life" (M.A. thesis, Department of Sociology, University of Pittsburgh, 1935), 30; John V. Anderson, "Unemployment in Pittsburgh with Reference to the Negro" (M.A. thesis, Department of Economics, University of Pittsburgh, 1932); Thomas Augustine, "The Negro Steelworkers of Pittsburgh and the Unions" (M.A. thesis, Department of Sociology, University of Pittsburgh, 1948); Floyd C. Covington, ''Occupational Choices in Relation to Economic Opportunities of Negro Youth in Pittsburgh" (M.A. thesis, Department of Economics, University of Pittsburgh, 1934); and Betty Ann Weiskopf, "A Directory of Some of the Organizations to Which People in the Hill District of Pittsburgh Belong" (M.A. thesis, Social Administration, University of Pittsburgh, 1943).

23. Glenn E. McLaughlin and Ralph J. Watkins, "The Problem of Industrial Growth in a Mature Economy," *American Economic Review* 29 (March 1939), pt. 2, supplement 6–14, cited in Roy Lubove, ed., *Pittsburgh* (New York, 1976), 112–21; John Bodnar, Roger Simon, and Michael P. Weber, *Lives of Their Own: Blacks, Italians, and Poles in Pittsburgh, 1900–1960* (Urbana, Ill., 1982), 117, 186.

24. Bodnar et al., *Lives of Their Own,* 55–82, esp. 59. See also Bodner et al., "Migration, Kinship, and Urban Adjustment: Blacks and Poles in Pittsburgh, 1900–1930," *Journal of American History* 66 (December 1979): 548–65.

25. Dennis C. Dickerson, *Out of the Crucible: Black Steelworkers in Western Pennsylvania, 1875–1980* (Albany, N.Y., 1986).

26. Linda Nyden, "Black Miners in Western Pennsylvania, 1925–1931: The National Miners Union and the United Mine Workers of America" (seminar paper, Department of History, University of Pittsburgh, 1974), 3, 41, and "Black Miners in Western Pennsylvania, 1925–1931: The National Miners Union and the United Mine Workers of America," *Science and Society* 41 (Spring 1977): 69–101. See also Gerald E. Allen, "The Negro Coal Miner in the Pittsburgh District" (M.A. thesis, Department of Economics, University of Pittsburgh, 1927).

27. Nyden, seminar paper, 39–46.

28. Peter Gottlieb, *Making Their Own Way: Southern Blacks' Migration to Pittsburgh, 1916–1930* (Urbana: University of Illinois Press, 1987), 185, 192, 118, 205f., the dissertation on which this book was based was completed in 1977. See also Gottlieb's "Migration and

Jobs: The New Black Workers in Pittsburgh, 1916–1930," *Western Pennsylvania Historical Magazine* 61 (January 1978): 1–16; and Russell Bogin, "The Role of Education in Black Employment in the A. M. Byers & Co." (seminar paper, Department of History, Carnegie Mellon University, 1981).

29. Reid, *Social Conditions,* 39–41, 58–63. See also Maryann Brice, "Vocational Adjustment of 101 Negro High School Graduates in Allegheny County" (M.A. thesis, Department of Social Work, University of Pittsburgh, 1938); Elsie R. Clarke, "A Study of Juvenile Delinquency in a Restricted Area of Pittsburgh" (M.A. thesis, Department of Sociology, University of Pittsburgh, 1932); Wiley A. Hall, "Negro Housing and Rents in the Hill District of Pittsburgh, Pa." (M.A. thesis, Department of Economics, University of Pittsburgh, 1929); Ruth M. Lowman, "Negro Delinquency in Pittsburgh" (M.A. thesis, Social Work, Carnegie Institute of Technology, 1923); Anna C. Morrison, "Study of 141 Dependent Negro Children Placed in Boarding Homes by the Juvenile Court of Allegheny County" (M.A. thesis, Department of Sociology, University of Pittsburgh, 1935); and Donald J. Richey, "The Legal Status of Education for Colored People as Determined by Court Decisions" (M.A. thesis, Department of Sociology, University of Pittsburgh, 1932). In addition, see Dean Scruggs Yarbrough, "Educational Status of Negro Public School Children as Reflecting Economic and Social Problems" (M.A. thesis, Department of Economics, University of Pittsburgh, 1926); Marion M. Banfield, "A Settlement House and Its Negro Neighbors" (M.A. thesis, Social Administration, University of Pittsburgh, 1941); Horace W. Bickle, "A Study of the Intelligence of a Group of Negro Trade School Boys" (M.A. thesis, Department of Psychology, University of Pittsburgh, 1930); Celia R. Moss, "Social and Economic Factors Affecting the Health and Welfare of a Group of Migrant Families: A Study of 29 Negro Families Migrating to Aliquippa, Pa., from Americus, Georgia, in 1936, for the Purpose of Employment at the Jones & Laughlin Steel Corporation" (M.A. thesis, Social Administration, University of Pittsburgh, 1943); Shirley A. Butler, "Attitudes of a Selected Group of Negro Women on the Selection of Medical Facilities in Pittsburgh" (M.A. thesis, Department of Social Work, University of Pittsburgh, 1948); and Juliata Martinez, "The Role of the Group Worker in the Area of Interracial Education" (M.A. thesis, Social Administration, University of Pittsburgh, 1944).

30. Bodnar et al., *Lives of Their Own,* 256. For a description of Bloomfield, see William Simon, Samuel Patti, and George Hermann, "Bloomfield: An Italian Working-Class Neighborhood," *Italian Americana* 7 (1981): 102–16. For other neighborhoods, see Alexander Z. Pittler, "The Hill District in Pittsburgh: A Study in Succession" (M.A. thesis, Department of Sociology, University of Pittsburgh, 1930); Delmar C. Seawright, "Effect of City Growth on the Homewood-Brushton District of Pittsburgh" (M.A. thesis, Department of Sociology, University of Pittsburgh, 1932); and Everett Alderman, "Study of Twenty-Four Fraternal Organizations and Clubs of the Larimer Avenue District, East Liberty, Pittsburgh" (M.A. thesis, School of Education, University of Pittsburgh, 1932).

31. Alonzo G. Moron, "Distribution of the Negro Population in Pittsburgh, 1910–1930" (M.A. thesis, Department of Sociology, University of Pittsburgh, 1933), 28–30.

32. See Joe Darden, *Afro-Americans in Pittsburgh: The Residential Segregation of a People* (Lexington, Mass., 1973), 13; and Karl and Alma Taeuber, *Negroes in Cities: Residential Segregation and Neighborhood Change* (Chicago, 1965), table 4.

33. Moron, "Distribution of the Negro Population," 29. Curiously, the overall index of racial segregation in Pittsburgh was still quite high.

34. The quotation is from Bell, "Commercial Recreation Facilities." Whites also moved out of the Hill district at this time; Italians and Jews moved to Bloomfield and Squirrel Hill, respectively. For the recollections of a Jewish resident, see M. R. Goldman, "The Hill District of

Pittsburgh as I Knew It," *Western Pennsylvania Historical Magazine* 51 (July 1968): 279–95. See also Kurt Pine, "The Jews in the Hill District of Pittsburgh, 1910–1940: A Study of Trends" (M.A. thesis, Social Administration, University of Pittsburgh, 1943).

35. Bodnar et al., *Lives of Their Own,* 197; Steven Sapolsky and Bartholomew Roselli, *Homewood-Brushton: A Century of Community-Making* (Pittsburgh, 1987). See also Geraldine Hermalin, "Recreational Resources for the Negro in the Homewood-Brushton Area, 1945" (M.A. thesis, Social Administration, University of Pittsburgh, 1945); Helen Judd, "A Study of Recreational Facilities for Negroes in Manchester" (M.A. thesis, Social Administration, University of Pittsburgh, 1945); Carole T. Szwarc, "Manchester: A Study in Contrast, 1930–1968" (seminar paper, Department of History, Carnegie Mellon University, n.d.); Hilda Kaplan, "Recreational Facilities for the Negro in the East Liberty District, with Special Emphasis on Tracts 7G 12 and 12E" (M.A. thesis, Social Administration, University of Pittsburgh, 1945); Ruby E. Ovid, "Recreational Facilities for the Negro in Manchester" (M.A. thesis, Department of Social Work, University of Pittsburgh, 1952); Pauline Redmond, "Race Relations on the South Side of Pittsburgh as Seen Through Brashear Settlement" (M.A. thesis, Department of Social Work, University of Pittsburgh, 1936); and Gertrude A. Tanneyhill, "Carver House and the Community: A Study of Twenty-two Families Served by Brashear Association in December 1940 and 1941" (M.A. thesis, Social Administration, University of Pittsburgh, 1942).

36. Jean Hamilton Walls, "A Study of the Negro Graduates of the University of Pittsburgh for the Decade, 1926–1936" (Ph.D. diss., University of Pittsburgh, 1938), 18 and passim.

37. Based on personal communications from several Pittsburghers to the author. This seating pattern might simply have been the result of dark-skinned newcomers joining an older and predominantly light-skinned congregation in which the established members continued to occupy seats toward the front.

38. Gottlieb, *Making Their Own Way,* 267. For the description of a storefront Pentecostal church in the Hill district, see Melvin D. Williams, "A Pentecostal Congregation in Pittsburgh: A Religious Community in a Black Ghetto" (Ph.D. diss., University of Pittsburgh, 1973), published as *Community in a Black Pentecostal Church: An Anthropological Study* (Pittsburgh, 1974). See also Noshir F. Kaikobad, "The Colored Moslems of Pittsburgh" (M.A. thesis, Department of Social Work, University of Pittsburgh, 1948); Dennis C. Dickerson, "Black Ecumenicist: Efforts to Establish a United Methodist Episcopal Church, 1918–1932," *Church History* 52 (December 1983): 479–91; Dickerson's "The Black Church in Industrializing Western Pennsylvania, 1870–1950," *Western Pennsylvania Historical Magazine* 64 (October 1981): 329–44; Haseltine T. Watkins, "The Newer Religious Bodies Among Negroes in the City of Pittsburgh" (M.A. thesis, Social Administration, University of Pittsburgh, 1945).

39. Majorie Allen, "The Negro Upper Class in Pittsburgh, 1910–1964" (seminar paper, Department of History, University of Pittsburgh 1964), 5 and passim.

40. The *Courier* had been established several years previously by Edwin Nathaniel Harleston, a guard at the H. J. Heinz food-processing plant. See Buni, *Vann,* 42–43.

41. *University Times,* February 19, 1987; Buni, *Vann,* 37–38, 80–81. Buni's excellent biography is rich in detail on the social and political history of black Pittsburgh from about 1910 to 1940. Frank Bolden, former reporter for the *Courier,* is a storehouse of information and insight. See also Miriam B. Rosenbloom, "An Outline of the History of the Negro in the Pittsburgh Area" (M.A. thesis, Social Administration, University of Pittsburgh, 1945); and Charles C. Berkley, "The Analysis and Classification of Negro Items in Four Pittsburgh Newspapers, 1917–1937" (M.A. thesis, Department of Sociology, University of Pittsburgh, 1937).

42. Buni, *Vann,* 107ff.

43. Wright, "The Negro in Pittsburgh," chap. 13, pp. 3, 62.

44. Charles J. Burks was the first black to be admitted to the University of Pittsburgh Medical School; he gained staff privileges at Montefiore Hospital (*University Times,* February 19, 1987); Dr. M. R. Hadley was the first on the staff of any Allegheny County hospital, having joined McKeesport Hospital in 1945 (*Pittsburgh Press,* Roto Section, October 17, 1982, 22). Bodnar et al., *Lives of Their Own,* 242; Martha B. Moore, *Unmasked: The Story of My Life on Both Sides of the Race Barrier* (New York, 1964), 59.

45. Ralph Proctor Jr., "Racial Discrimination Against Black Teachers and Black Professionals in the Pittsburgh Public School System, 1834–1973" (Ph.D. diss., University of Pittsburgh, 1979), table II-5, pp. 46–48. See also Barbara J. Hunter, "The Public Education of Blacks in the City of Pittsburgh, 1920–1950: Actions and Reactions of the Black Community in Its Pursuit of Educational Equality" (Ph.D. diss., University of Pittsburgh, 1987).

46. Walls, "Negro Graduates," 65.

47. Ibid., 105. Track and field was the only major sport open to blacks in the 1930s; those who did participate distinguished themselves. Everett Utterback was chosen team captain in 1931 (causing an uproar); John Woodruff and Herb Douglass won medals in the 1936 and 1948 Olympics. See Jim O'Brien, ed., *Hail to Pitt* (University of Pittsburgh, 1982), 246–47. Not until the 1940s were blacks allowed on the football and basketball teams.

48. Buni, *Vann,* 74, 176; Wright, "The Negro in Pittsburgh," chap. 5, pp. 70ff.

49. Buni, *Vann,* 62–63.

50. In 1939, one year before his death, Vann finally was invited to join the Chamber of Commerce (ibid., 122, 315).

51. Ibid., chap. 7.

52. Ibid., 91ff.

53. Ibid., 357 n. 75. By the late 1920s the *Courier* gave less attention to Pittsburgh, apparently reflecting Vann's disillusionment with local politics and his increasing interest in securing a position with Roosevelt's New Deal (ibid., 142ff.). Walter Tucker in 1930 was elected the first black state legislator from Western Pennsylvania (ibid., 356 n. 75). See also James Brewer, "Robert L. Vann and the *Pittsburgh Courier*" (M.A. thesis, Department of History, University of Pittsburgh, 1941); James S. Galloway, "The *Pittsburgh Courier* and FEPC Agitation" (M.A. thesis, Department of History, University of Pittsburgh, 1954).

54. Buni, *Vann,* 194, 272–73.

55. Ruth Simmons, "The Negro in Recent Pittsburgh Politics" (M.A. thesis, Department of Political Science, University of Pittsburgh, 1945), 38, 43, 140, and passim. See also James S. Galloway, "The Negro in Politics in Pittsburgh, 1928–1940" (seminar paper, History Department, University of Pittsburgh, n.d.).

56. Henry A. Schooley, "A Case Study of the Pittsburgh Branch of the NAACP" (M.A. thesis, Department of Sociology, University of Pittsburgh, 1952), 8, 58–59 and passim; Buni, *Vann,* 58–59, 200; Frank Zabrosky, "Some Aspects of Negro Civic Leadership in Pittsburgh, 1955–1965" (seminar paper, Department of History, University of Pittsburgh, n.d.), 9.

57. Arthur J. Edmunds, *Daybreakers: The Story of the Urban League of Pittsburgh, the First Sixty-Five Years* (Pittsburgh, 1983), 29ff. See also Ruth L. Stevenson, "The Pittsburgh Urban League" (M.A. thesis, Department of Social Work, University of Pittsburgh, 1936); Antoinette H. Westmoreland, "A Study of Requests for Specialized Services Directed to the Urban League of Pittsburgh" (M.A. thesis, Department of Social Work, University of Pittsburgh, 1938); and Katherine R. Wilson, "A Personnel Guidance of Negro Youth in the Urban League of Pittsburgh" (M.A. thesis, Department of Psychology, University of Pittsburgh, 1940).

58. "Homer S. Brown: First Black Political Leader in Pittsburgh," *Journal of Negro History* 66 (Winter 1981–82): 304–17; Simmons, "Negro in Recent Pittsburgh Politics," 39.

59. Proctor, "Racial Discrimination," 50–62, 75–79, and passim. In fact, the board's hiring also reflected a greater sensitivity to problems of interracial relations. See, for example, Anthony J. Major, "An Investigation of Supervisory Practices for the Improvement of Instruction in Negro Public Schools" (Ed.D. diss., School of Education, University of Pittsburgh, 1940); Kathryn R. Witz, "A Study of the Dispositions Given Negro and White Juvenile Delinquents at the Juvenile Court of Allegheny County" (M.A. thesis, Department of Sociology, University of Pittsburgh, 1949); Margaret D. Thomson, "The Role of the American Service Institute's Consultant on Interracial and Intercultural Problems for Summer Camps in Allegheny County" (M.A. thesis, Department of Social Work, University of Pittsburgh, 1949); Ignacia Torres, "Methods of Developing Interracial and Intercultural Practices in the Pittsburgh YWCA: A Descriptive Study of Three Departments" (M.A. thesis, Department of Social Work, University of Pittsburgh, 1947); Kenneth R. Hopkins, "Some Factors Involved in the Discontinuance of Participation of Selected Junior-Age Negro Boys in the Program of the Irene Kaufmann Settlement" (M.A. thesis, Department of Social Work, University of Pittsburgh, 1952); Lillian B. Hotard, "Problems of Implementing Agency Policy: A Study of Children in Inter-Racial Activity Groups in Wadsworth Hall Who Discontinued Participation During 1949–1950" (M.A. thesis, Department of Social Work, University of Pittsburgh, 1951); Elizabeth B. Jackson, "The Pittsburgh Council on Intercultural Education: A Study in Community Organizations" (M.A. thesis, Department of Social Work, University of Pittsburgh, 1948); and Albert G. Rosenberg, "Interracial Development in Hill District Agencies and Schools, 1944 to 1948" (M.A. thesis, Department of Social Work, University of Pittsburgh, 1949).

See also Arthur M. Stevenson, "Analysis of Five Agencies of Pittsburgh Providing Intercultural Services" (M.A. thesis, Department of Social Work, University of Pittsburgh, 1949); Carl B. Richard and William B. Weinstein, "The Curtaineers: A Study of an Interracial Dramatic Project of the Irene Kaufmann Settlement of Pittsburgh from Its Inception" (M.A. thesis, Department of Social Work, University of Pittsburgh, 1948); Goldie Gibson, "The Change of Policy in SoHo's Afternoon Program and Its Effect on Interracial Relationships in Groups" (M.A. thesis, Department of Social Work, University of Pittsburgh, 1950); Cuthbert G. Gifford, "The Hill District People's Forum: A Study of Social Action as Carried Out by the Forum from Its Inception in 1942 to March, 1947" (M.A. thesis, Department of Social Work, University of Pittsburgh, 1947; Anne M. Barton, "Ethnic and Racial Groups in Rankin, Pa.: A Study of Relations Between Them as Expressed Through Various Social Forces" (M.A. thesis, Department of Social Work, University of Pittsburgh, 1947). That black students had special needs is obvious from the studies of Helen M. Simmen, "A Study of the Graduates of the Fifth Avenue High School" (M.A. thesis, School of Education, University of Pittsburgh, 1928); Irene A. Thompson, "Everyday English of a Ghetto Group" (M.A. thesis, School of Education, University of Pittsburgh, 1929); and J. Allen Figurel, "The Vocabulary of Underprivileged Children" (Ph.D. diss., School of Education, University of Pittsburgh, 1948).

60. Race relations received increasing attention during the 1940s and were the subject of numerous master's theses. See Celia Bach, "The Pittsburgh Council on Intercultural Education: A Descriptive Study" (M.A. thesis, Social Administration, University of Pittsburgh, 1946); Bernard M. Shiffman, "The Development of Interracial Camping in Allegheny County" (M.A. thesis, Department of Social Administration, University of Pittsburgh, 1946); Marylyn E. Duncan, "Areas of Racial Tension in a Public Housing Project: A Study of Relations Between Building Location in Terrace Village and Racial Tensions, with Special Reference to Play Areas" (M.A. thesis, Social Administration, University of Pittsburgh, 1946); Thelma W. Smith, "The Selection of Foster Homes for Negro Foster Children of the Juvenile Court of Allegheny County" (M.A. thesis, Social Administration, University of Pittsburgh, 1942); Frances A. Zorn,

"Substitute Parental Care of the Negro Child" (M.A. thesis, Social Administration, University of Pittsburgh, 1941); Alberta W. Brown, "A Descriptive Study of the Negro Students Received in Transfer from the South at Herron Hill Junior High School from the Fall of 1943 Through the Fall of 1945" (M.A. thesis, Social Administration, University of Pittsburgh, 1946); and Francis J. Costigan, "Employment Opportunities for Student Leaving Herron Hill Junior High School" (M.A. thesis, Social Administration, University of Pittsburgh, 1944).

61. For an analysis of this trend nationally, see William J. Wilson, *The Declining Significance of Race* (Chicago, 1978); Frank Giarratani and David Houston, "Economic Change in the Pittsburgh Region," typescript, March 27, 1986, 12; *U.S. Census of Manufacturers, 1947,* vol. 3: *Statistics by States* (Washington, D.C., 1950); and *U.S. Census of Manufacturers, 1977,* vol. 3: *Geographic Area Statistics,* pt. 2, *General Summary Nebraska–Wyoming* (Washington, D.C., 1971).

62. Giarratani and Houston, "Economic Change," 27; L. Haley, president, Urban League of Pittsburgh, press conference, January 22, 1987. William O'Hare, a Washington, D.C., consultant, ranked metropolitan areas by comparing the economic status of local blacks to that of local whites; see *Pittsburgh Press,* February 8, 1987, B5. See also Institute for the Black Family, "Final Report of the Black Community Profile Study" (typescript, University of Pittsburgh, 1987), 8; Barry Wellman, "Crossing Social Boundaries: Cosmopolitanism Among Black and White Adolescents," *Social Science Quarterly* 52 (December 1971): 602–24; P. S. Fry and K. J. Coe, "Achievement Performance of Internally and Externally Oriented Black and White High School Students Under Conditions of Competition and Co-operation Expectancies," *British Journal of Education Psychology* 50 (June 1980): 162–67.

63. Roy Lubove, *Twentieth-Century Pittsburgh: Government, Business, and Environmental Change* (New York, 1969), 130–32.

64. However, the exodus by whites, already under way before urban renewal, was swifter than that of middle-class blacks. Homewood-Brushton, for example, went from 22 percent black in 1950 to 66 percent black in 1960. Destruction of the lower Hill probably increased residential segregation, although indexes of residential segregation show remarkably little change from 1930 to 1970. Darden, *Afro-Americans in Pittsburgh,* calculated that for each of those years, 70 to 75 percent of blacks (or whites) would have to change wards to desegregate the city. He also presents calculations showing that the segregation was due primarily to racial rather than economic factors. See also M. Ruth McIntyre, "The Organizational Nature of an Urban Residential Neighborhood in Transition: Homewood-Brushton of Pittsburgh" (Ph.D. diss., University of Pittsburgh, 1963); Suk-Han Shin, "A Geographical Measurement of Residential Blight in the City of Pittsburgh, Pa., 1950 and 1960" (Ph.D. diss., University of Pittsburgh, 1975); William S. J. Smith, "Redlining: A Neighborhood Analysis of Mortgage Lending in Pittsburgh, Pa." (M.A. thesis, Department of Geography, University of Pittsburgh, 1982); Jacqueline W. Wolfe, "The Changing Pattern of Residence of the Negro in Pittsburgh, Pa., with Emphasis on the Period 1930–1960" (M.A. thesis, Department of Geography, University of Pittsburgh, 1964); and Brenda K. Miller, "Racial Change in an Urban Residential Area: A Geographic Analysis of Wilkinsburg, Pa." (Ph.D. diss., University of Pittsburgh, 1979); Stanley Lieberson, *Ethic Patterns in American Cities* (New York, 1963). See, further, R. Jeffrey Green and George M. von Furstenberg, "The Effects of Race and Age of Housing on Mortgage Delinquency Risk," *Urban Studies* (Great Britain) 12 (February 1975): 85–89; Arnold J. Auerbach, "The Patterns of Community Leadership in Urban Redevelopment: A Pittsburgh Profile" (Ph.D. diss., University of Pittsburgh, 1960); Edmund M. Burke, "A Study of Community Organization in Urban Renewal: Social Work Method in a Non-Social Work Setting" (Ph.D. diss., University of Pittsburgh, 1965); Carol Buer and Joan Scharf, "A Study of Residents'

Attitudes Toward an Interracial Private Housing Development" (M.A. thesis, Department of Social Work, University of Pittsburgh, 1959); Gayle H. Dobbs, "Support Systems and Services Utilized by Parents in Beltzhoover" (M.A. thesis, Department of Child Development, University of Pittsburgh, 1980); and Rodney A. Pelton, "The Value System of a Large Voluntary Negro Civic Organization Within a Poverty Area: The Homewood-Brushton Committee Improvement Association" (Ph.D. diss., University of Pittsburgh, 1968).

65. Neil Gilbert, "Clients or Constituents? A Case Study of Pittsburgh's War on Poverty" (Ph.D. diss., University of Pittsburgh, 1968), 23, 119, 125; see also his "Maximum Feasible Participation? A Pittsburgh Encounter," *Social Work* 14 (July 1969): 84–92. Regarding other efforts, see David H. Freedman, "An Analysis of the Institutional Capability of the City of Pittsburgh to Provide Effective Technical Assistance to Black Businessmen" (Ph.D. diss., University of Pittsburgh, 1971); Colin De'Ath, "Patterns of Participation and Exclusion: A Poor Italian and Black Urban Community and Its Response to a Federal Poverty Program" (Ph.D. diss., University of Pittsburgh, 1970); Barbara B. Jameson, *A Study of the Social Services Program of the Housing Authority, City of Pittsburgh* (University of Pittsburgh School of Social Work, 1975); Norman J. Johnson and Peggy R. Sanday, "Subcultural Variations in an Urban Poor Population," *American Anthropologist* 73 (February 1971): 128–43; Shirley A. Ali, "A Case Study of Interracial Child Care Relations in a Residential Institution" (M.A. thesis, Department of Child Development, University of Pittsburgh, 1975); Larry V. Stockman, "Poverty and Hunger: A Pittsburgh Profile of Selected Neighborhoods" (Ph.D. diss., University of Pittsburgh, 1982); and Earl D. Hollander, "Utilization and Views of Available Health Care Among Residents in Three Poverty Neighborhoods in Pittsburgh, Pa." (Ph.D. diss., University of Pittsburgh, 1970).

66. Stanley Plastrik, "Confrontation in Pittsburgh," *Dissent* 17 (January–February 1970): 25–31; Irwin Dubinsky, "Trade Union Discrimination in the Pittsburgh Construction Industry: How and Why It Operates," *Urban Affairs Quarterly* 6 (March 1971): 297–318. See also Daniel U. Levine, "Research Note: Are the Black Poor Satisfied with Conditions in Their Neighborhood?" *Journal of the American Institute of Planners* 38 (May 1972): 168–71; and Norman D. Randolph, "Perceptions of Former Trainees of the Effectiveness of the Comprehensive Employment Training Act (CETA) Training Programs in Allegheny County" (Ph.D. diss., University of Pittsburgh, 1983).

67. Pittsburgh Board of Public Education, *Annual Report for 1965: The Quest for Racial Equality in the Pittsburgh Public Schools,* 7, 11, 14, 19, 21; David H. Elliott, "Social Origins and Values of Teachers and Their Attitudes to Students from Poverty Background" (Ph.D. diss., University of Pittsburgh, 1968); Louis H. McKey, "The Pennsylvania Human Relations Committee and Desegregation in the Public Schools of Pennsylvania, 1961–1978" (Ph.D. diss., University of Pittsburgh, 1978).

68. Rollo Turner, "Citizen, Freeman, or Elector: A History of Blacks in the Political and Electoral Process in Pittsburgh, 1837–1975," typescript, March 1987; *Pittsburgh Press,* October 27, 1986. Carter's quote appeared locally; my source is the *Dayton (Ohio) Daily News,* November 30, 1986, 3B.

69. Melvin D. Williams, "Belmar: Diverse LifeStyles in a Pittsburgh Black Neighborhood," *Ethnic Groups* 3 (December 19): 23–54; for a fuller description, see Williams's *On the Street Where I Lived* (New York, 1981).

70. Williams, *Community in a Black Pentecostal Church,* 4, 21, and passim.

71. *Board of Education, Annual Report for 1965,* 7 and passim; Proctor, "Racial Discrimination," chap. 3, tables 3, 4, 5, 9, and 1, 149–64; table IV-I. Proctor documents efforts by these teachers to promote black pride and improve race relations. See also Philip E. McPherson, "Coordination of Efforts for the Improvement of Race Relations in the Pittsburgh Public Schools" (Ph.D. diss., Harvard University, 1966); Theodore Vasser, "A Historical and Phe-

nomenological Study of Black Administration in the Pittsburgh Public School System Inclusive of the Years 1950–1977" (Ph.D. diss., University of Pittsburgh, 1978); Richard D. Gutkind, "Desegregation of Pittsburgh Public Schools, 1968–1980: A Study of the Superintendent and Educational Policy Dynamics" (Ph.D. diss., University of Pittsburgh, 1983); Chapman W. Bouldin, "An Analysis of How Black Americans Are Depicted in Eleventh Grade United States History Textbooks Used in the Secondary Public Schools from 1930 to 1979" (Ph.D. diss., University of Pittsburgh, 1980); Edward A. Suchman et al., *The Relationship Between Poverty and Educational Deprivation: Final Report* (University of Pittsburgh, Learning Research and Development Center, 1968); Edward S. Greenberg, "Black Children, Self-Esteem and the Liberation Movement," *Politics and Society* 2 (Spring 1972): 293–307; Jack L. Palmer, "A Case Study in School-Community Conflict over Desegregation" (Ph.D. diss., University of Pittsburgh, 1974); and Barbara Sizemore, *An Abashing Anomaly: The High-Achieving Predominantly Black Elementary School* (University of Pittsburgh, Department of Black Community Education, Research, and Development [Black Studies], 1983).

72. Giarratani and Houston, "Economic Change," 11.

73. Homer Brown was the first black appointed to the Board of Education, in 1943. At the University of Pittsburgh, during the 1980s the growth of black student enrollment leveled off and the number of black faculty actually declined. See the annual *Fact Book,* published by the Office of Institutional and Policy Studies. For an analysis of the impact of the UCEP, the special admissions program for minority students, see Diane D. Eddins, "A Casual Model of the Attrition of Specially Admitted Black Students in Higher Education" (Ph.D. diss., University of Pittsburgh, 1981); Wilma R. Smith, "The Relationship Between Self-Concept of Academic Ability, Locus-of-Control of the Environment, and Academic Achievement of Black Students Specially Admitted to the University of Pittsburgh" (Ph.D. diss., University of Pittsburgh, 1972); and Barbara K. Shore, "New Careers: Myth or Reality? A Study of Stirrings of Indigenous New Professionals" (Ph.D. diss., University of Pittsburgh, 1971). The universities also became more attuned to nearby black neighborhoods. See Ralph H. Holmes, "The University of Pittsburgh's Trees–Hall–Community Leisure–Learn Program, 1968–1982" (Ph.D. diss., University of Pittsburgh, 1983); Sheila L. Johnson, "The Ethnomusicology Program at the University of Pittsburgh: A Case Study" (Ph.D. diss., University of Pittsburgh, 1983); and Dorothy Burnett, "Black Studies Departments and Afro-American Library Collections at Two Predominantly White Universities: A Comparative Analysis" (Ph.D. diss., University of Pittsburgh, 1984). The relative performance of the nation's research universities was documented by Alexander Astin, *Minorities in American Higher Education* (San Francisco, 1982), 136. The ranking was based on a comparison of percentage black enrollment in a specific university to the proportion black enrollment in all universities in the state. Penn State University came out near the bottom nationally.

74. Edmunds, *Daybreakers,* 112–37. See also "Blacks in White: Affirmative Action in Health Services [in Pittsburgh]," *Urban League Review* 4 (Winter 1979): 65–71; and James O. Hackshaw, "The Committee for Fair Employment in Pittsburgh Department Stores: A Study of the Methods and Techniques Used by the Committee in Their Campaign to Secure a Non-Discriminatory Hiring Policy in the Department Stores of Pittsburgh" (M.A. thesis, Department of Social Work, University of Pittsburgh, 1949).

75. We very much need studies of black businesses in Pittsburgh. For one of the few case studies, see Kem R. Kemathe, "Selected Characteristics of Black Businesses in the U.S., 1969–1972, with Two Case Studies of Black Owned Businesses in Pittsburgh as Special Reference" (Ph.D. diss., University of Pittsburgh, 1978).

76. Patricia Prattis Jennings also was probably the first black to play for the orchestra in any capacity when she performed in 1956, with William Steinberg conducting. Personal communication, March 29, 1988.

CHAPTER EIGHTEEN

Public Housing, Isolation, and the Urban Underclass:
Philadelphia's Richard Allen Homes, 1941–1965

John Bauman, Norman P. Hummon,
Edward K. Muller

The underclass is a timely issue. In the past decade at least five books and dozens of articles examining the subject have been published.[1] Scholars define this inner-city population as physically and socially isolated. Individuals and families who experience sustained unemployment or may not even participate in the labor force, who may engage in criminal behavior, endure long-term poverty and are welfare dependent. These characteristics, moreover, are often associated with the large percentage of inner-city, minority families that are headed by women.[2]

The debate over the causes of the underclass locates its origins in the 1960s. In his acclaimed *The Truly Disadvantaged,* William Julius Wilson distinguishes today's underclass from post–World War II low-income black families who lived in stable communities with strong social networks and little social disorganization.[3] Indeed, many scholars, especially in the early

This chapter was first published in the *Journal of Urban History* 17 (May 1991): 264–92. Copyright © 1991 by Sage Publications Inc. Reprinted by permission of Sage Publications Inc. The authors want to thank Michael Weber, Laurence Glasco, and the reviewers of the original draft for their valuable suggests. Material found in this chapter is based upon work supported by the Samuel S. Fels Fund of Philadelphia, by the Center for Social and Urban Research of the University of Pittsburgh, and by the National Science Foundation under Grant No. SES-8208448.

1970s, emphasized the black family as an adaptive institution that enabled ghetto residents to endure the depriving inner-city environment. They argued that historically in every generation the black family has been forced to contend against monumental social and economic barriers. In the face of these obstacles, black families have been resilient and have made necessary adaptations, including, for example, broadening kinship networks and reshaping male and female roles.[4]

However, in our study of low-income black families living in the Richard Allen Homes, a large Philadelphia public housing project, we have evidence of a black population who, as early as the 1950s, displayed characteristics similar to the modern underclass.[5] In the 1960s, scholars and social commentators also described families in public housing whose ability to cope strained against the hardships of their ghetto existence. But these observers failed to recognize the importance of public housing policy itself, and the urban redevelopment program of which it was a part, as factors in this postwar era. They treated public housing projects merely as ghetto space, albeit federally designed space. In their conceptions, these families confronted hardships common to all ghetto residents, including neighborhood segregation, labor market exclusion, inadequate education, and poor access to social services.[6] We see postwar federal policy, particularly public housing and urban renewal policies, posing obstacles that intensified social isolation and impeded the adaptive strategies that had historically facilitated survival in the depriving world of the inner city.

The Low-Income Black Family in the Literature

It was not until the 1960s, in the wake of the rediscovery of black urban poverty, that psychologist Kenneth Clark's *Dark Ghetto* and Assistant Secretary of Labor Daniel P. Moynihan's *The Negro Family* refocused scholarly attention on black life in the city, and especially on the black family. If Clark's portrait of the socially stifling environment of the inner city, from which Moynihan borrowed, drew uniform praise, the young assistant secretary's call for governmental intervention in the black family attracted unmitigated controversy.[7] A year before his Department of Labor study of the black family, Moynihan and Nathan Glazer, in *Beyond the Melting Pot,* attributed black America's disadvantaged position in American society to structural defects in the black family, emphasizing the destructive legacy of slavery.[8] Moynihan's 1965 report expressly sought to explain why the civil rights victories of the late 1950s and 1960s would not be translated into black equality—why, that is, the 1964 civil rights legislation, the Manpower Training Act, and the Office of Equal Opportunity would not halt the breakup or diminish the number of black families on the welfare rolls.[9] He asserted that the cumulative effect of historic discrimination (including the slavery-induced matriarchal family structure and the destructiveness of rapid urbanization) rendered the black family too impaired to seize the opportunities afforded by the civil rights victories. "The fundamental problem," he wrote in 1965, "is that the Negro family in urban ghettos is crumbling." A middle class, Moynihan conceded, had saved itself, but the vast number of unskilled, poorly educated blacks had become enmeshed in a self-perpetuating cycle of poverty. Therefore, as early as 1965, Moynihan spotlighted the emergence of a black underclass, the same population that sociologists such as William Julius Wilson would rediscover in the 1980s.[10]

Like Wilson's rediscovery in the 1980s, Moynihan's earlier disclosure unleashed a whirlwind of debate. Following the lead of Kenneth Clark, Moynihan's report contained solid evidence about the state of the urban black family. He based his study on an analysis of 1960 census data that showed that blacks represented an increasingly large segment of the welfare population, that females headed 25 percent of black families, and that nearly a quarter of black babies were born out of wedlock. Therefore, despite gains during the 1950s in black employment, Moynihan revealed that the number of black female-headed families was rising ominously in tandem with black welfare dependency. He concluded that the black family was hopelessly entangled in a web of poverty. While Moynihan acknowledged the existence of a historical pattern of housing and job discrimination, "at the heart of the deterioration of the fabric of Negro society," he wrote, "lay the deterioration of the Negro family."[11]

Moynihan's nod to the upwardly mobile black middle class notwithstanding, many scholars viewed his report as a scathing indictment of black families in general. Rather than producing a consensus on how to attack inner-city poverty, as President Lyndon Baines Johnson had hoped, Moynihan's report on the black family stirred a decade of political and academic controversy. Not only were federal policies for achieving black equality at stake, but also scholarly positions concerning the nature and history of the black family. Ethnologists and historians who wrote about the black family in the 1960s and early 1970s hardly disputed Moynihan's linkage of fatherlessness and deepening poverty. What they challenged was his conclusion that this represented a pathological condition rooted in twentieth-century urbanization and discriminatory employment, as well as in the ravages of slavery and post–Civil War Reconstruction. Ardent defenders of the black family particularly assailed Moynihan's "tangle of pathology" thesis, first challenging the assistant secretary's use of statistical data, then attacking his use of race as an explanatory variable.[12]

Elizabeth Herzog and Hylan Lewis denounced Moynihan's insinuation of the black family in a culture of poverty. Rather than being embedded in a dysfunctional culture, lower-class black family behavior, they argued, originated in the travail of poor people burdened by discrimination, joblessness, and low pay. According to Herzog and Lewis, the socioeconomic indicators that Moynihan had used to define the culture of poverty—poor employability, low wages, crowded living conditions, and poor education—defined poverty not black culture. Moreover, they charged Moynihan with failing to recognize the great diversity of both incomes and lifestyles among black families. When controlled for income, argued Herzog, black and white family differences had largely disappeared.[13]

Studies of Syracuse (New York), and the Cardoza area of Washington, D.C., by Charles V. Willie, and of St. Louis by David Schulz and Camille Jeffers, found that, despite poverty, black families nourished middle-class aspirations. After a series of interviews in the 1960s with black mothers living in Washington, D.C., public housing, Jeffers reported that the black women there expressed the same hopes for their children and had the same solicitude for their welfare as middle-class mothers. All these mothers lacked, Jeffers stressed, was the money to help accomplish their goals.[14]

However, while rejecting his characterization of the black family as a "tangle of pathology," these ethnographers of the 1960s seemed to concur with Moynihan that society had erected social and economic barriers to the attainment of middle-class status that many lower-class black families found increasingly impossible to surmount. Although viewing poverty as situational, not cultural, they saw the chronically poor internalizing lower-class behaviors that made dependency harder to overcome. This latter point of view was especially pronounced in the sociological writings of Lee Rainwater and Elliot Liebow. Participant-observers Liebow and Rainwater analyzed the behavior of poor urban black families. Their studies described the form and operation of low-income black families as part of the subculture rooted in a depriving environment. In particular, this environment denied the black male the opportunity to perform effectively the crucial role of breadwinner. Liebow's ethnographic study of Washington, D.C., streetcorner men explored the world of inner-city black males whose low skills and pay foreclosed the kind of employment that would have enabled them to feed and clothe a family adequately. Work, marriage, fatherhood, even friendship, became occasions for failure, and this failure shaped their social interactions and behavior.[15]

Failure seemed just as ubiquitous and malignant among the black tenant households of St. Louis' notorious Pruitt-Igoe housing project, which Rainwater studied in the early 1960s. In both "The Crucible of Identity" and

Behind Ghetto Walls, Rainwater portrayed the low-income black family enmeshed in an invidious process of victimization, one that allowed family members to survive inside the ghetto but that thwarted their ability to succeed outside. Rainwater presented the environment of Pruitt-Igoe as fearful and despairing, a world described by many tenants as "full of troubles."[16]

To cope with this world, low-income black families, according to Rainwater, fashioned sets of adaptive norms that imparted meaning to their lives as victims. Pruitt-Igoe families were fully cognizant of the "good," or normative, life of marriage and family presumably existing outside the ghetto walls. However, given the reality of their unstable incomes, unstable families, and unstable friendships, these families adapted instead to "our life," where marriages normally failed and children succumbed to the lure of the streets.[17] Nevertheless, despite his somber outlook for the black family, Rainwater, like Willie, Jeffers, Liebow, and other Moynihan critics, rejected the idea of a black culture of poverty. Instead, they saw the black family adapting to historical discrimination and to a racially oppressive social and economic environment. But in this process, argued Rainwater, poor black families formed a world view and set of behaviors that, while presenting a formidable obstacle, did not foreclose successful adaptation to the outside world.[18]

For Robert Staples, Carol Stack, and Joyce Ladner, Liebow and Rainwater had rescued the low-income black family from the culture of poverty without recognizing its positive features.[19] Hylan Lewis in 1967 had written that the "behavior of the bulk of poor Negro families appears as a pragmatic adjustment to external and internal stresses."[20] Four years later in 1971, amid the milieu of black power and black cultural nationalism, Staples, Ladner, and Stack declared that black lower-class familiy behavior was not only pragmatic but also effectively adaptive and indisputably legitimate. Staples, for one, took exception to Liebow's and Rainwater's thesis that the only difference between black males and white males is that they are black and live under adverse social and economic conditions. "Such an analysis," Staples contended, "ignored the existence of a unique black culture, with its own beliefs, attitudes, and rituals, which constituted a lifestyle that gives every culture its own distinctive character."[21]

In a study of low-income young black women based on her research as a member of Rainwater's Pruitt-Igoe project, Joyce Ladner forcefully stated the case for both the legitimacy and the viability of the black family. Employing what she called the "sociohistorical" perspective, Ladner charged that the black family had always endured the ravages of institutionalized racism that excluded blacks from full participation in social, economic, and political life. Blacks could not conform to social norms because society withheld from them the resources to accomplish basic material and social goals. In her *Tomorrow's Tomorrow,* Ladner dismissed middle-class family norms as irrelevant for blacks, thus freeing the low-income black family from centuries of stigma.[22] For Ladner as for Carol Stack, whose *All Our Kin* examined black family life in a midwestern city, rather than being pathological, as the popular stereotype would have it, the black family was effective, resourceful, and resilient in the face of historic racism.[23]

While ethnographers addressed Moynihan's assertion of a tangle of pathology, historians examined his theory that what he espied as black family defectiveness could be traced historically to slavery and urbanization. In addition to his debt to the historian Stanley Elkins, whose book *Slavery* compared the culture-rending experience of the chattel slavery to the psychologically debilitating horror of Nazi concentration camps,[24] Moynihan had drawn heavily for his treatment of the black family upon historically grounded Chicago sociologists, Ernest Burgess, Saint Clair Drake, and Horace Cayton, and especially E. Franklin Frazier.[25]

In the wake of the Great Depression, with black urbanization unabating and the rate of black joblessness and poverty appallingly high, Frazier questioned the very survivability of the urban low-income black family that he deemed too disorganized and demoralized to cope with modern city life. An assimilationist who feared that lower-class folkways impaired black progress, Frazier traced this flawed behavior historically to American Negro slavery that permitted only the loosest ties of sympathy between black family members and households. By casting the weak slave family adrift, even emancipation, insisted Frazier, proved a shattering experience. Nevertheless, despite being burdened by a loose family structure, the black family weathered the serfdom of the Reconstruction era only to flounder following the great urban migration northward. Frazier blamed this perceived demoralization and breakup of the lower-class urban black family not only on a matriarchal family structure inherited from slavery but also on the economic discrimination blacks faced in the city.[26]

Surmising that both Moynihan and Frazier had constructed their case for the pathological black family upon an untested assumption that slavery had demoralized the black family, in 1967 two historians, Laurence Glasco and Herbert Gutman, set out to derive a more accurate picture of the black family. They theorized that if, as Frazier and Moynihan argued, slavery caused matrifocal black families, then such families should be visible in the census records of nineteenth-century cities. The two historians quantitatively assessed black families in nineteenth- and early-twentieth-century Buffalo, New York. But, rather than broken families, they found that consistently for the years between 1855 and 1925 double-headed kin-related households prevailed among black families. Moreover, their research also disclosed strong evidence of lively black institutions, suggesting that, contrary to the Frazier and

Moynihan argument, urbanization had not destroyed the fabric of black social life.[27]

Tantalized by the Buffalo findings, historians scoured nineteenth-century archival records in Boston and Philadelphia. Elizabeth Pleck, for example, looked at black households in nineteenth-century Boston and discovered that typical black families there in the 1880s included husband, wife, and children. Poverty haunted black families in Boston, where in 1880 such low-paying jobs as waiter, cook, laborer, laundress, and seamstress accounted for 74 percent of black employment. Moreover, a high male death rate, compounded by spouse desertion and voluntary separation, ensured that 18 percent of Boston's black households in 1880 were headed by one parent. Nevertheless, these harsh vicissitudes of urban life, notwithstanding, a conjugal pair headed 82 percent of black households in the Cradle of Liberty.[28]

In their Philadelphia research, Frank Furstenberg, Theodore Hershberg, and John Modell pressed further the implications of Pleck's demographic findings. Comparing 1880 data on Philadelphia's Irish, German, and African-American families, the authors found little variation in family composition; black families were slightly more extended and slightly more female-headed.[29] Therefore, the findings about nineteenth-century black Philadelphia, Buffalo, and Boston did not uphold Moynihan's and Frazier's slavery-specific hypothesis. Indeed, in the 1847–80 era, families of ex-slaves seemed more likely to be two-parent households. Rather than slavery, Pleck, Furstenberg, Hershberg, and Modell identified economic and particularly demographic factors as the best predictors of female-headedness.[30]

The historian's effort to vindicate the modern black family culminated in Gutman's highly acclaimed *Black Family in Slavery and Freedom*. Encompassing more than three centuries of black family history, 1620–1925, Gutman's opus concluded that the black family had survived both slavery and the initial process of urbanization intact. Despite the venality and malevolence of white slaveholders, slave husbands and wives acted often heroically to defend and preserve the bonds of marriage and family. Rather than causing disorganization, as Frazier contended, emancipation and the era of Reconstruction, in Gutman's view, confirmed the free black family's resilience and vitality.[31]

According to Gutman, black families coped with the grinding rural poverty of the post–Civil War era by increasingly extending and augmenting their households, a process that continued in urban America. Despite evidence of high rates of joblessness and poverty among New York City black families in the 1920s, Gutman discovered neither rampant disorganization nor exceptionally widespread matrifocality. Although two of five families were augmented in 1925, mainly by taking in boarders, 83 percent had a husband present.[32]

Most of this effort to extricate the historical black family from the tangle of pathology emphasized black household form and structure. Furstenberg, Hershberg, and Modell speculated only briefly about how the urban black family functioned. In contrast, James Borchert, in *Alley Life in Washington,* explored how the low-income black family functioned in the initial half of the twentieth century. Like Pleck, Furstenberg, Gutman, and Glasco, he also found little evidence that urban life spawned broken families and bred welfare dependency, rampant sexual promiscuity, and juvenile delinquency, as nineteenth-century reformers had charged.[33]

Borchert abjured normative language in describing the alley world and its families. He preferred instead to present life there and the constellation of family types visible in the alley world as creatively adaptive responses to either life-cycle changes or desperate social and economic conditions. Despite its complexity of lifestyles, the alley world, like the family, functioned as a supportive unit.[34]

Borchert contended that black families molded rural folkways to the demands of urban living. He understood the resiliency and adaptability that the poor black alley family displayed in forging strategies for survival amid the dire economic circumstances of low pay and high unemployment. He equally commended the physical merits or adaptability of alley space. The "secret world" of the alley, argued Borchert, operated ideally as usable space, enabling dwellers to engage in cottage-type industries, fashion nurturing kinship systems, and in other ways support a viable community life.[35]

While Borchert discussed the alleys of Washington, D.C., the kinds of black family adaptation and expedients for survival that he discovered there were also visible in the urban environment generally. Borchert may have painted alley life in too roseate hues. The prewar Philadelphia black community described by Allan Ballard, Ethel Waters, and in numerous reports of the Philadelphia Housing Association reeked of violence and abject poverty. Nevertheless, in defense of Borchert, the ancient alleys, courts, streets, and parts of streets where blacks lived tucked within the racial and ethnic quilt work of prewar Philadelphia afforded black families the opportunity to engage in most of the economic, familial, and community-building strategies apparent in Washington, D.C. After World War II, the changing urban environment—and especially, as we shall see, public housing policy—curtailed the use of the survival strategies discussed by Borchert.[36]

Social Change in the Richard Allen Homes

A quarter-century of scholarship has left the debate about the nature and origin of the black underclass unresolved; while Charles Murray condemns the failure of Johnson's Great Society, Wilson blames its successes. During the years 1965–90, from Moynihan to Rainwater, Ladner to Gutman and Borchert, scholars have wrestled with the issue of black culture versus the black situation in a racially oppressive socioeconomic system. Their studies either deplored the racist urban environment that compelled black families to shape a system of social norms different from those of the white middle class, or celebrated the resiliency of the malleable black household. However, with the exception of those historians, such as Gutman, Pleck, and Hershberg, who sought to exorcise the curse of slavery, few scholars of the urban black experience looked longitudinally at the forces molding the black family experience. None examined the critical period 1945–60, when heavy black urban migration, white suburbanization, the erosion of the urban industrial base, and the dual forces of urban renewal and public housing reshaped the physical and social contours of urban America.

Among the first cities to plan postwar urban redevelopment, Philadelphia as early as 1947 had targeted a sizable district north of downtown for large-scale renewal. This area of North Philadelphia was no newcomer to slum clearance. Several years earlier, in 1941, it had experienced demolition activity when it became the site for the building of the Richard Allen Homes, an impressive 1,324-unit human-scale housing complex for low-income black families.

Before clearance, the site consisted of a maze of small streets, alleys, and ancient courts. The Richard Allen Homes, one of the original three housing projects built in Philadelphia following passage of the 1937 Housing Act, replaced this quilt work of small businesses and residences with fifty-three three- and four-story, red-and-yellow-brick apartment buildings arranged on eight quadrangles. In addition to the bright new housing, Richard Allen featured a community building, housing management offices, workshops, a nursery, an auditorium, and grassy courts planted with trees and shrubbery.[37] Originally conceived in the 1930s as a waystation—or community of opportunity for a temporarily submerged, but potentially upwardly mobile working class—the Richard Allen Homes, like public housing projects across America, welcomed applications for occupancy from hardworking, albeit low-income, two-parent families. Following a "neighborhood composition formula," Richard Allen was racially segregated.[38]

World War II temporarily forced the Philadelphia Housing Authority to soften its rigid income limits for occupancy. Therefore, Richard Allen opened as housing for black war workers as much as for homes for the poor. Indeed, the wartime environment at the project reflected the optimism of a working-class black community. An article in the *Philadelphia Evening Bulletin* in 1942, titled "New Homes, New Wealth, New Fun, New Happiness," captured the tenants' exhilaration at the well-kept front lawns, safe play areas, and modern kitchens. One tenant bragged in the article that all her life she dreamed of having a pretty kitchen decorated in red and white. Now she had such a kitchen, and she dared anybody to "find a spot of dust."[39]

Project organizations flowered as luxuriantly as the rose garden planted in front of the community building. Some organizations, such as the Girl's Victory Club, were war inspired; but those such as Club Orchid, the Tu Wann Club, and the Stork Club mirrored the organization gestation attending a community's birth. A column "In and Around the Richard Allen Homes," which appeared frequently in one of the city's black newspapers, the *Philadelphia Tribune,* not only reported the project's Christmas party and the winner of the Allen's Most Popular Child contest, but also carried gossipy tidbits about the comings and goings of Richard Allen society, welcome-home parties for soldiers on leave, or showers for Allen's growing population of expectant mothers.[40]

The glow lingered two years after V-E Day, when a *Philadelphia Evening Bulletin* report praised Richard Allen as "a spic and span place so outstanding that the remainder of the city is extremely drab by comparison. What little trash there," stated the article, "blows in from the outside, and the residents are justifiably proud of the appearance of the area."[41]

However, only five years later the kudos and high expectations of the 1940s had vanished. The combination of housing authority tenant selection and occupancy policies, the 1947 federal directive forcing housing authorities nationally to purge from their projects households with incomes over the maximum allowable for continued occupancy, and regional economic forces, including a declining urban manufacturing base and the inception of urban redevelopment, produced a tenant population with a demographic and occupational profile much different from the wartime years.[42]

Change in the demography of the Richard Allen Homes revealed itself most profoundly in family structure and size. In 1943, soon after the initial acceptance of tenants, couples headed approximately 70 percent of the Allen families.[43] Almost half of these families had between three and four members; 40 percent had more than five members. Committed to the waystation model of public housing (that is, a temporary shelter and moral environment for the uplifting of the submerged working class) and therefore to middle-class family norms, management in the early postwar years (1945–52) enforced a policy of admitting married couples.[44] More than 80 percent of families entering the Richard Allen Homes during these years listed a married couple and children. By 1952, married couples with children still accounted for nearly 70 percent of Allen families, despite the increasing rate of marital dissolution in the project apparently caused by the growing unemployment

Built during the 1940s, the Richard Allen Homes was one of Philadelphia's most attractive public housing projects when it opened. Here teenagers play in one of the playgrounds within the Richard Allen Homes during the early 1950s. (Courtesy of the Urban Archives, Temple University)

of the immediate postwar years. The situation changed significantly over the next decade. Within five years only half of Allen households included a married couple, and by 1964 the percentage had dropped to under 40. A female headed 48 percent of Allen families that year.[45]

Accompanying this increase in the number of female-headed families was a corresponding decrease in the size of Richard Allen households. While one- and two-person households accounted for barely 11 percent of the project population in 1943, two decades later they composed 28 percent, reflecting both an increase in female-headed families and the aging of the population.

These demographic changes corresponded to a pattern of steadily worsening employability among Richard Allen tenants, which emphasized diminished labor force participation and female rather than male employment. In wartime, 80 percent of Richard Allen Homes heads of household found good, stable employment in the blooming Philadelphia job market. With the exception of the Korean War years, the percentage of employed heads of household fell after 1945 to 60 percent in the 1960s. More ominously, the percentage of heads of household not in the labor force doubled from about 11 percent in the 1940s to 23 percent in 1965.[46]

Both the place of employment and occupation of tenants confirm not only the city's weakening opportunities for low-skilled blacks but also the cyclical impact of war. The war had raised hopes that blacks would inherit a greater share of the central city's traditional pool of manufacturing jobs.[47] By 1945, almost a quarter of Richard Allen's male work force labored as skilled craftsmen, mostly in Philadelphia's large primary metals industry. Remarkably, in 1945 almost 60 percent of Allen breadwinners found work in either primary metals, metal fabrication, or transportation industries, areas in which few blacks toiled prior to World War II.[48]

Tragically, as experienced in other large rust belt cities, the rate of black male employment in Philadelphia's manufacturing, especially the skilled trades, plummeted in the wake of World War II.[49] The Richard Allen data mirror the trend. From a high of 54 percent in 1943, employment of Richard Allen workers in manufacturing had slumped to 25 percent by the 1960s. It revived briefly during the Korean War. The percentage of Richard Allen heads of household working in the craft occupations plunged from 23 percent in 1946 to 6 percent by 1962. This precipitous decline reflects especially the vacation of the Richard Allen workers from Philadelphia's metal-working industries. While 58 percent of Allen's male work force had labored there in 1945, fewer than 15 percent still did in the 1960s.[50]

The decline of Allen males in metal manufacturing was paralleled by a growing proportion of Richard Allen women employed in the city's textile and garment trades. Black women had entered Philadelphia's garments industry and the needle trades early in the 1920s.[51] During World War II, approximately 18 percent Richard Allen manufacturing workers, mainly women, toiled as operatives and general laborers in textile and garment factories. This number rose to between 35 percent and 40 percent in the 1960s.[52]

Likewise, an increasing number of Allen household heads labored in the retail, health, and other jobs in the city's growing service sector, a trend that attests strongly to a changing urban employment structure. Similar to the garment and needle trades, the service sector employed a large number of women. Between 1947 and 1956, approximately 50 percent of the Allen work force found employment in this area. But employment here grew even more rapidly after 1957, spurred by the influx of Allen women into the health and education industry. By the 1960s, more than 60 percent of Allen breadwinners worked as maids in department stores; as laundresses, orderlies, or aides in city hospitals; as matrons and teacher helpers in city schools; or in other service trades. This sizable post-1957 growth of Allen employment in the service sector reflected the growing importance of the health industry as a source of low-skilled, low-paid work. Less than 10 percent of Allen workers labored in the health trades during the 1940s and early 1950s; after 1955, between 14 percent and 18 percent worked there.[53]

Therefore, by 1965 a clear pattern of project demography and employability emerged in the Richard Allen Homes. From a place characterized in the 1940s and early 1950s by working two-parent families, Richard Allen became by the 1960s a place where women headed more than 50 percent of Richard Allen homes and where nearly a quarter of all household heads were not in the labor force. This change can in large part be attributed to weakening postwar employment opportunities for black males, which shattered the World War II illusion that Philadelphia's black population had at last found a secure job niche in manufacturing. During this twenty-year period, jobless or partially employed Richard Allen males gradually disappeared from the labor force, to be replaced as primary breadwinners by females. Concomitantly, more and more Allen workers occupied the low-paid service sector of the economy. These facts belied the touted waystation role of public housing and pointed instead to public housing projects such as the Richard Allen Homes as unwitting nurseries of an embryonic underclass. Indeed, after 1952, black housing projects such as Richard Allen rather than bustling havens of opportunity for the suppressed working class, as originally conceived, increasingly harbored families where breadwinners, who were often underemployed or jobless, barely survived on abysmally low paychecks or public assistance.[54]

Making Postindustrial North Philadelphia

These portentous changes in project demography and employability can be understood by looking both at Philadelphia's postwar economy and at the impact of urban renewal and housing policy. One of the most striking facts was the extraordinary wartime and postwar growth of the city's black population, especially the increase of the black population in North Philadelphia. Although by the 1970s North Philadelphia's black population had began to decline, an inner-city ghetto had emerged there amid the decay of a deindustrializing economy.[55]

During the 1940s, Philadelphia's citywide black population rose by

125,161, a 50 percent increase, and continued to grow over the next two decades, while the city's total population declined by 123,000. Thus, by 1970, blacks composed fully a one-third of Philadelphia's inhabitants. In North Philadelphia the black population became steadily more concentrated in a ghetto. The number of census tracts in North Philadelphia that were 75 percent or more black increased from three in 1940 to twenty by 1960, when they contained 82 percent of all blacks.[56]

At the same time that the black population was expanding, the postindustrial economic transformation was displacing traditional central city goods production and distribution activities with corporate headquarters and expanded university, legal, managerial, and investment banking functions. Many of the old industries moved to more spacious locations outside the city, while obsolete or noncompetitive industries disappeared altogether.[57]

Between 1947 and 1965, employment in Philadelphia's basic industries plummeted by one-quarter. Once the bellwether of Philadelphia's economy, textile and metal manufacturing had exhibited signs of decline in the 1920s. Although temporarily resurrected by the war economy, in the next two decades employment in metal manufacturing skidded downward 66 percent, while employment fell by a third in textiles. By 1963, for example, North Philadelphia's Budd Corporation, an important metal producer of truck trailers and railroad passenger cars, reduced its work force in the city by 47 percent; during the same period, employment dropped 37 percent at nearby Crown Can. But Philadelphia's manufacturing decline was general, not confined to metals and textiles. The city lost 20 percent of its jobs in chemicals, 26 percent in food processing, and 78 percent in tobacco manufacturing. Although tobacco manufacturing was never a large industry in Philadelphia, it was important for black employment. By 1963, Bayuk Cigar, an important employer of black women (some from the Richard Allen Homes), had cut its work force 70 percent since 1947.[58]

North Philadelphia in particular felt the full brunt of the city's eroding traditional economic base. In fact, one study has estimated that between 1928 and 1972 the area lost between 20,000 and 50,000 manufacturing jobs. It is not surprising that the number of North Philadelphians who reported employment declined by a half between 1950 and 1970, from more than 143,000 to under 72,000 in 1970.[59] Although total population declined during the same period, the ratio of employment to population also declined from 38 percent to 29 percent. In 1946 a potpourri of more than 450 businesses and industries had crowded North Philadelphia between Vine Street and Allegheny Avenue, and Front Street and the Schuylkill River. Among these establishments were breweries, plate-glass manufacturers, battery makers, and ice cream factories, as well as a generous distribution of ice yards and coal yards, warehouses, and laundries. Technology robbed the area of its plethora of ice and coal businesses, and a combination of obsolescence, suburbanization, and urban renewal tolled the death knell for many other concerns. For example, Stetson Hat and Bayuk Cigar ultimately went out of business, while Merck-Sharp and Dohme and Link Belt moved with the white middle class to suburbia.[60]

Therefore, during the 1950s North Philadelphia experienced an ominous transformation. While the white population declined precipitously and the black population rose by almost a third, the city's manufacturing economy was disintegrating. Even though urban renewal in North Philadelphia spurred a black population decline in the 1960s, employment dropped even faster. Where once a white ethnic population built communities around thriving textile mills and metal manufactories, blacks now competed for a dwindling number of low-paying jobs in manufacturing and the service sector.[61]

As elsewhere in America, urban renewal disproportionately affected the inner city's growing black population by clearing away thousands of low-rent units without providing sufficient replacement housing, or eradicating the patterns of residential segregation. North Philadelphia experienced the social cost of urban renewal. As early as 1939, Federal Housing Administration property assessors and local bank officials spotlighted it as a blighted area ripe for renewal. The first urban renewal maps appearing in 1947 targeted the Poplar and Temple University areas for redevelopment.[62] But while urban renewal between 1950 and 1965 scored some early successes, such as revitalizing East Poplar and persuading Temple University to remain in North Philadelphia, large-scale demolition proved catastrophic for the neighborhood structure of the area. In the late 1950s, residents living in the midst of the Poplar Renewal Area complained about abandoned houses, vacant building, trash-filled lots, noise, juvenile delinquency, and the proliferation of tap rooms.[63] By 1960, North Philadelphia urban renewal involved clearance and code enforcement activities covering more than 235 acres of land. As a result, more than 6,250 families and single persons were dislocated, and between 1950 and 1970 the number of dwelling units in North Philadelphia declined from almost 114,000 units to under 90,000.[64]

Urban renewal cleared businesses as well as residential structures. For example, during two years, 1962–63, some 633 small laundries, repair shops, groceries, garages, ice yards, bakeries, junk shops, and other small businesses which once dotted the North Philadelphia streetscape, vanished into rubble.[65] A 1957 survey of ninety-five households living around Twelfth and Poplar reported that these businesses had provided many jobs for neighborhood residents as handymen, washers, stock boys, garage attendants, ice handlers, and junk men.[66] This universe of occupations recalls the job structure that James Borchert saw forming as an economic bulwark against the traditional insecurities of low-income black life. Renewal and code enforcement, along with the flight of business and industry, were eroding the already frail economy of these poor black communities.[67]

While numerous businesses and residential structures disappeared from North Philadelphia, the people did not. More than 90 percent of displaced families and single persons reportedly moved back into North Philadelphia, ordinarily within a mile of their demolished residence.[68] Contemporary reports show that blacks composed two-thirds of the families and single persons displaced from North Philadelphia sites between 1958 and 1962. Most of these dislocated households were economically disadvantaged. More than 60 percent of these cases had annual incomes under $3,000, a third were either divorced, widowed, or separated, and 19 percent were single.[69] A 1963–64 study of 780 cases of displacement found almost half of these households dependent on welfare, child support, or pensions. Some 38 percent of the household heads were not in the labor force, and 39 percent of the households were headed by a female. These displaced households, constrained by poor employability, low incomes, non–nuclear-family structures, and discrimination, formed part of the expanding pool of North Philadelphia families seeking shelter in places such as Richard Allen.[70]

Public Housing and the Black Family

Between 1952 and 1970, uprooted low-income black families more and more frequently found refuge in public housing. However, housing policy created conditions in the projects that contrasted invidiously with the malleable world of the alley described by James Borchert. While before World War II these alley places facilitated adaptation to the harsh urban environment, after World War II public housing would systematically thwart it. In fact, in all three areas of black folklife discussed by Borchert—family, community, and work—public housing policy obstructed rather than aided adaptation.

Borchert argued that in the cloistered alley world common to twentieth-century Philadelphia and Washington, D.C., rural black migrants, like the transplanted European peasantry, adapted traditional rural culture and work routines to overcome limited economic opportunities and overcrowded living quarters.[71] Historically, urban reformers had denounced tenement houses bulging with kin as socially disorganizing. However, the same reformers, Borchert explained, were just as fearful that urban life was destroying migrant family life, a process they saw beginning with the change from the extended to the nuclear family. Borchert argued that such alley families only appeared nuclear to reformers. In reality, observed Borchert, the situation was more complex. While many families were nuclear, others were either extended or augmented by both actual or fictive kin, as well as by boarders and even the children of hapless neighbors. Although the presence of outsiders in the families could be seriously disruptive, expanded households often enabled economically embattled families to endure hardships while effectively performing vital family functions, such as nurturant socialization and the provision of adequate food, shelter, and member emotional support. Aunts, uncles, boarders, or even unwed fathers living within the household supplemented household income, attended to young children, and helped with daily chores.[72]

Public housing policymakers, on the other hand, described the ideal tenant family as two-parent without the cluster of kin who crowded the tiny ramshackle houses of urban courts and alleys. Project managers required prospective tenants to present a certificate as evidence of marriage and disallowed aunts, uncles, cousins, or other extended kin from even short stays in the apartments.[73] The alley dwellings described by Borchert teemed with family members, including the offspring of households that were temporarily incapable of caring for them. The overcrowding that resulted was anathema to nineteenth- and early-twentieth-century middle-class reformers.[74] So it was this extended family—and this familial overcrowding so vital to the socialization process and economic survival of alley households—that was actively discouraged in public housing. Ironically, when circumstances compelled management to relax admission requirements and admit single-parent families, the proscription against the expanded family often handicapped female-headed households most in need of an environment buttressed by family and nonfamily members.[75]

If public housing barred tenants from mobilizing kinship networks for survival, it even more vigorously discouraged the construction of viable community life. Borchert acquitted the alleys from charges leveled by progressive-minded housing reformers that they seethed with vice, crime, and other forms of social disorder characteristic of weak communities. Instead, he discerned "clear lines of social order." Alley dwellers, noted Borchert, treated space as social not private, and age and sex roles were "harmoniously integrated." Rather than fostering anarchy, as reformers charged, Borchert saw the alleys encouraging the formation of leadership and a sense of belonging as well as community control.[76]

Paradoxically, public housing policymakers intended to create a strong community structure. In fact, the ideological roots of American public housing can be traced in large part to the communitarians of the 1920s, people such as Catherine Buer, Lewis Mumford, Clarence Perry, and Robert Kohn.[77] However, post–World War II housing management policies, which enforced the eviction of tenants with overmaximum incomes, closely monitored tenant behavior, and even conducted unannounced inspections of tenant units to check on housekeeping practices or illegal residents, undermined the achievement of community. Rather than controlling their environment, public housing tenants faced, and sometimes capitulated to, a host of regulations resisted only at the cost of eviction. Under management orders, flower gardens were to be planted on time; hallways were to be swept daily. Required to disclose annually every penny of their income, spiteful tenants anonymously informed on neighbors suspected of concealing resources.[78] The bureaucratic quagmire subverted the traditional network of cooperation among women discussed by Carol Stack.[79] Within such an oppressive and socially distrustful environment, neither cooperation nor community leadership could endure for long before withering for want of nourishment. Moreover, for those leaders who did emerge, the over-maximum income requirement often forced their removal. This process had the further consequence of depriving the project of valuable role models, therefore deepening the social isolation that inexorably gripped the world of public housing.[80]

Finally, public housing policy dismantled the frail but vital structure of opportunity that had facilitated survival of families in the ghettos. The challenge of economic survival had always severely tested the resilience and adaptive strengths of migrant culture. But Borchert found that black alley dwellers often successfully fashioned entrepreneurial strategies to cope with economic hardship. They kept boarders, repaired secondhand furniture for resale, took in laundry, and collected junk for sale to salvagers. Clandestine illegal operations such as bootlegging, prostitution, and gambling also contributed to the alley economy.[81]

However, management forbade the use of project apartments and grounds for commercial purposes. In the battle to maintain middle-class decorum, it would hardly permit the storage on the premises of junk or the hanging out to dry of excessive loads of laundry. Naturally, management banned all forms of vice, prostitution, numbers games, and even gambling for pennies. Nor were tenants allowed to have boarders, regarded as one of the most universally employed working-class strategies to make ends meet.[82]

Therefore, while black migrants flooded North Philadelphia, manufacturing, together with the white middle class, fled, urban renewal demolished whole blocks of aging alley housing, and the contours of a new, more formidable urban environment appeared. Public housing made up an important part of this new environment, especially for the low-skilled, low-income black family. It was not the architecture or design of these housing megaliths that made them, in Lee Rainwater's words, fearful and forbidding places[83]—after all, Philadelphia's Richard Allen Homes was a low-rise project whose brick design was not that unsympathetic to the carpet of two- and three-story brick houses covering the rest of North Philadelphia. Rather it was, as Jane Jacobs later observed, the insensitivity of postwar housing policymakers to the uses and potential of the urban community, a failure to understand the need for malleable community structures that people could adapt to their social, political, and economic requirements.[84]

Public Housing, Isolation, and the Underclass

The world that did evolve at the Richard Allen Homes in the postwar era has significance for illuminating the current debate about the underclass. For one, it rolls back the chronological boundaries of the debate by the full decade, from the early 1960s to the early 1950s. Current debate, as outlined earlier, has focused on the mid-1960s, when Moynihan conceived the "tangle of pathology" and when the boom in federal programs, critics such as Charles Murray charged, spawned an insidious nexus between family assistance and family dissolution.[85] Although Wilson has assailed the "welfare queen" explanation for the underclass, he too grounds his theoretical exploration of the subject in the mid-1960s. According to Wilson, federal programs of that period guaranteeing affirmative action in hiring, and prohibiting discrimination in housing, engendered the upsurge of the black middle class and the consequent isolation of an underclass in the black ghetto lacking the bulwark of an economically integrated community to provide direction and support.[86]

But public housing had produced evidence of that phenomenon as early as 1952 at the Richard Allen Homes. By the early 1960s, scholars failed to distinguish public housing from black housing and the black community in general. The housing project in effect became a convenient surrogate for the black ghetto. These scholars neither underscored the uniqueness of public housing as a creature of public policy nor explained, as Stack later did, that many black families outside public housing successfully utilized time-honored family strategies to cope with poverty and discrimination.

Public housing did not singularly create a black underclass. However, we do argue that midway through the postwar era it functioned to isolate, socially and spatially, a growing segment of the black poor whose manifold disadvantages—"low aspirations, poor education, family instability, illegitimacy, unemployment, crime, drug addiction and alcoholism, frequent illness"—eventually became hallmarks of the underclass.[87]

The black poor have historically lived in American central cities and in physical proximity to both the black middle class and to many white ethnics. While the social interaction among these groups, especially white and black, was often fragmentary, it existed, nevertheless, in varying degrees. However, by the late 1950s, social, political, and economic forces were unraveling the fabric of inner-city neighborhoods such as North Philadelphia. An increasing proportion of low-income black families were rendered unemployable and dependent, and routine interaction with the wider urban community diminished. Urban renewal and public housing shape the new environment of the evolving postwar ghetto.

Public housing in the 1950s, as we have argued, fostered a condition of isolation analogous to the process of isolation described by Wilson. Not only was it frequently concentrated in the black ghetto, but its tenant selection and retention policies had the unintended consequence of concentrating low-income black families away from the more socially and economically diverse black community surrounding it. Furthermore, its waystation mission foreclosed the use of traditional family strategies for economic survival. Therefore, because it left residents unable to include kin within the project household or to use their residences for enterprising purposes—both critical, as Borchert pointed out, to black family survival—public housing, together with urban renewal and regional economic decline, became deeply implicated in the processes of underclass isolation and alienation that inexorably overwhelmed sections of the inner city after the mid-1960s.

Notes

1. Among these are William Julius Wilson, *The Truly Disadvantaged: The Inner City, the Underclass, and Public Policy* (Chicago, 1987); Charles Murray, *Losing Ground: American Social Policy, 1950–1930* (New York, 1984); Douglas Glasgow, *The Black Underclass: Poverty, Unemployment, and Entrapment of Ghetto Youth* (New York, 1981); Ken Aulette, *The Underclass* (New York, 1982); and Nicholas Lemann, "The Origins of the Underclass," *Atlantic Monthly*, June 1986, 31–55, and *Atlantic Monthly*, July 1986, 54–68.

2. Wilson, *Truly Disadvantaged*, 8. In his *Undeserving Poor*, Michael Katz charges that the term "underclass" itself is pejorative and represents yet another chapter in the timeless American preoccupation with categorizing the poor as either deserving or undeserving. The term, explains Katz, degrades the black urban poor as behaviorally deficient and ignores the structural forces, especially the dearth of good jobs for low-skilled black youth, shaping the social and economic contours of inner-city life. Nevertheless, the term has entered the modern poverty lexicon. Since this article is our contribution to ongoing debate about modern urban poverty, and since it especially seeks to address the ideas of William Julius Wilson, we continue to employ the term "underclass," fully recognizing Katz's legitimate objection that the term

perpetuates the "language of difference." Furthermore, we see our study as an opportunity to accept Katz's invitation to explore the changing nature of poverty, to look at "how poor people throughout American history actually survived from day to day." See Michael B. Katz, *The Undeserving Poor: From the War on Poverty to the War on Welfare* (New York, 1989), 185–235.

3. Wilson, *Truly Disadvantaged,* 3.

4. See Carol Stack, *All Our Kin: Strategies for Survival in a Black Community* (New York, 1974); and Joyce Ladner, *Tomorrow's Tomorrow: The Black Woman* (Garden City, N.Y., 1971). This literature is discussed more fully in Andrew Billingsley, *Black Families in White America* (Englewood Cliffs, N.J., 1968); and Robert Staples, "Toward a Sociology of the Black Family: A Theoretical and Methodological Assessment," *Journal of Marriage and the Family* 33 (February 1971): 119–37.

5. Richard Allen Homes Study (hereafter RAH Study). Data derived from an ongoing study of the vacant tenant files of the Richard Allen Homes housing project in Philadelphia, Pennsylvania. These records are on temporary loan to the University of Pittsburgh. This material is based upon work supported by the Samuel S. Fels Fund of Philadelphia, the Center for Social and Urban Research of the University of Pittsburgh, and the National Science Foundation under Grant No. SES-8208448.

6. For an example, see Lee Rainwater's studies of black families in St. Louis's Pruitt-Igoe housing project, including "Crucible of Identity: The Lower-Class Negro Family," *Daedalus* 95 (Winter 1966): 172–216; and *Behind Ghetto Walls: Black Families in a Federal Slum* (Chicago, 1970).

7. See Kenneth B. Clark, *Dark Ghetto: Dilemmas of Social Power* (New York, 1965); and Daniel P. Moynihan, *The Negro Family: A Case Study for National Action* (Washington, D.C., 1965).

8. Nathan Glazer and Daniel P. Moynihan, *Beyond the Melting Pot* (Cambridge, Mass., 1963).

9. Moynihan, *Negro Family.*

10. Ibid., 5.

11. Ibid. For an extensive discussion of "The Moynihan Report," see Lee Rainwater and William L. Yancey, *The Moynihan Report and the Politics of Controversy* (Cambridge, Mass., 1967); Wilson, *Truly Disadvantaged,* 20–29.

12. See Billingsley, *Black Families in White America,* 33, 198–202; Staples, "Toward a Sociology of the Black Family," 122–24; Hylan Lewis, "Culture, Class, and Family Life Among Low-Income Urban Negroes," in Arthur Ross and Herbert Hill, eds., *Employment, Race, and Poverty* (New York, 1967); and Elizabeth Herzog, "Is There a 'Breakdown' of the Negro Family?" *Social Work,* January 1966, 178–84.

13. William Ryan summarized the Herzog/Lewis complaint against Moynihan in *Blaming the Victim* (New York, 1971), 63–88.

14. See Charles V. Willie and the Research Staff of Washington Action for Youth, "Family Life Among the Poor in the Cardoza Area of Washington, D.C.," Camille Jeffers, "Mothers and Children in Public Housing," in Charles V. Willie, ed., *Family Life of Black People* (New York, 1969), 202; and David A. Schultz, *Coming Up Black: Patterns of Ghetto Socialization* (Englewood Cliffs, N.J., 1969), 95.

15. Rainwater, *Behind Ghetto Walls;* Elliot Liebow, *Talley's Corner: A Study of Negro Streetcorner Men* (Boston, 1967).

16. On the dangerous, distrustful world, see Rainwater, *Behind Ghetto Walls,* 69–73; and Rainwater, "Crucible of Identity," 166–83. Rainwater is most explicit about the dangerousness

of the Pruitt-Igoe world in his "Fear and the House-as-Haven in the Lower Class," *Journal of the American Institute of Planners* 32 (January 1966): 23–31.

17. On "our life," as opposed to "good life," see Rainwater, *Behind Ghetto Walls,* 46–55.

18. Ibid., 46–47.

19. See Staples, "Toward a Sociology of the Black Family," 123–25. See also Staples, "Myth of the Black Matriarchy," in *Black Scholar,* January–February 1970, 9–16; Stack, *All Our Kin;* Ladner, *Tomorrow's Tomorrow;* Jacqueline Jackson, "But Where Are the Black Men," *Black Scholar* 3 (December 1971): 30–41; and Paul Glick, "Marriage and Martial Stability Among Blacks," *Millbank Fund Quarterly* 48 (April 1971): 113.

20. Lewis, "Culture, Class, and Family Life Among Low-Income Urban Negroes," 170.

21. Staples, "Toward a Sociology of the Black Family," 132.

22. Ladner, *Tomorrow's Tomorrow.*

23. Stack, *All Our Kin.*

24. Stanley M. Elkins, *Slavery: A Problem in American Institutional Life* (Chicago, 1959). While a more general survey (not necessarily focusing on the black family), Kenneth Kusmer's "Black Urban Experience in American History," in Darlene Clark Hine, ed., *The State of Afro-American History: Past, Present, and Future* (Baton Rouge, La., 1986), provides a valuable introduction to the historical literature.

25. Ernest W. Burgess, "The Growth of the City: An Introduction to a Research Project," in Robert E. Park and Ernest W. Burgess, eds., *The City* (Chicago, 1967), 47–62; St. Clair Drake and Horace Cayton, *Black Metropolis: A Study of Life in a Northern City* (New York, 1945); E. Franklin Frazier, *The Negro Family in the United States* (Chicago, 1939).

26. Frazier, *The Negro Family.*

27. See Herbert Gutman and Laurence Glasco, "The Negro Family: Household and Occupational Structure, 1855–1925, with Special Emphasis on Buffalo, New York," unpublished paper cited in Herbert Gutman, *The Black Family in Slavery and Freedom, 1750–1925* (New York, 1976), xvii–xviii.

28. See Elizabeth H. Pleck, "The Two-Parent Household: Black Family Structure in Late Nineteenth-Century Boston," *Journal of Social History* 6 (Fall 1972): 3–23.

29. Frank Furstenberg, Theodore Hershberg, and John Modell, "The Origins of the Female-Headed Black Family: The Impact of the Urban Experience," in Theodore Hershberg, ed., *Philadelphia: Work, Space, Family, and Group Experience in the Nineteenth-Century City* (New York, 1981), 434–52.

30. Pleck, "The Two-Parent Household," 23; Furstenberg, Hershberg, and Modell, "Origins of the Female-headed Black Family," 451.

31. Gutman, *Black Family in Slavery and Freedom,* 430–31, 432, 447. Note that Gutman's somewhat idyllic view of the tenaciousness of the black family in post–Civil War America has been challenged. It perhaps could be more balanced in view of the enormous racial hostility and limited opportunity that black families confronted in rural and urban America; see David Brion Davis's review of Gutman's *Black Family in Slavery and Freedom* in *American Historical Review* 82 (1977): 744–45.

32. Gutman, *Black Family in Slavery and Freedom,* 447–60.

33. James Borchert, *Alley Life in Washington: Family, Community, Religion, and Folklife in the City, 1850–1970* (Urbana, Ill., 1980).

34. Ibid., 138–42.

35. Ibid., 140, 195, 237–38.

36. For a critical review of Borchert's *Alley Life in Washington,* see Elliott Rudwick's review of Borchert's *Alley Life in Washington* in *American Historical Review* 86 (1981): 657–58.

See also Allen B. Ballard, *One More Day's Journey: The Study of Family and a People* (New York, 1984); Ethel Waters, *His Eye Is on the Sparrow* (Garden City, N.Y., 1951); and Roger Lane, *Roots of Violence in Black Philadelphia, 1860–1910* (Cambridge, Mass., 1986).

37. See Philadelphia Housing Authority, *Home for War Workers: Annual Report of the Philadelphia Housing Authority* (Philadelphia, 1943). See also, on the origins and architecture of the Richard Allen Homes, John F. Bauman, "Black Slums/Black Projects: The New Deal and Negro Housing in Philadelphia," *Pennsylvania History* 41 (1974): 311–38, and "Safe and Sanitary Without the Costly Frills: The Evolution of Public Housing in Philadelphia, 1929–1941," *Pennsylvania Magazine of History and Biography* 101 (January 1977): 114–28.

38. Bauman, "Black Slums/Black Projects," 331–33. On federal policy, see Lawrence M. Friedman, *Government and Slum Housing* (New York, 1978), 123–26; on racially segregated public housing in other cities, see Arnold Hirsch, *Making the Second Ghetto: Race and Housing in Chicago* (New York, 1983); and Robert B. Fairbanks, *Making Better Citizens: Housing Reform and the Community Development Strategy in Cincinnati, 1890–1960* (Urbana, Ill., 1988), 124–45.

39. We discussed the effect of World War II on the Richard Allen Homes and other publicly built housing complexes in Philadelphia; see John F. Bauman, Edward K. Muller, Norman Hummon, "Federal Slum or Waystation? Black Families and Philadelphia Public Housing During the 1940s" (paper delivered at the Ninth Biennial Convention of the American Studies Association, Philadelphia, 1983). See also John F. Bauman, *Public Housing, Race and Renewal: Urban Planning in Philadelphia, 1920–1974* (Philadelphia, 1987), 72–74; and Joan Wolcott, "New Homes, New Wealth, New Fun, New Happiness," *Phildelphia Evening Bulletin,* August 1, 1942.

40. See Burton's weekly column, "In and Around the Richard Allen Homes," *Philadelphia Tribune,* November 11, 1942, December 14, 1942, and August 16, 1944.

41. "A Spic-and-Span Spot," *Philadelphia Evening Bulletin,* June 5, 1947.

42. *Philadelphia Housing Authority, Annual Report* (Philadelphia, 1947). See also Friedman, *Government and Slum Housing,* 126–27.

43. The percentage of married couples was lower than management desired. The 1939 public housing law required management to admit all site residents, and among those residents were a considerable number of elderly as well as nonelderly female heads of household.

44. RAH Study.

45. Females headed 58 percent of all households—that is, both families with children and widowed and/or elderly.

46. The rise in the percentage of heads of household not in the labor force reflected the increasing number of families headed by women. Male heads of household maintained a fairly stable level of employment in this era.

47. This is not to say that World War II eased interracial tension or raised hopes for a less racially segregated city. Hirsch, in *Making the Second Ghetto,* 40–67, uncovered heightened racial tensions in wartime Chicago. Fueled by the wartime housing shortage, race rioting erupted in Harlem and Chicago. However, this was also an era of increasing black solidarity, black activism, and hope, as Richard Dalfiume observed in "The Forgotten Years of the Negro Revolution," *Journal of American History* 55 (June 1968), 90–106. See also William H. Harris, *The Harder We Run: Black Workers Since the Civil War* (New York, 1982), 125. Joe William Trotter notes in *Black Milwaukee: The Making of an Industrial Proletariat, 1915–1945* (Urbana, Ill., 1985), 163–69, that the black alliance with the Congress of Industrial Organizations, the campaign for the Fair Employment Practices Commission, and the war's stimulus to industrialism helped "blacks fully regain their industrial foothold [in Milwaukee]." Likewise in

Philadelphia, the black experience involved tensions and opportunity; see Bauman, Muller, and Hummon, "Federal Slum or Waystation?"

48. RAH Study.

49. U.S. Census Bureau, *1950 Census of Population, Tract Data* (Washington, D.C., 1953); *1960 Census of Population, Tract Data* (Washington, D.C. 1963); Mollenkopf, *Contested City,* 12–46; Harris, *Harder We Run,* 125–42.

50. RAH Study.

51. See Ruth Francis Paul, "Negro Women in Industry: A Study of the Negro Industrial Women in the Clothing, Cigar, and Laundry Industries of Philadelphia," mimeographed, n.d., in Southwest Belmont YWCA Papers, Temple University Archives (TUA), Philadelphia.

52. RAH Study.

53. Ibid.

54. A number of studies commented on the changing composition of the tenant population of public housing, including Catherine Bauer in her famous "The Dreary Deadlock of Public Housing and How to Break It," *Architectural Forum* 106 (May 1957): 140–42, 219, 221. See also Rainwater, *Behind Ghetto Walls;* and William Moore, *The Vertical Ghetto: Everyday Life in an Urban Project* (New York, 1969). On Philadelphia in particular, see Subcommittee on Tenant Selection and Occupancy, Minutes, November 19, 1952, Box 230, Folder 3349, Housing Association of Delaware Valley Papers, TUA (hereafter HADVP); and memorandum from Drayton Bryant to Walter Alesandroni, June 3, 1953, in Box 230, Folder 3353, HADVP.

55. U.S. Census Bureau, *1940 Census of Population, Tract Data; 1950 Census of Population, Tract Data; 1960 Census of Population, Tract Data; Census of Population, Tract Data, 1970* (Washington, D.C.). See also Leonard Blumberg, "A Study of Recent Negro Migrants into Philadelphia," April 20, 1950, Box 12, File 207, Urban League Papers, TUA; and Mollenkopf, *Contested City,* 23–41. Although Katz recognizes the importance of the postindustrial transformation of American central cities, he like other authors emphasizes the years after 1960. We, on the other hand, see the transformation occurring earlier in the 1950s. Katz, *Undeserving Poor,* 128–37.

56. U.S. Census Bureau, *1940 Census of Population, Tract Data; 1950 Census of Population, Tract Data; 1960 Census of Population, Tract Data; Census of Population, Tract Data, 1970.*

57. Mollenkopf, *Contested City,* 23–41.

58. See Chamber of Commerce of Greater Philadelphia, *Greater Philadelphia Facts: Business and Civic Statistics, 1946–1965* (Philadelphia, 1946–66).

59. Temple University, Philadelphia, Social Science Data Library, maps showing manufacturing jobs lost within one mile of Central City, Philadelphia, 1928–72; U.S. Census Bureau, *1940 Census of Population, Tract Data; 1950 Census of Population, Tract Data; 1960 Census of Population, Tract Data; Census of Population, Tract Data, 1970.*

60. Franklin Survey Company, *Franklin's Street and Business Occupancy Atlas* (Philadelphia, 1946); Chamber of Commerce, *Greater Philadelphia Facts* (Philadelphia, 1949, 1957, 1962, 1966).

61. See Philip Scranton, *Figured Tapestry: Production, Markets, and Power in Philadelphia Textiles, 1885–1941* (New York, 1989); Stephanie Greenberg, "Industrial Location and Ethnic Residential Patterns in an Industrializing City: Philadelphia 1880," in Hershberg, *Philadelphia,* 204–29; and Eugene P. Ericksen and William L. Yancey, "Work and Residence in Industrial Philadelphia," *Journal of Urban History* 5 (February 1979): 147–83.

62. Home Owner Loan Corporation, City Survey Files, Pennsylvania, 1935–40, in Federal Home Loan Bank Records, Box 95, Record Group 195, National Archives, Washington, D.C.;

Kenneth Jackson, "Race, Ethnicity, and Real Estate Appraisal: The HOLC and FHA," *Journal of Urban History* 6 (1980): 419–53.

63. City of Philadelphia, Environmental, Sanitation, Housing, and Neighborhood Evaluation Program, Opinion Attitude Questionnaire (1957), Philadelphia City Archives, Philadelphia. See also Marto Lentz, "Impressions of Survey—Melon to Fairmount, 11th to 12th Streets," July 14, 1953, Neighborhood Guild Papers, URB 6, Box 96, File 298, TUA.

64. See Dorothy S. Montgomery, "Relocation and Its Impact on Families: A Paper Presented Before the National Conference on Social Welfare," June 7, 1960, in HADVP; and U.S. Census Bureau, *Census of Housing, 1950, Census Tracts; Census of Housing, 1960, Census Tracts; Census of Housing: 1970, Census of Tracts* (Washington, D.C.).

65. Redevelopment Authority of Philadelphia, *Annual Report, 1962* (Philadelphia, 1962); Redevelopment Authority, *Annual Report, 1963;* G. W. Bromley & Company, *Atlas of Philadelphia* (Philadelphia, 1922); Works Progress Administration, Social Base Map of Philadelphia, Project 20879, in TUA.

66. City of Philadelphia, Environmental, Sanitation, Housing, and Neighborhood Evaluation Program (1957).

67. Borchert, *Alley Life in Washington,* 166–95.

68. Community Renewal Program, "Characteristics of the Residential Relocatee, 1958–1962, by Project of Origin," mimeographed, 1964, in HADVP; Philadelphia Housing Authority, "Relocation in Philadelphia," November 1985, in HADVP.

69. Community Renewal Program, "Characteristic of Residential Relocatee, 1958–1962."

70. See "Summary of Shirley Wellenbach's Report at Housing Services Committee on Major Findings of CRP Report 'The Needs of People Affected by Relocation' by Elizabeth Wood, and the CRP Staff Report 'Future Relocation Caseloads-Problem Cases and Services Rendered' " (mimeographed, ca. December 9, 1964), in Box 299, Folder 3353, HADVP. What we see here is the emergence of the "second ghetto" discussed by Arnold Hirsch in his *Making the Second Ghetto.*

71. Borchert, *Alley Life in Washington,* xii.

72. Ibid., 140–42. It is important to remember that Borchert was probably understating the social problems in these alleys; see note 36.

73. Philadelphia Housing Authority, "Manual of Policy and Procedure, Subject 535—Eligibility Standards—PHA Aided Developments," Philadelphia Housing Authority Records. Tenants sometimes evaded management rules against augmented households by hiding actual or fictive kin. The extent of these evasions is not known, but the vigilance of management in this era probably diminished such practices.

74. Borchert, *Alley Life in Washington,* 57–99; on attitudes toward "the boarder problem," see John Modell and Tamara Hareven, "Urbanization and the Malleable Household: An Examination of Boarding and Lodging in American Families," *Journal of Marriage and the Family* 35 (1973): 467–79.

75. Katz, *Undeserving Poor,* 190–91, hypothesizes that urban renewal and economic change "attenuated' crucial familial and social support networks within inner cities. Our Richard Allen study evidences this hypothesis. On changing tenant admission policy in public housing in the late 1960s and 1970s, see Bauman, *Public Housing, Race, and Renewal,* 203–6; Arthur P. Solomon, *Housing the Urban Poor: A Critical Evaluation of Federal Housing Policy* (Cambridge, Mass., 1975); and Chester W. Hartman, *Housing and Social Policy* (Englewood Cliffs, N.J., 1975).

76. Borchert, *Alley Life in Washington,* 108–17.

77. Fairbanks, *Making Better Citizens,* 24–57; Schaffer, *Garden Cities for America,* 15–49; Bauman, *Public Housing, Race, and Renewal,* 3–21.

78. Philadelphia Housing Authority, "Manual of Policy and Procedure"; tenant letters, management file notes, and stated reasons for eviction depict the collapse of cooperative behavior (see RAH Study).

79. Stack, *All Our Kin.*

80. RAH Study. For a good explication of social isolation with the departure of middle-class families, see Lemann, "The Origins of the Underclass," 59–64.

81. Borchert, *Alley Life in Washington,* 57–58, 166–95.

82. Philadelphia Housing Authority, "Manual of Policy and Procedure." On regimentation in early public housing, see Dorothy Canfield, "I Visit a Housing Project," *Survey Graphic,* February 1940, 89–90. Of course, vice existed in the Richard Allen Homes, but management in this era vigilantly combated it; see RAH Study.

83. Rainwater, "Fear and the House-as-Haven in the Lower Class," 23–31.

84. Jane Jacobs, *The Death and Life of Great American Cities* (New York, 1961), 29–73. See also Herbert J. Gans, *The Urban Villagers: Group and Class in the Life of Italian Americans* (New York, 1962); and Martin Anderson, *The Federal Bulldozer* (New York, 1967).

85. Murray, *Losing Ground.* Our critique of housing and renewal policy must be distinguished from Murray's assault on Great Society transfer payments. We are neither blaming the victims nor advocating the shredding of the "safety net." Furthermore, we are not assailing public housing, but the policies that concentrated the most severely disadvantaged there.

86. Wilson, *The Truly Disadvantaged,* 125–57.

87. Ibid.

CHAPTER NINETEEN

Race and Neighborhood Transition

Elijah Anderson

Around the nation, urban residents feel intimidated by their streets, parks, and other public places, particularly after dark or when too many strangers are present. The national public problem of safe streets has become especially acute in urban areas adjacent to large ghetto communities undergoing racial, class, and cultural transition. Occasionally, the margins of these areas are becoming "gentrified," being slowly absorbed by the wider community, which is made up primarily of middle- and upper-income people who are for the most part white.[1]

The housing units in these areas are relatively inexpensive but promise high return on the initial investment. The housing is generally old, even of antique vintage, which for many is part of the attraction; the area's novelty and social diversity are also often valued. The newcomers and the wider society increasingly place high value on such older dwellings, particularly when they are beautifully restored to something approaching their original splendor and are inhabited by well-to-do people. It is significant that such people, because of their professional status and usually but not always their

Work for this chapter was originally supported in part by a grant (80-NI-AX-0003) from the National Institute of Justice. The chapter was first published in *The New Urban Reality,* ed. Paul Peterson. Copyright © 1985 by The Brookings Institution. Reprinted by permission.

skin color, are able to alter the general perception and thus the value of such areas by buying homes and moving into them. As they occupy and make visible use of the neighborhood, they imbue it with a certain social distinction and reputation. They join others of their class, and form through their individual purchases and collective residence a subcultural community of financially well-off people, who in time threaten to displace the original residents.

In such transitional areas, the financially well-off sometimes move in right next door to relatively poor people, and with the establishment of their presence they make social, cultural, economic, and territorial claims on the area which sometimes confuse and upset their neighbors. In time, property values rise and taxes follow. Formerly nonexistent home improvement loans become available, houses get refurbished, long-vacant apartment buildings are renovated, and the neighborhood is physically improved. The city services begin to be revitalized, and local schools become more attentive to their charges, although the newcomers only cautiously approach these institutions. What was an urban area on the verge of becoming a slum slowly turns around, in time to be redefined as quaint, historic—and desirable. And the poorer people, unable to keep up with rising taxes and property values, often find themselves moving into an adjacent ghetto area.

Meanwhile, residents of the general community are concerned about crime and safe streets. In their conversations with neighbors, residents presuppose the offenders to be young, black, and male; some refer to them as "kids." Yet they tend to think of the street criminal as someone who recognizes no bounds. It is money, and sometimes thrills, that he is after. Many know him as a figure lurking in the shadows of dark streets, hiding in a doorway or behind a clump of bushes, ready to pounce on a victim. Or they know "them" as a small group of young black males out to hit (mug) anyone who seems vulnerable; thus, it is important not to seem vulnerable. And residents—black and white, male and female, young and old—become suspicious of strange black males they encounter in public. Such black males evoke fearsome images that are often in the minds and on the tongues of residents as they venture into the streets at night, wondering if they or their loved ones will return home safely. Many residents at times wonder if they will be next. In trying to be careful, some residents agonizingly work to keep strange black males at a comfortably "safe" physical and social distance, succumbing to a kind of racial prejudice peculiarly adapted to public places in the area. Others appear comfortable with such distancing behavior, viewing it simply as an urban survival tool. While many middle-income white and black people simply give up and flee the area, apologizing to the neighbors and friends they leave behind and bewailing inadequate police protection and the frequency of crime, others tough it out, learning and adopting a peculiar etiquette for surviving in the streets and other public places.

A Community in Transition

A prototype of the urban areas facing the problems that accompany racial and class transition is "Village-Northton," a community of "Eastern City."[2] Northton is predominantly black and low income. The Village is at present racially integrated, but becoming increasingly white and middle to upper income. The history of both areas is interrelated with the growth and expansion of Eastern City.

Early History

The Village was first settled in the 1800s by well-to-do people who could afford to commute across the Tyler River to the center of Eastern City or to maintain summer homes along the river's western bank. The first landowners built large houses on their estates, but in time these holdings were cut up and additional homes were built on the properties. Neighborhoods developed, with general stores, churches, and schools. During the 1850s, 1860s, and 1870s, many fancy Victorian houses were built. Some inhabitants branched out farther west into an area that is to this day wealthy and suburban.

During the late 1800s and 1900s the area to the north and west of the Village was overtaken by industrial development. Small factories emerged, and nearby homes were built at a rapid pace. Accompanying the new industries were working-class neighborhoods, and the most prominent one was Northton, just north of what was to become known as the Village.

In many respects, Northton was like a company town, with its small, sooty, close-packed dwellings. The social history of the area is evident in its architecture, in the scale of the houses, in the size of the lots, and in the craftsmanship of the facades; much of Northton was built for a class who worked for, not alongside, the inhabitants of the Village. Northton became an area of settlement for newly arrived Irish and German immigrants who worked in the light industry of Northton and also as servants for the wealthy families in the large homes across Bell Weather Street [sic], which became a kind of social boundary separating the working class from the well-to-do.

During the early twentieth century, this boundary was often violated by middle-class Irish and German proprietors of shops and manufacturing concerns who were eager to obtain Village property. The well-to-do looked on the up-and-coming Northtonians as invaders, and with each inroad the social definition of the Village as a neighborhood for the wealthy was altered.

The advent of the steam engine brought about even greater change. Rails were laid along the bank of the Tyler River, not far from the Village. The trains left great billows of smoke and soot, and residents had difficulty keeping clothes and houses clean. The invasion of technology, along with the invading lower classes, encouraged the original inhabitants of the once-pastoral setting to seek out better places to live, leaving the somewhat sooty Village to the middle-class Irish and Germans and the remnants of their own group who would not move elsewhere.

Blacks from the South were attracted to Northton during and after World War II, when, often in search of a better life, many migrated north and settled in white working-class areas, at times despite strong physical resistance. The blacks eventually succeeded the Irish and the Germans and claimed Northton—and in time they threatened the border areas of the Village, where slumlords found they could make good money by renting them their divided mansions. But the whites of the Village offered great resistance and only slowly gave way to pockets of black settlement within the Village, often on the least desirable blocks. The immediate result was that white working-class and middle-class areas were coexisting with small enclaves and communities of blacks who had recently migrated from the ghetto of Northton. Moreover, Bell Weather Street increasingly became a geographic and social boundary separating races as well as classes. What had separated the lace-curtain Irish from the Irish working class now separated blacks from whites.

Meanwhile, the Village underwent great changes in density and appearance. As financial depressions took their toll, houses were sold, often to be cut up and rented out. The Village went from an upper-income neighborhood to one inhabited primarily by working-class and middle-class people. But though the stone mansions and townhouses were gradually turned into multiple-family dwellings, lot sizes tended to remain the same. The towering sycamore trees still provided a lush canopy over the cobblestone walks. What once was grand has now become quaint, but the neighborhood is still distinguishable as one whose residents' collective identity places them socially higher than their neighbors in Northton. Dingy and dilapidated rowhouses, sometimes facing abandoned factory sites, line the narrow, treeless streets of Northton, while elegant Victorian homes are being beautifully restored on the sycamore-lined streets of the Village.

Today Northton is almost totally black and has a vast array of urban problems, including high rates of crime, poverty, and illiteracy. The Village is racially mixed but is becoming increasingly white and middle- to upper-middle class. Recently a small group of Southeast Asian immigrants has settled in the marginal areas between the Village and Northton and has met with physical resistance and harassment from young black toughs. Community residents, including blacks and whites, have been outraged and have rallied to the defense of the new residents, but some of the Southeast Asians have fled the area.

Through successive invasions and settlements, some of the Village's past splendor has lingered and rubbed off on its working-class and middle-class residents, who can seldom resist making invidious distinctions between the Village and Northton.[3] The class difference between the neighborhoods persists, even though the social realities have changed drastically since the first Irish and Germans made their move into the Village. In the social effort to coexist, skin color has become increasingly significant for determining one's place in the specific status configurations that to this day relate the Village of Northton and Village residents to one another.

The Liberal Era

During the 1950s, when the Korean War was raging and the civil rights movement was a major political issue, a group of liberal and civic-minded Quakers established a cooperative in one of the grand old houses of the Village. They called themselves the Village Friends, and they passionately supported pacifism, racial integration, and economic egalitarianism. The Village Friends invited blacks and others to live in their communal dwellings. They condoned interracial and interethnic marriages among their members. The group even began buying dilapidated buildings in the Village, refurbishing them and renting them out to the "right kind of people," including university students of color and others who had difficulty finding decent housing in the Village or in the immediate area. It was the time of the "beat generation," and the Village Friends developed their own version of such Bohemian values, watered down to fit with their own commitments to liberalism on racial equality and other issues. In this regard they actively supported the civil rights movement, including open housing, school integration, and other issues. Because they were especially concerned with brotherhood and equality between the races, their most immediate mission was in the Village.

Their neighbors—the conservative middle-class Irish and German Villagers—looked on the Friends with suspicion if not outrage, calling them "communists" and "nigger lovers." But despite such criticism, the Friends adhered to stated goals: "to keep the Village from becoming a land speculator's paradise" and "to make the Village the kind of place where all different kinds of people can live."[4]

Meanwhile, the Bell Weather Street boundary was showing increasing signs of weakness. Numbers of poor blacks were concentrating on the periphery of the Village. The slumlords continued to buy rundown buildings, making a minimum of cosmetic repairs and renting them to the poorest class of blacks from Northton and other areas of the city. The middle-class Irish and Germans, as well as the Village Friends, could rally together against this trend, for neither wanted the "wrong kind of blacks" for neighbors. As the Friends negotiated with the other whites for control over Village resources, the hidden restrictions in their own notions of who and what kind of blacks were to be tolerated became evident. They were most hospitable to "educated" or "decent" blacks who would contribute to neighborhood stability and to an ambiance of racial integration and harmony.

An association of concerned Villagers, the Village Development Association, sprang up. Individuals and families contributed to the association's fund for buying up properties, renovating them, and selling or renting to desirable tenants, black or white. The association held integrated picnics, parties, and parades in the neighborhood, celebrating their progressive social attitudes and attempting to attract support from liberal whites and "decent" blacks from around the city. A neighborhood movement of sorts developed as the Village Development Association's members attempted to save the Village from the hands of the speculators and the "racists." One informant explained that some of the Irish "saw what kind of people we were bringing in, and they were tolerant, if not accepting." In time, the social and political environment was altered as some of the conservatives moved and others died off. With those who remained into the early 1960s there was some friction, but this eventually faded as new issues gained prominence in the neighborhood.

In time the Village Friends and their neighbors formed coalitions based on their common interests. Through their transactions, often carried out quietly, the Village Development Association accumulated numerous properties in the area and constituted an ecological invasion force, helping to change the character of the neighborhood to what it is presently: socially and culturally diverse and well integrated. As one 40-year-old black artist who lived through the 1950s and 1960s in the Village said proudly, "You know how it was everywhere else in the sixties? Well, it was like that in the Village in the fifties!" Such is the pride with which some old-time Villagers describe "the good old days."

With the advent of the Vietnam conflict and the protests against it, the Village became a magnet for dropouts from college, the armed services, and society in general. The Main Committee for Conscientious Objectors, with headquarters in the Village, attracted young men in need of draft counseling—and their friends. The workers from an underground print shop that specialized in phony identification for deserters seeking admission to Canada lived and housed clients in the roomy homes and apartments of the Village. An ethos of political radicalism developed, and the Federal Bureau of Investigation was reputed to be infiltrating the neighborhood. Concerned and sympathetic residents were on the lookout then as now, but for a different kind of enemy.

A rundown area that became known as the East Village was occupied by the disaffected young of this era. Some of the sons and daughters of the original Village Friends chose to "drop out" and join what became known as the "hippies" and "squatters" of East Village. In this context the Village Friends' generation appeared patently conservative. Residents of the East Village, as distinct from the more conventional Friends, saw their mission as bringing to fruition a true countercultural lifestyle. Food co-ops were begun—one still thrives in an old apothecary shop on the fringe of the Village and draws members from all over the Village, from Collegetown, and, to a lesser extent, from Northton. The smells of nuts, grains, and fruits take one back to the days of general stores, before supermarkets packaged, bottled, and froze their goods. The co-op sells no food that contains chemical preservatives. Moreover, it sells mainly products whose containers are biodegradable. Even the bulk dog food is "all natural." The spirit of the co-op is hard work, good nutrition, sharing, and equality. Its image in the neighborhood is of usually white though occasionally racially mixed groups of bearded or long-haired men and women, clad in blue jeans and driving old pickup trucks and leaving mixed-breed dogs tied to poles out front. It is doubtful that the co-op's image reflects a true picture of its several thousand working and nonworking members, many of whom appear to be conventional.

Important distinctions are made between those of the Village who own their own homes and those who rent—homeowners being supposedly more seriously committed to the neighborhood. But even more important social and economic distinctions are indicated by the issue of "squatting rights" in the empty buildings of the East Village. This issue often divided generations, rather than the older Irish and German inhabitants, from their former rivals, the Village Friends. Both factions of the old guard, after all, were primarily homeowners, an important characteristic in common.

"Squatting" was the way many Villagers, particularly homeowners, described the living arrangements popular in the East Village during the turbulent 1960s. The owners of some of the largest, most dilapidated apartment buildings were unable or unwilling to keep the premises empty, and the nonpaying tenants were simply called "squatters." Though plumbing, wiring, and other amenities were ancient, the apartments were large and charming, with their bay windows, fireplaces, oak floors, and sixteen-foot ceilings. They were inhabited by drug dealers, deserters from the armed services, runaway teenagers, and students. Such old urban dwellings, and the life experiences that then corresponded to them, were in marked contrast to the white middle-class suburban homes where many of the squatters had been raised. Group life revolved around getting high on dope or alcohol, good music, the politics of revolution, and sex.

Perhaps because so many saw it as a haven for political refugees, the Village claimed strong loyalties from its inhabitants. What some current Villagers refer to as the "good old days in the Village" still come to life as one walks the streets and learns "This was the 3820 Co-op" or "That's the old headquarters for the MCCO." Many praise the Village as the most liberal-radical part of the city and would never consider living in any other area. As some of the former squatters have been transformed into renters, they have moved numerous times to different buildings or houses within the Village. One informant said, "There's something about the Village and the Village person. This is the greatest place to live. I wouldn't live anywhere else. You couldn't pay me to live out there among the squares and burbs."

Under the influence of the Quakers and a tradition of liberal political and social values, the Village has developed a reputation in the wider society of being a laid-back area where a variety of people leading diverse lifestyles are tolerated, if not accepted and encouraged, including gays, hippies, students, interreligious and interracial couples, and political liberals and radicals. Among the longtime residents are college professors, architects, lawyers, garbage men, cleaning ladies, automobile mechanics, carpenters, dishwashers, taxi drivers, and factory workers. The Village has the well-deserved reputation for being one of the most ethnically and culturally diverse areas of the city. In line with this reputation, the Village has developed a seemingly endlessly mutable credo of "live and let live." Over the years, however, the Village's black residents have only slowly come to take part in this collective definition of the situation, and they are thus the ones who probably know best that the openness has its restrictions, the tolerance its limitations, and the espoused egalitarianism its shortcomings.

The New Invasion

Today [the mid-1980s] the Village is again being invaded, this time by young to middle-aged, primarily white, professionals often in search of elegant homes and promising real-estate investments. Many choose the Village because it is relatively close to the cosmopolitan center of the city, but also

Twenty-fourth and Cumberland Streets looking west, North Philadelphia, early 1970s.
(Photo by Jack T. Franklin. Courtesy of the Afro-American Historical and Cultural
Museum, Philadelphia)

because of its unique offerings of large yards and homes and the promise of
an urban setting in which to raise children, grow gardens, and have pets—all
important aspects of suburban life. Many of the newcomers to the Village
come from suburbs that as a general rule are ethnically and racially less
complex than the Village-Northton area.

The newcomers' presence in the area, both current and anticipated, has
contributed to a rise in real-estate values and rents, thus affecting the present
and future makeup of the Village. As housing values increase, institutions on
the periphery of the area expand, and investors and speculators seek to take
advantage of these developments, the area promises to become increasingly
middle to upper income and predominantly white—but within a local area
bounded on two sides by long-standing high-crime and economically depressed black ghetto communities of Northton.

Sharing the Public Space

Today, with the general perception of increasing black youth unemployment
and rising crime on Village streets, feeling safe on the streets and in one's

home has become a central concern for even the most devoted supporters of openness and tolerance. Residents must daily confront the fact that public space in the community must somehow be shared, sometimes closely, by all kinds of people, rich and poor, black and white, including the sometimes desperate. Such concerns become complicated by issues of race and class in the community. To many residents, race becomes confused with class. Interaction on the streets is often significantly influenced by a person's skin color and gender. The communal acknowledgment of these differences expresses itself not only in behavior in public places but also in sociability patterns peculiar to this racially and culturally diverse area.

What users of the Village streets usually want is safe passage—to and from work, school, and recreational areas where others of their own kind gather—but to effect this they must learn whom to trust, whom to avoid, and what preventive measures are appropriate for helping them to avoid trouble. In short, they must resolve the social problem of navigating the public streets safely. With this general goal in mind, as well as an often vague notion of "community," they closely observe public situations of everyday life, exchange social information about the streets and local neighborhoods, read the daily papers, and listen attentively to television and radio reports. From all of this, they often generalize and attempt to fit the information to their immediate experiences as they try to plan their itineraries to maintain safety for themselves and their loved ones.

Making Mental Notes

In attempts to learn and know the area, the streets and public places are used and carefully observed, and various types of people are mentally noted. Social information on various kinds of people and the areas they occupy and frequent, including the times they are likely to be there, may be stored. Through observation over time, people may be determined to have a place. Certain individuals may then be viewed as people to avoid, while others may be held in a kind of social reserve as potential future allies or friends on the streets or in the neighborhood more generally. This amounts to a process of social typing as a means of making sense of the public areas, which then provides a basis for trusting the immediate public environment.

The local urban environment of a highly heterogeneous population of unknown people inspires this process of mental notation, which prepares the foundation for trust between strangers, dictated by the situation and proceeding by means of repeated face-to-face encounters. This social process works to form what may be viewed as the basis of public community within the immediate neighborhood. In effect, residents and users of public spaces come to know and trust the territory, particularly the various kinds of people who come with the territory.

The process begins something like this: One person spots another walking down a certain street alone, with another person, or perhaps even with a few others. The person or persons spied might be engaged in some noteworthy activity, such as getting out of an unusual car, riding a bicycle, walking a particular kind of dog, taking the run of the grounds of a particular dwelling in the neighborhood, simply crossing a street at the light, or leaving a store with bags of groceries. People repeatedly engaging in such everyday activities help to convey what may be interpreted as a usual picture of public life, or what is to be taken as normal happenstance in the immediate area. In such circumstances, skin color, gender, age, dress, and styles of comportment can become important as markers, which then help to characterize and define the area.

At times, depending on an individual observer's biases, such specific markers can become the most important characteristics determining the status of those being observed, often superseding other meaningful attributes of the person in question.[5] The most important aspect of the situation is simply that the observer makes note of the other person: some significant social contact, not necessarily reciprocal, is made. It is in this way that the person spotted or the category he is believed to represent comes to be seen as an ordinary part of the common picture of this public environment.

Although such initial contact is important, it is not the most crucial element in publicly "knowing" others and ultimately feeling comfortable in the area. Rather, the initial contact situation helps set the social context for any meaningful subsequent interaction, unilateral or bilateral; this gives observers a sense of who may be expected here, and when. The primary significance of the initial encounter is contingent upon the kind and quality of subsequent meetings and interactions. If the person spotted is never seen or heard from again, then the initial spotting may gradually lose its power. On the other hand, if the observer spots the person again or is reminded by others of the kind of person seen, the impression has the chance of developing and becoming stronger. The strength of such impressions, nurtured through repeated encounters, observations, and talk with other residents, builds.

All of this serves to form a kind of social bond that slowly works to knit the highly heterogeneous neighborhood into a series of often overlapping public communities wherein people keep familiar others in mind as potential threats, friends, or even allies on the streets in times of need. Though initially superficial, this form of knowing, and the mental maps it helps to foster, allows strangers of diverse lifestyles and backgrounds to navigate the Village streets with a certain reserve of social knowledge that in time grows into trust.

For instance, a stranger may be first seen in one context, then in another, then a third. In time, the observer might say to himself "Do I know that person?" and answer, "Yes," for on a certain level he does know that person—if only by sight. He has mentally noted him many times in various contexts in the neighborhood, although perhaps unwittingly. But with each successive encounter he has become increasingly familiar with him and the class of others he may represent. Based primarily upon unilateral observations and perhaps visual exchanges, this familiarity has yet to reach the verbal level; the persons are not on speaking terms. They may have exchanged knowing looks or initial looks important enough to establish at least the minimal basis for trust. If asked directly, the observer might say, "Yeah, I've seen him around." But a particular stimulus or provocation is often required, say an emergency or a major coincidence, to bring such knowledge to the surface to help make a meaningful connection. And there is indeed a distinct possibility that the people involved will never reach speaking terms. Yet on a visual level, strangers may know one another and obtain a degree of territorial communion without ever having spoken a word.

But there are those circumstances in which the social gap between visual and verbal interaction in public is pressed and the relationship between incomplete strangers is required to go further. People sometimes feel silly continually passing without speaking to others whom they know well by sight. They may experience a certain discomfort that may be resolved either by greeting the other person or by avoidance. Many choose simply to speak and perhaps to unwittingly commit themselves to what may amount to a series of often obligatory public greetings.

Or when visual interaction becomes rich enough, when it has occurred repeatedly over time and a context has been established, then the stranger may be placed in a kind of social reserve until opportunity or need arises. Background information and knowledge, gradually built up and refined through communication, may become useful for social connection and possible subsequent interaction. Though the connection is made quite often by chance, it is of importance for an emerging sense of community within the area. For instance, during emergencies such as house fires, crimes on the street in which someone is clearly in need of help, or some other focus of attention in which incomplete strangers have an opportunity to gather and compare notes with their neighbors, they may stumble a bit and seem embarrassed, saying, "Hello. My name is _____."

A similar kind of introduction sometimes occurs when two people have been taking note of each other in the neighborhood for some time and then happen to meet inadvertently in a different part of town and, somewhat embarrassed, become constrained to greet each other like long-lost friends. Perhaps in the Village they had not yet reached the point of speaking but had only warily acknowledged one another with knowing looks, perhaps stolen looks, or even the customary offensive-defensive scowl usually reserved for keeping strangers distant. After a meeting and verbal exchange, say downtown, two such previously socially distant Villagers may begin to exchange verbal greetings on the streets of the neighborhood on a regular basis. It is in just this way that a basis for interpersonal trust can be established between strangers who may then come to know one another, sometimes intimately.

The social knowledge gained through this process of mental notation seems to be situation-specific, and until times of emergency or coincidence it usually takes on no great significance for the observer. It remains in a kind of mental reserve, to be recalled in situations that demand it. A Villager may call up such knowledge and experience when he shares with others certain tales of strangers noticed on the streets. Such group talk and shared stories often serve as a means of confirming and consolidating observations, contributing to a mental picture of the public culture of the community.

The primary consequences of so much mental notation is the building of familiarity with and trust of the local environment. A shared sense of public community and positive feeling about the area develops. Such feelings allow many to relax and to become cautiously open with others they encounter on the streets and in public places. But when a mugging, killing, or rape occurs in the neighborhood, residents often tense up and begin taking defense action on the streets again. For the moment, many distrust the area and feel uncomfortable on the streets, particularly after dark. They become especially suspicious of strangers they encounter, particularly black males. However, the environment is slowly reused, retested, and made note of again. Neighbors talk and socialize. After a period of time, when diverse kinds of people have repeatedly used the public space uneventfully, memory of the initial incident fades. Feelings of suspicion and distrust subside. Familiarity rebuilds, and a shared sense of trust is gradually restored.

In this way, social knowledge of the immediate area is refined. Context is gained as stories are shared and retold, and in the process a group perspective on the area gradually emerges. It is from this perspective and the necessity of dealing with actual encounters that a set of informal rules emerges among residents and users of the streets and public areas. These rules, discussed among friends and refined through practice, allow diverse kinds of people orderly passage with the promise of security or at least the minimum of trouble or conflict. The general result amounts to perhaps a deceptive appearance of an effortlessly ordered and racially tolerant public space. In fact, however, color, gender, and other considerations and prejudices are much at work in the public ordering of the community area.

Stereotypical Perceptions

By living in the neighborhood and partaking of its lore, residents develop very localized stereotypical attitudes and expectations about what certain kinds of people are likely to do on the streets. For instance, an unknown black teenager wearing sneakers and bouncing a basketball might dictate one course of action to a watchful resident; the same person without the basketball, loitering in front of a vacant house, might dictate quite another. In some areas of the Village, the police might be called, basketball or no, just to check things out. The time of day, the season of the year, the neighborhood's social history—of the past thirty years or even a few days—and involvement with the adjacent neighborhoods affect the meaning this black teenager has for the residents who watch and informally guard the local streets and other public spaces.

Throughout the Village, young black male street groups often predominate, some lounging on street corners, others casually moving about. The black youths are stereotypically thought to be unemployed, and often are. Some young black males often wear sneakers, "gangster caps," and sunglasses and carry large portable radios. In this uniform, suggestive of an urban underclass, these young men are generally presumed to be involved in criminal activity or to be up to no good until they demonstrate otherwise. These working conceptions and behaviors of the streets are a source of sometimes subtle but enduring racial and class distinctions, if not overt hostility, within the community.

The law-abiding members of the community tend to hold such youths responsible for street crimes in the vicinity. Particularly on dark streets, these young men and others who resemble them are held suspect in chance encounters by most others who use the streets, whites as well as blacks. Many of the youths are indeed unemployed and are left to gain money any way they can. Some of the most desperate are involved in the underground economy and are known to man certain street corners and to set themselves up as community protectors and gatekeepers, at times tacitly offering to ensure safe passage for money.[6] Many residents thus become intimidated and are inclined to limit their use of the streets to daylight hours, to remain indoors after dark, to travel in small groups, to walk with a dog, or even to arm themselves in order to navigate the streets in security.

Drawing Color Lines

Though the Village is generally viewed as perhaps the most racially tolerant area of the city, its public spaces and streets are places where distinctions are very often made along the lines of color. There is prejudice, to be sure, but it must be distinguished from a traditional kind of racial prejudice that was perhaps more deep-seated and profound in its total emotional content and effects on the general relations between the races.[7] The prejudice here seems to emerge not so much out of deep-seated racial hatred and hostility, but rather seems to become prominent as it is felt useful for safe passage and security on the public streets. But this situation can and often does degenerate into racial hostility when blacks feel they are being overly scrutinized by whites or when whites blame backs for feelings of humiliation and harassment as they are required to expend an enormous amount of psychic energy in figuring out and abiding by the informal rules of the streets—or suffer certain consequences.

Hence, in an unexpectedly practical manner, the residents' cognitive maps of the area tend to be color-coded, contributing a situation and selective aspect to their dealings with co-users of the public spaces.[8] To be sure, this color-coding has as a basis an inordinate fear of blacks and a very strong association of black males, especially youths, with street crime. And along with this fear, residents feel a need to place distance between themselves and others who might mean them harm. Black middle-income people often appear as eager as whites to prejudge, avoid, and even defer to strange black males in the interest of safe passage on the streets.

As a general rule of the public order, blacks tend to be more suspect than whites. The unknown or strange black male, particularly the youth, is to be heavily scrutinized. Not trusted, his commitment to civility is easily questioned. When he approaches, people sometimes cross the street. Women sometimes tense up and clutch their purses or move them around to their other side. The following fieldnote is relevant:

> At 7:30 on a sunny Thursday morning, I was jogging through the Village neighborhood. I am black, male, 5'11", and weigh about 180 pounds. Dressed in a blue jogging suit and running shoes, I was running on the sidewalk, as I occasionally do to avoid cars. I spied a young white man and a young white woman walking ahead of me, their backs to me, approximately thirty-five yards away. The man was walking on the inside with the woman on his left side and near the street. They looked over their shoulder and spotted me. Our eyes met. As I approached towards the outside, still a good twenty-five yards

away, the man immediately, and perhaps instinctively, traded places with the woman, pushing her to the inside, in a grand protective gesture. She clutched her pocketbook. As I passed, both people looked at me. I looked back over my shoulder. They were still watching me.

Still others, including some black females, often cut short their looks at black males, averting their glance and gazing at something apparently far away. As one young white female informant reported: "I must admit, I look at [male] blacks on the streets just for a few seconds. Just long enough to let him know I know of his presence, and then I look away."

While members of all groups are inclined to engage in defensive behavior toward the stereotypical black male, many blacks and streetwise whites attempt to be selective, deliberately and carefully choosing those blacks and others whom they will approach with caution. On the public streets, most are on the lookout for those displaying threatening symbols, including black skin color, youth, unconventional dress, and incivility. Many such symbols possess a certain ambiguity—and felt risk: people often say they don't know what to expect from strange black youth on the streets. Consequently, many whites, and an increasing number of blacks, tend to cast a broad net of defensive prejudice around themselves, thus holding suspect numerous black male strangers they encounter.

To be sure, black males are not equally distrusted. While younger males seem to warrant keen scrutiny in this area, those who are known stand to be trusted. Moreover, those who display the emblems and uniforms of the overclass (particularly suits, ties, briefcases, and books) and who conform to a certain level of propriety may be granted a measure of trust on the streets. Older black men tend to earn a greater degree of trust through their appearance and demeanor, suggesting maturity and even a caretaking role toward others on the streets. In fact, they often become guardians of the public peace, showing concern for the safe passage of others. They inform strangers about certain corners, at times warning them of where not to go. But most often, the advice they offer is only to whites who they presume are ignorant of the ways of the streets, yet it is offered out of sincerity and genuine concern.

It is clear that black males' presentation of self is crucial for gaining trust from their counterparts on the streets. Many black youth exude an offensive-defensive posture because they themselves regard the city streets as a jungle. And their pose is generally not intended for people who are not aggressive toward them; it is usually intended for people who may threaten them. And yet this pose encourages fear, circumspection, and anxiety by law-abiding residents, black and white, whose primary concern is safe passage on the streets. An overwhelming number of younger black males are indeed committed to civility on the public streets, but they tend to have a difficult time convincing others of this because of the social meanings often attributed to their youth and their color. Many youths simply give in to the negative stereotypes, becoming angered by the scrutiny and the presumptions they know others have about them; at times, they may attempt to get even by scaring or ridiculing those who clearly operate with such prejudgments. This is illustrated in the following narrative by a young white female.

> I went out for something at the store at about 9 p.m., after it was already dark. And when I came back, there was no place to park in front of my house anymore. So I had to park around the corner, which I generally don't do because there's a greater chance of getting your car broken into or stolen over there, since a lot of foot traffic goes by there at night. So I parked the car, turned out all the lights, and got out of the car. And I began walking across the street, but I got into a situation I don't like to get into—and I've been into it a couple of times before—of having there be some ominous-looking stranger between me and my house. So I have to go around him or something. And he was a black fellow between twenty and thirty, on the youngish side. He certainly wasn't anybody I knew. So I decided not really to run, just sort of double-time it, so I wouldn't meet him at close distance at the corner. I kinda ran diagonally, keeping the maximum distance between him and me. And it must have been obvious to him that I was running out of fear, being alone at night out in the street. He started chuckling, not trying to hide. He just laughed at what I was doing. He could tell what he meant to me, the two of us being the only people out there.

In response to such attitudes and behavior, many law-abiding and civil black males find themselves needing to publicly disavow criminality and incivility in their interactions with complete strangers. Middle-class blacks often feel a great need to distance themselves publicly from members of the black underclass. And consequently many males find themselves working hard to put other strangers at ease about their own presence on the streets as they attempt to manage their black skin color in the public places of the Village.[9] Such disavowals are in stark recognition of what seems to be a general rule of the public order: that trust for whites is an ascribed characteristic, while trust for blacks must be achieved, which is not easy to do.

Class Differences

Class seems to be significant in determining how residents approach strangers and how they adjust to the problematic Village streets. Middle-class people, regardless of color, seem much more cautious on the streets than those of the working class or those of the urban counterculture. Middle-class people, for instance, tend to be very careful with their children, even in broad daylight; they walk their children on a remarkably short, invisible tether. Middle-class children are also usually very well supervised at play. Working-class blacks, on the other hand, appear comfortable and at ease on the streets and allow their children to roam more freely. It may be that these differences are strongly associated with relative differences about the sense of respective life changes in society. To be middle-class in the Village, regardless of race, is to have some particular sense of program or outlook toward the wider society. It is perhaps this sense, and the future it promises, that brings the middle-class person alive to the physical and social precariousness of the public environment of the Village, even highlighting his sense of self-worth. With a strong sense of something of value to protect and to defend, he becomes acutely aware of those people and public situations that might threathen his opportunities for the good life.

As the working-class black person navigates the streets in a seemingly relaxed and carefree manner, it is not that he cares less for himself and his children than does his middle-class counterpart. Rather, in the general scheme of things, he may simply not possess the same heightened sense of self-importance, hopes, expectations, and returns on his investment in living. And to him, feeling he is among his own in the general area, the streets are somehow relatively less suspect and more tolerable, though never completely trustworthy. This difference in class and racial outlook makes for important differences in views of the precariousness of the Village environment.

The Hegemony of Blacks in Public Spaces

Another important reason for this relative difference in orientation to the street culture is the general feeling of public hegemony of blacks. White residents often defer to blacks in the public places of the Village. This is indicated in the following fieldnotes:

> It was a warm evening in May. A middle-aged white Villager was gardening in his front yard, which opens on relatively quiet Linden Avenue. The street was calm, for the real traffic had not yet begun. He went to his work, busily digging with his hand trowel. Suddenly, out of nowhere, three black youths appeared. One carried a large radio, turned off, one carried a basketball, and a third youth simply walked. They were dressed in jeans, light jackets, and sneakers. One wore a dark blue cap. They talked among themselves and appeared to

be enjoying one another's company. As the youths approached, the white man acted very much involved in his work, though he could see them from the corner of his eye. They noticed him but continued on their way. As soon as their backs were to the man, however, he stopped his gardening and took a long scrutinizing look, watching them until they were out of sight. Then he returned to his work.

And on another occasion:

Near the local high school, not far from the trolley tracks, stood five black teenage girls. The girls were lighting up and passing around a pack of cigarettes. Each took one and passed the pack on. On the other side of the street walked two white girls on their way to the Village. One of the white girls looked intently at the group of black girls. Then came this from one of the black girls: "What you lookin' at?" "Yeah," chimed in another. Laughter mixed with mean looks and scowls came from the group of black girls. Something had been started. The white girl immediately looked away, perhaps wishing she had never looked at the group. Visibly shaken, she and her friend hurriedly walked toward the Village.

And again:

On a warm summer day, my two-and-a-half-year-old daughter and I approached the local community minipark in the center of the Village. The park, which is understood to be open to all residents of the community, has a swing, old tires for climbing, and other play equipment for children. Sitting on the swing was a three-year-old white boy with his father close behind him. Near them was a white woman of about twenty-five with her four-year-old daughter, and a black woman of about thirty with her four-year-old son. My daughter and I acknowledged the others, and she began to play. Soon she was involved with the equipment and the little girl. This went on for about half an hour. Then two black boys of seven or eight arrived. In a while, a twenty-five-year-old black man and his four- and six-year-old daughters appeared. The group lasted for about five minutes after his arrival, which apparently tipped the acceptable balance between the races. At this point the whites began trickling away, and soon the park was totally occupied by blacks. My daughter and I stayed about thirty minutes longer and witnessed the arrival of two other black children, but no whites. As I spoke with residents about the park and observed it over time, the racial use of the park that my daughter and I had witnessed seemed to be a patterned occurrence.

While use of the park is not supposed to be restricted to any one race, there are differences in usage that seem racially determined. Often the people using the park are either all black or all white. It seems that when blacks are present whites somehow know they are to stay away. But when whites are occupying the park and using the equipment, it is not a signal for the blacks to stay away. Usually the blacks approach the park regardless of who is there, do what they want for as long as they want, and leave when *they* are ready. Consequently, blacks are put in the role of invaders and successors. The relative usage of the public space and the resulting social distancing behavior of whites toward blacks may be viewed in the context of some vague but generalized notion of accepted territorial prerogatives. The dominant community impression may be that blacks have a free hand with the public space, using it whenever they please, while whites are more limited in their use. Thus whites readily defer to blacks, forfeiting rights to public spaces at the slightest hint of contest. Interestingly, whites appear emboldened when they are in numbers (particularly young white males), when they walk their dogs, or when the police are generally present.

Race and Street Crime

It is important to remember that there exists a general assumption among residents, black and white, that young blacks are primarily responsible for street crime in the area, and the blacks are somehow not as likely to assault other blacks on the streets when whites are available. In reality, though, middle-income blacks in the Village, who often share a victim mentality with middle-income whites, appear just as distrustful of black strangers as their white neighbors, if not more so. They find themselves at parties and other gatherings discussing a recently experienced close call and then instructing inexperienced whites in the ways of the streets, at times taking on a certain strong sense of outrage mixed with moral guilt for the street crimes of young blacks. On the streets, blacks express this attitude as they work at maintaining a certain distance toward certain black strangers whom they know only too well.

A felt deterrent to black-on-black crime in this area is the possibility that the victim will recognize his assailant later. It may be that the possibility of recognition causes the potential black mugger, if only for a crucial moment, to think twice before robbing a black person. Not only may the victim bump into his assailant again, but there may be a chance the victim will recognize and, equally important, "take care of him" personally. Many a mugger would not like to carry such a burden, especially when there are so many whites around who are often assumed, if erroneously, to be easier to rob, unlikely to bump into and recognize him, and certainly not as likely to be after him. Further, there is a sense in which membership in the black community is presumed to transcend other considerations in potential stick-up situations. It may be that such a sense of racial group belonging allows blacks who walk the streets the pretense that they are less likely to become actual victims than their white counterparts.

But such a racial interpretation of cultural responses to crime is much too simple. It is a convenient confusion of blacks and street criminals, reifying a "we-they" dichotomy between whites and blacks. One could argue that the average mugger is more concerned with the prospective trouble or ease of taking his victim's property and perhaps secondarily with the possible personal consequences of his actions. Given the important differences in the economic and social circumstances of blacks and whites in the Village, and the mugger's interpretation of them, whites may be viewed as easier and better targets, race in itself notwithstanding.

The changing racial and class composition of the Village may also be a factor in the choice of victims of street crime: not only do the perpetrators of crime often view new people as invaders of the community, they also tend to see them as "people who got something" and yet as inexperienced in the ways of the street. And the new residents, because of their actual and supposed inexperience, their relative wealth, and to some degree their skin color, are viewed as easy marks and often easily become victims.

Yet many residents, black and white, succumb to the simple and convenient view of the street crime as primarily a racial problem, though many whites who feel this way are inclined to keep such riskily "racist" view to themselves unless convinced they are in sympathetic company. In this racially tolerant area, speaking in a racially mixed group in a way that associates young blacks with street crime seems to be a liberty reserved to blacks only, for the black person who voices such opinions is supposedly not capable of the prejudice so often attributed to whites. Such widely held opinions are thought to contribute to the general public conception of strange black youth as the primary perpetrator of street crime, especially against whites. But with a belief in their immunity from the charge of racism, Village blacks make some of the same, if not more incisive, public observations concerning blacks and crime in the streets.

That whites and blacks have common concerns about such issues suggests a certain social communality and co-presence in the same moral community. Such a view allows them the sense, albeit limited, that as residents of the same community area they have the same problems of street navigation. But this ultimately breaks down, affecting neighborhood trust and the social integrity of the community. For in fact the actual experiences and problems of a person with dark skin on the streets are often, though not always, very different from those of a person with white skin. The idea of a moral community gives individuals an interest in interpreting such experiences similarly. And black and white residents sometimes at community meetings entertain the fiction that "we're all in this together." But this fiction is strained, if not exposed, when people are required to figure out and adopt the appropriate etiquette in order to be safe on the streets. This effort at times requires enormous energy mixed with a certain humiliation and sense of harassment, which serves to generate prejudice and exacerbate racial tensions.

Street Etiquette

While the Village's neighborhoods are affected by citywide and even nationally held stereotypes, the area imbues its residents with a peculiar and very local code of street etiquette—its own system of behavioral prescriptions and proscriptions for handling others on the streets with a minimum of trouble. Such a code might well be viewed as a collective response to the common problems local people face each time they venture into the streets. How much eye contact to give or allow from what sort of person on what streets at what time of day, whom to talk with and what to say, where not to walk the dog, how to stand at the corner, the safest though sometimes quite indirect route to one's destination, how to carry one's pocketbook, how much money to carry (in case of a mugging), or the appropriate way to behave in a stick-up situation all have their place in the street code of the Village.

By closely observing everyday life in public places and exchanging social information and opinions about the way things happen and why they do, residents gain and elaborate a perspective on the public areas and the streets they must use.[10] It is primarily through neighborly talk and information exchange that inhabitants of the Village provide new arrivals as well as established residents with informal rules concerning the best approaches to the areas and the streets at different times of the day. But residents chiefly learn from the mental notes of their own experiences. It is with the give-and-take of conversations relating to such personal experiences, including close calls and horror stories, and their explanations that neighborly communion may be initiated and affirmed. It is in this way that a neighborhood perspective may be offered and gained.

A young couple moving in from the suburbs learns from an upstairs neighbor that the reason Mrs. Leggett, an elderly white woman, walks with a cane is not just that she is eighty-five years old. Until several years ago, Mrs. Leggett took her regular afternoon walk unaided by the thick wooden stick she now relies on to get up and down the stairs to her second-floor apartment. Then one afternoon she was knocked to the pavement by "a couple of kids" outside Mel's, the neighborhood market where black high school students from the Village and Northton stop for candy and soda and usually congregate on their way home from school. In the scuffle, Mrs. Leggett's purse was snatched. The police took her to the hospital, where it was discovered she had a broken hip.

Sincer her injury, Mrs. Leggett's gait is less steady. She still takes her walks, but she now goes out earlier and avoids Mel's at the time school lets out. When the new couple ask about the circumstances of her mugging, she is unwilling to describe the "kids" who knocked her down. She only smiles and gestures toward the small, low-slung cloth bag in which she now carries her valuables. "This one is mug-proof, they tell me," she says, a glimmer in her eye. It is a poignant lesson for the young couple: purse straps should be worn around the neck and across the chest, bandolier style, not carelessly hooked over the arm. And perhaps Mel's is worth avoiding at three in the afternoon.

As time goes by, the young couple will come to understand the special meaning of the term "kids," which Villagers, particularly whites, often use to avoid direct reference to a young assailant's blackness. The special social history of the Village helps make certain euphemisms or code words preferable to more openly racial descriptions. So "kids" used in a story about street mugging generally means "black kids," and Villagers know it.

Such words and phrases are generated and refined during neighborly social intercourse behind closed doors of middle-class Village homes. At various social gatherings, including block meetings, cocktail parties, dinner parties, and small get-togethers, Villagers gather and exchange stories about urban living in general and life in the Village in particular. The streets and crime are often prime topics of both pointed narratives and casual conversations. People are often found comparing their actual experiences and passing on hearsay. They commiserate with victims of the streets, casting themselves and others with whom they identify in the role of the oppressed. Recent stick-ups, rapes, burglaries, and harassments are subjects that make them sit up and listen, taking special note of where certain kinds of trouble occurred and in what particular circumstances.

By engaging in such talk and sociability, not only do they learn about the streets, but they also often affirm personal conceptions that city people are somehow special, deserving commendation for putting up with the many problems of being middle class in an environment that must be shared with the working class and the poor. As one middle-class, middle-aged white woman said while fertilizing the geraniums on her front porch: "I'm convinced that city people are just so much more ingenious. We *have* to be."

In contrast, city living, and the urban streets in particular, appear not to be the same problem for many blacks and former hippies in the Village. At their gatherings, the streets are seldom a central topic, but are discussed more casually. Working-class Village blacks see their neighborhood as "nice" and "decent" compared with the streets of Northton, where many were raised. The former hippies, on the other hand, who often view themselves as the vessels of the unique hip Village neighborhood identity, pride themselves on knowing the streets. They generally consider theft and harassment facts of life in the city, to which one must adapt in order to survive. Hence they display little interest in stories of "who did what to whom." Said one thirty-ish former draft counselor of a block meeting entitled "Violence in the Village" scheduled by concerned Villagers: "It's always a lot of who got mugged where and when." She did not plan to attend the meeting.

At times, the young blacks and young white former hippies even come together in apartments or spontaneous intrabuilding get-togethers and lament the recent influx of middle-class suburbanites, whom they see as responsible for rent increases and stricter standards of porch and yard maintenance. They talk about the newcomers as "squares" or "uptight," believing their fears about theft and violence are not to be taken too seriously. Many of these self-proclaimed veterans, and even the young blacks to a certain extent, act as public models and agents of socialization for the newcomers who so desperately need to get a handle on the streets.

But even if the dangers of the streets are played down by the hippies and the blacks, they, along with the newcomers, follow certain rules in order to navigate the streets in safety. Women, especially as they remain longer in the Village, tend to adopt a style of dress designed to negate stereotypical female frailty and to symbolize aggressiveness. Many attempt to desexualize their appearance. For many of the veterans, up to age forty, plain blue jeans are the mainstay of Village casual street garb. Denim jackets and unisex nylon parkas, heavy boots, sneakers, and unshaven legs are all part of the urban female costume.

Along with their appearance goes a certain demeanor or strategy intended to allow them safe passage on the streets. When walking alone at night, some streetwise women will keep up with strangers who seem to be "all right." Especially at night, they sometimes will walk toward the center of particularly dark streets and try to walk only on those that are well lighted, though such streets may be indirect routes to their destinations. They avoid high bushes, large trees, and dark doorways. Some carry whistles and Mace. When a large, dark figure is spotted approaching, many women will cross the street, walk up to someone's lighted porch, or even run. The following story by a twenty-eight-year-old black male is relevant:

> A white lady walkin' down the street with a pocketbook. She started walkin' fast. She got so paranoid she broke into a little stride. Me and my friends comin' from a party about 12:00. She stops and goes up on the porch of a house, but you could tell she didn't live there. I stop and say, "Miss, you didn't have to do that. I thought you might think we're some wolf pack [small groups of black youths who have been known to assault and rob people in public places]. I'm twenty-eight, he's twenty-six, he's twenty-nine. You ain't gonna run from us." She said, "Well, I'm sorry." I said, "You can come down. I know you don't live there. We just comin' from a party." We just walked down the street where she really wanted to go. So she tried to act as though she lived there. And she didn't. After we said "You ain't gonna run from us," she said, "No, I was really in a hurry." My boy said, "No you wasn't. You thought we was goin' snatch yo' pocketbook." We pulled money out. "See this, we work." I said, "We grown men now. You gotta worry about them fifteen-, sixteen-, seventeen-year-old boys. That's what you worry about. But we're grown men." I told her all this. "They the ones ain't got no jobs; they're too young to really work. They're the ones you worry about, not us." She understood that. You could tell she was relieved and she gave a sigh. She came back down the steps, even went across the street. We stopped in the middle of the street. "You all right, now?" And she smiled. We just laughed and went on to a neighborhood bar.

The longtime Village men, many of whom are between 30 and 40, also tend to wear jeans on the public streets to employ survival strategies similar to those of females. Many will attempt to display, in trying circumstances, a tough or masculine appearance. Some take to the streets with a determined set to their jaws, displaying a dead serious look that can be interpreted as something between a frown and a scowl; among black youths, this behavior is referred to as "gritting." In planting such looks on their faces to ward off undesired advances by strangers, they may ward off potential friends. This has implications for the emergence in public of spontaneous relationships.

In time, the newcomers accept and adopt the rules for avoiding crime in the area. As they adapt to what is thought of as a "high-crime area," the newcomers learn to park their cars on certain east-west streets (ones with relatively little traffic from Northton) to avoid having them broken into at night. They find themselves purchasing crime locks and hood locks for their cars, precautions people of the suburbs tend not to take. They buy chains for the bicycles, bars for their first-floor windows, and deadbolts for their back doors. Yet they continue to feel not quite secure. They constantly talk and worry about getting ripped off. They sometimes build high fences to supplement the quaint waist-high wrought iron fences from the early 1900s, when the well-to-do still claimed hegemony within the area. Furthermore, they learn the schedule of the nearby black high school, enabling them to avoid the well-traveled north-south streets when high school students are there in force.

In addition, the newcomers work hard to know the general area, which eventually pays off in a slowly building measure of trust, allowing them to feel somewhat more at ease. They come to recognize other Villagers and frequent visitors from Northton, even though they may not always be fully aware that they know them. The more general neighborhood color-coding, which people in racially homogeneous areas can more easily apply in making decisions about strangers, goes through a refinement process in the Village, due to the strong tradition of tolerance of diversity in lifestyles, class, and race.

Gentrifying community areas may be of importance for the American urban landscape for years to come. Though the ultimate consequences remain to be seen, the more immediate implications seem clear. With the invasion of young, predominantly white, middle- to upper-income professionals, the phrase "inner city" increasingly takes on a new meaning.

Before the onset of gentrification, the setting described in this chapter was probably the most socially diverse and tolerant area of the city. As the newcomers move in, their presence threatens to alter the heterogeneous character of the neighborhood many of them may want to preserve; in time the area is likely to become increasingly homogeneous. They also value the area's proximity to the cosmopolitan center of the city. But this means they must tolerate an urban environment whose security is uncertain at best and for which many of them are unprepared. Many sell out and move, often to the suburbs, when they are no longer able to stand the crime (which many blame on the diversity of the area), or they tire of living in such close proximity to "so many suffering people," or their children reach school age.

Those who remain adopt a peculiar public etiquette in order to navigate the streets and public spaces of the general area. This etiquette is color-coded and relies upon prejudicial thinking in encounters with young black males and other strangers. Such prejudice is often troubling to those who entertain it and is a source of tension with blacks of the area, though many blacks take similar precautions and make similar adaptations to the problems of street navigation.

The longer such people remain in the area, the greater the chance they have of coming to trust the public spaces they use repeatedly. As their numbers gradually increase, and as they make use of the streets and public areas, they pay close attention to others who make up the community, mentally noting fellow users of the public spaces in a variety of situations. In effect, they mentally document such experiences, store their impressions, and recall them to help make sense of an otherwise dubious public environment. With this method, they slowly grow to trust the area, feeling increasingly secure, though they find themselves required to explain this sense of security to friends, family, and other outsiders who lack familiarity with the area they have come to trust.

But when a serious crime, such as rape, mugging, or killing has been committed, they tend to tense up and may even question their decision to live in this area. They then take some extra precautions, and as time passes they become reaccustomed to the area, being mindful of the spot where the latest crime occurred. In time, many find themselves learning the area and getting to know their neighbors; they form a subculture of sorts and sometimes develop a sense of affiliation with the area and a respect for its unique diversity.

The new invasion profoundly affects the social definition of the area, not only in the eyes of its residents, but also in those of local business and government officials. For instance, mortgages and home improvement loans that would have been denied a few years earlier now become readily available. Further, the new residents press government officials for increased municipal services, including police protection, for the area. These demands are often met, and the area benefits. The once-segregated schools gain some white students, whose parents involve themselves in the schools and require them to be responsive to their needs. Thus the schools improve. But with all of these improvements, housing costs increase and so do taxes. The poorer people trickle out, unable to afford to live in the area they have helped to create. Additional middle- and upper-income people are attracted to the area, and the neighborhood is gradually but surely transformed.

For centuries, blacks and whites have resided in separate communities, a separation that has been institutionalized and even supported in law until only recently. Generally, the development of each group has been both separate and unequal. Today, those blacks and whites who come together and reside in inner-city areas do so almost by historical accident. Their communities may be referred to as "integrated," but this is often deceptive. Such areas are usually in transition, from black to white and from lower income to upper income. And the very few black professionals who reside in such communities and are presumed likely to remain with others of their class, color notwithstanding, must often resist the strong attraction of the suburbs and other residential situations. In time, this dynamic leaves the community area predominantly white, but as a consequence of class factors rather than primarily racial considerations.[11] As W. E. B. Du Bois so presciently said, "the problem of the color line" still exists in 1985, but it is a problem increasingly compounded by consideration of social class.

Notes

1. Howard J. Sumka, "Neighborhood Revitalization and Displacement: A Review of the Evidence," *Journal of the American Planning Association* 45 (October 1979): 480–87; Dennis E. Gale, "Middle Class Resettlement in Older Urban Neighborhoods: The Evidence and the Implications," *Journal of the American Planning Association* 45 (July 1979): 293–304.

2. "Village-Northton" and "Eastern City" are fictionalized names deemed convenient for description, since the real community in question has qualities of smallness, quaintness, and a certain intimacy so often associated with villages, and the area is located in a large eastern city. These names are used to maintain the privacy and anonymity of the community residents. The information presented here as history is based on accounts collected through extensive interviews with longtime residents of both the Village and Northton. Though the facts of the various accounts sometimes differ, it is coherence with regard to ideals and impressions that the fieldworker here is after. In a sense, the history presented here is a kind of lore that is remembered to be true—what has come down through the years as a guiding ethos and neighborhood identity.

3. These social processes are reminiscent of the human ecological processes of invasion-succession described by Robert Park and his students. See Robert E. Park, Ernest W. Burgess, and Roderick D. McKenzie, *The City* (Chicago, 1967); Harvey W. Zorbaugh, *The Gold Coast and the Slum* (Chicago, 1929).

4. As told to me by a longtime Village resident and informant who participated in the general movement.

5. See Everett Cherrington Hughes, "Dilemmas and Contradictions of Status," *American Journal of Sociology* 50 (March 1945): 353–59.

6. See Elijah Anderson, "Some Observations on Black Youth Employment," in Bernard E. Anderson and Isabel V. Sawhill, eds., *Youth Employment and Public Policy* (Englewood Cliffs, N.J., 1980), 64–87.

7. See Thomas F. Pettigrew, "Prejudice," in Stephen Thernstrom, ed., *Harvard Encyclopedia of American Ethnic Groups* (Cambridge, Mass., 1980), 820–29; and Herbert Blumer, "Race Prejudice as a Sense of Group Position," *Pacific Sociological Review* 1 (Spring 1958): 3–7.

8. For an elaboration of the concept of cognitive maps, see Gerald D. Suttles, *The Social Construction of Communities* (Chicago, 1972), 32–33.

9. See Erving Goffman, *Stigma: Notes on the Management of Spoiled Identity* (Englewood Cliffs, N.J.: 1963).

10. For a discussion of the concept of group perspectives, see Howard S. Becker et al., *Boys in White: Student Culture in Medical School* (Chicago, 1961), 36–37, notably: "Group perspectives are modes of thought and action developed by a group which faces the same

problematic situation. They are customary ways members of the group think about such situations and act in them. . . . Perspectives contain definitions of the situation." Note also the discussion of the differences of attitudes and values from the perspectives; perspectives are defined as situationally specific, including modes of action, as well as collectively arrived at out of a group's felt need. See also Tomatsu Shibutani, "Reference Groups as Perspective," *American Journal of Sociology* 60 (May 1955): 562–70.

11. For an elaboration of this point with respect to recent historical changes in American institutions, see William Julius Wilson, *The Declining Significance of Race: Blacks and Changing American Institutions,* 2nd ed. (Chicago, 1980).

List of Contributors

Elijah Anderson is Charles and William Day Professor of Social Sciences at the University of Pennsylvania. He is also the author of *Streetwise: Race, Class, and Change in an Urban Community.*

John Bauman is Professor of History at California University of Pennsylvania. His co-authored essay in this volume originally appeared in the *Journal of Urban History.*

R. J. M. Blackett is Professor of History at the University of Houston, Texas. He edited *Thomas Morris Chester, Black Civil War Correspondent: His Dispatches from the Virginia Front.*

John E. Bodnar is Professor of History at Indiana University. He is the author of *Immigration and Industrialization: Ethnicity in an American Mill Town, 1870–1940.*

Carolyn Leonard Carson received her Ph.D. degree from Carnegie Mellon University, where she is currently an instructor in the Department of History. Her essay in this volume originally appeared in the *Journal of American Ethnic History.*

Dennis C. Dickerson is Professor of History at Williams College in Massachusetts. He is also author of *Out of the Crucible: Black Steelworkers in Western Pennsylvania, 1875–1980.*

Gerald G. Eggert taught history at The Pennsylvania State University before his retirement in 1991. He is the author of *Harrisburg Industrializes: The Coming of Factories to an American Community.*

V. P. Franklin is Professor of History and Politics at Drexel University. He is the author of *The Education of Black Philadelphia: The Social and Educational History of a Minority Community.*

Laurence Glasco is Associate Professor of History at the University of Pittsburgh. He is also the author of several essays on Pittsburgh's African American community.

Peter Gottlieb is State Archivist at the State Historical Society of Wisconsin. He is the author of *Making Their Own Way: Southern Blacks' Migration to Pittsburgh, 1916–1930.*

Theodore Hershberg is Director and Professor of Public Policy and History, Center for Greater Philadelphia at the University of Pennsylvania. He edited the volume

Philadelphia: Work, Space, Family, and Group Experience in the Nineteenth Century; Essays Toward an Interdisciplinary History of the City.

Leroy T. Hopkins is Professor of German at Millersville State University. His essay in this volume originally appeared in the *Journal of the Lancaster County Historical Society.*

Norman P. Hummon is Chair of the Department of Sociology at the University of Pittsburgh. His co-authored essay in this volume originally appeared in the *Journal of Urban History.*

Emma Jones Lapsansky is Professor of History at Haverford College. She is the author of *Neighborhoods in Transition: William Penn's Dream and Urban Reality.*

Frederic Miller has taught at Temple University and he is now with the National Endowment for the Humanities. His essay in this volume first appeared in the *Pennsylvania Magazine of History and Biography.*

Edward K. Muller is Chair of the Department of History at the University of Pittsburgh. He is also the author of several essays on Western Pennsylvania, as well as co-editor of the *Atlas of Pennsylvania.*

Gary B. Nash is Professor of History at the University of California at Los Angeles and author of *Forging Freedom: The Formation of Philadelphia's Black Community, 1720–1840.*

Merl E. Reed is Professor of History at Georgia State University. He is the author of *Seed Time for the Modern Civil Rights Movement: The President's Committee on Fair Employment Practice, 1941–1946.*

Harry C. Silcox is Executive Director for the Institute for Service Learning at the Philadelphia College of Textiles and Science. He is author of *A Place to Live and Work: The Henry Disston Saw Works and the Tacony Community of Philadelphia.*

Eric Ledell Smith is an Associate Historian with the Pennsylvania Historical and Museum Commission. He is the author of *Bert Williams: A Biography of the Pioneer Black Comedian.*

Jean R. Soderlund is Professor of History at Lehigh University. She is the author of *Quakers and Slavery: A Divided Spirit.*

Janice Sumler-Lewis is a historian and attorney in Atlanta, Georgia. Her essay in this volume originally appeared in the *Journal of Negro History.*

Joe W. Trotter Jr. is Mellon Bank Professor of History at Carnegie Mellon University. He is the editor of the volume *The Great Migration in Historical Perspective.*

Index